ROBERT
BRUCE

In memory of my mother
MARJORIE STEUART BARROW

ROBERT BRUCE

&

THE COMMUNITY OF THE REALM OF SCOTLAND

G.W.S.BARROW

EDINBURGH
UNIVERSITY
PRESS

© G.W.S.Barrow 1988
Edinburgh University Press
22 George Square, Edinburgh

First edition published in 1965
    by Eyre & Spottiswoode Ltd
Second edition published in 1976
    by Edinburgh University Press
Reprinted 1982
Third edition published in 1988
    by Edinburgh University Press

Set in Monotype Ehrhardt
by Speedspools, Edinburgh
and printed in Great Britain by
Redwood Burn Limited
Trowbridge

British Library Cataloguing
    in Publication Data
Barrow, G. W. S.
Robert Bruce and the community of the
realm of Scotland.—3rd ed.
1. Robert I, *King of Scots* 2. Scotland
—Kings and rulers—Biography
1. Title
941.102'092'4   DA783.4
ISBN 0 85224 539 4
ISBN 0 85224 604 8 Pbk

Contents

Maps *p.*vii

Abbreviations   ix

Preface   xi

1. A Kingdom in Perplexity   1
2. Bruce of Annandale   20
3. Bruce *versus* Balliol   39
4. A Lamb among Wolves   54
5. Two Kinds of War   69
6. Experiments in Guardianship   90
7. The King over the Water   109
8. Defeat   132
9. Revolution   145
10. A King in Search of his Throne   165
11. The Turn of the Tide   187
12. Bannockburn   203
13. War and Peace   233
14. Good King Robert   262
    The Clergy   263
    The Nobles   269
    The Community of the Realm   292
15. In Search of Robert Bruce   312

Appendix   325

Notes to Chapters   329

Genealogical Tables   382

Table of Dates   385

Index   391

Maps

1. Scotland 1286–1329; physical features and communications   *p.*14

2. Scotland at the end of the thirteenth century   19

3. The Invasion of 1296   70

4. 1297 and early 1298   82

5. The Falkirk Campaign, 1298   97

6. The Rule of the Guardians, 1299–1302   111

7. The Invasion of 1303–4   125

8. 1306   147

9. 1307–9   167

10. The terrain of Bannockburn   205

11. The terrain of Bannockburn   213

12. Southern Scotland and Northern England to illustrate the Scottish raids, 1311–27   *pp.*234–5

13. Buchan and Formartine, showing changes in landlordship in the reign of Robert I   272–3

Abbreviations

Abbreviations conform in general to the *List of abbreviated titles of the printed sources of Scottish history to 1560*, published as a supplement to the *Scottish Historical Review*, October 1963.

In the notes, numerals which are set in roman capitals denote part numbers; those in lower-case roman, volume numbers; and those in arabic, page numbers, except that an arabic numeral preceded by 'no.' is the number of a document.

Abbreviations not included in the List published in the *SHR* include the following:

Annales Londonienses	*Annales Londonienses*, in vol.i of *Chronicles of the reigns of Edward I and Edward II*, ed. W. Stubbs (Rolls Ser., 1882).
Barrow, *Kingdom*	G. W. S. Barrow, *The Kingdom of the Scots* (1973).
Barrow, *Kingship*	G. W. S. Barrow, *Kingship and Unity: Scotland, 1000-1306. The New History of Scotland*, ii (1981).
BIHR	*Bulletin of the Institute of Historical Research.*
BL	British Library
Cal. Chancery Warrants	*Calendar of Chancery Warrants: 1244-1326* (1927).
Cal. Close	*Calendar of the Close Rolls.*
Cal. Inqu. Misc.	*Calendar of Inquisitions Miscellaneous.*
Cal. Inqu. P.M.	*Calendar of Inquisitions Post Mortem.*
Cal. Pat.	*Calendar of the Patent Rolls.*
Chron. Guisb.	*The Chronicle of Walter of Guisborough, previously edited as the chronicle of Walter of Hemingford or Hemingburgh*, ed. for the Royal Historical Society by Harry Rothwell (London, 1957).
Chron. Man	*The Chronicle of Man and the Sudreys*, ed. P. A. Munch and A. Goss (Manx Society, Douglas, 1874).
Chron. Rishanger	*Chronica Willelmi Rishanger*, ed. H. T. Riley (Rolls Ser., 1865).
Chron. Stephen etc.	*Chronicles of the reigns of Stephen, Henry II and Richard I*, ed. R. Howlett (Rolls Ser.).
EHR	*English Historical Review.*
Flores Historiarum	*Flores Historiarum*, ed. H. R. Luard (Rolls Ser., 3 vols, 1980).
Gesta Edwardi de Carnarvan	*Gesta Edwardi de Carnarvan*, in vol. ii of *Chronicles of the reigns of Edward I and Edward II*, ed. W. Stubbs (Rolls ser., 1883).

Le Bel, *Chroniques*   *Les vrayes chroniques de Messire Jehan le bel*, ed. L. Polain
                        (Brussels, 1863).
NLS   National Library of Scotland
Northumberland   *A History of Northumberland* (Northumberland
County History   County History Committee, 15 vols, Newcastle upon
                        Tyne, 1893-1940).
Parl. Writs   *Parliamentary Writs and Writs of Summons, Edward I
                        and Edward II*, ed. F. Palgrave (Record Commission,
                        2 vols., 1827-34).
PRO   Public Record Office, London.
PROI   Public Record Office of Ireland, Dublin.
Reid, *Monarchy*   N. Reid, 'The Political Role of the Monarchy in
                        Scotland, 1249-1329', University of Edinburgh
                        unpublished PhD thesis, 1984.
Scimus, fili   Bull of Boniface VIII, June 27th, 1299, in Stones,
                        Relations, no.28.
SHR   *Scottish Historical Review.*
SRO   Scottish Record Office, HM General Register House,
                        Edinburgh.
Stones, *Relations*   E. L. G. Stones, *Anglo-Scottish Relations, 1174-1328:
                        Some Selected Documents*, ed. E. L. G. Stones, 1965,
                        2nd edn, 1970.
Stones and Simpson,   *Edward I and the Throne of Scotland, 1290-1296*, ed.
Great Cause   E. L. G. Stones and G. G. Simpson (2 vols, 1978).
TRHS   *Transactions of the Royal Historical Society.*
Vita Edwardi   *Vita Edwardi Secundi monachi cuiusdam Malmesberi-
                        ensis: the Life of Edward the Second by the so-called Monk
                        of Malmesbury*, ed. and translated by N. Denholm-
                        Young (Nelson's Medieval Texts, 1957).
Watt, *Fasti*   *Fasti Ecclesiae Scoticanae Medii Aevi ad annum 1638,
                        Second Draft*, ed. D. E. R. Watt (St Andrews, 1969).
Watt, *Graduates*   D. E. R. Watt, *A Biographical Dictionary of Scottish
                        Graduates to AD 1410* (1977).

Preface

An author would be foolish as well as churlish if he turned down an invitation from his publisher to produce a completely revised version of a book to which over the years he has devoted much thought, even if the original work is nearly twenty-five years old. Such an invitation amounts to a vote of confidence. I am much indebted to Archie Turnbull not only for rescuing *Robert Bruce* in 1976 when it threatened to disappear from the bookshops altogether but most of all for giving me the opportunity, obviously final, to see how a study which had grown out of work done in the fifties could be harmonized with the state of learning in the eighties and also reconciled with its author's inevitable changes of mood, interpretation and approach.

In 1965, I wrote that what had first been conceived simply as a study of the life and career of one man had had to become, in addition, the study of an abstract idea. The central theme of this final edition of *Robert Bruce* remains the interplay and tension between Bruce himself on the one hand and, on the other, the concept of a Scottish nation, of which Bruce could and eventually did see himself as leader. That concept, as has been well demonstrated by Dr Norman Reid in his thesis on 'The Political Role of the Monarchy in Scotland, 1249–1329' (Edinburgh, 1984), was beginning to be articulated in the later decades of the thirteenth century. In the minds of contemporaries, it could not be distinguished from the kingship and the kingdom of Scotland: Scots were neither more nor less than the men and women owing allegiance to the *rex Scottorum,* who in turn was the person to whom the secular governance of the Scots had been solemnly entrusted. The king of Scots was one side, the community of the realm of Scotland the other side, of a single coin. It is possible to imagine a kingdom emerging in northern Britain during the early medieval centuries entirely separate from, or even wholly lacking, any concept of a Scottish nation. Nevertheless, that is not how the historical kingship of the Scots did in fact develop. The *gens Scotica* preceded the *regnum Scottorum.* At the same time it must be acknowledged that the kingdom of the Scots rapidly acquired ethnic, linguistic and territorial components which took it far beyond the Pictish and Dalriadic groupings from which it originally emerged. By the twelfth and thirteenth centuries the kingdom of Scotland and its ruling dynasty were themselves determining what made the Scottish nation.

There is nothing that we know of in Robert Bruce's character or career to suggest that he contributed much that was fresh or original to the political idea of the Scottish kingdom as it existed at the outset of the fourteenth century. That idea was already present in men's minds in 1286, and even the author of the Declaration of Arbroath of 1320 did no more than articulate the idea in strikingly memorable language. But if Bruce's contribution to political ideas was negligible, his role in the preservation of an actual political entity was decisive. He clearly shared with many of his contemporaries, whether laymen or ecclesiastics, the notion of a Scottish kingdom ruled by its lawful dynasty, sprung from the remote past, enjoying external liberty and internal liberties, identified by a common system of law and custom and capable of determining its relationship to the papacy and the secular powers of Europe. The chief shift of emphasis in this new edition has been to demonstrate more fully than before the continuity and unity of purpose which linked the efforts of church leaders, nobles and freeholders throughout the period from 1290 to 1329. These individuals conducted a remarkably single-minded campaign to defend the freedom and integrity of the Scottish realm against English claims and armed onslaught. This remains true despite the obvious flaws in Scottish resistance: in 1291 the reckless selfishness of the claimants to the throne and loss of nerve by the Guardians; in the later 1290s jealousy and feuding among the nobles; in 1302 the desertion of the national cause by Bruce himself; and from 1305 onward the deep schism between those who plumped for Bruce and those, increasingly a minority, who remained loyal to Balliol.

An unbroken thread can be seen in Scottish lobbying at the papal *curia* and the court of Philip IV, as well as in the maintenance of the idea of the community of the realm and in the armed struggle itself. The rising of Wallace and Murray in 1297 was in the name of King John, but it was backed by two of Robert Bruce's closest friends and supporters, Bishop Wishart of Glasgow and James the Stewart. Wallace's mission to Paris in 1299, for which the French evidence is discussed here for the first time, was clearly linked to a not yet discredited Balliol kingship, but the quarrel to which it gave rise at home shows that Wallace also had a foot in the Bruce camp. The figure of John de Soules provides a vital link here on the side of the laity, just as the bishops, Lamberton, Wishart, Murray and Crambeth, formed the ecclesiastical bridge from the days of Balliol (and even earlier) to those of Bruce. I would now be inclined to see Bruce's *coup* in 1306 as much more of an election on the part of those who saw themselves as the community's leaders than merely, or even primarily, a brutal seizure of power by one ambitious individual.

Bruce's remarkable lack of bitterness towards former enemies, as well as his patient reconstruction of the old Alexandrian kingdom, may also be seen as aspects of genuine national unity. Of course, propaganda outran reality. The declarations of 1309–10 and 1320 exaggerated, respectively, Bruce's military success and the heightening of Scottish political consciousness. But they did not invent either of these important realities. Throughout this period Bruce was intent upon throwing the English out of Scotland but also restoring the French alliance and winning back papal favour. I would now argue, on the basis of evidence only recently brought to light, that the Declaration of Arbroath in particular had a French as well as a papal dimension. Otherwise the book stands much as it did in the edition of 1976, but the opportunity has been taken to correct mistakes, to amplify the notes (now placed at the end of the text) and to bring the index up to date.

It remains to be said that the task of revising this book has been greatly eased not only by helpful comments from and discussions with many people over many years, but also more specifically by the publication in 1978 of the truly magisterial work of my friends Dr Grant Simpson and the late Professor Lionel Stones, under the title *Edward I and the throne of Scotland*, and by the completion by my friend Professor Archie Duncan of the fifth volume of *Regesta Regum Scottorum*, the *Acts of Robert I*. In all cases where it has been possible and has seemed appropriate my references to sources available in print are to these two works. Otherwise my debt has chiefly been to a steady output of editions, monographs and articles, too numerous to be specified here, to Dr Reid's doctoral thesis mentioned above, and to much correspondence and discussion, including that generated by my honours class on England and Scotland from 1286 to 1328. The staff of the Edinburgh University Press have greatly lightened my labours, while Mrs Doris Williamson reduced to order and clarity a complicated welter of manuscript additions and corrections. To all, my thanks.

G.W.S.B.
Edinburgh, 1988.

ONE

A Kingdom in Perplexity

On the afternoon of Monday, March 18th, 1286, the king sat in Edinburgh Castle, dining late with the lords of his council and drinking, we may suppose, some of the blood-red wine of Gascony for whose payment a Bordeaux merchant was to sue for many years in vain. It was a wild day, overcast by equinoctial storm and evil omens. In the past twelve months a story had gone round Scotland that this would be the Day of Judgement. It must have been known to the king, for he joked about it at dinner. He was occupied with a vision more profane and less sombre than that of judgement: the young Frenchwoman, Yolande of Dreux, his wife of less than six months, whom he had left at the royal manor of Kinghorn across the Firth of Forth, twenty miles away by bad roads and the sea ferry. Forty-four years of age, a king for thirty-six, Alexander III had out-lived his first wife, Margaret of England, his two sons, and his daughter, the queen of Norway. His blood survived precariously and distantly, across the North Sea, only in his three-year-old grand-daughter Margaret, whom the magnates of Scotland had, since February 1284, accepted as heir to the throne. Doubtless nothing more than an uncomplicated desire for his young wife prompted Alexander, against his barons' advice, to set off for Kinghorn in the teeth of a snow-laden northerly gale. Yet in the nature of things politics could never be very distant from the most private life of a thirteenth-century king. The land cried out for a more auspicious heir than the little 'damsel of Norway': a boy, present and in good health, unfettered by other dynastic claims, in place of a sickly girl overseas who might one day inherit the Norwegian throne. A husband's uxoriousness was also a long-reigning king's duty to his people.

When Alexander reached Dalmeny the ferry master urged him to go back. The king asked if he was afraid. At once he got the answer 'I could not die better than in the company of your father's son,' and was rowed across the two miles of rough water to the royal burgh of Inverkeithing. Landing in pitch darkness, with only three esquires for escort, the king was met by one of the bailies of the town, Alexander *le Saucier*, master of the royal sauce-kitchen. As bailie it would be his duty to meet the king and offer him hospitality. He was a married man and it can be assumed that his home was one of the substantial burgess houses of the town. He assured the king that he would provide him with honourable lodging until morning. In later ages it was common enough for men of all classes in Scotland, nobles, burghers and peasants, to address their sovereign with extraordinary bluntness. Something of this familiarity shows forth in the frank rebuke which Alexander the sauce-maker addressed to Alexander the king: 'My lord, what are you doing out in such weather and darkness? How many times have I tried to persuade you that midnight travelling will bring you no good?' But the king, again in character, brushed aside rebukes and invitations. Asking only for two countrymen to guide him, he and his escort set off along the rough coast road towards Kinghorn. What happened after that no one knows, save that escort and guides lost their master in the blackness of the night and the storm. Next morning he was found dead on the shore, his neck broken. A small feudal kingdom of perhaps half a million inhabitants had now, by a whole series of unlooked for calamities, been left leaderless, in a situation for which there was no precedent. For the best part of two hundred years it had been led and held together by vigorous, warlike kings commanding the allegiance of a feudally conservative yet quarrelsome and potentially violent nobility. The new sovereign, the 'lady of Scotland', was an ailing child who had never seen her kingdom. Her name, Margaret, was a name of good hope; but her age and sex aroused on every side doubts and fears.

What was this kingdom like, which Alexander III – the last of his line to rule in Scotland – had governed peacefully and faithfully since 1249? The first thing which modern historians, especially English, French and American historians, have learned to say about medieval Scotland is that it was a Celtic country, part of what F. W. Maitland called the 'Celtic Fringe' of the British Isles. This emphasis on the Celtic quality of Scotland, a standard feature of modern books, derives not from Scottish historians as a whole but from a line of scholars whose chief founder and greatest figure was William Forbes Skene. Skene revolutionized the writing of Scottish history by a brilliant book which he called quite deliberately *Celtic Scotland*. Since Skene it has been impossible for serious historians to ignore the importance of the Celtic element in medieval Scottish society. But it is well over a century since Skene wrote, and in the interval the sharply drawn simplicities of Skene's view have yielded to a subtler and more complex picture. The notion of 'Celtic Scotland' has taken hold more powerfully outside Scotland than among the Scots themselves. For some French historians the highlands begin at the English border; and in the view of some English and American writers the clan system was universal from Berwick to Cape Wrath.

Alexander III's kingdom was indeed a Celtic country, but saying that does not explain everything in thirteenth-century Scotland. Politically and constitutionally it explains few of the important things. Our picture of medieval Scotland will be false if we overlook or underestimate its non-Celtic elements. Nevertheless, the Celtic features of Scotland were deeply embedded in her social structure, her language and her customs, and it is well worth considering some of those features here.

In undisputed first rank among the nobility were the earls, about thirteen in all, and their special authority and dignity were directly inherited from the Celtic kingdom of the eleventh century. Their acknowledged doyen was the earl of Fife, whose hereditary privilege it was to place a new king upon the seat of royalty at its inauguration. Although the French and English words *comte* and *earl* were applied to them, the Scottish earls were successors of the *mormaers* – literally, 'great officers' – who had been primarily provincial governors and military commanders. In this they may have resembled the earls of pre-Conquest England, but they were unlike their counterparts in Angevin England, who were essentially great landowners, lords of vast feudal estates, on whom the title of earl had been bestowed as no more than a mark of special honour. There was no one in Scotland to compare with the English earl of Oxford whose territory was in Essex and Suffolk, the earl of Albemarle who would be found in Holderness, or the earl of Surrey whose lands lay in Sussex, Norfolk and Yorkshire. In Scotland the arrangement was more primitive and logical: the earl of Atholl, for instance, had his chief seat at Moulin (near Pitlochry), most of his lands were in the surrounding district, and, although he was a landowner in Aberdeenshire, it was only in Atholl that, as earl, he wielded appreciable political and military authority. The earls had the power to muster the 'common army' of Scotland within their own provinces; they wielded a jurisdiction in their own courts which fell only just short of the Crown's; and they laid claim to ill-defined rights in the matter of choosing a new sovereign whenever the king died.

Many other pieces of Celtic conservatism survived north of Forth and in the south-west, where Galloway had its own special laws, including the archaic system of the wergild or blood-price. In these regions, for example, there were at every court to which free men resorted certain judges, 'doomsmen', 'dempsters', sometimes hereditary, who served as repositories of unrecorded, immemorial law and custom. Much the same had been true of the Scandinavian parts of England before 1066, but a great deal had happened in England in the intervening two centuries, nowhere more than in the field of law. In this as in many other ways Scotland had remained more conservative. The English historians who for 'conservative' tend to write 'backward' tend also in this context to forget that England was conquered by a Norman ruling class who monopolised control at the top and eventually brought the country they had captured into a vast trans-Channel empire. It is not surprising that the England of Edward I was very different from the England of Edward the Confessor. Scotland, on the other hand, had had a half-hearted 'Norman Conquest' and was never joined to the continent. At almost every point development was slower and more gradual than in the south and began from different origins.

The most obvious way in which Celtic influence survived in Alexander III's kingdom was in language and social custom, especially in the matter of family relationships. In 1286 Gaelic had not been driven back within the highland line: it must still have been the language of the great majority of the peasantry north of Forth and Clyde, as well as in Galloway. No doubt it also survived among the gentry of these regions, but in the lowlands at least (with the probable exception of Buchan) the greater lords and the educated clergy would speak French or northern English, and there is little doubt that English and French prevailed almost exclusively in the towns. Even if Gaelic-speaking gentry survived in the north-eastern lowlands they would certainly have been in a minority. By 1286 many families of 'Norman' or English origin had won lands in the north, and all our evidence shows that outside the highlands these new settlers used the English tongue, with perhaps a smattering of French. Yet they found Celtic custom tenacious, and in their attitude to the family they surely came under its influence. It is true that the succession of heirs by primogeniture, unknown in Celtic lands, was imported into Scotland in the twelfth century and was accepted by the entire landowning class, Normans, English and native Scots alike. But the clannishness deep-rooted among the Celts can be seen in the mixed post-Celtic society of the thirteenth century and was to emerge very strongly in later medieval Scotland. The 'clan system' is one of the myths of Scottish history, but in the thirteenth century there were undoubtedly clans in the more purely Celtic parts of the country – the west highlands and Galloway – and traces of clan organization can be found elsewhere. More important than any 'clan system', with all its picturesque accompaniment of slogans, badges and tartans, was the indisputable fact that the family as a whole, rather than any single father-to-son dynasty, was the dominant social unit in Scotland. Even allowing for the small population, a remarkably small number of surnames sufficed for the landowning class. The Scots, in short, were a kin-based society.

Down to this point the written records give us clear evidence. They fail us almost completely when we seek the richer and more colourful texture of daily life, its dress, its sports and pastimes, its worship, the books read by the educated, the tales listened to in ale-houses, the gossip of the village. Yet even here we can feel sure without being able to prove that Scottish society in lowlands and highlands alike retained a Celtic flavour. There was something of a conscious revival of things Celtic in the middle of the thirteenth century, which went hand in hand with an attempt to give a distinctive personality to the Scottish kingdom and nation. The name *Scotia*, the land of the Scots, which a hundred years earlier had been confined to the country north of Forth, was now applied to the whole Scottish kingdom. At the same time old chronicles and genealogies were studied in an effort to write an intelligible, acceptable history of the Scots which could compare with the better-known, more firmly established histories of neighbouring nations. To make a nation conscious of its identity you must first give it a history. Before the thirteenth century the Scottish nation had meant the people of mixed Scottish and Pictish descent who lived north of Forth and Clyde. 'Histories' of this nation, such as they were, related to the Scots of the west and, to a noticeably lesser degree, to the Picts of the east. In the thirteenth century, therefore, the only available histories (apart from chronicles of the recent past) which were in any way suitable for the Scottish kingdom as a whole were Celtic histories, the deeds and feuds and sometimes doubtful genealogies of long lines of kings with names which even then must have seemed uncouth and improbable. To make up for this there was the splendid if partly obscure story of the Scottish church, the great antiquity of the Christian faith in Scotland, the lives of innumerable saints, the undeniable fact that of all the missionaries who had tried to convert the English people the Scots of Iona had had the most resounding success, and the more questionable assumption that the Scots nation of the thirteenth century was the sole heir of this Columban tradition.

Scotsmen of Alexander III's time might be of Pictish, British, Gaelic, Scandinavian, English, Flemish or Norman descent. However inappropriate, however ironical it might seem, they all took a pride in the Celtic past of their country. At the inauguration of Alexander III, which, by a custom already very ancient in 1249, was celebrated at Scone, an aged highland shennachie recited the young king's genealogy in Gaelic: 'God's blessing on the king of Scotland, Alexander mac Alexander mac William mac Henry mac David,' and so on, till he reached the first Scotsman, Iber Scot.[1] The string of non-Celtic Christian names separated by the reiterated *mac* merely serves to emphasize that the old man was rehearsing not only the antiquity but also the Celtic character of the Scottish monarchy. And King Alexander did not cease to be given reminders of Celtic custom after his inauguration. He kept a harper, Master Elias, who, whether or not himself a Celt, practised an art in which the Scots were acknowledged to excel.[2] Music was certainly important to the Scottish court, as it doubtless was in every court of medieval Europe. In 1242, a Scots royal minstrel travelling by way of Durham had his horses and clothing confiscated until he would agree to pay exorbitantly for his lodging.[3] When the king travelled by the high road through Strathearn, it was the custom for seven women to meet him and sing before him on the way, an entertainment that seems quite in keeping with the progress of a Celtic chief, and far removed from the world of the Capetians and Plantagenets.[4]

It was a nagging reminder of Celtic habits of thought which occupied King Alexander on the day of his death. Over fifty years earlier a bastard son of Alan, lord of Galloway, by name Thomas, had been chosen as their chief by the Celtic people of that province, rather than see their land divided among Alan's three daughters and their English husbands. King Alexander's father, Alexander II, put down the Gallovidian revolt with great severity, and the bastard Thomas was shut up in Barnard Castle, in charge of John Balliol who had married Thomas's second half-sister, Dervorguilla.

Now, in 1286, John Balliol's son and successor, another John, wished to
release Thomas from his long imprisonment, and sought the king of Scots'
permission to restore him to his native land. It was this request which came
before Alexander III's council at Edinburgh on March 18th.[5] If Thomas of
Galloway seemed like a ghost from the distant past, his case illustrated the
gulf between feudal society which rigidly excluded bastards from inheritance and Celtic society which might prefer a man of unlawful birth to
legitimate heiresses.

If Scotland was thus a Celtic country, it was also a country of non-Celtic
developments and anti-Celtic tendencies. It is one of the startling paradoxes
of Scottish history that the thirteenth century saw not only the first
emergence of 'Scotland' in a modern sense but also the decisive defeat of the
Scottish language – Gaelic – by a northern English tongue, which in the
course of time coolly adopted the name 'Scots' for itself. This Scots
language is now retreating fast, save in poetry and as the speech of country
districts, especially in the north-east. Gaelic, though confined within an
ever-decreasing area, still has plenty of life left. But in the thirteenth century
Scots was an aggressive tongue, slowly but surely ousting Gaelic, more than
holding its own with French, confident of its future as the official and
literary language of the Scottish kingdom. Why this displacement happened
is not at all clear. It is true that since the tenth century there had been a
sizeable population of English race and language within the Scottish
kingdom, concentrated in the south-east, in Lothian, Tweeddale and
Teviotdale. It cannot have remained confined to this corner of the country,
and there is plenty of evidence that English-speaking people could be found
in the thirteenth century in Dumfriesshire and Ayrshire, in Clydesdale, and
in many parts of Scotland north of Forth. It was neither lairds nor scholars
but ordinary farming and fishing folk who in the first half of the thirteenth
century were giving names like 'Whitefield', 'Midfield', 'Stanbrig' and
'Stinchende [Stinking] Haven' to places in Angus and Perthshire.[6]

This would explain the increase of English speaking in the northern parts
of Scotland but one has still to explain the fact that no contrary movement of
Gaelic into the south seems to have taken place. If the king's peace allowed
Saxons to settle among Britons and Gaels, why did not the same peace allow
Gaels to settle among Saxons? Perhaps the answer is to be found in the
attitude of the monarchy. From David I's time there was a growing
tendency for the king to treat Edinburgh as the capital, to reside there or in
other southern castles like Roxburgh and Stirling, and to hunt in the great
southern forest of Selkirk (or Ettrick as it is more usually called today).
Here too, in the south-east, was the biggest concentration of religious
houses, including some of the most famous, Holyrood, Melrose and Kelso.
Agriculturally the south-east was probably the richest and most fertile part
of the kingdom, and in Stirling, Edinburgh, Roxburgh and above all

Berwick it could boast towns whose equal was not to be found elsewhere. Since the economic and political centre of gravity was located in Lothian, where a basic population of Anglian stock was ruled by lords who despite their 'Norman' descent were doubtless already capable of speaking English, it is not really surprising that the native language as well as the customs of Lothian were providing a model to be copied by the rest of Scotland, save for the far north, the west highlands, and Galloway.

Celtic Scotland had been rebuffed in popular devotion as well as popular speech. In ancient times the patron of the Scottish nation was Columba or Columcille of Iona, and in the thirteenth century (and for long afterwards) it was his reliquary, the *Brecbennach*, which was borne by the Scots army into battle. But as early as the eighth century the cult of the apostle Andrew had been established on the east coast by a Pictish king. While Iona was ravaged by the Norsemen and fell upon evil days of obscurity and decay, Saint Andrew's shrine attracted pilgrims from Scotland, England and many other lands. In the twelfth and thirteenth centuries, in keeping with the eastward orientation of the country, Saint Andrew, universally known and revered but also an eastern saint in an east-coast setting, became the undisputed patron of the Scottish people. By the early twelfth century the locality of his shrine, Kinrymont, had changed its name simply to St Andrews. Along with Andrew other saints who were specially revered or became widely popular in the thirteenth century either stood, like Ninian, for an anti-Columban tradition, or, like Nicholas, had distinct associations with the east-coast and North Sea. The cult of Margaret, Malcolm Canmore's Anglo-Hungarian queen, was significantly anti-Celtic. She was canonized in 1250, when her remains were translated with great ceremony at Dunfermline Abbey. By the end of the century Margaret had taken her place among the very small company of saints for whom all Scots felt love and reverence.

It was unquestionably in the field of government and administration that the Celtic inheritance of Scotland had suffered its most permanent reverses. Royal government in the thirteenth century was based on a fairly simple structure that was imported from the feudal states of north-west Europe, especially England and France. The monarchy might be Celtic historically, possibly more Celtic in spirit than the surviving evidence would suggest, but to outward seeming there was little to distinguish it, save in opulence, from the feudal monarchies of England and France. Such central government as existed, apart from the king himself, was provided by the royal household. This was emphatically feudal, Frankish, non-Celtic in character. Its chief officers were the steward or stewart, the chancellor, the chamberlain, the constable, the butler and the marischal. The office of the steward had been heritable from its establishment by David i, the constable's office had been hereditary from the same period, and there was a marked tendency for the other offices (except the chancellor's) to become hereditary in the thirteenth century. The steward had general responsibility for the household and its management, and under him were senior clerks, of the Provend and of the Liverance, who had charge of the day-to-day running of the household. The chamberlain was primarily a financial officer, with a general oversight of the royal revenues. The functions of the constable and the marischal were chiefly military, the former being responsible for organizing the Crown's military resources as a whole, the latter having a more specialised role in charge of the cavalry element. The chancellor presided over the king's chapel, which in addition to being the king's personal place of worship served as his chancery or writing-office, keeping his seals, preparing letters and other written documents and issuing legal writs or 'brieves'. The chancellor, himself invariably a clergyman who could normally expect promotion to a bishopric at the end of his term of office, was assisted by numerous chaplains and clerks, some with specialised duties, for example, as custodian of the great seal. Besides these greater officers of the household, there were others, more or less important, more or less hereditary in character, such as the doorward (durward, *hostiarius*), the pantler, the foresters and hunters, and the serjeants or officers of the *dispensa* or *spence*, the sub-department of the household dealing with bread and wine.

Outside the household, the earls, as we have seen, provided a remarkable example of Celtic survival; but the role assigned to them *as earls* in the work of royal government was relatively small. The three chief administrative and judicial officers of the Crown were the justiciar of *Scotia*, responsible for Scotland proper, north of Forth and Clyde, the justiciar of Lothian, whose jurisdiction covered the whole of south-east Scotland, and the justiciar of Galloway.[7] The justiciars might happen to be earls, but their authority derived directly from the Crown. Below them were the sheriffs, some twenty-six in all, who were the principal royal officials in the local districts into which the kingdom was divided for the purposes of royal government. There was a marked tendency for the sheriff's office to become heritable, but under Alexander III the sheriff, whether hereditary or not, still constituted the pivot of royal administration, presiding over the court most in use by free men, collecting and accounting for royal revenue, and often having responsibility for the chief royal castle (or castles) in his own sheriffdom. The sheriff was an English import, distinctly scotticized north of the border. Another import, less specifically English, was the royal burgh, a unit at once social, economic, political, and useful for maintaining public peace. Royal burghs and their non-royal imitators became more deeply embedded in the heart of Scottish life than perhaps any other institution imported by the kings of the twelfth century. Historically speaking, Scotland has been a land of burghs rather than villages. If the lack of true villages is a Celtic legacy, the success of burghs derives directly from the virtual absence of real town life in pre-twelfth-century Scotland, and the pioneering enthusiasm and copybook methods of the first burgesses, many of them coming from England or from across the North Sea.[8]

Above all, Scotland was a North Sea country, looking eastward and southward to the other countries which faced the same sea and used it increasingly as the highway for their trade. However stubbornly Celtic custom might persist, Scotland under Alexander III had largely turned its back on the west and the Celtic past. There were, it is true, sea-port towns on the west coast, Renfrew, Glasgow, Rutherglen, Irvine, Ayr and Dumfries, carrying on trade with Ireland and western England, but much the larger number of rich and thriving burghs were on or near the east coast. Of these, a distinct northern group included Inverness, Elgin and Aberdeen. In the central group, the chief towns were Perth – then more of a sea-port than it is today – St Andrews, Dundee and Montrose. Lastly, there was what amounted, by Scottish standards, to an 'urban cluster', south of the Forth. Here were Stirling, Edinburgh (with its ports of Leith and Musselburgh), Haddington, Roxburgh, Berwick and others. Insofar as she was not self-supporting, Scotland lived by exporting hides, wool, timber, and fish, and it was the trade in these goods which built up the North Sea towns. Aberdeen was as close to the Elbe as to the Thames, and closer to Norway than either.

They hoysed their sails on Monenday morn
Wi' a' the speed they may;
They hae landed in Noroway
Upon a Wodensday.

Sir Patric Spens, admittedly, was a sailor of exceptional skill. But it is a fact that when Alexander III's daughter Margaret sailed to Norway to marry King Eric in 1281, her ship left Scotland on August 11th and reached Bergen early on the morning of the 15th.[9]

In the eyes of the North Sea peoples Scotland was far from being remote, unknown or unprofitable. In 1247, for example, a ship was built at Inverness for Count Hugh of St Pol, whose wife was a relative of the Scottish king. This ship, designed to transport crusaders from the Pas de Calais to the Holy Land, was so large and fine that it caught the attention of the English historian, Matthew Paris.[10] But the Inverness shipyards could never have built such a vessel if Count Hugh's order had been unique. The links between Scotland and the Low Countries went back over a century and were vitally important for the Scottish economy. The vast flocks of sheep which grazed on the Southern Uplands produced fine wool which was shipped direct to Flanders from Berwick and other eastern ports. On a certain date in 1297 Scots merchandise seized at Sluys (on its way to Bruges) realized over £60, a fair sum for a presumably chance haul.[11] From the time of David I Flemish immigrants had been welcome in Scotland, and under Alexander III the Flemings were almost certainly the most numerous and important among the foreign trading colonies. At Berwick they had their own headquarters or 'factory', the Red Hall, held directly of the Crown on condition that they would always defend it against the king of England.[12]

The Flemings had no monopoly of Scotland's foreign trade, and by the end of Alexander III's reign they may have been meeting serious competition from the Germans of the Hanse towns. Various men of Cologne, Gottschalk, Gottfried, Alexander, Ingram and James, appear in Scottish record at the turn of the thirteenth and fourteenth centuries,[13] and the merchants of Cologne, like the Flemings, had their own Berwick factory, the White Hall in the Seagait.[14] A letter written eleven years after King Alexander's death, when Scotland was under English rule, states that some merchants of Lübeck, belonging to the company of merchants of that city, owed £80 in customs duty on wool and hides exported from Dundee.[15] The interest of this chance statement emerges in the sequel. Only a few months after it was written, William Wallace, having driven the English out of Scotland, wrote to the mayors of Lübeck and Hamburg explaining that his country had been liberated and that the Scottish ports were once more open to German traders.[16] German commercial activity in Scotland was certainly not the creation of either Edward I or Wallace: we can be sure that before 1286 it had come to play an essential part in the country's economy.

Apart from trade, royal marriages are a good index of a medieval country's external relations. Since 1160, the Scottish royal family had given brides to Brittany, Holland, England and Norway, and had taken brides from England, France, especially north-eastern France, and Flanders. Denmark, in fact, is the sole country bordering the North Sea with which Scottish connections in this period are difficult or impossible to trace. Political bonds, admittedly, are seldom exactly the same as the ties of trade, and it was an obvious necessity for Scotland to keep on good terms with England, not only her closest neighbour but also the only country in a position to inflict serious injury upon her. (As the English barons are reported to have said in 1244, their nation was powerful enough to wipe out the people of Scotland without the help of others[17]). But it would be a mistake to think that her relations with England, political, cultural and economic, were the only ones that mattered to Scotland, or that she counted in any way upon English protection and patronage. Enjoying no special favours, hampered by no special prejudices or hostility, the Scots of the thirteenth century were accustomed to earning their own living and making their own way in the community of North Sea peoples.

If we except the northern isles of Orkney and Shetland, Britain in 1286 acknowledged two sovereignties – that of the king of England, representing a Saxon monarchy of Wessex which had extended its power northward, and that of the king of Scotland, representing a Pictish monarchy of the Tay Valley which had extended its power southward. Only twenty years before there had been a third sovereignty, that of the king of Norway, which made 'foreign territory' of the whole north-western seaboard of Britain from the

Calf of Man to the Butt of Lewis. It was not the king of England but the king of Scotland who had annexed this Norwegian province and brought it under his rule. This had been a personal triumph for the young Alexander III in 1266, when Norwegian plenipotentiaries had come to Perth to put their seals to a treaty which gave up the Hebrides. But it was more than a personal triumph: it was the first notable alteration in the balance of power in the British Isles since the reign of Henry II, who had won back the north of England from the Scots and had taken the lordship of Ireland. Since England remained by far the wealthier country, the more homogeneous nation, the more experienced in war, surely it would be absurd to suppose that Alexander III's acquisition of Man and the Isles made one jot of difference to English strength? It may be doubted whether contemporaries saw things in this light. Englishmen of Edward I's time, certainly less aware than we are of the great disparity of wealth between the two countries, knew only that the king of Scots had at last rid his government of its biggest single source of weakness and had become master of an island which lay only thirty miles from England, fifty from Wales, and athwart one of the principal routes to Ireland. In so doing he had added to his fighting strength an unknown number of islesmen bred to the art of sea-warfare and sea-raiding.

It is of course an over-simplification and an anachronism to speak of two 'sovereignties' partitioning Britain in 1286. Not only would the vaguer 'overlordship' be more accurate than 'sovereignty', but we must recognize that the English Crown nursed ancient claims to a 'super overlordship' over Scotland. This was in no way comparable to the harmless eccentricity of later English sovereigns in using the title 'king of France'. From 1093 to 1124 the kings of Scotland were actually or virtually vassals of the kings of England, and from 1174 to 1189 Scotland had been brought into formal feudal subjection by Henry II. It is true that in 1189 relations were as formally restored to what they had been in the time of King Malcolm IV of Scotland (1153–65) but precisely what these relations were was something which had never been defined. In consequence, the thirteenth-century kings of England, John, Henry III and Edward I, did not always behave as though they recognized the political independence of Scotland. When the Scots kings tried to get the pope's sanction for the rite of anointing in their inauguration ceremonies, the English kings lobbied successfully at the papal curia to prevent it.[18] If they married English princesses, the English kings made this a pretext for interference north of the border. When the papacy decreed that a tax should be levied to support the crusade, it seemed normal to the English kings that they should be given the right to use the proceeds of this tax from Scotland as well as England, Wales and Ireland.[19] At each change of tenure in the English throne, it was usual for the king of Scotland to do homage to the new king of England. Since homage was never performed in the opposite direction, the English kings naturally regarded this usage as evidence of their feudal superiority. The practice may indeed have originated in Scottish admission of some degree of feudal dependence, but it is clear that from the time of David I the Scots kings wished to keep this so vague as to be meaningless, and that Alexander III denied it altogether. 'I become your man,' he declared to King Edward I at Westminster on October 29th, 1278, 'for the lands which I hold of you in the kingdom of England for which I owe homage, saving my kingdom.' The bishop of Norwich, William Middleton – an experienced canon lawyer – intervened, saying 'And be it saved to the king of England if he have a right to homage for it.' Which gave Alexander the opportunity to reply, speaking clearly, 'No one has a right to homage for my kingdom of Scotland save God alone, and I hold it only of God.'[20]

This account of King Alexander's homage comes only from a Scottish source, but even if partisan it may be well-founded. It was copied, c. 1320–30, into the cartulary of Dunfermline Abbey by a scribe who has copied beside it two documents of Ralph of Greenlaw, abbot of Dunfermline from 1275 to 1296, and we know that Abbot Ralph was one of those commissioned in 1291 to make an inventory of the royal archives in Edinburgh castle.[21] At the Roxburgh council held on October 2nd 1278, just before Alexander set off for Tewkesbury and Westminster, a royal letter was sealed in favour of Dunfermline Abbey.[22] Moreover, there is good evidence that King Edward employed the bishop of Norwich in confidential negotiations regarding the king of Scots' homage a few months after the ceremony on October 29th, for in February 1279 the English king sent letters-close to William Middleton, then on his way to the Scottish court, commanding him to enquire into the homage and attendant circumstances 'in as careful and confidential a manner as possible', but to attempt nothing without the king's special command.[23] Clearly King Edward took the matter seriously and had not got his own way – and indeed the much more guarded official English version of what took place might suggest as much.[24]

This personal declaration of independence was no mere posturing. King Alexander was the child of a marriage which had itself been a gesture of independence. His father's first wife, Joan of England, had been Henry III's sister. She had represented friendship with England, but also, unmistakably, the maintenance of the old tradition of Scottish dependence on England. She bore Alexander II no children, and after her death in 1238 he looked in a different direction for his second wife. On Whit Sunday 1239, at Roxburgh, Alexander was married to Marie de Couci, elder daughter of Enguerand, lord of Couci and peer of France, a great-grandson of King Louis VI. The marriage inevitably substituted French for English influence at the Scottish court. Couci adjoins the Vermandois and is not far from Vermand, and when in the year of the Couci marriage we find Master Richard 'Veirement' or 'Verment' acting for the king of Scots and a few years later holding the office of chancellor to the queen,[25] it is tempting to see in this man, who was prominent in the Scottish church for thirty years, a favoured dependant of the Couci family. Queen Marie's younger sister, Alice, married the count of Guines, in the Pas de Calais. Like their neighbour the count of St Pol, who had ordered his crusading ship from Inverness, the counts of Guines were not only near to England, they earned a useful income supplying the English king with mercenary troops. Their fief of Guines, feudally dependent on Flanders, was one of those North Sea territories with which it was natural for Scotland also to have connections. The Countess Alice's younger son, Enguerand de Guines, went off to seek his fortune in Scotland where his cousin, the young Alexander III, had become king in 1249 after his father's unexpected death. Enguerand found favour in his cousin's sight.[26] He was knighted, and the marriage arranged for him by the king made him one of the foremost barons of the realm. His wife, Christian Lindsay, was heiress of the main stem of the great house of Lindsay, which held large estates in the south of Scotland, especially in Clydesdale, and a good deal of land in England also.[27] In right of his lordship, Enguerand de Guines took his place among the earls and barons of Scotland on the major political occasions of the period – the recognition of the Maid of Norway as heir to the throne in 1284,[28] and the Treaty of Birgham of 1290.[29] But he belonged to a family which had a long tradition of friendship with the king of England, and with the outbreak of war between the Scots and Edward I it is not surprising to find Enguerand taking the English part. In 1311, somewhat unexpectedly, he succeeded to the lordship of Couci, and about this time, less unexpectedly, his great Scottish estates were judged forfeit by King Robert I. The story of Enguerand de Guines is perhaps a little untypical, but it shows that we must at least distinguish as carefully as possible between nobles who were genuinely Scottish and those, like Enguerand de Guines, whose 'Scottishness' was a technicality.

Alexander III's marriages followed the same pattern as his father's. His first wife was Henry III's daughter Margaret. Bride and bridegroom, the one eleven years old, the other a few months younger, were strictly subordinated to political necessity, in other words the desire of Henry III to have some say in Scottish affairs. This desire was first clearly expressed in the Anglo–Scottish crisis of 1244, and was a continuous factor in Scottish politics from the time of the young Alexander's wedding in 1251 until 1258, when a revolution in England ruled out, for the time being, any thought of an aggressive policy towards the Scots. Margaret of England, always the object of her father's love and anxiety, recovered from the acute misery of her early days in Scotland, when she had felt herself to be imprisoned in Edinburgh Castle, that 'dreary and solitary place'.[30] She bore her husband three children and died in 1275. Ten years passed before the tragically early death of all his children forced the king of Scots to marry again. So we are brought back to Queen Yolande, her marriage to Alexander on All Saints' Day 1285, and the ill-fated ride to Kinghorn five months later. Yolande of Dreux, like Marie de Couci, belonged to one of the great noble families of

Butt of Lewis

Cape Wrath

Pentland Firth

The Minch

Little Minch

L. Broom

L. Shin

F

F Moray Firth

F

F

B

Strathdon

Don

Dee

Findhorn

Spey

Loch Ness

Drumalban

L. Morar

Arkaig

L. Shiel

L. Oich

L. Ness

The Mounth

North Esk

L. Rannoch

Strathmore

S. Esk

Loch Tay

Tay

F

Firth
of Tay

Linnhe

Leven

Etive

L. Awe

Strathearn

B

B

Firth of
Lorne

Teith

Loch Leven

F

Loch
Lomond

B

F Firth of Forth

Clyde

B

Firth
of
Clyde

The
Forest

Ettrick

Teviot

B

Tweed

L. Doon

Nith

Dee

Cree

Fords of
Solway

Solway Firth

Calf of Man

0   20   40   60   80

Miles

Land over 1200 ft.

Principal Routes

Ford

B   F Ferry   Rivers

Bridge

1. Scotland 1286–1329; physical features and communications.

France; indeed, both were descended from Count Robert I of Dreux, a son of King Louis VI. Had Alexander III lived, this second French marriage might well have seen a second influx of Frenchmen into Scotland and a strong revival of French influence. Instead there followed only disaster and uncertainty.

As things stood, the acknowledged heir to the throne was Margaret of Norway. But it was rumoured that the queen was pregnant. Should she give birth to a son, the magnates would be forced to set aside Margaret's claims in his favour. One contemporary chronicler, whose writing is too deeply imbued with a pathological misogyny to be trusted on such a point, says that for several months Yolande deliberately pretended to be pregnant, with the intention of passing off an unknown baby as the late king's son.[31] In the meantime, the peace of the kingdom must be maintained, law administered, justice done. The great men of the land, the bishops, abbots and priors, the earl and barons, assembled at Scone about April 28th, 1280.[32] No doubt it was at this 'parliament', and not at the king's funeral a month before, that the magnates swore fealty to their lady, the king of Norway's daughter, and took a solemn oath, on pain of excommunication by the bishops, to guard and preserve for her the land of Scotland and to keep the peace of her land.[33] In accordance with the oath, the main business of the Scone assembly was the setting up of a provisional government.[34] The decisions taken, which were both careful and astute, make nonsense of any belief that after King Alexander's death Scotland disintegrated into anarchy. The realm was to be governed by six custodes, 'wardens' or (as it is usual to call them nowadays) 'Guardians'. This body was made up of two representatives of the earls, Alexander Comyn of Buchan and Duncan of Fife, two representatives of the bishops, William Fraser of St Andrews and Robert Wishart of Glasgow, and two representatives of the barons, John Comyn of Badenoch and James the Stewart. Not only was this division very much in keeping with thirteenth-century constitutional ideas, it also met the problem posed by the traditional division of the kingdom, since the first three magnates named above had special responsibility for the older 'Scotia', Scotland north of Forth, and the other three had similar responsibility for the south.[35] In electing Duncan of Fife, a young and inexperienced man, the assembly was really acknowledging the seniority of his earldom; in electing the Stewart it took into account the century-old primacy of the stewardship among the household offices. It appointed the two leading prelates of the Scottish church, and its choice of the two Comyns recognized the enormous influence of the most powerful baronial family in the land. Constitutionally impeccable, the election was also politically prudent. If the Maid of Norway should die and Queen Yolande not bear a child, the throne would be open to competition from a number of claimants. Of these the two strongest would be Robert Bruce, lord of Annandale, and John Balliol of Barnard Castle. It was clearly unwise to make either of these men a Guardian, but Bishop Fraser and the two Comyns supported Balliol (whose sister was John Comyn's wife), while Bishop Wishart, the Stewart, and, probably, Earl Duncan were supporters of Bruce.

According to a report preserved by Walter Bower, the Scone parliament appointed three envoys (the bishop of Brechin, the abbot of Jedburgh and Sir Geoffrey de Moubray[36]) to seek out Edward I in Gascony and ask for his advice and protection with regard to the Scottish kingdom and the Liberty of Penrith. The envoys set off on August 7th, found the English king at Saintes, and on November 25th, at Clackmannan, reported back to the Guardians, whom they found dealing with the difficult and delicate problem of the pregnancy of Queen Yolande, then lodged in Stirling Castle.[37] Ignored by most if not all modern historians, this high-powered mission in the summer of 1286 shows that the Scots leaders were anxious from the outset of the Maid's minority to enlist Edward I's support. But it tells against any notion that they were ready to concede, or Edward to demand, superior lordship over Scotland.

The situation which faced the Guardians was full of dangers and difficulty. Scotland was a feudal kingdom and her people were feudally minded. The members of the ruling class were bound closely to the Crown by social custom and the obligations of military service in virtue of which they held their land. A great deal of land, indeed most of the more fertile land, was held by knight-service and organized into baronies and knights' fees. The majority of the men so holding were men of fairly small substance, perhaps tenants-in-chief, more often freemen who held their estates of one or other of the great magnates. Whether tenants-in-chief or sub-tenants, many were holders of only single knight's fees or less. As such they were not separated from the peasantry, townsmen or lesser freemen of the country-side by any unbridgeable gulf, though in Scotland the fundamental medieval class distinction between noble and non-noble birth and rank was clearly understood. The Crown acted as the linchpin of this small society of men who were free and self-sufficient, yet at the same time feudally very conservative. Nothing and no one could be an adequate substitute for the king. If for some compelling reason the throne must be left vacant, the kingdom could only resolve itself into a collective entity, into the uni-versality of its freemen, or, in thirteenth-century language, into the 'community of the realm of Scotland' (*communitas regni Scotie*). Of course there was such a 'community' even when a king was on the throne, but in normal times, with an adult and vigorous rulers, the community would fade into the background. The king would take the initiative, would act or give orders as he thought best. In serious matters he would naturally take the advice of his council; but this council, in the theory of the time, was no other than a representation of the wider community.

Ideas of this sort had already been adumbrated in 1261 and now on Alexander III's death they sprang at once to the forefront. The Guardians invariably styled themselves 'appointed by common counsel' or 'elected by the community of the realm'.[38] The symbol of all government, the essential mark of authority, was the seal. The Guardians had a remarkable seal cut for their use, showing on one side a shield of the royal arms, on the other the figure of Saint Andrew on his cross.[39] The background or 'field' of these emblems, evenly sown with trefoils, repeated the design of the late king's seal and emphasized continuity with the immediate past. The seal bore two significant inscriptions, the first descriptive, the second emotional: 'the seal of Scotland appointed for the government of the kingdom' and 'Saint Andrew be leader of the compatriot Scots'.[40] While thus expressing the idea of the community of the realm, the Guardians were also at pains to appear as delegates or trustees of the Crown and the young queen. This we can most clearly see if we look forward a few years to the Treaty of Birgham (July 1290), entered into between Edward I and the community of the realm of Scotland led by the Guardians.[41] In this it was provided that once the Maid of Norway was made queen in the accustomed manner a seal should be cut for her with the usual arms and inscription of the name of the king of Scotland only. All relics, charters, privileges and muniments touching the Scottish 'royal dignity' and kingship were to be guarded securely within the realm of Scotland until the queen should have an heir, and in the meantime nothing pertaining to the 'royal dignity' was to be alienated or placed under subjection. But the Guardians' care for the rights and duties of the Crown had shown itself much earlier than this, especially in keeping the peace and in the defence of the realm, royal tasks *par excellence*. For example, James the Stewart, one of the Guardians, declared that public necessity had forced him to override Melrose Abbey's exemption from wapinschaws and military aid in Kyle 'because the peace and tranquillity of the realm were disturbed after King Alexander's death and the state was threatened by conflict'.[42] This must have been in line with a general instruction, for before Whitsun (May 25th) 1287, Earl Malise of Strathearn had raised men from among the tenants of Inchaffray Abbey 'to uphold the peace and tranquillity of the realm of Scotland'.[43] A writ preserved only in a later formulary possibly gives the gist of peace-keeping orders sent out at this time by the Guardians.[44]

In 1286 the gravest threat to the peace of Scotland came from Scotsmen, especially in the south-west, where it so happened that the two noblemen with the strongest claims to the throne, Balliol and Bruce, were both very powerful. Robert Bruce, lord of Annandale, and his son Robert, who held the earldom of Carrick in right of his wife Marjorie, gathered an armed force and seized the royal castles of Dumfries and Wigtown, and the lord of Galloway's castle at Buittle.[45] The revolt can only have been meant to strengthen the Bruce position *vis-à-vis* John Balliol, whose mother's lordship of Galloway – Wigtownshire and Kirkcudbright – was already hedged in by Bruce the elder in Annandale and Bruce the younger in Carrick, and stood to be encircled completely if the Bruces controlled Dumfries and the road north through Nithsdale. It has even been argued that when on September 20th, 1286, at Turnberry (the chief castle of Carrick) the Bruces, James the Stewart, two Scottish earls, the lord of Islay and several dependants entered into a 'band' or sworn agreement to support the earl of Ulster and Thomas de Clare against their adversaries, Bruce the elder made this the occasion of a deliberate claim to the Crown.[46] But the band merely saves the fealty of all parties to the king of England and to that person (man or woman) who shall obtain the kingdom of Scotland 'by reason of the blood of the late King Alexander'. With Queen Yolande possibly pregnant and Margaret of Norway not even in Scotland, still less formally enthroned, this cautious reservation is understandable. Whatever the grounds for Bruce's claim to the throne, they could not conceivably be 'by reason of the blood of King Alexander'.[47] The stir in the south west seems to have been put down peaceably, but it was an ugly defiance of the 'community of the realm'. More particularly, it showed that in the troubles which lay ahead the family of Bruce would not be content to cultivate its own garden.

⊙ *Seat of Sheriffdom*

Ⓔ *Earldom*

0   20   40   60   80
Miles

ORKNEY
(To Norway)

CAITHNESS
Ⓔ

SUTHERLAND
Ⓔ

LEWIS

HARRIS

N. UIST

S. UIST

ARRA

RUM

EIGG

COLL

TIREE

MULL

JURA

ISLAY

KINTYRE

ARRAN

ANTRIM

MAN

(To Scotland)

R O S S
Ⓔ
Dingwall ⊙   *Cromarty*

Inverness ⊙   *Nairn*   *Forres* *Elgin*   *Banff* ⊙

BUCHAN
Ⓔ

M O R A Y

BADENOCH

M A R
Ⓔ

Aberdeen ⊙

MEARNS

Kincardine ⊙

LOCHABER

GARMORAN

SKYE

D r u m a l b a n

The Mounth

Forfar ⊙

ATHOLL
Ⓔ

ANGUS
Ⓔ

A R G Y L L

LORNE

STRATHEARN
Ⓔ

Perth ⊙
Ⓔ FIFE   *Cupar* ⊙

MENTEITH
Ⓔ

Auchterarder ⊙

LENNOX

Stirling ⊙

Kinross ⊙

Clackmannan ⊙

Dumbarton ⊙

DUNBAR OR MARCH
Ⓔ

Edinburgh ⊙

L O T H I A N

Lanark ⊙

Berwick ⊙

BUTE

CUNNINGHAM

KYLE

Peebles ⊙

Ayr ⊙

Selkirk ⊙   *Roxburgh* ⊙

The Forest

CARRICK
Ⓔ

Dumfries ⊙

GALLOWAY

Carlisle ⊙

Newcastle upon Tyne ⊙

Wigtown ⊙

2. Scotland at the end of the thirteenth century.

TWO

Bruce of Annandale

For more than two centuries before the office and title of Warden of the March had been thought of, the Bruce lords of Annandale had been keeping the western march of Scotland. There were then, as there are now, two main routes between Scotland and England, by the east coast and by the west. Unlike its modern counterpart, however, the western route in the middle ages did not cross the Esk and Sark and enter Scotland at Gretna. Individuals or small groups may have gone that way, but it was too boggy for large numbers of men with horses and waggons, who had instead to ford the upper Solway at low tide and reach the Scottish shore almost as far west as Annan. Alternatively, they might strike eastward up the River Esk to enter Scotland near its junction with the Liddel Water, but this gave access only to difficult hilly roads through Eskdale or Liddesdale. For any strong force coming from the south and heading for central Scotland the natural route lay up the broad dale of Annan or further west, beyond Annandale, through Dumfries and Nithsdale. Annandale, therefore, was a gateway to Scotland, and its two castles of Annan and Lochmaben served as the gate.[1]

At the time the first Robert Bruce of Annandale was granted this territory by King David I, about 1124, it formed a border zone not only with England but also with Galloway. For King David the Galloway border needed watching as carefully as the English – indeed more carefully, towards the end of his reign, when he had won control of Cumberland and Westmorland. Galloway was a wild land which frightened and fascinated King David's French and English followers.[2] Around it he set a ring of military fiefs, each with its castle and its foreign lord.[3] Renfrew under the Breton, Walter Alan's son, first of the Stewarts; Cunningham under Hugh de Morville the constable; North Kyle, also placed under Walter the Stewart; South Kyle, reserved to the Crown; Annandale under Robert Bruce. Eastward again were Eskdale, the fief of Robert Avenel, and Liddesdale, given to Ranulf de Soules. These were men who had reason to serve King David with skill and loyalty. Most of them came from western Normandy and the borders of Brittany, a region in which David of Scotland, before gaining the throne, had been given lordship by Henry I of England. The first Robert Bruce – Robert de Brus – got his name from Brus or Bruis, now Brix, a few miles south of Cherbourg, where the family's home, 'Adam's Castle', has disappeared long since. Morville is not far from Brix; Soules – now Soulles – is farther south, near St Lô. The Stewart's family came from Dol, a short distance across the border in Brittany. The knightly families of this region supported Henry I in his early struggles, they won great reward at his hands, and they easily attached themselves to David of Scotland who was in many ways the most favoured of Henry's protégés.

Among those who gained a footing north of the border, this first Robert Bruce was the oldest and much the least dependent upon King David. He was lord of Cleveland in north Yorkshire, and he had long served King Henry as a 'justice', that is to say a chief royal agent, in the north of England. For all his origins in Normandy and his lordship over Annandale, this Robert Bruce must be seen as essentially a Yorkshireman, who on Cowton Moor in 1138, under Saint Peter's 'Standard' and encouraged by Archbishop Thurstan, fought stoutly even against King David to beat off a Scottish invasion. His body lies buried in the priory he founded at Guisborough. In Cleveland he was followed by his elder son Adam and a line of Yorkshire Bruces.

It was otherwise with his younger son, Robert, who fought against his father at the battle of the Standard and took his place among the great lords of Scotland. But in general the Scottish Bruces did not sever their connections with England. They held land in County Durham and family loyalty and piety kept their love for Guisborough Priory so strong that they never tried to found a monastery of their own in Annandale. Nevertheless, their lordship north of the border gave them Scottish interests and ambitions. Two of them married into the royal family, and from their castles of Annan and Lochmaben they ruled over a close-knit body of knights and lesser vassals who, whatever their origins, could hardly be distinguished from the other gentry of Scotland. From Gretna up to Moffat these 'knights of Annandale' – Johnstones, Herrieses, Jardines, Kirkpatricks, Dinwiddies, Crosbies and the rest – parcelled out the land amongst themselves and settled down as country gentlemen. They were a tough, prolific stock, sharing the management of their lord's fief, making sure of the best return from their estates, and prepared if need be to restrain the diocesan officials of Glasgow when their demands grew excessive.[4] Above all, in their conventional, feudal way they were loyal to the lord of Annandale. At the turn of the thirteenth and fourteenth centuries, when such territorial-cum-feudal loyalty was dying out in southern England and perhaps could not easily be paralleled in Scotland, the lairds of Annandale survived in stubborn anachronisms as a compactly united band.

At the date of Alexander III's death the Bruce lordship of Annandale, methodically divided into knight's fees and having its *caput* or legal and administrative headquarters at Lochmaben Castle, was already one of the older, more enduring features of the Scottish feudal landscape. It is against this background of five generations of Bruces and their knightly tenants that we should judge the value of the belief which even today is widely held that the Bruces were foreigners and strangers in Scotland, 'Norman' members of an alien 'Norman' baronage which had struck only shallow roots among a native Scottish population. This is the kernel of the 'Norman myth' in Scottish history, in its own small way as persistent and misleading as the 'Celtic myth'. A similar myth was once prevalent in books on English history also, but with a difference: a baronage which had wrested Magna Carta from the tyrant John and in the next century fought side by side with English bowmen against the French must have had its heart in the right place, even if its origins were in Normandy. Scottish historians, on the contrary, had no Magna Carta to deal with and had to explain the apparent fact that in the war of independence the nobility of Scotland were lacking in patriotism. If the nobility were not true patriots, it was some consolation to know that, after all, they were only Normans. In England, therefore, Norman ancestry was both picturesque and honourable, since the Normans had quickly effaced their defects of birth by acquiring the finest English qualities. In Scotland the Normans seemed suspect, willing to fight among themselves for the Crown and ready to betray their adopted country for the sake of estates across the border. In England the 'Norman myth' is long since dead. The Norman origin and character of the baronage of England from the Conquest to King John is never likely to be ignored or under-estimated by historians, but at the same time the thorough absorption of these men of Norman and other continental stock into a distinctively English society has long been recognized, and it would occur to no English historian nowadays to describe as 'Norman' the baronage of King Edward I. It is high time the Scottish 'Norman myth' died likewise. There is absolutely no evidence whatever that families such as Murray, Olifard, Comyn, Lindsay, Stewart or Bruce – to name only the most prominent among scores with 'Norman' origin – thought of themselves or were considered by others as differing in any way that mattered from the other noble families of the Scottish kingdom. The Normans were past masters at taking on the colour of their surroundings and north of the border they had adapted themselves to a Scottish coloration some generations before the time of Alexander III.

This of course did not mean that the Scots nobility were hostile to England and had no interests south of the border. On the contrary, many a Scottish landed family had, like the Bruces of Annandale, been founded by one of the younger sons of an established English family, and many Scots lords married the daughters, sometimes the heiresses, of English barons. Not only was family feeling strong, there was no barrier to inheritance on either side of the border, and marriage itself involved the transfer of land. It is not surprising that in 1286 a large amount of land in England was held by men and women who were normally domiciled in Scotland as subjects of the Scottish king, while in Scotland a proportionately even larger amount was held by English landowners. Nothing could be further from the truth than to suppose that it was only Scotsmen of 'Norman' descent who held English land. Along with more obviously 'Anglo-Norman' barons like Balliol and

Umfraville there were Scottish earls like Atholl, Buchan, Fife and Mar who either held or laid claim to estates in England. On the other hand, several Scots magnates whose continental origins were indisputable, such as Soules and the Stewart, owned little or no property south of the border.[5]

Robert Bruce, the fifth lord of Annandale and grandfather of the future king, was born *c.* 1220 and succeeded his father in 1245. Among the nobility of Scotland in the 1280s he may not have been a typical figure, but there was certainly nothing exotic or unnatural about the position he filled. His father was third in descent from the first Bruce of Annandale. His mother, Isabel, was the second daughter of Earl David, the youngest of King David I's three grandsons.[6] His background – it is the key to much of his grandson's conduct in the struggle with England – was at once aristocratic and royal. This Robert Bruce is known to history as the 'Competitor' or the 'Claimant', from the last phase of his career, when he staked nearly everything on a bid to become king of Scots. Contemporaries knew him as 'Robert the Noble' and before his bid for the throne he had already lived a long life rich in experience of high places, hard work and excitement. In 1237 the death of his uncle John of Scotland put his mother in possession of a third part of the vast Honour of Huntingdon and a third of the rich lordship which Earl David had held in Scotland, a lordship which included Garioch in Aberdeenshire and the growing burgh of Dundee.[7] All this property belonged to Robert Bruce by 1252.[8]

Apparently in 1238 – if we may believe a story which comes only from a Bruce source – King Alexander II, still childless and not yet married to Marie de Couci, caused Robert Bruce to be designated as his heir in a formal parliament of the magnates.[9] At that date, one year after John of Scotland's death, Bruce was the man nearest to the royal line. In the uncertain state of the law of succession to the throne, it is not impossible that the Scots magnates should have declared their preference for a man rather than a woman. But in 1238 or thereabouts Hugh Balliol was born,[10] the first grandson of the eldest of Earl David's daughters and surely a clear challenger of any son of younger daughters. And in any event, within a few years of the parliament which acknowledged Bruce as heir (if it ever met) the king's second wife had given birth to a son. In the meantime, in May 1240, Bruce himself married. His wife, Isabel de Clare, 'a tocherless lass wi' a lang pedigree', brought as her dowry a single Sussex manor.[11] But she was a daughter of the earl of Gloucester, a niece of the Earl Marshal. Now, by marriage as well as by descent from his mother, Bruce belonged to the small circle of the greatest aristocratic families of England.

During the fifties and sixties of the thirteenth century Robert Bruce was deeply involved in English politics. He was for some time governor of Carlisle castle.[12] Although the belief that he served in England as a royal judge is false, being based on confusion between Bruce and a more obscure

Robert 'de Briwes', the first Chief Justice of King's Bench,[13] nevertheless Bruce figured prominently in the disturbed period of baronial reform after 1258. In the relatively peaceful Scotland of Alexander III his affairs could no doubt be left to his son and other trusted agents. England was a different matter. The country was in turmoil, rent asunder for some years by a bitter civil war which brought bloodshed, disinheritance and the countrywide destruction of property. As long as the English baronage was largely united against Henry III, Bruce was on their conservative wing; when they split, he became a steadfast royalist. In April 1264 along with other Scots and northern English lords, he led a large force of men-at-arms to Nottingham to support King Henry and his son the Lord Edward.[14] A few months later the royalist army was smashed by Simon de Montfort at Lewes. Along with the king and the Lord Edward, Bruce was taken prisoner. His son, prudently left in Scotland, hurried south to arrange for his ransom and release. There was great slaughter at Lewes, but only (says an English chronicler) of 'insignificant men, common folk, especially Scots'[15] It is not hard to imagine the peasant lads from Annandale and Nithsdale along with highlanders from Galloway and Badenoch, unarmoured and bewildered, cut down by Montfort's fierce young knights or, if they tried to flee through the unfamiliar Sussex countryside, hunted down by the villagers. *Their* ransoms would not be paid. When Scots infantry next encountered English cavalry, more than thirty years later, Edward of England was on the other side. Nevertheless, they were to acquit themselves well, better, in fact, than Edward, with his memories of Lewes, could ever have expected.

Whatever else may be said of Bruce the Competitor, his stamina was astounding. At the age of fifty he left England in company with the Lord Edmund, Henry III's younger son, bound for Tunis and the Holy Land.[16] The crusade was brief and inglorious, but it acquainted the crusaders with the great shift of power in the Near East and even brought them into contact with the Mongol khan of Persia. It must have impressed on all of them the place of western Christendom in a larger world. On the one hand, Scotsmen like the knight Alexander Seton and his young esquire, who fell into Arab hands,[17] could come from their far north-western country and take their place beside the chivalry of Christendom. On the other hand, the crusaders' experience of the Mediterranean with its conflicting races and nationalisms, its rich, opportunist merchant states like Genoa and Venice, its even more opportunist kings like Charles of Anjou, must surely have given their minds some hint of social and political patterns very different from those familiar in their own corner of Europe.

On his way home from the east, probably in 1272, Robert Bruce paid a visit to the great Cistercian abbey of Clairvaux in Burgundy.[18] His purpose was to appease the anger of a man who had been dead for 120 years and to lift a curse which, if not oppressive, must have disturbed the lords of Annandale. The great Irish church reformer Maelmaedoc Ua Morgair (St Malachy O'Moore), while staying at Annan in 1140 or thereabouts as the guest of the second Robert Bruce of Annandale, had asked that a condemned robber's life should be spared, and was outraged when his host secretly hanged the man after promising to reprieve him.[19] The terms of the curse which Malachy then uttered on the house of Bruce and the town of Annan are unknown, but it has been well said that the imprecation of an angry Irish saint would have been 'thorough, comprehensive and devastating'.[20] The Bruces did not wither, but it is certain that somewhere about the turn of the twelfth and thirteenth centuries their chief castle, the Mote of Annan, was half washed away by a tremendous spate and the lords of Annandale were forced to move their headquarters to Lochmaben.[21] St Malachy had died at Clairvaux and he was buried in the abbey church.[22] We can picture Bruce the Competitor praying before his tomb. He gave the abbey an endowment of land in Annandale to pay for lights to burn for ever at the shrine of the Blessed Malachy.[23] We can only guess at Bruce's reasons for wishing so strongly for reconciliation. On May 3rd, 1273, very soon after he got home, he married for the second time, and the marriage may not have been welcome to his family.[24] His second wife, twice a widow, was Christian Ireby, daughter of a near neighbour, William Ireby, a Cumberland knight. Before taking a step which his son seems to have resented, Bruce may have thought it right to make his peace with the wrathful but holy Irishman.

Bruce's son and heir – the fifth Robert Bruce to hold the lordship of Annandale and the second of the three with whom we are chiefly concerned in this book – had meanwhile turned the family interests westward and gained a Scottish earldom. Neil, earl of Carrick – his name seems rather Celtic Niall than Norman Nigel – died in 1256, the last direct male descendant of Fergus, lord of Galloway in King David's reign. His heir was his daughter Marjorie, married to Adam of Kilconquhar.[25] Adam died at Acre on the crusade from which the elder Bruce returned safely, and about 1272 his widow married Bruce the younger who thus became, *jure uxoris*, the earl of Carrick.

This was indeed a marriage of Celtic with Anglo-Norman Scotland, though hardly in the protagonists themselves, since Marjorie was descended from Henry I,[26] her husband from Malcolm Canmore. But Annandale was settled by people of English or Anglo-Scandinavian speech, and thoroughly feudalized. Carrick was historically an integral part of Galloway, and though the earls had achieved some feudalization, the society of Carrick at the end of the thirteenth century remained emphatically Celtic. In acquiring Carrick the Bruces became involved in two further commitments: a close connexion with Ireland and an ancient rivalry between Carrick and the men of Galloway proper – modern Wigtownshire and Kirkcudbright. The Turnberry Band of 1286 is to be seen as a resumption of interference in the affairs of Ireland by which the lords of Carrick had profited hugely ever since the Norman conquest of Ulster.[27] The Countess Marjorie's grandfather Duncan, first earl of Carrick, had a grant from King John of England of the town of Ulderford (i.e. Larne), with the land stretching north from there to Glenarm. Earl Duncan in turn granted this estate to Thomas de Mandeville, ancestor of the Mandevilles of Antrim. Bruce the future king could thus look across from his earldom of Carrick to the Irish coast and rest his gaze on land of which he himself was feudal lord.[28]

It was not only the lords of Carrick who could win and exploit lands across the North Channel. Their rivals the lords of Galloway played the same game even more successfully.[29] The feud which went back at least as far as the time of Gilbert and Uhtred of Galloway, the two sons of Fergus, was still alive a hundred years later. The men of the south-west would not have forgotten that Uhtred had been savagely murdered on his brother's orders, nor that Gilbert had been ousted by Uhtred's heirs from land which he believed to be rightfully his. Marjorie of Carrick, who married Robert Bruce, was Gilbert's great-granddaughter; the great-granddaughter of Uhtred was the lady Dervorguilla, who married John Balliol.

Some two years after Bruce the younger's marriage to Marjorie of Carrick, and barely more than a year after the Competitor's second marriage, Robert Bruce the sixth, the future king, was born to the Countess Marjorie, probably at Turnberry Castle, on July 11th, 1274.[30] He may fairly be called a Scotsman, born among Scots. He was assuredly much more a Scotsman than his great adversary, Edward I, was an Englishman. It has been said that the Bruces were 'not themselves bred in the Gaelic tradition',[31] but the truth seems to be that Robert Bruce's upbringing was coloured by a mixture of traditions, of which the Gaelic tradition of Carrick and the west must have been one. In what is perhaps the earliest recorded appearance of the future king, we find him witnessing a deed of Alexander Macdonald of Islay in company with his father the earl of Carrick, the bishop of Argyll, the vicar of Arran and a clerk of Kintyre, as well as various personages of the earldom of Carrick.[32]

When Alexander III died, young Robert Bruce was well on his way to manhood. His birth, and for all we know his character as a boy and a youth, may have given a special stimulus to his tough old grandfather as he prepared to put forward his claim to the throne. The Competitor would hardly have fought so keenly for his spineless, colourless son: but already in the youngest Robert Bruce he must have beheld more fiery mettle.

In 1289 the number of Guardians was reduced by death to four. Inexplicably, the young earl of Fife was murdered at Pitpullox, two miles west of Brechin, by his own kinsmen the Abernethys along with Sir Walter de Percehay.[33] The earl of Buchan died full of years and honour.[34] There was no breakdown in government. The four remaining Guardians, Comyn of Badenoch, the Stewart, and the two bishops, Fraser and Wishart, did not formally replace the two earls, though they may have co-opted the assistance of Sir Andrew Murray of Petty and of Matthew Crambeth, who with their approval and possibly on their nomination had become bishop of Dunkeld in 1288.[35] Apart from day-to-day administration, which seems to have gone on as usual, the Guardians began the negotiations with England and Norway for the marriage of Queen Margaret, now six years of age, to the five-year-old Edward of Caernarvon, who had been King Edward's heir since the death of his elder brother Alfonso in 1284.[36] If all went well the Crowns of England and Scotland would both be held by the heir of this marriage. But there is no evidence, on the Scottish side at least, of any enthusiasm for a more organic union. The whole course of the negotiations which culminated in the marriage agreement called the Treaty of Birgham, July 18th, 1290 (confirmed by Edward I at Northampton on August 28th),[37] shows the Guardians anxious above all to do nothing which might impair the 'royal dignity' of Scotland or threaten the integrity of the Scottish kingdom. They asked that Margaret should be given certain lands in England as dower, that the Scottish kingdom should be 'separate, apart and free in itself without subjection to the English kingdom', and that there should be no fresh fortification of the English side of the border.[38] The business of Margaret's marriage and of union (in some sense) with England was too serious a responsibility to be borne by the four Guardians on their own. Not only were all their documents authenticated by the seal of regency, the 'common seal' or 'seal of Scotland' as it was called, but the Guardians were careful to associate with themselves the 'good men' of the realm.[39] By this they meant the men of substance and standing, the responsible men, the acknowledged leaders of the community as a whole. The words *bone gent* (singular) and *bones genz* (plural) which they used in French documents were translated by the Latin phrases *bona gens* and *probi homines*.[40] This last was even more of a technical term in Scotland than in England, for ever since the time of David I the kings of Scots had addressed their public pronouncements not, as did the English kings, to 'their faithful men' (*fidelibus suis*) but to 'all their good men' (*omnibus probis hominibus suis*). At its fullest the phrase no doubt covered all the king's free subjects; but essentially it referred to the king's substantial and responsible subjects, men of the landholding class, burgesses and beneficed clergy. Although these phrases, 'community of the realm' and 'good men', denoted political ideas they were not mere abstractions. The letter in which the Scots declared to King Edward their assent to the marriage and readiness to negotiate (Birgham, March 17th, 1290)[41] went in the names of the four Guardians, ten bishops, twelve earls, twenty-three abbots, eleven priors and forty-eight barons, speaking for the whole community of Scotland. This meant that the Guardians had been able to rally support from the bishops and earls and a thoroughly representative body of barons and heads of religious houses.

The Treaty of Birgham–Northampton[42] was the high-water-mark of this common endeavour by Guardians and community, but, as we shall see, it was not the last occasion on which their voice was heard. The treaty envisaged two feudal kingdoms, England and Scotland, ruled separately though in harmony by a king and queen respectively, whose sovereignties would remain distinct. The Scottish kingdom was to remain, as the Scots had stipulated, separate, free in itself and without subjection, and on certain vital points this freedom was explicitly defined. Elections of the clergy in Scotland were to be free of external interference, tenants-in-chief of the Scots Crown need do homage only in Scotland, persons who in Scotland had been accused of crime or sued at law should not have to answer in a court outside the country. The only valid symbol of Scottish government was a seal of regency, which was to be replaced by a new seal 'of the king of Scotland only' as soon as, but not before, Queen Margaret had been properly installed at Scone. The customary officers of the Scottish Crown should remain, and no writ of common law or letter of special favour should be issued save according to the accustomed process of the 'king's chapel' (i.e., the Scottish chancery) and of the Scottish realm. The emblems of Scottish royalty were to be kept under the seals of the great lords until the queen had given birth to a living child. No parliament dealing with Scottish affairs was to be held outside Scotland, and there was to be no taxation of the Scots except for Scottish needs. At King Edward's expense the treaty was to be confirmed by the pope, and the papal confirmation was to be handed to the community of the realm of Scotland for safe keeping.[43] The treaty has often been praised as a document of wise statesmanship and patriotism, but it was also something else. It was essentially a cautious, protective document. Temporary rulers of a conservative feudal kingdom, the Guardians were reluctant to take the full responsibility which could be borne only by king and council; and they were suspicious of English encroachment.[44]

The atmosphere in the summer of 1290 was hopeful, even joyful. There were shadows, one perhaps too faint for most Scots to notice. On June 4th, Edward I placed the Isle of Man in the charge of Walter Huntercombe, and took the Manx community into his protection.[45] It may be that the men of Man, who would remember well the great Manx revolt suppressed by Alexander III fifteen years earlier,[46] welcomed this action. It may also be true that since 1286 they had not enjoyed good government. It is only curious that their petition to the English king, in which they declared unanimously that they stood in need of protection by Edward as their lord, was made not before but after the English king had come to the same conclusion.[47] In his direct dealings with the Scots Edward I had not been high-handed; he had behaved reasonably. Yet now he had seized an island which was part of the Scottish kingdom and happened also to be strategically important to England, and he had done so apparently without consulting or informing the Guardians of Scotland, several months before he knew of the death of the Maid of Norway, the sovereign lady of Man.

A step which King Edward took at the very moment of ratifying Birgham (Northampton, 28th August, 1290) may have seemed more obviously sinister than his seizure of the Isle of Man. Going out of his way to emphasize the threat to the peace and tranquillity of the Scottish realm, he wrote to the Guardians to announce his appointment of the bishop of Durham, Anthony Bek, as lieutenant in that realm of his son Edward and of Queen Margaret, although they were not yet married.[48] The letter is unmistakably Edwardian in its mixture of courteous legality and thinly veiled menace. Bek is appointed to be lieutenant of the young couple and also 'to reform and set to rights the aforesaid realm in conjunction with the remaining Guardians, by the counsel of the prelates and magnates', although as far as we know the Scots had not requested that their country should be reformed. 'After admitting the bishop kindly and courteously', the king's letter concluded, 'for the purposes mentioned, you are to be obedient to him and put yourselves at his bidding in all matters needful for the government and peaceful state of the kingdom (of Scotland)'. Anthony Bek was an ambitious man, a powerful and militant prelate who ruled almost as a king within his own bishopric. His northernmost territory, Norhamshire, lay along the eastern Scottish border where it was conspicuously undefended, and his massive castle at Norham constituted a permanent threat to Scottish security which was hardly offset by Roxburgh and Berwick. Bek's appointment as lieutenant, not provided for in the cautious terms of Birgham, must have been unwelcome in Scotland generally, however much it pleased his friends.

The bad news from the north reached the Scottish government early in October.[49] Queen Margaret had died in Orkney on her way to Scotland, and her body had been taken back to Bergen for burial. There was, as we have seen, no undisputed successor and the news of her death set in train a struggle for the throne between a number of claimants of whom two were of outstanding importance: Robert Bruce the elder (who now earned his title of 'the Competitor') and John Balliol. The magnates were gathering at Perth, presumably for Queen Margaret's inauguration at Scone. Robert Bruce, in his seventieth year or thereabouts, had arrived unexpectedly with a strong body of armed men, and it was rumoured that his friends the earls of Mar and Atholl were raising their forces.[50] At the same time John Balliol, whose mother's death in the previous January had made him lord of Galloway, was styling himself 'heir of Scotland' and making private agreements with his friend and neighbour Bishop Bek, who as we have seen, was now King Edward's chief representative in Scotland.[51] It looked as though the guardianship would collapse and the question of succession be settled by open war between the claimants.

To the Scots as a whole such a prospect must have been detestable.

Bishop Fraser of St Andrews went so far as to write to the English king
(October 7th, 1290) asking for his intervention[52] – an act for which later
Scottish opinion has been less than fair to him. The bishop's news was that
the queen might be dead, though some said she had recovered. Bruce and
his friends were assembling under arms. If John Balliol should come to
Edward, the king would be well advised to reach an understanding with
him. If the queen died, Edward was urged to come to the border to prevent
war. This would enable the lords to keep their oath[53] and the rightful heir
could succeed peacefully, as long as he was ready to abide by Edward's
counsel. What has really stuck in the throats of later Scottish writers is the
fact that Fraser was an avowed Balliol man, but we must realize that in 1290
it was not in the least unpatriotic to be a Balliol man. Patriotism transcended
the question of succession, yet if that question were not settled quickly and
permanently, the kingdom, already virtually kingless for five years, might
well fall apart and patriotism become meaningless.

After the winter of 1290–91 and recovery from the sorrow of his wife's
death, King Edward moved swiftly. Each individual step he took may have
irked or dismayed the Scots, but still they welcomed his intervention, for the
alternative was civil war. As Bishop Fraser said in his letter, the community
was disturbed and losing hope. After some initial sword-rattling the
claimants themselves were probably not unwilling to have their case tried
under King Edward's powerful supervision. Whether they would all have
voluntarily submitted to his judgement as their overlord, had he not made it
quite clear that no other terms would satisfy him, is something we cannot
tell. Some would probably have done so, and others adhered to the
community. Edward I was almost certainly less concerned about the
individual competitors than about ensuring the peace of Scotland during
the vacancy of the throne and obtaining an authoritative admission by the
Scots of his feudal overlordship over the Scottish kingdom. Because of the
subsequent turn of events the legend rapidly established itself in Scotland
and survives, indeed, to the present day that Balliol was a puppet nominated
by King Edward to the Scots kingship in defiance of a national belief that
Bruce had the better claim. There is no evidence to support the first part of
this legend, and the second part is untrue. The legend obscures the true and
therefore really damaging charge against King Edward that he first took
advantage of the leaderless state of Scotland to extract something
approaching the admissions he required, and then harried the new king into
a relationship with himself which emphasized his new-found feudal
superiority in the most humiliating manner possible.

The spring of 1291 baffles the historian of Anglo-Scottish relations
though the comparative absence of contemporary record. No official document survives to prove or even suggest either that the Scots formally invited
Edward I to intervene or that Edward took the initiative himself. There is
good evidence that an English mission led by Bishop Bek came to Scotland

in January, 1291.[54] A well-informed but not unprejudiced English chronicler writes that the Scots asked not simply for Edward's advice but actually for his ruling (*ordinatio*, 'ordinance', 'decision').[55] We may at least accept that the crisis was discussed in Scotland at a full council or parliament, and that the Scots agreed with the English that a joint parliament to settle the succession should be convened for the early summer. There is explicit evidence that delegates were called to this parliament from the universities of Oxford and Cambridge [56] and it can be safely inferred that a good many English church notables and lay magnates were also summoned. This and other evidence adds up convincingly to proof that on the English side the assembly called for Norham on 6th May was an English parliament.[57] We can hardly doubt, in view of the solemnity of the occasion, that the Scots participation was also parliamentary. Had it been less formal and official than this, the encounter between Edward I and the Scots would have been even more unequal, and what is more, glaringly unequal, than it turned out to be. But weight should surely be given to an admittedly late (and odd) text purporting to be dated at 'Northampton' (read Norham) on 20th May AD 1291 'during a session of a parliament of both England and Scotland'.[58] It would be remarkable if the Scots plenipotentiaries and negotiators, who had already been through the long-drawn-out process of Salisbury–Birgham in 1289–90, had agreed to come to the border in May 1291 with any less authority than that of a Scottish parliament or (since there was no sovereign) an assembly of the estates.

There is little doubt that King Edward did not get all he wanted from the Scots in the summer of 1291. It is reasonable to infer that he wished for recognition of his feudal suzerainty from the community of the realm of Scotland in its fullest, most solemn, most representative character; the Guardians, prelates, earls and barons, and the whole community, speaking with the collective voice with which they had spoken in support of the Treaty of Birgham only ten months earlier. Edward I reached the bishop of Durham's great castle of Norham on the Tweed about May 5th, 1291.[59] He gave the Guardians and other Scots leaders – *les haus hommes de Escoce* – an assurance that if they came over the Tweed to meet him this crossing of the border to treat of Scottish affairs should not be turned to their prejudice or that of anyone in the Scottish realm.[60] When they appeared he confronted them with the demand for recognition of his suzerainty, once again stressing the need to establish peace and tranquillity.[61] The Scots asked for a delay to consider their reply. They were given three weeks, a short time indeed, but presumably the most that Edward could allow them, since he had summoned an armed force from the northern shires to meet him at Norham on June 3rd.[62] The king, framing his question characteristically as a skilled lawyer, had asked the Scots, not 'Am I the rightful suzerain of Scotland?' but 'Can you produce any evidence to show that I am *not* the rightful suzerain?' The reply of *les hauts hommes d'Escoce* to this demand came about

the end of May.[63] It was the last occasion on which the voice of the
community of the realm of Scotland was heard before enmity had succeeded
friendship between the two countries. Couched in courteous and memorable language, the reply, delivered as a letter written in French, thanked
King Edward for his great kindness towards the Scottish nation, and went
on to restate the king's claim to suzerainty and his promise to adjudge the
Scottish Crown to the rightful claimant. The letter continued:

> Sire, to this the responsible men [*la bone gent*] who have sent us here
> say that they know full well that you would not make so great a demand
> if you did not believe that you had good right to it; yet of any such right
> or demand made or used by yourself or your ancestors they know
> nothing. They answer, with such authority as they possess, that they
> have no power to reply in the absence of the lord [i.e., the king of Scots]
> to whom such a demand should be addressed and who could reply to it.
> For even if they did reply it would not increase your right nor take away
> from the right of their liege lord. But the responsible men of the
> kingdom are willing that whoever shall be king shall perform to you
> whatever right and law require, for he and no one else will have the
> power to do this. Meanwhile they can only refer to the oath they took
> after the death of the king [Alexander III],[64] saving your faith and
> theirs, and [? to the treaty] confirmed in your presence at North-
> ampton.[65]

It is known from English accounts, official and unofficial, that this reply
was given to King Edward 'in the name of the community of the realm of
Scotland'.[66] At the same time, no answer was given to him by the Guardians,
prelates, earls or barons as such, nor did the Scots furnish any evidence to
rebut the English claims.[67] Consequently, Edward's advisers said that the
reply contained 'nothing to the purpose',[68] and a modern historian has
called it 'evasive'.[69] But this surely is to miss the whole point which the
Scottish reply aimed to establish. It was a polite reminder to King Edward,
an expert in such matters, that in a feudal realm the most weighty decisions
affecting the very status of king and kingdom could be reached only by the
lawfully constituted king, acting with the council of his lieges. As the Scots
magnates said, even if they did give Edward an answer it could not validly
add to his rights or detract from the rights of the king of Scotland. King
Edward had been rummaging through the historical writings of England in
order to produce an extremely one-sided case in favour of his claim. It had
taken him a good deal longer than three weeks. Of course the Scots could
have done the same, but it would have been an irrelevant waste of time.
Because their answer gave no evidence, except to say that Edward's demand
was unprecedented, and no doubt because it was displeasing to the English
king, it was not enrolled upon the official record of the proceedings. Until
recently, all that was known of the reply was a brief summary in a less official
account.[70] As the Scots historian John Hill Burton wrote more than a

hundred years ago, 'though it did not seem to King Edward . . . to be to the point, yet would many people at the present day like to know what it was that the community of Scotland had to say against King Edward's demand'.[71] Time has now caught up with King Edward. In recent years, the late David Hunter Marshall and Professor Lionel Stones have brought to light the full text of the Scottish reply.[72] The older historians were under the impression that the 'community' meant the 'commonalty', the commons, as distinct from prelates and lords. The official record encouraged this mistake by its equivocal statement that King Edward was given no answer 'by' or 'in the name of' the magnates. It would be unfair to accuse the record of total dishonesty here, since to the clerks who compiled it the notion of the 'community of the realm' meaning the 'commons' would scarcely have been thinkable. It is clear enough both from the tenor and contents of the reply itself, and from the sense in which the word 'community' was used in contemporary Scottish documents, that the reply was as authoritative and official as King Edward could have received at the time, and his rejection of it out of hand now emerges clearly as the first thoroughly discreditable action in his dealings with the Scottish nation.

Foiled in his attempt to obtain the fullest possible recognition, Edward was successful in getting other recognitions which he evidently felt would serve his purpose. That he put pressure on the Guardians and the competitors to obtain them can hardly be contested. Both wanted the rightful claimant to be chosen quickly, and never was it more important that justice should not only be done but also be seen to be done. To Edward's legal and tidy mind the requirements were obvious. First, admission of his overlordship; second, physical control of Scotland, especially of the castles and strongpoints (this was both an expression of suzerainty and the necessary condition of a lawful tribunal); third, the tribunal itself, under his presidency, to decide between the claimants. During the first fortnight of June the majority of the competitors, among them Bruce and Balliol, issued formal instruments acknowledging King Edward's suzerainty and agreeing to abide by his judgement.[73] They also agreed that the king should be put in possession of the Scottish realm and especially of the royal castles. Since neither kingdom nor castles had been vested in the Competitors it is not easy to see what right they had to give them away.[74] In any case, their concession, far-reaching though it was, had not been unconditional. King Edward, while reserving his own rights as one of the competitors, promised the rest that within two months of awarding the Crown he would restore kingdom and castles to the rightful king, and that in future on the death of a king he would demand nothing but homage and the rights incidental to it.[75]

At what precise stage of the negotiations the English king was persuaded into this concession, and by whose urging, is impossible to say. Walter Bower has a story that when Edward confronted the Scots with his claim to suzerainty early in May, Robert Wishart, bishop of Glasgow, rebutted the

claim in words which echoed those put into Alexander III's mouth in 1278:
'the Scottish kingdom is not held in tribute or homage to anyone save God
alone', and went on (no doubt to Edward's exasperation) to quote the so-
called 'Prophecies of Gildas'.[76] Bower must have based his account on
record closely similar to that used by the Scots negotiators in the abortive
peace talks with the English envoys at Bamburgh in 1321. The record of
these talks, discovered in a manuscript at Córdoba by Dr Peter Linehan,[77]
gives a prominent place to Bishop Wishart in its narrative of the events of
1291. It reports Edward I as confronting the Scots inexorably with one of
three possible choices. They must concede his demand for overlordship,
which he had made as an assertion, not asked as a question; or they must
produce evidence to show that he was not their lawful overlord; or else they
must defend their independence by force of arms. Robert Wishart, according to this account, protested that even if the Scots nation, lacking any
lawfully appointed ruler, conceded Edward's suzerainty that could not bind
their ruler, once he had been appointed, nor add to Edward's right. As for
the second choice, the bishop objected that the Scots ought not to have to
prove a negative when positive proof of the English claim was contradicted
by their own laws (or rights). And Wishart concluded that it was not
compatible with the honour of so great a king as Edward I to invade and
attack a people so divided and defenceless. If he made such an attack his
declared vow to lead a crusade to the Holy Land would be nullified.

It is a striking fact that on June 14th Bishop Wishart, together with his
close colleague Bishop Crambeth of Dunkeld, caused to be drawn up and
issued under their respective seals an official copy of 'inspeximus' of
Edward's concession.[78] Along with this they included a copy of a declaration
that the competitors' recognition of Edward's overlordship had been made
with the consent of the Guardians – all named – and of the 'responsible men'
(les bones genz) of the realm.[79] No doubt this was intended to protect the
competitors in case they had acted ultra vires. There could be no clearer
demonstration that King Edward had the Scots in a cleft stick, and we can
almost see them squirming to escape the dilemma. It was very different from
the full and willing acknowledgement of overlordship which Edward surely
wished for and perhaps even expected. He had told the competitors – who,
after all, were only private men, very few of them Scotsmen – that there
would be no award unless they admitted his suzerainty. The competitors,
eager for an award, forthwith made the admission, but on certain important
conditions. At the same time, they sought to indemnify themselves with a
certificate that they had acted with the consent of the Guardians and probi
homines. Robert Wishart, one of the four Guardians (we may think that he
had much to do with the Treaty of Birgham and the community's letter of
May 1291), acting with a close colleague, saw fit to place on independent
record the concession made by Edward I and the indemnification of the
competitors.

From this point it was a short step for Edward to take over the government. The Guardians resigned their authority (June 11th?) and were
reappointed by the king with the addition of Brian FitzAlan of Bedale, an
English baron of more reputation than fortune.[80] They were no longer
'elected by the community' but 'appointed by the most serene prince, the
Lord Edward, by God's grace illustrious king of England, chief (or
superior) lord of Scotland'.[81] The seal of regency, however, continued in
use until judgement was given, though it was not always available to the
Guardians.[82] On November 19th, 1292, this fine symbol of independence
was broken in four pieces and these were carefully placed in the English
treasury 'lest, if the seal remained intact, doubts should arise about the
authenticity of documents, and as a sign of the king of England's full
sovereign lordship in the Scottish realm'.[83]

It is particularly regrettable that the official record of all these transactions, prepared for Edward I by his skilled notaries, the Norman John
Arthur of Caen and the Yorkshireman, Andrew of Tong, obscures, perhaps
of set purpose, the true course of events as they happened day by day. If we
try to pinpoint the precise moment at which the English king overcame
Scottish resistance to his demands for recognition, the surest guide is
probably given to us by the 'Rolls of Scotland' (*Rotuli Scotiae*), the earliest
entries on which are dated June 13th.[84] This record was carefully established by the English king and government to provide the documentation of
Scots affairs essential for their temporary administration of the northern
kingdom. To have begun the record before Edward I's rule over Scotland
was formally acknowledged would have overstepped legality, but once it
was acknowledged he or his officials are not likely to have delayed very long
before issuing and enrolling routine and other documents. But if this
apparently firm date is to be tied to Edward's take-over of the royal castles
we at once come up against a discrepancy in the notarial record. Some at
least, perhaps all, of the castle commanders refused to hand over their
castles to Edward on the grounds that they had not been entrusted with
them by the king of England but by King Alexander III, or the Guardians,
or the community of the realm of Scotland (*par la commune del reaume
d'Escoce*).[85] Of the four versions of Edward I's letter dealing with the
commanders, from which we learn these details, three date the surrender of
the castles 'Thursday *after* Saint Barnabas' (June 14th 1291), whereas the
fourth names the *previous* Thursday (June 7th). A compromise formula was
devised which allowed the commanders to give up their charges with a clear
conscience. They had all taken an oath of allegiance to whoever should rule
Scotland through nearness of blood to the late king, and would now entrust
the castles to King Edward simply as one of the claimants acting on behalf of
all. The letter already mentioned, dealing with the commanders, announces
a surrender in terms of this formula and is itself dated June 12th, the day
after the Guardians had agreed to transfer their authority over the castles to

the English king.[86]

A possible resolution of these difficulties and discrepancies might run as follows. The first week of June was occupied with English rejections of the Scots' reply to Edward I's initial demand for recognition as overlord, and with choosing assessors who would support the claims of Bailliol and Bruce, the strongest of the competitors. The three days from 8th to 10th June – allowing for the due observance of the Whitsun feast – are likely to have been taken up by hard talking between the Guardians and the English king's councillors, the former trying to salvage as much as possible of the treaty of Birgham, the latter insisting on an English overlordship so exalted that Edward I was to be styled not merely *superior dominus* (*soverein seignur*, 'sovereign lord') but *superior et directus dominus*, a sovereign lord endowed with overriding authority.[87] By June 11th, Saint Barnabas' Day, the Guardians seem to have capitulated, although they won important concessions. On the following day a batch of letters was promulgated referring to the Scottish surrender of the castles as though it had already taken place. An actual surrender on Thursday 14th would square well with the enrolled orders of Edward I the date of which, June 13th, is not in doubt,[88] directing the royal castles to be handed over to certain named individuals – orders which would scarcely make sense if the castles had been yielded as early as Thursday 7th.

The Scots' effort to salvage something from the treaty of Birgham is another feature of these negotiations to which the notarial record does scant justice. Indeed, if it were not for the early version of these events preserved in the sixteenth-century MS. now in Glasgow University Library we should have very little evidence at all of activity on the Scottish side. That manuscript contains copies of the three vitally important declarations made by King Edward, first (June 12th) that the award of the throne would be made within the kingdom of Scotland,[89] second (June 6th) that Edward would maintain the customary laws, liberties and usages of Scotland pending the award, saving only the homage of whoever should become king,[90] and third (June 12th) that Edward promised to restore the Scottish realm, including the royal castles to the successful claimant within two months of the award, provided that homage was rendered to the king of England by the new king for his kingdom, along with whatever belonged to homage, and that the sovereign lordship over Scotland and whatever belonged to it, should be reserved to the king of England.[91] The undertaking to maintain Scotland's laws and liberties is repeated. The penalty in case of default was a fine of £100,000 to be paid to the holy see in support of a crusade. Moreover the relics, charters and other muniments touching the 'royal dignity' of Scotland were to be placed in safe locations, under good guard, secured by the seals of custodians nominated by King Edward from among the noblest and most faithful of the Scottish realm. The claimants were promised that the trial of their claims would not be unduly delayed.

Finally, Edward promised that in future, on the death of any king of Scots leaving an heir whose rights were uncontested, no king of England would demand rights of custody and marriage or possession of the Scottish realm, but only homage and sovereign lordship. Possession and jurisdiction would be demanded only in the case of a contested succession.

The last two declarations incorporate substantial passages from the treaty of Birgham, in places lifted more or less word for word. They do not, admittedly, say that the Scottish realm is to remain separate, free in itself and without subjection to England, nor do they restrict business concerning Scotland to Scottish parliaments and taxation of Scots to purely Scottish needs. In these respects the Edward I of 1291 stood in sharp contrast with the Edward I of 1290. It was therefore a remarkable achievement for the Scots to have wrung from the English king and council promises that crossing the Tweed to discuss the succession was not to prejudice their independence,[92] that the award of the crown would be made on Scottish soil,[93] that (here following Birgham) the rights, laws, usages, liberties and customs of Scotland, both of holy church and of secular society, should be preserved, and that the emblems of Scottish royalty were to be in the custody of responsible Scottish magnates.[94] That the negotiators of 1291 had their eyes fixed fairly closely on the text of Birgham is shown not only by these concessions but also by the fact that they employed the Scots terms 'letters of common right' and 'letters of grace' to distinguish the routine from the exceptional productions of the royal chancery,[95] they added, from Birgham, the ambiguous proviso that Edward I's rights 'on the border or *elsewhere*' should be safeguarded,[96] and finally they lifted from Birgham the penalty clause of £100,000 – so astronomically large as to be symbolic rather than realistic.

On Wednesday, June 13th, 1291, at Upsettlington opposite Norham, in a green meadow beside the Tweed, the Guardians and other magnates present swore fealty individually to King Edward as, according to the record, 'superior and direct' lord of the kingdom of Scotland.[97] Besides the four Scottish Guardians, the great men whose names were judged worthy of record were as follows: Mark, bishop of Sodor and Man; (Alan bishop of Caithness, chancellor of Scotland?); Robert Bruce of Annandale, John Balliol lord of Galloway, Robert Bruce earl of Carrick, Patrick of Dunbar earl of March, Donald earl of Mar, John Comyn earl of Buchan, John of Strathbogie earl of Atholl, Gilbert de Umfraville earl of Angus, Malcolm earl of Lennox, Walter Stewart earl of Menteith, William de Soules, John de Soules, Patrick Graham, Thomas Randolph, Willaim Sinclair, Ralph of Hadden, Alexander Balliol of Cavers, chamberlain of Scotland, William Comyn, John Stewart, Ingram de Umfraville, William Murray of Tulli-bardine, Henry Pinkney, Walter Burdon, Ralph Crawford and Henry Sinclair, 'knights and barons of the realm of Scotland'.

During the next month and a half, an appreciable number of lords, gentry, freeholders, burgesses and heads of religious houses came in person to swear fealty to the English king, including the mayor and seventy-eight burgesses of Berwick on Tweed.[98] Edward made a short progress into Scotland by way of Edinburgh, Stirling, Dunfermline, St Andrews and Perth, before returning to Berwick in time for the opening session of the court of claims on August 2nd. At Stirling on July 12th special provisions were made for the general swearing of fealty to the king throughout Scotland. 'To save everyone toil and expense,' it was ordered that the fealties should be received at Perth by the bishop of St Andrews, John Comyn of Badenoch and Brian FitzAlan, at Ayr by the bishop of Glasgow, James the Stewart and Sir Nicholas Segrave, at Inverness by the earl of Sutherland and the local sheriff and castle commander, and in Galloway by the justiciar of Galloway, Sir William Sinclair, aided by William de Boyville and by the bishop of Galloway as soon as he had himself sworn fealty. Very short notice was given, for all the fealties had to be sworn by July 27th, and strict measures were to be taken against those who neglected or refused to take the oath.

Instead, therefore, of a full and unequivocal admission of his claims in 1291, King Edward obtained three lesser things: a full but qualified admission by the competitors (not in any sense a representative body within the Scottish kingdom); de facto resignation of authority and power by the Guardians; and the individual fealty and homage to himself, as lord superior, of the leading men and women of Scotland from the Guardians downward.

If this was far from what Edward I required, it was also far from being a sturdy stand for independence. Within a few years, the Scots were seeking to explain it, perhaps truthfully enough, as brought about by the fear which may seize even the most steadfast. Despite the concessions which they had won, the Guardians had fatally compromised their independence, especially in resigning and allowing themselves to be reappointed by Edward I and in authorising the surrender of the royal castles. The castle commanders had, perhaps with the Guardians' connivance, made at least a token show of resistance. Their gesture has a legalistic appearance, but it went to the heart of the matter of sovereignty and the constitution. The events crowded into the critical days of the first half of June, 1291 expose the weakness of the Scots' position. What sort of unity could they show against English invasion when the identity of their king had not even been determined? The stage was set for Scots and English, under the presidency of a king whom all now acknowledged to be the overlord (superior dominus, soverein seignur) of Scotland, to decide which claimant had the best right to the throne.

THREE

Bruce *versus* Balliol

King Edward had gained control of Scotland without a sword being drawn. A court was at once appointed to decide which claimant had the best right to the throne.[1] Its sessions were to be held on Scottish soil, and its scale was impressive: 104 auditors, under the king, a body modelled with conscious archaism on the *centumviri*, the court of 105 used under the Roman republic to settle questions of succession to property.[2] Twenty-four auditors belonged to Edward I's council, and of the remainder forty were nominated by John Balliol of Galloway and forty by Robert Bruce of Annandale. Flattering as it might seem to the Scots, the fact that claims were lodged by no fewer than fourteen competitors, two of them kings, did not really mean that the throne of Scotland was the most coveted prize of its time in western Europe. It looks as though the field was large, but in reality, while Balliol was favourite and Bruce heavily backed, the other entries were generally non-starters. Most of the competitors, in fact, were relatively obscure men, and all but four of the claims were lodged as a formality, chiefly for the sake of being put on record so that in future they could not be said to have gone by default. From the outset the real choice lay between four claimants, Balliol, Bruce, John Hastings of Abergavenny and Florence v, count of Holland, all of them direct and legitimate descendants of Henry of North-umberland, son and heir of King David I.[3] The first three were descendants of Henry's youngest son, Earl David. Count Florence was fourth in descent from Henry's daughter Ada. Normally a son's heirs would have a stronger claim than a daughter's, and the count's case would have carried no weight whatever had he not based it on a simple but radical allegation. He averred that in return for a grant of the Garioch (a district in Aberdeenshire) Earl David had resigned the right which he and his heirs might have in the throne to his brother King William the Lion and his heirs. At the same time (the count continued) King William had designated his sister Ada as heir, though subsequently he had had a son, the future Alexander II. Since this line had now failed and the count of Holland was Ada's great-great-grandson, the alleged resignation should have given him the Scottish Crown without further argument. But there was one snag. The count did not have copies of any of the relevant documents, especially Earl David's resignation and the record of baronial fealty to Ada as heir. It was said that they were in the treasury in Edinburgh Castle, or elsewhere in Scotland, and the count asked that a search should be made for them. With characteristic patience and thoroughness, King Edward adjourned the court for ten months, from August 12th, 1291, until June 2nd, 1292, so that the documents required by Florence of Holland might be found.[4]

The count's claim raises a host of puzzling questions. Let us, for the moment, consider only two of them. His great-great-grandmother, Ada of Scotland, who was married in 1162 to Count Florence III of Holland, had a sister Margaret, married in 1160 to the duke of Brittany.[5] Historians have usually assumed that Ada was the elder sister. There seems in fact to be no clear evidence which was the elder. In view of the girls' Christian names,[6] and the order in which they were married, it may be thought that Margaret was older than Ada. If so, her oldest direct male descendant, Humphrey de Bohun, earl of Hereford, would have had a better claim than Count Florence.[7] Yet the earl is not known to have put in a claim of any kind. Even allowing that Ada was the elder sister, it would be astonishing that the earl of Hereford had made no claim if the story of Earl David's resignation was widely known and believed. This brings us to what was really the crucial part of Count Florence's claim: King William's designation of Ada as heir and the Scottish barons' fealty to her. Without this, the count's claim by mere heredity would have been extremely shaky. Now, it so happens that we know on excellent authority that in 1195, three years before his son was born, King William the Lion did propose to set aside the claims of his brother Earl David in favour not of his sister but of his daughter Margaret, on condition that she married Otto of Brunswick (afterwards the emperor Otto IV).[8] Many of the Scottish nobles opposed the plan 'because' (we are told) 'it was not the custom of Scotland that a woman should have the kingdom so long as there was a brother or nephew in the family who could have the kingdom by right'. Yet in 1291 Count Florence asked the court to believe that the Scottish baronage had, before the proposal of 1195 was ever made, accepted as heir to the throne a woman who was not even the eldest daughter of the king but merely one of his sisters. Before going further with the count of Holland's claim it will be as well to take a closer look at the three descendants of Earl David, Balliol, Bruce and Hastings.

The composition of the court, with its eighty Scottish auditors chosen only by Balliol and Bruce, shows that for contemporaries these two were thought to be the really serious competitors. John Hastings, virtually unknown in Scotland, was grandson of Earl David's youngest daughter. Since he had no shadow of claim by primogeniture or by nearness of degree, it was no use his making a claim at all unless he could prove that Scotland was not a true kingdom, and that the 'royal demesne' was merely a landed estate like any other.[9] As such, by the feudal law recognized in both Scotland and England, it would be divided equally among the co-heiresses, and John Hastings would succeed to one third. This modest but destructive claim was pursued with ingenuity by Hastings' lawyers, who pointed out that the kings of Scots were neither crowned nor anointed and drew attention to other grave defects of Scottish kingship. The court was not convinced. It contained many of the leaders of the community of the realm of Scotland, and they were not prepared to be told by the attorneys of an English baron that the realm of Scotland had never existed.

Balliol and Bruce, the undisputed protagonists of this eighteen-month drama, each displayed the strength of his support in the body of influential sponsors which he had chosen.[10] Balliol's auditors unquestionably provided a weightier, more authoritative representation of the community of the realm than Bruce's.[11] It is true that whereas only four earls supported Balliol, five were sponsors for Bruce, to whom a sixth (his own son) might be added. But Balliol, himself lord of Galloway since his mother Dervorguilla's death in January 1290, also had on his side the lord of Argyll. Each of these lordships carried the prestige and influence of an earldom, in the south west and in the west highlands respectively. Of the bishops, Bruce had two, Glasgow and Dunkeld; Balliol six, including St Andrews and Aberdeen. Bruce, again, could count on only two heads of religious houses, Balliol no fewer than eight, including St Andrews, Dunfermline and Kelso, while one of his bishops had lately been abbot of Arbroath. Balliol's supporters were drawn evenly from the various provinces of Scotland, Bruce's show a striking but not surprising majority of notables from the south and south west. Finally, it can hardly be an accident that while Balliol preferred to nominate, almost exclusively, men of standing, earls, bishops, abbots and barons of renown, Bruce included as many as eight *magistri*, university graduates whose presence probably owed more to their legal training or experience of legal pleading than to their status in the community at large. Balliol, too, had his *magistri*, but he kept them in the background, as working deputies of the great men who had lent their names to his cause. In any case, these eighty auditors did not form a 'Bruce party' and a 'Balliol party', divided politically, as though they were backing candidates in an election. In reality, they were sureties or pledges, responsible witnesses that Bruce and Balliol were themselves responsible suitors demanding the judgement of a court.

The greater strength of Balliol's auditors surely reflected the simple fact that Balliol had the stronger case. There is no reason to think that Balliol's lawyers were inferior to Bruce's, but almost throughout the proceedings they used only two arguments. First, the kingship, the *regnum*, the 'royal dignity', of Scotland, together with all that went with it in demesne lands, revenues and so forth, was not divisible. Secondly, Balliol, as indisputably the senior descendant of Earl David by the strict rule of promogeniture, was the true heir to the Crown and office of king.[12] This economy in pleading was a sign of strength: the more numerous and various the arguments used by an advocate the weaker his case is likely to be. And the arguments put forward by Bruce's lawyers were indeed many and varied. Not only did they expend every shot in the locker, but Bruce himself, outside the court, seems to have used every possible means to bolster his cause. Surely the only satisfactory explanation of all his ingenuity, self-contradiction and even chicanery is that Bruce knew the exasperating, tantalizing truth that whereas politically he could count on powerful support, legally his case was weak.

His counsel began by taking a high line on the nature of monarchy. Succession to kingdoms was quite different from succession to landed property. It must be settled by reference to 'imperial laws' and the Natural Law. As a kingdom, Scotland was indivisible: Crown, royal honours and royal estates alike must remain in the hands of one man. They declared that according to the established customs and laws of Scotland, a living younger son, being nearer in blood to his father, had a better right to succeed than the son of a deceased elder son, who was one degree further removed. More-over, the *son* of a younger child would take precedence of the *daughter* of an older child. Bruce maintained that these rules should be applied to the present case. He was the son of a younger daughter of Earl David, Balliol the son of a daughter of the earl's eldest daughter. In addition, Bruce claimed that Alexander II had caused him to be designated heir to the throne at a time when the king was still childless and about to lead an expedition to the western isles.[13] This can only have been after John of Scotland's death in 1237 and before King Alexander married Marie de Couci in 1239. No royal campaign in the isles is recorded for that period, and it is unfortunate that the only accounts of the incident are to be found in two documents which both come from the *milieu* of the Competitor himself.[14] The weakness of this claim was that even if Bruce's designation had been an historical fact its only justification must have been that Bruce at that particular moment was the nearest male heir. In the intervening years the king had had direct descend-ants down to the third generation, and John and Dervorguilla Balliol had had several sons. In any event, the facts of Scottish history for the past two hundred years were against Bruce. The succession of kings from Edgar in 1097 to the acceptance of the Maid of Norway in 1284 – in which Bruce and his son had joined – demonstrated clearly that a tendency to prefer the most senior available heir had hardened into a rule.[15] The court of 1291–92 was surely right, and not merely overawed by Edward I and English influence, when it stated that Scottish royal succession was governed by the rule of primogeniture.

At the very end of the proceedings, when it was obvious that the court was going to uphold Balliol's claim of seniority, Bruce's lawyers threw over their high-flown arguments about the Natural Law and the indivisibility of the Scottish realm. They said that if the court had agreed to apply to the Scottish Crown the lower law which governed the succession to earldoms and other feudal honours, then of course Scotland was divisible, and Bruce should be guaranteed his third share of the income and land. At the very least, he should have a third part of the Liberty of Tynedale, which was dependent on, but not an integral part of, the Crown.[16] Many historians have been scandalized by this *volte face*, calling it a piece of effrontery, a 'shameless change of position' and the like. Admittedly, Bruce's lawyers weakened their case irretrievably by arguing for the indivisibility of Scotland on the grounds that it was a true kingdom and afterwards agreeing with Hastings that Scotland was not a kingdom at all. But surely they were only doing their duty by their client, and the claim was not without logic. The court was in fact dealing with an unprecedented situation, and there is no doubt that it actually made law on this point, and did not merely apply a law already clearly established. In rejecting Bruce's desperate last claim, the court gave Balliol all that his lawyers had asked for, since they had not only awarded him the Crown, i.e., the office of king, on the principle of *ainesse* (seniority) but had coupled with this the judgement that the kingdom of Scotland in the widest sense was indivisible. Consequently, when Bruce's counsel asked at the eleventh hour that he should be allowed a third share they were hardly acting more reprehensibly than Balliol's counsel when they for their part had first of all pleaded that the succession should be determined by the common law of England with regard to subordinate fiefs, and had then argued afterwards that if the court agreed that Scotland was indivisible Balliol should take the whole.

The failure of Bruce's main arguments brings us back to Count Florence of Holland. It was not until November 17th, 1292, only a short time before the court finally awarded the Crown to Balliol, that the count withdrew his claim.[17] We have seen how this claim struck at the root of the claims made by Balliol, Bruce and Hastings. Yet it has been said that 'there is no record of a direct contest between Bruce and the count during the pleadings'.[18] Why? We do not know for certain, and unless further evidence comes to light we shall never know. The answer suggested here, a simple answer which may perhaps be over-simple, is as follows. Although the count of Holland may have believed sincerely that he had some unsatisfied claim on the Scots, probably in connexion with his great-great-grandmother's marriage portion,[19] his claim to the Scottish throne itself was originally purely formal, not to say frivolous. As such it would have been comparable to the 'romanist' claim put in by King Eric of Norway. This harmless claim of the count's was seized on by Bruce and his supporters, and inflated for the sole purpose of defeating Balliol.

In the spring of 1290, Bruce was apparently trying to gain complete control of the Garioch, the largest of Earl David's Scottish lordships of which Bruce, Balliol and Hastings had each inherited one third. Exactly how he proposed to oust Balliol and Hastings from their respective shares is not clear. But on April 19th, 1290, a month after they had both attended the parliament of Birgham, Bruce made an agreement with Sir Nicholas Biggar, one of the most powerful and prominent magnates of Clydesdale.[20] According to this agreement, Sir Nicholas was to bring an action in the king's court (i.e., the court held by the Guardians) against Balliol and Hastings, by a royal 'brieve of right', to 'recover' for himself all Balliol's and Hasting's lands in the Garioch. Bruce would pay the whole costs of the action. Simultaneously, however, Sir Nicholas surrendered all his rights in the Garioch property to Bruce, so that the net result of the agreement, if it could have been implemented, would have been to make Bruce sole lord of the Garioch. In compensation, Sir Nicholas Biggar would be given by Bruce forty merks' worth of land in Scotland south of Forth, for the twentieth part of one knight's service – an almost nominal rent. The scheme would mean an appreciable addition to Bruce's Scottish estates, and more especially it would add to his influence in the north of Scotland, where he was the neighbour of his friend the earl of Mar.[21]

The deeper explanation of the scheme is not clear. It may have related to the marriage arranged between Gartnait, son and heir of Earl Donald of Mar, and Christian Bruce, sister of the future king, who is said to have received the Garioch as her tocher or marriage portion.[22] But this marriage can hardly have taken place so early, and it seems more likely that the Bruce-Biggar indenture should be connected with three further pieces of evidence. The first of these, the so-called 'Appeal of the Seven Earls', belongs to the winter of 1290–91 or spring of 1291.[23] The first part of this curious document is in the form of an 'open letter', though since it never seems to have borne a seal it cannot be regarded as a letter in any strict sense. This part of the document is addressed to Bishop Fraser and John Comyn of Badenoch, the two Guardians who supported Balliol, and also, in the first paragraph, to Balliol himself. These three magnates are accused of attempting to get Balliol made king of Scotland by a *coup*, aided and abetted by 'that small part (*particula*) of the community of the realm adhering to them'. There is no suggestion that Fraser and Comyn were improperly or unpatriotically using English influence; on the contrary, it is the authors of the 'Appeal' who declare that they are asking Edward I to intervene and uphold the rightful claims of Bruce of Annandale.

What gives the 'Appeal' its special interest is the fact that it calls itself the 'accusations (*appellationes*) of the seven earls of the kingdom of Scotland', and purports to state their claim in the appointment of a new king, as well as the claims of the 'community of the realm'. Some of the older historians, notably Palgrave and Skene, took the idea of the 'Seven Earls' seriously, but most were inclined to be sceptical. Nowadays the opposite is true. Most Scottish historians believe that the Seven Earls had a real existence – indeed, they have even been enumerated.[24] The truth seems to be rather that the Seven Earls were a mixture of fact and myth, and the myth surely outweighed the fact. The twelfth and thirteenth centuries were rich in the elaboration and even outright invention of ancient rights and privileges and constitutions – one is reminded of the claim of the citizens of London to elect a king of England,[25] and of the Seven Electors of Germany, with their 'ancient' claim (no older than the mid-thirteenth century) to elect a king of the Romans.[26] Indeed, Count Florence must have been well aware of the German example, for his father, William II of Holland, had been elected king of the Romans by a section of the electoral college in 1247. Bruce's allusion to 'imperial laws' referred to Roman Law, but he may have felt that the practice of the empire provided a good example of 'the law by which kings reign' when he asked King Edward as 'his sovereign lord and emperor' to award him the kingdom in accordance with this exalted law.[27] According to old chronicles, and some not so old, which were being keenly studied and rewritten in thirteenth-century Scotland, the country north of Forth was historically divided into the magical number of seven parts, ruled first by kings, then by mormaers under a single king.[28] The earls of these provinces represented the seven mormaers, and were the recognized leaders of the kingdom. The 'Appeal' declared that they enjoyed special rights in 'making' a king and placing him on the seat of royalty. Fraser and Comyn, by prejudging the issue of succession in Balliol's favour, had gravely infringed these ancient privileges.

We need not suppose that the 'Appeal' was based on complete fiction. It was an example of that semi-antiquarian revival of things Celtic which was not uncommon in thirteenth-century Scotland. As it stands, the document is highly tendentious and, when it speaks of alleged atrocities in Moray by officers of Fraser and Comyn, it becomes charged with an emotion which smacks of propaganda.[27] It is curious that the only earls mentioned by name in the 'Appeal' are the earl of Fife – a mere infant – and the earl of Mar. Anyone in 1290 who wanted to make up a list of suitable candidates to fill the Seven Earldoms could hardly leave out the earl of Fife, whose privileges at a royal inauguration were unchallenged. The earl of Mar probably had as good a claim as any other. But so too did the earls of Angus, Buchan and Strathearn, who were all supporters of Balliol. The real suspicion attaching to the 'Appeal' lies not in the fact that it mentions Earl Donald of Mar but in its quite disproportionate emphasis on his interests and grievances.

With the internal history of the earldom of Mar we are plunged at once into a tangle of confusions, obscure genealogies and blatant forgeries. Earl Donald was son and heir of an Earl William who had sought to confirm his disputed claim to the honour with a forged charter in favour of Earl Morgan who lived in the twelfth century.[30] At the end of the 'Appeal' is a memorandum upholding this forgery as proof of Earl Donald's rights and complaining that a large part of the earldom was still unjustly withheld from him. Still more significantly, there is a memorandum that Count Florence of Holland was with equal injustice being defrauded of the earldom of Ross which the 'old men of Scotland' declared to have been the princess Ada's marriage portion of 1162! (It is not surprising that William earl of Ross was a Balliol supporter). Most significantly of all, the 'Appeal' adds that these same old men – whom it unfortunately fails to identify – agreed that, should there be some failure in the heirs of David earl of Huntingdon, the count of Holland was the rightful heir by reason of King William's sister Ada.

The 'Appeal' begins by giving three quite distinct reasons why Bruce had a better right to the throne than Balliol: he was the choice of the Seven Earls and community, he was the male heir nearest in blood to Earl David, and he had been designated heir by Alexander II when that king 'had nearly reached senility' (he was forty in 1238). It ends by saying that if for some reason there was a flaw in the claim of Earl David's heirs the rightful claimant was the count of Holland. Even if the purpose of these arguments is not self-evident, the conjunction of Bruce and Count Florence and the story of Ada of Scotland should put us on our guard. Well before the competitors lodged their claims, the earl of Mar and Robert Bruce had also seen the possibilities inherent in the Dutch claim. As yet, these possibilities were all rather vague. The flaw in the inheritance from Earl David is not described, and Ada's claim as next heir is based on the testimony of the 'old men of Scotland'. But we now know that within a few months of the 'Appeal' a document was in existence which gave to these vital matters the precision they required.

In the second week of November 1291 two north-country prelates, the bishop of Moray and the prior of Pluscarden, formally set their seals to copies of the resignation of Earl David which Count Florence had made the basis of his claim in the previous summer.[31] An early copy of these 'certified copies' still survives at The Hague in what were formerly the count of Holland's archives.[32] The document purports to have been issued by David, son of Henry earl of Huntingdon. It records David's resignation of all right to the throne for himself and his posterity in exchange for the land of Garioch given by King William. It bears no date, which is what one would expect for the supposed period of its issue (1165–73), but it also has no witnesses, an omission which is scarcely credible for a twelfth-century deed of this important nature. Moreover, the phrases in which Count Florence's lawyers described the resignation to the court in November 1292 are too close to the phrases in the text of the resignation as we have it for the resemblance to be coincidence.[33] Either the count had seen the resignation and subsequently lost it, or he was able to 'quote' from it because he had invented it. In the present state of our ignorance it is hardly a point in favour of the count's honesty that he told the court that the document was being wrongfully detained by the Prior of Pluscarden, one of the two prelates responsible for the 'certified copies'. We do not know whose side the prior was on. He may have been acting against the count, but for all we know he may have been in league with him.

Whether the bishop and prior issued their copies in good faith, believing they had the original before them, or whether they were art and part in a piece of deliberate falsification, is something else we do not know. But one thing we do know is that the 'resignation' was a forgery.[34] Obviously it would be harder to prove this from a copy at second-hand than from the document which the forger would presumably have had to fabricate as the 'original'. The sort of criticism by internal evidence which is nowadays applied to historical documents was only in its infancy in 1291, when the normal tests of authenticity lay in the kind and size of parchment, in the seal, and perhaps in the handwriting. None of this could be examined in the copies made under the two prelates' auspices and sealed with their seals.

Had this document been available to Count Florence and put in by him as evidence, it is conceivable, though scarcely probable, that the court would have upheld his claim and ruled against the three competitors who claimed by descent from Earl David. How, then, could this have benefited Bruce, who was one of the three? The answer to this is contained in our third piece of evidence, the famous agreement of June 14th, 1292, between the count and Bruce.[35] This agreement was to be effective only if one or other of the two parties gained the throne. Whichever one was successful would, within four months, grant to the unsuccessful party one third of the royal demesne as a fief to be held for five knights' service. The new king was also to have first option of taking a lease of this third if the unsuccessful party should wish to let it for a rent. Moreover, if Bruce were successful, he was to grant the count of Holland lands in England equivalent to one third of the royal demesne of Scotland. There was no equivalent provision if Florence were to win. This hardly looks like an agreement made between competitors who were equally anxious to gain the Scottish Crown and conscious that their claims were evenly matched. The document surely tells us that Balliol was Bruce's only serious rival and that every device was worth using if it might help to defeat him. Hence the one-sidedness of the agreement, which seems to assume that Bruce would be successful. In that case Bruce could, at worst, take back on lease the lost third of the royal demesne, and, at best, buy it from the count of Holland by putting him in possession of a most desirable baronial estate in England. Annandale would still belong to Bruce, and if the agreement with Nicholas Biggar became effective he would also have the whole lordship of Garioch. It might still seem a heavy price for Bruce to pay, but the count's assistance was worth a good price. For his claim, if accepted, would defeat Balliol's strong single claim but could not defeat every one of Bruce's numerous claims. The expression in his agreement with the count, 'whoever shall recover the realm by judgement *or by private agreement* [*pacem*] or by any other method', may mean that Bruce still hoped to have the Great Cause settled politically rather than judicially, as some of his pleading suggests.[36] And the fact that there is no record throughout the pleadings of Bruce and the count being in conflict surely provides further evidence that they were in collusion.

Lastly, there is the question of timing. The court was required to decide between Bruce and Balliol, on the issue of seniority *versus* nearness of degree, before it dealt with the claims of the other competitors. It declared in favour of Balliol in pronouncements of November 5th and 6th, 1292.[37] On November 7th Bruce sealed what was in effect a special testament, resigning his claim to seek the Scottish throne to his son and heir and to his heirs after him.[38] The instrument of resignation was also sealed, for the sake of stronger testimony, by Gilbert de Clare earl of Gloucester, nephew of the Competitor's first wife and, since 1290, son-in-law of King Edward I. Two days later (Sunday, November 9th) the younger Bruce, to whom the claim to the throne had thus passed, himself resigned his earldom of Carrick (held in right of his wife Marjorie) to his own son and heir, the youngest Robert Bruce, the future king.[39] The precise meaning of this reshuffle of power within the three Bruce generations is not clear. Presumably the Competitor's resignation was made partly to ensure continuity of the Bruce claim in the event of his sudden death, partly to provide a formal declaration of the claim to be used as soon as a favourable opportunity arose. It certainly looks as though the Bruces had been well prepared for the court's decision in favour of Balliol on the strictly legal issue. It seems equally certain that they were determined not to abandon their 'right and claim to seek the kingdom of Scotland'. On November 14th, Bruce's lawyers made their final desperate plea for one third of the royal demesne or at least of Tynedale and the lands not comprised in the 'regality' of Scotland.[40] And it was only during this week, from Monday, November 10th, to Friday, November 14th, that Count Florence pressed his claim with all the ability and skill at his disposal.[41]

He was well aware of his disadvantages. He asked King Edward to bear in mind that he was a stranger and foreigner, against whom Balliol could range many supporters and maintainers. If a judicial enquiry were not made now into the truth of his story about Earl David's charter of the Garioch it never would be made, and the count's claim and right would be lost for ever. The count's touching picture of himself as a friendless alien among hostile natives should not be taken too seriously. The Bruce faction, far from negligible, was behind him. It hardly seems likely that the count was really anxious for the Scottish throne. If he used his claim in order to defeat Balliol, the Bruces would reward him well. In the end, however, he seems to have withdrawn his claim in order to help Balliol. His fellow Dutchmen appear to have thought that Balliol had bribed him, presumably by offering a more tempting reward than the one provided in his agreement with Bruce.[42] But there is no certainty that Florence was bribed. In the four days or less which elapsed between the count's final statement to his claim and his withdrawal, it may have become clear for reasons now unknown that his claim would fail. After all, it depended on a document of resignation which he could not or would not produce, which in any case was undoubtedly a forgery. It was supported by vague, unverified statements that strained beyond credulity the powers of memory enjoyed by the 'old men of Scotland'. It was not difficult for Balliol's lawyers to pour scorn on the count's case, and their point about the absence of the alleged resignation must have seemed unanswerable: 'although the count has had since August 2nd[1291], over a year ago, to seek out his document and has not found it, it does not seem right that he should be heard merely because he says it exists.'[43]

The magnates and legal experts who composed the court of 1291–92, and the councillors outside the court who were consulted, 'were settling a point in law, not discussing political problems'.[44] The last occasion on which there had been a succession dispute in either kingdom was in 1199, on the death of Richard Coeur de Lion. On that occasion there had been neither court nor judgement. Backed by a few men of influence who controlled the key places and the machinery of government, Count John of Mortain, the youngest of Henry II's sons, had simply seized the throne to the exclusion of Arthur, duke of Brittany, the son of John's elder brother Geoffrey. Ninety years later, on the eve of the great Cause in Scotland, the English rules of succession to the throne were settled by Edward I. His ordinance of April 1290 made it clear that the kingdom of England could not be partitioned and that succession to this indivisible realm would follow the strict rule of primogeniture, preference being given to males in each generation. When the king came to give judgement in the Scottish case, on November 17th, 1292, he and the court were applying the same rules to the northern kingdom. Scotland was a true kingdom like other kingdoms. Since it was the peculiar property of a kingdom that it could not be divided, the kingdom of Scotland would be preserved intact. By the strict rule of primogeniture Balliol was the rightful heir, and would therefore rule over what Alexander, of happy memory, late king of Scots had ruled over – save, awkwardly, for the Isle of Man, whose slightly belated separate restoration to King John by Edward I (January 5th, 1293)[45] only served to highlight the odd circumstances of its original detachment from the Scottish realm.

The judgement in favour of Balliol was surely the triumph of law, common sense and respect for orderly procedure in the most important public act in which a medieval nation could join. We may regret that the Scots failed to win their point that the Great Cause should have proceeded freely, with the English king as arbitrator and not judge, but the two issues should not be confused, and the choice of Balliol was not something with which most Scots had any wish to quarrel. No doubt on personal or political grounds a number of Bruce's auditors, men like Bishop Wishart of Glasgow and James the Stewart, were dissatisfied. It is even possible that on more general grounds there were misgivings that the Crown had gone to a comparative stranger, a baron of great wealth and international connexions who yet remained an Englishman rather than a Scotsman. Balliol's sister Eleanor, it is true, was married to the Guardian, John Comyn of Badenoch, who was head of the senior branch – the 'Red Comyns'[46] – of the most powerful Scottish baronial family. Moreover Balliol was lord of Galloway

by descent from his mother Dervorguilla. If Galloway was thornily separat-
ist, regarded with suspicion by the Scotland of east-coast lairds and burghs,
there was no denying that it was in its own way intensely Scottish. But
Bruce, for all his rich estates and long sojourns in England, was completely
at home in Scotland, where he had held a place in the first rank of the
baronage for nearly fifty years. Balliol's following in Scotland was largely
the following of the Comyns, descendants of the old 'national' or 'patriot'
party of the 1250s. Bruce's following was more of his own making, and
consisted of long-standing family or personal alliances with neighbouring
lords like the Souleses, Lindsays and Biggars, with the powerful church of
Glasgow, and with great magnates like the Stewart and the earls of Dunbar,
Lennox, Atholl and Mar. Nevertheless, Scotland was not a tribal society in
which personal considerations were uppermost. It was sophisticated
enough to carry on a governed existence during the prolonged absence of a
ruler, but at least there had to be a ruler. What mattered most was to end the
interregnum and to inaugurate a lawful king. There is no evidence that the
enthronement of Balliol on St Andrew's Day, 1292, failed to meet these
crying needs for the generality of Scots. In the view of the majority Balliol
had been the rightful candidate: Long live King John! The ceremony itself
was respectful of national tradition. It was held at Scone in the presence of
the great men of the realm, and though the earl of Fife was a child his right to
place the new king in the seat of royalty above the Stone of Destiny was
carefully delegated to Sir John de St John.[47]

It is true that in the following weeks and years there were some small signs
that ancient precedents were being deliberately flouted or at least not being
scrupulously followed. King John's seal styled him 'by God's grace king of
Scots', where all his predecessors from the time of King Edgar (1097–1107)
had been, with pleasing alliteration, 'king of Scots under God's governance'
(Deo rectore Rex Scottorum). This change at least was no accident, and the
English influence is obvious. King John's first chancellor was a Yorkshireman, Master Thomas of Hunsingore, who held the small parsonage of
Oldhamstocks in Berwickshire. He had been an Oxford don and guarantor
of good behaviour by Northerners and Scots in the university in 1274 after
they had fought the Southerners and Irish.[48] More often than not King John
kept to the time-honoured style 'king of Scots' in his official documents, but
sometimes he used the unfamiliar English type of style, 'king of Scotland'.
By December 1293, a treasurer of Scotland (Master Alpin of Strathearn)
had been appointed. Since there had never been a treasurer in Scotland
before, it seems reasonable to regard the appointment as a deliberate
imitation of English practice.[49]

If these were straws in the wind they did not amount to much. The
greatest contrast of the new reign was provided squarely, if not altogether
fairly, by King Edward. It is hardly a defence of the English king to say that
the line he now took should have been foreseen by the Scots leaders when, in

June 1291, they had been smitten by 'that fear which may strike even the stoutest-hearted'. They had taken refuge then in safeguards which now proved to be worth less than the parchment and wax of which they were composed.

For King Edward, however, the elaborately repeated homages and fealties obtained from Balliol, first after judgement had been given and then again after his enthronement, formed the concluding stage of a single process upon which he had embarked in May 1291. This was, characteristically, a process of definition, a piece of tidying up, whereby his own prejudged and highly questionable view of the relationship between the English and Scottish Crowns was to be given permanent force. In the summer of 1291 the Guardians and their colleagues had been harking back to the treaty of Birgham–Northampton of 1290, with its *leitmotiv* of Scottish separateness and independence. King Edward's mind was clearly moving in the opposite direction when in July 1291 he declared 'Through the blessing of the All Highest, the realms of England and Scotland are joined together, and consequently royal writs originating in Scotland and presented or returned to the (English) justices of Common Pleas may be dealt with by them.'[50]

It is surely somewhat naive, somewhat unrealistic, not to see in the case – or, rather, the cases – of Roger Bartholomew an essential part of the process by which Scotland was to be brought into a much closer union with England than at any earlier period.[51] Definition needs demonstration. It may not have been an ideal test case from Edward's point of view, but a test case of some sort was obviously necessary. It seems most unlikely that Bartholomew's appeals, the first appeals from the Scottish *curia regis* to the English, took either Edward I or the Scots leaders by surprise.

Master Roger Bartholomew was a burgess of Berwick who had been involved in litigation in the court of the Guardians. Even after their commission had been changed from an elective authority conferred by the community of the realm to a delegated authority conferred by the 'superior lord', their court still represented the Scottish *curia regis*. It was the highest secular tribunal to which Scottish litigants could have recourse. In three separate cases judgement had gone against Master Roger. He was executor of a deceased goldsmith whose widow sued him successfully for unjust detention of her dower and of money she had loaned to her late husband. He was, secondly, alleged to have deprived a fellow burgess of property in Berwick by the improper use of a brieve of right. And, finally, he was said to have frivolously accused one Gilbert of Dunbar of injuring him in the eye with a stick. Dissatisfied with the Guardians' adverse judgements, Master Roger complained to King Edward at Berwick on December 7th, 1292, one week after Balliol's enthronement. Edward had no wish to impose English law on the Scots. At Newcastle he consulted with the experienced Scotsmen in his company before giving judgement on December 22nd. In the case of the alleged assault, judgement was reversed in Roger's favour; in the property case it was confirmed, saving Roger's right to bring a further action; the case of the widow's money was settled by a compromise. That only a fortnight elapsed between the appeals and final judgement suggests strongly that if Bartholomew's case was not deliberately brought as a test case it was certainly expedited by Edward I's council in order to demonstrate the English king's right to hear appeals from Scottish litigants. On January 6th, 1293, King Edward paid £1 13s. 4d. to Bartholomew and £3 6s. 8d. to Philip of Rydale (another burgess involved in the case), which looks suspiciously like prompt settlement of expenses.[52]

The speed with which King John and his advisers reacted to the affair suggests that the Scots for their part were well prepared for a test case. As soon as judgement had been given on the Bartholomew appeals, four Scots magnates and supporters of Balliol, Bishop Fraser, John Comyn earl of Buchan, Patrick Graham and Thomas Randolph, together with others unnamed, lodged a petition on behalf of their king asking that Edward should keep his promise to preserve the laws and customs of Scotland, including the promise (in the Treaty of Birgham) that Scottish lawsuits should not be dealt with outside Scotland.[53] At first, the reply was that the Scots had specially requested Edward to cut short legal delays so that justice might be done quickly; but this surely applied to outstanding business, not to the revival of cases settled and done with. It was added more plausibly that the Guardians (after June 1291) were responsible solely to Edward as overlord, who therefore had a perfect right to review their judgements. Finally, however, it was declared on Edward's behalf that any promises he had made during the interregnum were only 'for the time being', and had no binding force now that a king had been created. When on the last day of December King Edward himself, speaking personally in French, repeated that he would in no wise be bound by any promises, concessions, ratifications etc. which he might have made previously, so far as appeals were concerned, but on the contrary would hear whatever appeals might be brought and if necessary summon the king of Scotland himself, the Scots could not have been given a clearer answer to the question of what Edward understood by homage and the rights that went with it.[54] We know now that the moral shabbiness in Edward I's dealings with the Scots went back to June 1291. There was scarcely any attempt to disguise it in the pronouncements of December 1292. As if they were not enough, King John was made to issue two instruments, one in Latin, one in French, on January 2nd, 1292, by which he solemnly freed Edward from all obligations and promises which the English king might have entered into with the Guardians and responsible men (*probi homines*, *la bone gent*) of the Scottish realm, declaring null and void any written evidence of such promises and explicitly annulling the Treaty of Birgham–Northampton.[55] In Edward's view this was no more than a marriage contract; in Scottish eyes it had been a sheet-anchor of their country's independence of the southern kingdom.

The course of events since King John's enthronement would have seemed ominous to any of his subjects who knew their country's history. It was not the first time an English ruler had made promises to the Scots which he afterwards repudiated. In 1149 Henry of Anjou had sworn before King David that if he became king of England he would leave Northumberland and Cumberland in Scottish hands.[56] Eight years later he went back on his word, and the Scots attempt to restore the *status quo* in 1173 led directly to an Angevin overlordship which lasted for fifteen years and saw English garrisons in Scottish castles and subjects of the king of Scots asking for the English king's direct protection. Edward I was not a man of less deter-mination than his great-grandfather. North of the Border, on the other hand, an idea of the community of the realm had grown from experience of feudal monarchy. Concepts of legal rights, concepts of nationality, concepts of kingship had all become sharper, and there was less room for manoeuvre than in the relatively casual days of the twelfth century. The last fourteen years of Edward I's life were, in proportion, more violent, more destructive, fraught with a more bitter hostility in Anglo-Scottish relations, than the last fifteen years of Henry II's.

FOUR

A Lamb among Wolves

After nearly seven years of uncertainty the Scots had a king again. No matter how competent or conscientious the Guardians may have been – and our evidence tells us they were both – they could not govern the feudal kingdom indefinitely nor satisfy all its needs. At best they could only be caretakers. Now, once more, 'full' parliaments could be held, charters confirmed and granted, foreign relations resumed, administrative improvements put into effect, military service performed without the suspicion of aiding private faction, vexatious lawsuits heard and determined. Vexatious lawsuits: here was the rub. The king had been regarded in former times as the very fount of justice, whose kingly duty it was, above all other duties, to punish wrong-doers and judge equitably between subject and subject. For administrative convenience or from a desire for maximum solemnity and publicity it had been usual for this ultimate jurisdiction to rest with the king and his 'full court', that is, with king and parliament. This practice, honoured by long usage, detracted nothing from the king's prerogatives. It was an entirely different matter if appeals were to be allowed from the Scottish courts to the king of England. If King John's capacity as supreme secular judge were diminished, his position was open to challenge from all sides. He might be regarded as a provincial governor or else a privileged feudatory enjoying ancient rights and revenues but possessing only the shadow of real power. He would certainly not be a king.

Modern historians sometimes suggest that in Edward I's view the Scottish kingdom resembled the duchy of Aquitaine, which he himself held as a vassal of the king of France. Whether Edward ever made the comparison we do not know; it is in any case one that cannot really be sustained. It is true that Aquitaine enjoyed almost complete independence of the Capetian kings of France as long as they were too weak to assert and exploit their rights of overlordship. At the same time the duchy had not developed for two hundred years as a self-contained kingdom with an increasingly centralized government, a distinct ecclesiastical organization, and a steady enhancement of royal authority. Power and judicial authority in Aquitaine remained stubbornly decentralized, and this made it relatively easy for Gascons to seek justice now from their duke, the king of England, now from the king of France in the *parlement* of Paris. In Aquitaine Edward I, however grudgingly, had come to accept appeals from his vassals to the French king, while at the same time offering attractively speedy and accessible justice in his own court. Even so, Anglo-French relations might be strained to breaking point over the question of appeals, despite the gradual way in which the custom of appeal had grown and despite the evident feudal subordination of the duchy to the French Crown. How much more was this likely to be true of Anglo-Scottish relations, where the practice of appeals from Scotland to England was unheard of until the case of Roger Bartholomew.[1]

The matter went far beyond a technical question of law and its administration. If King John's parliament was not to have the last word in secular causes, his authority and power in many other spheres would be called in question. How far was he free to enter into independent relations with foreign rulers, to make trade agreements with the merchants and communities upon whom Scotland partly depended for her income, to fortify and garrison castles (especially those on the Border), to harbour English fugitives, to keep in his active service subjects who might, on account of their estates in England, be required to appear in English courts or act as judges or jurors south of the Border? At every step he took, the new king would have to pause, examine its implications, and find out whether it could be allowed under the new régime. Yet there was work in plenty for a king of Scotland to do without having to look over his shoulder all the time to see what English reactions were. It was John's misfortune that he had succeeded to a kingdom which could not have been ruled by anyone forced to walk such a narrow tightrope. At least he made a worthwhile effort at government. We must, in fairness, get behind the powerful legend of Balliol the ineffectual puppet, laughed off the throne by scornful Scots and spurned at last by his own manipulator. It is true he was not a forceful man and certainly no match for Edward I. But he was not a complete nonentity nor altogether lacking in dignity.

Far-reaching legislation can hardly be expected from a king whose effective reign lasted only three and a half years. There is, indeed, very little record of legislation of any kind. Yet there survives one brief ordinance on new sheriffdoms in the west which proves that some sensible, constructive thinking was being done in government circles and that the king possessed the will to apply it. If this ordinance had ever had the chance to take effect, it might have gone far to solve the difficult problem of governing the Hebrides and the mainland country west of Drumalban and the Great Glen. By the terms of the ordinance,[2] Lewis, Uist, Barra, Skye and the Small Isles were to be grouped with Wester Ross and Kintail to form the sheriffdom of Skye, of which the earl of Ross was to be sheriff. South of this, most of what is now Argyllshire, except for Kintyre, was to become the sheriffdom of Lorn, administered by the lord of Argyll, Alexander Macdougall, as sheriff. His castle of Dunstaffnage made an ideal headquarters for the sea-borne government of this area, reaching as it did from Ardnamurchan and Morvern in the north to Islay in the south. Finally, James the Stewart, already hereditary lord of Bute and the Cumbraes, was to be sheriff of a third new sheriffdom comprising those islands together with Kintyre and, presumably, Arran, to be known as the sheriffdom of Kintyre. This scheme, though clearly in line with the 'forward policy' followed in the west highlands and isles by the two Alexanders, was a notable advance on anything they had achieved. The names assigned to the sheriffdoms suggest that for the first time royal authority was to be firmly based in the west and government represented by royal agents stationed at local centres. To that extent, one is reminded of the three new shires of Anglesey, Caernarvon and Merioneth set up under Edward I's Statute of Rhuddlan of 1284. Admittedly, two of the new highland sheriffs, the Stewart and the earl of Ross, had their chief interests outside the west. But it looks as though Alexander Macdougall – who, like Balliol, was a brother-in-law of John Comyn of Badenoch – had previously been entrusted by the king with a 'lieutenancy extending over the three sheriffdoms probably with powers wider than those of a sheriff'.[3] Within his new sheriffdom he could obviously use his hereditary power and prestige to advantage. It was Alexander whom King John commanded to bring Angus Macdonald lord of Islay and two other islesmen to do homage after Easter 1293, and to receive to the king's peace all those willing to take the king's lands in Lorn at farm.[4] Since, as far as we know, the Crown had no lands of its own in Lorn save for Loch Awe, it seems that Alexander Macdougall was to be the principal agent in a piece of forcible feudalization, by which the barons of Argyll could remain in the king's peace as long as they agreed to hold their estates of the Crown for a rent.[5]

This short excursion into the west is in no sense a digression. The interest which King John took in the west highland problem proves that he or his advisers had a good grasp of political and strategic realities. Orientated as she was towards the east, thirteenth-century Scotland could not ignore her western approaches. No able king could afford to neglect a wild terrain from which raiders might descend without warning, like a pack of winter wolves on a sleeping village, returning by trackless *bealachs* to some remote glen. No national defence was complete if it failed to provide for a coast of innumerable lochs and islands, where scores of galleys could lie hidden. For their part, the native chiefs of the west, most of them descended from Somerled, who was virtually independent lord of Argyll under David I, had been forced since 1266 to look eastward, to make unaccustomed and uncomfortable journeys to Scone or Edinburgh, to take a more active part in domestic Scottish politics. There are not many points at which it is useful to make any comparison between the kingship of John Balliol and the kingship of Robert Bruce, but in his concern for Argyll Balliol foreshadowed the exploits which were to make his successor a legend in the west. It was not necessary for a king in Edinburgh to take to the heather in order to grasp the essential truth that one who was not master of the highlands was not master of Scotland.

The impression is sometimes conveyed that King John's monarchy foundered on the question of appeals, and the name of Macduff – perhaps because it is so easily memorable – has filled a disproportionately large place in Scottish history. There was in fact no rush by Scots to appeal from their king's jurisdiction to that of the king of England. To say that the appeals were mostly brought by foreigners and malcontents might be putting it rather strongly, but it would not give a misleading impression.

Three of the appellants were subjects of the king of England. John Mazun was a Bordeaux wine merchant with whom King Alexander III had run up a large bill. Both king and Guardians had attempted to settle his claims, but his wayward and intemperate behaviour, coupled with the fact that he was beset by creditors, made settlement difficult. He had certainly not improved his case by procuring the arrest in Yorkshire (1289) of Bishop Fraser of St Andrews, then a Guardian, while the bishop was on his way to Gascony to discuss with King Edward the Maid of Norway's marriage.[6] The abbot of Reading, William Sutton, had perhaps a stronger case. He complained that his predecessor had unlawfully sold to Bishop Fraser the priory of May or Pittenweem, a dependency of Reading Abbey: in making the purchase the bishop, so he alleged, had abused his position as Guardian. Since Reading was a royal foundation, it was only to be expected that the abbot would appeal to his patron. King John was repeatedly summoned before the court of King's Bench to answer the abbot's complaint. He ignored these summonses. The case was already before his own parliament, but stood adjourned because Bishop Fraser had himself appealed to the papal court.[7] The other non-Scottish appellant was Anthony Bek, bishop of Durham, the trusted servant and friend of King Edward, who presented a grotesquely frivolous claim to the towns of Berwick and Haddington as being ancient possessions of his see.[8]

Of the six Scottish appellants (including Bartholomew), three were Manx or Hebrideans. One of these, Alexander Macdonald of Islay, was the heir of Angus Macdonald who had failed to do homage to King John by February, 1293. He was perhaps already a supplier of *gallóglach* (gallowglasses or mercenary infantry) to northern Ireland, and he and his father had joined the Bruces in the Turnberry Band of 1286, which almost certainly presaged some Irish adventure. Although married to Alexander Macdougall's daughter, he was bitterly opposed to the lord of Argyll, who was a loyal adherent of Balliol and the Comyns. The dispute between the two chiefs had already come before King Edward in 1291, when both parties had agreed to a postponement, evidently for the sake of keeping the peace in the 'isles and outlying territories'.[9] The struggle between Macdougalls and Macdonalds for land and power was the dominant feature of Hebridean 'politics' in the century from 1250 to 1350, and it was almost inevitable that Alexander of Islay should try to outflank his rival by appealing afresh to

Edward I against his rival's relative and patron, King John.[10] The other Hebridean, Malcolm, had the surname 'son of the Englishman' or simply 'the Englishman' (*le fiz le Engleys, le Engleys*), and was said to be a tenant in chief in the sheriffdom of Perth, which included Argyll so long as Balliol's ordinance of 1293 was not in force.[11] Malcolm was perhaps the same man who will appear later in this book as Malcolm MacCulian, but neither origin nor identity is known. Since his appeal was an hereditary claim to Kintyre, it may be that he was related to the family of Mac Sween or Sweeney, which had held the lordship of Knapdale and lands in Kintyre until 1262, when they were dislodged by the earl of Menteith.[12] They nursed a grievance, and between 1301 and 1310 John Mac Sween was understandably active with his galleys in the English service, and still keeping alive his claim against the Menteiths.[13] In 1300 Malcolm 'le fiz le Engleys' was similarly harassing the Scots with men and galleys.[14] The third appellant from former Norwegian territory was a lady named Affrica, cousin of Magnus the last king of Man, who died in 1266. Clearly, she thought the new régime an opportunity of raising an hereditary claim to Man which had probably seemed hopeless under Alexander III.[15]

The remaining three Scottish appellants were Bartholomew, whose case has been dealt with, Simon of Restalrig and Macduff of Fife. The Scots parliament had placed in wardship the barony of Restalrig because its holder was an idiot, and Simon's complaint was that during the wardship (which had not been given to him) Sir Patrick Graham had improperly persuaded Simon's mother to alienate some lands of the barony. Nothing more is known of this case.[16] Far and away the most famous appeal was that of Macduff, a younger son of Malcolm earl of Fife (died 1266). He complained that he had not been allowed peaceful possession of the lands of Creich and Rires settled on him (as he claimed) by his father, but on the contrary had been put in prison for a time by Balliol. Macduff's name, another instance of Celtic revival, seems to have puzzled at least one historian, who took it to be a surname and looked in vain for a Christian name to go with it.[17] The Fife family was evidently conscious that its members formed the 'Clan Macduff', ultimately descended from some unidentified Duf, possibly King Duf who had ruled briefly in the late tenth century. There is nothing to suggest that Macduff resorted to Edward I's superior lordship as a matter of principle. He was a man with a chip on his shoulder. In 1297 he and his sons joined Wallace,[18] and Macduff himself was killed at Falkirk the following year,[19] fighting for the very king whose judgement he had called in English help to overturn. By then he was a 'false traitor' in King Edward's eyes.

King John was summoned before King's Bench to answer for his failure to do justice in the Mazun case (May 8th, 1293)[20] and the Macduff appeal came before King's Bench at Trinity (May 24th) whence it was adjourned to the Michaelmas parliament.[21] The king refused to appear or defend his judgement through attorneys, and Edward's council, evidently prepared in advance for this contumacy, drew up a set of carefully worked out rules to cover these and future cases of appeal from Scotland to England.[22] The rules were drastic. They involved the personal attendance of the king of Scots to answer for his judgements, a requirement which Edward's advisers must have known would be intolerable for a ruling monarch, and, among other equally onerous terms, the forfeiture of the Scots king's lordship over an appellant's fief if its custody pending an appeal had been interfered with. Almost the only record we have of this year 1293 is official record. It shows a mixture of firmness and pliancy on King John's part which may actually reflect the king's own character but is more probably the result of occasional pressure from more forceful councillors. For example, in the John Mazun case, King Edward wrote to Balliol on the appellant's behalf, and after the case had been heard in the Scottish parliament received a reasoned answer not from Balliol himself but from the bishop of St Andrews, as principal executor of Alexander III.[23] On the other hand, humble petitions sent to Edward at this time by Balliol do not show much spirit, and the English king's gracious replies conceded very little save the news that the litigious John Mazun had died and his lawsuit was therefore void.[24]

The critical moment in this calculated oppression and provocation was reached after Michaelmas 1293, when King John at last appeared in person before the English parliament and was treated like a defaulting debtor.[25] At first he showed surprising courage and dignity. He said he neither dared nor was able to answer in an English court on a matter affecting the kingdom of Scotland without consulting the *probi homines*, the responsible men, of his realm. He could not admit any adjournment, for that would imply recognition of English jurisdiction. It is clear that so far he had been well briefed, and that the same minds were at work here as in the Treaty of Birgham and the protestations of 1291 and 1292. But the Scots leaders had reckoned without Balliol's personal weakness, the psychological effect of a browbeating from Edward I (in the following year this was to give a dean of St Paul's heart-failure) and the humiliating high-handedness of a hostile English parliament. The king of Scots was judged to be in King Edward's mercy for contempt of court, and sentenced to lose his three chief castles and towns (presumably Edinburgh, Roxburgh and Berwick) until he made amends. Under this threat Balliol collapsed. He renewed his submission and homage in abject terms, and asked for a delay until the next English parliament.[26] 'We have no power', the Scots lords had declared in 1291, 'to reply in the absence of a king to whom such a demand should be addressed and who could reply to it.' Now, all too clearly, their king had given his reply.

Far from supporting any belief that appeals from Scotland to England became popular in King John's reign, the evidence suggests that the Scots were indifferent or hostile to the new facilities. Of course, for all we know, litigants may have been discouraged from appealing by John and his council, though if that had been so we should have expected a protest from Edward I. The historian, however, cannot have it both ways. He cannot say in the same breath that the Scots found the procedure of appeal attractive and yet regarded the practice as an unwarrantable restriction of their independence. The truth is that Anglo-Scottish relations, which on the whole had been remarkably good under the two Alexanders, were wrecked not on particular instances of appeal, not even on Edward I's stubborn insistence on his right to hear appeals, but on a wholly different principle or attitude which the English king had introduced into these relations ever since June 1291. Appeals were merely one aspect of what a Yorkshire chronicler of the time describes bluntly as the 'yoke of servitude which the Scots deserved'.[27] For there is no question that however correct and legalistic King Edward himself was, his subjects looked at the matter much less subtly. They made the inevitable comparison between what Edward had recently accomplished in Wales, which in 1284 had been annexed to the English Crown, and the claim of sovereign or direct lordship which he made in Scotland. To the ordinary Englishman it was the great glory of his king that he had defied Philip the Fair of France and reduced the treacherous Welsh and the 'fickle and unstable'[28] Scots to servitude. He was mourned after his death as 'the conqueror of lands and flower of chivalry',[29] not as a lawyer-king who had been scrupulous about his own rights and those of others.

The Scottish leaders were clearly alarmed at the consequences of their own weakness as early as December 1292, when they made their formal protestation to Edward I on King John's behalf. With each of Balliol's successive acts of defiance and subsequent surrenders their alarm must have grown. Scotland was a small country, smaller even than its geographical area would suggest. Its leading men formed a correspondingly close-knit group, sub-divided of course by family ties and by faction but still small enough for its members to know one another well and see one another frequently. In the record of public assemblies and acts of state the same few names occur over and over again. After the court of Berwick had adjudged the crown to Balliol it was only a matter of weeks before many of the auditors reassembled at Scone for the inauguration. Around Christmas an appreciable number were still gathered together, and just over a month later John held his first parliament at Scone,[30] where most of the same magnates must once again have been present. Among the auditors in November 1291, for example, had been Bishop Fraser of St Andrews, the earl of Buchan and Sir Patrick Graham. These, with Sir Thomas Randolph who had been Dervorguilla Balliol's executor, were King John's spokesmen in the protest of December. Again, Bishop Wishart of Glasgow, Sir Andrew Murray of Petty and Master Nicholas of St Andrews (*alias* of Balmyle) were also auditors in November.[31] In the following February, at John's first parliament, they are to be found sealing or witnessing an agreement made under the aegis of the bishop of Glasgow between his Dean and Chapter and Sir Andrew Murray's brother, Sir William Murray of Bothwell, 'pantler of Scotland', one of the most powerful barons of the country and known popularly as Sir William 'le riche'.[32] Nearly all these men played leading parts in the events of the next few years. Nothing of their conversation has been handed down to us, but we may be sure it was not taken up with mere pleasantries. Though they belonged to a conventional, hierarchical society, the nobles of that age were used to great frankness, outspoken expression of opinion, graphic and often ribald abuse of one another. They were no fools, and knew perfectly well that King Edward entertained, as Sir Maurice Powicke has put it, 'no exalted ideas about the nature of Scottish kingship'.[33] Nor, it may be added, about Scotland itself. Sir Thomas Grey, the fourteenth-century Northumberland knight and chronicler, says that when King Edward handed over the seal of government for conquered Scotland to John de Warenne at Newminister (beside Morpeth) in September 1296 he exclaimed jokingly 'A man does good business when he rids himself of a turd.'[34]

The Scots leaders also knew well enough that if King John continued to lead his subjects along the path he had taken in October 1293, they would very soon spring the trap which Edward had set for them. Powicke believed that 'gradually the legend grew that Edward, a foe in the guise of a friend, had struck down a trustful and defenceless people', and cites as evidence that 'masterpiece of political rhetoric', the Declaration of Arbroath of 1320.[35] If the legend had really taken thirty years to gain concrete expression its growth would indeed have been gradual. But its substance appears quite plainly in the letter *Scimus, fili* which Pope Boniface VIII addressed to King Edward in June 1299.[36] The contents or substance of this letter must have been prepared, and very carefully prepared at that, with the help of the Scots themselves, probably some while before the formal date of its issue.[37] After summarizing the Treaty of Birgham and Edward's assurance of May 1291 that the visit of *les haus hommes* of Scotland to Norham should not prejudice the liberties of the realm, the bull continues:

> It is said that at the time when the realm of Scotland lacked a defender, certain novel matters were, contrary to custom, introduced touching the state of that realm and the liberty it had formerly enjoyed, either by the magnates of the realm who were, so to speak, without a head and lacked the guidance of a leader and steersman, or else by him to whom the government had (though improperly) been committed by you.[38] Nevertheless, these novel matters, exacted as it were by force and by that fear which could have smitten even the constant,[39] ought in no circumstances to remain in force by right nor redound to the prejudice of the kingdom.

Bearing in mind that this bull was expedited after King Edward's sack of

Berwick and his 'abolition' of Scottish monarchy, after the battles of Stirling
Bridge and Falkirk, the statement, far from embodying a legend, seems an
astonishingly sober, cautious, and in the main accurate account of what
happened in 1291–92.

The immediate origins of the Scottish war of independence lay in the
struggle which broke out in June 1294 between Philip IV of France and
Edward I over the conditions on which Gascony could continue to be held as
a fief of the French Crown. If the Scots were to regain their independence
they too would have to make war. They must have a specific *casus belli*, and
above all they must have allies. Since the king would not take the initiative,
the 'responsible men' must take it for him. It is not difficult to feel sympathy
for the wretched Balliol, ground between the upper and nether millstones of
an overlord who demanded humble obedience and a community of the
realm whose leaders insisted that he stand up manfully for their independence. A contemporary English writer, conflating Saint Luke and Isaiah,
compared him to a lamb among the wolves, who dared not open his mouth.[40]
The suspense which had mounted in the eighteen months from John's
accession came to an end almost overnight with the outbreak of war between
France and England. All at once the Scots regained their nerve.

The sequence of events which precipitated the Scottish decision to defy
King Edward was as follows. On May 19th, 1294, Philip IV confiscated
Edward's duchy of Aquitaine. On June 24th Edward renounced his homage
as duke and sent his formal 'defiance' to the French king. He embarked
upon an elaborate scheme of military alliances to encircle France. This
included Germany and the northern Spanish kingdoms, especially Aragon,
but concentrated, by long-standing tradition, on the principalities of the
Low Countries, Holland, Brabant, Gelders, and even Flanders itself, a fief
of France, which was brought in because the count, Guy de Dampierre, had
a personal quarrel with King Philip. At the end of May all sea communication between England and the continent was put under strict royal control.
On June 2nd King John was ordered to apply the same prohibition to
Scottish shipping and report as soon as he had done so.[41] The English feudal
host was summoned to be at Portsmouth on September 1st, ready to embark
for overseas service. At the end of June a similar summons went out
demanding the personal service of the king of Scots, ten earls of Scotland,
and sixteen barons, headed by James the Stewart and Bruce of Annandale
the Competitor, now over seventy years of age.[42] Here was 'superior or
direct lordship' with a vengeance. Not since 1159, when King Malcolm IV
had joined Henry II's expedition to Toulouse, had a king of Scotland
performed overseas military service for a king of England. On that occasion
King Malcolm had come home to find the earls of Scotland angry at what he
had done. They had, indeed, banded together to make sure that he would
never again leave his kingdom to go on a mere adventure of chivalry. In 1294
the Scottish magnates were determined that their king should not be given

the chance to perform military service even if he was ready to. Balliol was present at the emergency great council convened by Edward in mid-June, and is said to have promised to give aid.[43] In fact neither he nor any of his barons appeared in response to Edward's repeated summons, but instead made various excuses. In August the newly-conquered Welsh were called on to fight in Gascony. So sure was Edward of their loyalty that arms were distributed among them while they were still at home. In September almost the whole of Wales broke into fierce revolt. Local leaders were found everywhere, and in Madog ap Llywelyn of Merioneth a national leader. The king's castles, even great Caernarvon, were seized and destroyed. In January 1295 a spectacularly successful ambush of Edward's baggage train between Conway and Bangor halted the English winter campaign. Although we know of no liaison between Madog and the Scots, his rebellion, continuing until March 1295, must have impressed the Scots leaders profoundly. Already, before December 1294, they had apparently taken the highly significant step of obtaining from the simple-minded old Pope Celestine v (Peter Morrone) absolution from any oaths exacted from them under duress.[44]

To seek French as well as papal aid was an obvious course. It is often said that the Franco-Scottish treaty of 1295 was the beginning of the Auld Alliance. In fact it was nothing of the sort. Ever since 1173 (to go back no further) it had been the normal, one might almost say the routine, practice for a French king at war with England to call upon Scottish support, and for a Scots king at odds with England to look for help from France. It was the inevitable consequence both of the entry of Scotland into the community of North Sea nations and of the development of her independent monarchy. We do not know who took the initiative in 1295: the first move could as easily have come from Paris as from Edinburgh. Nor do we know the exact moment at which negotiations began. All we can be sure of is that in March 1295 King Philip still viewed the Scots as enemies along with the English,[45] while two months later he held them 'not as enemies but rather as our friends'.[46] By early July the Scots leaders' resolve to fight for their independence, and their mistrust of Balliol, had pushed them to the point of a sober constitutional revolution. At a parliament held at Stirling the government was taken out of Balliol's hands and a council of twelve elected to manage the direction of affairs.[47] Walter of Guisborough and the Lanercost Chronicle both draw across their account the red herring of a comparison with the Twelve Peers of France, but the former adds the really significant fact that the council consisted of four bishops, four earls and four barons – a doubling of the two bishops, two earls and two barons who formed the regency council of 1286. Tout rightly compared the twelve to the council of fifteen elected to take over the government of England from Henry III in 1258,[48] but he missed the vital point of difference, namely the symmetry of representation on the Scottish council. Highly characteristic of late-

thirteenth-century Scotland, this arrangement continued to express the
idea of the community of the realm. So far there had been Guardians during
a minority and Guardians during an interregnum. Now there were to be
Guardians during the 'incapacity' or 'incompetence' of the sovereign.[49] The
revolutionary nature of this step should not be underrated. In 1258, when
the English baronage – not for the first time – were placing their king under
constraint, the Scottish baronage, much more conservative and feudally-
minded, told the Welsh leaders with whom they had concluded a treaty that
they would try to persuade their king to give it his support, but that they
would have to go back on their word if the king strictly ordered them to do
so.[50] Unlike the English, the Scots of the thirteenth century were not
habitual king-breakers. That the Scots nobles in 1295 had at last caught up
with the English nobles of forty years before is proof not of the back-
wardness of Scotland but of the strength of Scottish hostility to Edward I.

The council of twelve had two urgent tasks, to negotiate the French treaty
and to put the country into a state of defence. At the July parliament four
commissioners were appointed to go to Paris.[51] The senior commissioner
was William Fraser, bishop of St Andrews, whose long experience of
government included seven years as chancellor of Scotland and six years as
Guardian. Uncle of Simon Fraser of Oliver Castle on the upper Tweed, who
died in 1291, the bishop belonged to a baronial family of the second rank
whose various branches held land in East Lothian, Stirlingshire and
Tweeddale. No doubt Fraser and the second commissioner, Matthew of
Crambeth, were members of the twelve.[52] Matthew, previously dean of
Aberdeen, was appointed bishop of Dunkeld at the instance of the Guardians in 1288. This see, whose diocese was composed of many separate pieces
of territory dispersed across central Scotland from Drumalban almost to
Berwick, ranked third in seniority after St Andrews and Glasgow. We have
seen already how Bishop Matthew co-operated with Wishart of Glasgow to
issue a formal copy of the guarantees obtained from Edward I in 1291. Like
Wishart he was one of Bruce's auditors in the Great Cause. Despite his
clerical orders, Matthew was heir to the small barony of Crambeth, now
called Dowhill, whose ruined tower-house of a later date still stands on a
slope of the Cleish Hills overlooking Kinross. The two lay commissioners
were younger sons of great baronial families. Sir John de Soules was brother
of William de Soules, hereditary butler of Scotland and lord of Liddesdale.[53] He had already been an envoy in Paris, in 1285, when he negotiated
Alexander III's marriage to Yolande de Dreux. He too had been an auditor
for Bruce. Sir Ingram de Umfraville was probably a cousin of the earl of
Angus, and was related to the Balliols.[54]

These four were sent to France, and the treaty with King Philip followed
on October 23rd.[55] It provided for an offensive and defensive alliance
between John and Philip, towards whose people the community of the realm
of Scotland was said to be well affected. As long as hostilities continued

between France and England the Scots were to wage war on the English by land and sea, not only the king but also the prelates (as far as appropriate), earls, barons, knights and the urban communities – all these groups were to notify the French in writing of their assent as soon as possible. On the other hand, if Scotland was invaded the king of France would begin diversionary activity or send suitable aid to Scotland. If Edward 1 left England (for the continent), the Scots were to mount a large-scale invasion by land (*bellum campestre*). Neither side would make a separate peace. The alliance was to be cemented by a marriage between King John's son Edward and Jeanne, daughter of Charles of Valois, King Philip's brother. Thus the French would be given a stake in the survival of the Balliol dynasty, since Edward, described as 'future king of Scotland', was guaranteed to be the heir by the Scottish envoys. The treaty was ratified by the Scottish king and parliament on February 23rd, 1296. From the names of those who set their seals to the ratification we may infer that the four bishops of the council of twelve were St Andrews, Glasgow, Dunkeld and Aberdeen,[56] and the four earls Buchan, Mar, Strathearn and Atholl. Of the eleven barons who sealed, it is reasonable to assume that the first two named, John Comyn of Badenoch and James the Stewart, were also of the council. Possibly the next two, Alexander Balliol and Geoffrey Moubray, made up the dozen.

The treaty was one leg of a triangular alliance which brought together France, Scotland and Norway. It has been shown how some serious differences between the Scots and Norwegians were temporarily laid aside as the result of King Philip's busy diplomacy.[57] Though there was no direct Scoto-Norwegian treaty, the Scots were accessory to the Franco-Norwegian treaty completed on October 22nd, 1295, the day before their own treaty with Philip. Both countries agreed not to attack one another so long as they were helping France against England. The Norwegians could hardly invade England, so their part in the scheme was the provision of a large fleet of galleys, which would reinforce the ships Philip had both obtained direct from Genoa and was building in Normandy with skilled Genoese assistance. The French encircling alliance with Norway and Scotland seems an obvious counterpart of Edward 1's encircling alliances with Germany, Spain and the Low Countries. Yet for the Norwegians it meant reversing a policy of good relations with England. The Maid of Norway's father, King Eric, had been on good terms with Edward 1 at the time of the treaties of Salisbury and Birgham–Northampton, and this harmony survived the rejection of Eric's far-fetched claim in the competition for the Scottish throne.

On November 9th, 1292, Robert Bruce, the Competitor's son, resigned the earldom of Carrick, which he held in right of his wife Marjorie, to their son and heir the young Robert, the future king, then eighteen years old. Next year he went to Norway by leave of Edward 1 to give his daughter Isabel in marriage to King Eric.[58] By refusing homage to Balliol, Bruce had kept open his father's claim to the throne; by marrying Isabel Bruce, King

Eric renewed his Scottish interests and (since the Bruces were loyal friends and supporters of Edward) increased the ties of friendship which bound him to the English king.

The marriage of Isabel Bruce in particular and the position of the Bruces in general bring us to the second task confronting the council of twelve: the defence and security of Scotland. The Bruces were the most powerful of the magnatial families who were likely to be disloyal to the Balliol régime. Old Bruce, the Competitor, died at Lochmaben on Maundy Thursday 1295, before the storm broke. His last public act, characteristically, was a double defiance of Balliol. In 1294 he secured the appointment of his clerk and protégé, Master Thomas Dalton of Kirkcudbright, as bishop of Galloway.[59]

Episcopal appointments were the concern of the Crown, and King John protested against Master Thomas's election.[60] Thomas had been elected by the prior and canons of Whithorn, the cathedral church of the diocese. The king did not contest their right to perform the election, but he alleged that there had been bribery, and there can be little doubt that his accusations were really aimed at the Bruce faction. Indeed, ancient rivalries were involved in the affair. The lords of Galloway regarded themselves as special patrons of the see, and Balliol's protest had actually been addressed to the archbishop of York from Buittle, the chief residence of the lords of Galloway. Moreover, the election had taken place in an atmosphere of clerical dissension within the diocese, which itself seems to have reflected the Bruce-Balliol conflict. The chapter's right to exercise the bishop's spiritual jurisdiction during a vacancy was disputed not only by the archdeacon Henry, an elderly, blind man, but also, more vigorously and capably, by the archdeacon's nephew, Master John 'the Nephew' (*Nepos*) who had probably been for some years the most influential clergyman in the diocese. It can hardly be a coincidence that this man was one of Balliol's auditors in the competition for the throne, along with the previous bishop of Galloway.[61] Owing, presumably, to Balliol's reluctance at this stage to alienate the Bruces and their friends altogether, he climbed down in the summer of 1294, and Thomas Dalton was duly consecrated in October. But the affair had been a serious rebuff. The Competitor's family was strongly entrenched. His son succeeded to Annandale and his grandson had been confirmed in his mother's earldom of Carrick at the Stirling parliament of August 1293, sponsored by his family's friends James the Stewart and the earl of Mar.[62]

The acid test for all the nobles and gentry in Scotland who, for one reason or another, put their loyalty to Edward I before their loyalty to King John was the decision to call out the host, in accordance with the terms of the French treaty. The order went out presumably early in 1296, for a 'wapinschaw' (inspection of arms and equipment) and was followed by a summons to the host to assemble on March 11th.[63] Here, as elsewhere, we can see how much store the Scots set by the punctilious observance of tradition. The host was to meet at Caddonlee, where the Caddon Water joins the Tweed some four miles north of Selkirk. Evidently this was the correct starting-point for an army operating south of the march. The chronicler of an earlier Anglo-Scottish war wrote of King William the Lion in 1173,

> Now the king of Scotland has made ready his host,
> At Caddonlee they were assembled.[64]

The actual writ of summons has not survived but we know from the writ probably issued by the Guardians in or after 1286[65] that a national call to arms would require 'free service' and 'Scottish service'. Free service was military service *par excellence*, performed by free men – barons, thanes, knights, serjeants and other freeholders – who according to their rank and wealth would be equipped either with a knight's full armour or the rather lighter armour of a serjeant, and would be mounted on 'barded' horses, heavily built *destriers* protected by mail, or else lighter, weaker horses wearing coats of *cuir bouillé* – leather steeped in warm oil and wax. Scottish service or 'Scottish army' was demanded from the earldoms north of the Forth. It meant the attendance of able-bodied men from the 'horseless classes' – peasant farmers, herds, drovers, shepherds and hunters, fighting on foot and wearing no body armour. Indeed, if they were highlanders they would wear an early version of the kilt, producing an effect of nakedness about the lower quarters of the body which had long struck foreign observers with amazement. The weapons used by these foot soldiers were chiefly the long spear and long-handled, pointed 'Lochaber axe'. The men from Selkirk Forest were skilled archers, but presumably they used the short bow which was soon to be outclassed by the deadly Welsh or English long bow. Walter of Guisborough's words suggest that the summons of 1296 was for the landholding and propertied classes only.[66] Certainly it was only the Scottish 'host' in this narrow sense, the feudal cavalry, which the English defeated. But the speed with which Andrew Murray and William Wallace raised their infantry force in the following year suggests that the machinery for summoning and training the non-feudal 'common army' was not rusty from lack of use.

The Bruces, at all events, refused to answer the summons. In the eyes of Walter of Guisborough the Bruces (whom he knew well as the patrons of Guisborough Priory) were simply like the numerous other English nobles holding land in Scotland who remained faithful to the English king. North of the border such men had become enemies of the community. Those who had not already fled were expelled and their land given to others. Annandale was placed under the earl of Buchan, to become a base for raids on Cumberland.[67] We know too that English clergy were ejected from their Scottish livings lest they form a fifth column. In Bishop Fraser's absence the St Andrews diocese was administered by two vicars-general, Master William of Kinghorn and Master Peter de Champneys. On the orders of the council of twelve they removed twenty-six English clerks from their benefices in the diocese, and doubtless similar action was taken throughout the country. Even some English members of religious orders in Scotland were expelled.[68]

Things had gone badly for Edward in Gascony and were to go worse. The French commanders, Charles of Valois and Robert count of Artois, were more than a match for the inadequate English forces under the earl of Lincoln, John of Brittany and John de St John. First the Welsh, then the Scots, prevented Edward from leading his troops in person and sending enough men and arms. The cost of the war mounted as hopes of English success faded. But despite the Gascon failure we must not underestimate the formidable war-potential of Edward I's England. The country was rich and until 1297 was as fully united behind its king as any country in that age could be. The Welsh wars of 1277, 1282–83 and 1294–95 had revolutionized the English army, and the experience and confidence which they had given to commanders and men would prove of immense value to them in Scotland. For King Edward the years of greatest danger and difficulty were from 1297 to 1303. He rode out the storm, his will-power, force of character and relentless energy surpassing those of any of his subjects. For the last four years of his life he was back on top, master of every situation save that which broke him in the end, the rising of Robert Bruce. In 1295 neither the stubborn resistance of the Scots nor the part to be played by Bruce would have been credible to Edward. Not only did he know Scotland from personal visits in the 1260s, but his acquaintance with many of the Scots nobility and gentry must have been extensive and in some cases of long standing.[69] He believed that he had the measure of his Scottish opponents. He had seen their commoners cut to pieces at Lewes, he had thrown their nobles into confusion at Norham. 'What matter if both Welsh and Scots are our foes?' he exclaimed at Falkirk, 'let them join forces if they please. We shall beat them both in a day.'[70] But he moved with characteristic patience. In October 1295 he demanded that the border castles of Berwick, Roxburgh and Jedburgh should be handed over till the end of the French war, and asked that no French or Flemings should be allowed to enter Scotland.[71] When the Scots replied that their country was free and they would admit whom they pleased he was astonished, and when a report reached him that some English merchants had been killed at Berwick he was shocked and indignant, saying 'Who could believe such wickedness and treachery?'[72] In February 1296 the French treaty was ratified in the Scottish parliament. It was a declaration of war; but long before this the feudal host of England had been summoned to meet at Newcastle on March 1st.[73]

FIVE

Two Kinds of War

Characteristically, the Scots were much too confident. The border was in good hands. The earl of Buchan held Annandale, Nicholas de Soules (John de Soules' nephew) held Liddesdale, and the two most important castles of Roxburgh and Berwick were commanded respectively by the Stewart and Sir William Douglas.[1] Some of Edward I's measures against the Scots had been mere pinpricks. In October 1295 he ordered land held in England by Scots to be seized, and in April 1296, he followed this up with an order that Scotsmen in England should be arrested. The order is interesting chiefly for the light it throws on the question of nationality. Contrary to a common belief, the concept of Scottish nationality and the fact that it was distinct from English nationality were clearly understood in the late thirteenth century. At the remote north Hertfordshire village of Bennington, for example, an entire colony of Scotsmen was discovered, including the rector, Henry of Adderston. They had all lived there many years.[2] At Stebbing near Dunmow the sheriff found a son of Sir William Douglas, born in England and nearly two years old. This dangerous young Scot was arrested till the king should send further instructions.[3] The difference in nationality is well shown by the story of Robert de Ros,[4] lord of Wark-on-Tweed, an Englishman who went over to the Scots because of his love for a Scots-woman whom he wished to marry. When he brought men from Roxburgh for a surprise attack on Wark they used a password to tell friend from foe – an English phrase of course, since southern Scots and Northumbrian English spoke the same tongue. The Northumbrians found it easy to pick up the password themselves, and so escaped. But already between the English-speaking Scot and the English-speaking Englishman, subjects of different kingdoms, a mental and emotional line of division was fixed which ran as clear as those ancient boundaries the Tweed and the Redden Burn.

The war began towards the end of March with de Ros's treachery and King Edward's rapid advance to relieve Wark. This done, he waited for the celebration of Easter (which fell this year on Lady Day) before laying siege to Berwick. Meanwhile, on Easter Monday, seven earls of Scotland and John Comyn the younger of Badenoch, the Guardian's son, crossed the fords of Solway from Annandale with a large infantry force, burning the villages from Arthuret to the suburbs of Carlisle and trying to take the city itself by storm. Ironically, the commander of Carlisle castle since October 1295 had been Robert Bruce, lord of Annandale and previously earl of

Elgin (26-28/7)
The Enzie (in tents) (24/7)
Cullen
Banff
Rothes
?
Fyvie (21/7)
(Cantilupe, Hastings & Co.)
Kintore (20/7)
Kildrummy (1/8)
B a d e n o c h   M a r
Aberdeen (14-19/7)
Lumphanan
(Bishop of Durham)
?
Durris
Kindrochit
Cairn o'Mount
Kincardine
T h e   M o u n t h
Brechin (4/8)   Montrose (8-10/7)
Clunie   Forfar (3/7)
Arbroath (5/8)
Dundee (6/8)
Perth (21-24/6)
St. Andrews (11/8)
Auchterarder
Stirling (14/6; 14-15/8)   Dunfermline
Edinburgh (6/6; 17-18/8)
Dunbar (28/4)
X 27/4
Berwick 30/3-27/4 (sacked); 22/8 (Parliament 28/8)
Lauder
Coldstream (28/3)
Caddonlea
Wark
Roxburgh (7-23/5; 1/6)
The Forest   Jedburgh
Route of Edward I
—·—· Northward
·········· Southward
Dates of Edward I's sojourns shown thus: (28/3)
—S→ Scots earls, March-April, 1296
Wheel
-S
-S
Castleton (25/5)
Corbridge
0   10   20   30
Miles
-S
Arthuret
Hexham
Newcastle upon Tyne
Carlisle

3. The Invasion of 1296.

Carrick, who with his young son, the future king, adhered to the English king. Although a fire started by the Scots caused great damage in the town, they lacked siege engines and made no headway against the inhabitants' stout resistance. After barely one day's 'siege' they withdrew to Annandale, and we know that the earl of Buchan at least had retired as far west as Sweetheart Abbey by April 1st.[5] Two days earlier (Friday, March 30th) the English army was arrayed in front of Berwick. The largest and richest town of Scotland was defended only by a ditch and timber palisade. The invaders swept over this at their first assault, taking the townsmen so much by surprise that they put up almost no fight at all. Only the thirty Flemings in the Red Hall fought to the last and were burned to death or suffocated when the building went up in flames. The castle garrison surrendered on terms, which included the condition that Douglas should be kept with the king's household till the end of the campaign.[6] Edward's magnanimity did not reach far beyond the knightly class. The men of Berwick were burgesses, merchants, artisans. By the conventions of the age, above which Edward himself never rose, such men could expect little mercy from feudal armies. Besides, they had committed outrages upon English merchants and had taunted the king himself with ribald rhymes and gestures. He gave the order that no one should be spared, and the Berwick men were killed in such numbers that their corpses became a dangerous nuisance and had to be thrown in the sea or buried in deep pits.[7] The slaughter, for which the king alone must be held responsible, went on until the frantic pleading of the clergy of the district moved him at last to pity. Their gesture was sincere enough no doubt; it was also conventional enough for Edward to understand.

In April another grim convention was observed across the hills from Berwick, in Redesdale, Coquetdale and Tynedale. The Scots earls, now based on Jedburgh, came over the Cheviots and raided purposelessly far and wide in Northumberland, burning villages, churches and monasteries. According to an English propaganda draft, they burned alive some 200 schoolboys at Corbridge,[8] a figure which seems too large to credit. Walter of Guisborough, who was not slow to relate Scottish atrocities, confines their crimes to arson.[9] Whether viewed as a reprisal or as a tactical diversion, the raid was a failure. Edward methodically set about the refounding of Berwick as an English town with English burgesses, comparable with the new towns he had built in Wales and with the *bastides* or fortified new towns of Gascony. Henceforth Berwick was to be the headquarters of the English administration of conquered Scotland, and the home of a special exchequer established for this purpose. Eventually (September 6th) a senior royal clerk, Hugh Cressingham, who had recently been chief itinerant justice in the northern counties, was put in charge of this exchequer as treasurer of Scotland.[10]

The Scots had failed to save Berwick, but their main force had not yet engaged the invaders. There is nothing to show that the Scottish leaders had any but the most conventional ideas on how to fight the war. A cavalry army must be confronted with cavalry in the open field. The rules required pitched battles and sieges, and the rules must be observed. Dunbar, seat of the earls of Dunbar or March, was the next obstacle in Edward's path. He was in no hurry to complete the conquest of which he was confident, and it was not until April 23rd that he sent forward a cavalry force under John, Earl Warenne, to take Dunbar.[11] Earl Patrick of Dunbar was opposed to the patriots and a firm adherent of Edward. But while he was with the English king his countess, a Scottish loyalist, managed to hoodwink her husband's garrison and opened the castle to a Scottish force commanded by three other earls.[12] On Friday, April 27th, Warenne's knights, who had begun the siege of Dunbar, were attacked by the main body of King John's army, the 'feudal host' of Scotland.[13] They came up shortly after noon, a brave sight which so cheered the Scots within the castle that they raised their banners and shouted at the besiegers 'Tailed dogs, we will cut your tails off'. (The accepted way to infuriate an Englishman in the middle ages was to remind him of the popular belief that the English had tails.) Warenne set his junior officers the task of preventing the garrison joining up with the main Scottish army, and with his veterans in good heart turned westward to confront it himself as it came over the brow of Spottsmuir. To reach the Scots the invaders had first to descend into the steep den cut by the Spott Burn. As they deployed to cross the burn, their ranks thinning or even out of sight altogether, the Scots thought they were fleeing. Yelling in their excitement and blowing horns loud enough to waken the dead, the Scottish horsemen left their commanding position and poured down the hill to give chase. Warenne's men were not in flight. Forming up in good order they threw themselves on the broken ranks of the Scottish host, overwhelmed them at the first onslaught and sent them swarming back across Lammermuir towards the shelter of Selkirk Forest forty miles to the west. Sir Patrick Graham stood his ground and was killed, and there were heavy casualties among the foot soldiers on the Scottish side.[14] But Dunbar is chiefly notable for the large number of distinguished prisoners taken and for the devastating proof it had given that the feudal host of Scotland – the Crown's official military machine, on which it had depended for a century and a half – was now utterly inadequate. Viewed as a whole it was a disorderly rabble, and its members completely failed to make up for their excessive individualism by any real experience of war. With the exception of the 'battle' of Largs in 1263, in which the Scots army cannot have been numerous, there had been no serious warfare in Scotland since Alexander II's Galloway campaign in 1235.[15]

The rules of feudal warfare required that the side which had been beaten should acknowledge the fact. Then, in a gentlemanly way, terms could be discussed and ransoms arranged. There was, consequently, very little resistance to Edward I after Dunbar. The Stewart surrendered Roxburgh, Edinburgh Castle held out for only a week or so, and Stirling Castle, disgracefully, was completely abandoned, only the porter being left to hand over the keys to the invaders.[16] In the west highlands Alexander Macdougall, lord of Lorn, put up enough resistance for a while to call forth a small expeditionary force of Irish troops.[17] King John and the Comyns retired northward, without any set purpose, and at Midsummer sent messengers to Edward at Perth begging to be received to his peace and asking for surrender terms.[18] The Scots were bidden to come to Brechin Castle, where Bishop Bek of Durham told them of the harsh but surely not unexpected conditions which Edward required. John was to resign his kingdom, his seal was to be broken, and he and all his council were to renounce the French treaty.

Constitutionally or legally, Edward I was in a curious position. In his own belief he was the superior lord who had been forced to take a fief out of the hands of a tenant or vassal because the tenant had rebelled and allied himself to the lord's mortal enemy (Philip the Fair). The defaulting vassal must therefore resign the fief, which would remain in the king's hand unless he chose to grant it to another vassal. But although much that happened in 1296 can be explained by this line of reasoning, some of the king's most striking actions and one of his best-known utterances belie the notion of a feudal lord recovering possession of his fief. In the early summer of 1296 he ordered the removal from Edinburgh to London of the regalia and a mass of plate, jewellery and relics, including the Black Rood of Saint Margaret, the holiest and most venerated relic in Scotland.[19] After he reached 'Saint John's Town' of Perth, he commanded that the Stone of Destiny should be moved from the abbey church of Scone and presented to Westminster Abbey as a gift to his special patron, Edward the Confessor.[20] The Stone of Destiny, on which the kings of Scots had been enthroned since time immemorial, was the innermost sacrosanct mystery among the insignia of Scottish monarchy. These acts of plunder were the acts of a conqueror anxious for trophies and determined to crush the pride of an independent people. His own subjects recognized this and sang of his triumph.

> Their kings' seat of Scone
> is driven over down,
> to London led.[21]

> I'll tell you truly what the Stone of Scotland is . . .
> Now Edward king of England has taken it,
> by the grace of Jesus and by hard fighting.
> To saint Edward has he given it.[22]

And the voice of Edward the Conqueror rings out in the contemptuous reply with which he crushed the spineless Bruce of Annandale. After Dunbar, Bruce put forward a plea to be allowed to take the throne for which his father had competed in vain. 'Have we nothing else to do,' said Edward, 'but win kingdoms for you?'[23]

Flitting aimlessly from place to place in the valleys of the north and south Esk during the first fortnight of July 1296, King John presented a sorry enough figure. It seems that towards the end of June a 'form of peace' which would have spared the Scots king the worst humiliation had been put forward, perhaps drafted by Bishop Bek of Durham, who was Balliol's friend.[24] But by July 8th, if not sooner, the English had decided to insist on unconditional surrender. At the old royal castle of Kincardine, on July 2nd, Balliol confessed his rebellion in an abjectly humble document;[25] in the kirkyard of Stracathro (July 7th) he renounced the French treaty;[26] finally at the burgh of Montrose (July 8th), he solemnly resigned his kingdom and royal dignity to the king of England.[27] No detail of humiliation was spared. His surcoat or tabard was embroidered with a blazon of the royal arms. This blazon was stripped off, so that he should suffer a total loss of face. The act gave the Scots a merciless nickname for their wretched sovereign – Toom Tabard, the empty surcoat which denoted King Nobody.[28] In August Balliol followed the regalia and royal records to the Tower of London. Soon he was moved to the relative comfort of Hertford, where he was allowed a huntsman and ten hounds, and was not far from his own great manor of Hitchin.[29] A few of the most prominent Scottish leaders, among them the earl of Buchan and Comyn of Badenoch, were also sent to England, and required to stay south of Trent.[30] Many other Scottish barons, knights and esquires had been captured at Dunbar and were held prisoner in various castles of the midlands, the south country and Wales. Chief among them were the three earls (Atholl, Ross and Menteith) who had led the force which occupied Dunbar Castle. In recognition of their rank they went to the Tower, along with several other noted barons and sons of barons: John Comyn the younger of Badenoch, Richard Siward, John Moubray, John of Inchmartin, David Graham (son of Sir Patrick), Alexander Menzies (de Meners), and Nicholas, son of Sir Thomas Randolph. Altogether, we have the names of nearly a hundred captives whose rank put them in the ransomable class.[31] Although most came from the earldoms of the three earls who led them they formed a surprisingly representative cross-section of the Scots gentry, from the Aird and Glenurquhart west of Inverness to Nithsdale, Annandale and Berwickshire in the south. Among the names which we have met already was that of Sir Andrew Murray, brother of the pantler, Sir William Murray of Bothwell. Sir Andrew was lord of Petty in Inverness-shire, Avoch in the Black Isle and Boharm in Banffshire.[32] He had served, probably from 1289, as Justiciar of Scotia, i.e. Scotland north of Forth.[33] He went to the Tower in virtue of his office and his membership of one of the greatest Scottish baronial families. Among the names which we shall meet again was that of Sir Andrew's son and heir, Andrew Murray esquire. By chance – the sort of chance which now and again shapes the history of nations – young Andrew Murray was sent to Chester,[34] the nearest to Scotland of all the castles used to house the Scottish prisoners of war.

In July, while Thomas of Lancaster was escorting Balliol from Montrose to London, King Edward advanced steadily northward, making sure of his hold upon a conquered land and taking the homages of prominent Scots.[36] He crossed into Deeside by the Cowie Mounth, stayed for five days at Aberdeen, and then proceeded in short marches by way of Kintore, Fyvie, Banff and Cullen to the Spey.[36]; Elgin, which he reached on July 26th, was the furthest point of his progress; his lieutenants – like Agricola's twelve centuries earlier – could be trusted to secure the western parts of Moray and the far north. He himself turned south to Rothes. From here a force was sent up the Spey under John de Cantilupe and John Hastings 'to search the country of Badenoch.'[37] Comyn the elder of Badenoch had submitted to the king at Montrose, but it did not follow automatically that the men of Badenoch and Lochaber, the highland districts of which he was lord,[38] would remain peaceable. The king himself crossed the hills by Invercharach[39] at the head of the Deveron to the earl of Mar's secluded fastness of Kildrummy, and so back to the lowlands by Kincardine O'Neil and the pass of Cairn o' Mount. The bishop of Durham had accompanied or proceeded Edward all the way to Elgin. Throughout the campaign he had behaved more like an under-king than a prelate, with an army from St Cuthbert's Land which is mentioned by contemporaries as quite distinct from the king's army. From Rothes he was sent south by a different route – probably up Stratha'an and across the upper Don into the Braes of Mar, where at Kindrochit (now Braemar) the earl of Mar possessed another castle.[40]

By August 22nd the king was back at Berwick. In four months he had traversed the whole eastern part of Scotland, stayed at every burgh and royal castle of note, and demonstrated his might to the people. It was time to consolidate this brief summer's conquest. At the Berwick parliament an ordinance was drawn up for the government of Scotland. Apparently the kingdom was not abolished but remained in abeyance. Edward would rule it as direct lord, but he did not add the title 'king of Scots' or even 'lord of Scotland' to his royal style. The Earl Warenne, victor of Dunbar, was made lieutenant or 'keeper', Hugh Cressingham treasurer, and Walter of Amersham chancellor.[41] Justices were appointed, of whom the chief was William Ormsby, Cressingham's colleague on the northern assizes. Sheriffs were appointed or confirmed in office, and castles were committed to a small number of trusted officials. On the English model two escheators were appointed – officials with general oversight of the Crown's feudal rights and revenues, Henry of Rye for north of Forth, based apparently at Elgin, and Peter of Dunwich for the south, entrusted with Yester in East Lothian.[42] There was a host of lesser appointments, and different posts might be given to one official. The clerk William de Rue (Dru), for example, had custody of the bishopric of St Andrews because Bishop Fraser remained in France and would not submit to Edward, and the earldom of Fife because the earl was a minor.[43] He was also keeper of the customs of Dundee, and it was in this capacity that he encountered the Lübeck merchants who, as we have seen, were shipping hides and wool from Scotland.[44]

The more one reads or handles some of the vast quantity of records left behind by this burst of imperialist activity, the more one admires the calm ambitiousness and the extraordinary thoroughness of the thirteenth-century English monarchy as it set about governing a foreign country. Here was a feudal king, peripatetic and personally attentive to all the details of administration, ruling an empire and fighting a complex war by means of a handful of hard-working officials. It is staggering to think of the weight of responsibility that rested on such men as John Droxford, keeper of the Wardrobe, Ralph Manton, cofferer of the Wardrobe, John Sandal, Philip Willoughby, John Benstead and a few more. They had to see to the raising of vast sums of money, to the purchase of stores, weapons and equipment, to the garrisoning of castles, to a thousand and one details of day-to-day administration, for all of which they must render an exact account. There is no question that Edward I gained such success as he did enjoy in Scotland because he was able to back up his own forcefulness with the hard work of officials who in general were loyal and conscientious. Their hands were certainly not clean – corruption was more or less endemic in thirteenth-century government service – but they got the king's work done.

What of the Scots themselves? Edward was in no hurry to free the Dunbar prisoners, and with Balliol and the Comyns out of Scotland he may have thought all would be well. At all events his only major act, apart from this constraint on certain notable leaders, was somewhat legalistic, though certainly thorough. As in 1291, every substantial freeholder of land in Scotland was required to swear fealty to the king of England in his capacity – albeit unstated in his official style – of lord of Scotland. Many Scots swore fealty personally as the king made his progress to the north and back in July and August. But the vast majority of fealties, formally recorded on the 'Ragman Roll', are dated at Berwick on August 28th.[45] It is hard to believe – though most historians appear to believe – that all these persons were actually present together at Berwick on that or any other date. It was, to be sure, a parliament, no doubt attended by many men of substance. But to suppose that more than fifteen hundred of the gentry and clergy from every part of Scotland were assembled in such a manner not only strains credulity but seems to be based on a misunderstanding of Edward's intentions. It was not that, as Tout put it, 'a crowd of Scots of every class flocked to the victor's court and took oaths of fealty'.[46] Edward required formal, legal acknow-ledgement of his lordship from the appropriate persons, so that in future his subjects in North Britain should be on precisely the same footing as his subjects south of the Border.[47] Thus fealty was sworn not only by those

Scots notables, such as the Bruces, who were already in his peace before war broke out, but also by certain English lay magnates and ecclesiastics who held property in Scotland. Among those doing homage, therefore, we find Brian Fitz Alan of Bedale,[48] Sir John Swinburne,[49] the abbot of Alnwick,[50] and the prior of Durham (who actually tried to do homage in place of the prior of Coldingham).[51] We even find the Italian Giacomo de Vicia, parson of Idvies in Angus and presumably a kinsman of the famous Master Bagimond – Baiamundo de Vicia – who was collector of the Crusading Tenth in Scotland in the 1280's.[52] By no stretch of the imagination can these men be regarded as defeated Scots bowing before the conqueror. The truth seems to be not that a motley gathering of 'Scots of every class' rendered homage, but that certain limited and well-defined classes of persons who held property in Scotland were required to provide written and sealed instruments of homage and fealty. Tenants-in-chief of the Crown and their heirs, substantial under-tenants and their heirs, officers and burgesses of some leading east-country burghs, heads of religious houses, a high propor- tion of the beneficed clergy (especially those who were university graduates) – these are the classes who make up by far the greater part of the names on the Ragman Roll. A contemporary description says that there were present at the Berwick parliament all the bishops (in fact there seem to have been only three out of a possible total of twelve), the abbots, priors, earls, barons and the 'superiors' (*souverains*) of all the common people.[53] This, if true, would make a large enough gathering, but very many fewer than fifteen hundred.

To judge from the Roll it looks as though the names and fealties were collected on a basis of sheriffdoms, and it is likely that during July and August the sheriffs were responsible for taking the fealties and sending or bringing the instruments recording them to the English officials at Berwick. Several features of the consolidated list point to the fundamentally legalistic nature of the process. For example, a considerable number of names appear more than once. Sometimes, as in the case of Sir John Stewart of Jedburgh (the Stewart's brother), a man's name will appear once for each sheriffdom in which he held land.[54] At other times the repetition is hard to explain, but the presence of repeated names argues against the physical presence of the homagers. Again, among the Lothian names we find not only Simon of Restalrig, heir to the barony of Restalrig, but also his father John who (as we have seen) was in fact *non compos mentis*. Was the idiot laird of Restalrig actually brought to Berwick to perform his homage?

One feature of the Roll has always interested historians: the absence of the name of William Wallace. In truth, a more surprising thing is the absence of the name of his brother, Malcolm, since it was he, evidently, who held land in Elderslie as a vassal of the Stewart. William Wallace may not have been judged a landholder of enough substance to justify obtaining fealty. But the list of names from the Stewart's great Lordship of Renfrew and Paisley is uncommonly full and thorough, including such apparently humble and obscure men as Thomas Brewster of the Forest of Paisley and Thomas the Wright of Blackhall (in Paisley).[55] It is possible that the sheriff of Lanark was unable to obtain the homages of Malcolm and William Wallace because they deliberately chose not to perform them. Such a refusal would not only be in line with Wallace's whole conduct throughout the war, it would also explain why he was regarded as an outlaw when the rising of 1297 began. This indeed, seems to be implied by Walter of Guisborough.[56]

In conquered Scotland the treasurer Hugh Cressingham quickly gained control of the occupation régime. He was the busy man on the spot, whereas Warenne, his nominal superior, disliked Scotland so much and took such a casual attitude towards his duties that he remained on his estates in Yorkshire.[57] Cressingham seems a typical enough example of his kind, though personally perhaps more obnoxious than most. Officious, smooth, with the pushfulness which often characterizes men of illegitimate birth, he had made his own way in the king's service.[58] Scotland might have been the stepping-stone to higher things. As it turned out, his rich Yorkshire living of Rudby, his many prebends and his little property in Hendon and Finchley, suitable for a civil servant's retirement, were as far as he ever got.[59] The Scots despised and hated him, and dubbed him the 'treacherer'.[60] His task was to raise the Crown revenues, to oversee the English administration, and to keep the peace. We have few details of his administration. Among his measures was a proclamation that all stores of wool throughout Scotland should be seized for the king's use and sent to the nearest seaport; but there is no evidence that the government did not intend, eventually, to pay for the wool thus seized.[61] Edward believed firmly that the Scottish problem was solved. The details could be left to his ministers. He himself returned to more pressing affairs, the resumption of the war against France, the development of the Flemish alliance and the most serious political crisis of his reign, the stiff clerical, mercantile and baronial opposition which occupied his attention from the close of 1296 until after his departure for Flanders on August 22nd, 1297.

Events were to prove that the English, from their king downward, had seriously misjudged the Scottish situation, though not without good reason. Ever since the reign of Alexander II, the leadership of the community of the realm of Scotland, especially in acts of resistance to English encroachment, had rested with the prelates of the church and with a large section of the feudal nobility among whom the great family of Comyn had played a dominant role. In a sense, the war of 1296 had been the war of the Comyns, assisted by the bishops of St Andrews and Glasgow. It had been fought according to their notions of warfare, and they had been decisively defeated. The Comyns themselves, the king in whose name they had fought, and a large number of the military leaders of Scotland who had adhered to them, were all *hors de combat*. The church, by contrast, was much less affected by the defeat. Fraser of St Andrews and Crambeth of Dunkeld remained in France, out of Edward's reach. Wishart of Glasgow, it is true, had been compelled to do homage. It is doubtful if he set much store by this, and it must in any case be noted that out of a possible total of twelve bishops of Scotland only three are known to have done homage to Edward – Wishart of Glasgow, Henry Cheyne of Aberdeen, and Thomas Dalton of Whithorn, who was a protégé of the Bruces and a suffragan of the archbishop of York.[62] The ageing Archibald of Moray may have done homage, though it is not recorded.[63]; Three bishops were overseas, three bishoprics were vacant, nothing is known of the bishop of Argyll, and the bishop of Sodor and Man seems to have been hostile to Edward I.[64] All the same, even though the church had conspicuously not been won over to the English king,[65] a handful of bishops could not start a fresh war. At best they could fire others with courage and determination and keep the Scottish cause warm at the court of Philip the Fair and at the papal *curia*. The stark fact remained that many of the Scottish nobles were prisoners, and that a number of others – among them Bruce of Annandale, his son the younger earl of Carrick, and the earls of Angus and Dunbar – were on the English side.

It is more than eighty years since Evan Barron, in his book *The Scottish War of Independence*,[66] showed us how big a part the north of Scotland played in the rising of 1297, taught us to see Wallace in perspective instead of regarding him as an isolated folk-hero, and stated that the Edwardian occupation, though doubtless the occasion, was emphatically not the cause of the Scottish bid for independence. It may be doubted if popular opinion has yet caught up with Dr Barron or even wishes to catch up. For his pugnacious and convincing criticism of the received view appeared to deprive Wallace of his heroic stature, and by spreading the action of the play across a wider stage he lessened the dramatic tension. There is much deeper emotional satisfaction in the story of David and Goliath than in a complex account of the community of the realm, bereft of leadership, struggling and stumbling to regain it. The popular view remains closer to that expressed by G. M. Trevelyan in his *History of England*.

> Deserted by her nobles, Scotland discovered herself. The governors whom Edward I left behind him were incapable and cruel and the foreign soldiery made the Scots feel their subjection . . . A guerilla chief of genius, a tall man of iron strength who suddenly appears on the page of history as if from nowhere, defeated at Stirling Bridge end an English army under its blundering feudal chief the earl of Warrenne . . . Edward I had thought that he was going to yoke Scotland to England through the ordinary feudal apparatus of the time. His mistake was very natural, for by the accepted standards of the day his proceedings were less abnormal than Wallace's amazing appeal to the Scottish democracy to save the Scottish nation . . . Society was divided, not

perpendicularly into nations but horizontally into feudal strata. *And Edward I had the feudal magnates of Scotland mainly on his side*. Anglo-Normans, owning estates in England as well as Scotland were excusably lukewarm in their Scottish patriotism and anxious not to quarrel with England's king, from whom they held their English lands.'[67]

In this stricture on the Scots nobles, Trevelyan was echoing the classical statement by Patrick Fraser-Tytler of what must surely be one of the hardest-dying half-truths of Scottish history. 'At the very time when an honest love of liberty, and a simultaneous spirit of resistance, could alone have saved Scotland, its nobility deserted their country.'[68]

In fact, the Edwardian conquest of 1296 had been too easy and the occupation which followed it was too superficial. It may be doubted if more than a handful of leading Scots (other than those already committed to Edward I when war broke out) had resigned themselves to a permanent English occupation and overlordship. We can be certain that neither Bishop Fraser, down to his death at Auteuil near Paris on August 20th, 1297,[69] nor his colleague Matthew Crambeth of Dunkeld, had given up the struggle. In Scotland, Bishop Wishart of Glasgow had lost none of his influence or animosity towards English rule. No homage to Edward was ever done by Sir John de Soules, who perhaps remained in France and whose career shows continuous and consistent support for the Scottish cause.[70] What is often thought of as Wallace's rising in 1297 was in truth a general resumption of resistance on a national scale, but with an inevitable shift in leadership. Since the Comyns and most of the earls were temporarily discredited and not free agents, the lead was now taken largely by men who had supported the Competitor Bruce against Balliol and the Comyns. Chief among them were Robert Wishart and James the Stewart. Of the Guardians of 1286–92, they were the only two left in Scotland. Although both were great lords in the lower Clyde valley, office and connexions alike made them national rather than local figures. Wishart belonged to an old east-country family whose seat was Conveth in Mearns, an estate which then gave its name to the parish now called Laurencekirk.[71] The family's origins are unknown, but the surname – Guiscard, Wiscard, Wishart, 'cunning' – is Norman-French. Robert's uncle William, a graduate of Oxford and perhaps of Paris also, had been archdeacon of St Andrews, chancellor of Scotland and bishop of St Andrews. Robert himself had become bishop of Glasgow as long ago as 1273, and by the 1290s an unmistakably east-country and Wishart influence was at work in the diocese. The dean of Glasgow was Thomas Wishart, the archdeacon very possibly John Wishart, and the archdeacon of Teviotdale was Master William Wishart. The sub-dean of Glasgow, Master Thomas of Dundee, was a relative of Ralph of Dundee, a prominent clerk of King Alexander III. Thomas of Dundee held the deanery of Brechin, and in 1296, no doubt on the initiative of the council of twelve of whom Bishop Wishart was one, he was appointed bishop of Ross. The chancellor of Glasgow was

Master William Lamberton, almost certainly one of the Lambertons of Linlathen near Dundee.[72] It is presumably a mark of Wishart's influence that in the last year of Balliol's rule the Official of Glasgow, Master Alexander Kennedy, had been made chancellor of Scotland in place of the Englishman Thomas of Hunsingore.[73] Agile, perhaps rather plausible, fertile of ideas, Wishart was not of the stuff of which martyrs and heroes are made, though by the close of his long life he had suffered deeply in the cause of Scottish independence. Again and again he bent under English pressure, but he never broke. There was something indefatigable about the man, and it is no wonder that the English found him exasperating.

The Stewart presents a different problem. We cannot get as close to James Stewart as we can to Wishart, yet something of his character seems to emerge, however dimly, from his conduct. Cautious and devious, possessed of a recognisably 'Stewart' canniness, inclined to actions rather than speech, he was not a man to make the first move, yet neither was he an ineffectual figure. In 1297 he seems to play a double game, but there is no doubt where his inclinations lay. He was certainly among the nobles of whom Walter of Guisborough wrote that their hearts were far from the English king, no matter where their bodies might be.[74] The distinction of his office and the size of his lordships, Renfrew, Bute and Kyle Stewart, as well as lands in Teviotdale, Lauderdale and Lothian, made him one of the greatest magnates of Scotland. In addition, his marriage (1296) to Gelis de Burgh, the earl of Ulster's sister, gave him a stake in northern Ireland. If, instead of impugning his patriotism as lukewarm, we ask what the effect would have been had he thrown his influence on the side of England, we can better appreciate the value of his part in the Scottish struggle. But there is more to it than that. William Wallace, far from being a 'man from nowhere', belonged to one of the knightly families that made up the Stewart's feudal following, and came, what is more, from the parish of Paisley which was at the very centre of the great Stewart fief. Many of the families which had composed this fief when it was founded in the twelfth century still survived at the end of the thirteenth, and the Wallaces, doubtless of Shropshire origin like so many of the others, were among them.[75] It would, of course, be absurd to set James Stewart on the stage of history beside Wallace, one of those rare immortals who tower head and shoulders above their contemporaries. But in 1297 Wallace owed such standing as he possessed in the community of the realm of Scotland to his place among the feudal vassals of James Stewart. The Lanercost Chronicle, indeed, states plainly that Wishart and the Stewart plotted the revolt and instigated Wallace to the open violence which they dared not resort to themselves.[76] This cannot be the whole story. Wallace, still a very young man, must already have performed some feats of daring and laid the foundations of his immense popular reputation. But it can hardly be doubted that Wallace was closely involved with Wishart and the Stewart, nor that at the outset he owed much to the

Southern limits of Wallace's
invasion of Northern England

0   20   40   60   80
              Miles

Banff

Avoch   Elgin   The
              Enzie
Castle   Inverness
Urquhart

M o r a y

Spey

Mar

Dee   Aberdeen

The   M o u n t h

A r g y l l

Dundee

Scone   St. Andrews

11 Sep. 1297

Stirling

Glasgow   Haddington
      Torphichen
Paisley   Berwick
      Lanark
Irvine   Stobo   Roxburgh
            The Forest   Bolton
      Ayr   Ancrum
                              Rothbury
                        Rothbury
      Annandale   Forest
Nithsdale

                  Carlisle   Hexham   Newcastle
                                            upon Tyne
                                  Corbridge
            Cockermouth

4. 1297 and early 1298.

fact that the Stewart was his patron and friend. His ties with Wishart are shown by two interesting details. When the bishop surrendered in July, Wallace was so enraged that he emerged from Selkirk Forest to make a raid on Wishart's palace at Ancrum and carry off his belongings, arms, horses and even his family.[78] The emotion behind this act speaks of close relations between the two men. Later, when Wallace had driven the English out of all but a few castles, he sent his men to besiege Roxburgh expressly because the bishop of Glasgow was imprisoned there, and evidently too valuable, in Wallace's view, to be left in English hands.[78]

The rising of 1297 was partly spontaneous, partly organized. Early in the year there were disturbances in the west highlands, not necessarily anti-English but all grist to the patriots' mill.[79] Rather later, probably by the beginning of May, there were outbreaks of violence in Aberdeenshire and Galloway.[80] Some time during May Wallace slew the English sheriff of Lanark, William Hesilrig, and this gave the signal for a general revolt.[81] Wallace's followers are supposed to have been outlaws like himself, peasants and common folk. Perhaps most were, but for his next much bolder exploit he must have had horses and horsemen. The English justiciar William Ormsby was holding his court at Scone. He was set upon by Wallace with so little warning that he barely escaped with his life and left the Scots valuable booty.[82] This daring raid had the effect of shutting up the English north of the Forth inside a few castles. Sir William Douglas, whose movements after the surrender of Berwick are not recorded, joined Wallace for the raid upon Scone. Douglas was a rough and reckless man. He had been in trouble with Edward I for abducting and forcibly marrying an English widow while she was staying with relatives in Scotland.[83] He had flouted the Guardians by imprisoning three of his own men without trial, beheading one and letting another die in jail.[84] He had shown contempt for King John by keeping the royal justiciar's officers in Douglas Castle for a night and a day against their will.[85] Though Douglas may have been violent and unruly, there was no denying that he was also a nobleman. The lords of Douglas had been tenants-in-chief for a century and a half and were kin to the great family of de Moravia or Murray. William Douglas himself, before he carried off Eleanor Ferrers, had been married to Elizabeth Stewart, James the Stewart's sister. He had therefore a natural place among the south-western magnates who came to the fore in the summer of 1297, and his leadership in a revolt plotted by Wishart and his former brother-in-law is quite understandable.

Less easily understandable, yet profoundly significant, was the fact that along with Wishart, the Stewart, his brother Sir John, Sir William Douglas, Sir Alexander Lindsay and William Wallace, we find as a leader of the native resistance the young Robert Bruce, earl of Carrick and king to be. He was twenty-two years old and had lately been serving Edward I along with his father. His family had been expelled from Scotland by the council of twelve, and it was the English conquest which put them back in possession of their lands. Surely young Bruce had everything to gain by loyalty to Edward, everything to lose by supporting the hopeless and reckless enterprise of Wishart and the Stewart, for all they were old friends of his family? Yet he joined the Scots. It was the crucial decision of his life, far more crucial than his similar decision in 1305 or 1306 to defy King Edward and send the fiery cross through Scotland. Walter of Guisborough says that when the Scots revolt began the bishop of Carlisle had misgivings about Bruce's loyalty and made him take a special oath of allegiance.[86] He goes on to say that Bruce then joined the Scots because he was a Scotsman. This explanation is too simple for modern historians, who believe it impossible because they hold that Scottish nationalism was the product rather than the cause of the war of independence. Nevertheless, it seems to be no more than the truth. After making a mock attack on Douglasdale to deceive the English, Bruce assembled his father's vassals, the knights of Annandale, and told them that his Carlisle oath had been given under duress. 'No man holds his own flesh and blood in hatred and I am no exception. I must join my own people [that is, the men of Carrick] and the nation in which I was born.' He asked the knights to follow him, but they were unwilling. Their lord, Bruce of Annandale, remained with Edward I. As he had chosen, so would they. It was thus that the young Bruce, who as earl could contribute the traditional 'army' of an earldom to the common cause, threw off his father's tutelage and made the first independent political decision of his life. It was apparently said that he already aimed at the throne. Whatever the truth of this, there is no evidence that any such idea inspired the movement of Scottish resistance as a whole until after the collapse of 1304.

Militarily speaking, Wishart, the Stewart and Bruce were fumbling and inept. Henry Percy[87] and Robert Clifford[88] quickly recruited levies from the English border counties and moved with great dispatch through Annandale and Nithsdale to reach Ayr by the end of June.[89] The Scots, chiefly foot soldiers and much weaker than the English in mounted troops, were at Irvine a few miles north. As soon as Percy's cavalry came in sight the Stewart and Douglas sent envoys to ask if the English were empowered to receive a formal surrender, an act of funk which so disgusted one of the Scots, Richard Lundie, that he promptly changed sides. But it is the Scots' political tactics, not their lack of military skill, which are important. The Scots leaders spun out the surrender negotiations for the best part of a month and even then Bruce did not submit.[90] It is clear, moreover, that Wishart, Bruce and the Stewart – one bishop, one earl, one baron – regarded themselves as spokesmen not only for themselves and their immediate following but also for 'the whole community of the realm of Scotland';[91] Guardians in fact if not in name. They talked in political terms about ancient rights and customs, and declared that the 'middle folk' of Scotland would be ruined by Edward's demands for overseas service.[92] Although the bishop and Douglas were imprisoned before the end of July and although the Stewart seems to have given some assurances of good behaviour, their attitude was not merely bravado. In the first place, the delay was of enormous value to Wallace, who, left to his own devices, was having much greater military success. Secondly, at the very time that Wishart and the rest were beginning negotiations, on July 10th, Hugh Cressingham, then at Bolton in Northumberland, wrote a private letter to the deputy treasurer in London. He explained why the sum of £2,000 he had persuaded the king to send him was needed urgently to meet expenses in Scotland. 'Not one of the sheriffs, bailiffs or officials of the Lord King appointed within that kingdom can at this time raise a penny of the revenues of their bailiwicks, on account of a multitude of different perils which daily and continually threaten them.'[93] A fortnight later he wrote to the king in even stronger terms. 'By far the greater part of your counties in the Scottish kingdom are still not provided with keepers, because they have been killed, besieged or imprisoned, or have abandoned their bailiwicks and dare not go back. *And in some shires the Scots have appointed and established bailiffs and officials.* Thus no shire is properly kept save for Berwickshire and Roxburghshire, and they only recently.'[94]

In other words, behind the high-flown stipulations of Wishart and the rest lay knowledge of a country-wide sabotage of the occupation régime and a methodical attempt to restore the independent administration of the realm. That all this was the unaided work of Wallace is impossible to believe. He was much too busy, gathering his men in the fastnesses of Selkirk Forest in July,[95] laying siege to Dundee Castle in August.[96] Barons, knights and clergy must have co-operated to get the native machinery working again. To be sure, after the capitulation of Irvine, Wallace's primacy of leadership could not be challenged. 'The common folk of the land followed him as their leader and ruler; the retainers of the great lords adhered to him; and even though the lords themselves were present with the English king in body, at heart they were on the opposite side.'[97] Wallace's audacity and success fired the people south of the Mounth with patriotic fervour, but to gather and train an army some revenue and an organized mobilization, however rough and ready, were surely needed. Hence the appointment of local officers. The 'free service' or knight-service of Scotland had largely disintegrated, but there was still the 'Scottish service' to which the able-bodied commonalty were bound.

While all this was happening in southern and middle Scotland, a strikingly similar rising broke out on the north side of the Mounth. Before the summer was over it had swept the English out of Moray and the country between Spey and Dee. This critically important revolt, the work of Andrew Murray who some time in the past winter had got away from Chester to his native heath, makes a stirring tale. Barron has told it so exhaustively that we need only recapitulate its main features here.[98] It began in May with an assault by Andrew Murray and the townsfolk of Inverness[99] upon the Loch Ness-side stronghold of Castle Urquhart. By mid-July the insurgents had the free run of the country as far east as the Spey. By early August they had seized the English-held castles of the north, Inverness, Elgin, Banff and the rest. A number of north-country Scots lords tried, somewhat half-heartedly, to quell the rising, which seems to have been strongly popular in character although its leader was the son and heir of a prominent baron. In June King Edward sent north the two Comyns,[100] John of Badenoch and John of Buchan, to help keep the peace. Their colleagues on the spot were the bishop of Aberdeen, Henry Cheyne (a consistent supporter of the English), Countess Effie of Ross, and the heir of Earl Donald of Mar, whose ancient Pictish name of Gartnait is further evidence of the 'Celtic revival'.[101] Guisborough, writing after the event,[102] and Cressingham writing at the time (August 5th),[103] both believed that the Comyns and most of the Scots earls were either sitting on the fence or had already jumped down on the Scottish side. The details we shall never know, but the indisputable fact is that by the end of August Andrew Murray and William Wallace, north and south of the mountains respectively, had gathered formidable armies of foot soldiers. By ancient tradition these men were accustomed to be mobilized and to serve in the 'armies' of their respective earldoms, unless they lived in districts like Moray or Gowrie where the Crown took the place of an earl. But when we find Macduff, son of an earl of Fife, joining Wallace,[104] Bruce of Carrick leading out the 'army' of his earldom; the earl of Buchan's loyalty to England at first suspect and soon proved worthless; and, finally, Cressingham writing to Edward that no one knows what is happening north of the Forth 'on account of the conduct of the earls who are there',[105] it is hardly rash to guess that with a degree of connivance from some of the earls Murray and Wallace recruited what they called the 'army of Scotland' by the customary methods of raising what had been known since time immemorial as 'Scottish army'. If the earls' patriotism seems lukewarm, we must not censure them too harshly. They had much to lose if things went wrong, not because they had lands in England but because their whole way of life was geared to settled residences, regular revenues and conspicuous consumption. It was hard for them to wage a war that was not essentially a matter of cavalry and castles.

We do not know exactly when these two young men, Andrew Murray the baron's son and William Wallace the knight's son, joined forces. It must have been towards the end of August. Warenne and Cressingham had at last bestirred themselves. They advanced from Berwick to Stirling with a respectable force of cavalry and a body of infantry, many of them Welsh.[106] The castle of Stirling and the crossing of the Forth which it guarded, formed the key which would unlock the two halves of Scotland. Murray and Wallace had drawn up their men on the south-facing slope of the Abbey Craig, one mile north of the narrow bridge across the Forth which stood less than half a mile below Stirling Castle. From the north end of the bridge to the foot of the Abbey Craig ran a causeway, on either side of which lay meadow and corn fields, not necessarily swampy as is sometimes said,[107] but very probably soft ground, not suitable for deploying heavy cavalry. Beyond this, on either side, flowed the river, for Stirling Bridge was sited near the southern tip of a great horseshoe loop. The bridge itself would take only two horsemen abreast. Warenne reached Stirling in the first week of September. He was met by certain Scots lords, among them James Stewart and Earl Malcolm of Lennox, who suggested that if they were given a little time they might be able to pacify the Scots. They returned on September 10th empty-handed, but promised to appear with forty barded horses on the following day. As they rode off, the earl of Lennox met some English troops foraging, and after high words one of them was killed. An angry murmur of treachery arose in the army, which Warenne had difficulty in quelling. At dawn the next day many of the infantry were sent over the bridge, but were recalled because Warenne overslept. When at length he rose, they were sent over again, but again recalled, this time because the Stewart and Lennox appeared and the English thought they had come with news of a Scottish submission. The opposite was true: they explained that they could not detach any of their own men from Wallace, but it may be doubted whether they tried very hard.[108] Finally, Warenne sent two Dominican friars to Wallace to ask if he would yield. 'Tell your commander,' was his reply, 'that we are not here to make peace but to do battle to defend ourselves and liberate our kingdom. Let them come on, and we shall prove this in their very beards.'[109]

If Warenne had shown tactical skill at Dunbar, it deserted him now. Sir Richard Lundie asked the earl to send him with a detachment of horse and foot up river a little to the wide Fords of Drip,[110] where sixty men could cross the river simultaneously. 'Once we get round to the enemy's rear,' he said, 'you can cross the bridge safely.' This was sound advice, but it was overridden by the treasurer Cressingham. As if he had not done enough damage by sending home reinforcements on grounds of expense, he now urged for the same reason that no more time should be wasted, but that battle should be joined at once. So Warenne gave the order to cross. As soon as they judged that enough knights and infantry had come over, Murray and Wallace sent their spearmen rushing down the hill, along the causeway and over the meadowland, to cut the English army in two at the bridge. The movement was brilliantly successful. The English north of the bridge were trapped, without room to manoeuvre, and their comrades south of the bridge were powerless to help them. They could only look on while a bloody massacre took place across the river, redeemed by some individual acts of presence of mind or courage, such as the escape of the Yorkshireman, Sir Marmaduke Tweng. Some of the Welsh, unencumbered by armour, swam to safety, but nearly a hundred knights were slain and a great many infantry.

The treasurer rode into battle like a knight and was killed by the spearmen. The Scots flayed his body and cut the skin into small pieces to be carried about the country as tokens of liberation from a hated régime of which Cressingham had been the symbol. For their part the Scots did not get off lightly, and it seems probable that the death of their brilliant leader Andrew Murray, which occurred before the end of the year, resulted from wounds he got during the battle.[111]

Warenne himself had not crossed the bridge. When he judged that all was lost he ordered it to be broken, entrusted Stirling Castle to Sir Marmaduke Tweng, Sir William Fitz Warin and others,[112] and then, heedless of the fact that he was an elderly man, rode for the Border in such haste that his horse was reputed to have had nothing to eat between Stirling and Berwick. The waggon-teams of the English baggage train, and the rank and file trying to escape, did not fare so well. They set off down the road to Falkirk, which followed a line over higher ground with woodland to the south and, not far to the north, the area known as 'The Pows'. This was the name popularly given to the flat, boggy carse beside the Forth, intersected by countless sluggish streams called 'polles' or (in later Scots) 'pows'. James Stewart and the earl of Lennox, as soon as they saw Wallace gaining the upper hand, withdrew to their men, who were lurking in the woods which bordered The Pows. From this shelter they emerged to kill the fleeing groups of English, seizing quantities of booty and leading away the laden waggons. It proved impossible, in the lagoons and marshes of the carse, for the invaders to get any waggons or sumpter horses away.[113]

From a long-term point of view, Stirling Bridge was not a decisive battle, but it would be difficult to exaggerate its importance in the struggle for Scottish independence. It is hard to convey the sheer shock of it. For the English, the impossible had happened – not once, but twice. First, a cavalry army of gentlemen-professionals had been defeated by an infantry army of peasant-amateurs. After Courtrai (1302) such events were to become commonplace, but in 1297 it was too much to stomach. Secondly, and surely an even more bitter blow, an English army had been defeated by the Scots. Such a thing had not happened on this scale since the early eleventh century. Now the whole character of the war was changed. At Dunbar the Scots behaved as though it was all a game. Henceforth they were in grim earnest, and the stage was set for Falkirk, the most dour and bloody battle of the entire struggle. Wallace was neither so humble nor so obscure as is sometimes made out, and Murray, his colleague, belonged by birth to the great lords. But it would be absurd to deny that Stirling Bridge was a popular victory, the triumph of the inarticulate, unchronicled 'poor commons' of Scotland. The men who stood, spear in hand, on the steep slopes of the Abbey Craig, waiting for Murray and Wallace to give the signal, were no doubt mostly landless men, hardly the *probi homines* on whose collective wisdom and experience the government of Scotland depended. Some of them indeed, as Wallace later admitted, were thorough-going rascals who could not be kept in order. But they were inspired by one of the deepest and most primitive emotions known to human beings, the urge to defend their native land against a foreign invader. Led by Murray and Wallace, they had given unmistakable proof that, along with the baronage and gentry, they too had their place in the community of the realm.

SIX

Experiments in Guardianship

Even for England as a whole, the battle of Stirling Bridge could hardly have come at a worse moment, but for the north it was an unmitigated disaster. The king was beyond the Channel, helping his ally Guy de Dampierre, count of Flanders, to conduct a futile campaign against Philip the Fair. For men in the south of England Scotland seemed very remote, and the plight of their fellow-countrymen beyond the Tees touched them scarcely at all. Those who were involved in public affairs were still preoccupied with the great quarrel between the king and 'the earls' (Norfolk and Hereford) which threatened to grow into a second Montfortian revolution. If the southern English chose at this moment of national peril to indulge in the luxury of a constitutional quarrel about the royal prerogative, so much the better for the French and the Scots. For the next seven years the guiding principle of Scottish history was the assumption that the events of the summer of 1296 should be wiped off the slate. John was still king, the community of the realm was still intact, the Franco-Scottish alliance was still in force. All this is obscured by the habit of portraying Wallace as the democratic leader in a war of precocious proletarian nationalism. In fact, the Scots, far from being in advance of the age, were intensely conservative. Unless this is understood, the events of the period make no sense whatever. Time and again we see the Scots struggling, often desperately, to maintain or restore the old, lawful order of things. Wallace was no exception in this: indeed, in some respects he was more conservative than the greater magnates.

Wallace, for one thing, made no attempt to seize the government of Scotland or set himself up as an independent ruler. Not only did he share the leadership with Andrew Murray until Murray's death in November,[1] but his consistent aim was, as he said to Warenne's envoys at Stirling Bridge, the liberation of *the kingdom*. On October 11th, Murray and he, then at Haddington, sent a letter to the mayors and communes of Lübeck and Hamburg[2] telling them that *the kingdom* of Scotland had been, by God's grace recovered by battle from the power of the English, and that in consequence the ports of Scotland were once more open to German merchants. (No doubt this was only one of a number of similar letters to the North Sea communities whose trading activity was vitally important to the Scottish economy, especially if weapons and other munitions were to be bought abroad). Even the English indictment against Wallace in 1305 seems to take care not to charge him with setting up a personal dictatorship.[3] It stated with evident truth that he sent out writs equivalent to writs issued by the sovereign [*superior*] of Scotland. But for Wallace the sovereign of Scotland was King John. It is yet more significant that, like the Guardians of 1286–91, like Wishart and the rest in July 1297, and like the Guardians after him, Wallace was fully aware that in the absence or incapacity of the lawful king the actual rulers must be responsible to the community of the realm and must derive their authority from its consent. This was true no matter how defective the machinery for getting that consent had become.

Only four writs and charters issued by Wallace survive. They are well written, expertly composed documents which prove, incidentally, that Wallace had clerks with him who knew something of the rules of the Scottish king's chancery.[4] The most interesting feature of the documents is the formal style which Murray and Wallace, and later Wallace alone, adopted. The letter to Lübeck and Hamburg begins, 'Andrew Murray and William Wallace, commanders of the army of the kingdom of Scotland, and the community of that realm . . .' A month later, a letter of protection issued by them for Hexham Priory[5] begins, 'Andrew Murray and William Wallace, commanders of the army of the kingdom of Scotland, in the name of the famous prince the lord John, by God's grace illustrious king of Scotland, by consent of the community of that realm . . .' Five months later Wallace issued a charter for Alexander Scrymgeour,[6] using this style, 'William Wallace, knight, Guardian of the kingdom of Scotland and commander of its army, in the name of the famous prince the lord John, by God's grace illustrious king of Scotland, by consent of the community of that realm . . .' Of course, these are all that survive of what was doubtless a large number of documents issued by Murray and Wallace. Few as they are, they are enough to prove that Wallace regarded himself as ruling on behalf of King John, and based his authority on the collective assent of the community. Just as the Guardians of 1286–91, and the Guardians of 1298–1304 held parliaments and assemblies, so also the holding of 'parliaments and assemblies' is expressly stated to have been one of Wallace's crimes in the indictment of 1305.[7] Just as the Guardians used a special seal of regency, so also did Murray and Wallace.

We know less about Wallace than we know about almost any of the great national figures of our history. Utterly fearless, violent but not lacking in compassion, possessed of a certain grim humour, Wallace impresses us most by his extraordinary singleness of mind and purpose. During the seven years of his active career he was never diverted from his aim of ridding Scotland of the English yoke. But he was not a revolutionary either in politics or as a soldier. Trevelyan has called him a 'guerrilla chief of genius',[8] but in fact Wallace used guerrilla tactics only while he had no choice. As soon as possible he gathered large armies and fought pitched battles. At Stirling Bridge, with Murray at his side, he won; at Falkirk, on his own, he was badly defeated. It might have been better for Scotland if Wallace had really been a *guerrillero*. Ironically, it was not the middle-class Wallace but the aristocratic Bruce who possessed the genius for guerrilla warfare. The fact is surely that Wallace had the defects of his qualities, and one of these was lack of imagination.

The three main achievements of Wallace's régime were the invasion of Northumbria, the filling of the vacant see of St Andrews, and the successful revival of the idea of guardianship. The retaliatory raid[9] which Wallace carried out south of the Border in October and November 1297 was a savage business, marked by ghastly atrocities which seem to have been due chiefly to the lack of discipline among the Scots. At first they plundered and slaughtered at will in Northumberland, making a lair for themselves in Rothbury Forest. Many of the people, including all the clergy, fled south of the Tyne to Saint Cuthbert's Land – County Durham, to use its more modern name. The invaders then ravaged the country far and wide, from Cockermouth to Newcastle. The cry 'The Scots are coming', taken up from village to village, spread such panic that even in the palatinate men began to flee southwards. Yet Wallace, having no siege engines or experienced troops, had failed to capture any of the castles save Stirling.[10] Edinburgh, Roxburgh, Berwick, Alnwick, Newcastle, Durham and Carlisle – all these garrisons defied him successfully. Baffled, and demoralized by snowstorms and frost, the Scots went back to their own country about the end of November. Guisborough's statement that they first handed over to the men of Galloway their share of the plunder is doubly significant.[11] It underlines the stubbornly persistent separatism of Galloway, and it at once calls to mind the Scottish incursions into Northumbria under David I, when the Gallovidians were singled out as perpetrators of especially barbarous atrocities. A story which Guisborough tells about Wallace at Hexham also recalls the campaigns of King David, and shows us, in a brief but piercing shaft of light, both the character of the great champion of Scotland and the essential weakness of his position.[12] Three of the Austin canons of Hexham Priory had plucked up courage and returned to the church. Some Scots demanded to be shown their treasures, and were told that their compatriots had already carried off everything. Wallace arrived, dismissed the intruders, and asked for mass to be celebrated. After the elevation of the Host, Wallace went out to lay down his arms. As the priest was washing his hands in readiness to take the bread and wine, the marauders returned and stole the chalice, cloths, altar ornaments and even the missal. When Wallace was told by the priest what had happened he gave orders that the thieves should be sought out and hanged, but his men made only a pretence of pursuit. 'These men are bad characters,' he said, 'they cannot be brought to justice and punished.' At the same time, he gave the priory a general letter of protection. The parallel and the contrast with King David's invasion 150 years earlier is noteworthy. In 1138 King David, in addition to giving Hexham

Priory a written protection, stationed five of his officers there to see that the peace of the church was not violated.[13] When the Galloway men came in search of plunder, two of them were executed on the spot and the rest fled in terror. Wallace might have defeated the English in pitched battle, something the great King David had never achieved, but that did not make him king nor give his commands the stamp of royal authority.

It may nevertheless be a fact that Wallace could count on some aristocratic co-operation for his invasion of Northumberland, just as he certainly enjoyed it in the following year at the time of the battle of Falkirk. The anonymous chronicle composed at the East Anglian abbey of Bury St Edmunds, though written far from Scotland, seems to draw on a source of authentic information for events in the north. The Bury chronicler writes that the Scots invaded Northumberland in 1297 and laid it waste 'under the leadership of a certain Maleis along with William Wallace'.[14] Although Malise was not uncommon as a personal name in thirteenth-century Scotland, the chronicler's 'Maleis' seems most probably to refer to Malise III earl of Strathearn, who had been a leader of the abortive Scottish raid on northern England in 1296. His father, also Earl Malise, had married one of the three coheiresses of Robert de Muschamp lord of Wooler, so that the family of Strathearn had considerable interests in north Northumberland.[15] If the otherwise mysterious 'Maleis' was really the earl of Strathearn the notion that Wallace's war was exclusively proletarian, already weakened by a dispassionate review of the evidence, would be fatally undermined. Moreover, it may have been on this occasion – rather than in March 1296, when there would hardly have been time – that Aymer laird of Hadden and Mary widow of William Melville raided the bishop of Durham's lands in Norhamshire, plundering and burning, 'at the beginning of the Scottish war'.[16]

A telling sentence in the English indictment against Wallace charges him with urging the prelates, earls and barons who were on his side to 'subject themselves to the lordship of the king of France and work with King Philip for the destruction of England'.[17] The appointment of a new bishop of St Andrews in place of Fraser was to some extent bound up with the active revival of the Franco-Scottish alliance. The Scottish Church (save for the outlying dioceses of Galloway and the Isles) formed a single province subject directly to the papacy. Consequently every new Scottish bishop had to have his election confirmed by the pope, and it was the usual practice in the thirteenth century for Scottish bishops to travel to the papal *curia* for confirmation of their appointment and for their consecration, sometimes at the hands of the pope personally, but more often by one of the cardinal bishops. The new bishop of St Andrews – and for that matter any other new bishop of a Scottish diocese – would have to run the gauntlet of a long North Sea passage to France or the Low Countries, sailing through waters patrolled by English ships on the look-out for enemy craft. Historians have not done justice to the courage of the Scots and foreign seamen and their passengers who during the long war with England undertook these perilous voyages. Sending a bishop-elect to Rome was a risky affair, and the journey was much too valuable to be devoted solely to the formalities of consecration. The new bishop would have to earn his passage by diplomatic activity in every friendly foreign court, especially at the papal *curia* itself and at Paris.

As soon as the news of Bishop Fraser's death reached Scotland, the leading clergy of the cathedral church of St Andrews entrusted the jurisdiction of the diocese (which during a vacancy belonged to the cathedral chapter) to Master Nicholas Balmyle, whom they appointed as Official.[18] Although this man keeps himself in the background of surviving historical record, we should be doing him no more than belated justice if we recognized that in these years he played a critically important part. It was of the utmost concern to the patriots that the majority they already commanded among the bishops at the start of the struggle with Edward I should be maintained and if possible increased. Glasgow and Dunkeld were already in good hands, but owing to the special pre-eminence of St Andrews in the Scottish Church it was urgently necessary that Fraser's successor should be a vigorous patriot. The five chief clergy connected with the cathedral were the prior, John of Haddington, an auditor for Balliol in the competition for the throne; the archdeacon of St Andrews, John Fraser, presumably a kinsman of the late bishop; the archdeacon of Lothian, Master William Frere; the Official, Nicholas Balmyle who, under the name Nicholas 'of St Andrews', had also been one of Balliol's auditors; and finally, Master William Comyn, the earl of Buchan's brother.[19] He claimed a seat in the St Andrews chapter in virtue of his office as provost of the highly privileged chapel-royal of St Mary, the successor to the ancient community of 'culdees' which had been attached to the church of St Andrews in Celtic times.[20] On November 3rd, 1297, while Wallace himself was in England but acting on his instructions, the St Andrews chapter elected as their new bishop the chancellor of Glasgow cathedral, Master William Lamberton.[21] The English afterwards accused Wallace of forcing the chapter to carry out this election.[22] On the contrary, we can be sure that the two archdeacons at least were eager to elect such a staunch upholder of the national cause as Lamberton, and that although he did not actually have a vote in the election Nicholas Balmyle used his doubtless considerable influence on the same side. It may well be true that Master William Comyn also, although he was denied a vote on technical grounds, supported Lamberton's election. Already, probably, his brother the earl of Buchan had come out openly on the patriotic side,[23] and in the following year King Edward I gave Master William's valuable provostry to one of his own favoured clerks, presumably on the grounds that William was a 'rebel'.[24]

At what date and by what means we know not, Lamberton travelled to

Rome, where he was consecrated on June 1st, 1298.[25] He returned to France to join the other Scots magnates staying at the French court, among them the abbot of Melrose, Sir John de Soules, and almost certainly Bishop Matthew Crambeth of Dunkeld.[26] Within two months of Lamberton's consecration Wallace had been defeated at Falkirk, and before the bishop got back to Scotland in the summer of 1299 the outlook for the patriots seemed gloomy indeed. But Lamberton and his colleagues had scored one small yet important success. As early as June and July 1298 the French king and Pope Boniface VIII both wrote to Edward I urging him to release Balliol and to cease his attacks on Scotland.[27] Now, a year later, at the very time that Lamberton and the others were waiting at Damme for a passage to Scotland, John Balliol was sent from Dover to Wissant and handed over by King Edward's officials to the bishop of Vicenza as representative of the pope.[28] At the urging of Boniface, King Edward had released Balliol on condition that he was kept in papal custody at a residence belonging to the papacy.

The Scots consistently maintained that Balliol was still their lawful king and that his enforced abdication could not be valid in the law of Scotland. But as long as Balliol was captive in England any scheme for his restoration seemed hopeless. His surrender, therefore, was a remarkable concession on Edward's part. But the pope went even further. The formal record of Balliol's transfer (July 18th, 1299) described him hopefully as 'called king of Scotland'.[29] On June 27th and 28th respectively the pope wrote to King Edward and to Archbishop Winchelsey of Canterbury condemning the English invasions of Scotland in the strongest terms, declaring that Scotland was subject to the papacy, and commanding that the dispute between Edward and the Scots should be laid before the pope for final judgement.[30] The French king also was still taking a strongly pro-Scottish line. On April 6th, 1299, he wrote from St Germain-en-Laye to the patriot leaders in Scotland.[31] He told them that he had received their new envoys, the abbot of Jedburgh (John Morel) and Sir John Wishart of the Carse, with warm friendship. He applauded the constancy and perfect loyalty which they had displayed towards the illustrious king of Scotland [Balliol] and the vigour and courage of which they had given proof in defending their native land against unjust invasion. He commended to them the bishop of St Andrews, who would be able to tell them by word of mouth what plans he had in mind for implementing the Franco-Scottish alliance and the treaty of 1295, which (added the king) he had not forgotten. Apparently King Philip would not accept the proposal which Lamberton is said to have put to him that Charles of Valois should be sent to Scotland with an expeditionary force.[32] But so far as diplomacy could achieve anything for their country's cause the bishop and his colleagues had done all they could, and when they ran the English blockade and won home safely in August 1299, they did not come empty-handed.

The Scots had done better at diplomacy than in war. Stirling Bridge had caught King Edward off guard, and with winter coming on not much could be attempted before the summer of 1298. Warenne and Sir Robert Clifford, it is true, began a modest counter-attack before Christmas. Clifford raided Annandale where the local peasantry, after jeering at his cavalry with the usual shouts of 'Tailed dogs!', were trapped in a bog and suffered heavy casualties. But after burning ten townships the English withdrew.[33] Over in the east Warenne achieved no more than the relief of Roxburgh and Berwick.[34] In the middle of February a letter reached him in which Edward I announced that he was returning from Flanders directly and telling him not to attempt a major campaign until Edward arrived to take charge personally.[35] Most of the Welsh foot were sent home, and the Scots obtained five months' breathing space.

As far as we can tell, Wallace spent this time consolidating his position and training his troops. Our sources show how important the control of Lothian, Tweeddale and Teviotdale seemed to the Scots throughout these years and how, time and again, they placed their forces where they could most easily threaten the English-held castles of Stirling, Edinburgh, Roxburgh and Berwick. Here, the wild country of Selkirk Forest – Ettrick Forest is its rather smaller present-day successor – was enormously useful. Wallace had lurked there in 1297, and a year later the bowmen of the Forest, fine-looking men of great stature, formed a prominent *corps* in his army, fighting under James Stewart's brother, Sir John Stewart of Jedburgh.[36] It is likely that in the spring and early summer of 1298 Wallace kept to the south of Scotland,[37] though no doubt he recruited men from all parts of the country to meet the full-scale invasion which he knew could not be long delayed. Before March 29th, one of the foremost earls of Scotland (according to a reliable English contemporary) had bestowed on him the honour of knighthood.[38] Militarily speaking he had won this at Stirling Bridge, but the important point was that the formal ceremony put Wallace, the younger son of a cadet branch of a not very prominent family, into the class of *nobiles* or *gentilhommes*, words which are scarcely translatable nowadays because in the late thirteen century there was none of the later distinction between 'gentlemen' and 'noblemen'.

The knighting of Wallace was no doubt connected with his election as Guardian, the date of which is unknown though like the knighting it must have taken place before the end of March.[39] The whole trend of events since 1286 made it virtually certain that the guardianship would be revived. It looked like being revived in 1297, not only by Bishop Wishart and his allies, but also by Murray and Wallace, who actually used a seal of guardianship. The special interest and problem of Wallace's election in 1298 is that he was sole Guardian and that he was obviously chosen because he had proved himself the military champion of his country. Between Murray's death in November and the battle of Falkirk in the following July, Wallace alone was in command. The great feudal magnates, far from being, as Trevelyan

5. The Falkirk Campaign, 1298.

believed, mainly on Edward I's side, were already mainly behind Wallace, but it is clear that if they joined fully in the common enterprise they had to submit to his commands. Edward I had taken to Flanders many of the distinguished Scots captured at Dunbar.[40] There they had served against the French, but while the king was at Aardenburg, on his way home, they reverted to their natural allegiance, gave Edward the slip and, much to his annoyance, joined the French king.[41] In effect, this can only mean that they joined Wallace. At home, the earl of Strathearn, Malise III, had been exceptionally busy with military activity during the winter of 1297-98. On February 11th 1298 he promised his vassal Sir William Murray of Tulli-bardine that the succour and aid in men-at-arms, horses and weapons which Sir William had rendered to the earl for the defence of the realm had been offered voluntarily, and was in addition to the 'Scottish service' which was all that Sir William strictly owed in respect of the lands he held of the earl.[42]

There may have been jealousy of Wallace among the nobles, there may have been jealousy between the Comyns on the one hand and the young earl of Carrick on the other. But the important point is that in this crucial year a large body of Scottish lords, representing both the influential Comyn faction and the friends of Bruce, were committed to the struggle against England. It would be misleading, in other words, to exaggerate the difference between Wallace's war and the war fought by his successors down to 1304. In neither was there any real danger that the idea of the community of the realm would be lost. But, though many nobles were engaged in the struggle before Wallace's defeat, most of the community's natural leaders had for a time failed to give the lead or to inspire the trust which by inheritance it was their responsibility to give and inspire.

King Edward meant business in 1298. He made York the headquarters of government. The exchequer and common law courts were moved there and remained for six years. It was probably at this time that the king issued a proclamation (referred to in an inquest of 1312, but otherwise unrecorded) that all English persons (save, presumably, those on active military service) must leave Scotland.[43] The army which Edward led into Scotland was formidable.[44] Of some 2,000 horse, about half were recruited by 'commissioners of array' from those who owed knight-service but were fighting for pay. The rest were brought by the great earls, who were more firmly united behind the king in the summer of 1298 than they were to be again for many years. They would bear the cost of their own contingents. There were also about 12,000 foot soldiers, a total more impressive on paper than in fact, for 10,000 were Welsh – 2,000 from Snowdon alone – and their loyalty was uncertain.[45] The shock of the Scottish rising had at last penetrated to English minds and had aroused powerful feelings of nationalism. To the king and the nobles in particular, the victory and high position of Wallace must have been especially galling. No words were too strong for vilification. Surviving written records, which are likely to be more restrained than popular speech, call him thief, robber, master of thieves, chief of brigands, man of blood, and so forth. In the English popular imagination, Wallace had become an ogre, a monstrous bogey who would skin an Englishman to make a baldric, force nuns to dance naked in front of him and, with a heartless jest, abandon his comrades like the ignoble coward they felt he ought to be.[46] We may suspect that along with all the horror and hatred went a good deal of fascinated curiosity; but there is no hint of admiration, however grudging. We need not doubt that the whole of England prayed fervently for the victory of King Edward as he advanced to crush Wallace and make an end of the Scottish war.

The cavalry was ordered to assemble at Roxburgh on Wednesday, June 25th.[47] Deliberately following in the footsteps of King Athelstan, Edward made a pilgrimage to the shrine of Saint John, patron saint of Beverley,[48] and joined his army at the beginning of July. The Welshmen must have arrived at about the same time, coming across country from Carlisle. The whole army then advanced into Scotland by the road through Lauderdale,[49] burning and laying waste the countryside but finding not a soul to tell them of the enemy's whereabouts. By July 11th they had reached Braid, two miles south of Edinburgh,[50] and a week later they camped in the parish of Liston on a manor belonging to the Knights of the Temple which is now called Hallyards.[51] The Master of the English Templars, Sir Brian le Jay, had formerly been preceptor of the order in Scotland, and his presence with the English host probably accounts for the choice of site. Moreover, adjacent to Temple Liston lay the lands of Kirkliston, belonging to the 'rebel' bishop of St Andrews, and a thorough plundering of that estate would neatly kill two birds with one stone. In truth, the army was badly short of food. Wheat transports due at Leith had been held up by contrary winds and when a few ships did arrive they unfortunately carried more wine than corn.[52] At Temple Liston the king learned that Dirleton and two other castles of East Lothian were held by the Scots.[53] He sent Bishop Bek to capture them. All the castles seemed formidable, and Dirleton was newly built. Bek had no siege engines and his men no food save peas and beans they picked in the fields. He sent Sir John Fitz Marmaduke to the king for fresh instructions. 'Go back and tell the bishop that as bishop he is a man of Christian piety, but Christian piety has no place in what he is now doing. And as for you,' the king added, clapping his hand upon Sir John, 'you are a bloodthirsty man, I have often had to rebuke you for being too cruel. But now be off, use all your cruelty, and instead of rebuking you I shall praise you. Take care you don't see me until all three castles are burned.' 'My lord king, how shall I do what seems extremely difficult?' 'That you will know when you have done it, and you shall give me a pledge that you will do it.' Sir John returned to Bishop Bek with this inexorable message, food ships suddenly arrived, and the heartened troops renewed the assault with such vigour that Dirleton surrendered in two days and the other two castles (one of which was probably Tantallon) were abandoned and burnt.[54]

Meanwhile the main body of the army faced starvation and many Welsh were already dying. Edward ordered wine to be given to them to cheer their spirits, an unwise move. The wretched Welshmen got very drunk and in a serious brawl with the English several priests were slain. At this the English knights charged the Welsh, killing eighty and putting the rest to flight. Next morning the king was told that the Welsh were threatening to go over to the Scots, but he was not impressed. Angry and unappeased, the Welshmen stayed at a distance, declaring that if they saw the Scots gaining the upper hand they would desert to them at once. It looked as though the whole ambitious and hopeful expedition would end in failure, and Edward decided to fall back on Edinburgh.

A measure of official English anxiety is seen in the order of July 19th to the sheriffs of Northumberland, Cumberland and Westmorland to spy out the country for Scots raiders and light warning beacons on the hilltops if the enemy were sighted.[55] For some weeks it seems that the English had lost all contact with the Scots and actually feared a counter invasion by the West March. But at this moment Earl Patrick of Dunbar and Gilbert de Umfraville, earl of Angus, two Scottish earls[56] who were (as they had always been) on the English side, brought to Edward a scout who gave him the welcome news that the enemy were only thirteen miles away, in the Wood of Callendar beside Falkirk. The news changed everything. Ordering his men to arm themselves, the king mounted and led the host westward along the road to Falkirk. That night they bivouacked just east of Linlithgow, on the Burgh Muir,[57] each man with his horse beside him. They passed through the town at dawn. The king was slightly injured during the night when a careless groom let his horse tread on him, but he promptly mounted and quelled rumours that he was badly hurt. Not long after leaving Linlithgow they could see many lances lining the top of a hill. But the spearmen melted away as the English hurried towards them, and it was not till they had pushed further west and tents had been pitched to let the king and the bishop of Durham hear mass that they saw, in the clearer light of morning, the Scottish host making ready for battle. It was the feast of Saint Mary Magdalene, Tuesday, July 22nd. After a month of searching in an empty land on empty stomachs, the English had at last found the dragon they had come to slay in the lair which he had prepared for the encounter.

More than anything, the Scots feared the disciplined, experienced heavy cavalry of England and Gascony. They feared it with as good reason and in a sense for much the same reason as in 1939 an army of riflemen would have feared an army equipped with tanks. It was because of this fear that the Scots resistance had crumbled at Irvine in July 1297, and that two months later Murray and Wallace had stationed their spearmen on a steep hillside ringed by the Forth. It underlay the request to Philip the Fair to send the veteran Charles of Valois to Scotland with a body of knights.[58] It was this same fear which explained Wallace's tactics at Falkirk. And the English were not only immensely superior in weight of cavalry. They had archers from Sherwood and Wales and crossbowmen from Ponthieu and Guienne whose killing power was much greater than that of the Scottish bowmen. Wallace had to convert his army into a human fortress and inspire it with enough steadiness to withstand a siege. In addition, he had taught his men to attack the cavalry at its weakest spot by killing the horses. Only four years earlier, at Maes Moydog, the English had proved that skilful use of cavalry interspersed with accurate crossbowmen could outfight an army of spearmen even though they were dense-packed and strongly placed.[59] Wallace, no doubt, knew all about Maes Moydog, but given the necessity of a pitched battle he had no alternative save to do what the Welsh had done on that occasion but try to do it better. He built his fortress of spearmen 'on hard ground on one side of a hill beside Falkirk'[60] facing south-east. Behind him lay Callendar Wood, while in front ran the Westquarter Burn and its tributary coming down from Glen. Near their confluence there was evidently a boggy loch, lying immediately in front of the Scottish battle line. The left flank of Wallace's army, protected to some extent by the valley of the Westquarter Burn deepening away to the north-east, covered the high road to Falkirk and Stirling. His right flank may have been protected by woodland and more broken ground to the west. Why did Wallace not repeat his movements of 1297? His position now was not so strong as it had been on the Abbey Craig, yet it was not badly chosen for the kind of battle he wished to fight. He arranged his spearmen in four great schiltroms, 'shield-rings', which Guisborough describes most exactly. Each was a thickly packed circle of spearmen, standing or kneeling with their spears slanting obliquely outwards towards the circumference, a hedgehog every one of whose spines was a long iron-tipped spear in the grip of a man fighting for the freedom of his country. The number of men in each schiltrom is not known; it may have been as much as one, it can hardly have been more than two, thousand. Round each schiltrom wooden stakes had been driven into the ground and roped together. In the spaces between the schiltroms Wallace placed the archers of the Forest under John Stewart. In the rear was the cavalry, contributed by the Comyns and the other earls who supported Wallace,[61] and including no doubt many of the gentry who appear in the next few years fighting against the English. Whether Robert Bruce was with them we do not know. It is virtually certain that James Stewart was one of the considerable body of knights present, most of whom fled the field, but a few of whom stayed to organize the infantry.[62]

Although the account of Falkirk in the Guisborough chronicle is by far the most detailed, we are not wholly dependent on it for knowledge of those who took part on the Scots side. Record preserved at Durham gives the names and property of some 40–60 freeholders of modest fortune in Coldinghamshire, on the coast north of Berwick, who were slain or wounded at the 'discomfiture' of Falkirk, or at all events were forfeited for taking part.[63] On September 25th 1298 Edward I forfeited Robert de Ros of Wark, Alexander laird of Folkerton in Lanarkshire, Sir Geoffrey Moubray, John Stirling, Andrew Charteris of Amisfield, Sir William Hay of Lochwarret (now Borthwick), Andrew Murray and Sir William Ramsay of Dalhousie.[64] In some cases the forfeiture was explicitly said to take effect on July 22nd, the date of Falkirk, clearly implying participation in the battle by those forfeited.

King Edward, who could show humanity and common sense, proposed that the army should halt until men and horses had eaten, for neither had had a meal since nine o'clock the previous morning.[65] But his commanders would have none of it. A halt was dangerous, for it seemed that only a small burn separated the armies. Roger Bigod, earl of Norfolk, Humphrey de Bohun, earl of Hereford (the king's two adversaries of the year before), together with Henry de Lacy, earl of Lincoln, pressed forward with the vanguard not knowing of the loch which lay between them and the enemy. The obstacle forced them to swing westward and delayed their contact with the Scottish right. On the English right wing Bishop Bek had under him thirty-six 'bannerets' – senior commanders of cavalry – to lead the second brigade or 'battle'. They of course turned east to skirt the loch. The bishop had difficulty in restraining his knights who were eager to be the first to reach the enemy. Ralph Bassett, lord of Drayton, told him roundly, 'It's not for you, bishop, to teach us knights how to fight when you ought to be busy saying mass. Go back and celebrate mass; we shall do all that needs to be done in the way of fighting.' The two wings then made contact with the outer schiltroms. The Scottish horse, disgracefully, fled the field without striking a blow, but there is no need to put this down to treachery. The fourteenth-century historian John Fordun felt obliged to do so because, in common with all Scots of his day, he had to show the Comyns in as black a light as possible.[66] It is more likely that simple panic seized them, as at Dunbar and Irvine. Guisborough says explicitly that a few Scottish knights remained to command the schiltroms, and there is no need to doubt Fordun's statement that Macduff of Fife, indisputably a nobleman, was killed at Falkirk fighting at the head of the men of that earldom.[67]

All now turned on the steadiness of the Scots peasantry and their capacity for exhausting the repeated cavalry rushes. It must have seemed now or never, and before the battle Wallace, addressing the schiltroms, had summed up the desperateness of the hour in a homely quip, half serious and wholly memorable: 'I have brought you into the ring: now see if you can dance.'[68] They did their best. We have a list of 110 English horses killed at Falkirk and that can hardly be the full reckoning.[69] But the English knights rode first at the bowmen, and from their leader Sir John Stewart downwards they were killed almost to a man. After this the schiltroms, though still unbroken, were isolated. The Welsh archers and foreign crossbowmen got to work, pouring in a deadly rain of arrows and bolts, and heavy casualties were inflicted by lobbing stones from slings. Gradually the gaps in the dense outer circles of spearmen grew too wide to be filled by their comrades in the centre. In each schiltrom the outer ranks fell back on the men behind. Choosing their moment, the troops of mail-clad knights charged in an irresistible mass, overwhelming the Scots by the sheer weight of their impetus. The battle, hard fought, long-drawn out, became a slaughter, many hundreds, perhaps thousands of Scots being killed and an unknown number drowned, presumably in the loch below the battlefield. King Edward's army lost only two men of high rank: Brother Brian le Jay, the Master of the English Templars, who chased some Scots into a bog and was surrounded, and Brother John of Sawtry, the Huntingdonshire knight who had succeeded Jay as Master of the Scottish Templars.[70]

William Wallace and the other Scots magnates escaped to 'castles and woods' – no doubt at first into the great Wood of Tor which stretched between Falkirk and Stirling.[71] If Robert Bruce was on the field he must have ridden straight to Carrick, for by the end of August when Edward I reached Ayr he found the town evacuated and the castle burned down on Bruce's orders, so that they would be of no use to the English.[72] Bruce himself may have hidden in the Carrick hills or gone north, for despite the outcome of the battle the Scots remained in control of the country beyond the Tay and even between Tay and Forth the English had achieved nothing more than burning the towns of St Andrews and Perth.[73] In the extreme south, most remarkably, Jedburgh castle was held against Edward till October, and the English king was forced to turn aside from his southward journey to supervise the siege.[74]

Like Stirling Bridge, Falkirk was not a decisive battle. But in several ways it marked a turning point in the Anglo-Scottish war. Not for another sixteen years did the Scots attempt a full-scale pitched battle against the English. Secondly, Falkirk meant the end of one experiment in guardianship and the start of another. However unfair it might be to judge a general by one defeat, Wallace could not expect to be given a second chance. He had no hereditary position as one of the natural leaders of the community, and must stand or fall on his military reputation. It seems to have been his own conservatism which led him to offer battle at all, instead of scorching the country and harassing the invaders. He gave up the guardianship, whether voluntarily or under compulsion is immaterial. Finally, though this is not a conclusion that can be proved by documentary evidence, there is little doubt that the psychological effect of Falkirk was tremendous. Just as Stirling Bridge had been a different kind of war from Dunbar, so at Falkirk the war entered yet again into a fresh phase, much grimmer than before, in which the Scots had their backs to the wall and knew it. There can hardly have been many parts of the country where there were not families who mourned a father, son or husband slain in that battle. The bloody slaughter of Falkirk must have made an indelible impression on the Scottish mind and, far from discouraging the Scots, done more to stiffen the will to resist than any amount of appeals to old history, encouragement from popes and kings of France, or efforts to restore Toom Tabard to the throne of Scotland. And the nobles, the feudal magnates who are supposed not have to been true to Scotland and to have been mainly on the side of Edward I, at once put themselves at the head of a five-year struggle to frustrate his ambitions. In this they were at first remarkably successful, and in any case, whether in success or in failure, they were certainly not half-hearted. There is, moreover, good evidence that King Edward, lacking the hindsight of modern historians, failed to realize that the Scots landowning class was on his side. In September 1298, after he had reached Carlisle, the king made grants of estates 'forfeited' by an appreciable number of Scottish lairds. The earl of Warwick, Guy de Beauchamp and Robert de Touny were among the magnates who benefited.[75] A St Albans writer says that the king proposed to distribute Scotland among his followers who, if single, were to marry only English women.[76]

The disaster of Falkirk forced the community of the realm to fall back once more on collective leadership. At some date between July and December 1298, Robert Bruce earl of Carrick and John Comyn the younger of Badenoch were elected joint Guardians, an uneasy marriage perhaps, yet proof of the Scots determination that the guardianship should survive.[77] Militarily the situation was grim but not hopeless. Famine and the restlessness of the English magnates compelled Edward I to leave Scotland in October, having taken the elder Bruce's castle of Lochmaben, hitherto held by the Scots.[78] He issued a summons to the host to reassemble on June 6th, 1299, but for various reasons no campaign was possible that summer, and the king was not in Scotland again till July 1300. From 1298 to 1303 Scotland can scarcely be said to have been under English occupation save in the south east where the English-held castles were much thicker on the ground than elsewhere and the country in between much easier to overawe. The Scots more than held their own in these years, yet it was to become increasingly clear that the old practice of joint or multiple guardianship would prove a failure. Apart from the transfer of Balliol to papal custody in 1299, the most hopeful features of the period were the effort, largely successful it seems, to get the normal machinery of government going again, and the ability of the patriots to keep and even extend their control over the leadership of the Scottish Church.

As far as central government was concerned, there was no break of any consequence in the guardianship between Wallace's election and the surrender of John Comyn in 1304. The Guardians recognised the legal validity of acts done by their predecessors. Bruce, for example, confirmed to Alexander Scrymgeour the constableship of Dundee 'as he held it by the grant of Sir William Wallace before I received the guardianship'.[79] All the Guardians ruled in the name of King John and associated with their rule the authority of the community. With William Wallace's style as commander and Guardian we may compare the style used by Bruce and Comyn, which we can reconstruct from the address of Philip IV's letter of April 6th, 1299: 'Robert Bruce, earl of Carrick, and John Comyn the son, Guardians of the kingdom of Scotland in the name of the famous prince, the illustrious King John, together with the bishops, abbots, priors, earls, barons and other magnates and the whole community of the realm.'[80] We know a few of the places where government documents were issued. Govan, Torwood and Inchaffray[81] may have a rustic look compared with the famous burghs and castles frequented by Alexander III, but there are also acts issued from Rutherglen, Stirling, Scone and St Andrews.[82] The justiciar of Scotland north of Forth (John Comyn, earl of Buchan) could still hold his court at Aberdeen in February 1300,[83] and in that year also we hear of two parliaments, called at properly appointed terms.[84] As for local government, the scanty surviving record gives us casual glimpses of sheriffs of Aberdeen, Forfar, Stirling, Lanark and even Roxburgh.[85] No doubt wherever the Scots had control of a sheriffdom, and sometimes where they had not, they would appoint a sheriff. There must also have been a more or less regular collection of revenues, however much depleted. Whenever the English won any Scottish territory they were able to use an established revenue-collecting and accounting system, and it would follow that the Scots likewise must have been able to keep this system in operation.[86]

Local government and military needs must often have gone hand in hand. The Guardians made use of, or were forced to pay attention to, local influence and local interests. We can see a clear illustration of this in the siege of Stirling, the biggest task undertaken by the Scots after they recovered from the Falkirk *débâcle*. Among the prominent landowning families of Stirlingshire were the Malherbes. One branch of this family was more commonly called Morham, from the East Lothian village which they also owned.[87] The Malherbe-Morhams held lands in the Carron valley, from Stenhouse up to Dunipace, Garth and Castlerankine.[88] In this period there were two prominent Morhams, a father, Thomas, and a son, Herbert. The elder was with Edward at Falkirk, his son on the Scottish side. Young Herbert Morham commanded the force besieging Stirling Castle in 1299,[89] a task which did not prevent him from ambushing King Edward's relative, Joan de Clare, dowager countess of Fife, as she was travelling from Stirling to Edinburgh with no better protection than an English safe-conduct.[90] Morham carried her off to his brother Thomas's house at Castlerankine and tried, without success, to force her to marry him.[91] In a document of this period Herbert Morham's kinsman Gilbert Malherbe, lord of Slamannan and Livilands, appears as sheriff of Stirling.[92] We can be fairly certain that he already held the office in 1299, for when towards the close of the year the English garrison of Stirling was at last starved into submission it was to Gilbert Malherbe, 'Scotsman' that the English constable John Sampson handed over the castle.[93] But if it was convenient to employ local potentates it was also true that such men might rate their local interests higher than the common enterprise. The Scots leaders committed Stirling Castle to the Perthshire knight Sir William Oliphant (Olifard), thereby provoking resentment among the Malherbes.[94] At all events, after the Scots generally had made peace with Edward I in 1304 it was to Gilbert Malherbe that the goods and chattels of Sir William Oliphant, who still held out, were assigned.[95] Afterwards Malherbe seems to have recovered the sheriffdom of Stirling from Edward II, but later still he was reconciled with Bruce, only to be forfeited and executed for his part in the Soules treason-plot of 1320.[96] Trying to keep pace with every shift of power could be a perilous occupation.

Co-operation between Bruce and Comyn had begun to break down by August 1299, soon after William Lamberton's return from France. The bishop arrived just in time to join the Scots leaders in a full-scale raid south of the Forth.[97] They went first to Glasgow and from there up into the Forest,[98] at whose north-western corner they would find a good base in the bishop of Glasgow's large manor of Stobo. Many of the greatest magnates joined in the raid. Besides Lamberton and the two Guardians there were the earls of Buchan and Menteith, probably the earl of Atholl also,[99] James the Stewart, Sir Ingram de Umfraville, Sir William Balliol, Sir David Graham (Sir Patrick's son), Sir David of Brechin and Sir Robert Keith, the Marischal. William Wallace was conspicuously absent, but his brother Sir Malcolm Wallace was there in Bruce's following.[100] They first planned to attack Roxburgh, but changed their minds when they learned how strongly the town was defended and how an attack would involve them in very heavy casualties – a striking illustration of the effect Falkirk had had upon Scottish strategy. Instead, Umfraville and Keith were ordered to stay in the Forest with a hundred barded horse and 1,500 foot, not counting the men of the Forest. There was a justifiable hope of winning over the most influential of the local lords, Simon Fraser of Oliver Castle, whose forebears had been sheriffs of Tweeddale, on and off, since the twelfth century. Fraser had been with the English since 1296. For a long time he dissembled his intentions, but it is virtually certain that the Scottish incursion into the Forest was made easier by the fact that Fraser was already inclined to come over to the patriotic side. The English constable of Edinburgh advised King Edward to beware of Fraser, who, so he had heard, in a parley with the Scots leaders, had eaten and drunk with them so that they had all been friends together.[101]

The Scots were powerful enough at this time to bring about an exchange of prisoners, and, with the help of Margaret, lady of Penicuik, and her son Hugh, to raid as far as the outskirts of Edinburgh.[102] Nevertheless, cracks had begun to show openly in the leaders' unity. Most of our knowledge of the raid into the Forest comes from a report sent to Edward on August 20th by the English constable of Roxburgh, Robert Hastang. Hastang had a spy –

one of the lesser folk – among the Scots army, and in addition to his useful military information, he had some startling news to tell of a council which the Scots magnates held at Peebles on August 19th.[103]

> At the council Sir David Graham demanded the lands and goods of Sir William Wallace because he was leaving the kingdom without the leave or approval of the Guardians. And Sir Malcolm, Sir William's brother, answered that neither his lands nor his goods should be given away, for they were protected by the peace in which Wallace had left the kingdom, since he was leaving to work for the good of the kingdom. At this, the two knights gave the lie to each other and drew their daggers. And since Sir David Graham was of Sir John Comyn's following and Sir Malcolm Wallace of the earl of Carrick's following, it was reported to the earl of Buchan and John Comyn that a fight had broken out without their knowing it; and John Comyn leaped at the earl of Carrick and seized him by the throat, and the earl of Buchan turned on the bishop of St Andrews, declaring that treason and lesemajestie were being plotted. Eventually the Stewart and others came between them and quietened them. At that moment a letter was brought from beyond the Firth of Forth, telling how Sir Alexander Comyn and Lachlan were burning and devastating the district they were in, attacking the people of Scotland (*la nacion Descoce*). So it was ordained then that the bishop of St Andrews should have all the castles in his hands as principal captain, and the earl of Carrick and John Comyn be with him as joint-guardians of the kingdom. And that same Wednesday, after the letter had been read, they all left Peebles.

The report shows us only one small eruption of rivalries which smouldered deep down below the surface. It would be hard to drive the northerners, the Balliol men *par excellence*, in the same harness as the south-westerners, Bruce and the Stewart among them, the group to which the Wallaces naturally belonged. The sinister report from the north concerned men of the Comyn faction. Alexander Comyn was the earl of Buchan's brother. Lachlan was Lachlan Macruarie, the west highland captain of galloglasses, who in 1297, in alliance with Alexander Macdougall, his son Duncan and Comyn of Badenoch, had been burning and devastating the lands and men of Edward I's friend Alexander Macdonald of Islay.[104] As yet, Lamberton was a neutral, moderating figure, supporting no faction but fighting only for the community of the realm and for the liberty of 'la nacion Descoce', to use the phrase of Hastang's spy. The bishop's career had linked him to Wishart, Glasgow, the south-west; but by family origins and now through his great bishopric, he belonged to the old Scotia north of Forth and Tay. As a result of the quarrel at Peebles and the bad news from the north, the ranks had been closed. For a little longer Bruce and Comyn would work together. Once again, the community had one bishop, one earl and one baron to rule them on behalf of their absent king. But surely there was something prophetic in the manner in which the Forest gathering broke up? While Bishop Lamberton remained at Stobo, the other great lords rode off toward their own homes. The two Comyns returned to the country beyond the Forth, Bruce and the Gallovidians headed for Annandale and Galloway – partly in order to attack the English-held castle of Lochmaben – while James Stewart and the earl of Menteith went back to Clydesdale.

SEVEN

The King over the Water

Unless we try to understand the events of the years from 1299 to 1304 we shall miss the significance of Bruce's bid for the throne. The struggle against Edwardian aggression was a single national effort, even when it revealed or gave rise to bitter rivalries and divisions between noble families or geographical regions. The Scottish leaders were not by any means a happy band of brothers, but for all that a dour and dogged persistence in the common enterprise distinguishes their actions from the battle of Falkirk to the submission of 1304. If this is acknowledged it becomes easier to understand the stubborn refusal of Oliphant, Soules and Wallace to surrender even then, easier to understand Bruce's decision in 1305 to resume the struggle, easier to appreciate the opinion of an observer at Forfar in 1307 that Bruce had never enjoyed the good will of the people so much as at that moment.

Bruce himself was the only leader of the first rank to desert the national cause in this period. He may well have debated for a long time whether or not to make his peace with Edward I, against whom he had fought consistently, if not always very effectively, since the summer of 1297. But the stages by which he reached his decision and his motives for reaching it are alike hidden from us. In November 1299 he was still Guardian with Comyn and Lamberton, waiting in Torwood for the English garrison of Stirling to surrender, and telling Edward I that, through the mediation of Philip the Fair, the Scots would agree to a truce.[1] The Guardian's constitutional position and the striking fidelity with which they adhered to the time-honoured forms of expressing it are shown in the style used in their letter to King Edward. 'William by divine mercy bishop of St Andrews, Robert Bruce earl of Carrick and John Comyn the younger, Guardians of the kingdom of Scotland in the name of the famous prince the lord John, by God's grace illustrious king of Scotland, appointed by the community of that realm, together with the community of the realm itself.'[2] The address on the seal-tag runs: 'To the lord Edward, by God's grace king of England, by the Guardians and community of the realm of Scotland.'[3]

The Scots were in a strong position and full of hope. Their great enemy was actually in Northumberland, yet he could not lift a finger to save the starving garrison of Stirling, and the castle was in Scottish hands by the end of the year.[4] The next step was to gain control of southern Scotland by wiping out pockets of native disaffection (chiefly in Galloway) and by recapturing the border fortresses. It was resolved to concentrate on the south-west, where Bruce held his earldom and where his father, firm in his English allegiance, still held the loyalty of the knights, if not of the commoners, of Annandale. It is not rash to guess that this south-western drive was connected with Bruce's resignation from the guardianship.

It also does not seem rash to guess that in this period Bruce failed to make good his ambition to enjoy a pre-eminent leadership within the Scots nation. We can be sure that he never for a moment lost sight of his claim to the throne. Although formally serving the absentee King John since 1297, Bruce's personal attitude towards the Balliols was surely ambivalent. For Bruce it was one thing to rule as Guardian on behalf of a king over the water who might be expected never to return to a country he apparently disliked and despised,[5] quite another to settle down as the obedient liegeman of this same king once he had actually been brought back to his kingdom. If this comes somewhere near the truth with regard to Bruce's attitude it would follow that he must have had mixed feelings about William Wallace's mission to France in 1299–1300. Wallace belonged personally to the south-western milieu which Bruce shared with Bishop Wishart of Glasgow and James the Stewart. But for Wallace patriotism rose above feudal or terri-torial allegiance. He accepted the legitimacy of King John as a representation of the legitimacy of a free Scottish realm. His mission to the French court was surely aimed as much to hasten the restoration of Balliol as to persuade Philip the Fair to give the Scots military support and bring pressure to bear on Edward I to desist from his schemes of conquest. Certainly the company who went with him to Paris seem to have Balliol associations and cannot have given Bruce much comfort. From November and December, 1299, we have record of loans and payments by the French king to Wallace and other 'knights of Scotland' by then in Paris, Roger Moubray, Richard Fraser, William de Vieuxpont, Edward of Leitholm and Hugh of Fotheringay.[6] Fotheringay had served John Balliol's mother as attorney in 1280,[7] Richard Fraser was one of his auditors in 1291–92,[8] Roger Moubray's family were aligned with the Balliols,[9] while in 1296 Edward of Leitholm was reported to be in France with Thomas Randolph, one of King John's chief councillors.[10] In the following year William de Vieuxpont was arrested by the English at Blaye near Bordeaux on suspicion of spying on English shipping. He was said to be 'of the company of William Wallace'.[11] What became of the rest of the company is not known, but Wallace himself stayed in France at least until the end of 1300 when the French king gave him a letter of recommendation to the papal court.[12]

In May 1300 the earl of Buchan (who was lord of Cruggleton in Wigtownshire and sheriff of the county) went to Galloway to try to win over the leading men to the national cause.[13] It was an uphill task. The Gallovidians were inspired by a traditional hostility towards Scotland in general and towards Carrick in particular. This did not mean that they were anxious for English rule, but Edward I consistently exploited their separat-

Route of Edward I in Galloway
campaign, 1300

Routes of Edward I and Prince
of Wales, summer and autumn of 1301

English Supply Fleet

English Supply Fleet

SCOTS ARMY 1301

St. Andrews

Scone

Inchaffray

Stirling (Scots 1299-1304)

Torwood

Linlithgow

Bothwell

Govan

Rutherglen

Stonehouse

Loudoun

Inverst

Ayr

Turnberry

Edinburgh

Peebles

Selkirk

The Forest

Berwick

Roxburgh

Carlisle

Lochmaben

Annan

Caerlaverock (fell 1300) (fell 1313)

Skinburness

Dumfries

Kirkcudbright

Whithorn

Cree
(Aug. 1300)

G a l l o w a y

L. Ryan

Newcastle upon Tyne

Miles
0 10 20 30 40

◆ Places at which surviving acts
   of the Guardians were issued

◆ Strong points held by the
   English after 1299 underlined

6. The Rule of the Guardians, 1299–1302.

ism. At the outbreak of the war in 1296 Bishop Bek of Durham had brought
out of his sixty years' imprisonment in Barnard Castle the pathetic figure of
Thomas of Galloway.[14] He had been condemned as long ago as the reign of
Alexander II for his part in the Gallovidian revolt of 1235. Now the poor old
man, eighty-eight years old, was shaved, given clean clothes, and sent back
to his native province armed with a special charter of liberties from the
English Justinian which, if generously interpreted, would have allowed the
men of Galloway to do pretty much as they liked.[15] To be sure, many
Gallovidians began the war fighting against the English: after all, Balliol was
lord of Galloway. Many more joined Wallace's raid on northern England,
but this was surely because it was traditional for Galloway men to take part
in these fearful plundering raids, not because they were heart and soul
behind the patriots. The fact is that for many years from 1297 the leading
men of Galloway, among them the MacCans and the Macdoualls, were
active on the English side.

    In preparation for the campaigning season, the remaining Scots magnates
(apart from the earl of Buchan) held a parliament at Rutherglen on May
10th.[16] Bruce must by now have resigned. Comyn of Badenoch said he
would serve no longer with William Lamberton. James Stewart and the earl
of Atholl – both Bruce partisans – took the bishop's side. In the end, it was
agreed that Comyn and Lamberton should remain in office, and the place of
Bruce should be filled not by another earl but by Sir Ingram de Umfraville,
Balliol's kinsman and an ally of the Comyns. The next parliament was to
meet at Rutherglen in six weeks' time, at midsummer. As it happened, or as
the Scots knew, this was the day appointed by Edward I for the gathering of
the feudal host at Carlisle.[17] Clearly, the geography of Scotland, coupled
with the hold the Scots still retained in the south west, dictated the zone of
fighting. For the first time since the Falkirk campaign, Edward had been
able to raise a respectable army. In its support, as it advanced through
'Solwayland' to its first camp at Annan, was a large fleet to guard supply
routes and keep watch on the Galloway coast.[18] Lochmaben, which Bruce
had attacked unsuccessfully after the Forest meeting in the previous
August, had apparently not fallen to the Scots.[19] Still held by the English,
under Robert Felton, it had suffered much from the Scots garrison at
Caerlaverock, that splendid castle at the mouth of the Nith, ten miles south-
west of Lochmaben. In a skirmish Felton's men had killed the young
captain of Caerlaverock, Robert Cunningham, and Felton had had his head
hoisted aloft on the great tower of Lochmaben. The report of this barbarity
greatly grieved the Stewart, for Cunningham was his sister's nephew and
belonged to his own following.[20] King Edward quickly relieved Lochmaben
and proceeded to the siege of Caerlaverock on July 10th, 'enraged as a
lioness who has lost her cubs' because the garrison had asked for honourable
surrender terms, saving life and limb.[21] Powerful battering-rams and
trébuchets (stone-lobbing engines) made short work of the castle, and rope

tied to the nearest trees made even shorter work of some of the hapless garrison.[22]

The king then advanced westward into Galloway, brushing aside overtures of peace put forward by Thomas Dalton, bishop of Whithorn.[23] The invaders reached Bridge of Dee and turned south to Kirkcudbright. A two-day parley took place here between Edward and the Scots leaders Buchan and Badenoch. The terms requested by the Scots probably reflect the work of diplomacy carried out by Wallace at the French court. In brief, they consisted of the restoration of King John, the recognition of Edward Balliol's right to succeed his father on the throne, and the right of Scottish magnates to redeem their estates (in England) from the Englishmen to whom the king had granted them. If this was refused, the Scots would defend themselves as long as they could. These not very extravagant terms apparently filled Edward with great indignation and the Scots withdrew.

While the king was staying at Girthon and Twynholm,[24] just west of Kirkcudbright, some of his foragers, with an escort, went off in search of provender as far as the Cree,[25] beyond which the Scots were lurking in an inaccessible glen. There was a skirmish and Sir Robert Keith the Marischal was captured. Next day the whole English army reached the Cree and found the Scots facing them across the tidal estuary, presumably between Cree-town and Newton Stewart. The archers on both sides exchanged shots across the river and when the tide went out the English infantry crossed over and harassed the enemy at close quarters. In each army the cavalry was grouped in three brigades. Edward, mistrusting snares and traps which the Scots were reported to have laid, wished to keep the English horse on the east side. But owing to a misunderstanding the earl of Hereford's brigade went over, whereupon the king and his son Edward of Caernarvon followed in support. At this the three Scottish cavalry brigades, commanded respectively by Buchan, Comyn of Badenoch and Umfraville, took to flight, many knights abandoning their horses and fleeing to the moors. The English regretted much that they had brought no Welsh troops with them to give chase in this wild country.[26] They had got the foxes into a cairn and now had no terriers. But in these Cree-side encounters they had at least captured two of their 'worst enemies', Sir Robert Keith and Robert Baird of Strathaven in Clydesdale, who were sent for safety to Bristol and Gloucester respectively.[27]

Frustrated at not coming to grips with the enemy and exasperated by the delivery at the hands of Archbishop Winchelsey of the pope's rebuke of June 1299, King Edward went back to England in the autumn of 1300, having given the Scots a truce on October 30th to last till the following Whitsun (May 21st).[28] The Scots had made a poor showing on the banks of Cree and had lost the castle of Caerlaverock. But, on balance, this jubilee year of 1300, in which their ally and patron Pope Boniface VIII reached the height of his power and prestige, must be reckoned on the credit side.

Edward I had raised an army as large as the one he brought to Falkirk and more representative than any he had led since he conquered Wales, nearly twenty years earlier. Yet set beside his hopes and intentions his achievement had been trifling. By far the greater part of Scotland remained under the Guardians' control. The English magnates had dispersed after a short campaign and the Scots had successfully persuaded the pope to send his letter of rebuke to Edward personally, though it was a year late and more than a year out of date. In their demands for a truce they had been supported by both Boniface VIII and Philip the Fair. It is clear that they were conscious of Edward's weakness from the conversation reported between their envoys and the English king, presumably at Dumfries in October when he granted the truce.[29] Edward laughed scornfully at their offers of peace. 'Every one of you has done homage to me as chief lord of Scotland. Now you set aside your allegiance and make a fool of me as though I were a weakling.' To which the Scottish envoys replied, 'You should not laugh; we offer peace in all seriousness. Exert your strength and see if might will triumph over right or right over might.' 'Take care,' was Edward's answer, 'that you do not come to me again.' And he declared with an oath that he would lay the whole of Scotland waste from sea to sea and force its people into submission.[30]

The combination of Lamberton, Comyn and Umfraville lasted until the end of the year. Like their predecessors they were 'Guardians in the kingdom of Scotland appointed by the community of that realm.'[31] But their tenure of office was the last experiment in multiple or joint guardianship. It had proved impossible in turn to get Comyn and Bruce, or Comyn, Bruce and Lamberton, or Comyn, Umfraville and Lamberton, to work together. The obvious inference, that young John Comyn was an impossible man to get on with, may be too simple. We have no clear evidence to support it. But there is little doubt of one thing: the Comyn leadership of the national cause, which went far back into the thirteenth century, would no longer be accepted without challenge and discontent. This is clear from the change of régime which characterized the years 1301 and 1302, and also from Robert Bruce's desertion coming at an unknown date about the turn of these years. Yet the timing of Bruce's desertion, as we shall see, suggests that his motive was more a refusal to go on fighting for the Balliols, John or Edward, than simple dislike of the Comyns.

Between December 1300 and May 1301 – most probably, indeed, early in 1301 – Lamberton, Comyn, and Umfraville resigned office and in their place a single Guardian was elected, Sir John de Soules.[32] Among the great men of the independence struggle Soules has been most undeservedly neglected. Fordun, writing seventy years later, calls him feeble and ineffectual.[33] This is unjust. Soules was older than Bruce, Comyn and Wallace, and though he had never been a Guardian he had a long experience in public affairs. A younger son, he was not himself a wealthy landowner, having only the upland barony of Westerkirk in Eskdale (held of Enguerand de Guines)[34] and, in right of his wife, the old barony of Ardross on the Fife coast.[35] But his family had held the lordship of Liddesdale since David I's time and their castles of Liddesdale and Hermitage controlled one of the routes from England to Scotland.[36] Soules's record of constancy in the patriot cause can stand beside that of Wallace. Perhaps his most valuable quality was that while his nephew married a Comyn and although his family were the neighbours and natural allies of the Bruces of Annandale, John de Soules himself held a neutral place. But Fordun, despite his unfair strictures, may provide the clue to the strength – and weakness – of Soules's position. He says that Soules was associated with Comyn in the guardianship by John Balliol personally.[37] This statement is part of the evidence which has led Dr Norman Reid to believe that the years 1301–03 saw a novel constitutional experiment, with Soules as chief Guardian, appointed by and responsible to King John, while Comyn was 'under-guardian' elected by the community.[38] Persuasive though this hypothesis may be in several respects, it does not seem completely convincing. The view taken here is that Soules was in fact sole Guardian and Comyn for a time resigned. Certainly Soules's term of office coincides with a marked change of policy with regard to Balliol which fits in well with Fordun's statement. If Soules was indeed appointed at the express wish of King John, the Scots may have welcomed him all the more readily as a moderator between factions. He was the much-needed secular counterpart of William Lamberton, and it is not surprising to find him working very closely with the bishop in 1301 and 1302.

His lengthy sojourn in Paris must have given John de Soules a clear understanding of the advantages for Scotland of the French connexion. Largely on his initiative, it seems, the military and diplomatic offensives were intensified, and a vigorous effort was made to restore King John to his throne. Despite the famous letter of the English barons to the pope,[39] which purported to come from the Lincoln parliament of January 1301, and which denied the pope's right to interfere in the Anglo-Scottish quarrel on the grounds that it was a purely domestic matter, King Edward did not in fact make light of the papal claim to arbitrate. In November 1300, at the very time that Wallace was being recommended to the pope by Philip IV, a powerful English delegation was appointed to go to the *curia*.[40] As in 1291, the cathedrals and monasteries were ordered to search their chronicles for evidence of English suzerainty over Scotland. One of Edward's expert notaries, the Yorkshireman Master Andrew of Tong, was busy from December 1300 till February 1301 preparing an elaborate legal brief to be used at the papal court.[41] This included charges against the bishops of St Andrews and Glasgow and a copy of the hundreds of oaths of fealty and homage by which in 1291 and again in 1296 the Scots had become King

Edward's vassals. This work bore fruit in the king's lengthy letter to Boniface dated May 7th, 1301,[42] and was followed up by the diligent lobbying carried out at the *curia* by the Dominican, Brother William of Gainsborough, and the king's confidential clerk, Thomas Wale. These agents were still hopeful in October 1301 that they could persuade Boniface to see the justice of their master's claims.[43]

The Scots, for their part, had everything to gain from a formal trial of the dispute at the papal court. Since 1294, when Celestine v had absolved their leaders from the oaths Edward had forced upon them, the papacy had been consistently friendly towards the Scots. Boniface viii's letter, *Scimus, fili* (Anagni, June 27th, 1299),[44] which had now been brought into the open, must have been drafted on the basis of information supplied by Scottish agents. It can hardly be a coincidence that the letter was issued the day before the consecration, at Anagni, of a new Scottish bishop who was to play an invaluable part in the national struggle. While joint Guardians, Bruce and Comyn had appointed to the bishopric of Moray (one of the more important sees) Master David Murray, parson of two livings formerly in Olifard patronage to which the Murrays had succeeded, Bothwell in Clydesdale and Lilford in Northamptonshire.[45] It is probable that David Murray was brother of Sir William Murray of Bothwell, the Pantler, and so uncle of young Andrew Murray who had led the Moray rising and was mortally wounded at Stirling Bridge.[46] For Murray as for Lamberton, the journey to Rome must have had a diplomatic as well as a spiritual purpose. On the very day of Murray's consecration Pope Boniface issued a letter to Archbishop Winchelsey on the same lines as *Scimus, fili*, condemning English interference in Scotland.[47] This Scottish lobbying at the *curia* must be connected with the mission to the French court led by Wallace in the autumn of 1299. As we have seen, Wallace and his companions had reached Paris by early November. Wallace himself seems to have stayed there at least a year, for there survives a brief letter of recommendation from Philip iv to his agents at the papal court telling them to assist 'our beloved William le Walois of Scotland, knight', and the letter is dated at Pierrefonds on November 7th, the year (unstated) being evidently 1300.[48] A week earlier two high-ranking English envoys to the papacy, the earl of Lincoln and Sir Hugh Despenser, were at Canterbury on their way to Rome.[49] There is nothing to suggest that Wallace did not go to see the pope. His mission may best be seen as the Scottish counterpart of the powerful English delegation.

The main Scottish effort at the papal court was exerted in May 1301, when the Scots were furnished with a *processus*, or brief, designed to counter the English arguments point by point, not only on ancient history but also, and more especially, on the events of the last few years.[50] There is, of course, a great deal of fable and bad history both in Edward i's letter and in the Scottish reply, though the respect which both pay to the value of historical evidence is remarkable. There are some telling points in Edward's letter, but there is little question that the Scottish reply is the more impressive document. It is better written, its 'pre-history', though fabulous, is in some respects curiously close to the known facts about Scottish origins, its handling of events in the twelfth and thirteenth centuries, though not free from serious errors, is less tendentious than Edward's, and above all it gains strength from the emphasis which it lays upon the events of the recent past, on the importance the Scots attached to the treaty of Birgham–Northampton and on the charge that Edward had taken advantage of the Scottish dilemma of 1291. At least one statement made by Edward in these representations was plainly false. In a letter given to his delegates in November 1300 the king declared: 'My enemies the Scots have recently acknowledged that I am chief lord of Scotland by hereditary right, *by a decree of their entire nation*'.[51] Not once in the course of Edward's dealings with Scotland had there been any recognition of his suzerainty, even under duress, that could be called an act of the whole Scottish nation.

One forceful point made by the Scots was that whereas Edward I had informed the pope that he was in full possession of Scotland the truth was that of the twelve 'cities' (bishops' sees), and twelve dioceses, existing in Scotland the English king did not have complete possession of any, 'but only of certain places in the dioceses of St Andrews and Glasgow'.[52] As to the rest of the Scottish pleading, there survives a summary made for King Edward at the time by one of his agents which because of its ability to convey the gist of the Scottish case in a few words deserves to be quoted in a full translation of its original French.[53]

Sire, the Scots, in the document sent from Rome, say three things. First, that your statement of claims sent to the pope ought not to have any validity since it did not reach him on the day assigned to you by summons [it was four months overdue] and if it contained anything in your favour this is already annulled and contradicted by the following contrary facts. In the second place, they deny that certain *gestes*, histories, chronicles and other matters which you have quoted are in your favour, and declare that others are in their favour. And they in turn call to witness for their side other histories and *gestes*, contrary to yours, to affirm that the condition of the kingdom of Scotland is free and not subject to you, and they have an answer to the papal bulls which you allege to be in your favour. In the third place, they attempt to prove that the kingdom of Scotland is free and in no way subject to you, and this in five ways, (i) by papal privileges, (ii) by the principle of common law that one kingdom ought not to be in any way subject to another, (iii) by prescription [i.e., independence dating back before the time of written laws], (iv) by the existence of independence at all times, and (v) by various instruments of the kings of England [especially Richard I's quitclaim of 1189 revoking the so-called 'treaty' of Falaise]. And so they pray that the pope will pronounce judgement on this affair between them and you, and that he will immediately forbid you to engage in any kind of warlike acts against them.

We know the identity of the man who was chiefly responsible for the impressive Scottish pleading at the papal court. Shortly after Whitsun (May 21st) 1301,[54] a letter was addressed to Pope Boniface by John de Soules, Guardian of the kingdom of Scotland, by the counsel of the prelates, earls, barons and other nobles of the community of the realm, giving formal authority to a delegation composed of Master William Frere, archdeacon of Lothian and professor of canon law in the university of Paris, Master William of Eaglesham, doctor of canon law, and Master Baldred Bisset.[55] Contemporary record and later chroniclers agree in assigning the lion's share in this business to Master Baldred, whom Andrew Wyntoun called approvingly a 'wys and cunnand clerk'.[56] In the 1280s Baldred Bisset, who seems to have belonged to the Stirlingshire branch of the Bisset family, was already a sufficiently experienced lawyer to be Official of St Andrews – president of the bishop's ordinary court and therefore enjoying a leading position in the administration of ecclesiastical law in Scotland.[57] He held the parsonage or rectory of Kinghorn, a rich living in Crown patronage.[58] After the collapse of the Scots in 1296, Edward I began to distribute to English clerks those Scottish benefices whose incumbents had not submitted to him. Bisset's name is as conspicuously absent from the Ragman Roll as Wallace's – very possibly he was abroad, at Bologna. Some time between 1296 and 1301 the English king gave the parsonage of Kinghorn to Peter of Dunwich, who was active in Scotland from 1296 as one of Edward's hated officials.[59] In 1302 or thereabouts Bisset protested formally to the bishop of Bologna against his deprivation, his protest being referred to Scottish commissioners.[60] A report made to Edward I on the situation in Scotland, which must surely have been written in 1301 or at latest 1302, gave the following news:

> The bishop of St Andrews is showing the people a letter under the king of France's seal (whether counterfeit or not the writer cannot say) asserting that there will be no peace between him and the king of England unless the Scots are included. The people are putting their faith in this and in the success which they hope will be obtained by Master Baldred, their spokesman at the court of Rome. They say for certain that the bishop is at the bottom of the whole affair.[61]

The mission to the papacy caught the popular imagination. If Scotland possessed in William Wallace a military champion she could also boast a forensic champion in Master Baldred Bisset.

In spite of the optimism of the English envoys, Bisset and his colleagues carried the day at Rome. The whole force of the Scottish diplomatic effort at Paris and Rome had been concentrated on the recognition of King John's legitimate title to kingship and the necessity of his restoration. As Bisset put it in his written pleadings before the pope, 'King Edward by force and fear extorted fealty and homage from our king, John Balliol, who had peacefully obtained the realm of Scotland, having succeeded to it by hereditary right, justly and lawfully, in accordance with the practices and praiseworthy customs of that realm, approved by all the inhabitants of the realm.'[62] Since July 1299, John Balliol had been kept in papal custody, first at Malmaison in the diocese of Cambrai,[63] then at the Burgundian *château* of Gévrey-Chambertin. During the summer of 1301 he was released from papal custody and installed by Philip the Fair in the ancestral *château* of the Balliols at Bailleul-en-Vimeu, in Picardy.[64] Balliol's movements had been accompanied by increasing marks of respect in the papal documents referring to him: 'called king of Scotland', July 1299; 'king of Scots', November 1299; and finally 'illustrious king of Scots' by September 1300.[65] Even Edward I, by the end of 1301, had been forced to admit the possibility either of Balliol's restoration or of the succession of his son Edward whom the English king had prudently kept as a state prisoner.[66] Scottish confidence in King John's restoration can be seen in a number of ways. Since 1297, official acts of government had been issued in the names of the Guardians or commanders of the army, though these officers had consistently claimed to be acting on behalf of King John. But in 1301 such acts began to be issued directly in the name of King John and were dated by his regnal years calculated from his accession in November 1292.[67] John de Soules the Guardian, instead of appearing at the head of these documents, took a more modest place as the first or only witness. A phrase in one surviving act of this type is particularly significant. 'King John', confirming (July 10th, 1301) to Alexander Scrymgeour certain rights belonging to his constableship of Dundee, concluded, 'these letters-patent to be valid at our will or that of our dearest son Edward or of John de Soules, Guardian of our kingdom'.[68] A new seal neatly symbolized the new position with the name and title of King John on the obverse and the name and arms of 'John de Soules, knight' on the reverse.[69] That King John of Scotland was once more a reality, at least in the French realm, is shown by the fact that in February 1301 an authenticated copy of the king of Scots' acknowledgement (Edinburgh May 16th 1294) of an obligation to meet the dower claims of Margaret of Flanders dating from 1284 was issued under the seal of the *prévoté* of Tours.[70]

The Scrymgeour document proves that the Guardians had restored or preserved at least one ancient function of Scottish royal government: the holding of inquests about property and the formal return of their findings to the king's chancery, or 'chapel' as it was called in Scotland. The traditional head of the chapel was the chancellor, and it was in keeping with the new policy that by January 31st, 1301, a chancellor of Scotland had been appointed.[71] He was Master Nicholas Balmyle, who – for the historian – has a way of turning up unobtrusively at a number of major occasions for which written evidence survives. An auditor at the court of claims in 1292,[72] he

attended King John's first parliament in 1293,[73] and was appointed Official
of St Andrews during the critical vacancy of 1297 when Lamberton was
elected bishop.[74] Now in 1301 he took his place with Soules and Lamberton
as one of the handful of key men who directed the national struggle. Indeed,
the first of the only two documents which prove that Balmyle was chancellor
shows him in the company of Bishop Lamberton and of two out of the three
members of the delegation to Rome, Archdeacon Frere and William of
Eaglesham. The second document referring to Balmyle as chancellor[75] is
interesting because it shows one way in which the Guardians were able to
pay the salaries of high officials in a period when the national revenue had
been badly dislocated. The rich abbey of Arbroath was made responsible for
paying Master Nicholas's fee as chancellor.

The Scots had hoped that before the truce expired on May 21st, 1301,
King Edward would give way under papal and French pressure and agree to
a permanent peace. In fact Edward had no mind to give way. He allowed
French envoys to come to Canterbury but he remained as stubborn as ever
about his claims in Scotland and long before the truce expired was busy
planning a fresh campaign. By contrast, the Scots attached much importance to the Canterbury peace talks. Nicholas Balmyle, the chancellor, was
one of their four representatives, and the others were men of standing: Sir
Adam Gordon (keeper of the West March for the Guardians in 1300),[76] Sir
John of Inchmartin, and Master Thomas of Bunkle, a prominent clerk from
Matthew Crambeth's diocese of Dunkeld.[77] In 1291–92 Master Thomas
had been one of Bruce's auditors along with Matthew Crambeth and Sir
Alexander of Bunkle, a substantial Berwickshire laird to whom Master
Thomas was doubtless kin. The envoys' efforts were in vain. The truce
expired at Whitsun with no sign of peace being any nearer.

In the midst of all this diplomatic activity and efforts to get Scottish
government working again along its accustomed paths, Soules did not
neglect his main objective, to beat the English in the field. He avoided
pitched battles but pursued harassing tactics with vigour. Edward I's
campaign in 1301 was intended to smash the position of strength which the
Scots had built up in the south-west, partly by direct attack, partly by
severing communications with the rest of Scotland. He was not yet strong
enough to recapture Stirling. Instead, he concentrated on seizing and holding the natural line formed by Tweeddale and Clydesdale. The army was
summoned for midsummer in two divisions, the larger at Berwick under
the king, the smaller at Carlisle under Edward of Caernarvon, now prince
of Wales. The prince's task was to attack the enemy in the south-west, so
that, in his father's words, 'the chief honour of taming the pride of the Scots'
should fall to his son.[78] The king's force moved up Tweeddale, taking
Selkirk and Peebles to seal off the Forest and nullify its peculiar usefulness
to the Scots, and then continuing down Clydesdale to lay siege in August to
the great castle of Bothwell. This castle, commanding the direct route from

northern Scotland to the south-west, had been the ancient stronghold of the Oliphants (Olifards) and in 1301 was the property of the three-year-old boy, Andrew Murray, son of Wallace's colleague, who was being brought up in Moray among King Edward's enemies.

The main Scottish army was busy in Dumfriesshire and Ayrshire, highly mobile, too strong to allow the prince of Wales the share of glory his father had planned. The prince kept to the Solway coast and got no further than Whithorn and Loch Ryan. Meanwhile the Scots, under Soules and Umfraville, made a bold attack on Lochmaben (September 7th and 8th) and using Comyn of Badenoch's estate of Dalswinton as base began to recruit men from Nithsdale.[79] While they hung on to the flanks of the prince's army they also found time to menace the main English force at Bothwell. Soules and the earl of Buchan gathered at Loudoun in Cunningham while Simon Fraser, Alexander Abernethy and Herbert Morham were reported at Stonehouse near Strathaven.[80] At one moment they were rumoured to be threatening the English communication line by a drive towards Roxburgh, at another they were said to be heading for Galloway. Bothwell had fallen by September 24th,[81] but Soules's vigour had thwarted the English pincer movement. Instead of the king and his son meeting at Inverkip as planned, the prince withdrew to the east after some of his advance units had helped to capture Turnberry.[82] The fall of this castle, the chief stronghold of the earldom of Carrick, was due in part to a force brought across from Ireland by Eustace le Poer and Thomas de Mandeville.[83] Eventually the prince joined his father who retired to winter at Linlithgow. The Scots could still break out of their south-western stronghold, and on January 26th, 1302, Edward I, under some pressure from the French, agreed to a truce for nine months.[84]

One reason why the south-west was a Scottish stronghold was that the earl of Carrick had been active on the patriotic side. His castle of Turnberry held out till September 1301,[85] and as late as October its new English garrison and their comrades in the castle of Ayr were gravely threatened by a great force of Scots operating in Carrick.[86] They were so numerous that they threatened to overwhelm such men of Kyle and Cunningham as were in the English peace. At least a part of this Scots infantry force must have composed the 'army' of Carrick which only Bruce, as earl, had the authority to call out. One reason why the Scots changed their strategy after 1302 was that Bruce deserted them and went over to Edward I. He changed sides before February 16th, 1302, giving himself up to Sir John de St John, English warden of Annandale and Galloway.[87] The making of the truce on January 26th no doubt provided the occasion of his surrender. Since the Scots had been led by Soules for almost a year, this drastic decision was surely not prompted merely by jealousy of the Comyns. It is more likely to have been due to the whole trend of events since 1299, culminating in the news from Rome that Balliol had been transferred from papal to French tutelage and to the rumour that Philip the Fair was sending him back to Scotland with a French army.

Bruce feared not only that restoration of Balliol and thus the likely succession of his son Edward would block his own claim to the throne but also, and perhaps more immediately, that restoration would jeopardize his position as earl of Carrick and his expectation of Annandale when his father died. The provisional peace of Asnières which Edward I had made with the French stipulated that till November 1st 1302 (if no final peace treaty had been concluded) lands of Scots opposing Edward and acquired in war by English armies should be held by agents appointed by Philip IV. The effect of this would be to put Bruce's earldom in French hands with no guarantee that it would be restored to him after a relatively short interval, or indeed at all.

There still survives among the Duchy of Lancaster records (into which the earlier Bruce of Annandale archives found their way in the fourteenth century because of English confiscation) the original memorandum in the form of an 'open writing' (not the same as letters patent, though bearing the privy seal) stating the terms on which Edward I would accept Bruce's submission. Translated from the original French, it runs as follows:

Be it remembered that whereas Sir Robert Bruce the younger, who was in the homage and faith of the king of England for the earldom of Carrick [i.e. from August, 1296 to the summer of 1297], rose in rebellion against the said king his lord, through evil counsel, and has submitted himself to the peace and will of the same king in hope of his good grace, the king, for the sake of the good service which Robert's ancestors and family have rendered to the king and his ancestors, and the good service which Robert himself has promised to render in the future, has declared his grace and will in this manner.

That is to say, that Robert and his men and his tenants of Carrick will be guaranteed life and limb, lands and tenements, and will be free from imprisonment.

If it should happen that by a papal ordinance, or by a truce, or by a conditional peace touching the war against Scotland or the war against France, the aforesaid Robert should be at a disadvantage, so that he may not be able to enjoy his own lands, of which he has possession at present in Scotland, the king promises to take his loss into consideration so that he may have reasonable maintenance, as is proper for him.

And the king grants to Robert that, so far as it lies in his power, he will not be disinherited of any land which may fall to him by right from his father, in England or in Scotland.

And the king grants to Robert the wardship and marriage of the earl of Mar's son and heir.

And because the said [king – or Robert – fears(?) that][88] the kingdom of Scotland may be removed from out of the king's hands (which God forbid!), and handed over to Sir John Balliol or to his son, or that the right [le droit] may be brought into dispute, or reversed and contradicted in a fresh judgement, the king grants to Robert that he may pursue his right and the king will hear him fairly and hold him to justice in the king's court. If, by any chance, it should happen that the right must be adjudicated elsewhere than in the king's court, then in this case the king promises Robert assistance and counsel as before, as well as he is able to give it.

And if, after the kingdom of Scotland is at peace in the king's hands, any persons should wish to do injury to Robert by [force?][88] the king will maintain and defend him in his right as before, as a lord ought to do for his man.

And in witness of all these points, the king has ordered this open writing to be made and sealed with his privy seal.[89]

The document gives us a fascinating glimpse of the anxieties of both King Edward and the future King Robert at the outset of the new century. The admission of a possible Balliol restoration is striking proof of Edward I's weakness in 1302. The 'right' which might be disputed or reversed in a fresh judgement seems here to be the right to the Scottish throne, awarded to Balliol in 1292 and revoked by Edward I four years later. Now it was feared – presumably by Edward, and ostensibly by Bruce too – that Balliol might vindicate his right after all, thus affecting Edward's capacity, even as overlord, to maintain Bruce in Carrick or Annandale. At least Bruce might pursue in Edward I's own court his claims to titles and estates denied him by a Balliol restoration, and if this proved ineffectual he could count on Edward's support in some other tribunal. Ultimately, however, Edward I contemplated enjoying peaceful, unchallenged possession of the Scottish realm, and once that situation was realised Bruce's rightful claims would be maintained by Edward, as any vassal could expect of his lord. A charter which Bruce himself, as king, was to execute twenty-six years later in favour of the younger Henry Percy is not altogether irrelevant here. Percy, a newly reconciled 'rebel', was restored to his paternal inheritance in Scotland, despite previous forfeiture, and the king granted that Henry and his heirs would not be excluded from pursuing their right, whether hereditary or otherwise, in the king's courts or in the courts of anyone else.[90]

It is perhaps idle to speculate further about Bruce's motives for submission, yet there is one more fact that should be considered. 1302 was the year of Bruce's second marriage. Since his new wife was Elizabeth de Burgh, daughter of Richard de Burgh earl of Ulster, one of King Edward's chief magnates in Ireland, it is certain that the wedding must have followed the submission. It is true that Edward failed to persuade Earl Richard to contribute a force to his Scottish campaign in 1301, and that the earl had some differences with the English king at this time.[91] But that can hardly mean that Richard de Burgh could have close and friendly relations, even to the extent of a marriage alliance, with a man who was one of the English king's chief enemies. Whenever, and by whatever prompting, the marriage took place, it implied a revival of the Carrick alliance with the chief magnate of Ulster and was in line with the traditional Bruce–Stewart friendship, since Elizabeth de Burgh was James Stewart's niece by marriage. The attractions of an Ulster alliance may have been enough to tip the scales of Bruce's indecision, already weighted by his growing disgust and frustration with a struggle which threatened to exalt the Balliols at the expense of his family's power and position.

Winning Bruce over was a triumph for Edward I, but his change of side was more Scotland's loss than England's gain. He had not only been a Guardian, he had, as earl, time and again raised the 'army' of his earldom on the patriots' behalf although there had been no national call-up. As Bruce, then at Maybole, wrote on March 11th, 1302 to the anxious monks of Melrose Abbey, 'whereas I have often vexed the abbey's tenants on their grange of Maybole by leading them all over the country in my army of Carrick although there was no summons of the common army of the realm, troubled in conscience I shall never again demand such army service, neither of many nor of few, unless the common army of the whole realm is raised for its defence, when all inhabitants are bound to serve'.[92] It is curious, to say the least, that Bruce's conscience did not trouble him until the beginning of Lent 1302, just in time to ensure that his army would be less use to Edward than it had been to the Scots.

A much worse blow befell the Scots in 1302 than the defection of Bruce. The history of the war of independence has no greater irony than the fact that the great upsurge of proletarian nationalism in Flanders which led to the massacre of the French feudal host at Courtrai on July 11th did more to make Scotland an English province than any other single event of these years. It knocked King Philip out of the fight for a time, and his quarrel with the papacy caused an ominous change of heart in Pope Boniface, of whose fickle and fortuitous support the Scots had up till now taken every advantage. But it was nearly two years before the Scots admitted defeat. The long truce of 1302 was primarily a truce between French and English. That the Scots benefited from it seems to have been due to the good work of Bishop Lamberton, who went to France in 1301 and returned in time to attend a parliament at Scone in February 1302.[93] The danger of an Anglo-French peace from which the Scots were excluded was so serious that an extra-ordinarily large and powerful delegation went to Paris in the autumn of 1302, probably with safe-conducts from King Edward. John de Soules himself was one of the envoys. Presumably he gave up his monopoly of the guardianship when he left Scotland, though his position as King John's special representative may not have been affected. His colleagues were Bishop Lamberton, the earl of Buchan, James Stewart, Ingram de Umfra-ville and William Balliol. Already at Paris was Matthew Crambeth, bishop

Kinloss Abbey (14/9)
Rathven (6/9)
Cullen
Banff (3/9)
Elgin
Mortlach (6/10)
Lochindorb (25/9)
Kildrummy (8-9/10)
Garten (1/10)
Cochran (10/10)
Aberdeen (23/8)
The   Mounth
Brechin Castle captured (9/8)
Strathmartine
Coupar
Arbroath (1/8)
Strathord
Perth (18/6-13/7)
Scone (22/10)
Dundee (17/10)
St. Andrews
Tullibardine (26/10)
Cambuskenneth
Stirling
Dunfermline (5/11) (Winter quarters)
Prefabricated Pontoon Bridge
Drymen
Linlithgow
Edinburgh
Roslin (24/2/03)
Berwick
Lauder
From King's Lynn
Peebles
Happrew
The   Forest
Roxburgh (May, 1303)
Newcastle (7/5/03)
Carlisle

Edward I's route
May–November, 1303
••••••• Northward
—•—•— Southward

0   10   20   30
Miles

7. The Invasion of 1303–04.

of Dunkeld, who had evidently served as permanent Scottish agent at Paris since as long ago as 1295.[94] The three Scottish envoys to the papal court in 1301 were probably also with the magnates in France. At home the direction of affairs was entrusted to John Comyn of Badenoch, who – according to the view of events adopted here – assumed the Guardian's office for the second time.[95]

One contemporary English chronicler, who at this point seems to know nothing of Comyn, Soules and the other leaders, states that in 1303 the Scots 'began to rebel, making William Wallace their commander and captain'.[96] It is certain that Wallace had come back into the fray by 1303, but there is nothing to suggest that he alone took the initiative, as though impatient of the slow peace negotiations. And it is of course absurd to speak of the Scots 'beginning to rebel' in 1303. When the truce expired in November 1302, the English king was not ready to campaign personally. Instead, he summoned the host for May 1303, and in the meantime sent his lieutenant in Scotland, Sir John Segrave, to carry out a probe in depth into the Scottish-held territory west of Edinburgh. Segrave was accompanied by Ralph Manton, cofferer of the wardrobe, one of the busiest and most responsible clerks then at work for the occupation régime. They had got as far as Roslin, south of Edinburgh, with a strong force of knights in three brigades, when on February 24th they were caught by a surprise attack.[97] Led by Comyn and Simon Fraser, a large party of mounted troops rode all the way from Biggar during the night and fell upon the leading English brigade, killing Manton and capturing many knights including Segrave, who was badly wounded. In a little while the second brigade rescued some of the prisoners, Segrave himself being freed by Robert Neville of Raby. But the affair had come near to being a major disaster for the English and the Scots were understandably jubilant. Despite Edward's campaign of 1301 the Forest was obviously still available to the Scots, perhaps not surprisingly as long as Simon Fraser was still active. Even the peel of Selkirk, newly built by the English, and in the charge of Sir Alexander Balliol of Cavers, was captured by the patriots early in 1303.[98]

It took a full-scale invasion in the following summer to avenge Roslin and expose the essential weakness of the Scots. In August 1302 Earl Richard of Ulster and eighty-two other lieges of Ireland were notified of the English campaign in Scotland planned for 1303, and urged to produce a mixed force of men at arms, hobelars (light horse), and infantry, eventually in the proportions 300, 400 and 2,000 respectively. The earl himself was to command the Irish contingent. Troops, horses and supplies crossed to England or Scotland in July 1303, some of them being given the task of taking the castles of Rothesay in Bute and Inverkip. By September they had fulfilled what Edward I required of them. Unpaid, unfed and reduced to robbery and pillage in order to survive, most of them left for home about the end of the month, leaving only Earl Richard and a handful of magnates with their retinues. They remained with the English king and his son until the surrender of Stirling (1304) and went back to Ireland at the end of July.[99]

Edward had three floating bridges prefabricated at King's Lynn and brought by sea to the Firth of Forth, so that the main army could cross directly into Fife. As it happened, this advanced technology was not put to any use, but nevertheless it was necessary to by-pass Stirling Castle, where Sir William Oliphant refused to surrender. The English reached Brechin at the end of July and laid siege to the castle there, which was held against them with great spirit and courage by Sir Thomas Maule. When he was killed on the battlements on August 9th, the garrison yielded, but its valiant resistance had made it necessary for Edward to strip the lead off Brechin Cathedral (for which he duly paid £17 18s. 4d.) and to have siege engines brought by sea to Montrose.[100] Edward continued his march northward, meeting no more recorded resistance, though later traditions, unsupported but not necessarily unfounded, claim that Urquhart and Cromarty castles were only captured after hard fighting.[101] In September the king reached Kinloss Abbey, the furthest point of his progress, and a month later, having sojourned at Lochindorb and Garten in Strathspey,[102] he was back in Fife, where Dunfermline Abbey formed his winter quarters.

All this time the Scots were not idle, but they could neither bring into the field an army which was remotely equal to a pitched battle with the English nor, as yet, push to its logical conclusion their half-learned lesson that scorched earth and incessant guerrilla attacks might make it impossible for the English to stay north of Lothian. Fraser's presence at Roslin proves that the military effort in 1303, though sadly lacking in strong central control, did not consist of Comyn and the great lords fighting one war and Wallace and the commoners fighting another. For we know that while Edward wintered at Dunfermline (probably in February 1304) he sent a mounted commando (*chevauchée*) into the Forest and 'the parts of Lothian', under Segrave, Clifford and Latimer, and this force routed Fraser and Wallace together at Happrew in Stobo, a few miles west of Peebles.[103] In the autumn of 1303 John Comyn was still in southern Scotland with as many as 100 mounted men and 1,000 foot, with whom he raided the Lennox as far as Drymen as well as harassing the Irish troops around Linlithgow.[104] But the individual acts of bravery could not prop up much longer the king over the water. The writing on the wall for this ghost-king, Toom Tabard, had been seen at Courtrai. His fate was sealed absolutely on May 20th, 1303, when a peace was made between France and England from which the Scots, despite all King Philip's promises and protestations, were excluded.

Since 1297 the Scottish effort had been informed consistently by a single forceful, even if conservative, principle. Under the direction of properly constituted Guardians, the totality of the feudal kingdom, the community of the realm, had fought to rid their land of foreign invaders and to restore their lawful king. Political strategy had been dominated by this legitimism, by the

Franco–Scottish treaty of 1295, by the belief that French military support was just round the corner, by a somewhat naïve confidence that once apprised of the facts Pope Boniface VIII would exert all the papal fullness of power to protect Scottish independence. These beliefs died very hard. On May 25th, 1303, the Scots magnates in Paris wrote to encourage Comyn the Guardian and all the faithful men of the community of the realm of Scotland.[105] It was true, they said, that firm peace had been made between France and England and the Scots had been left out. But the king of France had faithfully promised them that he would strive to bring Scotland into the peace, and was now in a better position to do so.

> Be of good heart. If the king of England agree to a truce, you should likewise agree, on the conditions to be brought to you by a man of our side who will be known to you. If the English king harden his heart, like Pharaoh, and refuse a truce, then, by the mercy of Jesus Christ, defend yourselves manfully and stay united, so that by your manful defence and with God's help you will prevail, or at least receive stronger support from us. For God's sake do not despair. If ever you have done brave deeds, do braver ones now. The swiftest runner who fails before the winning-post has run in vain.[106] And it would gladden your hearts if you could know how much your honour has increased in every part of the world as the result of your recent battle with the English [i.e., Roslin].

And they concluded, in striking testimony to the great part which John de Soules had played in the struggle, by asking that Soules's wife should be allowed peaceful enjoyment of the estate provided for her when the envoys went to France or else an equivalent provision in another suitable place, 'so that Sir John, who up to now has laboured loyally and diligently on the business of the realm, should not give up his efforts'.

This refusal to believe that all was lost animated the letters written by Bishop Lamberton (presumably when in France) to Wallace and to the officials of his own bishopric,[107] and it shows itself very clearly in the attitude of Sir William Oliphant, the young commander of Stirling Castle. Lamberton urged Wallace for the love Wallace bore him and with the bishop's blessing, to do all in his power to aid and counsel the community of Scotland, as he had done in the past, and to make war on King Edward and attack him and his men as before, as well as he knew how, and was able, to do it. To help in the good work, the bishop ordered his officers to supply Wallace with part of the revenues of his bishopric. Oliphant, when Edward I settled down to the serious siege of Stirling in May 1304, asked permission to send a messenger to his master, Sir John de Soules (by whom the castle had been committed to him), to find out whether he might surrender or whether he should defend it to the last.[108] King Edward could seldom bring himself to display towards Scottish castle garrisons the chivalrous decency which the age admired and which the Scottish Guardians had notably shown towards the starving English garrison of Stirling in 1299.[109] He rejected Oliphant's polite request, exclaiming: 'If he thinks it will be better for him to defend the castle than yield it, he will see.'[110] And when, after three tormenting months (May–July) in which every kind of siege engine and explosive material that the ingenuity of the time could devise had been used against them, the garrison at last submitted (July 20th), the king would not let them surrender with military honour but threatened them with disembowelling and hanging.[111] Only their abject abasement and the sympathy of those who were with Edward mollified him at last, and they were sent, about fifty in all, to various English prisons.[112] By a piece of cold-blooded cruelty which shows Edward in a singularly unattractive light, he had refused to accept the garrison's surrender, even after it was offered unconditionally, until the castle had been bombarded for a time by one of his new engines, the 'Warwolf', while the men inside made shift to defend themselves as best they could. The anonymous letter by an eye-witness which gave news of the king's intention, is confirmed by neutral exchequer accounts rendered by the engineers. Cable, rope, grease and stones were no longer required by July 20th for any of the siege engines save the Parson, the Berefrey and the Warwolf ('Low de Guerre') which were supplied continu-ously from July 19th to July 23rd.[113] The notarial instrument recording the surrender and listing the garrison was dated July 24th.[114]

The king's meanness of spirit and implacable, almost paranoid hostility were not shared by his subjects, who admired Oliphant for his courage and magnanimity. They did not think any the worse of the young man because he refused the terms accepted by Comyn and the rest, for as Sir Thomas Grey explained in a phrase full of significance, Oliphant claimed to hold Stirling 'of the Lion', that is to say, of the crown of Scotland.[115] Hence his punctilious desire to get orders from Soules, who had been a duly consti-tuted Guardian on behalf of that crown, or (as a document of 1306 puts it) 'Guardian for the community of Scotland'.[116]

All the prominent Scots leaders save Wallace, Fraser and Soules sub-mitted to King Edward some five months before the fall of Stirling. Those who had been in France returned under safe conducts, among them the earl of Buchan, the bishops of St Andrews and Dunkeld, James Stewart and Ingram de Umfraville.[117] On the Scottish side, the negotiations were conducted by John Comyn of Badenoch, doubtless in his capacity of Guardian. He would not surrender unconditionally and his demands that there should be no reprisals or disinheritance and that prisoners on both sides should be released free of ransom were accepted by Edward I, with some important reservations.[118] Much of the most interesting passages in the terms set forth by Comyn are those which show the defeated Guardian speaking, however, falteringly, the language of the Treaty of Birgham and of his own predecessors in the days when Scotland had powerful allies and enjoyed some success in arms. There was more dignity in Comyn's submission than there had been in Balliol's abject abdication eight years before. In 1304 the demands of the defeated side were made 'on behalf of the community of Scotland'.[119] The Scottish people 'should be protected in all their laws, usages, customs and liberties in every particular as they existed in the time of King Alexander III, unless there are laws to be amended, in which case it should be done with the advice of King Edward *and the advice and assent of the responsible men [bones gentz] of the land*'.[120] The terms on which Comyn actually surrendered (at Strathord, north of Perth, on February 9th)[121] did not amount to a restoration of things as they had been in the good old days of King Alexander, yet they were not excessively harsh. Varying periods of exile were imposed on the leading men, and the ageing bishop of Glasgow, Robert Wishart, was at first required to stay outside Scotland for two or three years 'on account of the great evils he has caused'. Exile was not intended to be a comfortable life in France plotting a future Scottish *risorgimento*, for the English king sought the expulsion of Scots from the French royal dominions.[122] But within Scotland there was to be no disinheritance, and forfeited estates could be redeemed by their former owners at a cost of two, three, four or (in Umfraville's case only) five years' value.[123]

Despite this apparent generosity, King Edward was not a big enough man to forgive all his enemies, even in this hour of triumph. The humanity of the surrender terms was marred by a relentless pursuit of Wallace which could only be aimed at his extermination and which bore every mark of a personal vendetta. Had such a concept been familiar in the fourteenth century, Wallace would no doubt have been regarded as a 'war criminal'. But the special enormity of Wallace's crime lay in his steadfast refusal to submit to foreign domination and in the fact that he had become a symbol of national resistance. 'No words of peace are to be held out to William Wallace in any circumstances whatever unless he places himself utterly and absolutely in our will ['will' being here contrasted with 'grace' or 'mercy'].'[124] 'The Stewart, Sir John de Soules and Sir Ingram de Umfraville are not to have safe conducts nor come within the king's power until Sir William Wallace is given up.'[125] And, most disgracefully, 'Sir John Comyn, Sir Alexander Lindsay, Sir David Graham and Sir Simon Fraser shall exert themselves until twenty days after Christmas to capture Sir William Wallace and hand him over to the king, who will watch to see how each of them conducts himself so that he can do most favour to whoever shall capture Wallace, with regard to exile or legal claims or expiation of past misdeeds.'[126]

The capture of Wallace would only be a matter of time. Apart from him and John de Soules, who either stayed in, or returned to, France, it seemed that the Scots had been finally crushed. Even Fraser had apparently submitted. Henceforth, in Edward's view, the 'kingdom' of Scotland no longer existed. The future could be assured by a carefully planned ordinance for the 'land' of Scotland, which would be brought into line with Wales or Ireland. Once again, we should give much to have some hint of the common talk in Scotland at the end of 1304 and during 1305. There were two things which might have disturbed King Edward's peace of mind, but he was too busy to be troubled by one, John de Soules' defiant refusal to surrender, and of the other, a secret 'band' between Bishop Lamberton and Robert Bruce, he as yet knew nothing. On June 11th, 1304, at Cambuskenneth, while they were with the English army at the siege of Stirling, and at the very time that Bruce was performing homage to King Edward as heir to his father who had lately died, the bishop and Bruce entered into a solemn bond of mutual friendship and alliance against all men – that is, potential enemies – under a penalty of £10,000.[127] Nothing was said about saving their faith to the king, nor, indeed did the band explicitly mention any purpose whatever. 'Coming together to talk over future perils which they wish as far as possible to avoid', the text runs, 'and in order to resist prudently attacks by rivals, they have agreed faithfully to be of one another's counsel in all their business and affairs at all times and against whichever individuals, and to provide help and succour to one another at all times and without any deceit. Neither Bruce nor Lamberton will attempt any major enterprise without consulting his colleague, and each will warn the other of any danger and try to obviate it.' The band is urgent, solemn – and vague. But there can be no question that between its lines we may read much deep and secret conversation. It meant, first, that William Lamberton had not given up the cause of a free Scotland, secondly, that he had been forced to realize that nothing short of revolution could now save his country. The bishop had made the essential leap from Balliol to Bruce. The two men henceforth faced a more perilous course of action than any they had yet faced. For Lamberton, the friend of Wishart, Wallace and Bruce, the past nine years of struggle, the perilous voyages to and from the continent, the strenuous diplomatic negotiations, the blood spilt at Berwick, Stirling Bridge and Falkirk, the palpable misery of a land where villages and whole towns were burned down, people homeless, churches roofless and desolate, religious houses razed to the ground, were not to go for naught, nor was their memory to be effaced by any ordinance of the conqueror, however moderate and methodical.

EIGHT

Defeat

The fall of Stirling marked the end of an epoch and the frustration of a remarkable experiment. Guardianship had failed. It had proved more successful when the monarch was a minor or an absentee than when (as in 1291) there was no king at all or when (as in 1296) the king was present but incompetent. Restored by Wallace and given fresh life and vigour, taken over by men of higher rank, among whom John de Soules best showed what the office was capable of, guardianship on behalf of the community succumbed to the combination of military defeat, defection of allies and the chronic hopelessness of King John. But if its wardens had failed, the community persisted. It was King Edward's task to alter the character of the community, to re-shape it so that it might take its place in his dominion in an orderly manner. It must cease to be the 'community of the *realm* of Scotland' and become the 'community of the *land* of Scotland'. It must cease to look for the restoration of its king over the water and reconcile itself to the fact that its king was present at Westminster and not in any need of restoration.

In his last years Edward became a hard man who believed that it was his duty to bend the Scots to his will. It would be wrong to think of him acting in Scotland as a mere tyrant, if by tyrant we mean a ruler whose arbitrary whims are law, who pays no regard to local feeling and opinion, or for whom cruelty towards his subjects has become settled policy. If we look at the situation in 1304 as it appeared to Edward, we must in fairness admit that his attempted settlement was both mild and statesmanlike. In his view, he had to deal with a nation which had rebelled against his lordship for many years, had given aid and comfort to his enemies, and had been decisively defeated in war. How many kings or governments emerging as the victors of long and bloody wars in the seventeenth, eighteenth or even nineteenth centuries treated their vanquished foes as prudently and leniently as Edward I treated the Scots in 1304 or 1305? The two main demands made by Comyn of Badenoch when he negotiated the Scottish submission early in 1304 were, first, that there should be an amnesty and restoration of estates for those who had fought against Edward, and, secondly (echoing, however faintly, the braver words of Birgham), that the Scottish people should be assured of all their laws, customs and liberties in every respect as they enjoyed them under King Alexander III. Such laws as must be amended should be amended only by the counsel of the king and the counsel and assent of the responsible men [*bones gentz*] of Scotland.[1] Edward's dealings with the Scots at the St Andrews parliament of March 1304,[2] and the final settlement – the Ordinance of September 1305 – were in harmony with Comyn's demands.

There was no scramble by the victors for the lands of the vanquished. Scotsmen came in and made their peace, did homage, and had writs ordering the restoration of their property, very much as in 1296. We have no Ragman Roll for 1304, but the names of a fair number of men who submitted are known, and we have at least two lists, the first containing the names of some eighty-nine or ninety landowners who did homage to the king of March 14th,[3] the second naming forty who did homage on March 15th.[4] It is a measure of the prejudice among historians against the Scottish nobility that Sir Francis Palgrave (by implication)[5] and Joseph Bain (expressly)[6] assigned the first list, dated March 14th with no year given, to 1296, that is, some days before war had actually broken out between England and Scotland. 'These persons,' writes Bain, apparently without surprise, 'probably foresaw the inevitable issue of the contest.'[7] What 'these persons' had in fact seen was almost eight years of bitter struggle, in which some of them, such as Malcolm, earl of Lennox, Sir Edmund Ramsay, Sir John of Cambo and Sir John Cameron, had taken a notable part. As might be expected in a list of homages performed at St Andrews, most of the landowners recorded on it came from the north and east, especially Angus, Fife and Perthshire. There are several names on the list which are worth remembering in the light of after events: Earl Malcolm of Lennox and John of Cremannan,[8] Walter of Alyth, Walter Barclay, Sir John of Cambo, Sir John Cameron of Baledgarno, Sir William Fenton, Patrick Graham, William Gourlay, Sir John de la Hay, Sir William Mowat, Sir William Murray of Drumsargard, Sir William Murray of St Fort, Sir Adam de Valoignes, Andrew Dempster ('le Jugeor') and Sir William Wiseman. Similarly, from the second list we may select for future reference the names of Walter of Bickerton, Alan Murray of Culbin, Ralph of Dundee and Hamelin of Troup.

The 130 men and women on these lists formed, of course, only a small proportion of those who must have done homage in March 1304 or thereabouts. But there is no reason to think that the process was any different for those whose names do not happen to be recorded. Among the most interesting surviving writs issued at the St Andrews parliament are those of which the following may be regarded as typical: 'The king commands the restoration to Hugh of Penicuik, a Scottish rebel who has come to his peace, of his lands and heritage in England'.[9] It was such men whose patriotism is supposed to have been lukewarm from fear of losing their English estates. In reality, it was they who, under the Guardians' leadership, bore the brunt of the struggle against England. To the great magnates also, with some notable exceptions, King Edward was ready to be generous. As early as May 1304 the earl of Buchan had his earldom restored to him with all its appurtenances, save for the castles of Old Slains and Balvenie.[10] In the same month Bishop Lamberton had his temporalities restored,[11] and Bishop Crambeth of Dunkeld, still absent through illness, recovered not only the temporalities of his see but also the lands which formed his personal inheritance, Bogie (Fife), Crambeth, Cockairney and Dalqueich (Kinross) and Auchrannie in Glenisla.[12] Arbroath Abbey got back its church of Haltwhistle in Tynedale and the bishops of Brechin and Aberdeen had small grants of timber from the king.[13] James Stewart had much longer to wait: he does not seem to have got back his vast estates until after November 3rd, 1305, the date of an instrument recording his abjectly humble submission to Edward's will and pleasure.[14]

The political wisdom of King Edward is shown by his resolve to consult Scottish leaders on the new constitution to be devised for the country and to give them some measure of responsibility for making it work. It has been objected that this was neither statesmanship nor generosity but merely 'policy'. Whatever label we choose to give the decision, its author deserves credit if it was clearly designed to lessen friction, resolve tensions and frustrations, and reconcile the community of Scotland as quickly and peacefully as possible to an indefinite period of English rule. Edward, in other words, had learned part of the lesson of 1296–97. As it happened, he had not learned the most important part, but it was no small achievement for this elderly, conventional, conservative, unimaginative man that he had learned anything at all. At the Lenten parliament of 1305 Robert Wishart, Robert Bruce and John Moubray (one bishop, one earl and one baron) were commanded to advise the king on the settlement of what Edward, for the last time in his reign, called the 'kingdom of Scotland'.[15] Their reply was that ten representatives should be elected by the Scottish community to attend the next English parliament and help to draw up a constitution for Scotland. With Sir John Segrave (lieutenant in Lothian) and John of Sandal (the English chamberlain of Scotland), the three Scottish leaders assembled a parliament in May at which the ten were duly chosen.[16] The symmetry of this commission has a familiar look. It was originally meant to consist of two bishops, two abbots, two earls, and two barons, together with one representative of the community north of the Forth and one for the south – who were, in fact, the two laymen envoys of 1301, Sir John of Inchmartin and Sir Adam Gordon.[17] The English parliament which they attended, postponed from three weeks after midsummer, met on September 15th.[18] Neither the bishop of Glasgow nor the earl of Carrick was among the ten, and (as Dr Barron has argued)[19] they both probably stayed in the north. It was at the September parliament that the Ordinance for the Government of the 'land' – no longer the 'realm' – of Scotland was drawn up and promulgated.[20]

The king's nephew John of Brittany was appointed lieutenant of Scotland. William of Bevercotes and John of Sandal remained as chancellor and chamberlain respectively, with Robert Heron as the chamberlain's comptroller. There were to be four pairs of justices (each consisting of an Englishman and a Scotsman) assigned, with sensible regard to history and geography, to the four principal zones: Lothian, Galloway (that is, the whole south-west), the country between the Forth and the Mounth, and country beyond the Mounth.[21] The sheriffs and constables appointed, some of whom were the hereditary claimants to office, were for the most part Scots. But the militarily crucial sheriffdoms and constabularies of the south-east, Edinburgh, Linlithgow, Haddington, Peebles, were kept in English hands, and the castles of Roxburgh and Jedburgh were under the lieutenant himself. Berwick, although by now almost an 'English' town, was to play a headquarters role similar to that given it in 1296. The only castles of first-rate importance entrusted to Scotsmen were Stirling, assigned to William Bisset, and Dumbarton, placed in the charge of Sir John [Stewart] of Menteith, the younger son of Walter Stewart who from c.1260 to c.1293 had held the earldom of Menteith in right of his wife. A Scottish council was appointed to advise and assist the lieutenant.[22] If it included all those named in a surviving draft it numbered twenty-two Scots, four bishops (including Lamberton), five earls (including Bruce and Buchan), and nine barons (including Comyn of Badenoch).[23] Whether from statesmanship or expediency three former Guardians were thus brought back into the government, albeit in a restricted capacity. But certain English councillors were added to their number, and despite the conversion of old enemies into new advisers, the real power was to be vested in the lieutenant, chancellor and chamberlain. They would have authority to remove any lesser officials and replace them, as they saw fit, by Englishmen or Scotsmen. In theory, at least, they could anglicize the entire Scottish administrative system without consulting Edward I. To say therefore that the official element was derived 'mainly from Scotland'[24] is true only in the rather unreal numerical sense. There was no escaping the fact that Scotland was once more what she had been in 1296, a conquered country, occupied by foreign garrisons and governed by the foreign officials of a foreign king.

The first task of the new régime was to be the holding of an assembly of the responsible men to review the laws of Scotland. The 'laws of King David I', together with subsequent amendments and additions, were to be rehearsed and, where necessary, redressed and amended, so that they would no longer contain anything 'openly contrary to God and reason'.[25] Difficult problems were to be reserved for the king at his next parliament. In only one respect did King Edward make a decision about Scottish law without consulting the community. He abolished the 'usage of Scot(s) and Bret(s)'.[26] It has been seriously suggested that by this act he destroyed the ancient Celtic law of Scotland.[27] In fact the provision referred to the custom which has come down to us in early manuscripts as the 'Law among Brets and Scots', which consisted chiefly of a tariff of wergilds or 'blood-prices' payable to the victim or his kindred in cases of wounding or slaying.[28] It is uncertain whether this archaic (and not specially Celtic) system was still in operation north of the Forth: it may perhaps have survived in the west highlands. It is most improbable that it survived anywhere south of the Forth save in Galloway, where it doubtless formed part of the 'special laws' of that province and where there were special grounds for preserving in the Gaelic *cro* and Welsh *galnis* the terms used for wergild respectively by the Scots of Galloway and the 'Brets', i.e. the Welsh or British, of Cumbria.[29] Whether operative, obsolescent or obsolete, the system was long overdue for abolition. If there had been no foreign conqueror with freedom to make drastic changes, the custom would no doubt have died out gradually. But in 1284 Edward I's Statute of Rhuddlan confirmed, by implication, the abolition of the *galanas* or wergild said to have been decreed by David of Wales (1240–1246). It was unthinkable that Edwardian rule would tolerate the survival north of the border of *cro* and *galnis*; it would be like expecting Lord William Bentinck to have preserved suttee in British India.

The settlement of 1305 was marked by few rewards and fewer punishments. Yet there was one punishment which, had there been no others at all, would have been more than enough. In August 1305, while King Edward was feeling his way towards a new relationship with the Scottish leaders which was surely intended to be based on mutual trust, William Wallace was captured, brought to Westminster for trial, and butchered judicially at the elms of Smithfield. Politically, it must always be a false economy to make one man pay with his blood for the deeds of a whole nation. The conspicuous leniency shown by Edward to his former enemies in 1305 gave his treatment of Wallace an unmistakably vindictive stamp. He was singled out for retribution, and what was meant, no doubt, to have been the inexorable working of justice and at the same time a fearful warning to possible imitators became instead a mark of signal honour.

The pursuit of Wallace had gone on relentlessly ever since the general Scottish surrender early in 1304.[30] His last recorded military action seems to have been a skirmish in September 1304 'below Earnside', that is below the northernmost extremity of the Ochil Hills by Abernethy and Lindores.[31] He was taken at last, on August 3rd, 1305, in or near Glasgow, by servants of Sir John Menteith, the keeper of Dumbarton.[32] Menteith had, during the period of guardianship, been a staunch fighter for the community of Scotland. After the general submission of 1304 he became a firm adherent of the English king.[33] If there was indeed treachery in the capture of Wallace it can hardly be laid at Sir John Menteith's door, for in handing Wallace over to the king he was but repaying the trust which Edward had for some time placed in him.[34] Led first to Edward, who refused to see him, Wallace was brought to London on August 22nd and lodged in the house of a well-known alderman, William de Leyre, in the parish of Fenchurch (Allhallows or St Gabriel's, Fenchurch Street).[35] Next morning, Monday, August 23rd, he was led on horseback to Westminster Hall in a procession which included the mayor of London and the other justices commissioned to try him, together with the sheriffs and aldermen.[36] As on the previous day, immense crowds collected to gaze on the greatest spectacle of that London summer. In mockery, they put a laurel crown on Wallace's head because of his alleged boast that one day he would wear a crown at Westminster.[37] The indictment charged him with treason and many other crimes, the murder of the sheriff of Lanark, atrocities in time of war, convening Scottish parliaments, and persuading the nobles to maintain or renew the Franco-Scottish alliance. Wallace denied the treason but admitted the rest. Most of the other charges, after all, were no more than proof that he had carried out his avowed aims with great success. The charge of treason, on the other hand, meant that he had betrayed and attacked his lawful and natural lord. To Wallace it seemed plain enough that King Edward had never been his lawful and natural lord, and at no time had he ever sworn allegiance or done homage to him.

The judgement, like the trial, was a formality. It was not really a judicial proceeding but an act of simple retribution dictated by a deep desire for revenge, which might be disguised or rationalized as political necessity. William Wallace, 'a Scotsman born in Scotland', was bound to a hurdle and dragged behind a horse for more than four miles, from Westminster to the Tower, from there to Aldgate, and thence finally through the heart of the city to the Smithfield Elms. There he was hanged, cut down while still living, disembowelled and then beheaded. The law was not content to make this the limit of the butchery. The heart and entrails were burned by the executioners, and what remained of the body was cut into four pieces. The head was hoisted above London Bridge, the quarters were distributed to Newcastle upon Tyne, Berwick, Stirling and Perth, to be exposed to the public gaze probably on the bridges at those four towns.[38]

Suddenly, seen against the whole circumstances in which Wallace was hunted down and met his death, Edward I, the greatest of the Plantagenets, a king most admired and feared and one who could show nobility of character, appears small and mean. He is measured against one of the great spirits of history and found wanting. In Wallace himself, who had fought and worked for seven years with a constancy and singleness of purpose remarkable in any age, and for a man of his time and class altogether extraordinary, who alone among the Scottish leaders had defeated a full-scale English army in the field, who had roused a nation to a new sense of its unity and freedom, all that Edward I and his subjects could see was an implacable foe (which he was) and a traitor unmindful of his fealty (which he was never).[39]

The tragedy of Wallace did not lie in the fact that he was a popular leader of proletarian nationalism betrayed by selfish aristocrats. It makes sense to call Wallace a democrat only if we mean by that description that he possessed the common touch, that he could speak to ordinary men in their own language and inspire them with courage and a sense of common purpose to which they could not normally attain. Politically and constitutionally, Wallace was a conservative, quite as much a part of the life of feudal society and breathing its air as the English king against whose might he pitted his own limited strength. Surely the real tragedy of Wallace lay in this, that he was thwarted and overthrown at last by the very same structure of society which he accepted without question. He set before himself the ideal of the community of the realm of Scotland, free and independent, owing allegiance only to its lawfully established king. If the king could not or would not act as its leader, the great feudal magnates and the prelates of the church must for the time being take his place. But if they failed, for whatever reason, to give the lead which it was their duty to give, it was for any one of the responsible men to take up the task. In a dark hour Wallace stood forth as the champion of Scotland – not in opposition to half-hearted and selfish nobles, but to do their work for them and show them that a member of one of the lesser knightly families could respond quite as well as the Comyns, Wisharts, Stewarts or Bruces to the call of the community and the defence of the royal dignity. But, like Wallace himself, Scotland was conservative. In the long run, only the king and great lords could be accepted as her rulers. Defeat and, ironically, the rallying of the magnates which resulted from his defeat, removed the justification for Wallace's remaining at the top. Yet he could not return to the life of an obscure knight. From Falkirk to Smithfield Wallace's career, though obviously far from negligible, was but a sad second best. The greatest achievement of this simple, single-minded man lay in the future, in his capture of the popular imagination of Scotland.

> Of his gud dedis and manhad
> Gret gestis, I hard say, ar made;
> Bot sa mony, I trow noucht,
> As he in till hys dayis wroucht.
> Quha all hys dedis off prys wald dyte
> Hym worthyd a gret buk to wryte
> And all thai to wryte in here
> I want bathe wyt and gud laysere[40]

But, as it happened, this task was never to be carried out in a manner worthy of the man.

The Ordinance of September 1305 contains one chapter which because of its oddity and its rather cryptic import has always caught the eye of historians. Sandwiched between chapters which provided for the exile, for half a year and four years respectively, of Sir Alexander Lindsay and Sir Simon Fraser, are the following words: 'Also it is agreed that the earl of Carrick shall be commanded to put Kildrummy Castle in the keeping of such a man as he himself will be willing to answer for.'[41] The position of this chapter may be due to the vagaries of fourteenth-century drafting, yet the Ordinance is a methodically arranged document. The association of the earl of Carrick with two patriot leaders towards whom Edward still bore rancour, coupled with the tone of mistrust conveyed by this enigmatic provision, may point to some changes in the king's attitude to Robert Bruce. It can hardly yet have amounted to open suspicion or Bruce would not have been included in the Scottish council which was to assist the lieutenant – a fact ignored by Dr Barron in his otherwise powerful arguments for believing that Bruce had 'fallen from favour'.[42] We know, of course, what Edward did not know in the autumn of 1305, that Bruce and Lamberton had entered into a secret 'band' to help each other in case of future perils. But when Wallace was captured there were found in his possession documents which included 'confederations and ordinances made between Wallace and the magnates of Scotland'.[43] These can hardly have included any agreement between Bruce and Wallace made after Bruce's change of sides in 1302, for if they had Edward would surely have taken action against Bruce at once. But there may well have been an earlier agreement. In 1299 Wallace's brother, Sir Malcolm Wallace, had been in Bruce's following,[44] a fact of some significance when it is remembered that the Wallaces' feudal superior was not Bruce but James Stewart. It was Bruce who defended Wallace in the Peebles *fracas*, and Wallace had always belonged to the south-western group of leaders of whom Bruce, Bishop Wishart and the Stewart were the foremost figures. Other, less directly incriminating, evidence may have been found among Wallace's papers.

It is probable that after April 1305 Bruce and Bishop Wishart remained in Scotland. Since the new lieutenant could not take up his duties till the following year, the temporary custody of the country had been committed, on October 26th, to Bishop Lamberton, John of Sandal, Sir Robert Keith and Sir John Kingston.[45] Their commission was actually renewed as late as February 16th,[46] 1306 – six days after Comyn had been murdered. Clearly, Edward did not suspect that anything was seriously amiss. If he had planned Bruce's *coup d'état* himself he could hardly have arranged matters better than to allow Bruce and Wishart complete freedom in Scotland and make Lamberton chief Guardian.

The later Scottish chroniclers, Barbour, Fordun and Wyntoun, tell a romantic story about the origins of Bruce's rising which finds no confirmation in any contemporary source. Some modern historians ignore it, presumably judging it to be pure fiction. Briefly (for there are variations in the tale) it runs as follows.[47] Bruce and the Red Comyn, indignant at Scotland's servitude, made a pact that Bruce should take the crown with Comyn's support and Comyn in return should receive Bruce's lands. The pact was recorded in reciprocally sealed indentures, whereupon Comyn promptly went to Edward and blabbed forth the plot. The king summoned Bruce (but not Comyn) to a parliament, confronted him with Comyn's half of the indenture and asked if the seal on it was his. Bruce asked for a night's respite, since he had foolishly forgotten to bring his seal with him. While he was at his lodgings, the earl of Gloucester (Raoul de Monthermer) sent him a messenger with a shilling and a pair of spurs – a nice touch. Bruce, tipping the messenger with the shilling (a still nicer touch), rode for Lochmaben as fast as he could go and then, finding Comyn at Dumfries, challenged him with his treachery. This tale must be regarded as a literary product, the final, satisfying version of an originally much simpler, or at least less romantic, story. There was no parliament in the period to which Bruce could have been summoned,[48] and there is no evidence that Bruce was with the king only a few weeks before Comyn's murder. The story credits King Edward with a trustfulness and simplicity which, however engaging, would have lost him his throne in a few years, while it attributes to Comyn a treacherousness which owes more to the necessity of giving the Comyns a bad name in post-Bruce Scotland than to anything we know for certain about Comyn's life and character.

But yet the tale cannot be totally fictitious. Walter of Guisborough, followed substantially by Sir Thomas Grey, gives a coherent, self-consistent account of Bruce's uprising and his dealings with Comyn of Badenoch.[49] Bruce, fearing that Comyn might hinder him in an attempt on the throne, sent two of his brothers from Lochmaben to Comyn's castle at Dalswinton, some ten miles to the west, asking him to come to the Franciscan convent in Dumfries to discuss certain important affairs. According to Grey, the brothers were secretly ordered to assassinate Comyn, but Guisborough says nothing of this, only that they were sent to Comyn 'treacherously'. In Grey's account, the brothers found Comyn so open and friendly that they could not bring themselves to kill him – an explanation so lame that we are on safe grounds in dismissing the brother's secret commission as embroidery. Comyn duly appeared at the Greyfriars' church, whereupon Bruce himself took charge and led Comyn up towards the high altar. Here again, Guisborough and Grey diverge. The one says that Bruce, after friendly words, suddenly turned on Comyn and accused him of treacherously reporting to Edward I that Bruce was plotting treason; the other says that Bruce spoke to Comyn of the unhappy plight of their country prostrate beneath the heel of the conqueror. 'Help me to be king and you shall have my lands, or give me yours and I will help you to win the crown.' But Comyn, in this story the soul of uprightness, would not listen to such treason. In their essentials, shorn of the accretions which gather so readily about public events which are both dramatic and secret, the accounts of Guisborough and Grey tally with the much briefer report of the affair made to the pope by Edward I in the course of his charges against Bishop Lamberton. This report, though obviously from a potentially biased source, is closest in time to the event of any that we have. 'When Lamberton was made chief Guardian, Bruce rose against King Edward as a traitor, and murdered Sir John Comyn, lord of Badenoch, in the church of the Friars Minor of the town of Dumfries, by the high altar, because Sir John would not assent to the treason which Robert planned to perpetrate against the king of England, namely, to resume war against him and make himself king of Scotland.'[50]

Without more evidence than we possess at present, it is impossible to reconstruct the sequence of events leading to Comyn's murder and from there to Bruce's coronation. We can note a few certainties and suggest one of what will always be several possible interpolations between the certainties. In order to do this, it will be as well to recapitulate some of the few known landmarks in Bruce's career since 1302, the year of his submission to Edward I.

At the time he went over to the English, Robert Bruce was twenty-eight, entering the prime of life and about to enter on his second marriage. His first wife had been Isabel, daughter of Donald, earl of Mar, his grandfather's friend and ally. The link with the Mar family was close, for Bruce's sister Christian had married Earl Donald's son and successor Earl Gartnait, and is said to have carried with her, as her marriage-portion, the Bruce share in the lordship of Garioch.[51] There was only one child of this first marriage, cut tragically short by Isabel's death in an unknown year: this was Marjorie, born before 1297[52] and named after her grandmother who had brought the earldom of Carrick into the Bruce family. Bruce's second wife, whom he married in 1302, obviously after his submission, was Elizabeth de Burgh, daughter of Richard de Burgh, earl of Ulster. As we have seen, his desire for this marriage may have been one of the reasons which led him to desert the national cause.. Yet at the same time it strengthened his ties with James Stewart, for James's wife Egidia (Gelis) was Elizabeth's aunt. More importantly, it preserved the ancient connexion between the lords of Carrick and northern Ireland. Ultimately, Marjorie Bruce was given in marriage to Walter, James Stewart's second son, who succeeded as heir because his elder brother Andrew died in their father's lifetime.

Between 1302 and 1304 Bruce took an active though never a brilliant or conspicuous part in the Anglo-Scottish war. He had not gained Edward's confidence sufficiently by the autumn of 1302 to figure in a schedule prepared on September 20th listing senior officers in Scotland and the men under their command.[53] Indeed, it is a striking fact that in this list, which contains no fewer than 508 names, only the merest handful were Scotsmen. The aristocracy which is supposed to have been supporting the English king is represented only by the earl of Dunbar (who was more of an Englishman than a Scotsman), and Sir Archibald Livingstone. It seems that Bruce's first public act as an adherent of Edward I was his attendance at the Westminster parliament in October 1302.[54] In the next year he served for a short period as sheriff of Lanark and Ayr and had the keeping of Ayr castle.[55] In the summer campaign of 1303 he was ordered to call up one thousand picked footmen from Kyle, Cunningham and Cumnock (which were within his sheriffdom of Ayr but not in his earldom of Carrick) and a further thousand, as he thought fit, from Carrick and Galloway.[56] These would be among the men he was accustomed to call out as his earl's army of Carrick. This, ironically, was to be done in collaboration with Gibbon MacCan and Dungal Macdougall of Galloway. They were to send their forces to join the main English army in the east, but in July 1303 we find Bruce himself still in association with Sir John de Botetourt, King Edward 1's bastard son, who was then English warden of the western march.[57]

At this time Comyn, Fraser and Wallace, holding out in the forest, were still free to raid Annandale, Liddesdale and the Cumberland border with a strong force of horse and foot.[58] But by the end of the year, as we have seen, their position was hopeless. Comyn and many others were on the point of surrender and it remained only to mop up the forces still holding out under Fraser and Wallace and to await the fall of Stirling. In January 1304 Bruce was still commanding the garrison at Ayr,[59] while Botetourt planned a large-scale foray against the patriots.[60] Not long afterwards, Bruce had crossed the country to join Segrave, Clifford and William Latimer in the mounted commando which left Dunfermline about the end of February and made a rapid surprise attack on the Scots leaders near Peebles. They failed to capture Fraser and Wallace, a fact which explains a phrase in the king's letter to Bruce on this occasion (March 3rd): 'As the cloak has been made well, make the hood also.'[61] Nevertheless, it is clear that Bruce had taken a strenuous part in the main English military effort which, though it failed to shut Wallace and Fraser up in the forest, did prevent them from breaking out north of the Forth in any strength.

Bruce's father, lord of Annandale and still by courtesy 'earl of Carrick',[62] died not far from Holm Cultram in Cumberland, while on his way to Annandale, on April 21st, and was buried at Holm Abbey.[63] A few days before his father's death Bruce was thanked by Edward 1 for sending siege engines to Stirling.[64] A fortnight later Edward issued the writs ordering the inquisitions *post mortem* on Bruce's estates. These were held about May 25th, and Bruce duly did homage for his English lands on or before June 14th.[65] We have seen him making his secret band with Bishop Lamberton on June 11th. Between August and October he seems to have been busy trying to recover Annandale and its liberties.[66] From November 9th, 1304, when he was at York,[67] until the Lenten parliament of 1305 his whereabouts and activities are unknown, but one fact about him at this time is clear enough: potentially he had never been richer or more favoured. Among the motives of his bid for the crown we may discount the desperation or bitterness of a disappointed man. He was earl of Carrick, lord of Annandale, lord of a great estate in England, a house in London and the pleasant suburban manor of Tottenham. In the far north he held part of Garioch and, as guardian of his nephew, the young Earl Donald of Mar, he had in his keeping the stoutly-built fortress of Kildrummy – which he must place in the charge of someone for whom he would be responsible. Also in the north he was keeper of at least three royal forests, Kintore, Darnaway and Longmorn.[68]

There is no evidence that Bruce was on bad terms with the young prince of Wales, who as all men now realized would very soon succeed his father on the English throne. Still only thirty himself, Bruce had brothers who were too young to expect to have reached a corresponding prosperity. But Edward, the eldest, was in the prince of Wales's household,[69] and for Alexander Bruce at least the future seemed bright. He had recently been a student at Cambridge[70] and the English king, probably at a date subsequent to his brother's submission and certainly before February 1304, had granted him in maintenance the living of Kirkinner ('Carnemoel') near Wigtown.[71] Alexander Bruce had had a brilliant career at the university. The Lincoln-shire poet Robert Manning of Bourne, who had known him at Cambridge, wrote admiringly: 'No one who read arts at Cambridge before or since his time ever made such progress. He was a master of arts before his brother was king of Scotland.'[72] Robert Bruce himself gave the traditional feast at Cambridge when his brother 'incepted' as M.A., probably in the spring of 1303.[73] Promotion came quickly and by 1306 he had been made dean of Glasgow.[74]

In the midst of all his prosperity, much of it new-found, there was one thing which Bruce could not forget. A great nobleman of royal descent, related to the greatest aristocratic family of England, son-in-law of the most powerful man in Ireland, his actions were swayed more and more by the knowledge that he inherited a claim to the Scottish throne. When put forward by his grandfather fourteen years earlier it had proved weaker than Balliol's. But the weakest claim may lie dormant to be reawakened when stronger claims are extinguished, and the Bruce claim, though weak against Balliol, was incomparably stronger than any other. In 1292, Bruce's grand-father had carefully resigned to his son all his possible claims to the throne, and now, since April 1304, Bruce had become the head of his family. By 1304 moreover, John Balliol had given every proof that his was the negation of true kingship. And Edward I was an old man, a prey to sickness, close to death. There was something else of which Bruce can hardly have been unaware but to which Edward was blind. The surrender at Strathord, the fall of Stirling, Wallace's execution, the Ordinance of September, had not abolished the Scottish kingdom or the idea of the community of the realm. So long as men like Robert Wishart, William Lamberton and John de Soules remained alive this powerful idea would survive and remain articu-late. This was the part of the lesson of 1296–97 which the English king had not learned, and it was vital. But how could the idea of the community be put once more into action? The old solution was guardianship, but a revival of guardianship – though it was to come again in 1329, in a dangerous hour – was clearly out of the question in 1305. The only possible answer was a revival of kingship. The Scottish kingdom must cease to be the disembodied ghost which it had been since Toom Tabard had been stripped of his insignia in 1296, and be turned again into a living reality. It was thus that out of defeat was born revolution. Judged from one standpoint, it was the private revolution of an ambitious man. But judged from another standpoint, and much more momentously, it was also the political revolution of the community of the realm.

NINE

Revolution

Behind the sudden deed of violence and sacrilege in the Greyfriars' kirk at Dumfries on February 10th, 1306, lay one fact of fundamental importance. The success of any revolution would depend on the full support or else on the elimination of John the Red Comyn of Badenoch. This was true not only because of what he was himself but more precisely because of the powers and tradition he represented. John Comyn was about the same age as Robert Bruce. He was head of the senior line of his family and his estates in Nithsdale, Tweeddale, Atholl and elsewhere, as well as his two highland lordships of Lochaber and Badenoch, placed him as a landowner in that small class which included the earls and the foremost barons. He was also lord of two large manors in Tynedale, a reminder of his descent from Waltheof of Tynedale, one of the ancient aristocracy of Northumbria, as well as from King Donald Bán (Donalbain of Shakespeare's *Macbeth*), whose daughter Bethoc married Waltheof's son. King John was his uncle, the earl of Buchan his cousin, the future earl of Pembroke his brother-in-law. The Comyns, who looked upon him as their chief, formed a powerful clan whose ramifications extended into almost every part of Scotland. Since the end of Alexander II's reign they had been peculiarly identified with leadership of the patriotic or anti-English faction among the Scots nobility. Not one of the men responsible for the conduct of the war against England had a more natural – one might say, a prescriptive – right to leadership of the community of the realm than John Comyn of Badenoch. His father had served as Guardian from 1286 to 1292 and was almost certainly one of the council of twelve in 1295–96. He himself had been Guardian from 1298 to the end of 1300, and again from 1302 until the general submission of 1304. In nearly every event of the war, save for the twenty-two months from April 1296 to February 1298, when he was King Edward's prisoner, Comyn had been in the forefront. His pedigree, connexions and career combine to make a brave story, but the harsh fact remains that he was an almost total failure. Nevertheless, revolution without or against the Comyns would be incomparably more difficult than revolution with their full support.

Ever since the secret pact with Lamberton Bruce must have been laying his plans for an eventual *coup*. No doubt he hoped for Edward I's death, no doubt he wished to gauge the degree of support on which he could depend among the great nobles, gentry and substantial freeholders. We have at least one glimpse of a part of Bruce's entourage in this period, from a grant which he made of land at Longforgan in the Carse of Gowrie. The charter for this survives at Glamis, in favour of Alexander Keith – possibly the Alexander Keith who held the Annandale parsonage of Hoddam in 1296.[1] The witnesses to the charter were not an Annandale or even a Carrick group. They included the earl's knights, Alexander Menzies (son of Alexander III's chamberlain), Walter Logan of Hartside, sometime sheriff of Lanark, Reginald Crawford, sometime sheriff of Ayr and Robert Boyd of Noddsdale, coroner of Ayr and Lanark. With these lairds, none of whom is known to have had inherited or personal ties with the earldom of Carrick or the lordship of Annandale, were Patrick of Skene in Aberdeenshire, Peter of Graden near Kelso and Robert of Annan. In this interestingly mixed group we can see a 'meinie' or retinue gathering round the earl, a vital cadre of support which could spring into action once the *coup* was launched. The charter gives precision to Sir Thomas Grey's comment about Bruce in this period that he 'retained a strong following through kinsmanship and alliance, always hoping for the establishment of his claim of succession to the realm of Scotland.'[2]

We can regard it as reasonably certain that in the autumn of 1305 Bruce had discussed revolution with Wishart and Lamberton.[3] In the following February he was at Lochmaben, while Comyn was at nearby Dalswinton. King Edward was ill and not expected to live much longer. It was the moment for action. It is contrary to everything we know of Bruce's character that he should have called Comyn to the Greyfriars' church with the secret intention of killing him. The place of meeting, the fact that King Edward's justices were holding their session in the castle at the time, and the kiss – though it was not the kiss of peace – with which the two men greeted each other all suggest that Bruce meant only to put some such plan to Comyn as Grey and Barbour believed him to have done. Had not his grandfather proposed a similar plan to Count Florence of Holland? But no doubt Bruce's intention was to take the throne himself, and give his estates to Comyn, rather than take Comyn's, vast as they were, and help his old rival, Balliol's nephew, to become king of Scots.

Comyn can hardly be blamed for refusing. As Bruce was to learn to his cost, there were many other great men in Scotland who could not throw over their lawfully constituted sovereign and accept Bruce. No matter how inept King John had been, he was still alive and had a full-grown son and heir. No king of Scots had been overturned in this way since 1097, when Donald Bán had been driven from the throne by Edgar with the help of an English army. This was hardly an auspicious precedent, even if it had been at all clearly remembered. But Bruce was fully committed and prepared. He would identify his own ambition with the inarticulate but nonetheless powerful desires of the community of the realm. As the two leaders stood together in front of the high altar, speaking of the future, all their old antagonism and jealousy sprang to life. Bruce urged the revival of Scottish kingship, Comyn

········· *Suggested routes taken by Robert Bruce after the murder of Comyn at Dumfries 12 Feb. 1306*

—·—·— *Suggested routes taken by Robert Bruce after the Battle of Methven, 19 June, 1306*

— — — *Queen Elizabeth, Earl of Atholl & Co.*

Orkney

0   20   40   60   80

Miles

Bishop of Moray

N. Uist

Carinish

S. Uist

Tain   St. Duthac's Sanctuary

Elgin

Barra

Kisimul

Garmoran

Castle Tirrim

Kildrummy

M a r   Aberdeen

The Mounth

Cairnburgmore Castle

Mull

Dunstaffnage

Kenmore

Methven 19/6/06

Scone 25-27/3/06

Perth

Cupar

Dail Right (? July 1306)

Scotlandwell

Stirling

Earls Ferry

Islay

Inverkip

Dumbarton

Kirkintilloch

Edinburgh

Rothesay

Glasgow

Rutherglen

Berwick

Rathlin

Dunaverty

Ayr

Roxburgh

The Roe

Antrim

Loch Doon

Tibbers

Dalswinton

Dumfries (12/2/06)

Lochmaben

Annan

Carlisle

Newcastle-upon-Tyne

Galloway

Skinburness

Man

8. 1306.

would have none of it. It may be that Comyn called Bruce a traitor, it seems certain that Bruce struck at Comyn with his dagger. At this, Bruce's companions attacked him with their swords. Mortally wounded, he was left for dead, lying on the flagstones before the altar. Sir Robert Comyn, John Comyn's uncle, rushing up to defend his nephew, was killed by a blow on the head from the sword of Christopher Seton, the son of a Yorkshire knight and the husband of Bruce's sister Christian. Soon the town was in an uproar, the Scots flocking to Bruce's support as he and his men-at-arms hurried to seize the castle. The justices, fearing for their lives, shut themselves in the hall where they had been holding their session, but surrendered when Bruce threatened to set the place on fire. It was then reported that Comyn was still alive: the Franciscans had carried him into the vestry to treat his wounds and administer the last sacrament. According to Guisborough (who seems here to be retailing a deliberately hostile embellishment to what was doubtless a substantially truthful account), Bruce had the dying man brought back to the altar steps and bloodily despatched there.[4] It was enough, surely, that Bruce had murdered him and that the deed had been done in a consecrated place. But there was evidently a general tradition, both in Scotland and England, that Comyn was killed in two stages, and it is this tradition which lies behind the famous but wholly fabulous tale of Kirkpatrick and his cry of 'I mak siccar'.

Six weeks elapsed between Comyn's murder and Bruce's inauguration. Although the murder itself was surely an act of unpremeditated violence, what followed must have been part of a pre-arranged plan. The fiery cross was never to be carried more urgently through Scotland than during February and March 1306. Castles were seized, the kinsmen of the lord of Badenoch fled before his murderer, and Englishmen rode as fast as they could to safe castles or to the Border. By a piece of extraordinary good fortune, there survives a copy of a newsletter written by an Englishman at Berwick not long before Bruce's inauguration, which gives us an invaluable glimpse of the movements of Bruce and his supporters during these critical weeks.[5] Since much of this information is to be found nowhere else, its reliability cannot be checked directly. But the writer's accuracy on points which can be checked inspires confidence in the whole of the admittedly incomplete story he has to tell. Certainly no one attempting to reconstruct the events of this period can ignore his urgent, almost breathless narrative.

Bruce's achievements in these few short weeks were remarkable, but he had not time to put himself in a commanding position militarily, save perhaps in the south-west. He and his friends seized the castles of Dumfries, Dalswinton, Tibbers and Ayr. Robert Boyd of Cunningham, who was to prove one of Bruce's staunchest companions, took Rothesay Castle by sea, and then laid siege to Inverkip.[6] At the southern extremity of the peninsula of Kintyre – the 'isle of Kintyre' as contemporaries called it[7] – stood on a sea-girt rock the castle of Dunaverty.[8] Apparently Edward I had been persuaded to grant this castle, without a proper inquest, to one Malcolm MacCoyllan (*alias* Malcolm MacCulian).[9] An attractive interpretation of the evidence would suggest that Malcolm MacCulian was identical with Malcolm le fiz Lengleys, to whom King Edward had given possession of at least a part of Kintyre in 1296, apparently without due process of law.[10] Malcolm MacCulian's origins are as yet a mystery. He has been claimed, doubtfully, as a MacQuillan of Antrim, and perhaps even more doubtfully as an ancestor of the Macleans. Whatever the truth of this may be, it seems that Bruce got Dunaverty from Malcolm MacCulian in exchange for another castle, and he took good care to stock Dunaverty and also his own ancestral castle, on the island in Loch Doon in Carrick, with plenty of victuals.[11] Finally, before going north to Scone, Bruce tried, without success, to persuade Sir John Menteith to surrender the castle of Dumbarton.[12] The attention thus paid by Bruce to five of the fortresses which commanded the Firth of Clyde is striking proof of his awareness of the 'western approaches'. The way must be kept open for allies and supplies to reach him from Ireland and the Outer Isles, while enemies from the same quarter, and also English fleets based on Skinburness, must find their approach routes barred.

Before going to Dumbarton and thence on to Scone, Bruce spent some time at Rutherglen and Glasgow, taking individual fealties, putting the populace on twenty-four hours' notice of mobilization,[13] and conferring with Robert Wishart, who is known to have been at Glasgow four days before John Comyn was killed.[14] The murder had been committed in Wishart's diocese. Far from excommunicating the guilty man, the bishop exhorted his flock to fight for Bruce as though his cause were a crusade.[15] He brought out from his episcopal wardrobe robes and vestments suitable for a new king to wear, and also a banner bearing the arms of the last king, which the indefatigable old man had been carefully hiding in his treasury for precisely this purpose and moment. It was a picturesque touch, and reminds us forcefully that the mind of Wishart had most probably been behind the drafting of the Treaty of Birgham, which sixteen years earlier had provided so elaborately that relics and muniments touching the royal dignity should be kept safely, under their seals, by the great magnates of the realm.[16] The writer of the English newsletter called Wishart the 'bad bishop' and considered that he was Bruce's chief counsellor. He goes on to give a highly interesting piece of information which though unsupported rings true enough. Wishart, he says, not only absolved Bruce formally for his sin in being a party to the killing of John Comyn, but made Bruce swear an oath to abide under the direction and with the assent of the clergy of Scotland. Once the oath was sworn, he might do what he could to secure his inheritance. Wishart worked for the freedom of Scotland, but he would assuredly not have supported a king who would not guarantee the freedom of the Scottish Church. Barely four months before the great rising of 1297, when he was supposedly administering his diocese peaceably under the English régime of occupation, Bishop Wishart sent a mandate to the dean of Christianity of Lennox, reminding him of 'the liberties of the Scottish Church hitherto enjoyed and granted by our lord the king'.[17] We can be sure that these liberties meant much to the bishop, and when he wrote with possibly careful anonymity of 'our lord the king' it is by no means certain that it was Edward I he had in mind.[18] The oath which Robert Bruce took in Wishart's presence in March 1306 may be seen as the oath of one who was soon to be *Rex Scottorum* to preserve and defend those same *libertates ecclesie Scoticane*.

Bruce was set upon taking the throne. The die had been cast before Comyn's murder, probably long before. Perhaps the decision dated from 1304, when Bruce and Lamberton had made their secret pact. Certainly Lamberton was ready when the time came. At the crucial moment of Comyn's murder, and for some weeks afterwards, he was at Berwick, trusted by Edward I, president of the council established under the 1305 Ordinance for the government of conquered Scotland.[19] Shortly before Bruce was made king, the bishop slipped away from Berwick under cover of darkness, crossed the Forth (no doubt by the 'earl's ferry' from North Berwick to Elie) and hurried to Scone to be present at the ceremony. We are not told how Lamberton had wind of Bruce's movements. It is clear from the newsletter that the English at Berwick realized that speedy enthronement at Scone was Bruce's objective, and there even seems to have been some communication between Bruce and the English. At this eleventh hour, Bruce made a formal demand to be recognized as king.[20] For their part, King Edward's council and his chamberlain ordered Bruce to hand over the castles he had seized, especially those belonging to the Red Comyn which had escheated to the English Crown! Bruce's answer was that he would seize castles and people and strengthen his position as fast as he could until King Edward had told him what was his will in response to his demand. If this were not granted, Bruce would defend himself 'with the longest stick that he had'.[21]

Guisborough, a hostile witness, speaks quite frankly of Bruce's coronation at Scone as a great public event, 'attended and consented to by four bishops, five earls and the people of the land.[22] A strong element of election or choice was involved. A curious parable put out at the time by some unknown English observer compares the choice of Bruce as king with the conspiracy of Abimelech in the Book of Judges – he too had assassinated his rivals in order to seize the throne, and was likened to the hurtful bramble elected as their king by the trees when the more benign and peaceful olive, fig and vine had each in turn declined.[23] Although this can partly be discounted as hostile gossip, and little faith can be placed in the writer's statement that 'the Scots' had first offered the throne in turn to the earls of Buchan, Ross and Dunbar, we can hardly dismiss the main implication of the story, namely that a group of people influential in Scotland in 1305–06 made public their approval of Bruce's bid for the throne and thus in effect 'elected' him king. And we might make a guess that the unidentified electorate included the bishops of St Andrews, Glasgow, Dunkeld, Moray and Brechin, and abbot of Scone, possibly the abbot of Inchcolm,[24] as well as a good many other senior clergy, two or three earls, Atholl and Lennox among them, and a large array of men of the lairds' class. It was three such men, Thomas Hay of Borthwick, Alexander Seton of that ilk and Neil Campbell of Lochawe, who about 1308 made a band to hold together in defence of their king Robert and of the liberty of his realm with their last breath.[25]

As to the full formality and solemnity of the inauguration there can be little doubt that Guisborough was right. He does not name the bishops and earls, and the available evidence suggests the attendance of three bishops and four earls. It seems that there were actually two separate ceremonies, and the explanation of this curious fact throws a fascinating light on the dilemma confronting the Scottish leaders: on the one hand the desperate need to have Bruce enthroned as soon as possible, on the other, the compelling arguments to make his inauguration follow the traditional pattern. He was actually made king on Lady Day, Friday, March 25th, 1306 the tenth anniversary of the outbreak of war between Edward I and the Scots. The Stone of Destiny was in Westminster Abbey, but the English king had not been able to remove Scone itself, the Moot Hill, or the Augustinian abbey which acted in some sense as the custodian of what was by far the most ancient seat of royalty still in use in Britain. Apparently the abbey church was the actual scene of the coronation itself, and after Bruce's first defeat Edward I requested the pope to authorize the wholesale removal of Scone Abbey to another diocese, presumably somewhere in England.[26] Abbot Henry of Scone willingly took part in the ceremony along with Lamberton, Wishart and David Murray, bishop of Moray. Maurice abbot of Inchaffray was almost certainly at the inauguration.[27] Three earls who are known to have been present were John of Atholl, Malcolm of Lennox and Alan of Menteith, and to them we may probably add the boy Donald earl of Mar, who was Bruce's ward. The most conspicuous absentee among the earls was, of course, Duncan of Fife. It might, indeed, have been denied that any ceremony could be valid without him. In 1292 a substitute had been carefully provided; now the earl was sixteen years of age, but completely in King Edward's power. His aunt, Isabel, perhaps in her late thirties, was wife to the earl of Buchan. For her, as for the countess of Dunbar ten years before, the call of patriotism, or of the ancient realm of Scotland, was stronger than wifely loyalty – although English accounts do not hesitate to say that she was, or wished to be, Bruce's mistress.[28] We do not know where the countess was staying at the time of Bruce's *coup*,[29] but it may not have been by chance that by the last week of March she was within reach of Scone. She had as part of her tocher a house near Balmullo in the west of

Leuchars parish,[30] from where a comfortable day's ride would take her to the inauguration. Sir Thomas Grey (who otherwise follows Guisborough or a source common to both of them) preserves the information that Isabel's husband was at his manor house at Whitwick in Leicestershire,[31] while Guisborough uniquely reports that she deliberately kept the earl's war horses (*destriers*) at her house so that she could play her part in the inauguration ceremony, and that she left her husband's company deceitfully.[32]

The reign of Robert I was reckoned to begin on March 25th.[33] It was evidently on this day, the feast of the Annunciation, that Isabel of Fife, standing in for her nephew and acting as head of her kin, performed the rite of enthronement.[34] Whether or not William Lamberton was present at this ceremony is unknown, but two days later, on Palm Sunday (March 27th), the bishop celebrated pontifical high mass for the new king.[35] On one if not on both of these solemn occasions a golden coronet was placed on Bruce's head.[36] Since at least the earlier twelfth century it had been customary for the bishops to assist at the inauguration of a new king. The special high mass would have been part of a determined attempt to make King Robert's enthronement conform as closely as possible to time-honoured practices. But it is possible that Lamberton had arrived at Scone by Lady Day, in time to perform some action intended to ratify Robert's kingly status, for this was included in the accusation the English were soon levelling against him.[37] And it is certain that the bishop swore fealty to the new king for the temporalities of his see. The more closely the evidence for Bruce's inauguration is examined, the more carefully it appears to have been stage-managed, however hastily the separate acts in the drama may have had to be performed.

There was no time to call a parliament. The country must be put in a state of defence. There would have been some proclamation, some declaration of right, by the new king, but no formal document issued by Bruce or on his behalf has survived from this time, or, indeed, from earlier than the third year of his reign.[38] Bishop Wishart, old as he was, plunged with zest into the struggle. The English had given him timber to repair the bell-tower of his cathedral, and with this he had siege engines made to use against the castle at Kirkintilloch. He himself seized the royal castle at Cupar in Fife 'comme homme de guerre', as the English complained.[39] The new king showed similar energy as he went to different parts of the country,[40] quelling Balliol and Comyn sympathizers, taking the homage of unwilling magnates like the earl of Strathearn (Buchan's brother-in-law) and seizing more castles. He returned to the south-west, no doubt to rally support, for the west-country element among his early followers is noteworthy. His sojourn in this region included a visit to Galloway to put hostile chiefs out of action.[41] But he could not approach the strongly-held redoubt of Lothian, guarded as it was by the great fortresses of Stirling, Edinburgh, Roxburgh and Berwick. And in the mean time the English, who possessed this enormous advantage, had not been idle.

King Edward was taken utterly by surprise, and at first he does not seem to have been sure that it was really Bruce who had risen against him. 'Certain Scots in malice have slain John Comyn,' he wrote, as though unwilling to credit such a preposterous enormity as that Robert Bruce, whom he regarded as being deeply in his debt, could have done this deed.[42] But by April 5th he had appointed as his special lieutenant in Scotland Aymer de Valence, his own half-cousin and Comyn's brother-in-law, and had armed him with wide and drastic powers.[43] He was, in Barbour's graphic phrase, 'to burn and slay and raise dragon',[44] to raise, that is, the terrible dragon banner which meant that no mercy would be shown and that none of the accepted restraints of fourteenth-centure warfare – few as these were – need be observed. This is confirmed by letters from the king congratulating Valence on burning Simon Fraser's lands in Tweeddale and admitting that he had originally ordered all prisoners to be killed.[45] He later modified these orders, partly to allow Valence to pardon the 'middling men', but partly because he wished to reserve for Bruce, Fraser and the earl of Atholl a more terrible fate than summary execution. Even in his great rage, Edward's eye for detail, his unsurpassed memory of individuals, did not desert him.

'Since we have not found in Sir Michael Wemyss' (the king wrote to Valence on June 19th), 'either good word or service, and he has now shown in deed that he is a traitor and our enemy, we command you to burn his manor where we stayed, and all his other manors, to destroy his lands and goods and to strip his gardens clean so that nothing is left, for an example to others like him. And as for Sir Gilbert de la Hay, to whom we showed much courtesy when he stayed with us in London recently, and in whom we thought we could place our trust, but whom we now find to be a traitor and our enemy, we order you to burn down all his manors and houses, destroy all his lands and goods, and strip all his gardens so that nothing is left, and if possible do worse to him than to Sir Michael Wemyss.'[46]

Armed with these extensive powers, Valence moved with speed and vigour. By June 9th, Bishop Lamberton, then at Scotlandwell in Kinross-shire, had made the first overtures of surrender,[47] though after this he apparently called out all his tenantry and sent them off to fight for Bruce, and for good measure sent him the boy Andrew, James Stewart's son and heir, who had been in the bishop's custody.[48] Wishart was captured in Cupar castle and the two bishops were sent south, along with the abbot of Scone, to be put in irons in Wessex dungeons.[49] Only their orders saved them from hanging.[50] By the early part of June Valence had secured the town of Perth and Bruce judged the moment ripe for an attack in strength. He approached from the mountains to the west of the town on June 18th.[51]

Failing to tempt the English out to fight, he bivouacked at Methven, in a wood on high ground south of the Almond. Unwisely, some of his men went off to forage, others were scattered to find sleeping quarters. Valence seized his opportunity, coming out from Perth before daylight and taking the Scots unawares. His men made a fierce onslaught and there was hard fighting at first, but Methven was a rout rather than a battle. Within three months of his coronation, King Robert was fleeing for safety with a few hundred men. Many of his most valuable supporters were taken prisoner, and of these very few could be saved by Valence's clemency from the vengeful wrath of King Edward. Yet the disaster was the saving of Bruce and his kingdom. If he had won, as he might well have done, he would almost certainly have met the English king in the field in a major pitched battle, eight years before he was ready for it.

Dr Evan Barron compiled a list of some 135 men who came out for Bruce in the spring of 1306, most of whom were with him at his coronation or had joined his standard before the fight at Methven.[52] Although it is not as complete as surviving evidence would enable us to make it, the list is a valuable starting point for our assessment of the scope and character of support for the revival of Scottish kingship in 1306. What follows owes much to a study of Barron's list, although the conclusions he drew from it do not seem to be tenable.

Before looking at the names on the list we ought to remember that the war for the survival of an independent Scottish kingdom had been waged for the best part of a decade before Robert Bruce made his bid for the throne. There had been plenty of time to sort out the convinced and committed patriots from the fence-sitters and defeatists on the one hand and the sincere supporters of English claims on the other. If he played his cards right, Bruce could fall heir to a tough tradition of (for the age) remarkably single-minded patriotism, and might also take advantage of disillusionment with Edward I in the ranks of English landowners. Among the obscure and humbly-placed we might notice Thomas, a priest of Edinburgh, William of Bolhope and Robert Scort. On the approach of Edward I's army in 1296 Thomas of Edinburgh took bell and candle and solemnly excommunicated the invading host, king and all, apparently as an expression of pure hostility. In the same period William of Bolhope, a Scot long resident at Alnmouth in Northumberland, hurried home to help defend his native land. Learning that King Edward was gaining the upper hand William took two swords and set off south again on a one-man counter invasion, only to be challenged and slain for refusing to declare his loyalty to the English king. Robert Scort was arrested in Cumberland as a Scottish spy in 1300 and hanged at Carlisle in the following year. He was said to have come into Edward I's peace 'once, twice and thrice', but always returned to the Scots to give them information about conditions in north-west England.

Among the English, or at least those with English property and connexions, we should remember Sir Henry Lathom of Lancashire appointed
sheriff of Aberdeen by Edward I in 1296 and aligned with the Scots by 1297;
Stephen Pesshun of Lincolnshire, in Scots service by 1298, Sir Christopher
Seton of Yorkshire, who became one of Bruce's most devoted followers,
Thomas Clennell and William of Burradon of north Northumberland
families, Simon de Cresseville of Attercliffe near Sheffield who held Jedburgh gallantly for the Scots in the autumn of 1298, long after Wallace's
defeat, and Walter of Barkston in the West Riding. Walter fought for King
John at Dunbar and by 1297 was reported still to be an adherent of the Scots
and an enemy of the English king and kingdom.[53]

These are only a handful of the persons who, from whatever motive,
decided to throw in their lot with the Scots defending their country's
freedom from 1296 onward. Much the same picture emerges when we look
at the situation in and after 1306. There were those who were personally,
feudally or territorially committed to Robert Bruce. There were many no
doubt who hesitated or felt reluctance at the prospect of renewed warfare
and devastation. In attempting a brief analysis, based on Barron's list but
ranging more widely, we may at least bear in mind that although Bruce's bid
for the throne amounted to a dynastic revolution, it did not totally transform
the nature of the war.

First of all, there are the men whose attitude represented and at the same
time ensured continuity in the struggle for the community of the realm; the
men, that is, who had been fully committed to King John and now rallied to
Bruce. They were going far beyond the cautious revolution of 1295 and
performing (no doubt in the community's name) nothing less than a
deliberate act of deposition and election. They were also taking a terrible
risk. Foremost among these men were the three bishops, Lamberton,
Wishart and Murray, and also John de Soules. Although Soules seems to
have stayed overseas, dying in France about 1310,[54] his support for King
Robert may have counted for much among men who did not belong to the
Bruce or Comyn faction. James the Stewart was another great magnate in
this group who supported Bruce. He had got his lands back only at the end
of 1305 and within a few months they had again been forfeited and were
given to the earl of Lincoln.[55] But the Stewart was an old man. Since King
Alexander's death twenty years before he had played a part which, though
far from negligible, was always secondary. He would neither hang for the
young king nor take to the heather with him. On October 23rd he made a
second abject submission to Edward I and the grant to the earl of Lincoln
was rescinded.[56] But by March 1309 (the year of his death) he was back with
King Robert, taking his rightful place as the senior officer of the royal
household.[57] Simon Fraser's movements are more obscure. The provisions
for his exile suggest that he surrendered in 1304 or 1305, and in October
1305 it was agreed that he might then recover his estates at three years'

purchase.[58] Yet he still faced a long exile.[59] At the time of Bruce's rising, he was apparently with the English at Berwick.[60] Landless, deeply aggrieved, he seems to have joined the new king at or just after his inauguration. He was present at Methven, but was soon captured, and was drawn and hanged in London on September 7th.[61]

Other leading men in this same group were the three earls, Atholl, Lennox and Menteith. John of Strathbogie, earl of Atholl, who had supported the common cause more or less consistently since 1296, had nevertheless always been a close friend of the Bruces. Like Bruce he had married a daughter of Earl Donald of Mar, and his estates in Stratha'an and Strathbogie[62] gave him as strong an interest in the north east as the lordship of part of Garioch gave to Bruce. Under the Guardians Earl John had served as sheriff of Aberdeen,[63] and in 1304, when he was Edward I's warden between Forth and Spey, he resented the fact that the Aberdeen sheriffdom had been given to Alexander Comyn, the earl of Buchan's brother.[64] He besought the king not to let Comyn have Aboyne Castle; 'Sir Alexander,' he wrote, 'already has two of the strongest castles in the north, Urquhart and Tarradale, and (as sheriff) he can use the castle at Aberdeen.'[65] He suspected that Comyn was still in league with the west highlander Lachlan Macruarie, as he had been in 1299. Atholl's plea was successful, but it was not quite disinterested. When he came out for Bruce two years later the authority in the north in which Edward had confirmed him must have been of much value to the new king of Scots. Of Menteith we know only that he surrendered after Methven, to be imprisoned and deprived of his earldom.[66] Lennox escaped with Bruce, to become, along with James Douglas, Neil Campbell and Gilbert de la Hay, one of his almost inseparable companions.

The earl of Strathearn was arrested. He pleaded that after Bruce's inauguration (which he had evidently not attended) Atholl, Robert Boyd and others had pursued and kidnapped him and compelled him to do homage to the new king on pain of losing his head. After Methven, he had sent his son to join in the pursuit of Bruce.[67] He was imprisoned at Rochester, but not in irons, and ultimately he recovered his earldom.[68] In truth, an appreciable number of earls were hostile at this time: Sutherland, Ross, Buchan, Angus and Dunbar; while Caithness and Fife were at best neutral. Alexander Macdougall, lord of Argyll, and his son and heir John, respectively uncle and cousin of the murdered John Comyn, were fiercely opposed to Bruce. So, for different reasons, were the leading men of Galloway. Between them, these magnates controlled a great proportion of the wealth and military resources of Scotland in castles and manpower, especially of the country north of Forth. The majority of them opposed Bruce not because they were on principle pro-English and held English estates but because they could accept neither the overthrow of the Comyns nor the claims of Bruce, in their view a plain usurper. If Bruce, therefore, had depended solely on the men who by rank and tradition stood at the top of Scottish feudal society, his revolution would have failed.

No doubt some men joined Bruce partly because English rule threatened to leave them landless, or much poorer than they believed was just. James Douglas was one such, the son of the rough Sir William, who had died in the Tower of London about 1299, still implacably hostile to the English king.[69] His lands were given to Sir Robert Clifford.[70] James Douglas was the nephew and perhaps also (because of the comparative rarity of his Christian name in thirteenth-century Scotland) the godson of James the Stewart.[71] He was to win so shining a reputation for chivalry as the bravest of King Robert's liegemen that John Barbour's great poem *The Bruce* is almost as much the story of Douglas as it is of Bruce himself.

> Thusgat maid thai thar aquentance
> That nevir syne, for nakyn chance
> Departyt quhill thai lyffand war.
> Thair frendschip woux ay mar and mar.[72]

Sir John, laird of Cambo in the East Neuk of Fife, was another man whom English rule threatened to deprive of property. Although his name is on the list of homagers to Edward I in 1304, he had been prevented from doing homage by Sir Henry de Beaumont, probably because he had acquired the revenues of the prosperous fishing town of Crail, to which Beaumont's sister, the lady de Vesci, claimed an hereditary right.[73] Lady de Vesci was confirmed in possession in June 1305, with reversion to her brother.[74] By the following summer Sir John of Cambo was listed among King Edward's enemies, and on August 4th he was hanged at Newcastle.[75] William Gourlay, who like John of Cambo figures on the list of homages to Edward I of March 14th, 1304,[76] was similarly frustrated by claimants supported by the English king, in his case over the land of 'Macfothel' (Pitfoddels?) in Aberdeenshire. The Aberdeen jury which rejected Gourlay's claim on December 14th, 1306, declared 'he is still an enemy of the king, adhering to Robert Bruce.[77] How many more men among Bruce's followers had lost or were under threat of losing their lands it is impossible to say. If we look at the petitions which Scotsmen presented to King Edward at the September parliament of 1305 we find the names of Gilbert Hay, Laurence of Strathbogie, Hamelin of Troup and William Gourlay. These four men, perhaps all disappointed of achieving their desires, were out with Bruce a few months later.[78] It would certainly be wrong to suggest that the grievances of disinherited landowners formed the mainspring of Bruce's revolt. But it is beyond question that we must look to men of the class of Sir John of Cambo, Sir James Douglas and William Gourlay if we wish to know who provided the backbone of the militaty effort on which Bruce depended both before and after the rout at Methven.

Among such men there were many who had fought for the common cause not only when Bruce had been one of the national leaders but also for two years after Bruce had gone over to the English. It is clear that Bruce did not rely solely on the support of men who belonged to his own lordships or lived within his sphere of influence. Admittedly there were many such men and they could be important. From Kyle, Reginald Crawford and Alexander Lindsay of Barnweill near Ayr;[79] from Carrick itself, Gilbert son of Roland and Roland Askeloc; from Nithsdale, Stephen of Closeburn, Thomas and Robert of Kirkconnel, and young Thomas Randolph, Bruce's nephew on his mother's side; from upper Clydesdale, the laird of Wiston and Simon Lockhart of the Lee; from Aberdeenshire, James of the Garioch: none of these men of the lairds' class was insignificant, and a few, like Alexander Lindsay and Thomas Randolph, belonged to well-known families. The knights of Annandale, whose loyalty to their lord we have remarked on when he was on the English side, ran true to form and, in the main, supported the young Robert Bruce when he made his bid for Scottish freedom. Ralph Herries, for example, was among those hanged at Newcastle on August 4th, 1306.[80] On October 20th the earl of Hereford was granted the forfeited lands of all those who held of Lochmaben Castle and of Annandale – that is, the knights and other freeholders of the lordship which had been possessed by the family of Bruce for nearly two hundred years.[81] But there were other landowners south of the Forth who had no territorial reason to be subject to Bruce's influence. Apart from James Stewart, John de Soules and James Douglas, there were two knights of Cunningham, Robert Boyd of Nodds-dale and Brice Blair. Hugh Lovel of Hawick, Simon Fraser and his brother Thomas, and their kinsmen and Somervilles, lords of Linton in Roxburgh-shire and Carnwath in Lanarkshire, do not seem to have been closely connected to Bruce. To them we may add Alexander Folkard of Folkerton in Lanarkshire; James, son of Sir Walter Lindsay, who held Thurston in East Lothian; William, son of Sir Alexander Menzies, who held Shielswood in Selkirkshire and the neighbouring lands of Harden in Roxburghshire; and the tenants of the royal castles and manors of Selkirk, Peebles and Traquair.[82]

It is particularly interesting to find among the middling men recorded as being with Bruce in 1306 several who had made their peace with Edward I only two years earlier, after long years as 'rebels' or enemies. Thus, in March 1304, the following men did homage to the king at St Andrews.[83] From Angus and Perthshire, Walter of Alyth, Walter of Rossie, Ralph of Dundee, Sir John Cameron of Baledgarno, Sir William Fenton,[84] Sir William Mowat, Sir Adam de Valognes, and Andrew Dempster; from Fife, Thomas of Balcaskie, Sir William Murray of St Fort, Alan Murray,[85] and Walter of Bickerton, laird of Kincraig; from Banffshire, Hamelin of Troup; from the Lennox, John of Cremannan. All these save the last-named were reported to be out with Bruce in 1306, and though John of Cremannan is not recorded as a rebel in that year, Thomas of Cremannan, a well-recorded Lennox baron, forfeited his lands for supporting Bruce, and we may suppose either that John was his kinsman or that the name ought correctly to

be Thomas.[86] The point was in fact well put in an English memorandum of
1306: 'The king has granted to Michael of Witton the lands *of his enemies in
the first war of Scotland*, who subsequently came to the king's peace *and have
now lately turned against the king.*'

In Scotland at the turn of the thirteenth and fourteenth centuries it was
usual for men of knight's or esquire's rank, even quite substantial men of
property, to attach themselves to some powerful magnate, an earl, a bishop,
or one of the richest barons, to belong to some 'following' or 'meinie'. Thus
John Cameron of Balnely was expressly said to be 'with' the earl of Atholl,[88]
and the same was very probably true of his kinsman Cameron of Baledgarno.[89] Sir John of Leny was no doubt in the following of the earl of
Menteith or the earl of Lennox. The Lennox men Sir John of Luss, Sir
Duncan son of Anelf (Macaulay?), Sir Thomas of Cremannan and
'Coweyn' [Ewen] Mackessan of Garchell in Drymen[90] would certainly have
been in the retinue of Earl Malcolm. It is noteworthy that Sir Alan
Durward, holding Fichlie beside Kildrummy, Sir Thomas of Monymusk,
adjacent to the Garioch and Sir Laurence of Strathbogie, whose name
connects him with the earl of Atholl, and who had been with the earl in 1296
and 1297,[91] were all among the new king's earliest supporters. It is
understandable that men should have come out with the lords to whose
following they belonged; it is more striking when we find men supporting
Bruce in opposition to their lord. The tenants of Henry de Pinkney, an
Englishman who was lord of Luffness and Ballencrieff in East Lothian, rose
against King Edward in 1300.[90] Another man who seems to have tried to
give a lead to his own leader was Sir Malcolm of Innerpeffray. Although he
had served as King Edward's sheriff of Auchterarder and Clackmannan, he
would almost certainly have belonged to the following of the earl of
Strathearn, yet he joined Atholl, Boyd and the rest when they pursued the
earl in the glens above Crieff trying to get him to do homage to King
Robert.[93]

We hear of hardly any early supporters of Bruce coming from north of
Inverness, from Lorn, Lochaber or Badenoch, from Buchan, or from
Galloway west of Nithsdale. The earl of Dunbar had been a consistent
adherent of the English king ever since 1296: his attitude must be part of the
reason why we find relatively few prominent men from East Lothian and the
Merse supporting either the Guardians or Bruce. Those who did had in any
case condemned themselves to many years of dispossession, a peculiarly
difficult sacrifice for men and women of that time. For most of the eighteen
years from 1296 to 1314 the country between Tweed and Forth was closely
held by large English garrisons based upon the strongest castles in Scotland.
Even so, the patriot leaders had been able to draw on substantial support
from Lothian and the Merse in the period 1296–1304. Much of the history
of Scotland for the past two hundred years, political, economic and
ecclesiastical, had been centred upon Lothian and Teviotdale. It is absurd

to suppose that all this was swept away overnight under the onslaught of Edward I, simply because the population of Lothian spoke English or had an alleged but wholly unverified predisposition to accept English rule.[94]

After Methven Bruce fled to Drumalban, the mountain country dividing Perthshire from Argyll. He put his trust in a handful of loyal followers and in his own extraordinary powers of physical endurance, moral courage and knightly prowess. He believed, in this dark hour, that he had the blessing of one of the most celebrated of the ancient Scottish saints, Fillan of Glendochart. He no more forgot this holy man of the sixth century than his grandfather forgot Malachy O'Moore. His generosity many years afterwards not only to Saint Fillan and his shrine in Strathfillan but also to Inchaffray Abbey surely sprang from earlier events than his alleged veneration of Saint Fillan's relics on the eve of Bannockburn and the exhortation of the Scottish army by Abbot Maurice of Inchaffray.[95] It is likely enough that as Bruce and his companions made their way westward from the field of Methven they were helped by the canons of Inchaffray, where Maurice had already been abbot since 1305.[96] To travel westward from Strathearn, as Bruce seems to have done, probably by Lochearnside and Glen Ogle into Glen Dochart, was to enter what might be called Saint Fillan's sanctuary. Here the chief men included Gilchrist and Henry of Balquhidder and Patrick (Macnab) lord of Glendochart,[97] heir of the ancient abbots of Glendochart who were Fillan's successors and custodians of his famous pastoral staff. We do not know how they received the new king of Scots; we know only that in later years Bruce granted the barony of Glendochart to one of the knights who were with him in 1306, Alexander Menzies of Weem in Strathtay.[98] This partial displacement of the Macnabs may mean that Patrick of Glendochart was Bruce's enemy.

At the head of Strathfillan, at a place called Dail Righ (Dalry), near Tyndrum, Bruce found his escape route barred by John Macdougall of Argyll, at whose hands he met his second defeat.[99] As a result Bruce and his men ceased to form an organized military force. The queen, the lady Marjorie (Bruce's daughter) and the other women of the party were given all the horses and sent across the Mounth, through the mountains of Atholl and Braemar, to Kildrummy Castle on Donside, in charge of the earl of Atholl, Neil Bruce (the king's brother), Alexander Lindsay and Robert Boyd.[100] Bruce himself and most of his men took to the mountains of Atholl and Breadalbane, little better than fugitives. It is impossible to construct anything like an exact chronology of their movements in the summer months of 1306. Fordun seems to put the battle of Dail Righ too late (August 11th).[101] It would be easier to understand Bruce's reported movements if Dail Righ were fought on July 13th (reading 'third of the ides of *July*' for Fordun's 'third of the ides of *August*'), or on July 30th (supposing Fordun's 'ides' to be a mistake for 'kalends'). For we have to account for the otherwise curious fact that Aymer de Valence, obviously pursuing either Bruce or some of Bruce's party, was in Aberdeen by August 3rd. This would be understandable if he had news that the queen, Atholl and the others had already reached, or were heading for, Kildrummy. In Barbour's account, Bruce after Methven made for Aberdeen by way of the Mounth, doubled back to Dail Righ across the mountains, and only then – when he must have known that the English were already in Aberdeenshire – sent the ladies to Kildrummy. But both Barbour and Fordun agree that the dispersal of Bruce's small party came after and not before the conflict at Dail Righ.[102]

Early in September Kildrummy fell to Valence and the prince of Wales, the garrisons being forced to yield when a traitor in their midst set fire to the store of corn in the great hall.[103] On the approach of the English army, the royal ladies had been sent hurriedly northward, in charge of the earl of Atholl.[104] Probably it was intended that they should reach Orkney, for Bruce's sister Isabel, dowager queen of Norway, was King Hakon v's sister-in-law, and Scoto-Norwegian relations seem to have been friendly through-out the seventeen years between the Franco-Scoto-Norwegian treaties of Paris (1295) and King Robert's first major piece of diplomacy, the Scoto-Norwegian treaty of Inverness (1312). But the party had only reached the sanctuary of Saint Duthac at Tain when they were seized by Earl William of Ross (a Balliol adherent) and sent to Edward I under escort.[105]

A brief reign of terror followed the rout of Methven and the fall of Kildrummy. Once again, the responsibility lay wholly with Edward I. Indeed, we must accept that the slaughter and persecution, which in their ferocity far exceeded anything previously seen in Edward's reign, marked a new and deliberate policy of terrorizing the Scots into submission. Simon Fraser was drawn, hanged and beheaded in London, his head being put above London Bridge on a pole beside that of Wallace.[106] Atholl, evidently captured at Tain, was the first earl to be executed in England for 230 years. It was pleaded on his behalf that he was King Edward's kinsman (his mother, a Kentish lady named Isabel of Chilham, was a granddaughter of one of King John's bastards).[107] Edward's response to this was an order that he should be hanged from a higher gallows than anyone else, and then decapitated and burned.[108] Neil Bruce was drawn, hanged and beheaded at Berwick, along with many others, including Sir Alan Durward of Fichlie.[109] Christopher Seton, captured in Loch Doon castle, suffered the same fate at Dumfries, where, with his brothers John and Humphrey, he had been art and part in the murder of John and Robert Comyn.[110] John of Seton, taken at Tibbers in Nithsdale, was drawn and hanged at Newcastle on August 4th, along with Bernard Mowat.[111] On the same day fourteen other adherents of Bruce were hanged (without having been drawn) at Newcastle, including two knights, David of Inchmartin (son of Sir John) and John of Cambo, and the king of Scots' hereditary standard-bearer, Alexander Scrymgeour ('le

Skirmischur').[112] Alexander Scrymgeour, the son of Colin, Carun's son, a Fife freeholder, had been granted the constableship of Dundee by Wallace in King John's name for the service of 'bearing the royal standard in the army of Scotland'.[113] He had served all the Guardians in this capacity and his adherence to Bruce is therefore especially noteworthy. Savage as these reprisals were, the peculiarly maniacal quality of King Edward's vengeance has always seemed most startling in his treatment of the women prisoners. Two of them, it is true, got off lightly. The new queen of Scots, who to Edward's approval had rebuked her husband at their coronation for playing kings and queens like children, was confined in the manor house at Burstwick in Holderness. She was allowed two women companions, 'elderly and not at all gay'.[114] Christian Bruce, formerly countess of Mar and now widow of Christopher Seton, was sent to the Gilbertine nunnery of Sixhills in Lincolnshire.[115] Mary, King Robert's other sister, whose reported remarks were perhaps less to Edward's liking than those of the queen, and the Countess Isabel of Buchan, who had committed the unpardonable crime of crowning or enthroning Bruce, were lodged in cages of strongly latticed timber and iron, especially made for the purpose and placed within towers or turrets of Roxburgh and Berwick castles respectively.[116]

The inspiration for this bizarre piece of cruelty may have come from Italy, for after the battle of Fossalta (1249) the Bolognese imprisoned Enzo (Henry) king of Sardinia, the brilliant bastard son of the Emperor Frederick II, in an iron cage, in which he died twenty-two years later. In medieval Italy it was evidently not uncommon for persons to be punished in this manner, the cages, of iron or timber, usually being placed on the tops of towers or other high buildings.[117] For several years the two courageous ladies remained in their cages, forbidden communication with anyone save the Englishwomen who brought their food and drink, exposed, so contemporaries believed, to the gaze of passers-by, treated for all the world as though they were beasts in a menagerie, save that they were allowed the convenience of a privy.[118] The countess was not released from her cage until June 1310, when Edward II allowed her to be removed to the house of the Carmelites in Berwick. In 1313 she was placed in the custody of Sir Henry Beaumont, who had married her husband's niece.[119] Mary Bruce also survived her ordeal. Still captive in Roxburgh Castle in 1310 (no longer, one hopes, in her cage) she was later transferred to Newcastle and freed at last after Bannockburn.[120] Bruce's daughter Marjorie, who cannot have been more than twelve years old, was at first ordered by King Edward to be kept in a similar cage in the Tower of London, and not to be allowed to speak to anyone, or be spoken to by anyone, save the Constable of the Tower.[121] Fortunately Edward revoked this horrifying decree, and Marjorie Bruce was sent to the Yorkshire Gilbertine nunnery at Watton.[122] Sir Maurice Powicke, who much admired King Edward, nevertheless wrote, rightly, of the king's 'peculiar ferocity' in regard to these women prisoners.[123]

Long before King Robert had any news of the terrible punishments inflicted on his family and followers it had become obvious to him that he must flee the mainland and perhaps flee his kingdom altogether. Somehow, before all the escape routes were stopped up, a way must be found. The east-coast ports were in enemy hands. In the north also there were enemies as well as friends, the actively hostile earls of Ross and Sutherland to be set against the friendly but now fugitive bishop of Moray. The west, guarded by John of Lorn, was full of dangers. Only towards the south west was there any gleam of hope. The earl of Lennox was loyal and the men of Lennox were loyal to their earl. As long as John Balliol had been king, the Macdougalls were patriots and the Macdonalds pro-English. Now a minor revolution had occurred in west highland politics. The Macdonalds could no longer hope for help from the English against their Macdougall rivals, for the family of Lorn were now sworn foes to Bruce and trusted adherents of Edward I and his son. Alexander, elder son of Angus Mór Macdonald, lord of Islay, may have died in 1299 or at latest by 1301, but his younger brothers Donald and Angus Og ('young Angus') seem to have emerged as staunch supporters of Bruce when he made his bid for the throne. Their sphere of influence evidently extended to Kintyre where they would have been able to protect the fugitives.[124] The Campbell brothers, Neil and Donald, were among the new king's most faithful supporters, and like Angus Macdonald they seem to have had influence in Kintyre, as of course did James the Stewart. Beyond Kintyre lay Ireland, and there the horizon will not have seemed wholly dark. It is true that the earl of Ulster, Bruce's father-in-law, was loyal to Edward I, at least after his fashion. It is also true that theoretically all the chiefs and people of Ireland owed allegiance to the English king and might have been expected to show hostility to Bruce. But Ireland is a country where the expected often does not happen. Bruce, let it not be forgotten, was lord of Carrick, and as such lord of, or claimant to, considerable estates on the coast of Antrim and Derry, including Olderfleet (now Larne), Glenarm, and lands near Coleraine and Port Stewart.[125] Twenty-two years afterwards, it was from Olderfleet that Bruce issued a mandate which still survives.[126] One of his closest friends and allies, James the Stewart, by marrying Egidia de Burgh, had acquired the lands and castle of the Roe on Lough Foyle.[127] Ireland cannot have seemed in any sense a foreign or unfriendly country to Robert Bruce, married to an Irishwoman and inheriting more than a century of family connexions with Ulster. In late August, therefore, or early September, the new king and his small party, keeping no doubt to hill tracks and hidden glens and corries,[128] travelled by way of the Lennox and Loch Lomond to Bute. From there they sailed to the temporary sanctuary of the castle of Dunaverty, built on a rock jutting into the sea not far from the Mull of Kintyre, which Bruce had prudently taken seven months earlier. News of his attempt to break through the English cordon must have reached King Edward or his lieutenants well before

September 22nd, by which date Sir John de Botetourt and Sir John Menteith were laying siege to Dunaverty and not finding the local population co-operative.[129] It is clear that they expected Robert Bruce to be inside the castle, but in this they were to be disappointed. Barbour may be right, and assuredly cannot be far wrong, when he says that Bruce stayed in Dunaverty no more than three days. Before his pursuers could reach him he had got clean away by boat, crossing the thirteen miles of open sea to the island of Rathlin and vanishing, for the next four and a half months, from the recorded knowledge of men in England and Scotland alike.

TEN

A King in Search of his Throne

The story of how Robert Bruce returned to Scotland, of how after many disasters and setbacks he slowly won the initiative, of how by a wonderful mixture of patience, sagacity and daring he made himself master of all but one of the great fortresses held by the English, until he was powerful enough at last to meet the challenge of a full-scale invasion led by the king of England in person, is the story of one of the great heroic enterprises of history. If it were cast in the form of a romance it would possess at least one of romance's essential requirements, incredibility. And if Bruce had done nothing else he would find an enduring place in history as one of its greatest adventurers. But in fact he survived his adventure to become for fourteen years one of the best of medieval kings, prudent, conscientious, vigorous and patriotic. His failings, it is true, were far from trivial. But his most serious failing, the encouragement he gave to that dissipation of royal power which was one cause of the weakness of later medieval Scottish monarchy, was very much a failing of his time. Hardly any king in western Europe in the fourteenth century successfully averted or overcame the tremendous pressures making for the disintegration of central authority.

Consciously or unconsciously, Bruce modelled himself, politically speaking, on his great adversary Edward I, in the shadow of whose example he had grown to manhood. The things for which Edward is remembered in English history are the things for which Bruce is – or ought to be – remembered in Scotland: a jealous regard for the royal dignity and prerogatives, the use of parliament as the supreme organ of government, the definition and statutory declaration of the common law, the attempt to heal the wounds of a bitter civil war, the absorption of a purely Celtic territory in the west – for Edward, Wales, for Bruce, the western highlands. In 1307 the accomplishment of these tasks lay far in the future. It was the product of an act of faith on Bruce's part, faith not only in himself but in the community of the realm of Scotland. His aims and achievements become credible and intelligible only when seen against the background of a long period of Scottish history. Three features of that history in particular were relevant to Bruce's *coup de force* and his policy as king. Firstly, there was the unbroken development of royal power and of the machinery of royal government since the days of Alexander I and David I. This gave to Bruce, enthroned at Scone with the help of the traditional representatives of the community, an immense advantage over his enemies within Scotland itself. Secondly, there was the long and prosperous reign of the king to whom Bruce referred over and over again in his charters as 'the lord Alexander, king of Scotland, of good memory, *our last deceased predecessor*'.[1] Finally – most importantly, yet at the same time most awkwardly for Bruce – there were the eight years of warfare during which the Scots had defied King Edward in the name of King John. John, it is true, had abdicated, he had been imprisoned and exiled and shifted about Europe like an object in an exhibition, until at last he settled down as an elderly *roi fainéant*. Nevertheless, down to 1304 the Scots had never ceased to look upon him as their rightful king, and even after 1304 the Comyns, Ingram de Umfraville, Alexander Abernethy, Adam Gordon, William Oliphant and many other leading men still believed that his claims or those of Edward Balliol were stronger than the claims of Bruce. Consequently Bruce must appeal to some other principle than dynastic legitimacy. He found it in the one overriding idea which had given continuity to Scottish politics since 1286, that idea of the community of the realm which had survived the Maid of Norway's death, the coming and going of Balliol, and experimentation with at least half a dozen assorted Guardians. And of course Bruce, however much his own genius and the death of Edward I bore him onward, could never have achieved success if many Scotsmen and Scotswomen had not shared this idea. Bruce, who could surely have lived honourably for the rest of his life in Scandinavia or on the continent, would have been mad to return to Carrick in 1307 unless he knew already that under the right leadership the people of Scotland would rise against the conqueror as they had risen in 1297. What could one man, whose friends and family had been butchered and jailed, who had hardly any money or troops, hope to do against the immense wealth and resources of the king of England, supported as he was by numerous powerful Scottish lords? But one man at the head of a nation could work miracles.

No evidence has yet been discovered to prove where Bruce spent the winter of 1306–07. Certain English writers of the fifteenth and sixteenth centuries believed that he was in the Norwegian king's dominions, perhaps in Norway itself, more probably in the Northern Isles.[2] Walter of Guisborough and the Lanercost chronicle give no support to this belief. Both say much the same thing, the one that Bruce was lurking 'in the furthermost isles of that country' (where 'country' means either Scotland or the west),[3] the other that he hid 'in the outer isles of Scotland'.[4] By the end of January 1307 King Edward evidently believed that Bruce's retreat was in 'the isles of the Scottish coast' and 'the isles between Scotland and Ireland'.[5] John Barbour believed that Bruce lay hidden in the small island of Rathlin, a few miles off the coast of Antrim.[6]

The fascination of this mystery, historically not very important, lies in the fact that though unsolved it does not seem quite insoluble. The case for a Norwegian refuge is that certain English chroniclers (admittedly writing

······ *Suggested route of Robert 1,*
February 1307 to May 1308

Important strongpoints held by English
throughout these years underlined

0   20   40   60   80

Miles

Orkney

Caithness

Lewis

Sutherland

L. Broom

Skelbo

Banff
Forres Duffus
Nairn Elgin Buchan
Tarradale
Inverness Auldearn Balvenie
Castle Slioch Inverurie
Urquhart (12.07) (23.5.08)

Uist

Barra G
Kisimul R Rum Eigg Aberdeen
Castle M (Captured June
Coll O or July 1308?)
Tiree R Castle Inverlochy T H E M O U N T H
Turim
Cairnburghmore Brander Forfar
Castle Mull (Aug. 1308?) L. Tay (Captured 25.12.08)
Dunchonnell Dunstaffnage Dundee
Castle Inchchonnel Perth St. Andrews
Jura Inchmahome Cupar (16–17.3.09)
Islay Dumbarton Stirling
Glasgow
Rutherglen Bothwell Edinburgh
Brodick Loudoun
(2.07) Hill Berwick
Kintyre Arran Ayr (13.5.07) (10.5.07)
Dunaverty Turnberry Roxburgh
Rathlin Ailsa Tibbers
Foyle Carrick Lochdoon Lochmaben Corbridge
The Roe Glentrool Dumfries Caerlaverock Lanercost Newcastle
Antrim Glenarm (April 1307) Buittle Carlisle Hexham
Olderfleet (Summer Burgh by Sands
1308) Skinburness

Man

9. 1307–09.

two centuries later) state that he went to Norway, that Bruce's sister Isabel
lived at Bergen, as the presumably influential widow of the late King Eric,
that Bruce's wife and family were caught at Tain, presumably on their way
to Orkney, that the bishop of Moray, one of his staunchest supporters, did in
fact take refuge in Orkney, and that Bruce's return to Carrick reveals an
ignorance of the state of affairs explicable only if he had been far away.
Bruce's later grant to St Magnus' Cathedral at Kirkwall is not relevant, for it
merely replaced an earlier grant made by some previous king or kings.[7] In
the absence of direct evidence, the appropriate line of enquiry is surely to
take into account opportunity, previous conduct, and motive. Here there are
three established facts. Bruce was last heard of at or near his own castle of
Dunaverty, in September 1306. The next definite news of him was that he
had landed in Carrick about the end of January or beginning of February
1307. In 1294, the last occasion on which Bruce had been driven from
Scotland by his enemies, he had gone (or had the intention of going) to
Ireland.[8] It is easy to understand how a desperate man, hard-pressed by his
pursuers, might leave Scotland at the Mull of Kintyre with the ultimate aim
of reaching Orkney or Norway. It is very much harder to believe that anyone
returning from Orkney to Scotland would land in Carrick. It becomes all the
more extraordinary if it is accepted that Bruce drew the bulk of his support
from the north, from Moray and Aberdeenshire. If he really wintered in
Orkney, why did he not make for the southern shore of the Moray Firth? On
the score of opportunity and past conduct, therefore, the bare facts suggest
Ireland and the southern Hebrides more strongly than they suggest Okrney
or Norway.

What of motive? The Norwegian theory is attractive on that score,
because of Bruce's family connexions with King Hakon, who, incidentally,
had given a safe-conduct to Wallace at a time when Wallace and Bruce were
friends.[9] Bruce had to make do at first without the French alliance, and it
was an early object of his policy to make an alliance with Norway. But there
were equally good motives for going to Ireland. The Bissets of the Glens of
Antrim, lords of Rathlin, were loyal to Edward I, but their conduct, from an
English point of view, was not altogether above suspicion. At the time of the
battle of Falkirk in 1298 Thomas Bisset of Antrim had crossed to Arran with
a force strong enough to overpower the islanders, intending 'as was
commonly said' to support the Scots, of whom Bruce was then a prominent
leader.[10] Only on hearing of Wallace's defeat did Bisset send messengers to
Edward I to say that really he had come to fight for the English, and claiming
the isle of Arran as his reward. In 1301, it is true, Hugh Bisset of Antrim was
on the English side.[11] But what may be more to the point is that he was then
in alliance with Angus Og and John Macsween against the Macdougalls of
Lorn. In 1307, the Macdougalls were Bruce's bitterest foes, and the man in
charge of operations against Bruce was Sir John Menteith, who was keeping
Macsween out of the lordship of Knapdale. In January 1307 Edward I

commanded Hugh Bisset to join the hunt for Bruce with as many ships as he could find,[12] but this is far from proof that Bisset was loyal to Edward through the autumn of 1306 or even that he joined in the search for Bruce wholeheartedly. He opposed Edward Bruce's invasion of Ireland in 1315,[13] but ultimately, in 1319, Bisset openly joined Bruce.[14] The significant fact, surely, is that in 1306–07 a powerful English fleet operating from Ayr and Skinburness in Cumberland was unable to intercept Bruce. And whether or not the Bissets were his foes, Bruce as lord of Carrick would no doubt have maintained connexions with the estates on the Antrim coast which had belonged to his ancestors, some of which may still have belonged to him, while to the west of Bisset territory there was James Stewart's estate and castlery of the Roe on Lough Foyle. Most important of all is the fact that Bruce was supported in this critically dangerous period by Angus Og Macdonald of Islay. The Macdonalds made their living partly by supplying galloglasses to fight in Irish wars.[15] Seen through their Hebridean eyes, Ireland must have seemed a very different country from the Dublin-ruled *dominium Hibernie* over which King Edward believed he had full control.

So much for the facts which are not in dispute, and the various possibilities to which they point. The narrative of chroniclers closest in time to the events of 1307 strongly supports an Irish or Hebridean solution of the mystery and gives no hint of refuge in Orkney or Norway. Guisborough, whose facts may be correct though his dating must be wrong, says that Bruce returned to Kintyre from the isles 'about Michaelmas' (September 29th, 1306) with 'many Irishmen and Scots', and from Kintyre sent agents across to Carrick to uplift the rents of his earldom for the Martinmas term (November 11th).[16] ('This is a detail which Guisborough can hardly have invented: Scottish rents, unlike English, were collected at Martinmas, and it is what we should expect of the penniless king, forced for so long to live on the generosity of his friends). He goes on to say that in the following Lent (which in 1307 began on February 8th) Bruce sent a detachment under his brothers Thomas (who 'had always hated the English') and Alexander (dean of Glasgow) who were quickly captured.[17] The Lanercost chronicle says that on February 9th Thomas and Alexander Bruce landed in Galloway with eighteen ships, in company with Reginald Crawford, *a certain Irish sub-king*, the 'lord of Kintyre' (Malcolm MacQuillan) and a large following.[18] They were captured by Dungal Macdouall, who beheaded the Irish kinglet and the lord of Kintyre on the spot and sent the more important prisoners to Edward I for the same terrible, quasi-judicial punishment which had befallen Wallace, Fraser and so many others. Barbour's story, though much more elaborate and exciting, is not substantially different.[19] Some of Bruce's party, led by Douglas and Boyd, left Rathlin for Kintyre, whence they crossed to Arran by night. There they seized valuable arms and equipment from a party which had come to reinforce the commander of Brodick Castle, John Hastings.[20] Bruce then joined them and sent a spy across to Carrick to see how the land lay. If all seemed well, the spy was to light a fire on Turnberry Point. In fact he judged that the English were too strong to be attacked. Their leader was Henry Percy, who had usurped Bruce's earldom and now commanded the garrison in Turnberry Castle. But it chanced that someone else lit a fire, and misled by this Bruce and his men came over from Arran. Finding the situation desperate, they attacked the village of Turnberry at night, killing many of Percy's men in their sleep.

The strongest confirmation of a Hebridean solution of the mystery come from Fordun, admittedly writing later in the century, but possessing important sources of information for Bruce's time which have not survived independently. Of King Robert's exile he says,

> He suffered these [hardships] alone for nearly a year, and at last, through God's mercy, with the help and by the power of Christiana of the Isles, a noble lady who wished him well, he returned to the earldom of Carrick, after much journeying in different directions, and after an infinity of toil, grief and adversity.[21]

By Christiana of the Isles, Fordun can only refer to the lady usually known as Christian or Christina of Mar, daughter and apparently sole legitimate child of Alan Macruarie, lord of Garmoran.[22] As Alan's heir, Christina of Mar was lady of many lands and islands of the west – Knoydart, Moidart, Arisaig, Rum, Eigg, Uist, Barra and Gigha. Christina had married Duncan of Mar, who was a younger son of Earl Donald of Mar and consequently a brother of Bruce's first wife and brother-in-law of Bruce's sister.[23] If family connexions meant anything, Christina had every reason for befriending Bruce in his time of need. And it can hardly be a coincidence that, just as Bruce granted to Inchaffray Abbey the church of Killin with the chapel of Strathfillan, so Christina of Mar granted to Inchaffray Abbey the lands of Carinish in North Uist with the chapel of the Holy Trinity of Uist – Teampull na Trianaide.[24]

On the strength of these facts and probabilities we may suggest the following outline of events in the winter of 1306–7. About the end of September 1306, Bruce and a few companions fled from Dunaverty to Rathlin. From there they may have visited parts of northern Ireland and almost certainly spent some time in various islands of the southern Hebrides. Towards the end of the year, Bruce sent agents to collect his Martinmas rents in Carrick. With the help of the Macdonalds, Christina of Mar, and friends in Ireland he gathered a force of Irishmen and Hebrideans, and about the beginning of February came to Kintyre. From there he crossed first to Arran and then to the Carrick shore near Turnberry. By this time he had divided his force, sending Thomas and Alexander Bruce to Galloway either from Kintyre or direct from Ireland. Their task may have been to divert attention from his own landing, or to put the Macdoualls and MacCans out of action. They met with complete disaster, and King Robert, who had already lost his brother Neil at Kildrummy, now lost two more of his brothers. Many years afterwards the English poet Robert Manning mourned the tragically short career of Alexander Bruce, the best scholar of his time at Cambridge, taken, badly wounded, from Galloway to Carlisle, and there, by King Edward's command, hanged and beheaded.[25]

How Bruce survived the next few months is a deeper mystery than where he spent the previous winter. This was the most perilous time of his career. He had landed in his own earldom, where the inhabitants might be expected to feel loyalty towards him. But all the castles in the country round about were in enemy hands, and the poorer people at least, if they were to come out against the occupation régime, would need more assurance of protection than the sight of Bruce and a handful of desperate men. One local lady of good family, Christian of Carrick, King Robert's kinswoman and perhaps also his mistress,[26] brought him (says Barbour) forty men, and also news of the fearful toll taken by Edward I of the king's followers. 'The king of England' (so runs Barbour's well-imagined version of Bruce's response to these grim tidings) 'thought that the kingdom of Scotland was too small for him and me, so I will make the whole of it mine. As for good Christopher Seton, who was of such noble renown, it was a great pity that he should have died save where his valour might have been proved.[27] At least Bruce could find consolation in the knowledge that to King Edward, already lying gravely ill at Lanercost, there could not remain many more days of butchery. Buoyed up by this knowledge, yet made desperate by circumstances, it was now that Bruce took a simple but momentous decision which changed the whole course and character of the war. He was the first of the Scottish leaders to accept the harsh logic of a situation in which the English would always have the upper hand in cavalry and siege machinery. For a great nobleman and a trained knight it was not only a revolutionary decision, it was proof of his genius and imagination. From the spring of 1307 to the short night which fell between the first and second days of the battle of Bannockburn, all Bruce's strategy was based on belief in the supreme virtue of guerrilla warfare. Speed, surprise, mobility, small-scale engagements, scorched earth and dismantling of fortresses – these were to be the hallmarks of his campaigns.

Bruce's plan of action in the months following his return is clear enough. Based on the hill country of Carrick and Galloway he would harass the enemy, spread panic among the English garrisons, recruit supporters until he was strong enough to break out towards the country north of Forth, where he could count on gathering many more followers and would have much more room to manoeuvre. The English commanders on the spot, under Aymer de Valence, were John Botetourt, Robert Clifford and Henry Percy; with these veterans were several prominent Scots lords, including John Menteith, Ingram de Umfraville, John Macdougall of Lorn[28] – John 'Bacach', 'the lame', as he was known – John Moubray and the earl of Atholl's son David. Their task was to hold Ayr and Turnberry, keep open communication between these castles and the east, and tempt Bruce into an engagement on favourable ground. Their master, though a dying man, was astonishingly alert and impatient to hear news of success. On February 11th he wrote to Valence and the others expressing his amazement at not hearing of Bruce's capture.[29] They are to tell the king at once what they are doing and what their plans are; for he suspects from their silence that they have acted timidly and wish to keep him in the dark. Try as they would, Bruce eluded them and slowly won the initiative. In April he penetrated far into Galloway, hiding in the Glen of Trool, a deep glen opening off the Cree valley, largely filled by the waters of Loch Trool.[30] This is wild country, dotted with suggestive place names – Murder Hole, Round Loch of the Dungeon, Loch Neldricken ('loch of the ambush'), Polmaddy ('wolf's burn') and so on. The English made a raid in force into Glen Trool, were caught in a natural ambush, and repulsed with heavy losses.[31] Bruce was now free to move north, by-passing Ayr, and encountered Valence at Loudoun Hill, a few miles east of Kilmarnock, about May 10th.[32] A skilful choice of site forced Valence to fight on a narrow front, so that his great superiority in cavalry and numbers was no advantage. Bruce and his men set upon the leading ranks so fiercely that the rear fell back in panic, and very soon Valence himself was fleeing to Bothwell. Three days later, Bruce struck hard at a force under Raoul de Monthermer, earl of Gloucester, and chased him back into Ayr.[33] Here at last was unqualified triumph, and the avenging of Methven. It had an immediate effect on popular feeling towards Bruce. On May 15th, within a few days of Loudoun Hill, a Scots lord on the English side (perhaps Alexander Abernethy) wrote an informative and highly revealing letter from Forfar.

I hear that Bruce never had the good will of his own followers or of the people generally so much with him as now. It appears that God is with him, for he has destroyed King Edward's power both among English and Scots. The people believe that Bruce will carry all before him, exhorted by 'false preachers' from Bruce's army, men who have previously been charged before the justices for advocating war and have been released on bail, but are now behaving worse than ever. I fully believe, as I have heard from Reginald Cheyne, Duncan of Frendraught and Gilbert of Glencarnie, who keep the peace beyond the Mounth and on this side, that if Bruce can get away in this direction or towards the parts of Ross he will find the people all ready at his will more entirely than ever, unless King Edward can send more troops for there are many people living loyally in his peace so long as the English are in power. May it please God to prolong King Edward's life, for men say openly that when he is gone the victory will go to Bruce. For these preachers have told the people that they have found a prophecy of Merlin, that after the death of 'le Roy Coveytous' the people of Scotland and the Welsh shall band together and have full lordship and live in peace together to the end of the world.[34]

From May to September Bruce seems to have stayed in the south west, much more aggressive after Loudoun than before. On July 7th the English king died at Burgh-on-Sands, at the beginning of his sixty-ninth year. Towards the end of his life he had had second thoughts about the wisdom of his policy of savage repression, enunciated in the previous winter. On this, Walter of Guisborough has some illuminating comments. Many men went over to Bruce, he says, who had been outlawed by the English justices sitting in the previous year. For since according to English law the Scots were to be burned, drawn at horse-tails and hanged, so with one accord they joined Bruce, preferring to die rather than be tried by English law.[35] The Lanercost chronicler remarks gloomily 'despite the fearful vengeance inflicted upon the Scots who adhered to Bruce, the number of those willing to strengthen him in his kingship increased daily'.[36] These words are strikingly confirmed by a letter which the king addressed on March 13th to Aymer de Valence and all the chief English officials and sheriffs in Scotland. 'As he understands that some have interpreted his recent ordinance for settling Scotland as too harsh and rigorous, which was not his intention, he commands it to be proclaimed that all who have been compelled to abet or give shelter to Robert Bruce under threat of force shall be pardoned.'[37] Barely a fortnight later Sir John Wallace, a brother of William, evidently captured while with Bruce's army, was sent to London to be drawn, hanged and beheaded.[38] In truth, it was too late for Edward to disavow any harsh intention in an ordinance which had decreed that all who were art and part in Comyn's murder should be drawn and hanged, that all found in Scotland without the king's leave should be hanged or beheaded, that all who took part in Bruce's rising should be jailed to await the king's pleasure, and even that the 'poor commons' of Scotland, though forced to join in the rising, should be held to ransom.[39] The view of Charlemagne as an epitome of the Christian king cannot have found much favour with the Saxons. It is easy to understand how the Scots likewise never came to share the belief that Edward I was a model of justice and magnanimity.

No concealment of the old king's death could hide for long the contrast between his masterful directing hand and the wilful *insouciance* of the new king, Edward of Caernarvon. The great expedition planned by his father had only reached Cumnock when, on August 25th, Edward II retired to England, not to show his face north of the border for three years. Valence remained in charge till shortly before October 12th,[40] and as long as he occupied the line of Clydesdale it is most unlikely that Bruce, reported in September to be raiding in Galloway,[41] would have left the south west. But on September 13th Edward II confirmed John of Brittany in the office of lieutenant of Scotland which he had been given in 1305 and in which Valence had superseded him for the emergency of Bruce's rising. It seems that Valence, who is recorded as holding a guardian's court at Rutherglen as late as September 17th,[42] must have left Scotland early in the following month. Here again, vigorous direction was replaced by feeble fumbling. Since there was no immediate danger from England, King Robert could plunge into the bitter but fairly brief civil war without which his kingship would never be a reality. He first attacked his foes in Galloway, so fiercely that many of their peasantry took refuge, with their cattle, in the Cumberland forest of Inglewood.[43] Next it was the turn of John Comyn, earl of Buchan. It is not known whether his castles of Old Slains and Balvenie had yet been restored to him. Even without them, Earl John, strong in his command of a compact north-eastern earldom with its castles at Ellon, Dundarg and Old Slains was a formidable obstacle to any Bruce conquest of Scotland.

Leaving a force under Douglas to recover, with brilliant success, Douglasdale, upper Clydesdale and the Forest as far as Jedburgh,[44] Bruce marched northward, probably about the last week of September. No doubt he gathered many recruits in the middle belt of counties, from the earldoms of Lennox, Menteith, Fife, Strathearn, Atholl and Angus. He would be anxious to perform notable acts of kingship, and one of these was almost certainly to bring about the promotion to the bishopric of Dunblane of Master Nicholas Balmyle, that key figure whose brief recorded appearances coincide with critical moments in the national struggle. Balmyle, already a canon of Dunblane, was elected by a committee of the chapter which included Bruce's friend, Abbot Maurice of Inchaffray, and Master William of Eaglesham, one of Bishop Lamberton's men and the colleague of William Frere and Baldred Bisset in 1301.[45] The new bishop-elect reached the papal court at Poitiers for his consecration shortly before December 11th. The patron of Dunblane diocese was not the Crown but the earl of Strathearn, a prisoner at Rochester. The pope's letter announcing Balmyle's consecration was addressed 'to Earl Malise *or another who may hold the place of the earl*'. We can be sure that Balmyle's appointment was King Robert's doing and had no support from the English. Bruce was short of good bishops. Wishart and Lamberton were in prison, Cheyne of Aberdeen, like the rest of his family, was still pro-English, so also were Dalton of Galloway (though a Bruce protégé), Farquhar Bellejambe of Caithness and Andrew of Argyll. Matthew Crambeth of Dunkeld was no doubt on Bruce's side, but had not many years to live. Besides him, the bishops on whose support Bruce could certainly or probably count were David Murray (Moray), Thomas of Dundee (Ross) and John Kinninmonth (Brechin). Balmyle's promotion to Dunblane was more than a reward for many years of service to the community of the realm, it was a most useful addition to King Robert's ecclesiastical councillors. It is a reasonable surmise that his election took place in the autumn of 1307 and at the new king's prompting.

The king's movements during the autumn and winter, though still not known in detail, have recently become much clearer thanks to the patience and skill of Dr Patricia Barnes in reading – deciphering would almost be the better word – a much-stained and worn letter sent to Edward II by Duncan of Frendraught, sheriff of Banff, probably in April 1308.[46] Duncan's letter gave the English king news of Bruce's operations apparently since the previous autumn, and told him of an earlier attempt to get news through to the south, frustrated when Duncan's messengers were killed in an ambush. Using this letter as our chief guide, and reinforcing its information with the long-familiar contributions of Fordun, Barbour and other sources, we may suggest, however tentatively, the following course of events.

At the end of September Bruce led his army northward into the highlands, making for Comyn of Badenoch's castle of Inverlochy in Lochaber. This bold march across the mountains was, it seems, backed by a corresponding movement of galleys up Loch Linnhe. In this way, John of Lorn felt himself threatened by land and sea and, knowing that no help would be forthcoming from the English, agreed to a truce. Inverlochy fell at an unknown date (October 8th, 13th or 21st are possible),[47] and the king's forces swept north through the Great Glen to take Inverness castle, which they razed to the ground, and burn Nairn. Castle Urquhart on Loch Ness was also destroyed. Bruce's audacity and speed took his enemies by surprise and the earl of Ross in particular seems to have been badly scared. Probably in November he sent a letter to Edward II which told of his plight.

> Be it known that we heard of the coming of Sir Robert Bruce towards the parts of Ross with a great power, so that we had no power against him, but nevertheless we caused our men to be called out and we were stationed for a fortnight with three thousand men, at our own expense, on the borders of our earldom, and in two other earldoms, Sutherland and Caithness; and he (Bruce) would have destroyed them utterly if we had not made a truce with him, at the entreaty of good men, both clergy and others, until Whitsun next (June 2nd). May help come from you, our lord, if it please you, for in you, Sir, is all our hope and trust. And know, dear lord, that we would on no account have made a truce with him if the warden of Moray had not been absent from the country, and the men of his province would not answer to us without his orders, for the purpose of attacking our enemies, so that we have no help save from our own men. Wherefore, dear lord, remember us and tell us what is your will on these matters of which we have given an account.[48]

The warden of Moray was Reginald Cheyne lord of Duffus and Inverugie, and the earl's remark about his absence and the refusal of his men to give support suggests some lack of unity among King Edward's friends in the north. But considering their isolated position the determination with which they resisted King Robert is remarkable. Secured by his truce with Ross, the king pushed eastward in November to attack Elgin, unsuccessfully, and threaten Banff. At this moment, when a decisive capture of the entire north of Scotland seemed within his grasp, Bruce was gripped by a serious illness. The strains and the rough living to which he had been exposed for the past year and a half were now exacting their price.

John Comyn earl of Buchan, David of Strathbogie earl of Atholl and John Moubray had by now mustered a respectable force and come to Duncan of Frendraught's assistance. Just before Christmas the king and his troops withdrew from the coastal lowlands south of Banff and took up a defensive position in boggy woodland at Slioch near Huntly. Winter weather sharpened the anxiety of Bruce's followers. Snow covered the ground and there was not enough food to fill the stomachs of 700 men. The king's sickness grew worse, no medicine was to be had, and they feared that he would not recover. On Christmas Day the earls' men came up and the archers of the opposing forces 'bickered' inconclusively. After a brief withdrawal, the earls returned more confidently on December 31st, only to find Bruce's force seemingly too strong to be attacked and in fact capable of retiring in good order, probably to the Garioch by way of Strathbogie (Huntly).

It is especially unfortunate that as Duncan of Frendraught's letter comes to deal with events of the first three months of 1308 its illegibility increases and we can glean only tantalizing fragments. The king evidently recovered sufficiently to attack the castle of Balvenie (doubtless before this date restored to the earl of Buchan) and destroy Cheyne's castle of Duffus after the interior had been fired. Striking still further west, Bruce took and destroyed the castle of Tarradale in the Black Isle and forced the earl of Ross and his son to withdraw either from that or some neighbouring strongpoint. William Wiseman, one of the king's northern supporters, seized the earl of Sutherland's castle of Skelbo near Dornoch. On Palm Sunday (April 7th) a second assault was made on Elgin castle but by the end of the month, through the timely intervention of John Moubray, the garrison had staved off the danger, at least for the moment.

A crucial problem in interpreting the patchy evidence of this period is the date, as yet uncertain, of the battle in which Bruce completely routed Buchan on the road between Inverurie and Oldmeldrum. Fordun places the battle in 1308, that is the twelve-month period running from March 25th, 1308 to March 24th, 1309. An anonymous verse chronicle inserted in some texts of Bower's *Scotichronicon* dates the event to the Ascension, 1308, a feast which fell that year on May 23rd. This date would agree well with two English official documents, the first[49] a letter of May 20th in which Edward II urged the earl of Buchan, Duncan of Frendraught and others to continue to defend the districts assigned to them until August, the second an undated memorandum,[50] drawn up some months later than the letter, from which it is clear that the English knew they had lost their hold over the north of Scotland. The only doubt which remains as to the date of Inverurie (apart from Barbour's placing it at Christmas, 1307, which is clearly wrong) turns on tactical probability. If the battle was not fought till May 23rd we have to accept the remarkable conclusion that Bruce was willing to leave Buchan unsubdued in his rear while he doubled back to harass the country west of Inverness and that then, after being repulsed before Elgin castle, he was nevertheless still able to take his army over the forty difficult miles eastward to Inverurie to tempt Buchan from his lair and defeat him. He not only defeated the earl, he laid waste the land of his earldom from end to end. Men still loyal to Comyn were killed, homesteads destroyed, livestock slaughtered, stores of corn burned. For fully fifty years, says the Aberdonian Barbour, men grieved over the 'herschip' (harrying) of Buchan.[51];

After this the new king's hold over the Moray Firth hinterland was unassailable. The earl of Buchan and his friends fled to the south. The earl of Ross's position was now fraught with peril. Menaced by the new king of Scots on the south and east, he was also defied in the west, in Skye and the other islands supposedly subject to him, by Lachlan Macruarie.

> We took the lands of the isles (the earl wrote to King Edward) from our lord the king, your father, on whom God have mercy. We assigned them to Lachlan Macruarie to answer to us for their revenues. Since he refuses, may it please you, dear lord, to command him to answer to us as justice requires. For we have answered to your chamberlain for the revenues of those lands. But Lachlan is such a high and mighty lord, he'll not answer to anyone except under great force or through fear of you.[52]

Earl William came of good highland stock and might have known better than to expect a Hebridean chief to obey orders from the east without good reason. Whether or not he won a renewal of the already broken truce beyond June 2nd, the earl must have reckoned that Bruce was unbeatable. He duly submitted on the last day of October, at the royal castle of Auldearn near Nairn.[53] The terms of submission show that Bruce felt it was worth winning the earl to his side by magnanimity and shrewd concessions. Ross confessed his trespasses, now graciously pardoned by the king, and acknowledged that he had got his own lands back and in addition the burgh of Dingwall and the land of Ferincoskry (Creich) in Sutherland. Subjecting himself to the 'royal dignity', he promised to serve the king well and faithfully – a promise which he fulfilled with distinction.

The sureties for his change of allegiance and future good behaviour were David Murray, bishop of Moray, and Thomas of Dundee, bishop of Ross. As E. M. Barron made abundantly clear, Bishop Murray played an outstanding part in the national struggle.[54] He had been a fierce and persistent opponent of the English since the time when he was appointed bishop by Bruce and Comyn as joint-Guardians. Like Wishart of Glasgow, Murray had exhorted his flock that fighting for Scotland was as good a cause as fighting against the Saracens.[55] He is not known to have surrendered in 1304 and two years later he was one of only three bishops present at Bruce's coronation. After Methven he fled to Orkney and stayed out of Scotland for

one year.[56] His lands were ravaged by the earl of Ross, and when he returned
– to come briefly, it seems, into Edward II's peace – he threatened to
excommunicate the earl unless the damage was made good. Now he had the
great satisfaction of seeing how, in Barbour's words,

> The king than till his pes has tane
> the north cuntre, that humylly
> obeysit till his senyhory.
> Swa that benorth the Month war nane
> that thai ne war his men ilkane.[57]

Bishop Thomas of Ross, if not so passionate a patriot as Murray, had been
firmly attached to the Guardians and the community. For the next eighteen
years these two bishops upheld the cause of King Robert in the prosperous
and populous country round the Moray Firth.

Apart from the dean and the chanter (precentor) of Elgin cathedral, most
of the witnesses to the submission were prominent landowners in Moray
and Ross, who had supported the Guardians before 1304 and had been
forfeited for supporting Bruce in 1306: William de la Hay, John Stirling,
William Wiseman (sheriff of Elgin in 1305), John Fenton, and David and
Walter Barclay. The most interesting name among the witnesses is that of
'Sir Bernard the king's chancellor', in his second earliest recorded appearance.[58] No doubt King Robert appointed a chancellor at his coronation, but
he had not had much time for letter writing since March 1306. Yet in the
struggle for Scottish independence the importance of written documents
cannot be exaggerated, and in Bruce's re-establishment of royal authority
the king's 'chapel' or chancery occupied a key position. In Bernard,
whatever his origins and education may have been,[59] Bruce was lucky to find
one of the really outstanding medieval royal chancellors. The last chancellor
of Scotland, Nicholas Balmyle, had been paid his salary from the revenues
of Arbroath Abbey. King Robert went one better, and (*circa* 1311) made
Bernard abbot of Arbroath, to hold both offices together.[60]

Within the course of a single year King Robert's position had changed out of
all recognition. A wide belt of territory from the Ayrshire coast to the
neighbourhood of Roxburgh and Jedburgh was under his control. Galloway
was paying tribute. Between the Forth and the Mounth the adherents of
Edward II were largely confined to defensible burghs and castles. North of
the Mounth (save at Aberdeen and Banff) the English had been expelled,
and it would not be long before Bruce's authority was unchallenged. The
last serious obstacle to be surmounted before he could concentrate all his
energies on ejecting the English garrisons was the inveterate enmity of the
Macdougalls, the ruling family of Argyll, and of the chiefs of Galloway, led
by the Macdoualls and the MacCans. King Robert, himself born in the west
and personally familiar with Argyll and the isles, never lost sight of the fact
that a ruler of Scotland must have command of the western approaches.

To Alexander Macdougall, an old man by now, and to his son John Bacach, lying sick in Dunstaffnage through the winter of 1307–8, the outlook cannot have seemed very hopeful. In some ways their position resembled that of the earl of Ross. Zealous part-takers with Balliol and the Comyns, they might fight for the community of the realm but they misliked Bruce. We have an undated letter written by John of Lorn to Edward II which, though gloomier and more prone to exaggeration, is parallel to Ross's letter quoted and describes much the same pattern of events.

I have received your last letter (dated, or received on?) March 11th, for whose contents I express my deep gratitude to your majesty (*vestre regalitati*). When it arrived I was confined to my bed with illness, and have been for six months past. Robert Bruce approached these parts by land and sea with 10,000 men, they say, or 15,000. I have no more than 800 men, 500 in my own pay whom I keep continually to guard the borders of my territory. The barons of Argyll give me no aid. Yet Bruce asked for a truce, which I granted him for a short space, and I have got a similar truce until you send me help. I have heard, my lord, that when Bruce came he was boasting and claiming that I had come to his peace, in order to inflate his own reputation so that others would rise more readily in his support. May God forbid this; I certainly do not wish it, and if you hear this from others you are not to believe it; for I shall always be ready to carry out your orders with all my power, wherever and whenever you wish. I have three castles to keep as well as a loch twenty-four miles long [Loch Awe], on which I keep and build galleys with trusty men to each galley. I am not sure of my neighbours in any direction. As soon as you or your army come, then, if my health permits, I shall not be found wanting where lands, ships or anything else is concerned, but will come to your service. But if sickness should prevent me I will send my son to serve you with my forces.[61]

Historians have tended to assume that this letter was written in 1309, and have believed that it was written shortly after March 11th.[62] It seems most unlikely[63] that it was written after Bruce's victorious incursion into Argyll which culminated in the battle of the Pass of Brander and the capture of Dunstaffnage Castle. By then John seems to have lost two of the three castles which he had had in his keeping.[64] And John would have had to be a master of the art of understatement, not to say downright mendacity, to describe the Brander campaign as a mere 'approach' towards his territories by Bruce. Dr Colin Macdonald, in his *History of Argyll*, is surely right to date the letter before the campaign of Brander, but he believes that this campaign was not fought until 1309.[65]

That an event of such importance as the Argyll campaign cannot be assigned beyond all doubt to a particular year is a striking illustration of the difficulties which face the historian of these early and critical years of Robert I's reign. On balance, the evidence seems to suggest that John of Lorn wrote his gloomy yet boastful apologia in March 1308. It is clear from the earl of Ross's letter that in the winter of 1307–08 Bruce already had a force numbering at least 3,000 men and probably considerably more, since the earl's own force of 3,000 was too small to withstand him. If by the end of May Bruce had reduced all the northern castles save Aberdeen and Banff he would have had plenty of time to prepare a major campaign against the Macdougalls to be launched in August. The refusal of the Argyllshire barons to support the lord of Lorn is significant and closely comparable with the refusal of the Moray landowners to support Ross. They may have been jealous of the Macdougalls; they certainly did not want an English conquest of Scotland.[66]

By mid-August 1308 any truce between John Macdougall and Robert Bruce would presumably have expired. Fordun states definitely that the king 'defeated the Argyllsmen in the heart of Argyll within the octave of the Assumption of the Blessed Virgin (between 15th and 23rd of August), and our manuscripts of Fordun place this in the year 1308.[67] It is true that Fordun has no annal for 1309, but before we can assume that he meant to assign the Argyll campaign to that year we should have to possess stronger evidence than we do for believing that it did not take place in 1308. It is, for example, under the year 1308 that Walter of Guisborough, after dealing with the English parliament on April 28th and the fierce quarrel over Piers Gaveston which broke out between Edward II and his barons, reports that 'meanwhile Robert de Brus returned from the isles and, being fully recovered from his protracted sickness by which he had been poisoned, began to launch numerous raids upon Northumberland.'[68] It is not easy to fit this report into any chronological context other than the summer and autumn of 1308, and a lengthy campaign by Robert I in the north and west highlands might easily have been mistaken at Guisborough for a sojourn in 'the isles'.

In his attack on Argyll the king followed the line taken by the modern road and railway to Oban. John of Lorn met him in the Pass of Brander, the narrow, treacherous pass where the southern flank of Cruachan (3,689 feet) falls precipitously into an arm of Loch Awe (118 feet). John himself, presumably still convalescent, kept to a galley on the loch.[69] His men were concealed along the hillside overlooking the track, lying in wait and aiming to do to Bruce what Bruce had done to the English in Glen Trool. The king was not to be caught so easily. He had many highlanders with him,

> Men that light and nimble were
> And light armour had on them there.[70]

A party of these light-armed men were sent under James Douglas to scramble even higher up the slopes of Cruachan than the enemy. As the men of Lorn began to attack the main body of the king's army with arrows and stones and with boulders rolled down the steep hillside, Douglas's men rushed down upon them, punished them severely with a hail of shots from their bows, and finally used their swords at close quarters. Assailed from below, taken by surprise from above, the Argyllsmen broke and fled to the only bridge across the formidable River Awe, hoping to destroy it once they were over. Bruce's men forestalled them, pursuing them so hotly that the bridge had to be left intact. The king himself was able to cross with his main body and pursued his foes to Dunstaffnage, which he at once besieged. According to Fordun, Alexander Macdougall surrendered the castle after a siege 'of some time',[71] according to Barbour it fell to Bruce's vigorous assault 'in short time'.[72]

John of Lorn seems to have slipped down Loch Awe to his castle at Inchchonnell – if this is to be identified correctly as the 'Loch Awe castle' of contemporary record.[73] For by October 4th, 1308, Edward 11 had received news that John was sending men and ships to England and Ireland to obtain supplies and munitions with which to replenish the castle of 'Lochawa' which John had in his keeping.[74] The fact that Lochawe is the sole castle named no doubt means that Dunstaffnage had already fallen, along with two out of the 'three castles' of which John of Lorn, according to his letter to Edward 11, had custody.[75] His father evidently came into Bruce's peace for long enough to attend the St Andrews parliament of March 1309.[76] But his submission cannot have been sincere. He soon left Scotland and was somewhere within easy reach of Berwick in October 1309.[77] He died in the English king's service about the end of 1310.[78] Alexander Macdougall's movements surely have some bearing on the question of whether the Argyll campaign was fought in 1308 or 1309. It would be understandable that Alexander should have gone to Bruce's first parliament virtually under duress, as the result of the battle of Brander and the fall of Dunstaffnage. It would be extraordinary if he had come to Bruce's peace before there had been any serious Argyll campaign, still more extraordinary if John Bacach had written his letter to Edward 11 a few days before his own father's appearance in the St Andrews parliament. On the strength of the scanty evidence we possess, the most probable course of events seems to be this.[79] In May or June 1308, Bruce turned from his successful Moray campaign to deal with the situation in southern Scotland and to organize an Argyll campaign. In mid-August he attacked the Macdougalls in strength, and as a result of his resounding victory on the slopes of Ben Cruachan Alexander Macdougall temporarily did homage to him, while John Bacach, after vainly trying to hold out in 'Lochawe Castle', fled to the English, to be joined by his father not later than the autumn of 1309.

Towards midsummer 1308, the king's only surviving brother Edward overran Galloway in an impetuous and savagely vengeful campaign.[80] The first phase of the reconquest of Galloway was evidently brief, and took the form of a devastating raid in which many Gallovidian natives were slaughtered or put to flight. Dungal Macdouall, who had much Scottish and Bruce blood on his hands, was driven out with all his kin, and many local chiefs were slain. Whether we prefer Barbour's version, which characteristically tells only of chivalrous warfare between brave knights – Edward Bruce on the one side against Ingram de Umfraville and Aymer de St John on the other – or the Lanercost-Fordun story of a ruinous harrying of the Galloway chiefs and peasantry, it is clear that Edward Bruce's summer campaign in 1308 was only a qualified success. The crucial battle was probably fought on the banks of the River Dee, not far from Buittle, mistakenly located by Barbour on the Water of Cree.[81] But Edward Bruce failed to eject the English garrisons from the castles marking a line of communication from which Galloway might ultimately be recovered – Lochmaben, Caerlaverock, Dumfries, Dalswinton, Tibbers, Loch Doon and Ayr. Barbour's statement that the reduction of these fortresses occupied an entire year must be read in the light of English record, which shows them still in English hands down to various dates between 1309 and 1313. Ayr Castle, for instance, probably under attack in June 1309, was in English hands as late as the following December.[82] The remaining south-western castles named above, together with Buittle, were also still held by the English in December 1309, their commanders being expressly ordered by Edward II not to take any truce from the enemy.[83] Unless subduing or putting to flight the native inhabitants may be taken as marks of lordship, it cannot be said that Edward Bruce succeeded before 1313 in justifying the title of 'Lord of Galloway' which his brother had conferred on him in or before March 1309.[84]

Nevertheless, by the autumn of 1308 the three provinces in which loyalty to Balliol and Comyn would naturally die hardest, Buchan, Argyll and Galloway, had been overrun by King Robert's forces. In the north Banff still held out against him, but the castle at Aberdeen had been forced to surrender in June or July, so that one of the safest and most accessible North Sea ports was brought under the king's control. It was part of the logic of these events that Forfar, the first major English-held castle south of the Mounth to fall into Bruce's hands, was captured at the end of 1308.[85] The credit for this success belonged to a local man, Philip, forester of the royal forest of Plater or Platan beside Forfar, who, as Barbour tells us, hastened to the castle with his friends, climbed over the stone wall by means of ladders erected 'all privily', and because no proper watch was kept had little difficulty in seizing the castle and putting the garrison to death. This happened on Christmas Day 1308, after darkness had fallen. In accordance with his normal practice, the king had the castle dismantled and the well filled in.

From the autumn of 1308 we begin to have surviving written acts of government issued by King Robert, a sure sign that the king was turning from ceaseless campaigning to the hard work of settled administration. The earliest of these acts were dated at Inchmahome (September 28th), Dunkeld (October 5th) and 'Perth' (October 14th),[86] the first presumably issued on the king's return from the Argyll campaign, and the third confirming Barbour's statement that after the fall of Dunstaffnage the king passed towards Perth.[87] His success had begun to reap its own reward. Before March 1309 he had won over to his side James the Stewart, James's nephew Alexander Stewart of Bunkle (Berwickshire), Thomas Randolph the younger (son of the king's half-sister, and a landowner in Nithsdale and Berwickshire), and John Menteith (Stewart on his father's side), who gave up the empty title of earl of Lennox bestowed on him by Edward I, apparently for the actual lordships of Arran and Knapdale.[88] The three Stewarts might have been expected to join or rejoin Bruce before long. Randolph, whose father had been closely connected with the Balliols, had been with Bruce at Methven, but changed sides after his capture. He held strong ideas about knightly conduct, despised Bruce's policy of guerrilla warfare as being unworthy of a gentleman, and told the king as much.[89] He was kept under constraint for a time until he had purged this contempt, but his ultimate adherence to the king was to prove of inestimable value. Another Lothian landowner, William Vieuxpont of Langton in Berwickshire, who had been active in France in 1299–1300 as a member of William Wallace's company, had joined Bruce by the end of 1308, if not sooner.[90] It is a measure of Bruce's strength at this time, or perhaps of Edward II's weakness, that in January 1309 the earl of Gloucester and two other English earls, together with papal envoys specially sent to treat of peace, were despatched to the Scottish court and arranged a truce to last until 1 November.[91]

On March 16th and 17th, 1309, Bruce was able to hold his first parliament.[92] Appropriately enough, it was at St Andrews, for among its business was the composition of a reply to a letter from King Philip IV of France, thus opening up the old North Sea lines of communication which had been out of use for some five years. As late as April 19th 1308 the French king was making a payment to John Balliol as 'king of Scotland',[93] but by July 7th 1309 he had evidently decided to recognise Robert I so publicly that he styled him 'king of Scots' even in a letter to Edward II.[94] Already, before March, King Philip spoke of his special love for King Robert, reminded the Scots of the old alliance between them and the French, and asked for Scottish help in a forthcoming crusade. To this the Scottish answer, put briefly, was 'first things first'. They were delighted to hear of Philip's affection for their king, they reminded him of the terrible ravages which English invasion had made across the face of their country, and they promised that when Scotland had recovered her 'pristine liberty' and was at peace, King Philip would find not only the king of Scots but all the natives of his kingdom ready to join the crusade with all their power.[95]

The resumption of Franco-Scottish relations was of fundamental importance. It had in fact been set in hand as early as the previous November by a French effort to secure a truce between Edward II and the king of Scots.[96]

But the most urgent task before the St Andrews parliament seems to have been, as we should expect, the solemn affirmation of Robert Bruce's right to the throne, and a declaration of loyalty and support from a body of magnates and prelates sufficiently representative to rank as the community of the realm. It is much to be regretted that, apart from the reply to King Philip and an original charter issued at St Andrews on March 16th,[97] our evidence for the proceedings at King Robert's first parliament consists of copies made in the seventeenth century of two original documents now lost,[98] and one brief abstract, made in the eighteenth century and printed in the nineteenth, of a third original which is likewise missing.[99] These precarious survivals combine to tell a consistent and inherently probable story, but as pieces of historical evidence they necessarily lack the authority which extant original instruments would possess. It seems that on March 17th, the day after the reply to King Philip's letter had been issued, the clergy present at the parliament, or their representatives, describing themselves as fully and solemnly as possible as 'the bishops, abbots, priors, and others of the clergy duly constituted in the realm of Scotland', gave their authority to a bold and radical declaration of right on behalf of Scottish independence and of Robert Bruce's claim to be king of Scots.[100] In its reference to the competition for the throne in 1291–92 we have for the first time a clear enunciation of the belief that Balliol had been made king of Scotland by Edward I *de facto* in defiance of a universal belief among the Scottish people that Robert Bruce the Competitor had a better title. The declaration then narrated the evils and disasters which had befallen Scotland by reason of English invasion and the capture and imprisonment of King John, until, through the working of divine providence, the people, not wishing any longer to bear the calamities which had been brought upon them through want of a captain and faithful leader, had taken for their king Robert Bruce, grandson of the Competitor, in whom the Competitor's right to the throne resided, and had raised him to the throne. Having been made king of Scots, Bruce had through Christ's mercy recovered and restored the kingdom, following the example of many former kings of Scotland by whom it had been won and held, 'as is fully related in the ancient and magnificent chronicles of the Scots, and as the warlike labours of the Picts against the Britons and of the Scots against the Picts clearly testify.'[101] And before concluding with a general affirmation of their loyalty to King Robert, the clergy's declaration added this cautionary statement: 'If anyone, in opposition [to King Robert], should claim right to the Scottish kingdom by means of documents sealed in the past and containing the consent of the people, be it known that all this was effected by irresistible force and violence, by manifold fears, bodily torture and other terrors, which could well pervert the opinions and minds of righteous men and strike fear into the stoutest hearts.'[102]

Apart from containing the earliest appearance of the powerful myth that John Balliol was merely an English puppet, the declaration is remarkable for two echoes. Its reference to the ancient chronicles of the Scots and to the wars in which the Britons had been driven out of Scotland by the Picts and the Picts by the Scots recalls the case presented to Boniface VIII in 1301 by Baldred Bisset and his colleagues, in rebuttal of Edward I's letter to the pope justifying his overlordship in Scotland.[103] The phrase in which the declaration seeks to explain the Scots' failure to defy the English claim of 1291 is not merely an echo, it is almost a *verbatim* quotation, of the words used in the bull *Scimus, fili* of 1299 and again in Bisset's pleading in 1301: 'the force and fear which can strike even the most steadfast' of the earlier documents becoming 'the force, violence and manifold fears which can strike even the most steadfast' of the later.[104] The continuity of argument which links the documents of 1299 and 1301 to those of 1309 is proof that Bruce, in his first parliament, had available to him the documentation produced by the earlier struggles of the community of the realm. It suggests, indeed, that he had with him some of the actual men who were responsible for, or at least well-informed about, the preparation of these earlier documents. No doubt Nicholas Balmyle, who had been chancellor in 1301 and was now bishop of Dunblane, was present at the parliament. It seems that Matthew of Crambeth, bishop of Dunkeld, also attended,[105] and it is reasonable to posit the attendance of the bishops of Ross, Moray and Brechin and of representatives of the bishops of St Andrews and Glasgow.[106]

Parallel with this declaration by the clergy there was apparently a similar – perhaps an identical – declaration by the nobles.[107] According to the brief eighteenth-century abstract which forms the only surviving evidence of this declaration, the nobles, addressing themselves to the king of France, affirmed that King Robert was the true and nearest heir of King Alexander last deceased. This was done 'at the city of St Andrews in the year of grace 1308, in the third year of King Robert's reign',[108] that is, between March 25th, 1308 and March 24th, 1309. We need have no doubt that it belongs, like the clergy's declaration, to the St Andrews parliament. It was evidently sealed by six earls or their representatives and by Edward Bruce as lord of Galloway. Whether it bore any title or endorsement we do not know, but the document put out by the clergy is said to have had the significant title: 'Declaration made by the community of the realm of Scotland that Robert Bruce, grandfather of the lord Robert king of Scotland, was the true heir of King Alexander, and that he ought to have succeeded to the realm on his death.'[109]

This brings us to the vital question of the composition of the St Andrews parliament. The lords, knights and other laymen whom we know to have attended or to have been represented at this first parliament of King Robert were the following:[110] the earls of Ross, Lennox and Sutherland; the 'communities' of the earldoms of Fife, Menteith, Mar, Buchan and Caithness, whose heirs were in wardship; the communities of the other earldoms of the realm except Dunbar; Edward Bruce, lord of Galloway; James the

Stewart; Alexander of Argyll; Donald of Islay; John Menteith; Gilbert de
la Hay, constable of Scotland; Robert Keith, marischal of Scotland;
Thomas Randolph, lord of Nithsdale; James Douglas; Alexander Lindsay;
Alexander (?Fraser); William Wiseman; John Fenton; David Barclay;
Robert Boyd; Edward Keith; Hugh, son of the earl of Ross; the barons of all
Argyll and the Hebrides (among them Gillespie Maclachlan and three
Campbells) 'and the inhabitants of the whole realm of Scotland acknow-
ledging allegiance to Robert king of Scotland'. The church leaders present
have already been mentioned, and to their number we must of course add
Bernard, the chancellor.

This makes an impressive list, but in some ways the gaps in it are as
striking as the names which are present. Ingram de Umfraville and his
kinsman the earl of Angus; the earls of Atholl and Dunbar; Alexander
Abernethy; John Moubray; Adam of Gordon; David of Brechin – these and
several other men of the highest rank, many of whom could show a notable
record in the war against England, were conspicuously missing. It was of the
utmost importance to Bruce that he should actually enjoy the support of
what could be called, without serious violence to the truth, the 'community
of the realm'. The phrase 'the inhabitants of the whole realm of Scotland
acknowledging allegiance to King Robert', used where all our reading of
such documents from 1286 onwards might lead us to expect the simpler
'community of the realm', must surely indicate doubt on the constitutional
point. The author of the rubric which is said to have been supplied to the
clerical declaration was bolder or less scrupulous. One of the most remarkable proofs of the power behind the concept of the community is to be seen
in the fact that in 1309 King Robert and his Scottish enemies both struggled
to capture this concept and to appear to act on behalf of the community. As
late as October 1309 'certain people in Scotland to whom the name 'the
community of Scotland' is given', who were presumably the not insignificant remnant of the old Balliol and Comyn party, petitioned Edward II to
restore and confirm the terms which had been granted by Edward I in the
peace he had made in 1304 with John Comyn of Badenoch and the rest of the
community.[111] The request was allowed, but whether or not it impressed
the English king is beside the point. The form of the petition is a forceful
reminder that the idea of the community of the realm remained very strong,
and that among the leaders of the Scottish nation King Robert had as yet no
monopoly of it. Nevertheless, even if at his first parliament Robert Bruce
could not claim with manifest truth to have the whole community behind
him, it may be fairly said that the search for his throne was at an end.[112]

ELEVEN

The Turn of the Tide

It is easy to regard the period from 1309 to 1314 as a mere prelude to Bannockburn, as though the Scots spent these years preparing themselves for an inevitable and decisive trial of strength with the English Crown. In truth, Bruce's famous battle was the least inevitable event in the whole war of independence. Bruce himself never seems to have been certain in his own mind that his crown and the independence of the Scottish kingdom would ultimately have to be vindicated in a single great trial by combat. An English observer in 1311 wrote that Bruce 'did not believe he was able to meet the [English] king's forces in a plain field',[1] an estimate which surely holds good for the whole period from Methven to the dramatic council of war held on the night of June 23rd–24th, 1314, between the first and second days of the battle of Bannockburn. Bruce's thinking was dominated by the principles summarized and made famous in later years in *Good King Robert's Testament*: dependence on infantry, scorched earth, guerrilla raids and sorties, and the systematic demolition of castles and fortifications; in short, caution in strategy, boldness in tactics. The English, in his view, must be so harassed and exhausted that they would come to feel that Scotland was not worth the effort and expense of conquest.

We must not exaggerate the success which Bruce had achieved by 1309, even while admitting that this success was extraordinary when we consider the almost ludicrous weakness of his position only two years before. The subjugation of Buchan, Ross and Argyll (a list soon to be augmented by Galloway), the resumption of communications with France, the winning over of many prominent nobles and lairds, the holding of a parliament at St Andrews – these were notable achievements, which bade fair to make 'King Hob' (as the English called him in ridicule)[2] a much more serious exponent of kingship than any but his most devoted followers of 1306–7 would have believed. But in 1309 he had still not won over the whole of Scotland. It is true that as the result of brilliant campaigns, his Scottish enemies no longer had any base for concerted action outside Lothian, and even Lothian had come under heavy attack as early as December 1308.[3] If Scotsmen still wanted to fight against Bruce, they must now do so simply as individual members of the English forces, and they were, indeed, described as 'English' by the later Scottish chroniclers. But Bruce had to recognize – as we also must recognize if we wish to grasp the significance of the years before Bannockburn – that an unmistakable change had come over the struggle with England since 1304. On the one hand there was defeatism, bred of the memory of actual defeat in the field and of material destruction and misery, and leading to a breakdown of order and to opportunist shifts of allegiance. On the other, there were the doubts entertained by many men of power and influence as to the lawfulness of Bruce's claim to the throne, the open belief or less articulate suspicion that he was a private man furthering a private ambition.

For many years King Robert's strength lay in the country north of Forth and in the 'middle west' – Lanarkshire, Ayrshire, Lennox and the Firth of Clyde. In 1311, for example, we are told on good authority that Piers Gaveston was sent to occupy Perth by Edward II 'so that Bruce who at the time was on an expedition towards Galloway *should not return north of Forth to recruit an army*'.[4] It was precisely in these regions that the English hold was weakest, not because of the exceptional hostility of the inhabitants but rather because of their remoteness from English bases and their excessively poor internal communications. Anyone attempting the recovery of Scottish independence in 1306 would have been obliged, if only for strategic and geographical reasons, to begin with the north and the west.

Looking at the struggle for Scottish independence as a whole, from 1286 to 1328, the balance of military and especially political importance was weighted much more towards Lothian and the south east. Before 1304, as we have already seen, not only was the south-east – Lothian, Tweeddale, Teviotdale and the Forest – repeatedly the scene of major campaigns, but many south-eastern landowners were prominent on the Scottish side. But even after Bruce's revolutionary *coup de force*, it is not true to say that the south east was unimportant or that all Lothian men remained hostile or apathetic until Bannockburn inspired or terrified them into patriotism. Between 1307 and February 1312 the following Lothian landowners had joined Bruce: William de Vieuxpont (Vipont) of Langton in Berwickshire; Sir Thomas Hay, Sir Robert Keith the marischal and (in Keith's following) Godfrey Broun of Colston (December 1308); Geoffrey Farsley (1308); Edmund Ramsay of Dalhousie (1309 or 1310); Peter of Pinkie and Aymer of Hadden (November 1310).[5] A series of fascinating documents from November 1312[6] throws a flood of light on the situation in Lothian a year and a half before Bannockburn, revealing it to be one of much complexity. These documents show us the plight of the communities of 'King Edward's men' – presumably including both the genuinely English and the Scots loyal to Edward II – in the sheriffdoms of Edinburgh, Roxburgh and Berwick. On one side the Scottish king was treating them exactly as he was treating the indisputably English communities of Cumberland, Northumberland and County Durham, forcing them to pay him swingeing sums of blackmail for immunity from burning, devastation and worse. On the other side, the English garrisons, especially at Edinburgh, Roxburgh, Jedburgh and Berwick, were brutally ignoring these dearly bought truces or *souffrances de guerre*. They refused to contribute their own share of the cost of a truce, and when local landowners took refuge inside these castles in order to evade their responsibilities, they refused to allow these evaders to pay the proper share due from their estates. Finally, they seized the goods and cattle of Bruce's own supporters in their sheriffdoms, when these were being brought to market peaceably under the terms of the truce. In consequence, not surprisingly, the 'civilian population' (if they may be so called) feared reprisals by Bruce because the truce had been violated. Nothing in the record of this time is more ironical than to see King Edward II sternly rebuking his own sheriffs and garrison commanders for attacking the enemy and for making life harder for Edward's own supporters. Nothing is more illuminating than to read in these official records of 1312 explicit reference to the men in Lothian 'who adhere to the side of the aforesaid Robert [Bruce]'.[7]

A passage in the Lanercost chronicle describing the situation at the turn of the years 1311 and 1312 strikingly reinforces the impression given by these official records.[8] The writer states that the men of the earldom of Dunbar, who had hitherto been in the English king's peace, were forced to pay very heavily for immunity from Bruce's attacks. We have already seen that the earl of Dunbar had been consistently pro-English throughout the Anglo-Scottish war. His attitude will easily account for the fact that his earldom was loyal to Edward II, but though it consisted of a large group of estates in East Lothian and Berwickshire the earldom of Dunbar was not Lothian. It may be relevant to add that the two magnates who were prominent in these years as leaders and spokesmen of the English party in Lothian were the earl of Dunbar himself and Sir Adam Gordon, who was a kinsman of the earls of Dunbar and held his principal estate, the village of Gordon in Berwickshire, as a member of the earldom. The Lanercost writer continues with these remarkable words:

> In all this fighting the Scots were so divided that often a father was with the Scots and his son with the English, or one brother was with the Scots and another with the English, or even one individual was first on one side and then on the other. But all or most of the Scots who were with the English were with them insincerely or to save their lands in England; for their hearts if not their bodies were always with their own people.'[9]

The men and women of south-eastern Scotland were, indeed, in an unenviable plight. If many of them remained in the increasingly ineffective 'peace' of King Edward, it would be unrealistic to attribute this to a lack of patriotic feeling. A few years later, when the triumphant Scots were raiding the English northern counties at will, many of the local inhabitants went over to the Scots. It does not occur to English historians (any more than it occurred to Edward II) to put this down to traitorous motives or lack of patriotism. They were prompted by stark necessity. No such necessity burdened the people north of Forth, where the majority were free to give effect to a patriotism which was neither more nor less pronounced than that which might be found in any feudal kingdom of comparable development.[10]

Fourteenth-century patriotism was not a total, all-embracing patriotism, any more than fourteenth-century warfare was total warfare, but both, for all that, were real enough. We must not be too surprised, therefore, if we find hard-pressed Lothian gentry supporting the English, or impoverished young men from the surrounding countryside serving in the enemy garrisons of Linlithgow or Bothwell, Perth or Dundee. Nor must we be too surprised if we find that a number of prominent men from districts well to the north or west of Lothian were conspicuously loyal to the English king and inveterate enemies of King Robert. It is a striking fact that the hard core of Scots who fought consistently against Bruce, who either never submitted, not even after the tide of victory had turned decisively in his favour, or submitted at the eleventh hour, was composed of men from regions at a considerable distance from the English border or with little or no experience of anglicization: Sir Dungal Macdouall of Galloway, Sir Alexander Abernethy of Abernethy (Perthshire) and Inverarity (Angus), Duncan of Frendraught (on the borders of Aberdeenshire and Banffshire), his father-in-law and brother-in-law, the elder and younger Gilbert of Glencarnie, from the highland parish of Duthil in Inverness-shire,[11] and John Bacach Macdougall, lord of Lorn.

The years from 1309 to 1314 were years not of orderly preparation but of dour and confused struggle. The elimination of concerted Scottish resistance to Bruce meant that the king's main efforts could be directed towards clearing his kingdom of English garrisons and re-establishing its independent position within the community of North Sea countries. Save for the summer and autumn of 1309, which he evidently spent traversing the west from Loch Broom in the north to Dunstaffnage in Argyll,[12] and the autumn of 1312, when he stayed for some weeks in Moray to witness the conclusion of the treaty with Norway, King Robert's time was chiefly spent in the centre and south of Scotland, or else beyond the border, raiding Cumberland and Northumberland. One further exception may be seen in the autumn of 1310 and earlier part of 1311, when he let an English army under Edward II, and latterly under Piers Gaveston, penetrate deep into Scotland to little purpose, since they found no Scots troops to defeat in open battle and not enough food to sustain either themselves or their horses.[13]

The chief castles still in enemy hands after the end of 1309 were concentrated in the south. On the line of the Tay the English retained Perth and Dundee. North of this line they held only Banff, which may have fallen to the Scots during 1310. Between Tay and Forth the English position was surprisingly weak: Cupar, which they still held in the spring of 1308, was lost not long afterwards, and only the small fortalice of Muckhart, belonging to the bishop of St Andrews, remained in enemy hands, apparently as late as 1311.[14] On the crucially important line of the Forth, or immediately south of it, the first-class castles of Stirling and Edinburgh were English-held, and precariously linked by the minor strongpoints of Linlithgow and Livingston. Already in 1309 the supply of these garrisons was proving difficult and dangerous. Food, stores and weapons were obtained from Berwick. Oddly enough, remote Banff and Dundee, because they could be supplied by sea, were easier to replenish than Stirling or Edinburgh. West of Stirling, 'English troops' (many of whom were actually Scotsmen) still controlled Kirkintilloch and Bothwell.[15] They must have felt increasingly isolated, though Bothwell, perhaps because of its exceptional size and strength, actually held out until the morrow of Bannockburn, when its Scottish commander, Walter, Gilbert's son, saw the light in time, handed Bothwell over to Edward Bruce, and survived to become the ancestor of the powerful Hamilton family. The still greater isolation of Ayr by December 1309 is shown by the fact that Edward II classed it along with Perth, Dundee and Banff as a castle whose commander was instructed to 'take what truce he could until Whitsun next (June 7th, 1310)'.[16] Rutherglen, which was being besieged in December 1308, was apparently taken by Edward Bruce.[17] Dumbarton may have been handed over to Bruce when its keeper Sir John Menteith joined him, before the spring of 1309.

The castles of the extreme south west could be expected to hold out longer, at least until the English lost their command of the Solway Firth. In these regions, moreover, a higher proportion of the local people were Bruce's enemies. It was thus some years before the Scots regained Lochmaben, Caerlaverock, Dumfries, Dalswinton, Tibbers and Buittle. As late as the autumn of 1311 an enemy garrison held Bruce's own island fortress of Loch Doon in Carrick. Although they were besieged, an 'English' force under David of Strathbogie, earl of Atholl, was making a strenuous effort to relieve them.[18] Dumfries and Caerlaverock were probably the strongest of these castles. Dumfries was at last surrendered, to King Robert in person, on February 7th, 1313, by his old enemy Dungal Macdouall.[19] With a clemency and respect for military honour conspicuously absent in Edward I's behaviour towards defeated garrisons, Macdouall was allowed to go free. He crossed to the Isle of Man and prepared to hold it against the king of Scotland, its lawful lord.

It was, of course, in the south east that the English position seemed, if not impregnable, at least formidably entrenched. It was not merely that they held, in addition to Edinburgh, three other first-class castles – Jedburgh, Roxburgh and Berwick – as well as numerous second-or third-rate strongpoints (Haddington, Luffness, Dirleton, Yester, Dunbar, Selkirk and Cavers).[20] Even more useful was the fact that the close, 'four-square' grouping of these castles, the relatively good communications between them, and the proximity of most of them to a North Sea coastline still dominated by English maritime power, combined to make the whole English position much less vulnerable in this area than anywhere else in Scotland. Bruce knew that there was no easy short-cut to victory here. Every single one of the major fortresses must be patiently invested, starved, and, when the right moment came, seized by a mixture of stratagem and daring. The methods of castle warfare used by the English were simply not available to Bruce, for he was woefully short of heavy siege engines and the skilled men to work them, and also of the food-supplies needed to sustain pro-longed sieges.

If the south east seemed to present obstacles which would not be easy to surmount, the south west offered a brighter prospect and was no less important. By the summer of 1310, if not earlier, the Scots had been peaceably received in Ireland and allowed to buy not only corn, meat and other foodstuffs but also sorely-needed iron and steel weapons and armour.[21] Since these can hardly have been Irish-made they were presum-ably re-exports from England or the continent. Scottish access to Ireland was made possible by the superiority which Bruce now enjoyed in Argyll, the isles and the seas between Galloway and Ulster. A persistent line of English strategy at this time was to encourage John Macdougall, the ousted lord of Lorn, to lead a naval expedition against the Hebrideans and Argyllsmen and try to win them over. For this Macdougall was appointed 'admiral and captain' of a special fleet in 1311, and given a base in one of the east-coast Irish ports, perhaps Dublin or Drogheda.[22] Here he could count on the support of dissident west highlanders such as John Macsween of Knapdale and his brothers Toirdelbach and Murdoch.[23]

As long as the English controlled the Isle of Man the south-western approaches of Scotland were vulnerable to attack on or from the sea. For their part the Scots had much to gain from pursuing an aggressive policy by preying on the English shipping routes to Ireland. Recovery of Man would be essential if this strategy was to succeed. Towards the end of 1310, Robert I was reported to be planning an assault upon Man with a fleet from the Outer Isles, and it was said that many Manxmen were already adhering to him.[24] For the English, the defence of Man had been complicated by the fact that Edward II had given the island to Piers Gaveston a few weeks after his accession.[25] The English baronage might well have preferred Man to be in Scots hands than see it serve as a possible bolt-hole for their king's hated lover. But by 1310 the island seems to have been once again under at least the nominal control of Anthony Bek, bishop of Durham, and administered by Bek's steward Gilbert Macaskill.[26]

Nothing came of King Robert's threat, Bek died in March 1311 and by May Edward II had transferred the island to Sir Henry Beaumont,[27] but since he too incurred the suspicion of the king's opponents, the Lords Ordainers, Beaumont's custody must have been brief. At some date before April 1313 Man was evidently seized in a baronial *coup* involving Simon

Montagu,[28] and it was evidently at this time that Dungal Macdouall was made commander of Rushen. These English vacillations were Bruce's opportunity. Gathering a large fleet, the king of Scots landed at Ramsey on May 18th, 1313, crossed the hills to Douglas two days later, and laid siege to the castle of Rushen (Castletown), nine miles to the south, on the 21st. On June 12th Bruce had the satisfaction of accepting Macdouall's second surrender of a castle in four months.[29] Once more set free, Macdouall became a veteran in the English king's service, dying about the end of 1327 and leaving a large family to become pensioners of the Westminster exchequer.[30]

Although Beaumont seems to have been restored in 1314 as custodian of the island, he cannot have made this good by physical possession, and it was not until early in 1315 that John Macdougall apparently wrested Man from the Scots.[31] Robert I then made a prospective grant of the lordship of Man to Thomas Randolph, whose reported efforts in July 1317 to recover the island for Scotland must have been successful, for it was evidently under Scottish rule from c. 1317 till 1333 and formally acknowledged to be so in 1328 by the English king and parliament.[32]

In the first half of Edward II's reign the English lost control of the western approaches. By the autumn of 1315 Scots ships, mostly under the command of Thomas Dun, had grown bold enough to raid English shipping at Holyhead.[33] Dun helped Edward Bruce while he was campaigning in Ireland, and in 1317 two new vessels, built and equipped in Devon or Cornish ports, were ordered to be used against him. This move was evidently successful, for Dun's capture was reported on July 13th, at the same time as Randolph was menacing the two islands of Man and Anglesey.[34]

The tactics of Bruce and the bold young men – Douglas, Randolph, Boyd and Edward Bruce – who under him were already forming a band of famous captains, would have astonished and amused Edward I. Castles must be surprised during the hours of darkness, and an entry must be forced at the most suitable point on the walls by means of rope ladders fitted with iron grappling-hooks. These simple but ingenious scaling ladders, evidently light enough to be carried by one or two men, may well have been used at Forfar and elsewhere in the north. The first occasion on which they are recorded was the attempt on Berwick, on the night of December 6th, 1312.[35] It is characteristic of the audacity of Bruce and his captains that the first big south-country stronghold to be attacked in earnest was the town nearest to the English border. The attempt was frustrated by the barking of a dog inside the walls, but in little more than a month Bruce was investing the town of Perth. Because of its strategic position, Perth (like Stirling) was of crucial importance to the English. Gaveston had been sent to hold and strengthen the town in February 1311,[36] during the campaign which

Edward II conducted in southern Scotland between September 1310 and August 1311. The Perth garrison was large, with a high proportion of Scotsmen.[37] Since October 1311 at latest, they had been commanded by the Perthshire knight Sir William Oliphant. As the brave young commander of Stirling castle on behalf of King John and the Guardians, Oliphant had won great renown. He had been in an English prison from July 1304 until December 1308, when he was released on condition of fighting against Bruce.[38] He had already given a gloomy report of the situation at Perth as early as autumn 1311,[39] and by January 1313 things must have seemed wellnigh hopeless. The town was surrounded by a stone wall with turrets, and by a water-filled ditch (except on the east where the River Tay gave protection). On the night of January 7th–8th, 1313 – 'a myrk nycht' says Barbour[40] – the garrison failed to keep a good watch, believing from Bruce's movements that the Scots had lifted the siege. Carrying their ladders and light weapons, the Scots waded through the moat in the darkness. To the astonishment of a French knight in his entourage, their king himself led the way through the black, icy water, which at one point came up to his throat, and with the help of his own rope ladder was the second man to scale the town wall. The men of Perth surrendered almost without a fight.

For some moments Bruce had clearly been in great danger; but it was during such moments as these that he won not merely the castles but also the hearts of Scotland. In most ages of history, the Scottish soldier (unless extremely well-trained) has not possessed the gift which has been the conspicuous mark of his English counterpart: the capacity to hold on coolly and philosophically, through thick and thin, regardless of either leadership or conditions. On the other hand, no one has responded more heroically to the inspiration of an oustanding leader, a Murray of Bothwell, a James IV, a Montrose, a Moore. And it seems undeniable that a successful leader of Scotsmen must have above all the power to kindle both affection and imagination. It is not normally the mark of a good general that he fights alongside his men. But Bruce had to be more than a good general; he had to be a Joshua, a captain of his people, one who could not only draw on existing loyalty but awaken dormant loyalty and win over to himself the loyalty previously given to his enemies.

The English in Perth were allowed to go free. The leading Scots burgesses were slain, though if we may believe Barbour the number of those killed was small.[41] The example – if such it was – proved effective, for we hear of no more cold-blooded killings. Slaughter of this kind, though common enough in the period, was highly uncharacteristic of Robert Bruce. As we have seen, only a month after the fall of Perth (February 7th, 1313) Dumfries Castle was starved into surrender. The king had taken personal command of the attack upon Dumfries, Caerlaverock and Buittle during the previous July, perhaps because he felt that his brother had not done well enough in this task. It seems likely that after the surrender of Dumfries the other two castles also fell into Scottish hands, and the West March with them. There was no mistaking it now: the tide had turned.

Stirling, commanded by Sir Philip Moubray, a Scot, was the next big castle to be attempted. Edward Bruce laid siege to it from Lent nearly to midsummer 1313, without success.[42] Then, by an act of characteristic chivalry and folly, he committed his brother to a pact which threatened to ruin all Bruce's cautious strategy and to change the very nature of the war Bruce had chosen to fight. The hard-pressed Moubray asked for a year's respite in which help was to arrive or else his position be proved untenable. This extremely generous term was conceded by Edward Bruce. If no English army came within three miles of Stirling to do battle for the castle before Midsummer 1314, Moubray would surrender. Possibly, in view of Edward II's struggle with his own great lords, embittered as it was by their judicial murder of Gaveston in 1312, Edward Bruce may have thought that Stirling would be cheaply bought. Yet faced by so public a challenge neither the king nor the barons of England could ignore the threat to their honour and the opportunity of ending the Scottish war once for all. King Robert was virtually compelled to meet the enemy in a pitched battle, the one thing he had striven to avoid since June 1306.

The affair earned Edward Bruce a sharp rebuke from the king,[43] but was not allowed to interfere with his plans to reduce the remaining enemy-held strongpoints. In the following winter Bruce turned to the two formidable strengths of Roxburgh – 'le Marche Mont (Marchmont)' in popular usage – and Edinburgh, 'le château des pucelles' or 'maidens' castle', clinging as stubbornly as lichen to its knob of volcanic rock. Well-guarded, these castles should have proved more than a match for ill-equipped besiegers. In fact, they fell within the space of a single Lent. On the night of February 19th–20th, 1314 (this was Shrove Tuesday and Ash Wednesday),[44] the Scots under James Douglas broke into Roxburgh castle and overwhelmed the garrison. Douglas and his men approached the walls at dead of night, crawling on their hands and knees, their body armour invisible under black surcoats. They carried the usual ingenious rope ladders, on this occasion apparently made by a man called Sim of the 'Ledows'.[45] Sim was the first man up. He made the way safe for the rest when he 'stekit upward with ane knyff' a sentry roused by the clatter as the grappling-hook of his ladder was lodged on the wall-head. Because it was Shrove Tuesday (Fastern's Eve) the garrison were relaxed, drinking and dancing. Taken utterly by surprise, many were killed or captured. Only their commander, a knight named Guillemin de Fenes from Bouglon in Gascony,[46] made any real resistance, shutting himself into a small turret. He surrendered the next day, however, and with his men was allowed to go freely to England.

Edinburgh castle was taken three weeks later by Thomas Randolph, obviously determined not to be outdone by Douglas.[47] The folk-hero in this case was William Francis, a local man whose father had served in the castle and whom the king afterwards rewarded with forfeited lands in Sprouston, Roxburghshire.[48] As a youth, Francis had had experience of climbing out of Edinburgh castle after dark when, without his father's knowledge, he was paying visits to his sweetheart in the town. On the night of March 14th, 1314 – once again, mercifully dark – a diversion was carried out at the East Port – 'the only place', says a contemporary, 'where an assault could be made'.[49] This sent the garrison rushing to the spot. Meanwhile, Francis and the other nimble leaders of the genuine assault party, rock-climbers before the art had been invented, inched their way in darkness up the steep and slippery north precipice, and swung their light siege ladders on to the masonry parapet. Up the ladders swarmed their followers, in numbers sufficient to overwhelm the astonished guards. The East Port was opened to admit the still larger force outside, and all was over. Most of the defenders fell in the fighting, but the commander, Sir Pierre Libaud (another Gascon), entered Bruce's service, only to be executed for treason soon afterwards. In accordance with his consistent policy, Bruce caused both Edinburgh and Roxburgh ('that fine castle', the Lanercost writer called it)[50] to be razed to the ground.

By their respective exploits at Roxburgh and Edinburgh, Douglas and Randolph set the seal on their already notable reputations. Already, in 1312, Bruce had demonstrated his confidence in Randolph and shown the value he set upon his support by making him earl of Moray and granting him, with wide powers, the lands of an earldom which had been in the possession of the Crown since 1130. Bruce, of course, was a man of his time. The greatest prizes in his gift went to men who were his own kin, like his nephew Randolph, or belonged to the circle of friends and allies of the Bruce family, like James Douglas and Walter Stewart, who had the greatest prize of all, the marriage of Bruce's daughter (and ultimate heir) Marjorie. His own brother Edward could hardly fail to be ennobled and honoured by Robert, but he and all the men to whom Bruce granted high office, noble titles and rich estates proved their worth during the reign.

It is impossible to calculate the total of castles captured by Bruce between the autumn of 1307, when he took Inverlochy, and the fall of Edinburgh six years later. On any showing, this must be reckoned one of the great military enterprises of British history. But the achievement appears even more remarkable when we set it in its context of activity in three other spheres. The first, keeping open the Irish supply line and recovering the Isle of Man, we have noted already. The two other spheres consisted of profitable raids south of the Border and the resumption of commercial and diplomatic links with towns and countries of the continent.

From 1311 onward, the English in England itself came to learn what Bruce meant by 'defending himself with the longest stick that he had'. His idea of defence was attack, again and again at the same place or at many different places in rapid succession. He gave the enemy no rest. As early as 1307

Gallovidians and the cattle inseparably associated with them were sheltering from Bruce in Inglewood Forest, along with men from Liddesdale. Very soon there was no safety to be found in Cumberland, or indeed in any of the northern counties of England. It is true that between February 1309 and March 1310 (mainly owing to French exertions) some pretence of peace was maintained along the Border by a series of precarious truces. But after the collapse of Edward II's expedition of 1310–11 and his withdrawal from Scotland (August 1311) Bruce became far more aggressive.

Two students of this period, the late James Willard and Jean Scammell, have examined the effect of the Scottish raids upon the north of England.[51] Willard's starting-point was the records of the central government, especially the exchequer. He showed that in 1307, for example, Northumberland paid its normal share of a national property tax: £916 18s. 11d. Two years later the county paid nothing, and in 1313 it was exempt. Much the same holds true for Cumberland and Westmorland. Working from the local north-country records as well as those of the central government, Mrs Scammell was able to fill in the grim details behind these bare fiscal facts. The 'community' of Northumberland, like the 'community' of Lothian, was forced to buy a truce from King Robert in 1311 and again from 1312 to 1313, each time for the colossal sum of £2,000. No one knew where the Scots would strike next – one month they poured across the fords of Solway to pillage and burn in Gilsland and the valley of the South Tyne; the next month they broke into Coquetdale and Redesdale, burning as far as Corbridge. There was no organized resistance. The English either tried to buy Bruce off or themselves resorted to burning to prevent the Scots getting supplies. What the Scots wanted more than anything was money, cattle and corn, the first two capable of being moved across difficult country with relative ease. Where possible they obtained what they wanted in the form of blackmail: for example, the men of the earldom of Dunbar won temporary respite in 1313 for 1,000 quarters of corn.[52] If blackmail was not paid they overran the country with fire and sword, though the killing of human beings was relatively uncommon and was not Bruce's object. In August, 1311, for example, the Scots in upper Tynedale slew only those men who offered resistance.[53] But in the following summer they penetrated south of the Tyne, surprising a great throng of folk at Durham on market day. Here they inflicted great destruction, burning the town and killing many of the local people.[54] A few leading gentry of the Bishopric at once acted on their own initiative, for the bishop, Richard Kellaw, was away in the south attending parliament. They met Bruce in person at Hexham (August 16th, 1312) and bought a truce till midsummer 1313 for two thousand marks, 450 to be paid at Holm Cultram abbey by September 29th, 1312.[55] Cumberland, Coupland and Westmorland also bought a truce for the same period, and since they could not raise the whole sum were forced to yield hostages. On the approach of midsummer 1313, the Scottish king notified the northern counties that if they did not buy a fresh truce they would be raided. The mere threat was enough to bring promises of payment from the county communities. But when Cumberland had failed to pay by April 1314, instead of injuring the hostages, the Scots under Edward Bruce established themselves at Rose Castle and ravaged the surrounding countryside for some days.[56]

These raids and truce-bargains were extremely well organized and far more profitable and effective than the wild ravaging of Wallace's incursion in 1297. The Scottish staff-work was excellent, and discipline, now under royal authority, was strictly maintained. Estates which had obtained no immunity were systematically plundered. Estates which had paid for a truce were left in peace. Only in one case, the town of Hartlepool (where the Bruces had held lordship for over a century),[57] did the king appear to show vindictiveness. In 1315, the men of Hartlepool could not buy any truce from the Scottish king, and were forced to take refuge out at sea while their town was sacked (though not burned) by James Douglas.[58] In general, however, the English could have peace if they paid heavily for it. The effort proved too much for Northumberland, an ill-organized county which in any case was too vulnerable once the national defence system had broken down. After 1314 it 'ceased to negotiate as an entity',[59] The palatinate bishopric of Durham was much tougher, but the price which it paid for immunity (some £5,000 between 1311 and 1329) was at least twice what it would normally have paid in taxes; and even then it was forced to allow the Scots free passage across the county to raid south of the Tees. By the time Edward II had gathered his large army in the summer of 1314 to meet the challenge of Stirling, the four northern counties of England were close to exhaustion, either devastated or impoverished or both. The money which they should have paid to the exchequer at Westminster had gone, with two-or three-fold increase, to fill Bruce's empty war chest. The men who should have joined Edward's army resented the appeals of a king who could not defend his realm. Some had no money left, some had been slain or put to flight, some had even gone over to the Scots. For some years the northern counties contributed little to the English war-effort and actually contributed more to that of Bruce, but we are not entitled to conclude that their patriotism was lukewarm. Given strong leadership and an adequate defence system the English borderers would once more give a good account of themselves, as they had done in the twelfth and thirteenth centuries.

The vigour and high morale infused into the Scots by their king were not enough. Scotland needed arms and armour from abroad, and allies in every quarter where English interests were vulnerable or where English influence might be damaging. It is doubtful if, during the whole course of the Anglo-Scottish war, there was ever any prolonged blockage of the lines of communication between Scotland and the continent. The chief single reason for this lay in the fact that Scotland's attraction for foreign merchants consisted in her wool, an annual crop which it was best to dispose of without delay. It was always in demand in the Low Countries because of its fine quality. It did not occur to Edward I or his son to stop the trade in Scottish wool altogether, but naturally in the districts they controlled such profit as it made for the Crown went to English, not Scottish coffers. Of course they did try to place an embargo on trade with Scots 'rebels'. But the Flemings, and perhaps still more the German or 'Eastland' merchants, with their ancient, well-established contacts with Scottish ports, showed no reluctance to trade with independent Scotland whether it was under the Guardians or under Robert Bruce. In December 1302, for example, a ship freighted with clothing, armour and other goods for independent Scotland, probably bound for Aberdeen and almost certainly coming from the Low Countries or a Hanseatic port, was captured off Filey in Yorkshire.[60] Merchants of St Omer were buying wool, hides and deerskins in Moray in 1303 or 1304.[61] In October 1309, Edward II complained bitterly to the count of Flanders that the Scots and their 'accomplices' the German merchants had been getting great help in succour from the Flemish towns.[62] Men of Hainault were involved in the Scottish trade in 1312.[63] We hear of a ship from the Baltic port of Stralsund being in alliance with the Scots some time before 1312, and of German merchants who before January 1313 had seized an English ship bound for occupied Scotland, sold the cargo at Aberdeen and taken the hull itself to Stralsund.[64]

It is true that our earliest record of formal relations between King Robert and continental powers, especially the Hanseatic, Flemish and other Low Country cities and principalities, comes from comparatively late in the reign. From 1321, for example, we have a royal letter to Lübeck and privileges issued in favour of Bruges:[65] from 1323 a letter to the count of Holland and Hainault.[66] It is not until 1316 that we have positive documentary evidence of the king negotiating with Genoese firms (then the best shipbuilders in Europe) for the supply of weapons and ships.[67] All this was after Bannockburn, and admittedly nothing succeeds like success. But it would be a mistake to think that foreign merchant communities waited for results before investing in the Scottish enterprise. Moreover, surprising as it may seem, the Scots found some of their best friends among English merchants of North Sea ports such as Harwich, Norwich, King's Lynn, Hull and English-held Berwick. The temptation to smuggle contraband to Scotland overcame both patriotism and fear of the harsh penalties threatened against those who trafficked with the 'rebels'.[68]

The evidence, though patchy and slight, is conclusive. During the early part of Bruce's reign the Scots and their North Sea associates were able to keep trade routes open, and supplies of foodstuffs, weapons and armour, iron and steel, all absolutely essential to the war effort, were reaching Scottish ports. Presumably these imports were being paid for by exports of

wool, hides and timber in sufficient quantities to imply a recovery of the
fairly simple Scottish economy from the dislocation and destruction of the
years before 1304 and of the period from 1306 to 1309. Of course, in these
years Scotland must have been even shorter of luxuries than usual, and prior
to Bannockburn Bruce certainly never had enough weapons and ships to
equip his forces as he would no doubt have liked. But, so far as these matters
are ever determined by purely technological considerations, the thin yet
steady trickle of vital imports seems to have made the difference between
success and failure.

The importance which Bruce attached to the resumption of continental
alliances is shown by his readiness to receive envoys from the French kings,
although the truces with England which were several times arranged
through their influence were not much to his liking. There is record of truce
negotiations of this kind, some of which may have been meant seriously to
lead to a peace treaty, in 1308–09, in 1309–10, and in January 1312.[69] In
January 1313, Abbot Maurice of Inchaffray, one of King Robert's most
loyal and trusted supporters, was given an English safe-conduct to visit
Edward 11,[70] presumably to discuss a truce or a peace, and later in the same
year representatives of King Robert (including Bishop Lamberton) and of
King Edward appear to have been appointed to negotiate truce or peace in
conjunction with the agents of the king of France and at his request.[71] We
shall see that six years after Bannockburn the French king was deeply
involved again in efforts to secure peace between Scots and English. There
is no reason to believe that Bruce's attitude towards these negotiations was
frivolous or cynical. But it is clear that he never allowed them to affect his
military and strategic dispositions, and also that any serious peace talks
would have to start from a recognition of his title to the Scottish Crown on
the part of Edward 11.

Long before there was anything which could be called a revived Franco-
Scottish alliance (as distinct from friendly intercourse) Bruce had taken
measures to preserve the good relations with Norway which had existed
more or less continuously since 1295.[72] Scoto-Norwegian friendship had
been threatened by a number of incidents. It seems that pirates from
Scotland had kidnapped the seneschal of Orkney, a Norwegian knight, after
he had collected the royal revenues and while the money was still in his
possession. He had been held to ransom both for himself and for his money.
In addition, there had been Scottish raids on Shetland. For their part, the
Scots complained that an esquire named Patrick Mowat had been arrested
in Orkney by a royal bailiff, beaten, chained, robbed of his goods and forced
to ransom himself for forty merks. Still more serious was the affair of some
Scots merchants, burgesses of St Andrews, who on arrival in Norway for the
purpose of trading seem to have been treated as hostages. Their goods,
worth £600, were seized, and they themselves suffered a lengthy imprisonment before they were allowed to sail home empty-handed. These incidents

may have an ugly look, but by the standards of international behaviour prevailing at the time none of them was atrocious. They can hardly have put Scoto-Norwegian relations in serious jeopardy, and for sheer horror cannot compare with an incident of 1316 which must have imposed a much greater strain upon relations between Norway and England.[73] Some English merchants from Berwick, having put in at a Norwegian port, invited aboard the provincial governor and ten other noblemen, who to save their hosts expense went unarmed and without servants. Instead of a second course, the merchants showered their guests with boiling water and hot cinders and then killed them with daggers and swords. Norwegian grievances against Scotland were probably less concerned with incidents, major or minor, than with the Scottish failure to maintain the terms of the treaty of Perth in 1266, by which the Scots kings were bound to pay a perpetual annuity to Norway of 100 merks. The agreement sealed at Inverness on October 29th, 1312, between King Robert in person and the envoys of King Hakon v, shows that both sides were anxious for a settlement and prepared to be sensible and statesmanlike. The Perth treaty was renewed without any alteration, and though nothing was said about past failures to pay the annuity its regular payment was promised in the future. The Scots agreed to pay 600 merks in final compensation for the kidnapping of the seneschal of Orkney; the Norwegians restored the goods taken from the merchants of St Andrews. The plundering of Shetland and the affair of Patrick Mowat were to be investigated by faithful inquest.

Among the few persons whom we know to have been involved in making the treaty of Inverness there are two clergymen, Farquhar Bellejambe bishop of Caithness and Bernard the chancellor, whose participation is worth noting. From the date of his appointment to the archdeaconry of Caithness in 1297[74] by King Edward i we have no evidence that Farquhar Bellejambe, who rose to be dean and then (1306) bishop of Caithness, played any positive part in political affairs or that he had supported the Guardians before the collapse of 1304. Nor does he seem to have come out in support of Robert Bruce in his early years, as the bishops of Moray and Ross had done. In 1312, however, Bishop Farquhar was one of the two Scots churchmen who took oath on behalf of King Robert for the security of the Inverness treaty, and it is clear that by this time, if not indeed earlier, the king had gained the allegiance of one more Scottish bishop. As for Chancellor Bernard, his importance to the king has already been emphasized. Between March 1310 and June 1311 there is no evidence that King Robert made use of his great seal to authenticate his written instruments.[75] Instead, he seems to have used the privy seal only. The great seal was, of course, kept by the chancellor, and used only on his own authorization. Now it was about this time that Bernard was made abbot of Arbroath,[76] and it can hardly be a coincidence that an abbot of Arbroath was absent in Norway on the king's business (and his own) at some unknown date within this general period.[77]

It is more than probable that Bernard was sent to Norway to conduct the negotiations which led to the treaty of Inverness. If so it would be a clear indication of the great store which King Robert set by the continuance of Norwegian friendship.

If, in the spring of 1314, Robert Bruce, now in his fortieth year, had taken stock of the situation in which Scotland found itself, his feelings could surely have been summed up as a sort of anxious satisfaction. Much, incredibly much, had been achieved in the vindication of Scottish independence. Scarcely one castle was left with a foreign garrison which could inflict serious harm on the surrounding inhabitants. Within the Scottish kingdom itself every province from Galloway to Caithness, from the Outer Isles to Buchan acknowledged Bruce as king. Beyond the Border, from Tweed and Solway southward as far as Stainmore and the Tees, the English had been made to feel the menace of a Scotland awakened and revivified under a new ruler. Armies had been raised under a new generation of young captains who were accustomed to victory instead of defeat, and who showed a flexibility in tactics and a readiness to depend upon properly trained infantry which was in the sharpest contrast with the kind of warfare waged by the Guardians. Something like the accustomed machinery of government was once again in operation, and it is fair to infer that judicial activity and the collection of royal revenue had been resumed on a national scale. Three parliaments had been held, at St Andrews in 1309 and at Inchture[78] and Ayr in 1312, and probably there were others of which we have no record. King Robert and his subjects were now taken seriously by foreign kingdoms such as France and Norway, and by foreign trading cities and industrial principalities, such as the Hanse and Flanders. If, at this point, the king of England and his barons had been capable of far-sighted statesmanship, there was surely nothing to prevent a resumption of the happier relationship which prevailed between England and Scotland during the reign of Alexander III. Alas, in Edward of Caernarvon England possessed one of the stupidest kings who have ever sat upon her throne, and among the ranks of his baronage and higher clergy (with the possible exception of Aymer de Valence, earl of Pembroke) one may search in vain for anything resembling statesmanship. Perhaps the nearest approach to peace had come in 1312 or 1313, after the collapse of King Edward's second Scottish expedition. The negotiations, though encouraged by Philip the Fair, had failed, and there seemed no possibility of the English king recognizing Robert Bruce's title to the throne of Scotland. The challenge of Stirling Castle was thus the occasion rather than the cause of a head-on clash between the forces of the two countries. Reluctantly perhaps, but methodically and with determination, Bruce began to prepare his troops for the greatest trial of strength they had yet faced.

TWELVE

Bannockburn

The immediate objective of Edward II's invasion of Scotland in 1314 was the relief of Stirling Castle. It is clear, however, from the scale of his preparations, from the size of the army he raised, and from the language of his writs of summons, that the English king's real purpose was 'to put down and suppress the wicked rebellion of Robert Bruce and his accomplices in the king's land of Scotland'.[1] In short, the outcome was to be conquest and the final settlement of the 'Scottish Question'. His last expedition, in 1310 and 1311, had been a failure. It was undertaken in the face of almost universal hostility, or at least lack of co-operation, on the part of the English baronage. In 1314 the political scene augured better. Contemporaries say that many barons went over to the king's side because of disgust at the killing of Piers Gaveston.[2] Certainly Edward was well supported by the young earl of Gloucester, by the earl of Hereford, and by Aymer de Valence, since 1307 earl of Pembroke. Valence, superseded in his wardenship of Scotland in September 1307, was reappointed warden in March 1314 with wide powers.[3] The most prominent figure among the king's baronial opponents, Thomas, earl of Lancaster, had already begun to lose such respect as might once have been accorded him in virtue of his five earldoms, his doubly royal descent and his possession of the largest private estate in England. Both Lancaster and another leading opponent, Guy Beauchamp, earl of Warwick, had been formally though not sincerely reconciled with the king in October 1313.[4] The higher ranks of the baronage were, temporarily at least, no longer the stumbling block in the path of Edward's admittedly erratic ambition to complete his father's work north of the Border.

During November 1313 the English government were looking to the defences and security of the castle and town of Berwick upon Tweed,[5] and as early as November 28th Edward II wrote to his remaining supporters in Scotland promising to have an army at Berwick before next midsummer.[6] This was in reply to a letter purporting to come from 'the people of Scotland'. In fact, it was sent by the earl of Dunbar and Sir Adam Gordon, evidently on behalf of the men of the earldom of Dunbar and its neighbourhood. They had been suffering greatly at the hands of English and Scots alike, and claimed to have paid £20,000 to Bruce in blackmail, though the figure is too large to credit. Edward's reply was perfunctory or absent minded enough to be addressed to 'archbishops' (among others), although Scotland had none. But it shows that already by the end of November

Edward was taking the challenge of Stirling seriously. A month later (December 23rd) writs of summons for military service, naming a rendezvous at Berwick on June 10th, 1314, were sent to Thomas of Lancaster, seven other earls, and eighty-seven barons.[7] During February Edward again declared his intention to lead an army against the Scots in the summer, and already his advice was that the campaign would be largely an affair of infantry.[8]

Accordingly, from about March 9th onwards he began to issue the stream of orders necessary to raise and equip a large infantry force and also to supply a full-scale land and sea expedition.[9] Ships and sailors were demanded from practically every English port of any consequence. If the summonses were obeyed more than sixty vessels should have appeared, to serve under John Sturmy and Peter Bard as joint 'captains and admirals of the fleet'. Many of the ships' names are known to us from the enrolled lists, such as the *Christopher* of Westminster, the *Plenty* of Great Yarmouth, the *Welfare*, the *Valence* and the *Blithe*. The king, like his father in 1303, hoped to raise considerable forces in Ireland and provided the necessary shipping to bring them over. Once again, Earl Richard of Ulster (Robert Bruce's father-in-law) was put in command of the Irish effort as he had been eleven years before. Summonses were sent to many chiefs of the native Irish, as well as to a fair selection of Anglo-Irish barons and knights. They were assured that service east of the Irish Sea would not be made a precedent. Several historians have cast serious doubts upon Irish participation in the campaign.[10] The earl of Ulster at least appears to have been with the English king at Newminster on May 29th, 1314,[11] and it is hard to believe he would have come empty-handed. The accounts available to Barbour fifty years later were that Edward II had with him 'a great following from Ireland'.[12] Ireland was also expected to provide bowmen and provisions.

About 5,000 infantry were called up from north and south Wales, probably a mixture of spearmen and archers respectively. The total is surprisingly small compared with twice that number of Welshmen who had been on the Falkirk campaign of 1298. On March 9th writs were sent to the midland and northern counties of England demanding some 4,500 men armed with bows. On March 24th this order was superseded by a more extensive call-up which demanded the levying of over 16,000 foot from thirteen English counties. A hundred crossbowmen and archers were called for from Bristol.[13] All told (including the Welsh but excluding any estimate of Irish foot and auxiliary groups such as masons etc.) the infantry required by Edward II for his invasion amounted to some 21,640 men, who were to gather at Wark-on-Tweed on June 10th.[14] Whether anything like this number actually turned up is, of course, another matter. Desertion was common at all stages of a campaign, and often sheriffs were simply unable to find the totals required. Lacking any documentary evidence we are forced to fall back on estimates which are not much better than guess-work. But at

10. The terrain of Bannockburn (1).

least we can try to make intelligent guesses. Dr J. E. Morris, basing his estimates on his extensive knowledge of Edward I's Welsh campaigns and of English campaigns in Scotland prior to 1314, suggested that Edward II may have succeeded in getting together some 15,000 foot.[15] Morris was in principle reluctant to accept the possibility of large concentrations of infantry in Edwardian wars, but he was not aware that in 1296 as many as 60,000 infantry were in pay at Newcastle ready for the campaign against Balliol.[16] Although it is virtually certain that nothing like this number was actually employed in the 1296 campaign, the fact that so large a force was collected at one time and place should put us on our guard against modern writers who pour scorn on all large estimates. One account of the Bannock-burn campaign, whose inclusion in the *Complete Peerage* has unfortunately given it undeserved authority, proposes to reduce the infantry available to Edward II in 1314 to a mere 5,000 all told.[17] This contrasts sharply with Morris's experienced and intelligent guess-work, and indeed hardly deserves serious consideration. But in any case, the actual numbers of infantry in the English army are not of great historical importance, for the battle of Bannockburn was a contest between Scottish infantry and English cavalry: the English foot, contrary to Edward II's surmise in February, played a very small part.

There are similar difficulties in estimating the cavalry, the really impor-tant element in Edward's army. As Morris points out,[18] there was no formal summons of the feudal host by parliamentary consent and in consequence we have no marshal's roll to guide us, and no later remissions of scutage. Nor have we any list of the valuable trained war-horses brought to the campaign, such as survive for several years between 1296 and 1314 when English cavalry was active in Scotland. We are told explicitly by contemporary chroniclers that all but three of the English earls refused to serve person-ally.[19] Taking their cue, presumably, from Lancaster and Warwick, they sent the minimum number of mounted troops required under their feudal obligation of military service. In Morris's view this might have been as few as sixty knights and men-at-arms from all these great noblemen together, a dismal performance by men bearing the proud titles of Lancaster, Warwick, Arundel, Surrey (Warenne), and Oxford. (Norfolk, the king's half-brother, does not seem to have served either, but he was only fourteen). The sheriffs were ordered to raise the feudal service due from the great ecclesiastical lords, the archbishops, bishops and abbots. If the bare minimum of service was rendered from this source it may have totalled some 150 mounted men. On the other hand, a large number of barons below the rank of earl were present willingly, and with them were Humphrey de Bohun earl of Here-ford and Constable of England, Gilbert de Clare earl of Gloucester, and Aymer de Valence earl of Pembroke. These magnates may be expected to have brought with them vastly more than the minimum number of knights and men-at-arms which they owed by way of feudal service. The Roll of

Scotland preserves copies of letters of protection issued to Pembroke, Gloucester and the rest to cover some 890 mounted soldiers (knights, esquires and the more lightly armoured men-at-arms).[20] Morris thinks it not unreasonable to multiply this figure by $2\frac{1}{2}$ or even 3 to arrive at the actual total of mounted troops present at the muster at Berwick on June 10th: some 2,000 or 2,500 men.[21]

To this provisional total we must add an even less certain figure of Scottish and Irish knights and of knights from Gascony and other continental countries. Their number was doubtless small, but there are no grounds for questioning Barbour's report that knights came to fight for Edward 11 from France, Brittany, Poitou, Guienne and Germany. The English king may have been a poor exponent of the art of government but he was not a poltroon. On the contrary, he was a tall, robust, athletic man of considerable physical courage. He was no general, but it is not true that he took no personal interest in the details of the campaign or in the men who were to fight under his standard. In August and October 1313, for example, he wrote no fewer than eleven separate letters to, among others, the *podestà* and city of Genoa and to both the emperors as well as to the empress of Constantinople, interceding for the release of one of his best knights, Sir Giles d'Argentan, who while going to fight at Rhodes had been captured by Christians and imprisoned at Salonika.[22] Sir Giles was duly released and came home to fight his last battle at Bannockburn. Barbour, who mourned his death there, tells us that he was accounted 'the third-best knight of his day'.[23]

Chroniclers' estimates of the number of English cavalry vary, but possibly not so widely as is sometimes alleged. The *Life of Edward II*, certainly written by someone with first-hand or authoritative information about Scottish affairs, puts the total at 'more than 2,000';[24] a Scottish verse account seems to say 3,100;[25] Barbour himself, though he speaks absurdly enough of 40,000 horse, says that there were 3,000 'barded' or 'covered' horse,[26] and if this is the realistic part of his estimate, actually referring to all types of cavalry, it tallies well enough with the other versions. Even if the total was as low as 2,000, that would still represent a very respectable cavalry force, roughly equal to the English cavalry which fought at Falkirk. And Morris is surely wrong to say that 'the English went into battle unprepared and untrained'.[27] They were in fact led by men like Hereford, Sir Hugh Despenser, Sir Henry Beaumont, Sir Robert Clifford, Sir Maurice Berkeley, Sir Marmaduke Tweng, Sir Pain Tiptoft, Sir Giles D'Argentan and many others who were veterans of both Welsh and Scottish wars. In their ranks were Scots, such as Sir Ingram de Umfraville, who had not only fought on the Scottish side but had held the highest positions of command. Above all, in Aymer de Valence the English had a leader who knew Scotland inside out and enjoyed the rare distinction of having been in command against Bruce himself in two pitched battles, the first in open country at Methven, where he won, the second on a narrow site at Loudoun Hill, where he was beaten. If excuses must be sought for the English defeat in 1314, they cannot be found in lack of experience or training. It is surely more sensible not to look for excuses but to acknowledge that for every victory there must also be a defeat. King Edward had an excellent army at Bannockburn, but it made some grave tactical errors and ultimately it was outfought.

King Robert also had an excellent army, but vastly different in character and composition from the English. It was excellent above all else in *morale*. Its core consisted of men who had fought continuously for the past seven years under Bruce himself or under Douglas, Randolph and other famous captains. Almost always they had had the best of the fighting, and their king had gained a European reputation. But they were essentially an infantry army, armed with long iron-tipped spears, with axes, swords, and (to a less extent) with bows.[28] Before 1314 Bruce had not tried to recreate the old 'feudal host' of Scotland. Not only had it been discredited by Dunbar and other events of the time of Comyn ascendancy, but even if Bruce had felt it desirable to reintroduce such a force the necessary armour and trained, large-boned war horses were not to be had in Scotland. These *destriers*, as they were called, were not bred in Scotland, where in winter there was no fodder for animals with such large appetites.[29] All that Bruce had were some 500 light horse under the Marischal, Sir Robert Keith. The rest fought on foot. Despite Stirling Bridge (which was not a battle of the first rank) and Courtrai (which might have been a fluke) the possibility that an army of spearmen could defeat heavy cavalry had still to be convincingly demonstrated. Moreover, in point of numbers it is very doubtful if the Scots could come anywhere near to matching their foes. Unfortunately there is absolutely no reliable evidence on which to base an estimate of Scottish numbers at Bannockburn. Barbour believed that the Scots' strength was about one third that of the English.[30] If this were so, they would have had some 6,000 men against an English army of 2,500 horse and 15,000 foot. But we have no reason to accept or reject Barbour's belief; he may have put the ratio too low, to enhance his hero's merits. We have seen that in 1308 Bruce was thought to have had 3,000 men in Ross and 10,000–15,000 (surely a gross exaggeration?) in Argyll. The forces employed in Bruce's raids south of the Border were too strong to be resisted by the local population, but in view of the breakdown of the Border defence system this is not very significant. If we are to make guesses at all it might be safer to work from estimates which put the total population of Scotland in Bruce's day at about 400,000.[31] This in turn, on a liberal calculation, might give us a figure for men of fighting age of 80,000–100,000. No medieval country could ever hope to raise, train and keep in the field more than a small fraction of its able-bodied males. A tenth would probably be a generous estimate, and this would allow Bruce not more than 10,000. To put the strength of the Scots army at Bannockburn at between 7,000 and 10,000 would be no more than a guess, but probably not a wild guess. Moreover, this would be a comprehensive figure, including many who would take no part in the actual fighting. In terms of effective participants, we may perhaps reckon on a light cavalry force of 500 and four brigades or 'battles' of 1,000 to 1,500 each; say, 5,000–6,000 men. On the other hand, we can scarcely put the Scots total any lower, for we know that the English cavalry was in fact repulsed by mere foot soldiers, and it is hard to believe this could have happened if the ratio of foot to horse had been less than 2 : 1.

The rendezvous appointed by King Robert was the Torwood.[32] This was the ancient woodland stretching from the banks of the River Carron west of Falkirk as far as the Bannock Burn, two and a half miles south of Stirling. In the twelfth century it had been known by the Gaelic name of Keltor (*coille torr*), 'wood of rocky outcrops'.[33] In Bruce's time, the area was referred to by persons writing in French as *les Torres*, and the Guardians had in fact dated one of their letters to Edward I in 1299 'at the forest *del Torre*'.[34] It was a well-chosen rendezvous, better than Wallace's position east of Falkirk in 1298. There was good cover; to the west were hills and broken country; to the north and east boggy 'carseland', that is, low-lying ground beside a tidal estuary. Through the forest ran the high road from Edinburgh to Stirling, on a line about 250 feet above sea-level, pioneered by the Roman soldiers who built a marching way from the Antonine Wall through to Strathallan and Strathearn. The enemy would have to traverse this road, as William the Conqueror and Edward the Conqueror had done before them. Bruce was gathering his men in the Torwood by the middle of May at latest, for on May 27th King Edward, then at Newminster in Northumberland, wrote to his sheriffs and recruiting officers to say that 'the Scots are striving to assemble great numbers of foot in strong and marshy places, extremely hard for cavalry to penetrate, between us and our castle of Stirling'.[35] He commanded them to urge the infantry forward as fast as possible, or else Stirling would have to surrender.

Bruce, however, did not mean to fight in the Torwood, and had not even decided whether to give battle at all. The English host left Berwick and Wark about June 17th.[36] Contemporaries described it as 'a very fine and large army', 'more than 2,000 armoured horse and a very large number of infantry', and wrote with amazement of the waggons carrying provisions and equipment: 'if they had been lined up end to end they would have stretched for twenty miles'.[37] The route taken was the same as Edward I's in 1298, up Lauderdale and over Soutra Moor to Edinburgh[38] – again on the general line, although not necessarily in the exact path, of a Roman road. Time was running short if the king was to keep his promise to be before Stirling by June 24th. The army was urged forward unsparingly during those warm midsummer days: 'short time was allowed for sleep, still shorter for meals'.[39] There was a brief halt at Edinburgh, reached about June 19th, and then on Saturday 22nd, when there would have been some nineteen or twenty hours of daylight, the whole army marched the twenty miles to Falkirk.[40] Fourteen miles and an army now lay between them and their goal. On this same Saturday the Scots were drawn up in the Torwood in four brigades, as for retreat.[41] Thomas Randolph, earl of Moray, led the vanguard, the brigade nearest to Stirling. The king, commanding the rearguard, covered the retreat at the extreme eastern end of the Scottish position. In between, side by side, were the other two brigades. One was nominally under the command of Walter the Stewart, the heir, though younger son, of James the Stewart. Since he was a mere youth, the actual command was held by James Douglas, Walter Stewart's cousin.[42] The fact that Douglas, who had already proved himself one of Bruce's most brilliant captains, should even nominally yield command to the hereditary Stewart of Scotland is a notable illustration of the conservatism of Scottish feudal society. But of course the arrangement did not prevent full use being made of Douglas's generalship. The other brigade was commanded by the king's brother Edward. Barbour gives us the composition only of the king's brigade.[43] It comprised the men of Carrick (although Edward Bruce was now earl of Carrick), the men of Argyll, Bute and the Isles,[44] many under Angus Macdonald of Islay, and 'ane mekill rout' of men from the 'playne land', presumably meaning the central lowlands and perhaps Fife and Strathmore. It is commonsense reasoning, not contemporary evidence, which suggests that Moray's brigade was made up of men from Moray and elsewhere in the north, Edward Bruce's of men from the south-west, including Galloway, and the Stewart-Douglas brigade of men from Strathclyde. During Saturday, as the English army made the last of its forced marches, the Scots withdrew from the Torwood to the next position chosen by Bruce, the wooded 'New Park',[45] a stretch of enclosed hunting preserve roughly one mile from north to south by two miles from east to west. At the point where the road entered it the New Park was set back half a mile north of the Bannock Burn, a fair sized stream which formed the only serious natural obstacle (apart from forest) between the Carron and Stirling. In the New Park they retained their order for retreat. The vanguard was now beside St Ninians kirk, only a mile or so from Stirling castle. Douglas and Edward Bruce were slightly to the south. The king's brigade halted at the 'entry' to the New Park. This was the point where the main road entered the woodland, on the edge of the higher ground overlooking the Bannock Burn from the north and west. Here, partly hidden by trees, King Robert and the men of his brigade took up their position towards evening on Saturday, June 22nd, and watched for the first signs of the great host which had now approached so near.

At this point our narrative too must halt. The battle of Bannockburn was a complex affair occupying two days. Its course cannot be understood unless we have some general knowledge of the terrain and some degree of certainty about the actual localities in which the successive phases of the conflict took place. At the risk of putting the cart before the horse it seems better to establish the site of the battle before resuming the story.

Historians have given serious consideration to four different sites. The so-called 'traditional' site, marked by a statue and Visitor Centre, is at the Borestone, between Milton and St Ninians. The Reverend Thomas Miller and Brigadier-General Carruthers proposed a small but important modification of this site, which would place the main battle about three-quarters of a mile further east, on the Dryfield of Balquhiderock.[46] According to Dr Mackay Mackenzie's revolutionary hypothesis, the main battle was fought right down on the Carse of Stirling, in the vicinity of Upper Taylorton and Muirton, between two and three miles north-east of the traditional site and the same distance due north of Bannockburn village.[47] General Sir Philip Christison has put forward a case for locating the main battle in the triangle formed by the Bannock Burn, its tributary the Pelstream Burn and the 50 foot contour, in what used to be called the Carse of Balquhiderock.[48] The Christison site (adopted as the most probable by the National Trust for Scotland) is about half way between the traditional and the Mackenzie site.

These suggestions can be weighed only if we have in our mind's eye some idea of the surrounding terrain. The country east and south of Stirling is divided into three clearly-marked zones, radiating from Stirling Castle like three successive segments of a circle. First, in the north, is the great Carse of Stirling, flat, boggy ground which in 1314 consisted in places, but apparently not everywhere, of a deep layer of peat lying on impervious clay.[49] This carseland is bordered on the north by the sinuous course of the tidal River Forth. The southern edge of the carse is clearly marked by a steep bank at the 50 and 100 foot contours, which follow a remarkably straight line south-eastward from Stirling. South-west of this comes the second or intermediate zone, some two to three miles wide, consisting of better-drained ground, firm though undulating, rising gradually from 100 to about 300 feet. Westward of this zone, sloping steadily upward from 300 feet, is broken country of poor soil, which rises without any break to the rough muirland and hills around the headwaters of the Carron and the Bannock Burn, 1,400 feet to 1,800 feet above the sea. It is vital for an understanding of the terrain as a whole and of the battle of Bannockburn in particular to realise that a considerable quantity of water drains off this hilly country through the intermediate zone and down into the carse, where in the fourteenth century it had somehow or other to make its way across peat and clay only a few feet above the level of high tide. In addition, a fair number of springs rise in the intermediate zone itself, and especially along its northern edge, at the foot of the bank marking the 50 foot contour. As a result, the carse was intersected by a large number of sluggish streams, some big, most of them little. These streams were known by the Celtic word *pol* ('pow' in later Scots) which in southern and central Scotland was widely applied to burns, especially those flowing sluggishly through carseland, often having deep peaty pools with crumbling, overhanging banks. Today the Carse of Stirling is relatively well-drained farmland, interspersed with disused coal mines and railway tracks. The pows have largely disappeared, but their presence in former times is betrayed by place-names. In the parish of St Ninians alone (where the battle of Bannockburn was fought) one may still list Polmaise, Cockspow, Drypow, Powdrake, Powside, Powbridge, Pow Burn and the *Pel*stream burn, while just across the Forth is the old estate of Powis.[50] Polmaise, indeed, which means 'sluggish stream in the plain', may well have been the ancient name of the Bannock Burn itself, for this stream is the largest of the pows between Stirling and the Carron. Not surprisingly, the entire Carse of Stirling was known in Bruce's time simply as *les Polles*, 'the pows',[51] the generic term for all these slow-running streams having become the colloquial name of a district, just as the district of the Torwood was known as *les Torres*.

Historians of Bannockburn have failed to grasp the fact that the carse was known as *les Polles* from the streams which intersected it, or else they have not seen the implications of this fact. On the contrary, most writers, especially Mackenzie and those who have followed him, not only supposed, quite mistakenly, that the *polles* were *pools*,[52] but have located these pools well to the north, in the 'buckle of the Forth', close to the tidal mouth of the Bannock Burn. Most modern sketch-maps of the battle are disfigured by a pimply rash of these imaginary pools. The point is important because the *polles* had their part to play in the battle and have been cited in various ways as evidence of where it was fought.

For an army approaching Stirling from the south-east, the choice of route was thus extremely restricted. The westernmost zone of moor and hills was quite impracticable. The northern zone, the *Pows*, was hardly less so, for although it was level enough it was boggy and intersected by countless streams of uncertain depth. These would be no obstacle to a man on foot, nor to small parties of horsemen; but cumulatively they would reduce a large army with its baggage train to helpless floundering. The advance therefore could only be by way of the intermediate zone of undulating wooded country; ideally, along the high road which naturally followed a line through the middle of this zone.

The New Park was merely a northerly continuation of the Torwood, from which it was separated by the open cultivated ground of the Bannock Burn valley. The park had been fenced in by King Alexander III as late as 1264 – hence 'New Park' to distinguish it from the older 'King's Park' just beneath Stirling Castle.[53] But despite what is shown on the maps of many modern historians, the New Park (as Miller made clear)[54] did not extend right across the intermediate zone from the hills on the west to the very edge of the carse

11. The terrain of Bannockburn (2).

on the north-east. It is true that the high road ran into the park, at the 'entry', and then through the park to St Ninians kirk. But east of the park were the lands of Balquhiderock, which were under cultivation for corn in 1215[55] and can hardly have been swallowed up by forest as a result of King Alexander's creation of the New Park fifty years later. Like most estates on the edge of the intermediate zone, Balquhiderock had a share of that zone, known as 'dryfield', and a share of the peaty carse.

The terrain in the neighbourhood of the Scots position, as it would appear to the English, may therefore be pictured as follows. On one side the main road ran down out of the Torwood and over some open country, to cross the Bannock Burn at Milton, and then up across more open ground to enter fairly thick woodland near the Borestone. On the other side, well to the east, there was a plateau of open cornland, some half a mile wide, between the woodland and the bank where the hard ground slopes steeply to the carse.

One further point must be insisted upon before this survey of the terrain is complete. Few historians have given it serious thought, yet it seems a point of crucial importance. The place where the Bannock Burn crosses the intermediate zone and, flowing here between high, steep banks in a minia-ture ravine, enters the carse was in 1314 an inhabited locality with a long history behind it. It was called Bannok, a name which must go far back into the Celtic past.[56] Perhaps we should not speak of Bannok as a 'village', with its implications of a close-knit huddle of houses along a village street. Nevertheless, Bannok was the name of a distinct inhabited place, an estate or group of estates, a social and agrarian entity within the larger parish of St Ninians. Moreover, Bannok was the name of a *place*, not of a *stream*. The stream known as the Bannock Burn was named after the place, not the other way round.[57] And even the name 'Bannockburn' was itself coming to be applied in the fourteenth century to the place called Bannok.[58] For about a century and a half the two names were used as alternatives, but from the late fifteenth century the name Bannok dropped out, being completely super-seded by Bannockburn. There is no reason to believe that the nucleus of this settlement is not represented today by the village of Bannockburn.

Bannok, *alias* Bannockburn, was large enough to have subdivisions. The upland part was Ochtirbannok, 'high ground of Bannok'. This was what later came to be known as Milton.[59] The part where the Bannock Burn entered the carse was known as Skeoch.[60] This tell-tale name shows that Bannok was associated by a cult dedication with an obscure saint called Skeoch, an Irishwoman of the sixth century.[61] Saint Skeoch was com-memorated at a holy well near St Ninians called after her Tibbermasko, 'Saint Skeoch's Well'.[62] At Bannok there was a chapel dedicated to the Blessed Virgin and called 'the chapel of Skeoch *alias* Bannockburn'.[63] It may be guessed that originally this was dedicated to Skeoch herself. On the Bannock Burn there seem to have been two mills, the first to be mentioned (1215) being the 'mill of Bannoc',[64] while we have later references to the 'mill of Bannockburn called "le mylne de Skeoch" or "Skeochmilne"'.[65] The mill of Bannok presumably stood at Milton (Ochtirbannok), where the main road crossed the burn; Skeoch Mill is half a mile further downstream. There was plenty of cornland in the Bannock Burn valley to justify these mills: record of 1215 mentions corn tithes payable from Skeoch, Balquhiderock and Ochtirbannok.[66]

It has been necessary to demonstrate at such length the existence of an old-established locality of Bannok or Bannockburn because historians have assumed that the battle of Bannockburn was named not after a place but after the stream. It is at least reasonable to suppose that if a geographical name is given to a battle it bears some relation to the actual site. The naming of the battle of Bannockburn is illuminating. At first, as one might expect, the battle was not given any name at all. None of our three best early chronicle sources, the *Life of Edward the Second*, the Lanercost Chronicle and the *Scalacronica*, refers to the battle by name; even Barbour, whose account is much the longest we have, does not give it a name himself, although this is supplied in a chapter-heading added much later. Next, there seems to have been a tendency, at least among those far from the scene, to refer to it as the 'battle of Stirling', obviously taking the name of the nearest well-known place, and of the castle for whose possession the battle was fought. This was used in south-country chronicles written at St Albans and London[67] and in letters written by Englishmen in the period 1314–1319.[68] But contemporary with this English usage we find, in Scottish sources only, that writers referred to the 'battle of Bannok', and events were actually dated '*ante* Bannok'.[69] It was possible, in Scotland, to write of the 'battle of Bannok' as late as the fifteenth century.[70] Almost, but not quite, as early to appear was the familiar 'battle of Bannockburn', invariably used in modern times. Two English chroniclers, John de Trokelowe and the canon of Bridlington, writing in the 1320s and 1330s respectively, already used this name,[71] and it occurs in an English inquest of 1357.[72] It was taken up by Scottish writers considerably later. John Fordun (1384–87) does not use it, but his fifteenth-century editors and continuators introduced it into their versions of his chronicle, and Andrew Wyntoun (c. 1420) speaks twice of the battle of Bannockburn.[73]

Lastly, we should note that some fourteenth-century writers tell us roughly where the battle took place, whether or not they give it a formal name. John de Trokelowe says that the battle was fought 'in the place called *Bannokesmora*' ('on the muir of Bannok').[74] A Welsh chronicle, the *Brut y Tywysogion*, in what is probably the earliest surviving reference to the battle, says it was fought in *y polles*,[75] that is, in *les Polles* or the Pows, the general name for the district of the Carse of Stirling. *Bannokesmora* would appear to be preserved today as Muir of Bannockburn, south of the modern village, an impossible site for the main battle. Alternatively this name might refer to the carse; but since it is unique, one cannot be certain what place was meant.

The Chronicle of Meaux ($c.$ 1406) says that the battle was fought 'in the field of Bannok near Stirling'.[76] The Oxfordshire clerk Geoffrey Baker of Swinbrook says merely that the battle took place in the district called Stirling; for him, even this name was outlandish.[77] Fordun, who writes of the 'battle of Bannok', implies that it took place when the English had got as far as Bannockburn, but it is not clear whether he meant the stream or the inhabited place. Walter Bower, who wrote an expanded version of Fordun's chronicle in the fifteenth century, tells an extremely interesting story in which Edward II's defeat is seen as a judgement for the cruel way in which the English treated Simon de Montfort.[78] The tale concerns a vision of a great battle 'at Bannockburn in Scotland', and an aged Scottish pensioner lodging at Glastonbury Abbey in Somerset explains to the abbot that 'Bannockburn is a place near to the royal burgh of Stirling in Scotland'.[79]

The evidence reviewed here shows that the battle got its name not from the stream (which would, in any case, be most unusual) but from the place at which it was believed to have been fought. If this is accepted, the site proposed by Mackenzie is ruled out of serious consideration. Had the battle really been fought around Muirton and Upper Taylorton in the 'buckle of the Forth', it could not have come to be known as the Battle of Bannok or Bannockburn, for two much better-known places, Stirling and St Ninians, are closer to the Mackenzie site than the obscure settlement made famous by Bruce's victory. The Welsh report of a battle in *y polles* has been taken to support the Mackenzie site[80] but cannot be taken in this way, because the *polles* were not pools and even if there were pools in the 'buckle of the Forth' these are strictly irrelevant. We are left with a choice from among the three remaining possibilities, the 'traditional', the Miller-Carruthers and the Christison sites. The 'traditional' site was successfully disposed of by Mackenzie, who in this has been followed by every serious student since he wrote. Consequently, we must choose either the Dryfield of Balquhiderock or the Carse of Balquhiderock. The narrative which follows is based upon a belief that the main conflict, on June 24th, took place on the Dryfield.

On Sunday, June 23rd, as we have seen, the Scottish army was drawn up in four brigades among the trees of the New Park. The vanguard, under Moray, was stationed by St Ninians kirk, at the northern end of the park. The rearguard, commanded by the king in person, was stationed at the 'entry'. Here it covered the main road, not only at the point where it entered the wood but also from that point down to the crossing of the Bannock Burn. The brigades of Douglas and Edward Bruce were somewhere in between. Their exact positions can only be guessed at, but Douglas was evidently nearer to Moray. King Robert knew that the position he had chosen was one of great natural strength. 'The enemy,' he said, 'are bound to try to pass through the New Park, unless they go below us across the marsh (i.e., the carse to the north). Thus, either way, we shall be at an advantage. On foot, among the trees, we shall get the better of mounted men; alternatively, the 'sikes' (i.e., the pows or streams of the carse) will put their cavalry out of action.'[81] But to make assurance double sure, Bruce used a device reminiscent of something he had done at Loudoun Hill in 1307, when he had compelled Valence to advance on a narrow front. At Loudoun his small force had stood athwart a road with treacherous mires on either side, and he built a triple earthwork to fill up the space between the bog and the road.[82] Now, in a similar situation, he had the ground on either side of the road honeycombed (the metaphor is Barbour's) with small pits or 'pots', covered with sticks and grass.[83] The modern analogy would be with a minefield, designed not only to cause casualties itself but to force the enemy to bunch at a single well-guarded spot.

Early in the morning the Scots heard mass.[84] Their day's meal was bread and water, for they kept the fast appropriate to the eve of Saint John Baptist. In good heart, they waited while Bruce sent Douglas and Keith with a party of horse to spy out the English advance. What these experienced soldiers saw disturbed them, but on their return Bruce ordered them to suppress their news of a vast and well-armed host, and instead to tell their men that the enemy was coming ill-arrayed. In truth, all was not well among the English ranks. Their mistakes began early. The cavalry pressed forward with reckless impetuosity. All our detailed accounts give an impression of the total absence of any single directing hand. King Edward, it is clear, neither took effective command in person nor delegated the sole command to any of his veteran officers. On the contrary, with tactlessness remarkable even in a Plantagenet, the king appointed as constable for the occasion the young earl of Gloucester, Gilbert de Clare, his own nephew.[85] This act gave needless offence to the much more experienced earl of Hereford, Humphrey de Bohun, who was not only Constable of England by hereditary right but also, as lord of Brecknock, an old and bitter rival of the Clare lords of neighbouring Glamorgan. Yet these two proud and quarrelsome noblemen held joint command of the vanguard, the *corps d'élite* of the English host and – since the English were drawn up in the order for advance – the leading brigade among the ten into which the mounted troops were formed. Early on Sunday, the governor of Stirling Castle, Sir Philip Moubray – presumably armed with a Scottish safe-conduct – rode out to meet the English king. He had a much clearer idea than anyone in the English army of the strength of the Scottish position, and urged the difficulty of a direct attack through the New Park, where the Scots had blocked all the narrow paths. In any case, as Moubray explained, honour had been saved now that the English king had come so near to Stirling by the appointed date: he would not now be obliged to surrender the castle.[86] Moubray's advice, we may guess, was 'Wait and see; the Scots may now retire and the castle be relieved without bloodshed'.

Gloucester and Hereford never got to know of Moubray's good advice.

Beyond reach of effective orders from the king they pressed on through the Torwood until, somewhere about Snabhead, they could see, across the valley, a number of Scots scattered in front of the New Park, apparently in the act of withdrawing.[87] The day must now have been well advanced. Impatiently, the young knights and esquires spurred their horses forward down the high road, crossed the Bannock Burn, and rode as hard as they could up the hill towards the enemy lines. In the very front were some of Hereford's retainers with their Welsh followers, presumably all mounted. It was now that an unbelievable opportunity of glory came to Sir Henry de Bohun, Hereford's nephew,[88] and endowed him with immortality. In front of him was one of the enemy soldiers, separated from his fellows, clad in mail, armed with a hand-axe, and mounted on a small sturdy grey. His helmet, covered by a leather crest, was surmounted by a high crown. To vanquish the king of Scots himself in single combat: such a feat of chivalry did not often come the way of an ambitious knight. Henry de Bohun rode at Bruce, lance at rest. Bruce pulled himself out of the path of the oncoming lance, so that, in Barbour's memorable line, 'Schir Henry myssit the nobill kyng'.[89] As he drew level, Bruce raised himself up in his stirrups and with a mighty effort swung his axe downward so fiercely that the blade pierced Bohun's helmet and split his head in two. Bohun's body fell to the earth beside him, and Bruce was left holding the stump of his axe-shaft, shattered by the tremendous impact. The Scots, gathered at the edge of the wood and witnessing this extraordinary scene, exulted in their king's prowess, still more in his safe emergence from the encounter. But their leaders rebuked him severely for risking his life and their whole cause in this reckless fashion. They were right, of course; but Bruce himself turned aside their rebukes, ruefully lamenting his broken axe-shaft. By rights, the incident ought never to have occurred; yet its effect on the highlanders, islesmen and others in the king's brigade can be imagined and the story, as it spread back through the rest of the army, would lose nothing in the telling. The Scots at the 'entry' surged forward to meet and repulse the oncoming English horsemen. The earl of Gloucester, well to the fore, was knocked off his horse in the mêlée. This was no minor skirmish, but a serious engagement in which Bruce's brigade took a full part and in which Edward Bruce's men may have joined also.[90] But after some fierce fighting at close quarters, in which the English van suffered sufficient casualties to make a lasting impression, the main body of cavalry withdrew south of the Bannock Burn, still intact. The Scots exultantly pursued them, but (the fact is a striking tribute to the discipline King Robert exercised over his army) they were recalled before any harm was done.

In the meantime, while Gloucester and Hereford were pressing forward impetuously to attack the Scots at the 'entry', another cavalry division under Sir Robert Clifford and Sir Henry Beaumont set off northward, towards the carse, in an attempt to by-pass the New Park altogether and force a way through to Stirling on the left flank of the Scots position.[91] Estimates of the strength of this division vary. Sir Thomas Grey, whose father, Sir Thomas Grey the elder, of Heaton on the Till, was one of its prominent members, puts it at 300;[92] Barbour says 800.[93] Probably Grey's figure is nearer the mark, for the cavalry, some 2,500 to 3,000 in all, were divided into ten brigades or squadrons which were presumably equal in numbers. On the other hand, Clifford and Beaumont, who had three bannerets under them,[94] may have commanded two of the ten cavalry brigades. It was obviously no mere patrol or raiding party, but a body of considerable fighting power. It has, indeed, been suggested that Clifford was carrying out a reconnaissance in strength;[95] his object that is, was to find out whether there was a practicable route by which the whole army could reach Stirling without going into the New Park at all. This may have been the case, but the suggestion finds no support among contemporary writers. What most modern commentators seem to forget is that until the very last moment the English were confident that the Scots would not fight a pitched battle in daylight. Their tactics were based on this belief, and can only be explained in accordance with it. Gloucester and Hereford attacked Scots 'who seemed to be in retreat'.[96] Clifford, according to the Lanercost Chronicle, 'wished to ride round the [New Park] to prevent the Scots escaping by flight'.[97] Barbour's explanation is that Clifford was put in command of a specially selected squadron whose task was to force a way through to the castle and relieve it:[98] in other words, its purpose was the same as that of the vanguard, only the route was different. Grey attempts no explanation. He merely says that Clifford and Beaumont rode round the New Park in the direction of the castle. The lack of discipline and direction in the English army was such that we cannot really be sure what Clifford's intentions were. For all we know, the king may have been as little consulted about Clifford's advance as he was about Gloucester's, while it seems certain that between Gloucester and Clifford there was no liaison whatever.

Clifford's party probably crossed the Bannock Burn near the present village and headed straight for Stirling. As Grey and Barbour both emphasize, they kept to the open country well clear of the New Park and its trees. Whether this took them down on to the carse, just below the 50 foot contour, or whether they crossed the higher ground between Balquhiderock and Broomridge, is not clear. Barbour says that 'they completely avoided the New Park, for they knew well that the king [of Scots] was there. They went below the New Park, until they were below the church [St Ninians kirk], all in company.'[99] Whatever their route, they cannot have expected an attack. A large body of mail-clad knights on powerful horses, moving in close formation across open country, could feel confident that the Scots spearmen would stay in the shelter of the wood. Indeed, they reached a point beneath St Ninians kirk without being molested. Whether or not they had crossed the boggy Pelstream Burn, they must by now have been sure of winning through to Stirling.

Bruce, however, had seen Clifford's squadron riding off northward to make a circuit of the New Park. It was to provide against just such a movement that he had stationed Moray near St Ninians kirk, to guard the road and prevent an enemy break-through on the Scottish flank. The way in which Bruce had arranged his brigades shows, incidentally, that the idea of an English cavalry advance right out on the carse never occurred to the Scots. It is easy therefore to understand Bruce's sudden anger when he realized that Clifford had drawn level with St Ninians without being challenged by Moray.[100] Indeed, at this moment, Moray was actually with the king, apparently unaware of the English advance. In a terse, graphic rebuke, the king told him that a rose had fallen from his chaplet; he had been stationed to 'keep the way', yet the English had slipped past him.[101]

Stung by the rebuke, angry with himself for a mistake that could cost the Scots the whole battle, Moray rode furiously back to his men. The situation was not quite hopeless. Clifford had still to advance across ground near enough to the wood for the Scottish footmen to reach it by a short march into the open. This is proved by Beaumont's immediate reaction as he saw the bristling hedgehog of spearmen coming out to meet the English knights. 'Let them come on,' he cried, 'give them some ground. We must draw back a little.'[102] Instinctively, he wanted the horse to have more room to manoeuvre. Sir Thomas Grey took a more serious view. 'My lord,' he said to Beaumont, 'give them what you like now; I'm afraid that in a short while they will have everything.' 'Flee then,' retorted Beaumont, 'flee, if you're afraid.' 'Fear will not make me flee, my lord,' was Grey's answer as he put spurs to his horse and, with Sir William Deyncourt, rode straight at the advancing line of spears. Deyncourt was killed at once, Grey was pulled from his mortally wounded horse and made prisoner. The battle that followed was fierce and exhausting. The spearmen sweated in the heat of the afternoon, and clouds of dust rose as the hooves of the heavy *destriers* churned up the dry earth. The whole object of Moray's schiltrom was to hold tightly together, presenting the mailed knights with an impenetrable hedge of spearpoints wherever they attacked. The horsemen for their part tried to rush the schiltrom, redoubling their efforts to find a weak point in its ranks so that they could pierce the whole formation and break it up. At Falkirk the cavalry had only been able to do this after archers had rained arrows and bolts down upon the infantry. Clifford had no archers, but at the same time Moray had a stiffer task than Wallace to keep his schiltrom unbroken. At Falkirk the schiltroms were static, dug in behind low palisades, whereas Moray's schiltrom was a freely moving group exposed and isolated on open arable. Training and discipline were to tell now, as never before on the Scottish side. Their own lances proving useless, the baffled knights hurled swords and maces, piling up a mountain of weapons inside the schiltrom. As at Falkirk, the Scots aimed their spears at the horses as much as at their riders. Most of the English casualties were no doubt caused by the unhorsing of knights encumbered with heavy armour. At last the impetus of the English attack was broken. The Scots, still holding together, pressed home their advantage, and the whole English squadron, or what remained of it, scattered and fled, some making for Stirling Castle, some (including Clifford) riding back the way they had come.

This hard fight between Moray and Clifford was the crisis of the whole battle, even though it involved relatively small numbers on both sides. Its critical character was understood by Douglas, Moray's colleague and friendly rival, and when the issue still seemed in doubt he implored the king to let him lead his own brigade to Moray's assistance.[103] With admirable coolness, Bruce held Douglas back. The day was late, admittedly, but there would be light for some hours yet. He could not be sure what further attempts the English would make. Bruce did, on the other hand, have confidence in his nephew's courage and soldierly skill. In the end, Douglas could contain his patience no longer, and led his men out of the wood, but only when all was over. The sense of chivalry for which he was famous made him halt, lest Moray and his sturdy spearmen should not enjoy all the glory earned by their exertions. Exhausted, soaked in sweat, Moray's men took off their helmets to feel the cool fresh air. Then they went to the king and reported their triumph, won with almost no casualties on the Scottish side. The rest of the army crowded round to congratulate them and salute the earl. His victory had in fact achieved two things of the utmost importance. It proved, firstly, that the schiltrom of spearmen in close formation could be used successfully as a mobile unit to attack armoured cavalry. Secondly, it stopped the English opening up a route to Stirling Castle; indeed, it seems to have stopped them making any but the most surreptitious contact with Moubray's garrison. It also greatly raised the spirits of the Scots and added enormously to the discomfiture of English *morale*. All our accounts agree that this second setback, coming after the repulse suffered by Gloucester and Hereford, spread gloom and confusion among the English.[104]

It was late in the day by the time Clifford and Beaumont regained the main body. No further attempts would be made before morning to penetrate the Scots position. Much the greater part of the English army had had no contact with the enemy, probably not even a sight of them. But all were exhausted by the heat and by hurried marches. Horses would have to be watered, and the men would need a meal and some rest. The aggressiveness of Bruce had alarmed the English into thinking that a night attack was not impossible, so proper sleep was out of the question. But a place had to be found where the army could rest and yet be ready to attack the Scots in the morning, if they were still there; a place, moreover, where men could bivouac and horses be given water. It was probably this last consideration that lay behind the dangerous decision to put all the cavalry and perhaps a part of the infantry across the Bannock Burn. Only Barbour and Grey describe this difficult and perilous manoeuvre. In modern English, what Barbour has to say is this.

> They bivouacked there that night, down in the carse, and made every man clean and prepare his weapons and armour to be ready for battle in the morning. And because there were 'pows' [sluggish streams] in the carse, they broke down houses and roofing and carried it off to make bridges by which to cross [the streams]. There are also some surviving who say that nearly all the men in the castle, knowing the difficulty the English army was in, came out after dark [that is, about midnight], taking with them doors and windows. In this way the English had before daylight bridged the pows, so that everyone crossed over and had taken up a position on horseback on the hard field.[105]

A translation of Grey's French gives this picture, different in some respects, yet not incompatible or contradictory.

> The king's host left the road through the wood and came into a plain in the direction of the River Forth, beyond Bannock Burn, an evil, deep marsh with streams, where the English troops unharnessed and remained all night in discomfort, being mortified and badly troubled by the events of the previous day.[106]

It is possible that Grey's words ought to be translated 'beyond Bannock Burn, an evil, deep, boggy stream';[107] either way, it is clear that the cavalry at least did cross the Bannock Burn during the night. On this point the Lanercost Chronicle and the *Life of Edward II* confirm Barbour and Grey, for the one states explicitly that the English had crossed the Bannock Burn before the battle, and the other implies it.[108] The *Life of Edward II* also confirms the impression of watchfulness, anxiety, and sleeplessness conveyed by Grey, for it says that when the English bivouacked they got no rest, spending the night without sleep in constant fear of a Scottish attack. And Barbour, with his account of pulling houses down, making bridges across the numerous pows, and getting arms and armour ready for battle likewise implies that the English spent a sleepless night. No doubt the main purpose of the bridges was to make sure that the heavy horses did not sink in the treacherous peat through which the streams, including the Bannock Burn itself, flowed. There was also the problem of transporting the king's household and tents and baggage across the carseland, for it cannot be supposed that Edward of Caernarvon, however brave and athletic, was forced to bivouac like a common knight.

These few hours of darkness between Saturday and Sunday contained all the suspense and drama of the battle of Bannockburn. For while the English were groping and floundering about down in the carse, wet, uncomfortable and depressed, their infantry drinking themselves into an unreal cheerfulness with cries of 'Wassail' and 'Drinkhail',[109] the Scots were actually proposing to withdraw altogether from their strong position in front of Stirling, and find a fresh base somewhere in the Lennox, a country too wild for the English army to reach.[110] So powerful and deep-seated was Bruce's inclination to avoid pitched battles and wage guerrilla warfare, an un-knightly policy which only harsh and bitter experience had taught him. But Grey says that during the hours of darkness a Scots knight in English service, Sir Alexander Seton, disgusted by the lack of leadership and dispiritedness among the English barons and knights, made his way to Bruce's camp and gained an audience of the king. 'My lord king, now is the time, if ever you mean to win Scotland. The English have lost heart; they are discomfited, and expect nothing but a sudden and open attack. I swear, on my head and on pain of being hanged and drawn, that if you attack them in the morning you will defeat them easily without loss.'[111] If Seton was the same man who allied himself with Neil Campbell and (Thomas?) Hay of Lochwharret, c. 1308–10, then he knew Bruce and his cause well from personal experience. The three men had taken an oath together to defend the liberty of the realm, and Robert lately crowned king, against all mortal men, English, French and Scots, 'till the very end of their lives'. Although this band has survived only in unsatisfactory sources,[112] we can accept that it was actually made. Its language is fascinating evidence of continuity between Wallace and Bruce, between the time of the Guardians and the Declaration of Arbroath [113] And Seton's actions in making the band with Campbell and Hay and in tipping the scales at Bannockburn underline the fact that the class of lairds, middling nobles, played a decisive rôle in the war with England, even more under Robert I than under John.

Barbour makes the debate on whether or not to stand and fight at Bannockburn take place in a public assembly after Moray's victory.[114] Although this artistically more satisfying story of Barbour's is probably largely invention, there is no reason to doubt the gist of what he says. The king asked his leaders if they should fight or not. With one voice their answer was 'Good King, as soon as day comes tomorrow order yourself and your army for battle. We shall not fail for fear of death, nor flinch at any suffering till we have made our country free.'

Both the days on which the battle of Bannockburn was fought were apparently warm and sunny. Unless the night was cloudy, there would have been no real darkness,[115] only some five hours of dusk blurring the sharp outlines of the landscape: across the Forth, the Ochils rising steeply out of the plain beyond the tower of Cambuskenneth Abbey and the abrupt bluff of the Abbey Craig; to the west, the rock of Stirling, and beyond it, in the far distance, the highland hills. At about a quarter past three by modern reckoning, the first light of Monday, June 24th, would have begun to spread into the sky over the Firth of Forth. Within an hour or so it would pick out more and more distinctly to English eyes the bank at the 50–100 foot contours, perhaps grown with trees and bushes, beyond which lay the New Park, where the Scots waited, hearing mass and eating a spartan breakfast.

When Barbour says that the English bivouacked 'down in the carse' and Grey tells us that they debouched into 'a plain in the direction of the River Forth, beyond Bannock Burn', we may conclude that the English cavalry got what rest they could somewhere in the area bounded by the Pelstream Burn, the Bannock Burn and the 50 foot contour. On the previous evening and during the night they had come down from the high ground by the Roman road, probably on a wide front, on to the Carse of Skeoch. At St Peter's Well in Bannockburn village, at another well beside the place where in modern times Bannockburn railway station was built, and also in the Bannock Burn itself, the horses could have been watered with little difficulty. We may then imagine the cavalry brigades picking their way slowly and uncertainly north-westward along the carse, negotiating the pows on bridges improvised out of beams and planks removed from the houses of Bannok. The Bannock Burn itself was probably too wide to be crossed this way. There would have been delay while the various units, still spread out on a wide front, waited their turn at the few existing fords. Even when they reached a resting-place, horses were kept bridled, and the men had their arms in readiness.

Neither Barbour nor Grey gives any support to the belief that the fighting on Monday took place here, where the English rested, in the boggy Carse of Balquhiderock. From this area the Scots position in the New Park would have been invisible. Before daybreak, says Barbour, the cavalry had reached the 'hard field',[116] and it was upon this 'hard field' or 'plain hard field'[117] – surely the firm ground between Balquhiderock and Broomridge – that he says the battle was fought. If the leading English brigades were not far above the 100 foot contour, where in daylight they could see the Scots, then it is true that several of the rear brigades, even though huddled altogether 'in one schiltrom', as Barbour says,[118] must still have been down on the carse, below the 50 foot contour. But at the outset, just before the fighting began, the opposing armies were in sight of each other. Baston, the Carmelite friar brought to glorify an English triumph in verse but compelled by the Scots who captured him to versify in the opposite sense, speaks of the battle on the *arida terra Strivelini*,[119] the dry arable of Stirling, which recalls the name 'dryfield' by which the ground above the 50 foot contour was known in earlier times.[120] Moreover, Grey, Barbour and the *Life of Edward II* agree that the battle was begun simply by the Scots advancing out of the 'wood' or New Park. If all the English had still been down on the carse, the Scots would have had to march more than half a mile before even coming in sight. Nor is there anything in contemporary accounts to suggest that the Scots were on appreciably higher ground,[121] as they had been at Stirling Bridge. What contemporaries do say or imply, without exception, is that the battle field was extremely constricted, indeed fatally so for the English. Admittedly, Barbour's phrase 'the great straitness of the place'[122] would apply to the Carse of Balquhiderock. But if in 1314 it was taken for granted that no one in his senses would fight a heavy cavalry action in carseland, the phrase fits the Dryfield of Balquhiderock quite as well, if not better.

The nearest we are ever likely to get to Robert Bruce's words at Bannock-burn is the speech attributed to him by his friend Bernard, abbot of Arbroath and chancellor. It is hardly to be doubted that Bernard was at the battle, for he was one of the king's closest councillors and in any case, as abbot of Arbroath, he would have been responsible for ensuring that the famous relic casket known as the Brecbennoch of Saint Columba (now the Monymusk Reliquary) was present, suitably attended, in the midst of the army.[123] According to Abbot Bernard, Bruce addressed his men early on the Monday morning, presumably just before battle was joined.

> My lords, my people, accustomed to enjoy that full freedom for which in times gone by the kings of Scotland have fought many a battle! For eight years or more I have struggled with much labour for my right to the kingdom and for honourable liberty. I have lost brothers, friends and kinsmen. Your own kinsmen have been made captive, and bishops and priests are locked in prison. Our country's nobility has poured forth its blood in war. Those barons you can see before you, clad in mail, are bent upon destroying me and obliterating my kingdom, nay, our whole nation. They do not believe that we can survive. They glory in their warhorses and equipment. For us, the name of the Lord must be our hope of victory in battle. This day is a day of rejoicing: the birthday of John the Baptist. With Our Lord Jesus as commander, Saint Andrew and the martyr Saint Thomas shall fight today with the saints of Scotland for the honour of their country and their nation. If you heartily repent for your sins you will be victorious, under God's command. As for offences committed against the Crown, I proclaim a pardon, by virtue of my royal power, to all those who fight manfully for the kingdom of our fathers.[124]

And Barbour tells us that the king also proclaimed a general remission of death-duties (reliefs and wardship) in respect of every man who might be killed in the battle.

At daybreak, King Robert gave the order to attack. The honour of leading the army went to the brigade of Edward Bruce, which had probably been stationed at the eastern edge of the New Park, half way between the Borestone and St Ninians. Next, on Edward Bruce's left, came Moray's brigade, so slightly to the rear that to English eyes the brigades seemed to be side by side. The Stewart's brigade, commanded by Sir James Douglas (both men newly knighted by the king,[125]) came out of the New Park on Moray's left, likewise slightly to the rear, so that the three schiltroms marched forward in echelon by the right. Once out in the open, in full view of the enemy, the Scots halted: every man knelt, saying the Lord's Prayer and commending his soul to God. King Edward had watched the infantry emerging from the wood. Even at this late hour he could not believe they would invite a pitched battle. 'What!' he exclaimed, 'will those Scots fight?' And then, still incredulous as he saw them kneeling to pray, he said: 'Those men kneel to ask for mercy.' 'You are right; they ask for mercy, but not from you. They ask it from God, for their sins.' According to Barbour, the answer was spoken by Sir Ingram de Umfraville, who among those present shared with King Robert alone the distinction of having once been a Guardian for the community of the realm of Scotland.[126]

Sir Ingram's opinion of the fighting qualities of Bruce's troops was too high for the liking of the younger men with Edward II. Apparently both he and the earl of Gloucester had advised the English king to postpone the battle, Gloucester for a whole day, Umfraville suggesting a feigned withdrawal beyond the English tents and baggage, so as to lure the Scots to destruction by tempting them with plunder. The earl was absurdly accused by the king of cowardice; Umfraville's advice, on the other hand, if correctly reported by Barbour, was surely disastrous, and King Edward did right to reject it. Honour and the tactical situation alike demanded that the English did not now refuse battle, even in pretence. They were in a tight corner and must get out of it as best they could.

The anonymous eye-witness whose story is given in the Lanercost Chronicle reported that the first actual fighting was a brief exchange of shots between archers on both sides, in which the Scots had the worst of it.[127] But there is no question that the first major clash came when the English vanguard, under Gloucester, charged the leading Scottish schiltrom across the short stretch of intervening ground. The movement was a spectacular failure. The mailed knights made no impression on the 'impenetrable forest' or 'dense hedge' of spears; the air was filled with the screams of dying horses and the sharp report of breaking spear-shafts. Soon after battle was joined the Scots killed the earl of Gloucester. Impetuous to the last, he was cut off from his household knights and esquires and borne down by the sheer press of spearmen. His was only the first name, though the noblest, on what was to prove a long and costly casualty list of English chivalry. Sir Pain Tiptoft, Sir Edmund de Mauley, Steward of the King's Household, the veteran Sir Robert Clifford, and Sir John Comyn, lord of Badenoch, son of the Guardian whom Bruce had killed in 1306, all seem to have been in the vanguard with Gloucester, and like him fell before the Scottish onslaught.[128]

While Edward Bruce was successfully holding the English vanguard, and perhaps forcing it to give ground somewhat, Moray and Douglas brought up their brigades and launched a general attack on the remaining nine English divisions, which were bunched in one single mass, 'all in a schiltrom' as Barbour puts it.[129] Again the Scots went for the horses as much as their riders, and by dint of keeping together in tight formation, as Moray's men had done the previous afternoon, all the Scottish schiltroms presented an impenetrable barrier to the lances and swords of the knights. Even making every allowance for the poetic effect at which Barbour strove, his impression of appalling tumult, no doubt gained from authentic tradition and eye-witness accounts, is surely true. He describes the clash of spears on the knights' helmets and 'birnies' (coats of mail), the shrieks of disembowelled horses, the panic stampede of riderless animals, and the grass made red with the outpoured blood of man and beast. The carnage was doubtless not so great at first as it had been at Falkirk, but it must be remembered that in cavalry actions casualties were not expected to be very heavy. Courtrai, in 1302, where the Flemish foot had virtually wiped out the French feudal host, had shocked Europe; and now Bannockburn was bidding fair to rival Courtrai.

Not until the English had taken great punishment was it possible for them to bring out on one flank a body of archers to harass the Scottish schiltroms by steady shooting against which they had little or no protection. Here, of course, was a cardinal error on Edward II's part. His archers should have been available in large numbers from the start, and their shooting should have been integrated with the short rushes of the cavalry. But in fact the larger part of the English bowmen seem to have been in the rear, and could only be brought up to the front with difficulty because of the narrowness of the battlefield. King Robert must have anticipated some such move, and to meet it he had held in reserve the only cavalry force in his army: some five hundred knights and men at arms, on light horses, under the marischal, Sir Robert Keith. Keith was sent to scatter the archers and prevent them from shooting steadily. In fact he did better: his charge was so fierce that the whole body of archers broke and fled, and many who tried to get back into the English ranks further in the rear were set upon and beaten up by men of their own side.[130] On which flank this took place matters little: from now on, the archers were no longer an element in the battle, which became solely a dour and strenuous contest, in the growing heat of a midsummer morning, between the spears and Lochaber axes of the Scots on foot and the lances, swords and maces or clubs wielded by mail-clad knights. The greater part of the infantry on the English side do not seem to have been engaged at all, and it may well be that most of them remained south of the Bannock Burn. The Scots evidently had sufficient numbers to occupy the English cavalry along virtually the whole width of the available ground between Balquhiderock and Broomridge; Barbour speaks of the three schiltroms of Edward Bruce, Moray and Douglas as 'all fighting very nearly side by side'.[131] King Robert seems to have known better than any of the English leaders how dangerous their archers might have proved if put to better use. Once Keith had routed them, he felt that the Scots were on top, the battle was theirs. He could not contain his jubilation; now, he told the officers of his brigade, was the moment; if only some extra pressure could be put on the English, defeat would quickly follow. There was evidently room to bring up his own brigade, presumably on the right flank of the three already engaged.[132] The highlanders, islesmen and others serving under the king's own standard, chafing with impatience (as one may imagine) at not yet having taken any part, now rushed upon the enemy in a rage.

> With all thar mycht and all thar mayne
> Thai layd on, as men out of wit;
> And quhar thai with full strak mycht hit,
> Thar mycht no armyng stint thar strak;
> Thai to-fruschit thame thai mycht our-tak
> And with axis sic duschis gaff
> That thai helmys and hedis claff.[133]

This, as the racy, excited, irresistible flood of his verse makes clear, was for Barbour the climax of the battle. No other source denies or contradicts him here. We accept his judgement or abandon any attempt at a detailed account. All four schiltroms, the whole effective strength of the Scottish army, were now engaged, fighting along one front. The English vanguard ceased to be a distinct unit; the entire English army now formed one huge schiltrom, packed so close that if one man fell he had no room to rise but was trampled under foot. Where men had once fought silently and grimly, saving their breath, emotions now inevitably got the better of discipline. The Scots were exultant, the English were beginning to be desperate. They had fought, and continued for some while to fight, stoutly; but they were fighting with the wrong tactics, the wrong weapons, and on the wrong ground. Amid the clash of arms and the groans of the wounded, battle cries 'hideous for to hear' sounded on every side. As the knights began to yield, the Scots shouted: 'On them, on them, on them, they fail!'[134] The Scots archers took courage, and added a cruel rain of arrows to the mêlée.

For the English, the battle was now past saving. In front of them the Scottish schiltroms still remained intact, a steadily advancing engine of destruction. Behind them were the gorge of the Bannock Burn and the treacherous carse with its innumerable pows, and on their flank the Forth itself, too wide and deep to be forded in safety. At this moment, there appeared in the rear of the attacking Scots a great mob of unarmoured, untrained lesser folk – yeomen, servants and labourers – bearing hastily improvised banners and armed with homemade weapons.[135] King Robert had kept them strictly apart from his fighting men, setting them to guard the supplies in a hollow, probably to the north of Coxet Hill.[136] Now, unbidden and having little or no effect upon the outcome, they streamed across the open ground with shouts of 'Slay, slay, on them hastily.' No blame if some of the hard-pressed English had really believed they were a second Scottish army, arriving vigorous and fresh when they themselves were near to exhaustion. King Robert himself could hardly have welcomed an undisciplined rabble who might kill English lords and knights indiscriminately so that their valuable ransoms would be lost. But in any event, the surviving

English leaders knew that the end had come.

The earl of Pembroke and Sir Giles d'Argentan were with the king, the latter in his personal bodyguard.[139] At all costs Edward must be got safely off the field. His death would have been a national disgrace, but his capture would have been far worse. His ransom alone would, economically speaking, put Scotland back on her feet, while the terms of his release could hardly have been less than unconditional recognition of Bruce's claim to the Scottish throne and of Scottish independence. King Edward had carried himself with notable courage, and protested as he was led from the field; but he was got away only just in time. As it was, he had one horse killed under him and had to be given a fresh mount, while the Scots captured Sir Roger Northburgh along with the king's shield which he had in his keeping.[138] Five hundred knights went with the king, not crossing the Bannock Burn, where the fighting was fiercest, but riding towards Stirling along the edge of the carse, in the vain and dangerous hope that they would find refuge in the castle. As soon as King Edward was out of immediate danger, Giles d'Argentan, 'the third best knight' in Christendom, declaring that his honour would not allow him to flee, returned to confront the schiltrom of Edward Bruce and plunged, gallantly but quite suicidally, into the forest of spears.[130]

In other circumstances, the king of England's personal presence should have been an enormous asset. Now it was to prove calamitous. His withdrawal was the signal for general flight, which, utterly uncontrolled as it was, turned defeat into stark disaster. Men fled in every possible direction, north-west to Stirling Castle, north to the River Forth in which most of those trying to cross were drowned, south-east to the Bannock Burn. It was here, in the gorge north of Bannockburn village, and presumably also in the peat-bordered stretch below the gorge, that the beaten army suffered its most terrible casualties.

> Bannokburn betwix the brais
> Of hors and men so chargit was,
> That apon drownit hors and men
> Men mycht pass dry atour it then.[140]

In more laconic fashion, Grey, the *Life of Edward II*, and the Lanercost Chronicle all bear out Barbour's account. The English, says Grey, 'recoiled upon the ditch of the Bannock Burn, tumbling over one another'.[141] The Lanercost account says 'a further misfortune befell the English, for since, a little while before, they had crossed a big ditch called the Bannock Burn, into which the tide flows,[142] and now, thrown back in confusion, they wished to retreat, many noblemen and others with their horses fell into this ditch because of the great press of men behind them. Some got away only with difficulty, but many never extricated themselves, so that 'Bannockburn' was on English lips for many years afterwards.'[143] The *Life of Edward II* has the same story, though it does not mention the Bannock Burn by name: 'While our people fled, a certain ditch entrapped many of them, and a great part of our army perished in it.'[144]

It is usually hard enough for a general to plan a battle so that it goes the way he wants it to go; it is only rarely that even the best of generals can steer the course of events after a successful battle so that he may reap the maximum advantage. Robert Bruce had won a brilliant victory, which rightly takes first place among the few decisive battles in the history of Scotland. It cannot tarnish the brilliance of his achievement to add, as a matter of historical fact, that in the battle's aftermath the English escaped more cheaply than they deserved. This was due largely to circumstances beyond Bruce's control. True, the English lost all their supplies and baggage and nearly all their arms and armour, amounting to an immensely rich haul for the Scots. King Edward lost his shield and his privy seal, both of which, with signal courtesy, King Robert returned to him.[145] He also lost all his personal equipment, clothing and other possessions, save what little he could carry with him. It is true also that casualties were heavy, proportionately heaviest among men of noble rank, that is barons, knights and esquires. One earl was killed: Gloucester, whom Bruce mourned as a cousin, and over whose corpse, decently laid in a nearby church, he made a night's vigil. It was then sent to King Edward at Berwick, along with the body of Clifford, who after Gloucester was the most high-ranking magnate to be killed.[146] Besides these and Tiptoft, Mauley and Comyn, at least thirty-four barons and knights are recorded as having been slain, including William, lord of Hingham (Suffolk), hereditary marshal of Ireland; Edmund Hastings, the younger son of John Hastings the Competitor; and John Lovel the Rich.[147] The family of Vieuxpont suffered heavily, losing an English and a Scottish representative, while Clifford was a Vieuxpont on his mother's side.

The English king, however, got away, and his escape was not due merely to good luck. When he reached Stirling Castle, its commander Moubray either told him that he was free to enter, in which case he would be taken by the Scots, or else (for the same reason) he raised the drawbridge and shut the gate against him.[148] Edward and his party thereupon turned about and made off through the King's Park, crossed the rear of the Scottish army, until, regaining the Torwood, they sped along the high road in the direction of Linlithgow.[149] Large numbers of the English followed the king to Stirling and scrambled vainly about the castle rock. But Bruce judged them too dangerous to be left in his rear, and kept a strong force to overpower them. Consequently, he ordered no serious pursuit of the English king. Instead, Douglas was allowed only sixty horse, with which he gave chase as best he could.[150] He had no real hope of doing more than harass a party nearly ten times as strong. Barbour tells how the English halted briefly at Winchburgh to feed their horses, Douglas's troop following suit a short way off. Then

away they rode again through Lothian, the Scots maintaining such a hot
pursuit that the English lords and knights, in Barbour's expressive phrase,
'had not even leisure to make water'. If any of them did lag behind they were
quickly captured. At last Edward reached the castle of Dunbar. It says much
for the sorely-tried loyalty of Earl Patrick that he received Edward hospitably and saw him safely on board the boat which took him to Bamburgh, and
so to the comparative security of Berwick. Most of the five hundred knights
reached Berwick by land. Earl Patrick must have submitted to the king of
Scots immediately afterwards, for the English records show that he was
forfeited as a traitor as from this date.[151]

A sizeable body of cavalry, under the earl of Hereford, fled to Bothwell
Castle on the Clyde.[152] The constable, Walter, Gilbert's son, though a Scot,
had hitherto been on the English side. He admitted Hereford and his party,
which included Robert de Umfraville earl of Angus, Ingram de Umfraville,
Maurice lord of Berkeley, John lord of Segrave, and Anthony de Lucy.
Once inside, he made them all prisoners, having presumably decided to go
over to Bruce if the English were defeated. Profitable ransoms were
obtained for these rich and important magnates. The earl of Hereford was so
great a prize that in October Bruce was able to exchange him for his queen,
his daughter the lady Marjorie, his sister Mary, and Robert Wishart, bishop
of Glasgow, now very old and blind.[154] On the other hand, Bruce behaved
with conspicuous generosity towards some of his prisoners. Sir Marmaduke
Tweng, for example, an old veteran of the English wars in Scotland,
surrendered personally to King Robert and was allowed to go home to
Yorkshire free of ransom.[155] Raoul de Monthermer, who had been styled
earl of Gloucester before the succession of his step-son Gilbert de Clare, was
likewise liberated without any ransom.[156] Such remarkable treatment for a
man of the highest rank suggests that there must be some kernel of truth in
Barbour's romantic tale of Earl Raoul saving Bruce from Edward I in 1305
or 1306.[157] Sir Philip Moubray, after surrendering Stirling Castle, was
allowed to change sides and came to King Robert's peace. The castle itself
was razed to the ground. It is not the hero-worshipping Barbour but a
hostile English writer who tells us that the bodies of Gloucester and Clifford
were restored to their families without any conditions or demands, and that
Bruce's behaviour towards the English captives was so humane and courteous that he completely won their hearts.[158]

The humanity, coolness and resolve which distinguished the Scottish
king's actions were not wholly absent on the other side. A large force of
Welsh infantry, perhaps several thousand in all, traversed the hundred
miles of difficult country between Stirling and Carlisle.[159] Though suffering
heavy losses at the hands of the Scots, the greater part of this contingent won
through to safety, and their escape must have been due to good leadership.
It was probably a member of this Welsh force who gave the news of
Bannockburn to some monastery in his own country, perhaps Valle Crucis,

whose chronicle contains what seems to be the earliest report of the battle that we have.[160]

If the Scots had had more horses at their disposal, if they had been rather more prepared than they were for such a resounding victory, if the earl of Dunbar had behaved like his counterpart at Bothwell,[161] then it is possible that the peace would have been won with the war. Robert Bruce, who was now recognized as king of Scots throughout his own kingdom and much of western Europe, might thus have gained the same recognition south of the Border. As it was, he had won the independence of Scotland, though the English were not yet prepared to admit the fact. In addition, he had triumphantly vindicated his claim to the Scottish throne and his revolutionary bid for leadership of the community of the realm. By the tests of the age, legality by hereditary right, legality by the acceptance of the people, and legality by God's judgement in a trial of battle, King Robert had now attained to a position of unshakeable authority.

THIRTEEN

War and Peace

Fourteen years separated Bannockburn from the Treaty of Edinburgh, which brought to an end the Scottish war begun by Edward I. By that time Edward of Caernarvon had been murdered and Robert Bruce was a sick man, within a year of his own death. The king of Scots' consistent objective during this period was to win from England recognition of his own position and a full renunciation of the English Crown's claims to suzerainty over Scotland. The efforts of Edward II and of most of the leading men of the community of the realm of England were directed towards avoiding or postponing these admissions. It is said that this was the price King Robert had to pay for his victory. Bannockburn, it is argued, was a mistake, because the English were bound to seek revenge. The reasoning seems curious; of the heads I win-tails-you-lose variety. It cannot seriously be maintained that the English would have been more ready to conclude a peace if Bruce had remained a *guerrillero*. As for the Scots, the effect on their morale if Bruce had lost Bannockburn or declined a pitched battle can easily be guessed.

There is no doubt whatever that Bruce had no wish to prolong the war. He would gladly have made peace at any time if his not very extravagant terms had been met. But he was confronted by a peculiar difficulty, arising from the historical structure of medieval England. The wealth of the country, its trade, its food production, its industries and its manpower, were all concentrated in the south and the midlands. To Englishmen south of Humber and Trent the Scottish war seemed immensely remote. It mattered little to them if Bruce extracted blackmail from the northern counties year after year and raided as far as Lancashire and Yorkshire. It is true that Bannockburn made a profound impression throughout England: it was, after all, the first time for six hundred years that an army led by an English king had been destroyed north of the Border. But the shock induced heart-searching rather than a desire for peace. It was harder for the southern English to learn the lesson of Bannockburn than it was for their descendants to learn the lesson of Yorktown. It was an additional but much smaller difficulty that of the two popes of this period, Clement V was a Gascon strongly predisposed in Edward II's favour and John XXII, who succeeded Clement in 1316, regarded Bruce as a sower of discord whose struggle was preventing England from taking her proper part in the crusade against the Turks.[1] Although the fact is not easy to explain, it remains true that the

12. Southern Scotland and Northern England to illustrate the Scottish Raids, 1311–27.

Scots gained more from the support given them by Boniface VIII before
1302 than they lost from the opposition of his successors between 1305 and
1323.

After Bannockburn, the Scottish raids south of the Border became so
regular and frequent that they amounted to the virtual subjection of
England north of Tees and involved the selective devastation of a still larger
area. Northumberland suffered heavy depopulation and was reduced to a
miserable anarchy. Ruffians such as Jack the Irishman and Gilbert of
Middleton, and English garrison commanders (e.g., at Bamburgh) did as
much harm as the Scots. Not surprisingly, many men in Northumberland
and northern Cumberland went over to Bruce and became 'Scottish', just as
many Lothian men had previously been 'English'.[2] The Scottish leaders
had three chief objects in view: revenue in blackmail; the recovery of
Berwick, now the only Scottish town and castle left in many hands; and
plain terrorization. All three objects were achieved, though it took time. A
conservative estimate would put Bruce's total income in blackmail at
£20,000, mostly received over a period of some ten years.[3] Berwick fell in
1318. And throughout northern England the mere rumour of a Scottish raid
sent peasants fleeing to the woods and moors while clergy and gentry made
joint efforts, as best they could, to buy immunity. Only in the exceptionally
strong castles of Carlisle, Norham, Newcastle upon Tyne and Richmond
(which never fell), and Berwick (which resisted stubbornly) did English
morale remain high.

No two raids were exactly alike, but they followed a pattern which was to
become only too familiar. The leaders were usually Sir James Douglas – the
'Good Douglas' – and Thomas Randolph earl of Moray, whose audacity and
skill grew with each new expedition. The raiders were mounted on sturdy
light horses, 'hobins', strong in wind and limb and sure of foot, and from
their hobins the men themselves derived their popular (and most misleading) name of 'hobelars'. In this they seem to have copied a military
fashion which had grown up in Ireland during the thirteenth century, when
men accustomed to cavalry warfare had been forced to adapt their tactics to
boggy, thickly wooded or hilly terrain.[4] They wore little armour, but took
with them the weapons appropriate for fighting on foot in schiltrom
formation. They lived rough and ate sparingly, every man carrying an iron
plate or 'girdle' on which he could bake himself oaten bannocks at the
bivouac fire.[5] We are not told how the large sums of blackmail were
transported, but presumably coin could be stowed in leather bags slung over
spare horses. Often the Scots were satisfied with promises that the money
would be paid later at some convenient point close to the Border, taking
hostages, however, to guarantee payment. A number of sumpter horses
must have accompanied the raiders, for we have the significant story of how
the Scots were overjoyed to find so much iron when they raided Furness in

1316, since iron was scarce in Scotland.[6] Most of the booty consisted of cattle and prisoners who would simply have to transport themselves; but the practice of driving off great numbers of animals had the consequence that whereas the raiders could strike with lightning swiftness when they were on their way south they were bound to be slower on the return journey.

Tough, brisk, grimly businesslike, these Scottish hobelars were exponents of a type of warfare not seen in Britain since the Danish raids of the ninth century. Set beside their highly professional operations, King John's cavalry at Dunbar and Wallace's spearmen at Falkirk seem to belong to a different era. It is hard to believe that some of the men accompanying Moray and Douglas had fought in the armies of 1296, 1297 and 1298. We know of few such men for certain, since most of those who have left their names in record have done so because they were captured, killed or executed. But Robert Baird of Strathaven, noted for his bitter hostility to the English, Sir Gilbert Hay of Errol whom Bruce made Constable before March 1309, and Sir Robert Keith the Marischal, all of whose military careers span the whole period from the Guardians to Bannockburn and after, were perhaps not untypical of that class of lairds and lesser nobles from which the patriotic cause drew so much of its strength.

The Scottish raids not only reached a new peak of effectiveness after 1314, they were also much bolder and penetrated much further south into the richer lowlands such as the Vale of Mowbray, Amounderness and even Holderness. In August 1314, Edward Bruce, James Douglas and John de Soules (great-nephew of Sir John de Soules the Guardian)[7] devastated Northumberland, passed through County Durham to raid in Richmond-shire, and returned by Swaledale with enormous plunder, burning Brough, Appleby and Kirkoswald.[8] In a second raid the same year, King Robert seems to have resumed the lordship of Tynedale held by Alexander III, for its men did him homage.[9] It is likely to have been on this occasion that the king granted the manor of Wark on Tyne to William de Soules for life. This grant evidently extended to South Tynedale, for its freeholders bargained with de Soules for as much as thirty-five pounds of silver to be left in peace for six months, and complained to Edward II that they were being preyed upon not by the Scots but by their compatriots from Cumberland and Westmorland who raided them by night and stole wine and other goods.[10]

Douglas and Moray raided in County Durham in the summer of 1315 and on July 22nd of that year King Robert laid siege to Carlisle.[11] Against the defenders' seven or eight stone-lobbing engines the Scots had only one, of little use. They built a 'sow' or shelter for the sappers undermining the fortifications, and an assault tower or 'berefrey', which sank in the soft earth when they tried to wheel it up to the wall. On the 30th they made a general assault, using the same stratagem of a diversionary attack by which Edinburgh had been won, but this time it did not succeed. They withdrew hastily on August 1st, leaving their siege equipment behind them and suffering casualties at the hands of some of the garrison, ably commanded by the sheriff of Cumberland, Sir Andrew Harcla (of Harcla, now Hartley, near Kirkby Stephen). Six months after this setback, King Robert and Sir James Douglas failed in their second attempt to capture Berwick.[12] The summer of 1316 saw the raiders once again in north Yorkshire and also, for the first time, in Furness.[13] Thereafter, the attempted conquest of Ireland under Edward Bruce diverted large numbers of Scots until 1318.

In Scotland 1316 and 1317 were by no means years of military inactivity. Douglas won great honour on February 14th 1316, in a sharp fight on Skaithmuir near Coldstream.[14] A strong party of horsemen from Berwick, including several Gascon knights, had been out raiding the Merse and Teviotdale to replenish their empty larders. Douglas was in Selkirk Forest when he heard of the raid, and promptly gave chase. The raiders turned about to meet him and in the fight which followed, reckoned the hottest encounter Douglas ever took part in, most of the Berwick men were slain, including Raymond de Calhau, apparently a nephew of Piers Gaveston. In this period also, Douglas inflicted heavy casualties on another raiding party, sent by the earl of Arundel, at Lintalee, south of Jedburgh.[15] In yet a third fray of the same kind, this time near Berwick, he routed a squadron of English knights and killed its leader, Robert Neville of Raby, the 'Peacock of the North'.[16] The reputation of 'Monsieur James', north and south of the Border, now stood very high, and it is not surprising that before King Robert and Moray went to Ireland early in 1317 Douglas was made warden or lieutenant of Scotland.[17]

North-country Englishmen, despairing of help from their king, collected a fleet in the Humber and on their own initiative attempted an invasion of Fife, probably in 1317.[18] They landed either at Inverkeithing or Donibristle and were half-heartedly challenged by a party under the sheriff of Fife and, if Barbour is right, Earl Duncan also.[19] One sight of the English invaders put such fear into the party that they turned back from the coast. Five miles away, at Auchtertool, a manor belonging to the see of Dunkeld, they were met by the bishop himself, William Sinclair, a brother of Sir Henry Sinclair of Roslin, one of Bruce's Lothian adherents. Indignant at their cowardice, the bishop, already in armour and mounted, put the knights to shame by seizing a lance and riding off to do battle with the enemy. His example was infectious, and very soon the English were driven back in confusion, many of them being killed, and many others, trying to escape in too small a boat, drowned.[20] By May 1317 the king was home again from his Irish expedition, and his return would discourage any further ventures of this kind.

The year 1318, which closed with the ominous defeat of the Scots at Dundalk and the death in battle of Edward Bruce, began with striking Scottish successes east of the Irish Sea. On the night of Saturday and Sunday, April 1st and 2nd, Douglas's men scrambled over the town walls of Berwick and got possession of the town after some fierce and confused street

fighting in which Sir William Keith of Galston distinguished himself.[21] The
entry had been contrived by an English burgess of Berwick, Peter of
Spalding, who had charge of a section of the wall.[22] Barbour's story is that he
was related by marriage to Keith the Marischal[23] and sent a message to
Keith saying he would admit the Scots at his part of the wall on a pre-
arranged date. Keith reported his treachery to the king, who decided to risk
the possibility that a trick was being played, and assigned the task of taking
Berwick to Moray and Douglas jointly. Berwick Castle was starved into
surrender about eleven weeks later.[24] The loss of Berwick was a severe blow
for the English, and it was followed by the capture of three lesser castles in
Northumberland, Wark on Tweed, Harbottle in Coquetdale and Mitford.[25]
About this time, or a little before, the king of Scots granted North Tynedale
to Sir Philip Moubray, who had once held Stirling castle for Edward II.
Moubray built a small fortalice at Falstone, while the lawless North-
umberland landowner Richard of Middleton, brother of Sir Gilbert of
Middleton, came into Bruce's allegiance and built another fortalice at
Houxty north of Wark.[26]

In May 1318, a big Scottish raiding party swept south into Yorkshire,
burning Northallerton and Boroughbridge. At Ripon the inhabitants shut
themselves in the minster, and the Scots accepted an offer of a thousand
marks as the price of not burning the city. Six citizens were delivered up as
hostages to ensure payment. More than two years later three-quarters of the
debt was still outstanding. Eventually the hostages' wives petitioned the
king to intercede on their behalf with the archbishop of York, as lord of
Ripon, to compel their heedless and callous fellow-citizens to pay off the
ransom. After leaving Ripon, the raiding party burned Knaresborough,
scoured the neighbouring woods for cattle, and returned home by Skipton
in Craven.[27]

Affairs had now gone so ill for the English that in 1319, for one brief and
unsuccessful campaign, King Edward and Earl Thomas of Lancaster
actually joined forces and besieged Berwick, where they were repulsed by
Walter the Stewart, to whom Bruce had committed town and castle.[28] The
English king, however, had a respectable-looking force of some eight
thousand men which Moray and Douglas were afraid to confront in open
battle. Instead, they took their hobelars to Boroughbridge, by the West
March, and began to ravage Yorkshire in the usual way. It was rumoured
that Douglas intended to kidnap the queen, then at York, and she was
removed to Nottingham. The mayor and citizens of York and its archbishop, the good and kindly William Melton,[29] raised such men as they
could (chiefly inexperienced townsmen and clergy) and went out to do
battle with the marauders, as Archbishop Thurstan had done in 1138. The
Scots met this motley company a few miles east of Boroughbridge, at
Myton-on-Swale, and made short work of them in a most unequal contest.
Though the affair hardly earned any glory for Douglas and Moray, the

'chapter of Myton' (as it was called in irony, from the great numbers of clergy slain or put to flight) did cause Edward II to raise the siege of Berwick and retreat south of the Trent. In consequence, Douglas carried out the most savage raid yet seen on the west side of the Pennines, waiting till after the harvest, about November 1st, and then burning all the corn and seizing large numbers of men and animals in Gilsland and Westmorland.[30]

At Christmas the English secured a truce for two years.[31] The truce negotiations took place at Newcastle upon Tyne in December, and the powers given to the high-ranking English commissioners, who included the earl of Pembroke and the chancellor John de Hothum, now bishop of Ely, allowed them to discuss a longer term peace if an opportunity was offered. The Scottish party at Newcastle, perhaps intentionally, was less distinguished, although it was led by William de Soules and included Alexander Seton, the greatly trusted Robert Lauder and two clerks James Ben and Walter 'of Galloway' (i.e. Twynholm) who were to become respectively bishop of St Andrews and king's chancellor.[32] The period 1320-22 was to prove the decisive turning-point in King Edward's reign and life. In future, there would be no possibility of his leading a concerted attack upon Scotland with even a majority of the baronage behind him. In the meantime Moray and Douglas grew in strength, King Robert himself surmounted the most serious political crisis of his reign, the Soules conspiracy, while the community of the realm of Scotland met reiterated fulminations from the papacy with the famous letter addressed to Pope John XXII in 1320, usually called the Declaration of Arbroath.[33]

It may have been partly as a consequence of that letter that papal pressure was brought to bear on the English king rather than on Bruce to agree the terms of a permanent peace instead of a mere truce.[34] To papal was added French pressure. Early in 1321 Edward II appointed envoys to treat for peace with the Scots, but still, as is abundantly clear from the documentation, on the old outworn, arrogant terms of English overlordship. The actual negotiations were to take place in March and April, at Bamburgh, only a few miles from the border and the recently recovered burgh and castle of Berwick which King Robert was building up as a major stronghold. For a brief period the little town of Bamburgh with its hilltop castle must have teemed with prelates, barons, knights, men at arms, along with learned clerks and notaries with their bundles of parchment and works of legal or historical reference. From Philip V came Guillaume Durand bishop of Mende, John lord of Varennes and the lawyer, Mr. Bertrand Boniface; from Edward II the bishops of Worcester and Carlisle, the baron Bartholomew Badlesmere and Mr. Robert Baldock. Pope John entrusted the papal representation to Rigaud of Assier bishop of Winchester and William of Landun. The Scots envoys are nowhere named in the extant record, but must have included or at least made use of persons well schooled in the history of Anglo-Scottish relations, especially since 1286.

The gist of the Scottish arguments employed against the English in 1321 has been preserved, by an unexpected piece of good fortune, in a four-teenth-century manuscript at Córdoba. The earliest history, aimed at countering the surprisingly unimaginative English repetition of the story of Brutus of Troy, is lifted virtually *verbatim* from the brief prepared by Baldred Bisset in 1301. In that year one of Bisset's two colleagues pleading the Scots cause at the papal *curia* had been Mr. William of Eaglesham. In 1321 Mr. William was archdeacon of Lothian, in which office he had been succeeded between 1324 and 1327 by Mr. Alexander Kinninmonth who, as we shall see, was active in pleading the Scots cause at the papal curia in the summer of 1320. The connexion between these two, both trusted clerks of Bishop Lamberton, is seen also in the fact that in 1322 Kinninmonth succeeded Eaglesham in the Aberdeenshire parsonage of Kinkell. It would not be unreasonable to suggest that both were involved in preparing the Scottish brief for the Bamburgh peace talks. There are several telling echoes of the Declaration of Arbroath in the 1321 brief: the Scots have preserved their pristine liberty under 113 kings without subjection to any foreigner; at the hands of Edward I and his son they have suffered oppressions and tyrannical severity; it would be intolerable for the Scots to accept English overlordship so long as there was within their realm one man who would fight to the death for the liberty of the realm and the clergy; and in defending their independence the Scots might have to make the same sacrifices as the holy Maccabees. In much of its phraseology, however, the brief of 1321 followed the wording of the papal bull *Scimus, fili* (1299), Bisset's *processus* (1301) and the statements originating in the 1309 parlia-ment – most strikingly, perhaps, in its dismissal of the English recitation of Scottish surrenders obtained through force and the fear which may assail even the most steadfast.[35] It would be hard to say whether the brief of 1321 literally echoes the letter of 1320 or whether both documents derive material from a common stock which the Scots intelligentsia had been building up for twenty or thirty years.

Not surprisingly, there was no meeting of minds at Bamburgh in March or April 1321. 'From the Scots we have heard many declarations that they desire peace above all things, but in practice they have little to say which suggests it, rather the contrary; and finally, after they had caused great delays, they would agree only to a long truce, for example of twenty-six years, to which we and your other envoys would not agree without informing you'.[36] The English envoys, in giving this account of their proceedings to their king, disingenuously omitted to explain that in persist-ing with the overlordship claim they were merely making deadlock inevitable. And the Scots for their part were being somewhat unrealistic if they imagined that either the pope or the king of France could influence the obdurate Edward II to the extent of relinquishing his claims and making a lasting peace. Their recorded arguments (if actually deployed) were scarcely tactful, since they claimed that the entire Norman and Plantagenet dynasty was illegitimate, stemming from the foreign usurpation of William the Bastard in 1066, when it was well known that the royal house of Wessex (represented, of course, by Robert 1!) was the lawful English dynasty. Indeed, they alleged that when Malcolm III Canmore invaded England after the Conqueror's death the population in the English west country welcomed him as their saviour from Norman tyranny.[37]

The conflict which broke out in Wales later in 1321 between Humphrey de Bohun earl of Hereford and other marcher lords on the one hand, and the king's favourites, the Despensers, on the other, foreshadowed the disorder and upheaval in which Edward II's reign came to its end six years later. The king's relations with Lancaster had gone from bad to worse, a fact of which the Scots took full advantage. At the end of 1321 Lancaster entered into secret negotiations with Douglas and Moray in which Lancaster was quaintly referred to as 'King Arthur'.[38] Lancaster had little to offer in return for Scottish help. It is doubtful if Bruce took these negotiations very seriously. It was obviously in his interest, from a short-term point of view, to encourage civil war in England, but he is said to have remarked about Lancaster's overtures: 'How will a man who cannot keep faith with his own lord keep faith with me?' Certainly the negotiations were not allowed to hinder military plans. Barely had the two-year truce expired than Douglas and Moray were over the Border (January 6th, 1322) and plundering Teesside. While Moray stayed at Darlington, Douglas raided Hartlepool and Cleveland and Walter Stewart (by now a hardened veteran) went to Richmondshire and sold immunity to its inhabitants at a heavy price.[39]

All this time Lancaster, although he was present in south Yorkshire with a sizeable force of armed men, did not lift a finger against the Scots. King Edward's immediate concern was to deal with Lancaster and his other baronial enemies, Hereford among them. He failed to prevent the two earls joining forces, but succeeded in driving them from the position they had taken up at Burton on Trent (March 10th) to block the royal army's passage of the river. The earls retreated northward, meaning to join the Scots. Their plan was utterly frustrated by a brilliant and unexpected move on the part of Andrew Harcla. While the Scots were in Teesdale Harcla raised the levies of Cumberland and Westmorland, by-passed Moray, and took up a position covering both the ford and the bridge at Boroughbridge, where Lancaster would have to cross the River Ure. In the battle that followed (March 16th) Harcla's tactics were a deliberate and masterly imitation of Bruce's at Bannockburn.[40] Hereford was killed on the bridge, Lancaster, after a night's delay, was taken prisoner and soon afterwards executed. The Scots prudently retired north of the Border. This copybook victory, which he had not deserved, brought out the worst in Edward II. His capacity for learning and forgetting nothing might have been the envy of a Restoration Bourbon. Boroughbridge led directly to the aggrandizement of the Despensers which in turn led to Edward 11's downfall in 1327.

One immediate result was that it gave Edward 11 sufficient confidence to lead another expedition into Scotland. It proved to be his last. It was entirely fruitless and for the king personally nearly ended in a worse disaster than Bannockburn. The expedition, which crossed the Border about the beginning of August, followed a particularly provocative Scottish incursion led by Bruce himself. On July 1st, 1322, the king of Scots progressed down the west side of Cumberland, plundering as he went, crossed the Duddon Sands into Furness (which bought immunity with only partial success) and finally crossed the sands of the Kent estuary to burn Lancaster and Preston. The entire Scottish party was back over the Border in less than four weeks.[41] Edward 11's answer was to march through Lothian as far as Edinburgh, but Bruce had ordered all cattle to be removed and food stocks destroyed. The main Scottish army was withdrawn to Culross, north of the Forth. The English sacked Holyrood Abbey but early in September famine forced them to withdraw, with very heavy loss.[42] The story went that in the whole of fertile Lothian they had found only one lame cow, straying in the cornfield of Tranent, of which the earl of Surrey remarked: 'This is the dearest beef that I ever saw; surely it has cost a thousand pounds and more!'[43] On their way south they attempted the sack of Melrose Abbey, but part of the army was surprised by Douglas, who in his usual way had been lurking in the Forest and rushed down amid shouts of 'Douglas! Douglas!' inflicting severe casualties.

The English king's retreat was the signal for Bruce to launch an exceptionally bold and dangerous raid, for which he had recruited a great host of men from north and south of Forth as well as from Bute, Argyll and the western isles. They entered England over the fords of Solway and presumably followed the familiar Eden valley route into north Yorkshire.[44] Knowing that Edward 11 was retiring southward, they struck out boldly across the North Riding towards the Hambleton Hills, apparently making for the region of Sutton Bank ('Blakehoumor') where they had never been before.[45] They were at Northallerton about October 12th, when Edward was still lodging in Rievaulx Abbey, fifteen miles to the south east.[46] Learning of the English king's whereabouts, Bruce moved swiftly towards Rievaulx, to find his direct route blocked by a considerable English force under the earl of Richmond, John of Brittany. Richmond was evidently occupying the western edge of Scawton Moor, overlooking Sutton Bank and Roulston Scar, a steep and partly rocky hillside, up which only a rough path gave access to the summit.[47] The only way to Rievaulx was round by Helmsley, some fourteen miles. If they delayed, the king would certainly escape. Douglas and Moray at once began a fierce attack straight up the hillside. Sir Ralph Cobham, 'the best knight in England', was taken prisoner, and with him Sir Thomas Uhtred, better than the best, for he had held his ground longer than Cobham. At the critical moment, King Robert

ordered his highlanders and islesmen to climb the precipitous cliffs to one
side of the path so as to take the English on the flank. Before long, Richmond
and his knights, assailed by Douglas and Moray on their front and unable to
break the wild highland charge across the top of the high ground, gave way
and fled in confusion. Richmond himself was captured, and with him a
noted French lord, Henry de Sully, butler of France. Many others were
killed or made prisoner. The Scots failed to achieve their main objective, for
King Edward had just enough warning to make his way first to Bridlington
and then to York.[48] For the second time in eight years, he was forced to
abandon his personal possessions and equipment, silver plate, jewellery,
horse trappings and harness.[49] It was only by the merest good luck that he
eluded his pursuers, who followed hot on his heels to the very gates of the
city. Nationally speaking, the affair was not a disaster like Bannockburn, but
for the king the humiliation was far greater.

Baulked of their prey, the Scots – or a large party of them – coolly crossed
the Yorkshire Wolds to Beverley, where they levied blackmail as usual.
They returned to Scotland on November 2nd. Richmond, a close friend of
Edward 11 and apparently the object of Bruce's special dislike, was not
ransomed for two years. It was not Bruce's intention to antagonize the
French, and consequently, after giving a hospitable welcome to Sully and
the other lords from France who had been captured with Richmond, the
king of Scots sent them home free of ransom. Before returning to France,
Sully assisted in the negotiations which led eventually, in May 1323, to the
conclusion of an Anglo-Scottish truce intended to last for thirteen years.
This truce, to be discussed in more detail shortly, was the nearest the
English had come since Bruce's coronation to making a firm peace with the
Scots. It was a measure of the success which King Robert had achieved after
seventeen strenuous years. But neither Bannockburn nor the rout near Old
Byland had taught Edward of Caernarvon good sense or moderation, and he
began the truce negotiations with a letter that referred only to the 'people of
Scotland' and ignored their king altogether. Bruce's own comment on this
letter, as expressed to Henry de Sully the go-between, shows both dignity
and a sense of humour in the face of such an exasperating opponent.

> Robert, by God's grace king of Scotland, to the most noble Henry, lord
> of Sully, knight, his good friend, affectionate and loving greeting. You
> will recall, my lord, how it was stated in our letters sent to the king of
> England, and how also we informed you by word of mouth, that we
> desired and still desire at all times to negotiate with the king of England
> on a final peace between him and us, saving always to us and to our heirs
> our realm free and independent, and also the integrity of our allies. If
> the English king had been agreeable, we were willing to make a truce
> until Trinity (May 22nd). Regarding this, my lord, we have received
> your letters and transcripts of letters from the king of England
> declaring that he has 'granted a truce to the people of Scotland who are

at war with him'. To us this is a very strange way of speaking. In earlier truces, even though the English king has not deigned to call us king, we have at least been named as the principal on one side, as he has on the other. But it does not seem advisable to us to accept a truce in which no more mention is made of us than of the humblest man in our kingdom, so that we could demand no more than any other if the truce were to be infringed wholly or in part.[50]

The long delay between Bannockburn and the peace treaty was not due solely to the pride of Edward II and the indifference of the southern English to the sufferings of their fellow-countrymen in the north. Peace would have come much sooner if King Robert had enjoyed the support of the papacy, an advantage from which King John and the Guardians had benefited greatly down to 1302, and also more positive friendship from the French crown than was shown him by Philip IV's successors. Philip the Fair died in the year of Bannockburn. It was a misfortune for the Scots as well as the French that his long reign was followed by the three short reigns of Louis X, Philip V and Charles IV. Although Charles IV did not die until 1328, a year before Bruce's own death, his reign lasted only six years, and his brothers ruled for still shorter periods. From 1303 until the outbreak of the petty 'war of Saint-Sardos' in 1323, relations between France and England, although hardly cordial, were never so bad as to lead to open war and thus incite the French kings to support the Scots with direct military intervention. And after the Saint-Sardos affair had been settled (1325) the English queen Isabella and her lover Roger Mortimer, from whom Bruce might have some hope of obtaining peace, became as obnoxious to the French as they were to Edward II. Consequently, although as early as 1309 Philip the Fair had recognized Bruce as king of Scots, and although in 1320 and 1321 there had been considerable diplomatic assistance from the French, there was no relentless pressure from Paris to persuade Edward II to make peace. All that Bruce could achieve was the formal renewal of the Franco-Scottish alliance in 1326.

With the papacy the position was rather different, for here Bruce had to contend with outright opposition and, indeed, the most stringent condemnation. John XXII was not naturally predisposed to favour the English kings, as Clement V had been, but he wished for peace among the powerful monarchs of Western Christendom so that they might join forces in a crusade against the Turks. Neither the pope nor anyone else in the fourteenth century would have denied the reality of patriotism as a political force, or refused to acknowledge that it might be the motive of a just war. But the age of Bruce saw nothing especially sacred in patriotism or nationalism in themselves. In the minds of most men trained in law, philosophy or politics, patriotism could never transcend loyalty and obedience to lawfully constituted authority. Everyone would have agreed that defence of the realm was a fundamental duty and a legitimate *casus belli*. But to fight for one's *nation* or for one's *country* simply because one belonged to it and wished to preserve its integrity was quite a different matter, and might, indeed, be unlawful rebellion. To the ordinary man, it is true, the concept of patriotism, or of a racialism and xenophobia more primitive than patriotism, was clear and compelling. Members of the ruling class knew how to exploit it when necessary. Edward I, for example, in his summons to parliament in 1283, had inveighed against the wickedness of the Welsh nation (*lingua Walensium*) whose men had taken the lives of English people.[52] He had been even more explicit in 1295, accusing the French king of plotting to exterminate the English nation (*lingua Anglica*), 'which God forbid'.[53] Bishop Sinclair of Dunkeld's reported words, when he shamed the cowardly knights of Fife in 1317, were 'Whoever loves his lord *and his country*, follow me!'[54] But only with difficulty could Robert Bruce have justified himself and his cause before the bar of contemporary opinion if his aim had been nothing more than 'Scotland for the Scots'. Philip the Fair, admittedly, had praised the Scots in 1299 for bravely defending their 'native land' (*defensionem natalis patrie*) but this defence was coupled with firm loyalty to King John.[55] Similarly, King Robert, once he had been, and could manifestly be seen to have been, chosen by the community of the realm of Scotland, was at pains to emphasize that his war with Edward II, even his fearful incursions beyond the Border, were in defence of his kingdom and of that same royal dignity of Scotland which had inhered in the monarchy of Alexander III and had been so carefully preserved by the Guardians.

It was difficult, naturally, to persuade the pope to accept this. Down to 1304, the Scots had acknowledged John Balliol as king. He had never been formally deposed by the Scots, and the parliament of 1309 which affirmed Robert Bruce's right had not been clearly a full and representative assembly of the community of the realm. What was worse, Bruce himself had begun his reign by murdering his chief rival in church. Even if Pope John had been utterly impartial and not in the least disposed to listen to English propaganda, he could scarcely be blamed for being in no hurry to recognize Bruce's title, even although Bruce, as a private person, had been absolved in 1310 from the sin of killing John and Robert Comyn.

The record of Pope John's attempt in 1317 to compel the Scots to observe a two-year truce with the English contains the clearest statement of Bruce's position and, incidentally, what Lord Hailes called 'the best original portrait of Robert Bruce which has been preserved to our times'.[56]

In August or September 1317, after much difficulty, the two legates sent by Pope John to Britain, John Gaucelin cardinal priest of SS. Marcellinus and Peter and Luke cardinal deacon of S. Maria in Via Lata, succeeded in making contact with King Robert by means of envoys. The cardinals and their party had been ambushed and robbed at Rushyford south of Durham by the ruffianly Northumberland laird Sir Gilbert of Middleton. The bishop-elect of Durham, Lewis brother of Sir Henry Beaumont, who was in the cardinals' party, was actually kidnapped and held to ransom.[57] Once they reached the border, however, the pope's envoys were honourably received and the king listened attentively to their proposals for peace. Then, after taking the advice of his councillors 'like a wise man', the king declared that he did indeed desire to have a firm and lasting peace. But without the advice of his whole council and other lords, he could not say definitely whether he would hold talks with the cardinals so long as they continued to address him merely as 'Governor of Scotland'. Bruce's ironic remarks at this point are best put into direct speech. 'We cannot,' he told envoys, 'say anything in reply to the cardinals' letters which are not addressed to us as king. There are several Robert Bruces who, in company with the other barons, are 'governors of the kingdom of Scotland'. We will inspect and have read out to us the pope's open letters [which bore only a general address], but we will not open the pope's sealed letters, for they carry no royal title and are not addressed to us.' But the king's councillors assured the envoys that the king would gladly negotiate with the cardinals if they addressed him correctly.

The envoys reported to the cardinals that even the official news of Pope John's coronation had been kept out of Scotland because the relevant bulls did not use Bruce's royal title. To Bruce himself they tried to excuse the pope's omission of his title by explaining that as long as a case was *sub judice* the papal see did not wish to say or write anything which might prejudice one or other of the parties. They thereby laid themselves open to the king's unanswerable retort that if the papal see did not wish to prejudice one party [Edward II] by calling Bruce king it was not clear why it should prejudice the other party [himself] by not doing so. 'Especially,' Bruce added, 'since I have possession of the kingdom, my royal title is acknowledged throughout the kingdom, and foreign rulers address me as king. Our father the pope and our mother the church of Rome seem to be showing partiality among their own children. If you had brought letters such as these to other kings you might have had a rougher answer.' The reply was firm, but the king's tone was friendly and his expression remained unclouded. King Robert knew how to administer a stinging rebuke, but mercifully he was not afflicted by the sudden convulsive rages to which the Angevins, especially Edward I, were notoriously prone.

The pope's two-year truce should have run from 1317 to 1319, but it was not observed by the Scots, who captured Berwick in defiance of it. They ignored excommunication, a general interdict imposed on all Scotland, and a prohibition of all Bruce's adherents, and their relatives to the second degree, from holding ecclesiastical office.[58] The two-year truce which Edward II was fortunate to obtain at the end of 1319 was duly observed, but it brought a firm peace no nearer. We have seen that although much effort and expense were devoted to the Bamburgh peace talks in March and April 1321 they proved abortive.[59] Lancaster's treasonable negotiations in 1321 and 1322 were too much the intrigues of a slippery customer bent on his own selfish policies to be a constructive step towards peace.

The next negotiations were held at Lochmaben on January 3rd, 1323, between Bruce himself and Sir Andrew Harcla, who since his victory at Boroughbridge had been earl of Carlisle. These also were a piece of private enterprise, undertaken without Edward II's knowledge. Consequently, they were held to be as treasonable as those of Lancaster, and Harcla, like Lancaster, was accused of furthering his own ambition, even of seeking a marriage alliance with the Bruces. Harcla may have been ambitious, but it is much easier to excuse his treason than Lancaster's. The rout near Old Byland had convinced men in the north of England that Edward II was incapable of defending them. Yet he would not adopt the only alternative policy and treat for peace. A contemporary observer on the spot, who seems to have heard his last speech from the scaffold, said that Harcla, realizing that Edward II could not rule, judged that it would be better for the communities of both kingdoms that each king should possess his kingdom freely and peacefully, without homage, rather than that every year there should be so much slaughter, burning and depredation, so many people made captive and so much land laid waste.[60] Harcla's mistake was to put into action, too soon and on his own initiative, thoughts which must have been in the minds of many contemporaries. At least his trial and the horrors of his execution (March 2nd, 1323) were not in vain if they helped to pave the way for the thirteen-year truce which was concluded two months later.

Harcla's abortive peace negotiations are worth looking at briefly, for they show better than the thirteen-year truce the way King Robert's mind was working on the terms of a final settlement. Unfortunately, the surviving texts of the Bruce-Harcla treaty represent two different versions, and it is not certain which was meant to be binding. According to the best text, preserved at Copenhagen,[61] the two kingdoms would be distinct and separate, each having its own king 'of its own nation', and governed according to its own laws, customs and rules. The earl promised the king and the community of the realm of Scotland to do everything in his power to implement the treaty and to secure King Robert and his kingdom in their independent status. For their part, King Robert and the whole community of the realm promised to promote and maintain the common advantage of the English kingdom. Twelve arbiters, six from each country, would be appointed to settle differences of detail and interpretation between the king and the earl. If the Scottish king brought an army to England under the terms of the treaty he would not harm the earl's property, nor would the earl harm the king's property in the [unlikely] event of his taking an army into Scotland. If Edward II could be persuaded to accept these terms within a year, Bruce would (1) pay him 40,000 merks, in ten annual instalments; (2) found a monastery in Scotland with an income of 500 merks *per annum*, for the souls of those killed in the war; and (3) give the English king the right to choose a wife from his own family for Bruce's male heir, provided that Bruce and Harcla and the twelve arbitrators deemed this desirable in the interests of both kingdoms. If, however, Edward II did not accept the terms within a year, Bruce would not be bound by these last three conditions. Finally, neither king would be forced on the conclusion of peace to receive back into his own kingdom anyone who had fought against him, or to restore his lands.

The other version of the treaty survives in copies kept in England.[62] They presumably represent a text originally in Harcla's possession, and used against him at his trial; but it is possible that they are not to be regarded as final and definitive. The chief difference between the 'English' version and the Copenhagen version is that the former seems to have envisaged the twelve arbiters becoming a body of regents or guardians who would decide matters for the common good of both realms; moreover, the great lords would be sworn to carry out the decisions and commands of the twelve. Nothing was said about Bruce bringing an army into England. It must be remembered that this agreement was made only seven months after the parliament of York, in which the Ordinances of 1310–11 had been annulled. It is tempting to suggest, therefore, that Harcla took back with him to England a slightly watered-down version of the agreement which kept silent about Scots military intervention in England but gave prominence to a baronial body that might seem attractive to those who sympathized with the Lords Ordainers and wished to revive the Ordinances. But it would be unwise to exaggerate the differences between the two versions of the treaty. The points of overwhelming importance – the independence of Scotland, the generous price offered for Edward's acceptance, the marriage alliance and the refusal to rehabilitate men of either side who had forfeited their estates in Scotland or England – all these were present in both versions.

Bruce's generosity was undoubtedly the most remarkable single feature of the treaty. In 1189, William the Lion had paid 10,000 merks for his independence, but this was after his defeat in war and fifteen years of subjection. In 1266, Alexander III, after a single battle, militarily quite inconclusive, had paid Magnus of Norway 4,000 merks plus a perpetual tribute of 100 merks a year in return for Norway's surrender of any title she might have to the Western Isles. Now, after a bloody war of nearly thirty years, during the last half of which Bruce had won victory after victory, he was prepared to pay nearly £27,000 in return for the English Crown's renunciation of all claim to suzerainty over Scotland. This was an appreciably larger sum than that ultimately accepted by the English in 1328.

The thirteen-year truce was concluded at Bishopthorpe, near York, on May 30th, 1323, and confirmed by Bruce at Berwick on June 7th.[62] It touched on hardly any points of fundamental importance for a final Anglo-Scottish peace, but it lessened friction on the Border and produced a reasonably calm atmosphere for the serious peace talks of 1324 at York. These talks, however, like those at Bamburgh three years earlier, foundered on the question of suzerainty, for Edward II still refused to concede points which involved what he called 'the manifest disinheritance of our royal crown'.[64] Under the truce, no new fortifications were to be built in the border counties of either country, there were to be special wardens to control crossing of the Border, to settle disputes, and to report unresolved disputes to the two kings. Sensible provisions were made to protect the shipping, Scottish and foreign, trading to Scotland, most of which had to run the gauntlet of the English coast.

One important clause provided that Edward II would not hinder the Scots from obtaining absolution from the pope and the lifting of the sentences of excommunication and interdict. Yet in the very next year (1324) Edward II sent a powerful mission to the papal curia, headed by the newly-appointed bishop of Winchester, John Stratford (afterwards archbishop of Canterbury), whose chief purpose was to secure the continuation and if possible the intensification of the papal sentences against the Scots. With staggering effrontery, the English king demanded, among other things, that no one in Scotland should be made a bishop in the Scottish church, 'for it is the prelates of Scotland who encourage the nobility, gentry and people (*status*) in their evil acts'.[65] In particular, he asked that John of Egglescliffe, an Englishman who had been made bishop of Glasgow in 1318 through English influence (and who, of course, had never been able to set foot in Scotland) should not on any account be translated to a see outside Scotland. The pope's reply to these demands, remarkable in view of the fact that Scotland was under an interdict and her king excommunicate, was that since no Englishman could enter Scotland the people would have no bishops, a state of affairs he could not tolerate.[66] The pope did, however, agree to Edward's request that when a new bishop was appointed in Scotland the papal bull authorizing the sovereign to deliver to the new bishop the temporalities of his see should be addressed to Edward 'and not to any other person', a practice which Edward quite mistakenly claimed had always been followed in the past.

In 1325 the English king got his way. Pope John rejected Bruce's plea that he and his kingdom should be freed from excommunication and interdict, and duly received Edward II's profuse thanks.[67] But at least Bruce had been able to obtain papal recognition of his royal title. Late in 1323, the earl of Moray went to the papal curia and in the pope's presence argued most shrewdly the case for recognizing Bruce as king of Scots. On January 13th, 1324, the pope wrote to Edward II to explain, half-apologetically, that he had decided to address Bruce as king in future, for to do so 'could not diminish your right and honour, nor add to Bruce's', but would help to bring peace nearer.[68] What King Robert made of Edward II's dishonourable behaviour during these years we are not told. From his point of view the truce was of very little value unless it quickly led to a peace settlement. It is only surprising that Bruce agreed to a truce for as long as thirteen years,

when he must surely have counted upon a peace treaty being concluded long
before that period had ended. And, as though his intrigues at the papal curia
were not sinister enough, Edward II took another step in 1324 (July 2nd)
which must have appeared to the Scottish king in the worst possible light.
Edward Balliol, son and heir of King John, who since his father's death in
1313 had been living on the Balliols' ancestral estates in Picardy, was
commanded to come to England and given a safe-conduct to do so.[69]

It was some compensation for all this English activity that in 1326 Bruce
was able to renew formally the alliance with the king of France. The
negotiations were conducted on the Scottish side by the earl of Moray,
Master James Ben (Lamberton's successor in the see of St Andrews),
Master Adam Murray and Master Walter of Twynholm (Abbot Bernard's
successor as chancellor). Their mission to the French court resulted in the
treaty of Corbeil (April 1326) whereby each country undertook to give
military aid to the other against the king of England.[70] The revival of the
formal Franco-Scottish treaty must be seen in the light of the little war of
Saint-Sardos, which, although it did not break out until the summer of
1324, originated in an outrage committed in October 1323. When Charles IV
embarked, in the spring of 1324, on action which would surely lead to war
with England, he must have regretted the absence of any firm commitment
on the part of the Scots. Even so, and in spite of the truce of Bishopthorpe, it
was apparently believed in English government circles that the Scots would
intervene if there were to be an Anglo-French war. The papal nuncio in
London, Hugh of Angoulême, wrote to John XXII at Avignon on May 22nd,
1324: 'He who acts as king of Scotland (Robert I) has held his solemn
council in a certain castle called Berwick. Although what was discussed is
not known, it is generally believed that if there should be war, which God
avert, Bruce will come to Charles IV's aid by every means in his power.'[71] It
is a matter of great interest that Robert I decided against intervention at this
moment; but he was soon embarking on the negotiations which led to
Corbeil, and the initiative may have been as much French as Scottish.[72]

In the event, final peace was to come only after further warfare and under
a new king of England. Edward II was deposed on January 20th, 1327, and
Edward III, fourteen years of age, was crowned on February 1st. The Scots
chose the very day of Edward's crowning to mount a dangerous assault upon
Norham Castle, which might well have succeeded had not a Scotsman in the
garrison got wind of the attack and warned the castle commander. This
dramatically-timed assault was surely meant as a reminder to the new
English government that if they chose to supplant one king by another they
must face the consequences. The thirteen-year truce was between Robert I
and whoever was lawfully king of England. At the outset of 1327, Robert I
was in no hurry to recognise the deposition of Edward II and coronation of
his son as lawful acts. The attack upon Norham was no more than a
reminder, for it was not followed by any further hostile acts, but it

succeeded in its purpose. The new rulers of England were a council of regency, of which the chief was Henry earl of Lancaster, brother of the executed Earl Thomas, and in whose counsels the queen-mother Isabella and her lover Mortimer had a considerable, though indefinable, influence. One of their first acts (February 15th) was to ensure that the truce was kept on the English side of the Border.[73] Then they proceeded to confirm the truce unilaterally (March 6th).[74] There is evidence which suggests fairly strongly that the English government sincerely desired peace, though it is true that in April troops were collected in the north. The Scots seem to have suspected English intentions,[75] and it is likely that King Robert's patience was close to exhaustion. There is no question that Bruce had ample ground for holding that the English had broken the truce since 1323, for (as Barbour says and as contemporary English records confirm)[76] Scottish and other ships had been seized on the high seas, cargoes stolen, and Scots people (including women and pilgrims) massacred, all without redress. But this does not explain why the Scottish king chose the summer of 1327 as the right moment to mount an invasion of England. It is possible that Moray and Douglas, who, as in the old days, actually led the raid, were in favour of a much more aggressive policy than their ageing and gravely ailing master. Yet Bruce's illness, so serious at this time that one hostile reporter declared that he could not last another year, did not prevent him crossing to Antrim, apparently at the invitation of certain Irish leaders. By an agreement forced upon Sir Henry Mandeville, the seneschal of Ulster, at Glendun on July 12th, 1327, King Robert secured food supplies delivered free at Larne, and compelled the pro-English gentry of Ulster to remain inactive until Whit-sun of the following year.[77]

The main force of Scots crossed the Border on June 15th, probably through the Kielder Gap and down the North Tyne.[78] Besides Moray and Douglas, they had as leaders Earl Donald of Mar (a strong sympathizer with the deposed Edward 11),[79] James Stewart, younger brother of Walter the Stewart who had died in 1326, and Archibald Douglas, Sir James's younger brother. They ravaged Weardale and another unidentified valley which Barbour calls 'Cokdaill' (Cockdale). The young king of England left York on July 10th with a large army, including many Hainaulters in the following of John of Hainault, to whose niece the king was betrothed. One of these Hainaulters, John le Bel, has left a graphic account of the campaign. On the 18th the English, then at Durham, could see smoke from the fires kindled by the raiders and set off in pursuit. For two whole days they marched across boggy moorland, probably by way of Blanchland,[80] but the Scots never came in sight. We might have some chance of explaining the odd failure of the two armies to make contact if we could identify the place Barbour had been told of when he wrote:

> The Scottis men all Cokdaill
> Fra end till end thai heryit haill.[81]

For it seems clear that it was the Scots' decision to move to this valley from Weardale that misled the scouts of Edward III. The understandable suggestion that 'Cokdaill' was the lengthy valley of the Northumberland Coquet must surely be rejected, for it would put the Scots fifty miles north of the Wear. It may be suggested, tentatively, that 'Cokdaill' was the valley of the little River Gaunless, a large part of which is occupied by the ancient parish of Cockfield.

At all events, the failure of their intelligence caused the English army to make a grave blunder. Its leaders decided on a forced march to the Tyne to cut off the Scots' retreat, and the cavalry reached Haydon Bridge on the evening of the 20th. That night it came on to rain heavily, and the rain continued for a week, sending a spate down the burns and rivers, making the going difficult and living conditions utterly wretched. Morale sank very low. It was not until the 31st, when the English army was probably somewhere in East Allendale,[82] that an esquire, Thomas Rokeby, who had gone out to look for the Scots, reported that he had found them nine miles away. He had been captured, but joyfully released because the Scots were as pleased to hear the whereabouts of Edward III as he would be to hear of theirs. The English camped that night at Blanchland, and on August 1st marched to the Wear, beyond which, on the south side, the Scots were drawn up in a very strong position on the steep slopes of a hill. Moray and Douglas refused to leave this position to do battle on more open ground, and deadlock might have been reached had not the Scots, during the night of the 3rd, suddenly decamped and, apparently crossing the Wear, taken up a second position in Stanhope Park, one of the bishop of Durham's hunting preserves.[83] On the night of the 4th, Douglas audaciously raided the king's own quarters, inflicted heavy casualties and very nearly succeeded in capturing Edward himself. But the alarm was quickly raised and the king's personal servants put up a stout defence, his chaplain being among those killed. On the 5th the English were led to expect a night attack and prepared themselves accordingly. Their intelligence, however, must still have been extremely inefficient, for during this same night the entire Scottish force, doubtless much smaller in numbers than the English, but all well-mounted, slipped away unnoticed from Stanhope Park across a treacherous moss, and by the morning they were out of reach, well on their way to the Border. King Edward wept with mortification, and it cannot have been much consolation for him to write from Stanhope on August 7th that 'his enemies had stolen away by night secretly, as if vanquished'.[84] Once again, energy, discipline and experience of the countryside had scored, and an English king had been put to shame in his own land.

In this campaign the Scots had been twisting the English lion's tail. The reverse suffered in Weardale amounted to a military defeat and must have been deeply humiliating. It led at once to Edward III's withdrawal to York. This was bad enough, but King Robert followed up the Scottish success with a massive incursion into Northumberland.[85] In August and September he mounted an elaborate siege of Norham Castle, while Douglas and Moray made less sustained attempts to capture Alnwick and Warkworth. The entire countryside of Northumberland was ravaged. Marcher districts which were relatively fortunate bought a truce till the following Whitsun (May 22nd, 1328) for a large sum of money. These included the Palatinate of Durham (except for Norhamshire), Richmondshire and Cleveland in the North Riding, probably Cumberland and Westmorland, and possibly Allertonshire. It was believed that the king of Scots was now bent upon the outright annexation of Northumberland. It seems more likely that Bruce meant only to terrorize the enemy into agreeing to make peace. But colour was given to the rumours of annexation by the serious efforts he made to capture Northumbrian castles and by the fact, which appears to be authenticated, that he began to grant lands in Northumberland to his supporters by charter.[86]

All this aggressive activity on the Scottish side, coming on top of the Stanhope Park fiasco, the dismissal of the Hainaulters, and the growing insecurity of the queen-mother and Mortimer, at last compelled the English government to begin negotiations for a firm and final peace. It was idle for Isabella and Mortimer to issue any further writs for military service, although they did so in the first week of October, more for form's sake than from any real hope of saving the situation.[87] On October 9th, two experienced English envoys, Henry Percy lord of Alnwick and William of Denum, a well-known common lawyer, were appointed to treat for a final peace.[88] They sought out the king of Scots while he was still engaged on the siege of Norham. At Berwick on October 18th Bruce sent a reply containing six points which he required Edward III to grant under his great seal.[89] These six points, intended to form the basis of a final peace, were as follows. (1) King Edward and his baronage must acknowledge that Robert I and his heirs for all time to come should have the kingdom of Scotland free, quit and entire, without rendering any kind of homage. (2) King Robert's son and heir [David, born on March 5th, 1324] would be married to King Edward's sister [Joan of the Tower, born on July 5th, 1321], who would receive as dower a sum to be agreed on. (3) No person in the faith of the king of England or of his adherents might demand land or tenements in Scotland, nor might any person in the faith of the king of Scots demand land or tenements in England. (4) King Robert and his heirs would give military aid to the king of England against all, saving the alliance between the kings of Scotland and France. Similarly, the king of England and his heirs would give military aid to King Robert and his heirs in Scotland against all, 'as good allies'. (5) King Robert would pay £20,000 within three years of peace being made, giving reasonable security. (6) It would be ordained by the king of England and his council and by King Robert and his council that the sentence of excommunication pronounced at the papal curia against King

Robert and his people should be formally repealed as soon as possible, and that King Edward would give aid and counsel to put this into effect.

If the king of England would inform the nobles of Scotland under his great seal that he was willing to confirm all six points and treat on these lines for a final peace, King Robert would command his envoys to go to Newcastle upon Tyne under sufficient safe-conducts from the English king, to negotiate with the English representatives.

On October 30th King Edward, then at Nottingham, agreed that negotiations should be started at Newcastle on the basis of a marriage between David Bruce and Joan of the Tower and a Scottish payment of £20,000.[90] The question of a military alliance and the peculiarly difficult problem of the 'disinherited' – the lords whose lands in either kingdom had been forfeited because of their allegiance during the war – were to be discussed by the envoys. If King Edward were satisfied on these points he would admit Robert Bruce's independent title to the kingdom of Scotland. It will be noted that the English reply was couched in language which still made it appear that King Edward 111 was a magnanimous victor and Robert Bruce a defeated rebel humbly suing for peace. But despite this form of words it was a great advance on anything that had gone before. The six points were sufficiently acceptable to the English to form the core and substance of the treaty of peace concluded in March 1328. The envoys negotiated at Newcastle during November and part of December. They must then have broadened their discussions to take in other matters on which one side or the other (or both) felt strongly, such as the limits of the Scottish kingdom, Scottish security in the Isle of Man, English security in Ireland, the restoration to Scotland (for cancellation) of all muniments purporting to show that the English Crown enjoyed a feudal superiority over Scotland, and any other documents touching on the liberty of Scotland.

The striking feature of these six points of October 1327 is their similarity to the chief points of the abortive 'treaty' made between King Robert and Andrew Harcla in 1323. According to the terms of the Harcla treaty the two kingdoms were to be separate and independent; indeed, the very same words were used, for in the Harcla treaty Robert was to 'hold' the kingdom of Scotland '*francement, entierement et quitement*', and to 'have' his kingdom '*frank et quit*', while in the points of October 1327 he was to 'have' the kingdom of Scotland '*frank*', *quit*' et entier'.[91] Again, by the Harcla treaty King Robert agreed to let the king of England provide a wife from any suitable member of his own family for Bruce's male heir. In 1327 this offer was repeated, naturally more specifically, since by this date a son had been born to Bruce and his queen. In 1323 the Scottish king was prepared to pay 40,000 merks (nearly £27,000) for the recognition of independence. In 1327 this offer was admittedly reduced, but not by very much. The remarkable thing is that the Scottish proposals remained so generous. If Edward 11 and the Dispensers had accepted peace on Bruce's terms in 1323 the English would have fared better than they did five years later, when Isabella and Mortimer and the young king, Edward III, at last agreed to bring the war to an end.

The negotiations at Newcastle must have been largely successful. In February 1328 Scottish representatives came to York, where King Edward was holding the third parliament of his reign. In this parliament, on March 1st, the English king issued letters-patent, endorsed 'by the king himself and council in parliament', which at long last gave the Scots what they had been striving to obtain in some thirty years of warfare.

> 'Whereas we,' King Edward declared, 'and some of our predecessors, kings of England, have attempted to gain rights of rule, lordship or superiority over the kingdom of Scotland, and terrible hardships have long afflicted the realms of England and Scotland through the wars fought on this account; and bearing in mind the bloodshed, slaughter, atrocities, destruction of churches, and innumerable evils from which the inhabitants of both realms have suffered over and over again because of these wars; and having regard also to the good things in which both realms might abound to their mutual advantage if joined in the stability of perpetual peace, and thus more effectually made secure, within and beyond their borders, against the harmful attempts of violent men to rebel or make war; *we will and concede for us and all our heirs and successors, by the common counsel, assent and consent of the prelates, magnates, earls and barons and communities of our realm in our parliament that the kingdom of Scotland shall remain for ever separate in all respects from the kingdom of England, in its entirety, free and in peace, without any kind of subjection, servitude, claim or demand, with its rightful boundaries as they were held and preserved in the times of Alexander of good memory king of Scotland last deceased, to the magnificent prince, the lord Robert, by God's grace illustrious king of Scots, our ally and very dear friend, and to his heirs and successors.'*[92]

The letter, having thus concurred by implication in the Bruce doctrine that John Balliol had not been rightful king of Scots, went on to renounce any right the king of England and his predecessors might have sought in the Scottish kingdom, to cancel any obligations or agreements made by any of the kings or inhabitants of Scotland concerning the subjection of Scotland or of any of its inhabitants, and to declare null and void any documents which might subsequently be discovered relating to such agreements. It is virtually certain that the letter was not made public on March 1st, for an alternative version of the same date was prepared which spoke of the boundaries of Scotland *at the time of Alexander III's death*, thus explicitly including Man and the Hebrides within the Scottish kingdom.[93] The final version (as given above) was presumably not decided upon until the peace treaty was concluded sixteen days later. Its ambiguity might be manipulated in England's favour, though a fair and reasonable interpretation would surely have left the boundaries of Scotland as they stood in March 1286. The question of boundaries was a minor point when set beside Bruce's main achievement. His representatives at York had the immense satisfaction of knowing that the king of England in parliament had at last admitted the independence of Scotland in unambiguous terms. Moreover, by admitting Bruce's claim to be king, Edward III had acknowledged Scottish independence twice over, for it was abundantly clear that Bruce's title did not derive in the slightest degree from any English judgement, whereas John Balliol's title, however soundly based in law, had been established by a court one of whose chief purposes was to make manifest Edward I's sovereignty over the Scottish realm.

As a final demonstration of Bruce's achievement, the treaty of peace was concluded, not in England, nor even upon the Border, but on Scottish soil, at Edinburgh, which for perhaps a century and a half had enjoyed some claim to be regarded as the principal town and castle, if not the capital, of Scotland. An imposing delegation had been sent north from York by Edward III.[94] It was led by Henry Burghersh, bishop of Lincoln and treasurer, William Ayermin, bishop of Norwich, Sir Geoffrey le Scrope, chief justice of King's Bench, Henry Percy of Alnwick and William de la Zouche of Ashby. These commissioners had had experience of Scottish affairs, including the peace negotiations of 1321 and 1324, and it may be noted in addition that Percy and Zouche were themselves interested parties, being two of the 'disinherited' with claims to land in Scotland. They reached Edinburgh on March 10th, with full powers to conclude and proclaim a final peace and to command its observance by subjects of the English king. Bruce had once more been laid low by sickness since his strenuous campaigning of the previous summer. He was confined to bed, and it was in fact 'in a chamber within the precincts of the monastery of Holyrood in Edinburgh where the lord king was lying' that the peace was concluded, after a bare week of final discussion, on March 17th.[95]

Naturally enough, since the king himself was present, there was an impressive gathering of notables on the Scottish side. Many of the traditional spokesmen and leaders of the community of the realm were present in a properly constituted parliament, to conduct or approve the last negotiations and to witness the sealing of the documents which brought the long war to its close.[96] We can hardly doubt that Bruce himself, even on his sickbed, dominated the scene. The force of his personality, his strength of character, the magic of his name and reputation, would have ensured as much, even if he played little or no part in the actual business. But there were men with the king who would be accounted great in any age and company. Thomas Randolph and James Douglas, the two men who apart from Bruce had done more than any others to win the war and spread the fame of Scotland among the nations of Christendom, were both present. If they were unmatched in feats of war, their experience of negotiation and statecraft could be equalled by that of Bishop Lamberton of St Andrews, who could look back over thirty years of service to the national cause. Besides Lamberton there were six other bishops, John Lindsay of Glasgow, William Sinclair of Dunkeld, John of Pilmuir of Moray,[97] Maurice of Dunblane, Roger of Ross and Simon of Wedale of Galloway. Besides Randolph there were five earls, Duncan of Fife, the doyen of the earls of Scotland, Patrick of Dunbar or March, Murdoch of Menteith, Hugh of Ross and Donald of Mar (a future Guardian).[98] Geographically, these six earldoms were broadly representative of Scotland, but the list – for various reasons – shows notable omissions, e.g. Buchan, Angus, Atholl, Strathearn and Lennox. Only one other Scots magnate, Sir Robert Lauder, justiciar of Lothian, appears by name in the official records of the treaty,[99] but the writ of summons called for all the magnates,[100] and we can tell from charters and other royal acts issued at Edinburgh at this time that members of the king's household in attendance included the chancellor, Abbot Bernard of Arbroath, Gilbert Hay the constable, Robert Keith the marischal, and Andrew Murray of Petty and Bothwell, the pantler (the son of Wallace's colleague); while of the unofficial baronage there were present Sir Alexander Seton – whose role at Bannockburn had been so crucial – Sir Alexander Fraser of Touch Fraser (the king's brother-in-law), Sir Robert Menzies, Sir David Barclay, Sir David Lindsay of Crawford, and Sir William Muschet of Cargill and Kincardine-in-Menteith, and no doubt this list is very incomplete.

The terms of the final treaty show clearly that it was based on Bruce's six points of October, which in turn had derived from the abortive Harcla treaty of 1323. But there were some notable differences which prove that although both sides were keen to reach agreement their negotiations cannot have been easy and were not, in the end, entirely successful. Some matters of great moment were passed over, apparently being insoluble. The main provisions of the treaty were contained in five formal documents, all dated at Edinburgh on March 17th, 1328.[101] The main substance was published in two indentures, one in Latin and one in French. Next, there were two notarial instruments in which King Robert bound himself to pay the £20,000 he had previously offered. Finally, there were King Robert's letters-patent on the subject of the marriage settlement. It will be convenient to summarize these main provisions in the order of the six points of October 1327, as given above.

(1) King Edward's solemn renunciation of all claims to lordship, suzerainty, or sovereignty over Scotland, made in the York parliament on March 1st, was embodied *verbatim* in the text of the Latin indenture. (Perhaps this was the reason why this indenture was written in Latin and not in French.)

(2) A marriage was contracted between David Bruce and Joan of the Tower. They were to wed as soon as this could duly be done, having regard to their tender age. King Robert promised to make available to Joan before

the following Ascension Day (May 12th) a dower of landed estates worth £2,000 a year, guaranteed for the term of her life. Should Joan die before the marriage could be solemnized, the English king would be free to arrange a marriage between David and someone else of the English blood-royal. Similarly, if David were to die before the marriage, King Edward would be free to arrange a marriage between Joan (or some other suitable princess) and the heir-male of the king of Scots.

(3) No part of the final treaty dealt with the vexed question of the 'disinherited'. In the previous October, Bruce had very wisely proposed that no one dispossessed because of the war, on either side, should be reinstated. But on the English side the pressure exerted by certain disinherited lords, notably Henry Beaumont (who had married an heiress of the earldom of Buchan), Henry Percy and Thomas Wake of Liddel, was evidently very strong. Presumably this question was among those discussed, to no avail, at Newcastle in November and December 1327. In view of the presence of Percy and Zouche, we may guess that the subject was again raised at Edinburgh in the following March. But it is pretty certain that Bruce was determined not to risk the peace being wrecked by the bitter feuds which old property disputes might so easily beget, while it seems clear that on the English side there were several lords, both Scots and English, selfish enough to press their claims regardless of the public interest.[102]

(4) There was to be a military alliance between England and Scotland, saving the Franco-Scottish alliance of 1326. If their French allies drew the Scots into war, the English would be allowed to make war in return, notwithstanding the terms of the treaty. The bare proposals of 1327 were modified by two provisions showing where English and Scottish anxieties lay. If anyone in Ireland made war against the king of England, the Scots were not to help him. Likewise, if anyone in Man or the Hebrides made war against the king of Scotland, he was not to be helped by the English.

(5) King Robert bound himself to pay to King Edward £20,000 'for the sake of peace'. The money was to be paid at Tweedmouth in three annual instalments. It has been suggested that this sum may represent approximately the amount taken by Bruce from the northern counties of England in blackmail.[103] But since the king had been prepared to pay nearly £27,000 for the recognition of independence as early as 1323, the suggestion can hardly be accepted. However unjust or illogical it may seem, it was not uncommon for one party to a dispute to pay to have its lawful rights acknowledged by the other party. The two sums offered by Bruce at different times may be seen simply as the price he was prepared to pay to silence for ever the ancient quarrel between English and Scottish kings over feudal superiority. Had the English observed the terms of the treaty of Edinburgh – and Bruce had every reason to believe they would – then the sum of £20,000, large as it was for a poor country like Scotland, would surely not have been too great a price to pay for the permanent healing of this old sore.

(6) The English king and his council would do all they could to have the papal sentences of excommunication against Bruce and his subjects lifted. This Edward proceeded to carry out in good faith, and the sentences were in fact repealed by a bull of October 1328.

So much for the points in the treaty which can be compared with the preliminaries of October 1327. With one notable exception, all Bruce's six points had been incorporated in the final settlement. The heart of the matter was the English renunciation of sovereignty and – as a *quid pro quo* – the marriage alliance, which Edward III regarded as vital, because otherwise the future David II would undoubtedly have found a bride at the French court. As a corollary of the renunciation, King Edward agreed to restore to the Scots all documents touching on English claims to superiority. As a guarantee of the marriage, King Robert agreed to pay the impossibly large sum of £100,000 if by Michaelmas 1338 the marriage between David and Joan had not been solemnized. The point of this arrangement was that David Bruce would not reach the age of fourteen – the legal age for giving his consent to the match – till March 1338, and at any time before that date the Scots might repudiate the contract (or so the English feared).[104] Bruce was therefore given the fairly generous period of ten years, plus six months grace, in which to have the marriage solemnized. In fact, however, the Scots had no intention of defaulting on this part of the agreement. The English queen-mother travelled north with her daughter early in July 1328, and on July 12th Joan of the Tower and David Bruce, though minors, were married at Berwick on Tweed, in the presence of a great gathering of magnates of both realms.[105]

The king of Scots himself was either too ill or (more probably) too punctilious to travel to Berwick for the wedding, but Isabella and Mortimer took the opportunity, nevertheless, of reopening discussions on the subject of the disinherited. It seems that at this point the English government had the sensible idea of restoring to the Scots the Stone of Destiny and the Black Rood of Saint Margaret, looted by Edward I more than thirty years before.[106] Probably this action was meant as a softener to persuade the Scots to make concessions to the dispossessed lords who claimed estates north of the Border. Unfortunately, both the Black Rood and the Stone of Destiny remained at Westminster. It is said that the London mob prevented the stone's removal. But despite this it may have been on the occasion of the wedding that the Scots – perhaps because of the king's illness – imprudently conceded (though not as part of the formal peace treaty) that Beaumont, Percy and Wake should get their Scottish estates back.[107]

Thus, within a year of his own death, Robert Bruce at last achieved the object for which he had fought so long: peace between Scotland and England on the basis of mutual independence. The Treaty of Edinburgh of March 17th, 1328, was formally ratified on the English side at the parliament of Northampton on May 4th. It was a remarkably fair, honourable and statesmanlike settlement, considering the length and bitterness of the struggle which it brought to an end. It has been rightly said that 'it would indeed have been well for both countries if the agreement of 1328 had governed their relations for the rest of the middle ages'.[108] But with how much greater force might it be said that if Edward I had chosen to abide by the spirit of that earlier agreement, the treaty of Birgham, which he ratified at Northampton in the summer of 1290, the later agreement, which his grandson ratified at Northampton thirty-eight years afterwards, would never have been necessary, and there would have been no occasion for the dark years of carnage and destruction, and the breeding of hatred between two nations who for the past century had been learning, not without success, to be friends.

FOURTEEN

Good King Robert

Had Robert Bruce done no more than defy the power of Edward I, restore the monarchy and win the battle of Bannockburn, he would still be reckoned among the Titans. But his fame among contemporaries and with posterity has always rested on a broader and more profound achievement. He was known to later generations of his countrymen as 'Good King Robert'. The epithet has been most sparingly distributed among Scottish sovereigns. Contrary to what might be supposed, the title 'good' was not bestowed automatically upon every king of Scots who defeated the English. Its attribution to Bruce sprang from a popular, instinctive feeling that he had achieved a *rapport* with the community of the realm which was closer, more securely established than any comparable relationship experienced by his predecessors or successors, even by James IV at the height of his popularity. Much of this instinctive feeling must have been derived ultimately from a direct, personal knowledge of Bruce which is denied to us. We see him only through the opaque and sometimes distorting glass of record and chronicle. We may be disappointed, even disillusioned, to see the hero and champion of his people acting very much as a man of his time: a conservatively feudal prince, an exponent of a particularly brutal and destructive form of warfare, a dynast prepared to defend his inherited claim to the throne on occasion at the expense of national unity, and use his country's resources in furtherance of family aggrandizement in Ireland, an accessory, if not a principal, in a deed of plain assassination. But the feet only seem to be made of clay if we choose to idolize the man. Record and chronicle, which show us the defects and shortcomings of the king, also give abundant proof of his courage, prudence and magnanimity. Perhaps, indeed, it was above all the king's humanity which won the affection of his people, the humanity so remark-ably exemplified in the story Barbour tells of how once, in Ireland, retreating in perilous circumstances, Bruce halted the entire army to give protection to a poor laundress in labour, until she could be safely delivered of her child.[1] The stature and the statesmanship of King Robert I appear enhanced rather than diminished when we see him grappling with political difficulties and often failing to find an easy or brilliant solution. He had to manage rough and unruly noblemen who did not all go in awe of him; he had to manage churchmen who, however much they might be his loyal sup-porters, owed allegiance to the Church and to its own monarchy the papacy. Above all, he had to manage the community of the realm, impalpable, inarticulate, yet always a force to be reckoned with; wayward to lead, yet impossible to drive. King Robert's problems in government can best be understood, his success best measured, if we look in turn at his relations with the clergy, the nobles, and the community as a whole.

The Clergy

In 1324, as we have seen, Edward II complained to the pope that it was the prelates of Scotland who were chiefly responsible for encouraging the nobles and people to make war upon the English. Beyond any question, the part played throughout the war of independence by the Scottish bishops was crucial. But it would not be true to say that Bruce always had the Church behind him. Only three bishops attended his coronation. Of these, Wishart and Lamberton were old hands at the game, former Guardians, while David Murray was deeply involved in the national cause, and belonged to a family which, perhaps more than any other, was identified with the fight to preserve Scottish independence. It was to be some years before Bruce could count on the support of a majority on the bishops' bench, equal to that enjoyed by the leaders of the nation between 1296 and 1304.

Down to 1302, thanks to a benevolent papacy (especially under Boniface VIII, 1294–1303), the Scots had normally been able to secure the consecration of bishops favourable to the patriotic cause: Matthew Crambeth (Dunkeld, 1288), Thomas of Dundee (Ross, 1296), William Lamberton (St Andrews, 1298), John Kinninmonth (Brechin, 1298), David Murray (Moray, 1299). But King Robert found it extremely hard to persuade a hostile papacy to confirm the episcopal appointments that would have met with his approval. True, in 1307 he seems to have got Nicholas Balmyle made bishop of Dunblane. But even on an interpretation of the evidence which is most favourable to Bruce, he cannot be allowed an attendance of more than five bishops at his St Andrews parliament in the spring of 1309. His biggest difficulty was in connexion with the two bishoprics of St Andrews and Glasgow, which were pre-eminent both ecclesiastically and politically, and together made up nearly half the population of Scotland.

Robert Wishart, who had already held his see for thirty-four years, was imprisoned in irons in 1306, and the English kings made strenuous efforts to have him deprived of his office by the papacy. In 1308 Wishart, escorted by the bishop of Poitiers, was allowed to go to the papal curia to answer the charges against him. Two years afterwards he was still at the curia, and in January 1311 Edward II argued the case against his return to Scotland in a bitterly-worded letter.[2] Some months later, King Edward requested the pope to remove Wishart from his see and put in his stead Master Stephen Segrave.[3] Pope Clement V, to his credit, neither suspended nor deprived Wishart, but he would not use his influence to have him set free and restored to his diocese. The bishop returned to English custody until after Bannockburn, when, much aged and going blind, he came home to Scotland (along with the royal ladies) in exchange for the earl of Hereford. He died on November 26th, 1316, indisputably one of the great figures in the struggle for Scottish independence, the statesman of the period 1286 to 1291, the patron and friend of Wallace and Bruce, the persistent opponent of Plantagenet pretensions, an unheroic hero of the long war.

For most of the years during which the English had possession of the bishop, King Robert had possession of his diocese. He could not afford to see its organization fall apart and its rich revenues dissipated. By April 1309 he had appointed a high-ranking governmental commission to take charge. Bernard the chancellor and Master Stephen of Dunnideer, a canon of Glasgow who was already king's chamberlain, were made vicars and lieutenants of the see on Wishart's behalf. Dunnideer, formerly associated with Bishop Lamberton, had also been parson of Laurencekirk, a parish owned by the Wisharts, although the living was in the patronage of St Andrews cathedral priory.[4] Soon after Wishart's death, the king tried to get Dunnideer promoted to the Glasgow see, but under pressure from Edward II the appointment was refused by the pope. Dunnideer, having vainly sought a reversal of this decision, died at Paris in 1317. In this or the following year Edward II succeeded in getting an English Dominican, John of Egglescliffe, 'elected' bishop of Glasgow. He was never in possession, and by March 1323 had been 'translated' to Llandaff. Meanwhile, King Robert's candidate for the see was a nobleman, Master John Lindsay, perhaps grandson of Philip Lindsay who had been chamberlain to Alexander III. Although his election (c. 1317) was not at first recognized by the papacy, Lindsay was treated in Scotland as bishop-elect, and eventually, with the bettering of relations between Bruce and Pope John XXII, he was consecrated in 1323. Thus, for fifteen years there was no consecrated bishop in possession of the see of Glasgow; only from 1314 to 1316 and again from 1323 to 1329 did King Robert have a bishop in this large and important diocese on whose co-operation and loyalty he could depend.

At St Andrews the situation was rather different; less dramatic, but still for a time troublesome. William Lamberton shared imprisonment with Wishart in 1306, but he was clearly not regarded by Edward II as an incorrigible recidivist. Possibly he had friends, such as the earl of Pembroke, in high places. In August 1308 he made his peace with the English king, although still under penalties, and in return was given a partial freedom, so long as he remained within the diocese of Durham.[5] By stationing himself on the Tweed, Lamberton could now be in direct contact with at least that part of his own diocese which was still in English hands.

There can be little doubt that Lamberton regarded his submission to the king of England as an unpleasant necessity, extorted under duress. At some date between November 1308 and March 1309 he wrote a letter to Philip IV which has never been published but deserves to be widely known. It is worth recalling that this was the very period when King Philip was switching his support from Balliol to Bruce. The French king had sent some instructions to Lamberton, now lost, which the bishop duly acknowledged in his letter. After commending the archdeacon of Therdonne and Ferricus Tascher who had brought King Philip's letter, Lamberton continued 'I do not wish to conceal from your revered excellency the fact that after I suffered many varied tribulations, oppressions, dangers and blows for the realm of Scotland in times past, I was harshly imprisoned by the famous prince the lord king of England, of good memory [!], on account of the love which I have felt towards you and towards my native land (*nathale solum*, a phrase used by Ovid), deprived of almost all my property and stripped of my revenues. Nevertheless, despite these countless tribulations and dangers I have been unable to win my freedom from the most serene prince my lord king of England who reigns now (your own son-in-law) until I made a bargain with him for £6,000 sterling payable at fixed terms for my redemption. If I am bound to pay this sum I shall not have enough to live on. Only through your help do I see any possibility of having this debt reduced. I therefore humbly beg your most worthy excellence – in whom, after God, I place my trust – that when you have your conference with the king of England at Amiens after next Easter you would obtain from him a remission of my debt'.[6] In this semi-private letter we surely see Lamberton's true sentiments, as in his band with Bruce in 1304 and in his part in Bruce's inauguration two years later.

At the end of 1308 the bishop took part in truce negotiations involving the English, French and Scots.[7] At the turn of 1309–10 he acted as an 'English' envoy in truce negotiations, along with John Lindsay the future bishop of Glasgow.[8] In February 1310 he was present at a court held in King Robert's name in Fife.[9] In this same year he had been able to hold one synod at St Andrews on June 11th, and was proposing to hold another one at Holyrood.[10] In July 1311 the English king was informed that Lamberton was in Scotland and gave him leave to remain there. He was again Edward 11's agent in 1312, and even in the following year, when he went to the court of Philip 1v, it seems to have been as much on Edward 11's as on Robert 1's behalf. By now, the English garrison in Berwick did not view him with much favour and actually threatened him with violence. In fact, Lamberton seems to have returned definitively to the Scottish fold in the spring of 1312, when he came to the Scottish king's camp during the successful siege of Dundee.[11] Bruce was obviously ready to receive him back into favour, and there is no suggestion that Lamberton, in his collaboration with the English, ever betrayed Bruce. For the rest of his life the bishop was busy and prominent in public affairs and in the administration of his great diocese. It was quite in vain that Edward 11 tried to oust him from his see in 1318, by now writing much ill of him to the papacy in somewhat hysterical letters.[12] The culminating point in his episcopate came on July 5th, 1318, when, in the presence of King Robert himself and a vast concourse of magnates, clergy and people, he consecrated the now completed cathedral church of St Andrews, begun by his predecessor Arnold as long ago as 1162.[13] Lamberton died in 1328. In politics, his role from 1299 to 1304, and again in 1306, was of crucial importance. He seems to have been a moderate, conscientious man and an able diplomat. Sincerely and consistently patriotic, not for nothing had Lamberton been the nominee of Wallace and the secret confederate of Bruce. He was also a notable churchman who has left abundant record of a busy and respected episcopate.[14]

The remaining ten dioceses presented similar problems. At Dunkeld Matthew Crambeth may have lived long enough to attend the St Andrews parliament in 1309, but must have died soon afterwards. In 1311 William Sinclair (of a prominent Lothian family) was elected to succeed him and was consecrated in 1312. But Sinclair cannot have been an effective bishop in independent Scotland until 1313 at the earliest, for in February of that year we find Edward II giving him a grudging safe-conduct to go to Scotland to be installed, but only as far as Berwick and on condition of not holding any converse with the enemy.[15] Sinclair must have eluded the English and soon became one of Bruce's staunchest supporters: 'my bishop', the king used to call him. Henry Cheyne of Aberdeen was appointed in 1282 and lived until 1328, when he was surely a very old man. He might have been expected to prove a stumbling-block, for he had never shown opposition to English rule. Like the other prominent members of his family (the elder and younger Reginald Cheyne of Inverugie in Buchan and Duffus in Moray) the bishop had often been active on behalf of the English government. But after the fall of Aberdeen in 1308 Cheyne's position cannot have been easy. His decision to change sides may not have been taken for some years, but on April 7th, 1312, he attended King Robert's parliament at Inchture,[16] and for long afterwards he remained loyal to the king.[17] As far as we know, Bruce could always count on the support of John Kinninmonth, the bishop of Brechin. By contrast, the bishop of Argyll, a Dominican friar named Andrew, although appointed under the Guardians in 1300, was possibly a protégé of the Macdougalls and therefore Bruce's enemy. At all events, he remained in the protection of England until 1314.[18] Nothing seems to be known of the political leanings, in Bruce's early years, of Alan of Galloway, bishop of Sodor and Man. By the date of his death in 1321, and probably by 1314, Bishop Alan was firmly in the king's peace. Finally, the bishop of Galloway, Thomas Dalton, although he had originally owed his appointment to the king's grandfather, the Competitor, remained hostile to Bruce for several years.

Gradually the situation began to shift in Bruce's favour. It would be safe to say that almost all the new episcopal appointments made during his reign were of men approved, if not actually nominated or suggested, by the king. In Moray, for example, on David Murray's death in 1326, there was elected in his place John of Pilmuir, son of a Dundee burgess and nephew of a Cistercian monk from Coupar Angus, who had served the king in 1321 as an envoy in peace negotiations.[19] Dalton of Galloway was succeeded in 1321 by the abbot of the royal abbey of Holyrood, Simon of Wedale, whose consecration was blocked until 1327.[20] Nicholas Balmyle died some time in 1319 or 1320, and his successor at Dunblane was the king's old friend Abbot Maurice of Inchaffray. Presumably Roger, an Augustinian canon of Abernethy, chosen to follow Thomas of Dundee at Ross in 1325, was *persona grata* with the king. It is remarkable that several of these new bishops were regular, not secular, clergy, but it seems impossible to say whether the reason for this lay in the troubled conditions of Bruce's earlier years.

The bishops formed only a tiny minority of the clergy as a whole, but they had constant and direct dealings with the Crown, and if they were able and conscientious and possessed strong personalities their influence among the clergy and people of their dioceses might be very great indeed. For administration they depended on the services of highly trained, experienced clerks, many of whom were university graduates. Since a century was to elapse before there was any university in Scotland, there was a good chance that her educated clerks would rid themselves of any undue insularity. After a period spent in a bishop's *familia* or household such clerks would normally be promoted to the various offices of diocesan administration, especially those of archdeacon – the chief administrative officer of the diocese – and of Official, that is, president of the archdeacon's or the bishop's ordinary court of jurisdiction. The same class of educated clerks might also find preferment as dignitaries of cathedral churches, as deans, sub-deans, chancellors, treasurers, and chanters. All these offices, often lucrative in themselves (especially the archdeaconries), might be regarded by the ambitious, able or merely well-connected clergyman as rungs on the ladder leading upward to the higher office of bishop.

In the Scottish Church during the war of independence this class of educated clergy was relatively small. Its members formed a close-knit, interconnected group, moving easily from diocese to diocese, often holding several offices simultaneously in different dioceses, exerting an influence out of all proportion to their numbers. Their common experience of long years of study at one or more of the great continental universities must have given the graduates among them a genuine *esprit de corps*, perhaps a sense of superiority. They were familiar with Paris and Cologne, and there seems to have been a strong Scottish connexion with Bologna, the centre of legal studies. This connexion dated from long before the outbreak of the war with England and continued into the fourteenth century. Among Scottish clerks found at Bologna University in the late thirteenth century[21] were Robert, bishop of Ross (Thomas of Dundee's predecessor), Hervey of Dundee, bishop-elect of Caithness, Ralph of Dundee, Master Michael of Dundee, Thomas of Dundee, bishop of Ross, Master Alpin, archdeacon of St

Andrews, treasurer of Scotland under king John and almost certainly son of an earl of Strathearn, John of Berwick (parson of Renfrew), William of Twynholm, and most famous of all, Master Baldred Bisset. With the exception of the Franciscan philosopher Duns Scotus, Bisset was surely the most remarkable of all the Scottish clergy of this period below the rank of bishop. He seems to have spent a good many years at Bologna and to have been a professional jurist of truly international distinction.[22] We have already seen the outstanding part he played in 1301, when the Scots were pleading their case against Edward I before Pope Boniface.

With such a background, it would not be surprising if the educated Scottish clergy of Bruce's day displayed a high *morale* and possessed a keenly-developed sense of their own liberties and privileges. They were well aware of the special status of the *Ecclesia Scoticana* within the western church as a whole, consisting as it did of a group of bishoprics directly dependent, *nullo mediante* in the historic phrase of the bull of 1192, upon the papacy. These self-confident clergy formed perhaps the biggest single obstacle to English pretensions north of the Border, and Edward I and his son were entirely justified, from their own point of view, in attempting to anglicize the Scottish Church, even though it cost them much energy and money.[23]

If the earlier years of the struggle had produced outstandingly able clergy such as Robert Wishart, Nicholas Balmyle and Baldred Bisset, the clerical hero of Robert I's reign was unquestionably the king's chancellor Bernard, better known as Abbot Bernard of Arbroath, less well known as Abbot Bernard of Kilwinning, least well known of all as Bishop Bernard of Sodor and Man, a see to which he was unaccountably promoted in 1328 and held until his death in 1331. It has been supposed that Bernard was the principal author of the Declaration of Arbroath of 1320. A different candidate for authorship will be put forward in the next chapter, but that is in no sense to lessen Bernard's share in the literate aspect of King Robert's government. He must have been perfectly familiar with the manifesto supporting Bruce's claim to the throne published at the St Andrews parliament of 1309, even if he was not actually its author. It would hardly be rash to guess that Bernard had some hand in the production of one puzzling version of this manifesto, which survives in an original and is dated 'in a general Scottish council held in the church of the Friars Minor of Dundee on February 24th, A.D. 1309, in the fourth year of [King Robert's] reign', i.e., February 24th, 1310, by modern reckoning.[24] Like the clerical version of the manifesto dated at St Andrews in March 1309,[25] this 'Dundee' version purports to come from 'the bishops, abbots, priors and remaining clergy holding office in the realm of Scotland', and its text is identical with the St Andrews document. We may assume that 'general Scottish council' meant a provincial council of the Scottish Church, and not a national general council, but it has been objected that no such assembly could have met in the Greyfriars of Dundee at a date when both castle and town were in English hands, certainly not to approve a document so seditious from an English standpoint.[26] If the objection is sound, the dating clause is fictitious; we should have to suppose that the version was produced at some later date, or elsewhere, and for some unknown reason deliberately ante-dated or given the wrong place of issue. But it is conceivable that during the Anglo-Scottish truce which prevailed at Dundee and elsewhere during the early part of 1310 a group of Scottish clergy did in fact hold a council at Dundee, to which, despite its possible incompleteness or irregularity, they gave the name *concilium generale Scoticanum*.[27] The opportunity would then have been taken to re-issue the St Andrews manifesto in an effort to prove that it had the full support of the Scottish Church. In any case, we know that the manifesto – an enormously useful and vitally important document – was re-issued considerably later than 1309. For we possess, also in the original, another text of the manifesto which, instead of emanating vaguely from the prelates and clergy, purports to have been issued by the twelve bishops of Scotland. They are all named, and the document apparently bore their seals.[28] It seems to be authentic. It cannot be earlier than 1312 (for William [Sinclair] appears as bishop of Dunkeld) nor later than November 1316 (for Robert Wishart appears as bishop of Glasgow). In fact, it can hardly be earlier than 1314, since one of the bishops named, Andrew of Argyll, seems to have been in exile in England until March of that year, and was presumably not reconciled with Bruce until after Bannockburn.[29] It may, therefore, be taken as reasonably certain that at some date between Bannockburn and Wishart's death a provincial council of the Scottish Church was held, partly to signalize the full reconciliation of the entire bench of bishops with the king. At this council, the St Andrews manifesto was evidently issued in the names of all the bishops, with the fullest solemnity and publicity. Whatever their private feelings may have been, the bishops of Scotland were now ranged solidly behind King Robert I.[30] It can hardly be doubted that Abbot Bernard played a principal part in the process by which, in the face of severe penalties of excommunication, the clergy came to present a united front of patriotism to the papacy, to England, and to the other nations of western Christendom.

The Nobles[31]

It cannot be said too often that Scotland in the thirteenth and fourteenth centuries was an intensely feudal and conservative kingdom. This fact more than any other governed the relations of King Robert with the nobility. Before these relations can be properly appreciated, we must clear away two myths which threaten to entangle the main thread of Scottish political history between 1286 and 1329. The first myth has already been encountered: the belief, derived at best from a mere quarter-truth, that the war of independence was fought and won by the common people in defiance of aristocratic apathy or hostility. The story of the struggle as it has been unfolded in the foregoing pages should give ample proof of the absurdity of this belief. At every stage of the struggle save in 1297 the Scottish nobility, as was only to be expected, occupied a leading place. Even in 1297 many of the nobles were deeply involved in the national rising, although for nearly a year most of the historic names were in the background, and the giant figure of Wallace bestrode the stage. But from 1298 to 1304, for good or ill, the nobles were back in command. When Bruce made his revolutionary bid in 1306, he was supported by a few earls, a fair number of great barons, and a considerable following of the lairds or gentry. It is one thing, and true enough, to say that the noble class was rent asunder by feuds and factions difficult or impossible to heal. It is quite another, and certainly false, to say that the nobility as a whole lacked the will and effectiveness to conduct the war against England.

The second myth that needs to be demolished is that the war of independence, and particularly the reign of Robert I, saw the overthrow of so many of the old aristocratic families that a virtually new ruling class came into being, composed of 'new men', adventurers even, who gambled on Bruce's victory and were consequently showered with lands and favours. Like so many of the conveniently simple and picturesque accounts which find their way into history books, this generalization is not wholly untrue. But, by over-simplifying, it seriously distorts the truth. It can be corrected only by stating the relevant facts. The first fact of real importance is that throughout his reign, even after November 1314,[32] King Robert held fast to the principle that there should be no disinheritance of men and women claiming property by hereditary right, provided that they were prepared to swear allegiance to him and come into his peace fully and without any reservations. From 1314 this meant that they could no longer be English landowners as well. For the first time since the eleventh century men and women of this class must choose to be either Scots or English: they could not be both. The 'disinherited' whom King Robert wisely wished to exclude from the peace terms in 1328 were those who wanted to have it both ways, to enjoy their Scottish lands and yet be subjects of the English king or vice versa. The second fact of significance is that the king's dealings with regard to property and the services rendered by its holders were informed by a spirit of conservatism and restoration. There were undoubtedly changes, but the remarkable thing is not that change occurred but that the changes which took place were not very much more radical in their character.

It will be as well to start with the earls of Scotland, whose ancient history and special position we have already seen. In 1286 the earldoms numbered about thirteen. There were no more than this at the time of King Robert I's death in 1329, for though the king created – or rather revived – the earldom of Moray in 1312, he virtually suppressed the earldom of Buchan. The part played by the earls of Caithness and Sutherland in Bruce's reign is almost unrecorded. At the date of the St Andrews parliament in March 1309,

William earl of Sutherland, previously a supporter of the English crown, was evidently in King Robert's peace, perhaps through the influence of his powerful neighbour the earl of Ross. The earldom of Caithness, held jointly with the Norwegian earldom of Orkney, was in wardship. In 1320, Earl Magnus of Caithness was included among the magnates of Scotland who addressed the letter to Pope John XXII. Presumably the earl was in King Robert's peace then, but little is known of his activities, and he died before the end of the reign. Earl William of Ross, an auditor for Balliol in the competition for the throne, began the reign of Bruce as a firm opponent. He was won over as early as 1308 and became one of the king's staunchest supporters. The earl's elder son Hugh (who succeeded to the earldom in 1323) was held in special favour by the king. Royal grants and confirmations of lands and offices made him before the end of the reign one of the richest magnates of the kingdom, and next to Thomas Randolph unquestionably the greatest potentate in the north. The sheriffdoms and burghs of Dingwall and Cromarty, the burgh of Nairn, vast estates in the Black Isle and elsewhere in Easter Ross, baronies and thanages in north-eastern Scotland, the Isle of Skye – all these came within the lordship of Earl Hugh, and as a final mark of favour he was given in marriage Maud Bruce, one of the king's sisters. His younger brother John (who died childless) was given in marriage Margaret Comyn, niece and co-heir of John Comyn, last earl of Buchan, and with her came half the earl's lands. Hugh of Ross was certainly no *novus homo*; his descent was direct in the male line from Farquhar MacTaggart, possibly hereditary lay priest of Tain or Applecross, whom King Alexander II had made earl of Ross about 1225.

John Comyn earl of Buchan, constable of Scotland, another of Balliol's supporters in 1291, died childless at the end of 1308. He was an irreconcilable enemy, but the king had no intention of exterminating the Comyns root and branch. Nevertheless, the ancient earldom of Buchan, whose lands were overrun and harried by Bruce and his brother Edward in 1308, was virtually dismembered during the next twenty years. As we have seen, half went to Margaret Comyn, one of Earl John's two co-heirs, daughters of his brother Alexander, and to her husband John of Ross. The other half escheated to the crown because Margaret's sister, Alice Comyn, wife of Sir Henry Beaumont, had become irretrievably English.[33] This half seems to have been sufficient to enable the king to grant away large tracts of land in Buchan to faithful followers. The biggest share went to the Keiths. Sir Robert Keith the marischal was given Aden and many other estates in the heart of Buchan; his brother (and heir) Edward had grants of much land in what are now the parishes of Methlick, Monquhitter, New Deer, Ellon, Longside and Foveran. Sir Gilbert Hay of Errol (who held the constableship of Scotland which had been Earl John's) was granted the lands, and presumably also the castle, of Slains, with which his family was to be so closely associated for some centuries. Archibald Douglas got Crimond and Rattray

*Landlords before: (Comyn)
and after: Keith, the forfeiture
of John Comyn, Earl of Buchan, 1308*

⊚ *King's burghs and other*
🏛 *royal centres*

🏛 *Castles*

0 1 2 3 4 5
|—|—|—|—|—|
Miles

BANFF

GLENDOWACHY
Ross
(in thanage)

B

NETHERDALE
John Bruning

✝ Turriff Hospital

River Deveron

HATTON •
John Bruning

• TOWIE
Barclay

(Strathbogie)
STRATHBOGIE
Gordon

(Frendraught)
• FRENDRAUGHT
Stewart

FYVIE
Thanage of
Dereleye
(Darley)

✗ *Slioch
(November, 1307)*

F o u d l a n d   H i l l s

Bogie

🏛 DUNNIDEER

Barra
(23/5/08)

INVERURIE •

🏛 KILDRUMMY

KINTOR

13. Buchan and Formartine showing changes in landlordship in the reign of Robert I.

with its harbour, Sir John de Boneville got Collieston, and Hugh of Ross, Sir Walter Barclay and Sir Philip Meldrum had grants of similar size and value. Not one of these men appears to have been in any sense an upstart or adventurer. Comyn's loss, to be sure, was their gain, but they had not started from nothing. What is more, the infeftment for military service of the king's constable and marischal in this strategically important coastal province forcibly recalls what King David 1 had done in the south west nearly two centuries earlier, when he planted his Stewart in Renfrew and North Kyle and his Constable in Cunningham.

The history of the earldom of Mar provides a striking illustration of the king's patience and of his reluctance to admit failure in his efforts to win the nobles to his allegiance. The links between Bruce and the Mar family were very close. Young Donald of Mar, who had a clear expectation of succeeding to the earldom at his father's death about 1302, was the king's nephew and had been his ward. He may have fallen into English hands at Methven or Kildrummy; at all events, he was brought up at the court of Edward of Caernarvon, to whom he became strongly attached. He was brought to Newcastle in 1314 to be returned to Scotland along with other exiles, but refused. He did not rejoin the Scots until after King Edward's deposition. With possibly misplaced generosity, Bruce not only restored his earldom but allowed him to take a leading part in the invasions of England during the summer of 1327 and also to intrigue in England against Isabella and Mortimer on behalf of the imprisoned Edward of Caernarvon.[34]

The case of Robert de Umfraville earl of Angus was even more remarkable. Neither his father Earl Gilbert (who had sponsored Balliol in 1291 and who died in 1307) nor Robert himself had ever shown the least inclination to join forces with the Scottish patriots. They were emphatically Englishmen, lords of Coquetdale and Redesdale in Northumberland, with an inherited distrust of aggressiveness north of the Border. Although the earldom of Angus had been theirs by marriage since 1243, the only member of the family who ever looked like striking roots in Scotland was Sir Ingram de Umfraville,[35] who after many years of loyalty to the cause of John Balliol came into King Robert's peace (perhaps reluctantly) from about 1314 until 1320. Earl Robert died in 1325, leaving as heir a young son Gilbert who was completely in the power of the English king. Despite the obvious Englishness of the Umfravilles, Bruce forebore to confiscate the earldom until the every end of his reign. Then, convinced at last that they would never become Scots, he granted it to Sir John Stewart of Bunkle, grandson of Sir John Stewart of Jedburgh who fell at Falkirk.[36]

King Robert was also personally related to the earls of Atholl. John of Strathbogie earl of Atholl had married as his first wife Marjorie, daughter of the elder Earl Donald of Mar, so that for some years Atholl and Bruce were brothers-in-law. Earl John, a Bruce supporter in the Great Cause, had played a strenuous part in the national struggle down to his capture and execution in 1306. It might have been expected that his son and heir David of Strathbogie would have become one of Robert Bruce's firmest adherents. But his wife was a daughter of the murdered John Comyn of Badenoch, and he gave his allegiance, for what it was worth, to the English king. Down to 1312 he was active in the war against Bruce, who, as usual, was in no hurry to have the earldom forfeited. Earl David changed sides before October 1312, his earldom was restored to him, and he was even given the office of constable of Scotland. This was a signal proof of Bruce's anxiety to win over yet another Scottish earl, for he had only recently granted this office, provisionally at least, to Gilbert Hay of Errol, whose loyalty and good service had been conspicuous from the very beginning of the reign. Though Earl David played a notable part in the capture of Perth,[37] the king's generosity was sorely misplaced. There was bad blood between the earl and the king's brother Edward Bruce, who had seduced the earl's sister Isabel and had then deserted her for a daughter of the earl of Ross. Earl David chose to take a treacherous revenge. On the very eve of Bannockburn he attacked the Scottish supply depot at Cambuskenneth Abbey, killing the officer in charge, Sir William of Airth, and many of his men, and carrying off stores of food.[38] This act could not be forgiven. His earldom lands were granted to Sir Neil Campbell and to the king's sister Mary, whom Sir Neil married after her release from captivity in 1314. Stratha'an in Banffshire, which he held of the earl of Fife, was given to Earl Malcolm of Lennox. His patrimony of Strathbogie in Aberdeenshire was granted to the prominent Berwickshire magnate Sir Adam Gordon, no doubt as part of the price of winning him over and also as reward for his part in delivering the Declaration of Arbroath to Pope John XXII and arguing the Scottish cause at the curia.[39] Earl David was dead by 1327, leaving a line of Strathbogie 'pretender' earls of Atholl recognized only in England. The earldom passed first to the Campbells, then to the Stewarts. In November 1314, in the parliament which approved the forfeiture of David of Strathbogie, the constableship of Scotland was restored to Gilbert Hay. This time the office was granted heritably, and it has been held by the Hays of Errol and their descendants ever since.

Malise earl of Strathearn, an auditor for Balliol in 1291, had done homage to Bruce in 1306, evidently under compulsion. Speedily reconciled with Edward II, he served against Bruce until the fall of Perth in January 1313. Barbour says that he was in the Perth garrison when the Scots captured the town, that he was brought to King Robert by his own son, the younger Malise, who was already on Bruce's side, and that because of the son's loyalty Bruce gave the father back his earldom. This story may well be true. At least it is not contradicted by the evidence of record,[40] which shows the younger Malise of Strathearn in receipt of English pay down to January 1310, but not thereafter. As for the elder Earl Malise, all we know for certain is that he disappears from the English record at the end of 1310, and he seems to have died about 1313. His son, recognized as earl, was definitely in King Robert's peace in March 1317,[41] and he seems to have remained a loyal adherent. Here again, therefore, we see a family of ancient Celtic descent successfully retaining its hereditary earldom throughout the Anglo-Scottish war.

At the end of the thirteenth century, the two earldoms to the south-west of Strathearn, Menteith and Lennox, were also held by old families of partly Celtic descent and strongly Celtic tradition. Walter Stewart, earl of Menteith in right of his wife Mary, had supported Bruce in 1291. His son Earl Alexander had taken an active part in the war under Balliol and the Guardians. Alexander's son Earl Alan had come out in support of Bruce at his coronation. He surrendered to the English, was deprived of his earldom, and died, probably in captivity, some time between November 1306 and March 1309, leaving as heir a young son of the same name, evidently in English hands.[42] The younger Alan died too soon to succeed to the earldom, which for most of Bruce's reign was in custody, at first on young Alan's behalf, afterwards on behalf of his sister Mary.[43] Eventually, perhaps in 1323, the king granted the earldom, on its resignation by Mary of Menteith, to her uncle Sir Murdoch of Menteith, brother of her father Earl Alan. Murdoch of Menteith had been with the English until 1317, possibly until 1320, the year of the Soules conspiracy against Bruce. He is said to have got wind of the plot and told the king. For this he got lands which had belonged to the conspirators, and it may be that the earldom also was in the nature of a reward.[44] At all events it remained in the possession of the old family of Menteith, although not in the direct line of descent. Lennox, the neighbouring earldom to the west, presented a more straightforward case. Earl Malcolm, who had sponsored the Bruce claim in 1291, was an old and tried friend. The king indeed owed his very survival in the dark days of 1306 to the loyalty of the earl and his followers. Malcolm of Lennox played a full part in King Robert's reign, and had several grants of land and office, notably the hereditary sheriffdom of Clackmannan and the sheriffdom and castle of Dumbarton, which his ancestors had previously held but which King Alexander II had prudently annexed to the crown.[45]

Carrick was not one of the ancient earldoms, yet it represented in part the older and larger lordship of Galloway of the twelfth century. Robert Bruce had held it since 1292 by inheritance from his mother, and it was only to be expected that he would settle it on a member of his family. His brother Edward and his nephew Thomas Randolph might both be thought to have some claim upon it.[46] For Randolph, however, other awards had been made or were in store, and by October 1313 Edward Bruce had become earl of Carrick. At first sight this looks a poor exchange, for early in the reign Edward Bruce had been given Balliol's more ancient title of 'lord of Galloway'. But down to 1313 the lordship of Galloway can hardly have been more than an empty title, whereas the earldom of Carrick, secure in Scottish hands, was an honour with tangible profits. Moreover, the lordship of Galloway, if historically greater, was technically inferior to any earldom. On Edward Bruce's death in 1318 the earldom of Carrick came back into the king's hands. It was given first (1328) to his son, young David Bruce, and afterwards to David's cousin Alexander Bruce, the bastard son of Edward and Isabel of Strathbogie, daughter of Earl John of Atholl. It is a mark of the special position accorded by the Bruce-Stewart dynasty to this western principality that before the end of the fourteenth century it came to be regarded as the peculiar appanage of the heir apparent to the Crown.

The earl of Dunbar (or March) Patrick IV, had supported Bruce the Competitor in the Great Cause. From 1296 until his death in 1308 he had given his allegiance faithfully to the English crown. His son and heir, Patrick V, at first followed suit, though from 1309 onwards his loyalty was maintained at great and increasing sacrifice. It was to this Earl Patrick that Edward II owed his escape after Bannockburn, and it seems to have been at this very time – immediately after allowing Edward and his company to take ship for Bamburgh – that the earl came over to the patriots.[47] His earldom and estates, including those held of him by tenants still in rebellion, were restored, and thereafter his loyalty to Robert I never wavered.

So far we have passed under review twelve earldoms, in only two of which had the king, by the end of his reign, installed an earl who did not belong to the family which had held the earldom before 1286. Considering the upheavals to be expected from almost thirty years of continuous warfare, some of it civil war, this was a most remarkable feat of conservation. Bruce's sole innovation among earldoms was his creation, probably in the summer of 1312, of an earldom of Moray in favour of Thomas Randolph.[48] Even here, neither earldom nor earl can be considered an upstart or raw intruder. The earldom consisted of most of what the crown had held in Moray since David I's time, including the Red Comyn's lordships of Badenoch and Lochaber.[49] But this was more or less equivalent to the lands and rights of the old mormaers of Moray, and the province would almost certainly have grown into a normal earldom had it not escheated in 1130 on the death of Angus, daughter's son to King Lulach. As for Randolph himself, his father was of an old-established landowning family in Roxburghshire and Nithsdale, while through his mother he was a potential heir to the earldoms of Fife and Carrick.[50] Even if he had not been one of the king's two indispensable lieutenants, his candidature for earl's rank would have seemed perfectly legitimate. He progressed from 'lord of Nithsdale' (c. 1306–12?) through 'earl of Moray and lord of Annandale' (1312) to 'earl of Moray, lord of Man and Annandale' (1313).

Fife, which in many ways gave the king his most intractable problem among the earldoms, has been left to the last. By common consent it was the senior earldom of Scotland, and its holder had the unchallenged privilege and duty of placing a new king of Scots on the seat of royalty at Scone.

Without this ceremony, indeed, a king's title might be called in question. The young Earl Duncan (a posthumous child) was about sixteen years old when his paternal aunt Isabel crowned Robert Bruce.[51] He was brought up a ward of the English Crown. It was a momentous decision on his part to wrench himself from English tutelage in 1315, to leave behind his childless wife, the young Marie de Monthermer, and to come into King Robert's peace. For the king his change of allegiance was crucial. The earl appears to have met King Robert's representatives at Crichton in Midlothian on August 23rd, 1315.[52] He agreed to surrender his earldom to the king, in order to receive it back on certain conditions. Failing any lawful heirs which Earl Duncan might subsequently beget, it was to be entailed upon the king himself and any of his lawful heirs to whom he chose to assign the earldom, in such a way that the persons of king and earl of Fife should always be distinct, and the arms of the earldom always distinct from the royal arms. If the king were to die without a lawful heir to whom the earldom could be thus assigned, it would revert to Earl Duncan's cousin Alan, son of Earl Alan of Menteith.[53] This tailzie or entail was made in order to ensure that there would always be a holder of the earldom of Fife, because, as the agreement frankly stated, 'the earl's wife is detained [by the English] and he might die without heirs of his body' and, further, because 'kings of Scotland ought to be made (i.e., inaugurated) by whoever is earl of Fife'. On these terms the premier earl of Scotland, at the age of twenty-five or thereabouts, was restored to his earldom with all its lands and honours intact. He was also confirmed in possession of the three baronies of Kinnoull, Kincardine Oneil and West Calder, which belonged ancestrally to the earls of Fife though not as part of the earldom.[54] In this case, reversion was in favour of Thomas Randolph who, like Alan of Menteith, had some claim of inheritance from the former earls of Fife. The agreement with Earl Duncan is a remarkable instance of the king's anxiety not to offend the great nobles by disinheriting one of their number, and it shows the importance which he and his council attached to the observance of ancient constitutional custom.

The pattern revealed in King Robert's treatment of the earls was repeated with variations in his dealings with the lesser nobles and the gentry. We find the same patient conservation and restoration, the same reluctance to overthrow ancient rights or to offend feudal susceptibilities. The king might, to be sure, display a sense of humour in this delicate process of rewarding both the faithful and the prodigal. The fate of the barony of Manor in Tweeddale is a case in point.[55] It had belonged since Alexander III's time to the family of Baddeby. Alexander Baddeby, who held it in the early years of Robert I's reign, was forfeited for adhering to the English, and in the St Andrews parliament of March 1309 the barony was granted to the king's retainer (*valletus*) Adam the marischal. Baddeby returned to Scottish allegiance probably after Bannockburn, and in April 1315 the king divided the barony in two, leaving half in possession of the faithful Adam and regranting the other half to his former enemy Baddeby. This generous arrangement did not satisfy Baddeby, however, and in 1323 he petitioned for the restoration of the whole. To this King Robert replied: 'I have given Alexander Baddeby half of Manor of my own grace. It is open to him to choose between resting content with that arrangement or surrendering his half to me and submitting the whole matter to the judgement of my court.'[56] Baddeby declared himself perfectly content with the king's gracious award.

Undoubtedly there was forfeiture of property among the noble and gentry class, but much the largest part of the total of forfeited estates consisted of lands, lordships and privileges held by a very small minority of irreconcilables. It is not often realized what an enormous amount of property was placed at the king's disposal through the forfeiture of only six men: John Balliol, John Comyn of Badenoch, John Comyn earl of Buchan, Alan la Zouche, William Ferrers and Enguerand de Guines. The last three were not Scotsmen, but they had inherited (or in the third case married into) very large Scottish estates. Enguerand de Guines, husband of Christian Lindsay, who succeeded to the great French lordship of Couci in 1311, never became King Robert's man. After forfeiture, he himself (but not his widow and family) passed from the Scottish scene for good. This meant that the king could grant away lands in Berwickshire and East Lothian as well as the baronies of Skirling, Durisdeer, Staplegordon and Westerkirk.[57] Yet Staplegordon did in fact descend to John Lindsay, the future bishop of Glasgow, as heir of Philip Lindsay, and although their exact relationship is obscure we can be sure that John Lindsay was a close kinsman (perhaps, indeed, the son) of Enguerand de Guines from the fact that he displayed the arms of Couci as well as Lindsay.[58] It is true that John Lindsay resigned the barony, but this was because he was a clergyman. Westerkirk remained in the hands of the Soules family (who had held it as tenants of de Guines) until William de Soules forfeited it in 1320.[59] Durisdeer went first to James Stewart (a younger son of James the Stewart who died in 1309) then to his sister Gelis and her husband Sir Alexander Menzies. In any event, the forfeiture of de Guines cast no blight on the fortunes of the Lindsays as a great landowning family. Pro-Bruce heirs of other anti-Bruce Lindsays might inherit despite forfeiture, as when in 1321 Sir John Lindsay (nephew of the Philip Lindsay mentioned above) received Wauchope and lands in Annandale as heir of his father Simon Lindsay, who had been forfeited as 'the king's rebel and enemy'.[60] And of course there were some Lindsays, like Sir Alexander of Barnweill in Ayrshire, who had been active in support of the Guardians and had then been 'out' with Bruce from the beginning, having, indeed, been art and part in the murder of John Comyn.[61]

In the same way, there was nothing vindictive in the king's treatment of men and women who bore the names of Balliol and Comyn. Although John Balliol and his son Edward and their kinsmen Alexander Balliol of Cavers and Richard Balliol of Yetholm suffered forfeiture, Sir Henry Balliol, submitting to Bruce, was able to get Branxholm (forfeited by Richard Lovel of Hawick) 'saving the land granted by the king to Walter Comyn'.[62] The widow of Edmund Comyn of Kilbride was provided for 'until she can recover her rightful dower according to the assize of the land'.[63] The respectable, if never dominant, place occupied in the north of Scotland during the later middle ages by families of this name proves that Bruce pursued no clan vendetta against the kinsmen of the Red Comyn and the earl of Buchan. In truth he had no need to, for the lands and lordship of Comyn of Badenoch by themselves gave plenty of scope for royal generosity. Thus, in Nithsdale Thomas Randolph got the lordship of the whole dale, temporarily at least,[64] to go with his ancestral barony of Morton, while Walter the Stewart and Robert Boyd divided Dalswinton between them. Elsewhere, James Douglas got Bedrule, Walter son of Gilbert got Machan in Clydesdale, Malcolm Fleming got Kirkintilloch, and the Red Comyn lordship of Badenoch was included in Thomas Randolph's earldom of Moray.

The forfeiture of John Balliol meant the redistribution of three groups of property – first, his lordship of Galloway, secondly his inherited third share of the Scottish lands of Earl David, brother of King William the Lion, and lastly his similar inheritance from the old Moreville and de Quinci lands in Lauderdale, Cunningham, Fife and East Lothian. The rest of Earl David's estates had passed to Bruce himself and to Edmund Hastings, a forfeited English lord, while the remaining Moreville-de Quinci lands had fallen to two other English lords, Alan la Zouche and William Ferrers, and to the earl of Buchan. Thus the whole of this vast feudal complex was available for regranting, or was already in Bruce's possession. The lordship of Galloway, as we have seen, went to Edward Bruce, who died without lawful issue in 1318. Perhaps from policy the king let the lordship lapse, but in 1325 he made a grant of its historic *caput*, Buittle in Kirkcudbright, to James Douglas, with jurisdictional liberties which just stopped short of the 'four pleas of the Crown'. Moreville-de Quinci property ranged widely, in every sense, embracing lordship of large tracts like Lauderdale and Cunningham, respectable burghs like Irvine and Lauder, and collieries like that known as 'Wawayne's Pot', in the East Lothian coalfield. It would take too much space to give an account of the redistribution of all this land, but it is worth noting that the two men who seem to have received the largest single shares were both very close to the king. The faithful James Douglas got the constabulary of Lauder, while the king's young grandson, Robert Stewart, born in 1316, was granted 'all the king's lands in Cunningham',[65] that is, whatever property in Cunningham was available through forfeiture after deducting estates already given to others, such as Kilmarnock, given to Robert Boyd.

It should not be thought that the forfeitures of men like Balliol, Comyn, Guines, Ferrers and Zouche were untypical of the transfers of property under King Robert I. On the contrary, if a generalization is permissible, it would be roughly true to say that the king forfeited only those non-Scots who had no intention of becoming his subjects and only those Scotsmen who proved irreconcilable enemies. The second class was small and (if we except the Comyns) did not represent any significant amount of property. The chief Scottish baronial families which either never made their peace with the king or came into it only temporarily included the Macdougalls of Lorn, the Macdoualls of Galloway, the Lovels of Hawick, the Siwards of Tibbers and Aberdour (Fife) and the Moubrays, whose lands were widely scattered across southern and central Scotland. Conversely, King Robert had no objection to rewarding Englishmen with lands in Scotland if they left the English king's faith and came into his own. Thus, his brother-in-law, the Yorkshire knight Sir Christopher Seton, who was executed in 1306, was regarded as virtually a Scotsman, held land in Annandale,[66] and had a chapel founded at Dumfries in his memory. The English burgess of Berwick on Tweed, Peter of Spalding, without whose help the Scots would probably not have captured the town in 1318, was given an estate in Angus which put him in the knightly class.[67] At the surrender of Edinburgh Castle its Gascon commander, Pierre Libaud, became Bruce's man and was granted consider-able estates in Lothian, though he soon lost them and his own life by turning traitor. One interesting grant of this type was that made to Sir William Blount 'in renunciation of any claim on which he might base a demand against the king by reason of the treaty made between the king and the late Andrew Harcla, earl of Carlisle'.[68] Admittedly, the Lanercost Chronicle calls Blount 'a knight of Scottish nationality'[69] (he was perhaps one of the Blounts of Esbie) but when he fled to Bruce, at the time of Harcla's downfall in 1323, he was thoroughly anglicized and one of the earl of Carlisle's 'special cronies'.[70] Like Spalding, Blount was given an estate in Angus, far from the Border where the memory of his treachery might have made life impossible for him.

If we turn from those who lost land to look at those who gained it, a study of the confused welter of detail reveals a few facts of overriding importance. One is that the men whom the king rewarded with really large grants of land and power were very few in number and were almost entirely his own close relatives. In other words, they were the men who would almost certainly have benefited even had there been no war and no forfeitures. Besides Edward Bruce and Thomas Randolph they included Sir Neil Campbell, who married the king's sister Mary and whose son John became earl of Atholl, and Sir Alexander Fraser of Touch-Fraser and Cowie, second cousin (once-removed) of Sir Simon Fraser, who married Mary Bruce on Sir Neil's death about 1316. Campbell and Fraser had been with the king throughout the early desperate days when he had taken to the heather. Merely to be given a lady of the royal house in marriage was itself a mark of special favour. It put a nobleman into a small and distinguished class to be the king's brother-in-law. But it did not automatically bring lands and privileges. In contrast with Hugh of Ross (married to Maud Bruce and showered with favours) Andrew Murray, the son of Wallace's colleague and grandson of Andrew Murray of Petty, does not seem to have had any really notable grants from the king, although he became the third husband of Christian Bruce when she was already the widow of Earl Gartnait of Mar and Sir Christopher Seton. As heir of his father and of his uncle (Sir William Murray 'the Rich' of Bothwell) Sir Andrew Murray of Bothwell, hereditary 'panetar' (*panetarius*) of Scotland, was in his own right one of the most powerful nobles in the kingdom. He was marked out as one of the leaders of the community of the realm by his descent, his wealth and his marriage to a Bruce, and understandably became Guardian of Scotland in 1332 after the disaster of Dupplin.

By far the most favoured of the king's kinsmen were the Stewarts. James the Stewart died in July 1309, ending his days – in the spirit of 1286 or of 1297 – as a firm and public supporter of the 'royal dignity' and the community of the realm. Since his eldest son Andrew had died (evidently in English custody), his heir was his second son Walter, who is said to have been 'but a beardless lad' in 1314.[71] Yet in 1315, nine years before the birth of his son, the king took the momentous step of giving to Walter Stewart in marriage his daughter Marjorie, then his only legitimate child. The royal house of Stewart was thus in a very real sense the creation, or at least the legacy, of Robert Bruce. The marriage of his eldest child to Walter Stewart must be seen in the light of the close friendship between the families of Bruce and Stewart which is abundantly illustrated between the date of the Turnberry Band of 1286 and the field of Bannockburn, and in fact went back much further. With his wife (who was a few years his senior) Walter Stewart received the barony of Bathgate and other lands.[72] He also got three-quarters of Comyn's barony of Dalswinton. His son Robert (born in 1316) had a grant of most of Cunningham as well as five forfeited baronies in Roxburghshire. The Stewart's kinsmen figure prominently among bene-ficiaries of Robert I's charters. The Stewarts of Bunkle (descended from James the Stewart's brother John who fell at Falkirk) having acquired Kimmerghame, Garleton, Elvingston and Ethie Beaton, ended the reign holding the earldom of Angus. Other branches of the family got forfeited lands in Ayrshire, Dumfriesshire and Aberdeenshire. If the Comyns had dominated the pattern of landownership in the thirteenth century, the Stewarts bade fair to succeed them in the fourteenth.

Among the king's closest relatives, at least one of his bastard sons, his namesake Sir Robert Bruce, was well provided for. In 1321 he was granted the small border barony of Sprouston (forfeited by the heirs of the de Vesci family) to be held 'in regality' as it had apparently been held under Alexander III by the lord de Vesci. About the same time he had a grant of the great and strategically important border lordship of Liddesdale, with its fortress of Hermitage,[73] forfeited by William de Soules. The regalian privileges of Sprouston, absurd though it may seem in the case of a small country parish, meant that the king's officers had no right to enter for any official purpose. The lord was answerable solely to the king, and possessed his own justiciar, chamberlain, chancellor and coroner. There is very little evidence of any tendency under the two Alexanders to initiate or encourage the growth of such regalities, and Sprouston scarcely makes an impressive regality, however it is regarded. It is Robert I's use of the precedent of the regality that gives interest to its existence in Scotland before 1286. For it cannot well be denied that a few of King Robert's grants gave a fillip to the process by which the crown lost power through excessive delegation, even to the point of dissipation. Some of the king's predecessors had done much the same, it is true. William the Lion had even proposed to grant away the whole of Lothian to Otto of Brunswick.[74] But in the twelfth century, when royal government was comparatively ill-developed, delegation of power was quite a different matter from what it might become in the fourteenth century, by which time centralized government had made great advances and there were signs of the beginning of an organized state in the modern sense. It must be emphasized that in Robert I's time there was no opening of the floodgates to let in the excesses of bastard feudalism or the overmighty subject. On the contrary, military feudalism seems to have undergone a fairly rigorous overhaul in the interest of more efficient service to the crown, while there is good evidence of the king's successful defence of his prerogative. Nevertheless, his creation of the earldom of Moray as a true 'regality' in which his nephew Thomas Randolph was to exercise all the powers of the crown and be answerable only to the king was an unfortunate reversion to the old 'palatinate' concept familiar in Norman England. Palatinates were little more than confessions of failure by the crown to exercise direct control throughout its dominions. The regality of Moray was echoed, perhaps anticipated, on a smaller scale in the regality of Annandale, created when the old Bruce lordship of Annandale was made over to Randolph about 1312. Even the more restricted jurisdictional liberties given to James Douglas by the 'Emerald Charter' and the charter of Buittle contrast markedly with the policy generally pursued by Edward I and Philip the Fair of controlling and restricting feudal privilege. In this respect Robert I, stronger and more effective as a ruler than Edward II, showed himself hardly different in kind. As long as he himself reigned, no Scottish feudatory would try to act the part of Thomas of Lancaster, Hugh Despenser or Roger Mortimer. But the fact remained that King Robert could not, even if he wished, resist the overwhelming pressures – paralleled in contemporary England, France and Germany – towards fragmentation of royal power.

A second fact to emerge from a study of the nobles who either made or improved their family fortunes under Bruce is that besides the king's close relatives there was a small group of specially trusted, specially favoured men, who though not personally related to the king were obviously his intimate counsellors, prominent in every department of the royal service, military, diplomatic and judicial. Some had been his companions in adversity in 1306 and 1307. Among them, rivalled only by Randolph as the recipient of royal favour, Sir James Douglas stood supreme. Alone with Randolph he shared the duties and honour of guardianship of the realm in Bruce's time. No other man save Randolph had grants of land and power to compare with his. He had, of course, a charter of Douglasdale and Carmichael, his own inheritance.[75] He was granted numerous forfeited estates, Buittle in Galloway, Lauderdale, Cockburn, Bedrule, Staplegordon, and half of Westerkirk. He was also given the royal burgh and castle of Jedburgh with the lands of Bonjedward. In two cases the service was reduced to a nominal honorific *reddendo*: Douglasdale (which must have been held for military service) and Buittle would in future render only gilt spurs annually. The 'Emerald Charter' (1324) gave him wide powers of justice in all his lands in recompense for over four thousand merks he had forgone when three French knights he captured at Byland in 1322 were repatriated free of ransom by the king.

The other members of this small group of key men were Sir Robert Keith the marischal, Sir Gilbert Hay the constable, Sir Robert Boyd, Sir Alexander Seton, Sir Robert Lauder and Sir John Menteith. Keith had been marischal since King John's time, his family having held the office for over a century. He was active on behalf of the Guardians until he submitted to Edward I evidently at some date in 1303. From King John Keith had bought the right to arrange the marriages of Susan and Alice Crawford of Loudoun, heiresses of Andrew Crawford who had succeeded a family of Flemish origin holding the lands of Draffan in Clydesdale, Loudoun in Cunningham and Lochmartnaham in King's Kyle with an island castle. To Edward II, just after the old king's death, Keith complained that the brothers Neil and Donald Campbell had carried off the two heiresses and married them (or arranged their marriages) in defiance of the laws of Scotland. But he also begged the English king to release from prison Fergus of Ardrossan (by 1320 loyal to Robert I) and, out of compassion, to free Countess Isabel of Buchan from her cage. Keith was shameless enough also to beg for a reward of land worth £200 a year.[76] It is unlikely that this 'worst enemy' of Edward I received much satisfaction from his son, and at Christmas 1308 he joined Bruce, thereafter becoming one of the king's indispensable commanders and administrators. We have seen something of his rewards in grants of land, which removed the main centre of his family's interests from Keith in East Lothian to the north east of Scotland. But he was perhaps not unknown in the north as early as 1305, when Edward I's Ordinance made him one of the two justices between the Forth and the Mounth. After his reconciliation with King Robert, Keith evidently retained or resumed this very same office, for in February 1310 he is to be found presiding over a court at

Lindores in Fife as 'justiciar between Forth and the Mounth'.[77] His commission was afterwards extended, and by October 1312 he was justiciar from Forth to Orkney.[78]

Sir Gilbert Hay of Errol and Sir Robert Boyd of Noddsdale in Cunningham had been with the king since the start of his reign, and both outlived him by a few years. Hay got the hereditary constableship, to which he had no substantial claim by inheritance, and considerable grants of land in Aberdeenshire. As a mark of special favour, his estates were exempted from the duty of paying relief and from liability to wardship at his death.[79] But he was not in any sense a *novus homo*: his family had held the barony of Errol for knight service since the early years of William the Lion's reign. Robert Boyd probably owed rather more to royal favour, for the grants he got from Robert I undoubtedly enabled the Boyds to rise from the position of fairly modest knightly tenants in Cunningham to holding one of the most powerful lordships of south-western Scotland. Robert Boyd himself was given a good deal of forfeited land, West Kilbride, Ardneil and Kilmarnock in Cunningham, Trabboch in Kyle, and parts of Dalswinton and Bridburgh in Dumfriesshire and of the Glenkens in Kirkcudbrightshire.[80]

Sir Alexander Seton must hold a rather special place among those who were rewarded. Pro-Bruce in 1310, he became his enemy until the night of June 23rd–24th, 1314, and his defection from the English at that critical moment was of decisive importance. Like Hay and Keith, he was already by descent and inheritance a baron of some consequence in eastern Scotland, one of his ancestors having been given Seton in East Lothian by William the Lion for knight-service. Regularly in attendance on the king after 1314, Seton, as steward of the household, played a notable part in the reception of the papal nuncios at Oldcambus in 1317, and was an envoy to the Anglo-Scottish peace talks planned for the early part of 1320.[81] His rewards were substantial, though not spectacular: Tranent, Myles, Elphinstone and Falside in East Lothian (all these were out of old de Quinci land), burghal status for Seton itself, and the East Mill of Haddington together with land beside the burgh. Seton's near neighbour, Sir Robert Lauder, was one of the very few men rewarded by King Robert with substantial grants of land and high office who really seems to have been raised from obscurity. He was among those who benefited from the redistribution of Pierre Libaud's forfeited lands, getting Cowden in Dalkeith from his source. He also received Pencaitland and Nisbet in East Lothian and Larbert Mill in Stirlingshire from forfeited estates. The chief proof of the trust reposed in him by the king, apart from his fairly frequent appearance as a witness to royal charters, is the fact that Robert I had made him justiciar of Lothian by 1321, and employed him as an envoy in the peace and truce negotiations of 1320 (when he was still only a 'yeoman', i.e. royal servant) and of 1323. He was one of the magnates who took oath to maintain the truce of 1323, and had the distinction of being the only person to take oath on the king's behalf as surety for the general provisions of the Treaty of Edinburgh in 1328.[82]

Perhaps it will never be possible to free Sir John Menteith from the infamy which gathered about his name and memory in later generations because he handed over the fugitive Wallace to King Edward I. At the time of Wallace's capture, in 1305, Menteith had been in King Edward's service for some two years. Not to have surrendered Wallace would have meant publicly defying his acknowledged king and lord at a time when in Scotland itself not a single other Scotsman of note was resisting the king of England. Menteith joined Robert Bruce before March 1309, perhaps some while before. It is doubtful if he then suffered from any stigma of treachery, popular or otherwise. He became a close counsellor of the king, who confirmed him in his strong position as a lord of the Firth of Clyde region, and probably made it still stronger by granting him Glenbreackerie in Kintyre and other land called 'Aulesai'.[83] He was frequently named as a witness to the king's charters, acted as an envoy in the peace negotiations of 1310, put his seal to the Declaration of Arbroath in 1320, as 'tutor of the earldom of Menteith', and was one of the magnates who took an oath to maintain the thirteen-year truce of 1323, his name being given third among the barons after the Stewart and Sir James Douglas.[84]

At the end of Robert I's reign, the nobility of Scotland, with a few notable exceptions, was still the old nobility, the nobility of the thirteenth, even of the twelfth century. If the families remained the same, can this also be said of their relationship to the Crown, and of the terms by which they held their land? It is not an easy question to answer. There is evidence that in the field of tenure and service King Robert was as much of a conservator and restorer as he was in respect of the feudal lords themselves. Yet there was some change and innovation which was neither haphazard nor sporadic. A study of the charters of land granted to noblemen and gentry leaves an ineffaceable impression of a deliberate royal policy of strengthening, while at the same time modifying feudal military service. One result of this policy was a sharp divergence, for the first time since the twelfth century, between Scottish and English development. At a time when the formal enfeoffment for knight service or some form of military serjeanty was being abandoned in England, and forces were being raised either by commissioners of array in the shires or by private indenture, the king of Scotland adhered to the older practice of attaching military service permanently and hereditarily to the holding of land. Since Robert I, of all men, was the least likely to be negligent, ultra-conservative or merely inept in the matter of military service, we must conclude that in his view the twelfth-century model – with certain modifications – was best suited to the conditions of Scottish society even in the fourteenth century.

The explanation, surely, lay in the king's own experience of Scottish warfare. Because of the relative poverty of the country, the 'feudal host' of Scotland, which had failed at Dunbar, could not maintain a place in Scottish military organization comparable with the place once held by its counter-part in English military organization. Robert I could without regret shift the emphasis away from knight service, in the old sense of heavy-armed cavalry, and place it instead upon knights who would normally fight on foot, and still more upon bowmen, who constituted a vitally important arm in which Scotland had been conspicuously deficient. Knight service was therefore restricted to an even more select minority of landowners than it had been in the previous century. The typical grant – among those which actually mention the service required – stipulated for the service of an *architenens*, a bowman.

There is positive evidence that knight service was converted into archer service. The barony of Manor in Tweeddale, for example, had formed one knight's fee in the thirteenth century. Robert I, regranting it in 1309, asked for ten archers.[85] When the barony was divided into two in 1315, one half was granted for the 'services used and wont' under Alexander III, but since the barony had never been divided before 1315 it looks as though the very common formula 'services used and wont' was here no more than a royal safeguard. Again, an estate in Whitsome (Berwickshire) was held of King John for half a knight's service. Robert I divided the estate in two and demanded the service of half an archer from each half.[86] The barony of Cessford in Roxburghshire had almost certainly been held for knight service under the Alexanders. Robert I regranted it (in two parts) for a total of five archers.[87] Bridburgh in Nithsdale had also probably been a knight's fee: Robert I got archer service from it.[88] The barony of Tranent in East Lothian had been a knight's fee and remained so; but Robert I, in regranting its component members, stipulated for one archer's service from the part forfeited by William de Ferrers.[89] Longforgan rendered knight service in the twelfth century, and when a third part of it (ex-Balliol) was granted out by King Robert the *reddendo* was the service of half an archer.[90]

Regardless of the extent to which knight service was converted into it, archer service for hereditary tenure increased unmistakably in Robert I's time. Significantly, we find the great tenants in chief themselves sub-infeudating for archer service.[91] The king's eagerness to secure bowmen is shown by his grants of hereditary annual pensions or 'money fiefs' in return for archery. Occasionally he even put on a feudal basis the ancient pre-feudal service of 'a man on foot with spear and sword'.[92] But if the charters are to be taken at anything like their face value, knight service was not a thing of the past by 1329. It was, indeed, too deeply embedded in the framework of Scottish feudal society and its landed estates to be eradicated, but there is nothing to suggest that Robert Bruce wished to eradicate it. Probably its incidence was often reduced, for in Scotland the increased financial burden of equipping and maintaining a heavily armed cavalry soldier and his *destrier* must have been relatively greater than in England, where it was already felt to be oppressive. It seems likely that when King

Robert's charters speak of *servitium militis* they refer not to any precise technical requirement but to a vaguer obligation that the tenant holding by this service will furnish one or more trained warriors possessing the best available weapons and horses.

Between 1306 and 1329 there was a marked tendency for knight service to be confined to the rich, and in the case of fees answering for more than one knight the tendency became an absolute rule. Thus great magnates like Randolph, James Douglas, Walter the Stewart and his son Robert, and substantial barons like Robert Boyd, Edward Keith, and Malcolm Fleming, are to be found holding fiefs for which the service was one or more knights. Fractional knights' fees tended to be the characteristic holding of men of rather less wealth and standing. There is a remarkable conservatism in at least some of the surviving knight service grants. For example, Thomas Randolph was granted Annandale for ten knights, the very service required when William the Lion confirmed this lordship to Robert Bruce before 1174. Loudoun in Ayrshire, which had formed a single knight's fee in the twelfth century, was granted to Duncan Campbell for one knight's service. Robert Stewart was granted the lordship of Cunningham for three knights' service, a figure which may be compared with the two knights for which (we may infer) Irvine, the *caput* of the honour of Cunningham, had been held in the thirteenth century.[93] James Douglas got Lauder and Lauderdale for the services used and wont, which appears to mean that he owed six knights, since in 1296 one sixth of this fief owed one knight.[94] William the Lion had granted Lenzie in Dumbartonshire to William Comyn for one knight's service. When Robert I gave this same barony, then known as Kirkintilloch, to Malcolm Fleming, the same service was required. It is not clear whether this evidence points to a genuine conservatism or means that the concept of knight service was in process of becoming merely honorific.

The truth may be that wherever estates were broken up or regrouped it was easier for the king to innovate and introduce archer service. When, however, ancient estates were regranted or confirmed with their boundaries intact it was perhaps harder to impose fresh services and customs. This would explain grants which have an obviously antique flavour. For example, Hugh, afterwards earl of Ross, got the old thanage of Glendowachy (the north-east extremity of Banffshire) for the service of eight horses for carting once a year from each arable unit of the estate. When Henry Butterwambe was given land at Clunie near Dunkeld, his *reddendo* was put in language of the period 1180–1250: 'one serjeant, horsed and in an haubergel'.[95] It would also explain many of the knight-service grants, in which the service would have been simply a survival from earlier times. But the king, as we know, could on occasion impose knight service on a newly-created fief, for he required eight knights' service from Randolph's earldom of Moray. In view of the fact that the ancient earldoms were not as a rule held in return for knight service, this suggests strongly that for King Robert knight service was not purely ornamental or honorific but real and desirable.

This impression of a strengthening – one might fairly call it a revival – of military feudalism under Robert I is decisively confirmed if we look at the king's dealings with the barons of the west highlands and islands. In the west the typical unit of military service was not the mounted knight nor the bowman but the 'birling' or galley of twenty, twenty-two, twenty-six or forty oars. Hebridean chiefs had served with birlings for generations before Bruce's time, but prior to the reign of Alexander II none of them had held his land as a fief in return for a fixed amount of military service. Indeed, down to the end of the thirteenth century most of them still held by Celto-Scandinavian tenure, and contributed to a general levy with ship service assessed on the quantity of productive land on their estates. Robert I brought many (perhaps all) of these men into a direct feudal relationship with the Crown by confirming or regranting their estates as fiefs in return either for fixed numbers of birlings of a stated capacity, or else (but much more rarely) for knight service.

This feudalized Hebridean and Argyll ship service is proof of the vitality and flexibility of military feudalism under Robert I. It was also bound up with the whole problem of the west, to which the king had always shown himself particularly sensitive. South of Skye, where the earl of Ross was installed in power, the western seaboard had no lord of earl's rank nor, indeed, any single dominant lord, for Comyn of Badenoch and Lochaber had been killed in 1306 and John of Lorn put to flight two years later. The king would have to woo, to cajole, to placate, and yet withal to overawe the leaders of the native aristocracy. He began with a solid advantage: he virtually inherited the support of the Campbells and of the Macdonalds, the ruling family of Islay and Kintyre. The precise origin of the Campbells is not known. There is no doubt that their greatness as territorial lords dates from King Robert's reign. But they were certainly not landless adventurers and seem to have had close links with Ayrshire, where Stewart and Bruce interests were especially strong. Colin Campbell (possibly with his son and heir Neil) had been one of the auditors for Bruce the Competitor in 1291, along with the clerical Master Neil Campbell, clearly a kinsman.[96] In 1296, Colin's son Sir Neil was bailie of the crown lands of Lochawe and Ardskeodnish (i.e. Kilmartin parish);[97] he may have had an hereditary claim to these lands, and been compelled to hold them of the crown at farm by King John's ordinance. They were confirmed to his son Colin in 1315 as a free barony, for a birling of forty oars.[98] Sir Neil Campbell was one of that small band of noblemen without whose help in 1306 and 1307 Robert Bruce would hardly have survived, let alone recovered the kingdom. Until his death about 1315, Sir Neil was one of the king's most trusted counsellors. First married perhaps to the Ayrshire heiress Alice Crawford, Neil Campbell became the husband of Mary Bruce, Robert I's sister. His kinsmen shared in the family's rise under the new régime, being given large tracts of land forfeited by John Macdougall of Lorn. His brother Donald got part of Benderloch for one ship of twenty-six oars, and of Donald's sons, Dugald got the isle of Torsa and many other lands, while Duncan had the lands of Duntrune. In addition, Donald married the other Crawford heiress, Susan, and with her acquired many Ayrshire estates. Other Campbells who supported Bruce in his early years included Thomas, whose son Duncan was confirmed in his fief for a birling of twenty-two oars, and Sir Arthur, who was granted land in Benderloch, together with the Macdougall strongholds of Dunollie and Ardstaffnage, for the quarter of a knight's service.

Thus, by a drastic revolution, those baronial neighbours whom (as he told Edward II in 1308) John of Lorn could not trust swept in to take possession of his lands, and laid the foundations of Campbell dominance between Loch Fyne and Loch Creran. Not that all families dependent on the Macdougalls succumbed. John Macdonleavie (or Maclay) seems to have been an adherent of John of Lorn in 1304;[99] Robert I confirmed to James Macdonleavie seven and a half old merklands in Kintyre for one twenty-six-oared birling.[100] No doubt, also, there was some sheer opportunism, as men shifted their allegiance in order to scramble for the lands of those who fell from power and favour. Thus Gillespie Maclachlan, a prominent baron of Argyll in 1293, petitioned Edward I for land in 1306, apparently the barony of Strath Eachaig in the parish of Dunoon, whose owner, Molbride the younger, had joined Bruce.[101] Yet within three years this same Gillespie attended Bruce's first parliament as one of the loyal barons of Argyll, and at some point in the reign got a charter from the king either granting or confirming to him the estate of 'Shirwachthyne', now Shirvan in Kilmichael Glassary.[102] The relative lawlessness of the west was also apt to throw up from time to time a buccaneering predator who played solely for his own hand. Such may have been Lachlan Macruarie, the bastard son of Alan Macruarie, lord of Garmoran, and half-brother of King Robert's relative and protector Christina of Mar. A shadowy figure, Lachlan flits in and out of the record of the Anglo-Scottish war, always in the background, always a troublemaker. He defied in turn and with impunity King John, King Edward I, the Guardians and the earl of Ross. In his own esteem he may well have ranked as a king of the Isles, after the time-honoured style of the Gaidhealtachd. At last, in 1306, he appeared before the English king at Ebchester in County Durham to petition for the lands (probably in the west) of Patrick Graham. Soon afterwards he disappears from history, surely regretted by no one save his own followers. His brother Ruairi seems to have stepped into his brogues, but only on condition of becoming King Robert's feudal vassal. By an arrangement which proves the extent of Macruarie power, Christina of Mar surrendered Glenelg, Knoydart, Moidart and the islands which made up the lordship of Garmoran to her half-brother Ruairi Macruarie. The conditions were that if Ruairi had no male heir, the lordship would revert to Christina's son, another Ruairi, who was required to marry one of his uncle's daughters. The service for his archipelagic lordship was to be only one birling of twenty-six oars. In view of the king's debt to Christina the whole settlement seems curious. Yet it put Garmoran into the hands of the man whom its warriors probably already regarded as their chief, and it brought that chief into direct feudal dependency on the Crown.[103]

Rewarding Angus Og and his family and strengthening their position was an obvious and straightforward step. Angus's motive in supporting Robert Bruce may have been partly his inherited enmity towards the Macdougalls, but his conduct rose above mere opportunism. His father had been linked with the Bruces in the Turnberry Band of 1286. The Macdonalds' control of Islay and Kintyre was of crucial importance in 1306–07, and so too, in all probability, were their connexions with northern Ireland. We may accept that Angus had an older brother who attended the St Andrews parliament of 1309, for it is virtually certain that he is to be identified with the 'Donald of Islay' recorded as being present. He, and Angus after him, must have been confirmed in possession of Islay and the Macdonald lands in Kintyre, though no charters to this effect are recorded. Robert I made over to Angus the Comyn lordship of Lochaber, and he had a charter of the adjacent districts of Morvern ('Cenel Badin')[104] and Ardnamurchan, probably his own inheritance. His nephew Alexander of Islay got the Isles of Mull and Tiree, formerly in Macdougall hands.

The result of the king's west highland policy may be summed up as follows. Skye and Wester Ross were under Earl Hugh; Garmoran was converted into a fief held for ship-service; what became the modern county of Argyll was parcelled out among friends and supporters, in particular, Angus Og Macdonald, John Menteith and the Campbells. Robert Bruce knew the highlands and the west from long personal experience. He succeeded with the chiefs doubtless because he understood them and possessed the gifts which they admired. He captured their imagination by bold encounters such as the battle of Brander and by gestures which appealed to their sense of tradition and prophecy, such as having himself, in 1315, borne across the *tairbeart* or isthmus between Knapdale and Kintyre, from East Loch Tarbert to West Loch Tarbert, in a galley with the sails hoisted.

> And quhen thai that in the Ilis war
> Herd tell how the gud Kyng had thar
> Gert schippis with the salys ga
> Out-our betwix the Tarbartis twa,
> Thai war abasit all utrely.
> For thai wist throu ald prophesy
> That he that suld ger schippis swa
> Betwix the seis with salys ga,

Suld wyn the Ilis swa till hand,
That nane with strynth suld him withstand.[105]
Above all, King Robert grasped the strategic and, by implication, the
political importance of the highlands and islands. He was the first king since
David I to be able to take islesmen with him on an invasion of England. He
used their birlings constantly to keep open communications with Ireland,
and to menace and then re-conquer the Isle of Man. In his days the highland
nobility were not, in the main, disaffected. Anticipating in the wildest
terrain of his realm the alleged ambition of his descendant James I a century
later, King Robert made 'the key keep the castle and the bracken-bush the
cow'.

The king handled the nobles conservatively, but with consummate skill and
a strong sense of justice. Before concluding this review of the relations
between Crown and nobility in his reign we should note one innovation.
Almost certainly, it strengthened the solidarity which undoubtedly existed
by the end of the reign between the king and the nobles as a class. Robert I's
charters granting or confirming landed estates of major importance made
regular use of the formula *in liberam baroniam*, 'in free barony'. The
adoption of this novel standard formula was not accidental and can hardly
have been a trivial matter of chancery procedure. It must be seen as part of a
deliberate policy of defining and stereotyping feudal rights as well as
obligations. Baronies had existed since the twelfth century, but under
Robert I it is clear that only a feudatory who held explicitly 'in free barony'
had the rights of jurisdiction which custom ascribed to the true baron: the
right to hear all suits arising among the lord's own tenants (saving appeal to
the sheriff court) and 'pit and gallows', the graphic phrase covering a very
full competence in criminal cases where the crime had been committed
within the barony or concerned its men and property. It may happen that a
new term introduced to denote old customs and institutions will itself
produce, through regular use, a fresh and standardized concept of these
customs. Before Robert I's time, the concept of 'barony', though familiar,
had been vague and ill-defined. King Robert gave it a new precision. He
emphasized, on the one hand, the doctrine that barony, like regality, stems
only from the Crown. On the other hand, he did not whittle away feudal
privileges as such. The nobles surely welcomed not only this new certainty
but also the security that went with it.

The Community of the Realm

In an unavoidably brief review of King Robert's relations with the community of the realm as a whole, it may be useful to look at the reign in terms
of the king's elementary duties towards the community and of the community's obligations to the king. We shall look in turn, therefore, at the
succession question, at royal administration, legislation, parliament and

taxation. Finally, we must try to judge the importance of the personal element in Robert I's kingship, and the degree of national unity to which Scotland attained at the close of the reign.

It was not much use restoring the monarchy if the king could not ensure its perpetuation. In this matter Bruce was dogged by ill luck. His first marriage, to Isabel of Mar, cannot have lasted more than six years or thereabouts, and as far as is known the only child born to Isabel was Marjorie, who would have been about ten or eleven years old in 1306 and hardly more than twenty-one or two when she died in 1317. Bruce's second marriage, to Elizabeth de Burgh in 1302, was marred by eight years of enforced separation when the queen was a prisoner of the English. There were, nevertheless, four children of this marriage, two boys and two girls. Of the sons, one died a child and the other, David, born as late as March 5th, 1324, was the king's sole surviving male heir of the body.

It must have seemed an urgent necessity from the very start of the reign that the succession should be settled. But the first formal provision was not made till the Ayr parliament of April 27th, 1315.[107] This was a month before Edward Bruce's expedition to Ireland to win for himself and his heirs the crown of Ireland offered him by the king of Tyrone with the support of various Irish underkings and chiefs. It was also shortly before the marriage of Marjorie Bruce and Walter Stewart. The tailzie, or entail, of the Scottish crown published in the Ayr parliament provided, with the consent of Marjorie Bruce, that if the king died without a male heir the crown should go to his brother Edward, 'as a man of great prowess in warlike actions for the defence of the rights and liberties of the Scottish realm'. This drastic and possibly unjust reversal of the succession policy laid down by Alexander III in 1284 is a measure of what the conservative community of the realm had suffered in the intervening years. Not only would it upset the principle of seniority, it would contemplate a union of the crowns of Ireland and Scotland about which many Scottish magnates might well have deep misgivings. Marjorie would succeed only if both Robert and Edward Bruce died without male heirs. If she died before marriage, the reversion would pass to the king's nearest heir by lineal descent, but in the same breath it was provided that Marjorie should marry, with her father's consent. If on the king's death the heir to the throne were a minor, Thomas Randolph earl of Moray would be Guardian of both child and kingdom, until such time as the community of the realm (or its greater part) deemed the heir fit to rule. Randolph was likewise to be Guardian if Marjorie died a widow, leaving an heir under age. Finally, if the king and Edward and Marjorie were all to die without leaving any heirs, Randolph was to be Guardian until the leaders of the community could take counsel among themselves on the choice of a new king.

There was clearly deep-seated rivalry between the rash and arrogant Edward Bruce and Thomas Randolph. Randolph's guardianship offset

Edward Bruce's irresponsibility. Moreover, in September 1316, after Edward had been crowned king of Ireland, Randolph was specially secured by King Robert and the Scottish magnates in his possession of Moray and the Isle of Man, the security being made 'by the consent of Edward, by God's grace king of Ireland', and for good measure bearing his seal.[108]

The death of Edward Bruce at the battle of Dundalk on October 14th, 1318, made fresh arrangements necessary. By this date Marjorie was also dead, but in 1316 she had given birth to a son, Robert Stewart. The new tailzie, promulgated in the parliament held at Scone on December 3rd, 1318,[109] provided for Robert's succession should the king die without male heirs. Once again, the guardianship of kingdom and heir (if a minor) was committed to Randolph or, if he died, to Sir James Douglas, until the time when the community or its wiser majority should deem the heir fit to govern. 'Randolph and Sir James', so runs the act, 'took this guardianship upon themselves with the approbation of the whole community.'

After David Bruce had passed his second birthday, surviving the most dangerous period for any child of the period, it was necessary for the leaders of the community to do him homage and swear fealty. Although the tailzie of 1318 did not require renewal, it was no doubt thought advisable to confirm it by a second parliamentary declaration, and the renewal of the Franco-Scottish alliance in April 1326 may have been the prime factor in this decision. At all events, the Cambuskenneth parliament of July 15th, 1326, witnessed the publication of a tailzie which was probably a simple re-issue of that of 1318, no doubt with the name of the lord David taking precedence of the vaguer 'male heirs of the king's body lawfully procreated.'[110] However favourably we may assess the monarchy of David Bruce in the last fourteen years of his long reign, and his style of government has certainly found vigorous defenders,[111] it is surely incontrovertible that the birth of an immediate male heir so late in Robert I's reign was a tragedy for the Scottish kingdom and people. Minorities had not been happy periods in the past, and such precedents as existed were not auspicious. If David had not been born or had not survived infancy, his nephew Robert Stewart would have begun to rule at thirteen, on the brink of fourteenth-century manhood. If the reigns of Malcolm IV and Alexander II were to be followed, there would have been no minority. It is at least arguable that the situation in Scotland would not in that event have seemed to the country's enemies such as Edward III, or to the dynasty's enemies such as Edward Balliol, so tempting as it did seem in the 1330s with Robert Bruce, James Douglas and Thomas Randolph removed from the scene and the throne occupied by a child.

Providing for the succession was only one primary duty to the community of the realm. The country looked to the king to give good and abundant governance, by proper administration of justice, by making and confirming good laws, and by the frequent holding of parliaments. King Robert claimed to be the immediate successor of Alexander III. In the administrative field he worked, in the main, to restore Alexandrian government. The early years of his reign are veiled by a deep obscurity which could only be cleared if we possessed vastly more evidence than we do. A few hard but unconnected facts stand out, like mountain peaks rising above the sea of mist. Among the major offices under the crown, a chancellor and a chamberlain, as we have seen, had been appointed by 1309. If the appearance of Keith the Marischal early in 1310 as 'justiciar from Forth to the Mounth' is anything to go by, we may infer that something like the Alexandrian system of justiciarships – as modified in Edward I's Ordinance of 1305 – had already been restored. It was certainly fully restored by the middle of the reign. There were possibly subordinate justiciars also, such as John, son of Adam Bruning, who acquired a good deal of land in the north east in the later years of the reign.[112] Desperate circumstances, however, called for novel measures, and the same document which shows us Keith holding his justiciarship shows us Randolph acting as 'the king's lieutenant from Forth to Orkney'.[113] These special positions of responsibility were created because of military necessity. The best example is the king's appointment, when he crossed to Ireland to help his brother in 1316, of Sir James Douglas and Walter the Stewart as 'wardens in his absence'.[114] 'Lieutenants' would perhaps be a better description of their position.

There is evidence that the system of sheriffs and sheriffdoms was continued with relatively little upheaval from 1306 into the years when King Robert had control of the north and west, and eventually into the period when he was master of the entire kingdom. Only one new sheriffdom was created in the reign: Argyll, which seems to have come into existence between 1315 and 1325.[115] It is not clear how much of the sheriffdom of Perth was carved away to form the new sheriffdom, but its creation was clearly an implementation, if only in part, of the sensible ordinance of 1293. The king's interest in the western approaches led not only to this sheriffdom but also to an extraordinary development of Tarbert, between Knapdale and Kintyre, as a royal castle, seaport and burgh. Under King Robert the sheriff remained the crucial figure in royal administration, as he had been in the thirteenth century. As soon as surviving record allows us to see the king governing at all, we find typical governmental activity, often involving the sheriff, in every part of the realm. Brieves or writs were 'retoured to the chapel' – returned to the chancery or writing-office – as in King Alexander's day. Freeholders were served heir to their fathers or other lawful predecessors; inquests were held by local juries into unlawful dispossessions, or to determine an estate's rightful boundaries by the ancient process of 'perambulation'. As far as administration and procedure go, it is clear that under Robert I what were called in the Treaty of Perth of 1266 'the laws and customs of the realm of Scotland' remained substantially in force.

It seems likely that the 'king's chapel', the royal writing-office, was the first of the organs of royal government to be restored to pre-war vigour.[116]

Since 1296 there had been no single hiatus of more than two years during which a writing-office under the control of the Scottish government had ceased to function, and no doubt there were available to Robert I at or soon after his enthronement a number of clerks with chancery experience. Already in the earliest surviving records of the reign we find the essential points of continuity. The king is once again *Rex Scottorum*; once again, he addresses 'all his good men', *omnibus probis hominibus suis*; once again he is styled, round the circumference of the great seal, 'king of Scots under God's governance', *Deo rectore rex Scottorum*. But if the Tironensian monk Bernard, the new chancellor, took care to restore the time-honoured forms of Alexander III's reign, he also introduced fresh practices. For one thing, there was a notable increase in the use of letters-patent and simple unwitnessed letters, more informal means of communication than the older charter. For another, a new type of charter, the inspection, came to be used to confirm the titles of holders of old rights, property and privileges. The inspection recited the older title-deeds at length, instead of merely referring to them as had been the case with the typical charter of confirmation before 1286. If in Bernard's time the handwriting of royal clerks showed a change for the worse, that was the fault of a new fashion characteristic of the period as a whole. The biggest innovation of the reign was probably the acceptance of the fact that the king's chapel could no longer travel with the king wherever he might go. It was therefore given a more or less fixed headquarters, located at Arbroath Abbey. This innovation meant that very much greater use had to be made of the privy seal, which would normally be kept by an official in the king's company. The privy seal could thus be used to authorize the king's immediate commands, while the great seal remained with the chancellor.

Robert I's reign marks a turning point in the development of written instruments of government. Under Abbot Bernard's direction, the chapel was strengthened and became more flexible. At least some classes of royal 'out-letters' had been systematically enrolled since the turn of the twelfth and thirteenth centuries. In the disturbance of the years from 1296 to 1306, and fundamentally because of Edward I's attempt to conquer Scotland, most of these archives were lost. Under King Robert, rolls began to be kept once more, and a small portion of these are still extant. It was especially important to enrol copies of the grants which the king made to loyal supporters of property forfeited by enemies, and most of the surviving enrolments are in fact concerned with forfeited lands.

There was a similar mixture of continuity and novelty in legislation. The principal statement of the laws of 'Good King Robert' was promulgated in the parliament which met at Scone on December 3rd, 1318, and on the days following.[117] A few of the enactments were obvious, not to say platitudinous: the 'fredomis of haly kirk' (Chapter 1) and the promise of equal justice to rich and poor (Chapter 11) were repetitions, almost verbatim, of laws said to have been passed by William the Lion in the twelfth century. Other enactments were novel only because they were necessitated by a period of prolonged warfare. Thus goods and money were not to be exported without royal licence (Chapter XXIV), provision was made for the punishment of soldiers who broke the law while serving in the army, and careful rules were drawn up to regulate the way in which the army obtained food and other necessaries (Chapters IV and V). The 'assize of arms' (Chapter XXVII) might have been issued at any period, but obviously had a special relevance in 1318. By it, every man whose goods were worth ten pounds or more must have a stuffed leather jacket, a basnet, a mail coat, an iron hat and 'gloves of war'. Poorer men, possessed of goods worth one cow, must have a good spear or a good bow with a sheaf of two dozen arrows.

In the field of property law there was appreciable reform. It is, admittedly, not easy to be sure whether any particular law was an innovation or not. For example, Chapter XXV, which laid down the principle that no one may be ejected from a freehold without the king's brieve (i.e. the brieve of right) was based on a ruling of English law which became established under Henry II. Although the laws of William I and the two Alexanders make no mention of it, there is a remarkable piece of evidence which proves that it was well-known in Scotland before 1296.[118] But it seems certain that the procedures of the old-established possessory actions of novel dissasine and mortancestry, borrowed from Henry II's laws in the thirteenth century, were altered in favour of the dispossessed pursuer. Thus, by Chapter XIII the action to recover property of which the pursuer had been dispossessed could in future lie not only against the sitting tenant (who might, of course, be innocent and unaware that he had dispossessed anybody) but also against the original perpetrator or perpetrators of the act of dispossession, wherever they could be found. Anyone caught ejecting a freeholder by force of arms would be very severely dealt with. Sitting tenants, however, got some protection from Chapter XIX. This provided that a pursuer trying to recover land, whether by a brieve of right or by brieves of novel dissasine or mortancestry, must state the whole of his case first, before the tenant need make his defence in court. Mortancestry – the recovery of a lawful inheritance from feudal superiors who might try to withhold it – also figures in Chapter XXIII, which extends the 'ancestors' from whom one could claim an inheritance to include grandfathers and grandmothers, along with parents, brothers, sisters, uncles and aunts.

Very few of the statutes of 1318 touch upon criminal law, which suggests, therefore, that it underwent little change. There was a provision against interfering with tracker dogs hunting for criminals (Chapter VII) and anyone found guilty of this offence was to be treated as conniving at the original crime. No one save those lords who had such a privilege granted in the past was to take 'theft-boot' (compensation for theft, payable by the thief or his kin) on pain of severe penalties. Here, no doubt, the object was to discourage still further the private subject's participation in criminal justice. There were a few other miscellaneous laws, some too technical to be summarized briefly, others, of more or less importance, which are interesting if only because of their variety. Thus the great nobles are strictly enjoined to keep the king's peace – a more realistic measure in 1318 than it would have been before Bannockburn (Chapter xx); conspirators and rumour-mongers are to be punished (Chapter xxi) – had there been already some presage of the Soules plot of 1320? – and the owners of cruives or fish-traps in salmon rivers are not to make the meshes so small that smolts and fry cannot pass freely up and down stream (Chapter xi). The old law enforcing a close season for salmon fishing was re-enacted.[119]

The statutes of 1318 were of course by no means the whole of King Robert's law-making. They say nothing about Galloway. In 1324, the king renewed for the benefit of the men of Galloway a provision apparently first made by Alexander III about 1285.[120] This extended to Gallovidians the options of having their guilt or innocence decided by a 'good and faithful assize' (i.e. jury) after being arrested and charged by a serjeant of the peace in the manner customary in Galloway. The privilege had been made standard practice for the rest of southern Scotland in 1245, when Galloway had been excluded, 'having its own special laws'. The laws and liberties of Galloway as they existed before 1234 had been confirmed to the province in 1296 when Edward I restored Thomas of Galloway. Whether these included the practice of individual serjeants making arrests and indictments and summarily hanging red-handed criminals is not clear. By about 1304 or 1305 the Galloway men were petitioning King Edward to abolish 'accusation of serjeants' (*surdit de sergaunt*) but we do not know whether he did so or not. Thanks to King Robert, from 1324 a Gallovidian could enjoy 'English law', and 'thole the good and faithful assize' of his neighbours instead of submitting to the arbitrary and perhaps tyrannical proceedings of an individual royal or feudal officer. Gradually thereafter whole districts of Galloway were permanently freed from the burden of being subject, and giving hospitality, to serjeants, and were allowed to adopt the jury system.[121] The king also had available a standard form of commission appointing the chief of a clan in Galloway 'in accordance with the laws and customs of Galloway hitherto in use'.[122]

There are three surviving formularies which contain texts of many official documents of King Robert I.[123] Several of these constitute legislation or quasi-legislation. For example, at an unknown date, most probably early in 1320,[124] the king took stringent measures to control the spread of a serious disease of sheep, variously called scab, 'pilsoucht' or 'pluk'. Local juries were to find out what sheep were infected in their own districts. Infected beasts must be slaughtered within eight days of notice given, on pain of a heavy £10 fine. There was an absolute prohibition on the movement of livestock, and any sheep found to have been moved from one pasture to another were to be forfeited to the Crown. In another semi-legislative act, the king provided a standard form for the reception of his former enemies into his peace. After Bannockburn former enemies must have been summoned to return to the king's faith and peace, and in the Cambuskenneth parliament which met in November 1314, those who had not yet done so were declared disinherited (perhaps with one year's grace).[125] This decree was not absolute, however, for after its promulgation many men of note were reconciled and restored to favour. We know of individual issues of 'remission of rancour' by the king. Gilbert of Carrick, for instance, chief of the Kennedys, had incurred the royal wrath because his son-in-law Arthur had surrendered Loch Doon castle to the English in 1306, thus letting the king's brother-in-law and great friend Christopher Seton fall into enemy hands and be executed. Gilbert had been granted a remission of rancour by 1309.[126] Henry Cheyne, bishop of Aberdeen, was evidently granted remission of rancour – presumably for opposing the king between 1306 and 1312 – but unfortunately the surviving letter of remission cannot be authentic as it stands.[127] The formularies show that by a routine letter men who wished to become King Robert's subjects could have their property restored and enjoy a remission of rancour incurred by 'trespasses committed in war against the king and his royal dignity'.

Legislation was closely linked to the holding of parliaments. In addition to the assembly at his coronation, we have record of ten or more parliaments held by King Robert. It is more than likely that our record is incomplete, for even allowing for the disturbances caused by constant warfare, fewer than a dozen parliaments in twenty-three years seems low for the early fourteenth century. Edward II, in a disturbed reign of twenty years, held at least twenty-six parliaments. 'Under Robert I record of parliament is for the most part concerned with great issues of state.'[128] Parliament was obviously the proper occasion for approving and promulgating major political acts, such as the declaration of the king's right in the St Andrews parliament of 1309, the ratification of the Franco-Scottish treaty in July 1326, and the ratification of the final peace with England (Edinburgh, 1328). The succession settlements of 1315, 1318, and 1326 were all made in parliament. It was in parliament that the estates announced their consent to major measures of taxation. Parliament was the supreme secular court of justice, terminating numerous lawsuits of whose record probably only a very small fraction survives. In 1320, for example, the 'Black Parliament' gave judgement on the Soules conspirators; in 1323 a Scone parliament settled the lawsuit Abbot of Dunfermline v. John Campbell; in a parliament of 1325 sentence of forfeiture was passed on Ruairi of Islay; and in 1327 parliament confirmed an agreement between Randolph and Sir William Oliphant. Connected with parliament's judicial role is the fact that more charters and like documents were issued for private subjects in or about the time of parliament than at any other period of equal duration. Such charters were no more valid than others, but at parliament one might secure more witnesses of good standing, and there were doubtless more skilled lawyers and clerks available in time of parliament than at other times. Long before the reign of Robert I, parliament, or its thirteenth-century ancestor (often called a *colloquium*), had become the most solemn occasion for expressing the will and opinion of the community of the realm. Under King Robert this position was immensely strengthened.

The men who were summoned to parliament by the king represented in themselves or by proxy the estates of the realm which with the king made up the community. In his first parliament (1309) there were bishops, earls and barons individually and lesser clergy and 'communities' of the earldoms presumably by some form of representation. At the Inchture parliament of April 1312, there were very probably present, in addition to the magnates, burgh representatives, who received an insurance that all the king's dealings with burghs would be through the chamberlain.[129] At various parliaments between 1312 and 1326 the higher ranks present were named and the description of the assembly was then rounded off with some such phrase as the 'remainder of the community' or 'the whole community of the realm'. Unless these words are to be regarded as a mere flourish, we must presume that some form of representation of men below baronial or knightly rank was in force.[130] The Cambuskenneth parliament of July 1326 used to be taken as marking the first appearance of burgesses in parliament. This view would not now be generally accepted, and, indeed, the attendance of certain burgh representatives at the parliament early in 1296 which ratified the French treaty, even if they were there only to underwrite Scotland's financial obligations, is proof that burgess representation as such was already thirty years old in 1326. Moreover, it is now certain that the burghs were represented in the Edinburgh parliament of February and March 1328. The summons to this parliament has miraculously survived, and it is worth quoting the list of those called: 'bishops, abbots, earls, barons, freeholders and six sufficient persons of the various burgh communities specially empowered for the purpose'.[131]

The burgesses coming to parliament were only one example of the extremely close links between the burghs and the Crown which emerge in the reign of Robert I with a force and clarity not to be found in record of earlier times. The king obviously set great store by the burghs, and the burgesses looked to him for protection and encouragement. Surviving evidence leaves a strong impression of the important part the burghs played in the war with England, but it does not fill in the details. Perhaps some were more to the fore than others in the national struggle, burghs such as Inverness, Aberdeen, Dundee and Berwick, which early or late or throughout the long war made a notable contribution. Perhaps also the fierce and sometimes bitter rivalry between neighbouring burghs tended to throw one town into the arms of the English if its rival were firmly committed to Bruce.

Perth and Dundee might offer a possible instance, but this is mere surmise which might be confirmed or wholly contradicted by fuller evidence. The overriding picture is of burghal solidarity in the patriotic cause.

King Robert therefore favoured the burghs, readily confirming the ancient privileges or granting fresh ones. But he expected a good price in return. The towns formed a vital source of crown revenue. Hence the burgesses summoned to the Cambuskenneth parliament in the summer of 1326, and to the Edinburgh parliament a year and a half later. By an indenture drawn up on the earlier occasion,[132] the community of the realm contracted to pay the king for the remainder of his life a tenth of rents and income from land and property held directly as well as from land held by tenants. The contribution, which was clearly intended to be exceptional, was to be paid throughout the realm, burghs and private liberties being included along with the rest of the country. The tenth was to be reckoned according to what was called the 'old extent', the valuation of land current in Alexander III's reign. If land had been wasted by war, allowance would be made after an inquest had been held by the local sheriff. In return for this sizeable grant, the king promised to forego other irregular sources of income, especially prises, that is summary or arbitrary seizure of goods and chattels, sometimes without payment. It was provided that money from the grant would pass through the king's Chamber or financial office. The grant would cease immediately the king died, or if he granted any exemptions, and would be without prejudice either to the king or to the community of the realm: the *status quo* would simply be resumed. The tenth was confirmed at the Edinburgh parliament of February–March 1328. This assembly witnessed the conclusion of the final treaty of peace with England, with its heavy stipulation of a payment 'for peace' of £20,000. To raise so large a sum in only three years a fresh effort was called for, and the king obtained a further tenth of income from the community, although the burghs compounded for their share with an annual payment of five hundred merks. The money was, in fact, paid off on time, but only with the help of loans.[133]

The best illustration of royal policy towards a burgh is to be seen in the difficult case of Berwick on Tweed. Down to 1296 the richest – and to traders perhaps the best-known – of Scottish mercantile centres, Berwick, having lost most of its native population by slaughter or flight, was carefully built up by Edward I and thoroughly anglicized, even though it was not transferred from one country to the other. Steadily shrinking to little more than a beleaguered garrison town during the years after Bannockburn, Berwick was recaptured by the Scots in April 1318. It is striking testimony to the favoured economic position the town enjoyed that King Robert not only repaired the castle but also repaired the town walls to a height of ten feet[134] and set about restoring Berwick's predominance as a Scottish trading community. By a long and important charter granted in 1320, the king confirmed to the mayor and burgesses the old boundaries of their burgh.[135]

The Berwick community was to enjoy all the usual customs and privileges of a free burgh, to go toll-free throughout the realm and to have a monopoly of buying and selling wool, woolfells and hides in the sheriffdom of Berwick. The burgesses were to have a merchant gild as in former times and, by a somewhat uncommon privilege, one of their number would act as king's coroner within the burgh. There was to be a market every Monday and Friday, and a fair during the summer months when foreign merchants came to trade. The annual farm which Berwick was to render to the king in return for all this was 500 merks. King Robert followed up this charter of privileges by measures designed to encourage men of substance from all over Scotland to take up residence in Berwick on favourable terms. He made a grant for the cleansing of Berwick after its decay and partial destruction, and a contribution was levied from Scotland north of Forth for the re-stocking and maintenance of the burgh.[136]

In common with a number of other Scottish towns, Berwick proved remarkably resilient through all the vicissitudes of war and occupation. Families from both sides of the border who had been established in Berwick in the golden age of Alexander III succeeded in many cases in holding on to their property in the burgh or at least to their claims which could be made good by later generations.[137] During most of the longest period of English occupation (1296–1318), an apparently Scottish merchant, Thomas of Coldingham, was able to ply a fairly steady though modest trade, dealing almost exclusively in wool.[138] In the last year of Robert I's reign the degree to which the export trade of Berwick had recovered may be measured by a customs account referring to 1,503 sacks and eleven stones of wool, 39,107 woolfells and fifty-eight lasts, fifteen dickers of hides with one singleton, all spoken of as having paid customs and being stowed away on board ship.[139] The future of this busy community, however, was not bright. In 1347, despite efforts to maintain the impetus of trade and prosperity between 1333 and 1342 under renewed English occupation,[140] Berwick was said to be 'like a desert for want of population'.[141]

Robert Bruce and the community of the realm of Scotland were never to be challenged by another crisis as severe as Bannockburn, but in the relationship between the king and his lieges the year 1320 was in some ways as decisive as 1314. It was in 1319 and 1320 that Pope John XXII's fulminations against King Robert and his senior clergy were at their most menacing, prompted partly by Edward II's revival of his father's vituperative campaign to have Bishop Lamberton ejected from his see and replaced by the English Franciscan Thomas Rivers.[142] Lamberton himself and three other bishops, Sinclair of Dunkeld, Cheyne of Aberdeen and Murray of Moray, were cited to appear at the curia by letters of November 18th, 1319.[143] They ignored the summons and were eventually (June 16th, 1320) excommunicated, along with the king of Scots.[144] Although the Scots had almost certainly taken a tough line in the truce negotiations at Christmas

1319, a hardening of the papal attitude towards them and especially towards King Robert personally called for nothing less than a national response.[145] Three letters were sent to Pope John about the end of May 1320, one from Bishop Lamberton, another from the king, and a third from the earls, barons, freeholders and the whole community of the realm. It is probable that all three letters were inspired by a common policy decision hammered out at a lengthy session of the king's council held at Newbattle Abbey a few miles south of Edinburgh in the second half of March. A common motivation for the letters is not ruled out by the fact that the king's letter dealt chiefly with such matters as the pope's refusal to recognise his royal title, the objection to accepting an English candidate for the see of Glasgow, and unjust treatment of Scots clergy at the curia. This may be inferred from the pope's reply, dated August 16th, which, like the reply to Bishop Lamberton of the same date, carried the welcome news that sentences of excommunication, suspension and interdict would be postponed at least until April 1st, 1321.[146]

In 1317 the pope had attempted to enforce an Anglo-Scottish truce in furtherance of his crusading plans. Robert I had defied the pope in the matter of the truce, pressing on successfully with his planned recovery of Berwick. More than that, he had protested, with dignity, at the pope's refusal to recognise his kingship and the independence of his kingdom. In 1320 it was part of the king's defence of his conduct that his barons would not allow him to make peace with the English, even had he wished, unless they recognised his title and Scottish independence. A model of sorts for this mock shifting of responsibility would have been familiar to Bruce and many other leaders of the Scottish community. This was the response of Edward I and his baronage to the pro-Scottish censures of Pope Boniface VIII in 1299–1300. In 1301 the barons of England rebutted papal claims to act as special guardian or protector of Scotland by means of a lengthy historically-based protest denying the pope's jurisdiction over the political relations between the king of England as feudal lord of Scotland and his Scottish vassals.[147] In the spring of 1320 the barons of Scotland gave their collective authority to an equally historically-based protest asserting the independence of Scotland since ancient times, condemning the aggression of Edward I and Edward II and respectfully beseeching Pope John to use his authority to bring this aggression to an end. To that extent, the Scots of 1320 were taking a leaf out of the English book.

The barons' letter, which ought more properly to be thought of as the community of the realm's letter, has long been renowned, and has become generally familiar in modern times as the Declaration of Arbroath. The copy sent to the pope at Avignon is lost, but by an astonishing piece of good fortune a duplicate fair copy, preserved for over two centuries at Tyninghame House in East Lothian, has survived, faded, fragile and much injured, yet rightly cherished as the most precious single item in the national archives of Scotland. The letter runs in the name of Duncan earl of Fife, Thomas Randolph earl of Moray and six other earls, and Walter the Stewart, William de Soules the hereditary butler, James lord of Douglas and twenty-eight other barons, and bears the date 'at the monastery of Arbroath in Scotland (Scotia) on the sixth day of the month of April in the year of grace 1320', and the fifteenth year of King Robert's reign. The seals and more particularly the folded foot of the document and the seal-tags, on which names were inscribed, show that at least eleven barons and free-holders who were not listed at the head of the letter were associated with those who were. This total of some fifty leading laymen in the community compares closely with the figures of sixty-two earls, barons and other laymen who, along with forty-six clergy, sealed the letter to Edward I in March, 1290 announcing their consent to what became the treaty of Birgham. The papal court would have had no reason to doubt that as far as the laity were concerned (and the clergy were perhaps inhibited by papal citations and sentences) the letter of April 6th represented the voice and mind of the community of the realm as truly as contemporary conditions allowed.

The substance of the letter would have been discussed and agreed by the council assembled at Newbattle in March, which of course included Bishop Lamberton and other leading clergy even though their names are not to be found among the senders. Why the letter was dated at Arbroath rather than at Newbattle or even Edinburgh we do not know. The most likely explana-tion seems to be that for much of the time that Bernard the chancellor was abbot of Arbroath the *capella regis* or chancery was located at the abbey. Many official documents authenticated by the king's great seal were actually (or by a convenient fiction were stated to have been) issued at Arbroath. It is possible, on the evidence at present available, that the document despatched to Avignon, and its file copy kept in Scotland (presumably in the chancery), although they did not of course bear the great seal, were prepared, engrossed and sealed at Arbroath, but if so we should have to assume that the chancery took charge of most of the seal matrices for long enough to apply them to the red and green wax placed on the tags in rows which neatly observed the social or political hierarchy. For it is hardly realistic to suppose that thirty or forty magnates were assembled at Newbattle in mid-March and then within a week or two rode north to Angus merely to seal two documents they had already agreed upon. It is surely more reasonable to regard the Arbroath dating as conventional, a gesture of deference towards the fact that the chancellor was abbot of Arbroath and the king's chapel was in the abbey. It is of course possible that for reasons of safety or availability of shipping Arbroath was the port at which the messengers embarked for the continent, but that would hardly have influenced the choice of place-date.

If April 6th was the true date at which the letter was finally produced there must have been an unusually long delay before it reached Avignon towards the end of June. This delay may have been due to difficulties in finding shipping, for the Anglo-Scottish truce would hardly have permitted safe passage through England for a document so damaging to English interests. Alternatively, it may have arisen from the need to provide exceptionally trustworthy ambassadors.[148] One of these was Sir Adam Gordon, a substantial laird in Berwickshire and principal tenant and vassal of the earl of Dunbar, whose seal was on the letter. Gordon was a man of mark whose experience of government, war and diplomacy went back twenty years or more. He had been keeper of the West March in 1300, an envoy to England with Nicholas Balmyle in 1301, a parliamentary commissioner to England in 1305 after the general Scottish submission, and joint-justiciar of Lothian under Edward 1's abortive Ordinance of September 1305. His fellow envoy to Avignon was for Robert 1 an unusual, yet at the same time entirely appropriate choice. This was Sir Odard de Maubuisson, a French lord of great experience in administrative, military and more especially naval affairs. Maubuisson had been active against the English in Gascony as long ago as 1296. Commander of Calais in 1303–04, he was then an admiral of the French fleet under the Genoese Rainier de Grimaldi and in that capacity had inflicted much damage on English shipping in the narrow seas and up the east coast of England. If anyone possessed the skill and experience required to ensure a safe delivery of the Scottish diplomatic offensive it was surely Odard de Maubuisson. But for the historian it is the French connexion that is important. Only with Philip v's approval could Maubuisson have been employed by the Scots, and we should see the Scottish lobbying at the curia in 1320 as part of the gradual Franco-Scottish *rapprochement* which had developed over the previous eleven years.

King Robert's ambassadors had at least one, but more probably several audiences of the pope at which they strenuously pleaded the cause of Scotland. They had, as we should expect, a clerical colleague; and indeed the position of the Scottish church, 'special daughter' of the holy see, was one of the chief matters in debate. This third envoy was Mr Alexander Kinninmonth, a papal chaplain and lawyer with considerable experience of the workings of the curia as auditor of causes and in other ways. Most probably he belonged to the old East Fife family of Kinninmonth of that ilk, and if so was the kinsman of the bishop of Brechin John Kinninmonth. We have seen that he succeeded William of Eaglesham (another of Bishop Lamberton's entourage) first of all as parson of Kinkell (autumn 1320) and then as archdeacon of Lothian (1323).[149] Such rapid promotion points to outstanding ability and royal favour, and indeed Kinninmonth was actually chosen to succeed as bishop of St Andrews on Lamberton's death in 1328, only to find himself thwarted by a fellow-clerk of the late bishop's *familia*, Mr James Ben, who had the advantage of being at the papal curia when news of the vacancy arrived.[150] Nevertheless, Pope John almost immediately compensated Kinninmonth with the vacant see of Aberdeen, without the formality of an election. In 1320 Kinninmonth and Maubuisson remained at Avignon until the end of September when they got papal safe-conducts to return to Scotland. Although they did not return with papal recognition for King Robert in their satchels, their mission had certainly not been in vain. Most notably, the series of letters issued from the papal chancery on August 28th, which included a polite but evasive reply to the Scottish barons, contained also an exhortation to all parties involved in the Anglo-Scottish war to observe the truces duly made under papal auspices or with papal approval, and this exhortation refers unequivocally to 'Robert illustrious king of Scotland'.[151]

The Declaration of Arbroath, which with the accompanying letters of Robert I and Bishop Lamberton formed the basis of the envoys' case, was and remains a masterpiece. The Latin in which it is written is the work of an accomplished stylist, well versed in the rhythmic prose employed for letters issued in the pope's name. It wastes scarcely a word, yet succeeds in summarizing in much less space almost everything of importance in the lengthy *processus* of Mr Baldred Bisset (1301). It adds a brief account of how the people of Scotland came to make Robert Bruce their king in 1306. For the early history of the Scots the author had available two versions, one derived from Nennius which brought them from Egypt (Scota, Pharaoh's daughter) to Ireland and then across to Scotland, another which located the Scots originally in Scythia and navigated them through the Tyrrhenian Sea and between the Pillars of Hercules to Spain (Iber Scot) and so to Scotland. He first chose the Nennius story used by Bisset but changed his mind at the last minute and used the version incorporating the old tradition that Picts (and presumably the Scots also through slight verbal similarity) had come from Scythia.[152] No doubt this was done to make more plausible the letter's bold claim that the Scots had been converted to Christianity by the apostle Andrew, brother of Simon Peter. The second-century church historian Eusebius stated that Andrew had preached to the Scythians, and at Rome Andrew, next only to Peter and Paul, was held in the highest reverence. With consummate tact the letter of 1320 says 'Nor would Our Lord Jesus Christ confirm the Scots in his faith save by the most gentle Andrew, first of his apostles by calling (though second or third in rank),[153] brother of the blessed Peter, whom he wished always to be their patron. The holy fathers, your predecessors, mindful of these events, have bestowed many favours and privileges on the Scottish realm and people, as being the special concern of Saint Peter's brother.'

Although it was official and served the purposes of the Scots king and his government, the Declaration of Arbroath was indisputably national and not merely governmental. Worlds away from the normal documentary output of chancery and other royal administrative authorities, the letter is strongly academic, even didactic, in tone. With notable confidence its author pillaged the account of the Catiline Conspiracy by the Roman historian Sallust and the books of holy scripture, especially the Maccabees, for apt quotations which might be rearranged and even reworded to meet not merely the technical requirements of the papal *cursus* (rhythmic prose) but also the message he wished to convey. Thus, before Judas Maccabaeus' last battle it was said that many had stolen away from his camp so that there remained but eight hundred men. The Arbroath declaration improved on that, and the pope was told that as long as but *one* hundred men remained – or, in the final version, one hundred remained alive – the Scots would never submit to English rule. Thus also, Sallust makes an ally of Catiline say that, denied the laws of their ancestors, the conspirators fight neither for dominion nor wealth but for freedom which no honest man gives up but with his life; Catiline complains that he and his friends have been deprived of glory, riches and honour. The 1320 letter selects and compresses all this with unerring skill, even to the extent of first trying a version which included ancestral laws as part of what the Scots were defending and then omitting them. The crucial need for the Scots was to justify their repudiation of Balliol and adoption of Bruce. They had thrown over Balliol ostensibly because he was not the true heir but really because his performance as defender of the realm was calamitous. Logically King Robert might also be rejected, not because of his lineage but because, however improbably, he might fail in his duty as captain and ruler. The whole passage in which this argument is set forth is only one of several (though the finest) which are markedly didactic and even minatory in tone.

But from these countless evils we have been set free, by the help of him who though he afflicts yet heals and restores, by our most tireless prince, king and lord, the lord Robert. He, that his people and heritage might be delivered out of the hands of our enemies, met toil and fatigue, hunger and peril, like another Maccabaeus or Joshua, and bore them cheerfully. Him, too, divine providence, his right of succession according to our laws and customs which we shall maintain to the death, and the due consent and assent of us all have made our prince and king. To him, as to the man by whom salvation has been wrought unto our people, we are bound both by law and by his merits that our freedom may be still maintained, and by him, come what may, we mean to stand.

Yet if he should give up what he has begun, and agree to make us and our kingdom subject to the king of England or the English, we should exert ourselves at once to drive him out as our enemy and a subverter of his own rights and ours, and make some other man who was well able to defend us our king; for, as long as but a hundred of us remain alive, never will we on any conditions be brought under English rule. It is in truth not for glory, nor riches, nor honours that we are fighting, but for freedom – for that alone, which no honest man gives up but with life itself.[154]

It is usual for theory to dance attendance upon fact, but that is not to say that theory is unimportant or that the articulation of theory cannot also be a fact of history and exert a powerful influence on contemporaries and the future. In 1295 the community of the realm had taken the government of Scotland out of the hands of the ineffectual King John. In 1306 a group of magnates, lairds and clergy had in effect elected a new king to resuscitate a community threatened by extinction. In 1320 king and community combined to produce a clear statement of their mutual relationship which was at the same time a declaration of the independence of Scotland, the most eloquent statement of the case for national independence to be produced anywhere in medieval Europe.

The authorship of the community's letter to Pope John still eludes us. Inevitably we speculate, although the truth may always be out of reach. At all events, it does not read as though it had been composed by a committee. Since the eighteenth century it has been usual to give the credit of authorship to Bernard the king's chancellor. We certainly need to look for a single author, a clerk of thorough academic training, accustomed to handling legal and political arguments, steeped in the *ars dictaminis* or rhythmic cadencies of the papal chancery, aware of the importance of history though poorly attuned to historical probabilities, possessing a sound knowledge of the bible and of at least one of the classical Latin authors. His work had to commend itself to Pope John and if it did he was likely to be rewarded with rapid ecclesiastical promotion. We might add, too, that our unknown author had enough clerical self-confidence to be able to tell a king that he could be deposed and a pope that he might imperil his immortal soul. No doubt there were sound reasons why in 1320 Master Alexander Kinninmonth was a member of the Scottish embassy to Avignon, just as there were when he was commissioned by Robert I in 1329, along with the bishop of Moray, to argue (successfully) before the pope that future kings of Scotland should be anointed at their coronation. But the soundest reason for sending him in 1320 may have been simply that he was the author of the community's letter and that there was no-one better qualified either to present it to the pope or to expound its message.

The list of names on the Declaration of Arbroath deserves a brief analysis even although the abnormal conditions of war may have made it hard to assemble fifty noblemen and lairds in any manner which could be described, politically or geographically, as balanced or representative. The small number of highland magnates is striking, although several of the earls as well as the Stewart, Sir John Menteith, and Donald and Arthur (or Martin?) Campbell were landowners north of the highland line, some on a large scale. Noticeable also, and more surprising, is the shortage of names from the south west generally – no Boyds, Kennedys, Crawfords, McCullochs or Kirkpatricks[155] to keep company with Fergus of Ardrossan and John Duraunt. This geographical imbalance bears out the notion that preparing and sealing the letter were matters of urgency, those keeping guard on the south-east marches or otherwise within comfortable reach of Newbattle being disproportionately represented. Household office and enjoyment of the king's highest confidence did not necessarily mean inclusion. Andrew Murray of Bothwell, for example, the hereditary panetar,[156] was expected to be present. His name was duly entered on a draft, but it was omitted from the final text presumably because neither he nor his seal was within reach. Alexander Seton was steward of the household and ought surely to have been listed. His name is indeed there, but it has been argued that since it occurs very low on the list it must belong to his son and heir.[157] Robert Lauder, by 1321 justiciar of Lothian, was greatly trusted by the king, but in 1320 he was not yet a knight, only a *vallettus* or 'yeoman', i.e. a personal servant or officer of the king,[158] so the absence of his name may be due to his lowly social rank.

A more intriguing aspect of the list of names than the highland and south-western absentees is the relatively large proportion of men who had belonged (or whose families had belonged) to the old Balliol–Comyn party. David Brechin and Roger Moubray were prominent among this group, which would also have included Ingram de Umfraville, William Oliphant, William of Abernethy, David Wemyss, Eustace Maxwell and possibly David Graham. Beside these names we might put those of the earl of March and Reginald Cheyne, whose fathers had been conspicuously pro-English during the long years of war from 1296 to 1314. It would be agreeable if we could look on these names as clear proof that Robert I's policy of moderation and leniency had begun to pay off, and that the letter to Pope John was truly an expression of national unity even for a divided baronage. Unhappily, the mysterious de Soules plot rules out any optimism of this kind. We might, indeed, speculate that certain magnates had been chosen deliberately to join in the letter to Pope John as a test of loyalty. Whatever the truth of this may be, at the very time the Scottish letters were under consideration at the curia a charge of treason was being brought against several of the men who sent it. Former (and in some cases future) Balliol supporters, they had gathered round the somewhat colourless figure of William de Soules, the hereditary butler, whose name and (evidently) seal were on the Arbroath letter.[159] Whether or not he was a mere figurehead in the plot he was certainly still in the king's confidence at the turn of the years 1319–20 when he headed the Scots team of truce negotiators.[160]

Odd as it may seem for men who supposedly believed in Balliol legitimacy, the plotters aimed to set de Soules on the throne – he was, after all, the son of one of the competitors of 1291, and great-nephew of the illustrious Sir John de Soules. Two Northumbrian writers state that Murdoch of Menteith disclosed the plot to the government, the one, Thomas Grey, saying that Murdoch returned to Scotland after a long sojourn in England expressly to reveal the conspiracy, the other, John of Tynemouth, alleging that Murdoch was himself a conspirator but decided to betray his comrades. The latter claims that as a reward the king gave the earldom of Menteith to Murdoch, who was a son of Earl Alexander and seems last to be found in Scotland in the 1290s.[161] Grey says merely that Murdoch got the earldom through the resignation of his niece. Barbour's story is that the de Soules plot was revealed by a lady, of whose identity he was ignorant.[162]

De Soules himself, David Brechin and Roger Moubray were convicted of treason in the parliament which met at Scone on August 4th. Moubray had in fact died before parliament met and his corpse was brought before the judges on a litter. This was done because conviction and sentence involving perpetual disinheritance could be pronounced and put into execution only on the body of the convicted person.[163] On the king's personal intervention Moubray's corpse was spared mutilation and allowed decent burial.[164] De Soules was let off lightly with perpetual imprisonment and the same sentence was passed on the countess of Strathearn, possibly widow of the Earl Malise who had fought for King John and rebuffed King Robert. Patrick Graham and Eustace Maxwell, both named in the Arbroath letter, along with Walter Barclay sheriff of Aberdeen, Hamelin of Troup and Eustace of Rattray, were accused with the rest but acquitted. Alexander Moubray, reported by John of Tynemouth to be in the plot, fled to England.[165] The other conspirators were the shifty opportunist Gilbert Malherbe of Stirlingshire,[166] John Logie (whose custody while a minor Malherbe had been prevented from enjoying by Earl Malise),[167] and a squire named Richard Brown. They were sentenced to be drawn, hanged and beheaded. Sir David Brechin (descendant of Earl David of Huntingdon), a gallant knight who had distinguished himself in Balliol or English service against Bruce before Bannockburn, was not himself a plotter, but he had been privy to the plot and failed to report it.[168] For this he too was condemned to hanging and beheading at Perth, a sentence which so disgusted Sir Ingram de Umfraville that he left Scotland for good.[169] Thus four out of the fifty sponsors of the Declaration were lost to King Robert's service within a few months of its date of issue, and two more had come under suspicion of treason. In view of the fact that there must have been numerous barons in Scotland of proven loyalty whose names could have adorned the Declaration of Arbroath, men such as Andrew Murray of Bothwell, Angus Macdonald or Robert Menzies, it looks very much as if the authorities responsible for the document deliberately cast their net wide, and tried to bring into the leadership of the community men associated for years with opposition to the Bruce régime. If this was indeed done it was surely a sound move, politically speaking, even though it did not wholly succeed. The letter to Pope John remains an impressive piece of work. Certainly we shall find no clearer statement of Scottish nationalism and patriotism in the fourteenth century. Equally certainly, no finer statement of a claim to national independence was produced in this period anywhere in western Europe. In this respect, the conservative community of the Scottish realm stands out in advance of the age.

FIFTEEN

In Search of Robert Bruce

It is easy to strip away the legend surrounding some notable figure from the distant past, but clearing away the legend does not necessarily reveal the man. Nothing that has been stated as a fact about Bruce in the foregoing pages, nor any speech or writing attributed to him, is legendary in quality. But it must still remain doubtful whether we have come much nearer to the king's true personality. To some extent our view of Bruce will always depend on how much credence we give to Barbour. If we choose to ignore Barbour altogether, as we may, we shall be left with a jejune assortment of glimpses in record and chronicle, and a few authentic utterances. These might carry more weight than Barbour, but they would not add up to a portrait. Barbour is far from being legend, but we need to remember that for him Bruce was the hero of a work of art. Consciously or unconsciously, he emphasized the chivalrous qualities in Bruce, and in Douglas, his other hero. More seriously than this, he over-emphasized the chivalrous qualities of the age in which Bruce and Douglas lived. It was an age in which a king of England was murdered with a red-hot iron plunged through his rectum into his bowels, in which two knights at the court of Philip IV, because of an affair with the king's daughters-in-law, were flayed alive – one of them having been extradited by Edward II for the purpose, much to the indignation '(may it be said to their credit) of ordinary English people. It was, though not of course uniquely, an age of horrors, of brutality, of intrigue and squalor. Much of this Barbour passes over. He touches on the miseries, but he dwells on the splendours.

Nevertheless, on the score of general reliability Barbour must be reckoned a biographer, not a romancer. How much would we feel we knew of Dr Johnson were it not for Boswell? It would not be absurd to ask a similar question with regard to Bruce and Barbour. Of course, Barbour lacks the pages of dialogue re-called *verbatim*, the mass of convincing detail, which constitute the chief reason for reading Boswell and believing his portrait to be a very close approach to truth. But Barbour, though only a boy when Bruce died, was a most careful and exact recorder, especially of names, personalities, incidents and points of detail. We shall not be on unsafe ground if we accept Barbour's portrait of the king, even though we must correct it by more reliable evidence wherever that is necessary and possible. He shows us a man at once humane and kingly, generous and firm of purpose. Barbour was not often embarrassed by the need to excuse or explain away some act which detracted from his hero's stature. The execution of the burgesses at Perth in 1313 was played down by Barbour in the words 'bot thair wes few slayne', which were vague enough not to be untrue.[1] The apparent fact that the king singled out the Scots for deterrent punishment, letting the English go free, is actually contradicted by Barbour's statement 'that thai war kynde to the cuntre he wist, and had of thame pite'.[2] The king's refusal to intervene to save Sir David Brechin's life clearly troubled Barbour, and he passed rapidly on from this sorry business to tell an anecdote of Bruce's unusual generosity towards Sir Ingram de Umfraville.[3] In these somewhat pathetic evasions or discomfitures of Barbour lies one of our surest pieces of evidence of Bruce's essential goodness.

The king's sense of humour comes out even in dry official documents, but is best remembered in his reply to the nobles who rebuked him for risking his life in the encounter with Sir Henry de Bohun at Bannockburn.[4] His immense courage is attested by the whole of his career. Patience, on the other hand, he was forced to learn, yet once learned it became his most dominant characteristic. Men trusted his word and his judgements, so that decisions and laws made by him were respected and, in after years, invented in order to be respected. In a period when there were virtually no professionals, generalship was not of a high order. But modern military experts agree that Bruce's handling of Bannockburn was masterly. The secret of his success here lay in the fact that behind his tactical brilliance and superlative gifts of leadership Bruce had an exceptionally good grasp of strategy: he always knew what should take priority. Directly or indirectly, Barbour's portrait gives us these qualities. His terms of reference forbade him to write of shortcomings, such as the evident rashness and hot-headedness of Bruce's earlier years. Barbour hardly brings out Bruce's ambition, yet it cannot be doubted that from young manhood Bruce was determined to play a leading part. The truth about his submission to Edward I in 1302 has now been established in sufficient detail to disprove the old charges of treachery and double-dealing, yet the fact remains that Bruce did change sides two years in advance of his colleagues. Nothing but frustrated ambition will easily account for his conduct. Barbour also fails to mention, presumably because word and concept were alike lacking in his time, one of Bruce's greatest gifts, the imaginative quality of his mind which allowed him to be revolutionary in more than just the political sense.

Finally, we must return to Robert Bruce's kingliness. It was suggested earlier that the key to much of his conduct may be sought in the background, at once aristocratic and royal, in which his grandfather was brought up and lived out his long career. There is an unmistakable assurance about the manner in which Bruce assumed kingship even though he reached the throne by a revolutionary *coup*. Even his flight in the heather did not snuff out his claims to royalty, though the news of it inspired mocking ballads in England[5] and became common gossip as far away as Italy.[6] The *regia dignitas* of Scotland was never in safer hands than those of King Robert I. Barbour convincingly makes the magnates gathered at his deathbed mourn their lord as a great exponent of kingship and kingliness: 'for better governour than he mycht in na cuntre fundyn be.'[7]

Let us look at two brief letters of which King Robert was at least the official author. They have not been mentioned earlier, and one was scarcely known at all until Professor Duncan brought it to light. The first was addressed to Edward II at some unknown date, the second to the kings and people of Ireland, probably in 1315, preparatory to Edward Bruce's expedition.

> To the most sincere prince, the Lord Edward, by God's grace illustrious king of England, Robert, by the same grace king of Scots, sends greetings in Him by whom the thrones of rulers are governed.
>
> Since while agreeable peace prevails the minds of the faithful are at rest, the Christian way of life is furthered, and all the affairs of holy mother church and of all kingdoms are everywhere carried on more prosperously, we in our humility have judged it right to entreat of your highness most earnestly that, having before your eyes the righteousness you owe to God and to the people, you desist from persecuting us and disturbing the people of our realm, so that there may be an end of slaughter and shedding of Christian blood. Everything that we ourselves and our people by their bodily service and contributions of wealth can do, we are now, and shall be, prepared to do sincerely and honourably for the sake of good peace and to earn perpetual grace for our souls. If it should be agreeable to your will to hold negotiations with us upon these matters, let your royal will be communicated to us in a letter by the hands of the bearer of this present letter.[8]

> The king sends greetings to all the kings of Ireland, to the prelates and clergy, and to the inhabitants of all Ireland, his friends.
>
> Whereas we and you and our people and your people, free since ancient times, share the same national ancestry and are urged to come together more eagerly and joyfully in friendship by a common language and by common custom, we have sent over to you our beloved kinsmen, the bearers of this letter, to negotiate with you in our name about permanently strengthening and maintaining inviolate the special friendship between us and you, so that with God's will our nation may be able to recover her ancient liberty. Whatever our envoys or one of them may on our behalf conclude with you in this matter we shall ratify and uphold in the future.[9]

Does either of these letters give us the real Bruce? Are they, in the most personal sense, authentic, or are they both merely the products of an embryonic 'foreign office' with an eye to the main chance? In view of the extremely personal quality of royal government in the fourteenth century, it would probably be wrong to put these letters too far from the king himself. At the very least they show two aspects of his policy, and give examples of his method of approach. There is no reason to suspect Bruce's sincerity in his professions of peace towards England, so long as it was peace between independent monarchies and not simply submission. And it seems typical that he should write direct to the only person who could take the initiative on the other side. If Professor Duncan is right in thinking that the letter to Edward 11 belongs to the period of the Declaration of Arbroath, possibly composed by the same author, then the seriousness of purpose underlying the Scottish king's appeal would be confirmed.

The letter to Ireland is a very different matter. The invasion of Ireland hangs over Bruce's career as a large question-mark. Some English historians dismiss it as nothing more than deliberate trouble-making, and dwell upon the horrors and miseries that followed from King Robert's perilous and futile march to Limerick and from the Scots' whole sojourn in Ireland between May 1315 and October 1318. One or two even contrive to suggest that this unique and shortlived Scottish invasion ended a halcyon period of Anglo-Irish harmony, and introduced a note of altogether unusual barbarity into the history of a nation which had hitherto been ruled and protected by the English Crown with motherly solicitude.[10]

The question must nevertheless be asked, was Bruce's motive plain aggression, the sort of aggression upon which successful revolutionary nationalism so often embarks? The affair hardly admits of any simple explanation. A powerful resurgence of Celtic tradition and Irish national feeling would have caused an explosion regardless of Scottish intervention. Behind the obvious propaganda appeal of Bruce's letter lay important truths.[11] Scotland and Ireland did share in part a common ancestry and culture, and the Irish did yearn to be free of foreign rule. The example set by Bruce in his own kingdom was bound to be infectious, and it was understandable that some of the Irish leaders should fancy that an answer to all their pent-up aspirations lay in Edward Bruce and a few thousand veterans of Loudoun Hill, Brander and Bannockburn.

Equally, there is no doubt that contemporary observers, both in England and in Ireland, believed the Scots were bent on conquest.[12] Their invasion threatened to wrest the lordship of Ireland totally from the control of the king of England and create a fresh kingdom of Ireland under a Scottish king, Edward Bruce. Moreover, in May 1315 when he crossed to Ireland to embark on his three-year adventure, it must have seemed well within the bounds of probability that Edward Bruce would succeed to the throne of Scotland.[13] Robert I had an acute awareness of the dangers of a hostile, of the value of a friendly, Ireland. For three years from 1315 a significant part of the military resources of Scotland (chiefly veteran commanders and soldiers, but also weaponry, shipping and supplies) was diverted to the Irish enterprise. Thomas Randolph was involved from the outset, and when the

Scots invasion appeared to be penned within the borders of Ulster Randolph went back to Scotland to fetch reinforcements (December, 1315)
whose numbers enabled the invaders to penetrate as far south as north
Leinster. Had the Scots intended merely to secure their western flank by
neutralizing Ulster this southward push would be hard to explain. It is true
that after outfacing, near Ardscull in Co. Kildare, an Anglo-Irish force
weakened by rivalries and jealousies, Edward was compelled to withdraw
northward again.[14] But on May 1st 1316 he was duly crowned 'king of
Ireland' at Dundalk, a move supported by Domnall O'Neill and clearly not
meant to limit Scots activity to Ulster.

Stalemate ensued, but instead of Robert I's deciding to cut his losses and
abandon his brother to the common fate of so many invaders of Ireland he
personally led an army of veterans to Ulster in January, 1317, and in
company with Edward and Randolph undertook a bold and dangerous
operation the aim of which was clearly to rouse the clans of central and
southern Ireland in support of 'King Edward' and to amass sufficient forces
to drive the English government out of Dublin. A winter of dearth and
disease was not well chosen for this venture, which with hindsight seems
more desperate than it may have appeared to those who were there. Save in
Ulster, where a few families such as Mandevilles, Bissets and Logans fought
on the Scottish side for some of the time,[15] the Anglo-Irish opposed the
Scots, only isolated dissidents like the Lacys of Meath or Gilbert de la
Roche joining Bruce because of private quarrels. The Dublin administration, whether under Edmund Butler or more vigorously under Roger
Mortimer, could afford to wait, making a Fabian virtue out of financial
necessity. For the Scots everything depended on the Irish kings, greater and
lesser, uniting in the common cause of Irish independence and being
motivated by a shared enmity towards the English. But of this they were
quite incapable. O'Neill merely excited jealousy, rival branches of the
kingly family of Connacht could not both receive satisfaction from 'King
Edward', and on the banks of the Shannon near Limerick the Scots army
was confronted by a hostile Muirchertach O'Brien where they had hoped to
find friends and allies. By May 1317 the king of Scots, his force decimated
by sickness and hunger, judged it prudent to return home.

It has been said that 'when Robert [Bruce] sought the backing of 'all the
kings of Ireland', he was asking for a unity quite foreign to Gaelic Ireland'.[16]
It is not easy, however, to accept that the king of Scots was so naïve, so
ignorant of the truth about Irish society and politics, that the failure of the
Irish kings or chiefs to rally behind his brother took him utterly by surprise.
Robert I was a realist, born and brought up among people who knew Ireland
well and, indeed, thoroughly at home in a region of Scotland, Carrick and
Galloway, which must have resembled northern Ireland very closely. The
establishment of his brother as king of Ireland would certainly have suited
Robert I's book. If the English government were drawn into costly diver-

sions of Irish resources which they would otherwise use against the Scots, if the English could be harried not only in Ireland itself but by an Irish-based invasion of north Wales, above all if the subjugation at least of Ulster could, along with the recovery of Man, secure for the Scots unchallenged command of the narrow seas between Ireland and Scotland, then a substantial, though not reckless, investment of ships, troops and leadership in Ireland would pay off.[17]

As for the long term, and the deeper implications, that seems a different matter. In the fifteen years between Bannockburn and King Robert's death he devoted a mere few months to personal interventions on Irish soil, and the Scots as a whole were active in Ireland for only three years. Had Ireland and its relations with England and Scotland been 'in the mainstream of Scottish policy, not regarded as a temporary diversion of it',[18] the Scots would surely have given Ireland closer and more continuous attention than appears to have been the case. This is not to say that King Robert did not take Ireland seriously. Geography alone would have guaranteed that the Irish situation could never be of temporary interest to Scotland. Bruce never forgot Scotland's Irish frontier. There was even a belief in Scotland (unsupported by any known evidence) that if only Edward Bruce had postponed the encounter with John Bermingham at Faughart (October 14th, 1318) 'till the morrow', his brother would have come to his aid with a large army.[19] Improbable as this may seem, Bruce could not afford to let English power become firmly established in Antrim or Down. In the very last years of his life, although suffering from a crippling malady, he crossed to Ulster twice, first in 1327 to make sure that Edward III got no help from Ireland, and secondly, in the summer of 1328, for an unknown purpose.[20] There is absolutely no question that Scottish policy throughout Robert I's reign embraced the exercise of a decisive influence upon the situation in northern Ireland. But when it came to the notion of a 'Celtic empire' in the west, fulfilling in part the popular prophecies of Merlin, the Scots seem to have been opportunistic. It would be wrong to sentimentalize the relations of the two peoples. They made use of each other when it suited them, and since under Robert I the Scots were better organized the advantage, as long as he lived, lay with them.

To the modern Scottish mind, largely protestant or post-protestant, there is one element in Robert Bruce's nature which has seemed unfamiliar and unattractive and has consequently been omitted from standard and popular works, or played down. This is the king's piety and devoutness, especially his devotion to certain saints of the church. Perhaps he was in no way exceptional in this respect among the kings of his time. But one is left with a strong impression that religious feeling at this level had a much more dominant place in his life than in that of Edward II, even if it meant less to him than it had done to Henry III. Certainly no picture of the king would be complete if it did not take this into account. Bruce seems, for example, to have felt a special devotion towards Saint Fillan, one of the most renowned of the Scoto-Irish saints. He granted Fillan's chief church and sanctuary (Killin and Strathfillan) to Inchaffray Abbey, evidently with the intention that a daughter-house of Inchaffray should be founded at Strathfillan, and this daughter-house he endowed with land in Glendochart.[21] The story goes that he venerated Saint Fillan's arm bone on the eve of Bannockborn and invoked the saint's help; and in the year of his death his natural son Robert Bruce of Liddesdale made a gift of £20 towards the fabric of Saint Fillan's church. Robert I is the first king known to have invoked Saint Andrew publicly as the nation's patron, and in thanks for his great victory he granted the cathedral priory of St Andrews an annual endowment of a hundred merks, afterwards exchanged for the patronage of the church of Fordoun in Kincardineshire.[22] Saint Cuthbert attracted his love and reverence, just as he had inspired the devotion of the twelfth-century kings of Scots.[23] Saint Thomas the Martyr of Canterbury, in whose honour William the Lion had founded the splendid abbey of Arbroath, was invoked along with Saint Andrew, Saint John Baptist, and the saints of Scotland (doubtless including Columba) at the outset of the battle of Bannockburn. It must be remembered that the chancellor Bernard, who tells us this, was abbot of Arbroath and would watch over Saint Thomas's interests with special care. But there is little doubt of King Robert's reverence for the martyr, for he granted very numerous charters to his abbey and, only a few days before he died, wrote on its behalf to Edward III to ask for the restoration of Haltwhistle parish church in Northumberland, given to Arbroath 150 years earlier.[24] He did not forget Saint Malachy, whose wrath his grandfather had tried to placate in 1272. In the Cistercian abbey of Coupar-Angus – the daughter of Melrose, the daughter of Rievaulx, the daughter of Clairvaux where Malachy had died – the king provided for a candle and a lamp to burn perpetually at the altar of the Blessed Malachy.[25]

The king's observance of his religious duties was occasionally linked to his strong sense of fitness and justice. In 1306 Earl William of Ross had evidently seized Earl John of Atholl in the sanctuary of Saint Duthac at Tain, where he had taken refuge with the royal ladies after their flight from Kildrummy. Since Ross had handed Atholl over for execution, one condition of his being received into King Robert's peace was that he should maintain at his own expense six chaplains to say masses for Earl John at St Duthac's church.[26] The king's brother-in-law Sir Christopher Seton, perhaps the man he loved best of all among his friends, was hanged at Dumfries after his capture at Loch Doon. When his widow, the Lady Christian Bruce, founded a chapel of the Holy Rood at Dumfries in memory of Sir Christopher, the king arranged that £5 towards its upkeep should be paid by the barony of Caerlaverock, temporarily forfeited by Sir Eustace Maxwell who was an adherent of the English.[27] Sir Neil Bruce, hanged in

1306 like Atholl and Seton, had been taken in Kildrummy. By a charter granted in 1328, the master and brethren of the hospital of Turriff, a house formerly under the patronage of the king's enemy the earl of Buchan, were required to find a chaplain to celebrate masses for Neil Bruce's soul.[28]

The clearest evidence of Bruce's religious devotion is provided by the long-drawn-out and surely painful pilgrimage which he undertook in the last few months of his life to the shrine of Saint Ninian at Whithorn in Galloway.[29] He was at Girvan in southern Carrick on February 6th, 1329. From there he was borne slowly southward to Inchmichael (the present Lochinch), where he stayed for over a month, and so by way of Glenluce and Monreith to Whithorn, reached by April 1st. Some four days at least were spent at Whithorn, seeking the intercession of Saint Ninian – who in Bruce's time was perhaps just approaching the height of his popularity among the Scots – before the royal party returned, with rather better speed than on their outward journey, to the king's house at Cardross.

About three years before his death, King Robert, who had caused every royal castle in Scotland to be destroyed save Berwick and Dumbarton, began to build a house for himself where he could find some comfort and relaxation. He chose for the site of this house the village of Cardross, on the north shore of the Firth of Clyde and on the right bank of the River Leven, immediately opposite the burgh of Dumbarton.[30] In some ways it was a remarkable choice. The Crown had virtually no demesne land in the Lennox, and the king had to go out of his way to acquire the necessary ground at Cardross by compensating the two existing landowners. The earl of Lennox, from whom he bought about two hundred and eight acres, received instead the lands of Leckie near Stirling.[31] Sir David Graham, who seems to have owned the bulk of the Cardross property, was given Old Montrose in Angus, an exchange which gave rise to the historic association between the names of Graham and Montrose.[32]

The king's house at Cardross has long since vanished, and only archaeo- logical investigation could now reveal its size and character.[33] It was not a 'castle', as it is sometimes called locally, but a *manerium*, which in Scotland meant a dwelling-house. There is no evidence of fortification of any kind, although a stone wall was built beside the king's chamber. The house was planned on a reasonably generous scale, with a hall, queen's chamber, chapel, kitchen and larder. The roofs were thatched. In 1328 there was an apartment called the 'new chamber' (perhaps the same as the 'king's chamber') which evidently had plastered and painted walls and glazed windows. Beside this new chamber was constructed the 'new gate'. Apart from the house itself there was a garden, for which we read of seeds being bought, and a park for the king's hunting, under the charge of Gillis the hunter and various parkers, William, Gilchrist and Gilfillan. A special building, surrounded by a hedge, housed the royal falcons. Material for the manor house was in fact brought considerable distances. A hundred 'large boards' for repairs to Cardross park were shipped from Tarbert on Loch Fyne in 1326, and two years later 400 boards were brought as far as Lamlash in Arran, presumably *en route* for Cardross. The large quantities of provisions bought by the constable of Cardross, Adam, Alan's son, show that the king lived and entertained comfortably and hospitably, though not lavishly. A fishing coble in the Leven, which was attached to the estate, may have helped here. In addition to hunting and falconry, Bruce seems to have taken an interest in sailing and boat-building. He kept ships at Cardross (as did his nephew Thomas Randolph) and we read of eighty stones of iron being bought for their repair in 1328. The king had more than one ship, but we read most of his 'great ship', and of at least one occasion when she sailed to Tarbert and back. At one time this ship was drawn up out of the water into the burn beside the house, and her tackle and equipment were carted and carried 'into the manor house', presumably into its precincts or outbuildings.

The site of this house is now unknown. A belief once held locally and perhaps not yet extinct is that it stood on Castlehill, about half a mile west of the River Leven. It is here that it has been thought fit to commemorate publicly Bruce's close connexion with this part of Cardross parish, now within the district of Dumbarton. Public commemoration is only right, and perhaps it does not matter greatly what site is chosen for it. It must be pointed out that the belief that Bruce died at Castlehill rests not just upon insufficient, but upon positively invalid evidence. This consists chiefly of two erroneous assumptions, first, that the royal residence must have been a 'castle' because no king would live in anything else, secondly, that the old name Castlehill obviously marks the site. In fact, the mound at Castlehill, which requires investigation, could not possibly be the site of King Robert's *manerium*. The contemporary evidence, whose implications were stated many years ago by David Murray,[34] points to a site closer to the River Leven. There is still beside the river, half-way between Dumbarton Bridge and Dalchurn, and now a little way south of the new line of the A82 trunk road, the farm of Mains of Cardross. By analogy, the 'mains' (= 'demesne', *dominium*) of Cardross would be at or close to the lord's dwelling. We recall that the king's great ship was drawn up out of the river (*ab aqua*) in a burn beside the house. Not only does this prove that the house cannot have been far from the river, but the only burn of any consequence between the mouth of the River Leven and Dalchurn is that which rises above Dalmoak and enters the river just north of Mains of Cardross. In 1362 the lands of 'Pelanysflat' – the last element denotes level arable or meadow – lay between Dalchurn and the king's park of Cardross.[35] An undated eighteenth-century map by Thomas Kitchin shows 'Pilinflait' south of Dalchurn and slightly north-east of Dalmoak, suggesting that it was situated just to the north of Mains of Cardross.[36] Between Mains of

Cardross and Dumbarton Bridge the ground has been much disturbed, partly by changes in the line of the River Leven, partly by industrial and road building. But it seems certain that the exact position of the house in which Bruce died is to be sought either at Mains of Cardross or somewhere in the half mile which separates the farm from the modern railway bridge over the Leven.

The king's choice of Cardross as the home of his last years raises a larger question, which has been postponed from an earlier stage of this study. Whether or not Bruce was bred in the Gaelic tradition, he certainly chose to die in a strongly Gaelic district. As far as Bruce himself is concerned, his decision to make a home for himself at Cardross certainly seems evidence of his love of the west, of his belief – against the current of fourteenth-century Scottish history – in the importance of the western approaches, the gateway to Ireland, the sea lanes which formed the only adequate communication with the powerful and potentially dangerous lords of Islay, Lorn and Garmoran.

There is surely a clue here to one abiding quality in Robert Bruce. Historians have found it hard to place the patriot king in a firm and believable context before 1306, or even before 1314. An Anglo-Norman unsympathetic towards a conservatively kin-based Celtic-speaking society; a nobleman who cannot have possessed the common touch enjoyed by Wallace; a trained knight who could feel only distaste for guerilla warfare – how could such a man have undergone the drastic metamorphosis required to make him a national hero? But in his own time Bruce was unlikely to have been forced into any of these categories. Born to Marjorie of Carrick, grandson of Neil son of Duncan son of Gilbert son of Fergus 'king of the Gallovidians', Bruce became earl of Carrick at eighteen and took care to associate the earldom with his family until his death in 1329. As far as we can tell neither Annandale nor the English Honour of Huntingdon meant much to him. The Firth of Clyde, however, and the Scottish islands and Ireland seem to have rated highly. Bruce was no Anglo-Norman fish out of water, grassed on a Celtic river bank. If we think of his masterly exploitation of the Clyde coast and islands in 1306 and 1307, of his astonishing march in October 1307 to overwhelm Inverlochy and Castle Urquhart, of his surprise attack on the Macdougalls in the Pass of Brander and his sea-borne expedition from Loch Broom in 1309, of his brilliant recovery of the Isle of Man with a great fleet of galleys, of his welcome at the hands of the lady of Garmoran, Christian MacRuarie, of his choice of Tarbert as the seat of a completely new royal sheriffdom, then we see in Bruce a potentate in the immemorial mould of the western Gaidhealtachd, inured since youth to a rough country and to rough warfare by land and sea. That was assuredly one aspect of Robert Bruce, even if it does not tell the whole story.

If this book has attempted anything, it has been to demonstrate that the most stubborn, persistent, tenacious resistance to foreign domination came from the old Scottish kingdom of the twelfth and thirteenth centuries, fed by a tradition of deep-rooted loyalty to the Crown and by a sense of political nationhood expressed in the term 'community of the realm', which was employed over and over again in a great variety of contexts, yet almost always with the same meaning. This does not seem to have been a monopoly of any distinctive element in Scotland, whether regional, cultural or racial. In truth, thirteenth-century Scotland formed a society too complex to allow us to project into it sharp divisions of race and culture possibly appropriate to the country a thousand years earlier. For historical reasons largely unconnected with racial factors the essential 'heartland' of the feudal kingdom of Scotland, as it was built up by the kings of Scots from the first to the third Alexander, stretched on the east from Dornoch to Berwick and Roxburgh, on the west from the Great Glen to Ayr. It is instructive to apply this fact to the events of 1286–1329. The least consistent support for the community of the Scottish realm during this period, and the most consistent support for the English kings, came from certain areas outwith this heart-land: Caithness, Islay, Lorn, Galloway and the Isle of Man. The heartland itself showed more consistent support for the community and less for English rule. Yet even if this rough and ready conclusion is acceptable, there were notable exceptions to warn us of the danger of giving too much weight to any broad generalization. The clash between Macdougall and Macdon-ald, for example, was strictly irrelevant to the Scots' long struggle for freedom, yet it proved of immense importance to Robert Bruce. The division of ancient Galloway into two parts was another irrelevance, but in the end it too played a vital part in Bruce's success. The prolonged and effective English occupation of most of Lothian and part of Teviotdale makes difficult any direct comparison between this region and the rest of Scotland. The biggest single weakness suffered by the community of the realm was not any racial or linguistic animosity but the dilemma of a disputed succession from which the war itself had arisen. Even Robert I did not solve this problem of schism, as was to be made painfully clear a few years after his death, when many Scots who had been identified with the national movement did homage to Edward Balliol as king, and later, after the catastrophe of Halidon Hill, an even greater number submitted to Edward III. Although many of these men had been traditionally members of the old 'Balliol' or 'Comyn' party, this was by no means true of all.

Robert Bruce died at his house in Cardross on June 7th, 1329, at the age of fifty-five. For at least two years he had been suffering from a serious illness. The existing evidence is apparently insufficient to enable medical experts to determine its character with certainty.[37] In two independent English accounts, the Lanercost chronicle and Sir Thomas Grey's *Scalacronica*, which are generally well-informed and which may without hesitation be trusted to give at least the popular belief, the king is said to have contracted leprosy and died of it.[38] In another independent account, Jean le Bel says that in 1327 the king was a victim of *la grosse maladie*,[39] which is usually taken to mean leprosy. The difficulty here is to judge how much, if any, meaning these statements possess, in view of the ignorant use of the term 'leprosy' by fourteenth-century writers. Almost any major skin disease might be called leprosy. Moreover, it cannot be proved, though it may be thought probable, that Bruce died of the disease he was known to have contracted. Our earliest mention of this disease is to be found in an original letter written by an eye-witness in Ulster at the time the king made the truce with Sir Henry Mandeville on July 12th, 1327. The writer of this letter reported that the Scottish king was so feeble and struck down by illness that he would not live till the following August, 'for he can scarcely move anything but his tongue'.[40] Yet Bruce recovered sufficiently to play a not inactive part in the northern English campaign of the late summer. He was present, though evidently confined to bed, at the Edinburgh parliament of March 1328, and was even able to cross once more to Ulster in August.[41] He was obviously ailing gravely when he made his pilgrimage to Whithorn in the following year, yet the significant fact from the point of view of the seriousness of his illness is that he was able to go through with it. The Scottish historians do not speak of leprosy, but this could be explained by a natural reluctance on their part to attribute to a hero-king a disease regarded with superstitious dread and loathing. On the other hand, Barbour writes of the king's illness without trying to minimize its seriousness, and his explanation is that 'it began through a benumbing (of the king's body) brought on by his cold lying' during the months of wandering from 1306 to 1309.[42] There does not seem to be any evidence as to what the king himself or his physicians believed his illness to be. Nor is there any sign of an attempt in his last years to segregate the king, even moderately, from the company of friends, family, courtiers or foreign diplomats.[43]

He had always wished to take part in a crusade, to fight the 'Saracens' in the Holy Land or elsewhere. On his deathbed he asked that his heart should be taken from his body, embalmed, and carried to the Holy Sepulchre by a warrior able to do battle with the enemies of God. The honour was given, either by the king himself or by the nobles who were with the king when he died, to the faithful Douglas. The king's body, with the heart removed, was borne to Dunfermline, where most of the Scottish rulers since King Edgar had been buried. It was laid beneath the middle of the choir in the abbey church, and over it was placed a 'fair tomb' which the king had ordered to be made in Paris. Douglas, with many Scottish knights, sailed from Montrose to Flanders early in 1330, and from there to Spain, armed with letters of protection from Edward III and a letter of commendation from the same king to King Alfonso XI of Castile and Leon. King Alfonso, based on Seville, was conducting a campaign against the Moors of Granada who were strongly reinforced by contingents from Morocco. Sir James Douglas was given the command of a division of the Christian army – perhaps, as Barbour says, consisting of all the knights from England, Scotland and other foreign lands. Bearing Bruce's heart, Douglas went into battle at Tebas de Ardales on March 25th, 1330. Deceived by the Moorish tactics of making a feint attack, the Scots found themselves cut off from the main body and helpless against a superior force of Moorish cavalry. Douglas himself, Sir William Sinclair, and Robert and Walter Logan were among the slain. The heart of Robert Bruce and the bones of the Good Sir James were brought back to Scotland by Sir William Keith of Galston, the former to be buried at Melrose Abbey,[44] the latter in the parish kirk of Douglas, where in after years Sir James' natural son, Archibald the Grim, erected a noble alabaster tomb.

In accordance with the terms of the tailzie of 1326, Thomas Randolph earl of Moray assumed the office of Guardian of Scotland. As lord of Badenoch the earl was patron of the kirk of Saint Drostan of Alvie, whose large mountainous parish stretches north and south from Loch Alvie, half a mile north of the River Spey. On October 18th, 1331 Earl Thomas, acting in collaboration with John of Pilmuir bishop of Moray, granted to the perpetual chaplains serving the chapelries founded in Elgin cathedral by the earl and others the patronage of this small highland kirk. The surplus income from this kirk, together with the revenues of the bishop's kirks of Altyre and Birnie, was assigned by Bishop Pilmuir to the chaplains to augment their stipends, on condition that each chaplain should celebrate a requiem mass once a week for the health during his life and soul's weal after death of Earl Thomas, and 'for the soul of the most noble prince, the lord Robert, of good memory, king of Scotland'. Daily throughout the year they were to make a special commemoration for the soul of King Robert (and likewise for those of Earl Thomas and the bishop and his parents) in their prayers and masses. The whole arrangement was set forth in and confirmed by letters of grace issued at Avignon by Pope Clement VI on June 12th in the jubilee year of 1350.[45]

Appendix

Scottish landowners forfeited by Edward I in 1306 for supporting Robert Bruce,
with the names of those who petitioned to have their lands

This list is based on the roll printed in Palgrave, *Docs. Hist. Scot.*, 301–18; cf.
ibid., 319. It will be noticed that a good many names of forfeited landowners
occur more than once; either because they held lands in more than one
sheriffdom or because their lands were sought by more than one petitioner. It
has been thought best to keep the entries in the order in which they appear on
the roll. This is not a complete list of those known to have been Bruce's
supporters in 1306. (S) after a petitioner's name indicates a Scotsman.

Forfeited landowner	Lands	Petitioner
HAY, Gilbert de la	(Errol?)	Hugh Despenser
CARRICK, earl of (Robert Bruce)	Annandale	earl of Hereford
ATHOLL, earl of	Atholl	earl of Gloucester
SETON, Christopher	in Annandale	Robert Felton
CLOSEBURN, Stephen of	(Closeburn?)	John Cromwell
LOGAN, Walter	(Hartside, Upper Clydesdale?)	John Cromwell
CAMERON of BALEDGARNO, John	Baledgarno	Hugh, son of earl of Ross (S)[1]
FRASER, Richard	Touch Fraser	John de Luk
FRASER, Alexander	Cornton	John de Luk
FRASER, Thomas (brother of Simon Fraser)	?	Thomas Grey
BICKERTON, Walter	Kincraig, Fife	Thomas Grey
FRASER, Alexander, son of Andrew Fraser	?	Thomas Grey
Tenants of Henry Pinkney	in Luffness and Ballencrieff	Henry Pinkney
RANDOLPH, Thomas	Stichill	Robert Hastang
SOMERVILLE, John	?	Robert Hastang
SOMERVILLE, Thomas	Linton, Roxburgh Carnwath, Lanarkshire	Robert Hastang
LOGAN, Walter	?	William Mulcaster, John Bisset
FRASER, Richard	?	Alexander Balliol (?S)
MENZIES, Alexander	?	Alexander Balliol (?S)
CRAWFORD, Reginald	in Ayrshire	Robert Haustede[2]
LENNOX, earl of	Lennox	John Menteith (S) Aymer de Valence[3]

STRATHEARN, earl of	Strathearn	Aymer de Valence[4]
SOMERVILLE, John	Clifton, Roxburgh	John Weston
WEMYSS, Michael	in Midlothian	John Weston
SOMERVILLE, William	in Midlothian	John Weston
FRASER, Alexander	in Midlothian	John Weston
LINDSAY, Alexander	in Midlothian	John Weston
RANDOLPH, Thomas	Garlies in Minnigaff Kirkcudbright Morton in Nithsdale, Dumfriesshire	Thomas Paynel
SOMERVILLE, John	Hedgeley, Northumberland	Robert Hastang
LOCKHART, Simon	Lochwood, Ayr The Lee, Lanarkshire	Robert Hastang
LOVEL, Hugh	(Hawick?)	Robert Bures
FENTON, William	?	Duncan of Frendraught (S)
ROSSIE, Walter of	in Angus	John Lutton[5]
DEMPSTER, Andrew the	in Angus	John Lutton
ATHOLL, earl of	Stratha'an, Banffshire Strathbogie, Aberdeen	Alexander Abernethy (S)
MURRAY, William	St Fort, Fife	Alexander Abernethy (S)
MURRAY, Alan (cousin of preceding)	(Culbin, Moray?)	Alexander Abernethy (S)
CARRICK, earl of	Lands north of Forth[6]	Alexander Abernethy (S)
BALCASKIE, Thomas of	Balcaskie, Fife	Alexander Harcaz
BOYS, Thomas de	?	John Autry
VALOGNES, Adam de	(in Angus?)	John Autry
SIWARD, John	in Mearns	Richard of Denmuir (Fife) (S)
(ARBUTHNOT ?), Duncan of	(in Mearns?)	Richard of Denmuir (Fife) (S)
NEWTIBBER, Richard of	in Angus	John (son of Richard) Comyn (S)
BEN, Robert	?	John Comyn (S)[7]
CAMERON of BALNELY, John	in Perthshire	Simon Warde
CUNNINGHAM, Robert of	in Perthshire	Edmund de Beyville
RIEL, Henry of	(Northumberland ?)	John Wigton
COMLONGON, laird of	in Dumfriesshire	John Wigton
ASKELOC, Roland	in Kirkcudbrightshire[8]	John Wigton
KIRKCONNEL, Thomas of	in Dumfriesshire	Henry Malton
KIRKCONNEL, Robert of	in Dumfriesshire	Henry Malton
BOYS, Walter de	(in Dumfriesshire?)	Adam Swinburne
CORRY, Nicholas	(in Dumfriesshire?)	Adam Swinburne
CALDECOTE, Robert son of Geoffrey		Adam Swinburne
COCKBURN, Peter	in Peeblesshire	Michael Witton
SOMERVILLE, Thomas and his son (nephew of Simon Fraser)	(in Roxburgh and Lanark?)	Walter de Moncy
CARRICK, Gilbert (i.e. Kennedy) son of Roland of	in Ayrshire	Gilbert Elsfield

RANDOLPH, Thomas	?	Maurice le Brun
MACCULIAN, Malcolm	in 'the isle of Kintyre'	John Ferrers
FRASER, Richard	Arkelton, Dumfries	John of Bristol
GRAHAM, Patrick	(in Lothian or West Highlands?)	Lachlan Macruarie of the Isles (S)
DALLAS, Thomas of	Dallas, Moray	Alexander Seton (S)
WISTON, Walter of	in Lanarkshire	Henry Prendergest (S)[9]
MURRAY, Austin	in Lanarkshire	Henry Prendergest (S)
NESBIT, Robert	in Lanarkshire	Henry Prendergest (S)
INCHTURE, Robert of	in Perthshire	Henry Prendergest (S)
SLEGH, Andrew, of Aberdeen	in Aberdeen	William le Jettour
BISHOP, Andrew, burgess	in Aberdeen	William le Jettour
CHAPEU, Adam, burgess	in Aberdeen	William le Jettour
RATTRAY, Eustace of	in Perthshire	John Thirlwall
CAMPBELL, Neil	(in Argyll or Ayrshire)	John Dovedale
ALYTH of the BRAE, Walter	in Perthshire	Adam Brunyng (S)
COKYN, John	?	Adam Brunyng (S)
INNERPEFFRAY, Malcolm of	in Perthshire	Adam Brunyng (S)
FOLKARD, Alexander	in Lanarkshire	Walter Gylling
ANELF, Duncan, son of (Macaulay)	in Lennox	Walter Gylling
LUSS, John of	in Lennox	Walter Gylling
DUNDEE, Master Ralph of	(in Angus or Argyll?)	John Hayward
WISHART, John	Conveth in Mearns	John Hayward
ANGUS, Laurence of	(in Angus?)	John Hayward
HAY, Gilbert de la	Errol	John de la Mare
MURRAY, William, of St Fort	Kinermony, Banff-shire	John de la Mare
BLAIR, Brice	in Ayrshire	William of Cambo
LOVEL, Hugh	Enoch and Drumcruilton in Nithsdale[10]	John Daniel
ST MICHAEL, John of	in Roxburghshire	John Alegate
MELVILLE, William	in Roxburghshire	John Alegate
FORBES, John	?	Robert Chival
MURRAY of DRUMSERGARD, John	in Lanarkshire	Robert Chival
CAMPBELL, Donald	(in Argyll or Ayrshire?)	Stephen Deepham
INCHTURE, Robert of	in Perthshire	William de Stroir
STOIL, Roger	?	William de Stroir
FRASER, Thomas	?	Robert de Repples
AUCHTERGAVEN, Donald of	in Perthshire	Richard Wollaston
DALLAS, Thomas of	(Dallas), Moray	Aliain (?)
CREMANNAN, Thomas of	in Lennox	Nicol de Boys
LENY, John of	in Menteith	Robert de Sapy
MACKESSAN, Coweyn (Ewen?)	(Probably Garchell in Drymen, Stirling-shire)	Alexander the queen's chandler

RANDOLPH, Thomas	Morton in Nithsdale	William son of William Latimer
HAY, Gilbert de la	Errol	William son of William Latimer
(FRASER)	'Ughtrothere-strother' (Struthers in Ceres, Fife)	Thomas Grey
HAY, John de la	in Inverness-shire	Oliver Avenel
KEITH, Bernard	in Ayrshire	Thomas and Herbert de Borehonte
LINDSAY, Alexander	Barnweill, Ayr	Roger de Borehonte
SOULES, John de	Old Roxburgh	Richard Lovel
(CREMANNAN ?), Thomas of	(in Lennox?)	Geoffrey Segrave
CUNNINGHAM, Robert of	in Ayrshire	Geoffrey Segrave
KNOCKDOLIAN, John of	in Ayrshire	Geoffrey Segrave
MONTGOMERY, John of	(Ayrshire or Renfrew?)	Geoffrey Segrave
GRADEN, Peter of	in Berwickshire	Randolf de Charron
STRATHBOGIE, Laurence of	in Caithness and Sutherland	Cristyn of the Aird (S)
PILCHE, Alexander, burgess	in Inverness	Cristyn of the Aird (S)
LINDSAY, James, son and heir of Walter	Thurston, E. Lothian	Thomas Convers
FRASER, Alexander	Drip, Stirling	William Montfichet (S?)
DURWARD, Alan	Fichlie, Aberdeenshire	William Montfichet (S?)
FORBES, John	(in Aberdeenshire?)	William Comyn (S)
DALLAS, Thomas of	in Moray	earl of Sutherland (S)
DURWARD, Alan	?	David of Brechin (S)[11]
TROUP, Hamelin of	in Banffshire	William de Hustweit
BARCLAY, Walter, of Kercock	in Perthshire	Gilbert Peche
MONYKEBBUCK, Walter (Barclay?) of[12]	in Aberdeenshire	Gilbert Peche
WAUCHOPE, Robert	in Fife	Richard de Lisle
FENTON, John, son of William	in Midlothian	Geoffrey of Ledes
DURWARD, Alan	Fichlie	Thomas de la Greve
MONYMUSK, Thomas of	Forglen, Banff	Thomas de la Greve
CARRICK, Maud of	in Cumberland	Henry Touke
BOTHWELL, Eustace of	in Cumberland	Henry Touke
MENZIES, William, son of Alexander	Shielswood and Harden, Selkirk and Roxburgh	John de Lisle
LOGAN, Walter	?	John de Lisle
FRASER, Alexander	?	John de Lisle
HATTELE, Alexander of	?	John de Lisle
NESBIT, Robert	?	John de Lisle
MURRAY, Austin	Wiston, Lanark	John de Lisle
MOWAT, William	Kinnettles, Angus	John de la Mare
MOLBRIDE the young	Strat (Strath Eachaig?)	Gillespie MacLachlan (S)
[BOYD, Robert	Coronerships of Ayr and Lanark	Dungal Macdouall (S)][13]

Notes to Chapters

CHAPTER ONE
A Kingdom in Perplexity

1. *Chron. Fordun*, i, 294-5.
2. *Cal. Docs. Scot*, ii, no.131. Master Elias was a tenant of the earl of Fife, *ibid.*, 224. For the Scots' reputation as harpists, see Gerald of Wales, *The history and topography of Ireland*, translated by J. J. O'Meara (Penguin Books, 1982), 104: 'in the opinion, however, of many, Scotland has by now not only caught up on Ireland, her instructor, but already far outdistances and excels her in musical skill. Therefore people now look to that country as to the fountain of the art.'
3. *Cal. Docs. Scot.*, iv, 475.
4. *Miscellanea of the Surtees Society*, ii (1916), 57-8.
5. *Chron. Lanercost*, 116.
6. G. W. S. Barrow, *The Anglo-Norman Era in Scottish History* (1980), 30-50, 201-3.
7. For these officers see Barrow, *Kingdom*, 83-138.
8. See Barrow, *Kingship*, 84-104.
9. *Chron. Lanercost*, 104-5.
10. Matthew Paris, *Chronica Majora* (ed. Luard, Rolls Series), v, 93.
11. *Cal. Docs. Scot.*, ii, 264.
12. *Chron. Guisb.*, 275.
13. Stevenson, *Documents*, ii, 96, 154; *Melrose Liber*, ii, no.372; *Foedera*, i, 772a; *SHR*, xxvii, 153.
14. James W. Dilley, 'German merchants in Scotland, 1297-1327', *SHR*, xxvii, 153-4; Stevenson, *Documents*, ii, 154, holdings of Alexander of Cologne in the Seagait. Professor Dilley's article is a most useful survey of the evidence of German trading activity in Scotland.
15. PRO, E.159/71, rot.30, dorse (K. R. Memoranda Roll).
16. Stevenson, *Wallace Docs.*, 159.

17. Matthew Paris, *Chronica Majora*, iv, 378.
18. P. E. Schramm, *A history of the English Coronation* (transl. L. G. Wickham Legg, 1937), 130; cf. M. Bloch, *SHR*, xxiii, 105-6; Stones, *Relations*, no.5.
19. A. I. Dunlop, 'Bagimond's Roll', *Miscellany* of SHS, vi, 6-7; W. E. Lunt, *Financial relations of the papacy with England to 1327*, 292, 296, 334, 338.
20. *Dunfermline Registrum*, no.321; Stones, *Relations*, no.12(b) and p.76.
21. *Dunfermline Registrum*, nos. 320, 324; *APS*, i, 112-13.
22. *Dunfermline Registrum*, no.87.
23. *Foedera*, i, 11, 565. *Chron. Bower*, ii, 124 reports a conference to discuss the Border, held at Berwick and attended by the bishops of Durham and Norwich as well as those of St Andrews, Glasgow and Dunblane. This is dated mid-Lent, i.e. 12 March 1279. Stones, *Relations* no.12(a). See also *Cal. Docs. Scot.*, v, nos. 39-41.
24. Barrow, *Kingdom*, 218-20.
25. Theiner, *Monumenta*, no.100; *Cal. Papal Letters*, i, 220.
26. *Cal. Docs. Scot.*, ii, nos. 209, 239, 241, 267; *Scots Peerage*, iii, 5.
27. *Ibid.*, 5-6. The English land was chiefly in Westmorland, part of the Honour of Kendal.
28. *APS*, i, 424.
29. *Ibid.*, 441.
30. Matthew Paris, *Chronica Majora*, v, 505.
31. *Chron. Lanercost*, 117-18.
32. *Chron. Bower*, ii, 138, 'a fortnight after Easter'.
33. Palgrave, *Docs. Hist. Scot.*, 42. *Chron. Lanercost*, 117, calls the Guardians *pacis custodes*.
34. *Chron. Fordun*, 310; *Chron. Bower*, ii, 136, 138.

35. The scheme had been foreshadowed by the arrangements to safeguard Queen Margaret's first-born child in 1261: *Cal. Docs. Scot.*, i, no.2229; D. E. R. Watt, 'The Minority of Alexander III of Scotland,' *TRHS*, 5th Ser., xxi, 21.

36. Lord of Dalmeny, and a supporter of Balliol, who had appointed him justiciar of Lothian by 22 September, 1294: *Kelso Liber*, no.192.

37. *Chron. Bower*, ii, 138. Virtual proof that such a mission reached Edward I in Gascony is found in his letter dated Saintes, September 15th, 1286, staying proceedings on the Border at the Guardians' request, Stevenson, *Documents*, i, no.11. In Bower's text, *Sanctum Johannem Evangelistam* is perhaps a copyist's error for *Sanctum Johannem Angeliacensem*, i.e. S. Jean d'Angély. King Edward was at S. Jean d'Angély on September 11th, 1286, and at Saintes from September 13th to 16th; J. Trabut-Cussac, in *BIHR*, xxv, 168-9. Moreover, we know that Bishop Fraser and Alexander Comyn earl of Buchan, were at Stirling on November 27th, 1286; *Arbroath Liber*, i, no.293.

This mission must be distinguished from a lesser mission consisting of two Dominicans sent by Bishops Fraser and Wishart at the time of Alexander III's funeral (March 29th, 1286: Stevenson, *Documents*, i, no.3), presumably to give Edward the news of Alexander's death, and ask for his good pleasure. *Chron. Lanercost*, 125, seems to refer to a later mission (1289?) when it speaks of the Scots asking Edward I to assist them in their leaderless state.

38. For the style *de communi consilio constituti*, see Stevenson, *Documents*, i, *passim* between no.14 and no.123; for the less common *per communitatem ejusdem regni electi*, *ibid*.,nos. 15, 27 and cf. no.89.

39. W. de G. Birch, *History of Scottish Seals* (1905), i, 31-3 and illustrations nos. 14 and 15.

40. SIGILLVM SCOCIE DEPVTATVM REGIMINI REGNI ; ANDREA SCOTIS DVX ESTO COMPATRIOTIS.

41. Stevenson, *Documents*, i, no.108.

42. *Melrose Liber*, no.396.

43. *Inchaffray Chrs.*, no.117.

44. *Formulary E: Scottish Letters and Brieves, 1286-1424*, ed. A. A. M. Duncan

(University of Glasgow, Scottish History Department Occasional Papers, 1976), no.89, referring significantly to army service due to the 'royal dignity' after the death of the king.

45. Palgrave, *Doc. Hist. Scot.*, 42 ('Bot . . .' and 'Wygge . . .' stand for Buittle and Wigtown). Cf. *Exch. Rolls*, i, 35, 39.

46. Stevenson, *Documents*, i, no.12. E. M. Barron, *Scottish War of Independence* (2nd edn), 112, states as a fact, and W. C. Dickinson, *Scotland from the earliest times to 1603* (1961), 144, implies that the Turnberry Band upheld Bruce's claim to the throne. Incidentally, the band does not say 'in accordance with hereditary rights' (Dickinson, *loc. cit.*) but *ratione sanguinis . . . Alexandri regis*, something rather different, which points to the Maid of Norway or a possible child born to Yolande.

47. F. M. Powicke, *The Thirteenth Century*, 598n., suggests, surely rightly, that 'some Irish enterprise was the occasion of the pact' at Turnberry. Thomas de Clare was the brother of Earl Gilbert of Gloucester and thus the nephew by marriage of Bruce the Competitor. Thomas (whose Irish interests lay in Thomond or North Munster, far from Ulster) and the new earl of Ulster, Richard de Burgh, were busy with military expeditions against the Irish of Connacht in 1285 and 1286 respectively (G. H. Orpen, *Ireland under the Normans*, iv, 73-5, 112; G. W. S. Barrow, 'Robert Bruce and Ayrshire', *Ayrshire Collections*, xiii, 2 (1980), 82-4).

CHAPTER TWO
Bruce of Annandale

1. R. C. Reid, 'The caput of Annandale', *Dumfriesshire Trans.*, 3rd ser., xxxii, 155-66, esp. 159ff.

2. R. L. G. Ritchie, *Chrétien de Troyes and Scotland* (Zaharoff Lecture, 1952), 17-24.

3. Barrow, *Kingdom*, 281, 322-6, 339-51.

4. Charters showing that the office of steward of Annandale was held at various times by members of different tenant families are in *Cal. Docs. Scot.*, i, nos. 197, 706, 1683, 1685. For the Annandale gentry's behaviour as landlords, cf. *Chron. Lanercost*, 99-100.

5. K. J. Stringer analyses Anglo-Scottish proprietorship in *Earl David of*

Huntingdon: a study in Anglo-Scottish history (1985), 177-211.

6. See Genealogical Table I and *Yorkshire Archaeological J.*, xiii, 226-61.

7. *Chron. Bower*, ii, 114, gives Bruce's cognomen as *Nobilis*; *Scots Peerage*, ii, 430, wrongly attributes it to his father. For Earl David's Scottish estates see Stringer, *Earl David*, 56-79. For the events of 1237 see *Complete Peerage*, iii, 169, vi, 647; *Cal. Docs. Scot.*, i, nos. 1369, 1384.

8. *Ibid.*, no. 1870. Much of the estate must have come to him in 1245 on his father's death, but Writtle and Hatfield Broadoak in Essex would not have passed to him until after his mother's death in 1252, *Complete Peerage*, ii, 358.

9. Palgrave, *Docs. Hist. Scot.*, 29.

10. *Northumberland County History*, vi, 49.

11. *Complete Peerage*, ii, 359; *Cal. Docs. Scot.*, i, no.1498.

12. *Ibid.*, nos. 1994, 2472; apparently not always a conscientious governor, *ibid.*, no. 2034.

13. C. A. F. Meekings, in *Notes and Queries*, clxii (1932), 278, 436.

14. R. F. Treharne, *The Baronial Plan of Reform*, 140, 323, 335; *Flores Historiarum*, ii, 400.

15. *Cal. Docs. Scot.*, i, no.2358; *Chron. Stephen etc.*, ii, 544.

16. *Cal. Docs., Scot.*, i, no.2575. See Alan MacQuarrie, *Scotland and the Crusades, 1095-1560* (1985), 57-62.

17. *Chron. Melrose*, 145-6.

18. *Chron. Lanercost*, 161; R. C. Reid, *Dumfriesshire Trans.*, 3rd Ser., xxxii, 155-66.

19. *Chron. Lanercost*, 160; cf. J. Wilson, *SHR*, xviii, 69-82, esp. pp.78-80.

20. R. C. Reid, *Dumfriesshire Trans.*, 3rd Ser., xxxii, 157.

21. *Ibid.*, 163-6.

22. Migne, *Patrologia Latina*, clxxxii, 1095-6.

23. *Ibid.*, clxxv, 1759-60, 'Esticroft', unidentified (correct reading from original in Archives départementales de l'Aube, Troyes, of which a photograph was kindly supplied by Dr A. MacQuarrie).

24. G. O. Sayles, *Select Cases in King's Bench*, iii, 91-2; cf. *SHR*, xxv, 388ff. The Competitor's son attempted unsuccessfully to withhold his step-mother's dower on the grounds that her marriage to his father was unlawful.

25. There is strong though inconclusive evidence that Adam, lord of Kilconquhar, was son of Duncan of Kilconquhar, son of Adam son of Earl Duncan I of Fife (died 1154). Cf. D. W. Hunter Marshall, 'The parentage of Thomas Randolph, earl of Moray', *Scottish Notes and Queries*, 3rd Ser., viii (1930), 2-5; and for the personnel of the supposed Kilconquhar pedigree, see *St Andrews Liber*, references in index under Adam filius and frater comitis, Adam filius Duncani, Duncanus filius Ade (de Kilcunkath), Kilkuncwauch (Dunecanus de); *North Berwick Carte*, nos. 3, 6; *Dunfermline Registrum*, nos. 145, 179, 196. The feudal superiority of Kilconquhar vested in the bishop of St Andrews, but the fief was held of the bishop by the earls of Fife. *Chron. Bower*, ii, 152, in mentioning the Macduff appeal, gives Kilconquhar as the estate in question, this being an alternative name for Rires. The link between Earl Adam and Thomas Randolph earl of Moray in the lordship of Scoonie is shown by charters of the two earls: *The Study of Medieval Records*, ed. D. A. Bullough and R. L. Storey (1971), 131 (Balgrummo); *Dunfermline Registrum*, no.357; *RMS*, i, App. II, no.104 (Mountflourie)

26. Roger Howden calls Uhtred son of Fergus of Galloway a cousin of King Henry II (*Gesta Henrici Secundi Benedicti Abbatis*, ed. Stubbs, Rolls Ser., i, 80), a relationship which is best explained on the supposition that Fergus married a bastard daughter of Henry I. The suggestion in *Scots Peerage*, s.v. 'Galloway', that Gilbert, Uhtred's brother, had a different mother is contradicted by *Cal. Docs. Scot.*, i, no.480, where King John calls Duncan of Carrick his cousin.

27. R. Greeves, 'The Galloway lands in Ulster', *Dumfriesshire Trans.*, 3rd Ser., xxxvi, 115-21, esp. 116; Robin Frame, 'The Bruces in Ireland, 1315-18', *Irish Historical Studies*, xix, 16-17.

28. PROI, Press Copies of Certified Copies, I, f. 121. Dr Kenneth Nicholls of University College, Cork, kindly provided this information.

29. *Dumfriesshire Trans.*, 3rd Ser., xxxvi, 117-20.

30. The cautious words in Dunbar, *Scot. Kings.*, 127, 'born – it has been supposed at Writtle, near Chelmsford in Essex, become a categorical statement in *Scots Peerage*, i, 7. They are based on a passage in the chronicle of Geoffrey le Baker of Swinbrook (ed. E. M. Thompson, 1889, p.38), which says that Alexander (III) had three daughters but no son, that the first daughter married John Balliol, the second John Comyn and the third Robert Bruce 'English by birth, born in Essex (at Writtle)' who later became king. It is hard to know what to make of a statement so full of error and confusion, but there may have been a sound tradition that Bruce's father was born at Writtle. *Chron. Guisb.*, 296, reports that Robert Bruce the future king referred to Scotland and (probably) Carrick as his native country; and the Harcla Treaty of 1323 refers to England (under Edward II, born in Wales but clearly not Welsh by nation) and Scotland (under Robert Bruce) each having a king of its own nation. In 1310 Bruce was absolved for his part in Comyn's murder as 'layman of Carrick in the diocese of Glasgow' (*SHR*, xix, 325). The erroneous story of Alexander III's daughters is found in French narratives of this period: *Chronographia Regum Francorum*, ed. H. Moranvillé (Paris, 1891-3), i, 75; *Chronique de Richard Lescot*, ed. J. Lemoine (Paris, 1896), 32.

31. M. McKisack, *The Fourteenth Century*, 42. Edward Bruce was educated with an Irish potentate, probably Domhnall Ua Neill king of Tyrone (1283-1325), Stevenson, *Illustrations*, 3.

32. *Paisley Registrum*, 128-9.

33. *Chron. Bower*, ii, 148 (under 1288, wrongly). *Chron. Lanercost*, 127, explains his murder by calling the earl 'cruel and greedy beyond the average'. Earl Duncan's latest appearance in record is in a brieve of August, 1289. (Stevenson, *Documents*, i, no.69), and the murder probably took place on September 3rd or 10th of that year. See G. W. S. Barrow (ed.), *The Scottish Tradition* (1974), 37-8. Earl Duncan was buried at Coupar Angus abbey: *Cal. Docs. Scot.*, iv, 375.

34. *Ibid.*, ii, no.366; *Scots Peerage*, ii, 254-5.

35. *Chron. Bower*, ii, 138, 148. They were not co-opted officially as Guardians, and Bower's statement about Murray may have been only an inference from Sir Andrew's part in bringing the earl's murderers to justice. But this is sufficiently explained on the supposition that Sir Andrew had succeeded the earl of Buchan (not Fife) as justiciar of Scotia (Scotland north of Forth), an office he certainly held *c.* 1293 (*Family of Rose*, 29). We know, in any case, that a permanent council of magnates was associated with the Guardians: *Aberdeen-Banff Illustrations*, ii, 129-30.

36. A short account of the negotiations is in F. M. Powicke, *The Thirteenth Century*, 598-9 but for detailed discussion of the entire period from 1286 to 1290 the best guide is Norman Reid, 'Margaret Maid of Norway and Scottish Queenship', *Reading Medieval Studies*, viii (1982), 75-96. Bishop Fraser attempted to visit Edward I in Gascony, but it is uncertain whether he ever reached the king. The treaty providing for the transference of Margaret from Norway to Scotland 'free of any marriage contract' was sealed at Salisbury on November 6th, 1289, the Scottish plenipotentiaries being the bishops of St Andrews and Glasgow, Robert Bruce of Annandale and John Comyn of Badenoch, Stevenson, *Documents*, i, no.75.

37. *Ibid.*, no.108.

38. *Ibid.*, no.106.

39. As in the letter of March 17th, 1290, *APS*, i, 441. Cf. also the Treaty of Salisbury of the previous November (Stevenson, *Documents*, i, no.75), whereby the good men (*bona gens, la bone gent*) of Scotland promised not to arrange any marriage for the queen without the advice and consent of Edward I and the consent of King Eric of Norway.

40. *Bona gens = la bone gent* in the Treaty of Salisbury (see previous note) and, in the accompanying letter of Edward I of November 6th (*Foedera*, i, 721), the words *probi homines* appear as equivalent. In a letter of King John, January 2nd, 1293, *probis hominibus* translates *as proudes hommes* once and *a la bone gent* once, *Foedera*, i, 785 (Original edn, ii, 597b, 598a, 599a). In a charter of Robert I translated into French the formal address *omnibus probis hominibus totius terre sue* becomes *a toutz les bones gentz de toute sa*

terre (*RRS*, v, no.148). In Edward I's parliament of Michaelmas, 1293, King John dared not act without consulting his *probi homines* (Stones, *Relations* no.21); in 1305 King Edward declared his intention of settling the government of Scotland *a les bones gentz de la terre d'Escoce* (*ibid.*, no.33).

41. *APS*, i, 441. The contemporary letters-patent issued at Birgham three days earlier (Stevenson, *Documents*, i, no.92) went in the names of the four Guardians, ten bishops, ten earls, twenty-three abbots, eleven priors and forty-eight barons. Perhaps the earls of Lennox and Ross arrived too late for the Birgham parliament.

42. Stevenson, *Documents*, i, no.108.

43. *Ibid.*, i, no.172. The provision suggests strongly that the 'community of the realm' stood in effect for the feudal kingdom, a political entity whose properly constituted authority could arrange for the receipt and safe-custody of the treaty. And this meaning of the phrase is equally suggested by the earl of Angus's statement that the castles of Dundee and Forfar had been entrusted to him by the community of the realm of Scotland: Stones and Simpson, *Great Cause*, ii, 101, no.2.

44. Dr Norman Reid shows that the terms insisted on by the Scots at Greenwich in 1543, when it was planned that the child Queen Mary should marry the English Prince Edward, followed the terms of Birgham very closely: *Reading Medieval Studies*, viii, 84-5, 88-9.

45. Stevenson, *Documents* i, no.103.

46. *Chron. Man.*, i, 110; *Chron. Stephen etc.*, ii, 570-1 (which shows that Alexander III was supported by Alexander Macdougall of Lorn and Alan Macruarie lord of Garmoran).

47. *Foedera*, i, 739. Even this declaration seems as much concerned with the possibility of Manx disaffection from Edward I as with the desirability of having the English king's protection.

48. *Ibid.*, i, 737 (date corrected in *Cal. Docs. Scot.*, ii, no.446).

49. *Cal. Docs. Scot.*, ii, no.459; Dunbar, *Scot. Kings*, 106. Margaret seems to have died about September 26th; she died in the arms of Narfi bishop of Bergen and was buried in Bergen Cathedral in the north aisle of the choir; Anderson, *Early Sources*, ii, 695.

50. *Nat. MSS. Scot.*, i, no.70.

51. Stevenson, *Documents*, i, no.125; above, n.48. Bek's lieutenancy should have lapsed with the queen's death but it is not certain that Bek was scrupulous enough to observe that nicety.

52. *Nat. MSS. Scot.*, i, no.70.

53. The oath of April 1286, to keep the peace of the realm, Palgrave, *Docs. Hist. Scot.*, 42.

54. Stones and Simpson, *Great Cause* i, 101.

55. *Ibid.*, ii, 4.

56. *Ibid.*, ii, 5.

57. *Ibid.*, i, 103-4.

58. See *Fritz Saxl, 1890-1948: Memorial essays*, ed. D. J. Gordon (1957), 125. It would be extraordinary if a fifteenth-century forger had fixed by chance on such a unique event as a joint Anglo-Scottish parliament and dated it correctly.

59. Stones and Simpson, *Great Cause*, i, 109; see also *Cal. Docs. Scot.*, ii, no.474. Norham was no doubt chosen as being one of the traditional places for Anglo-Scottish conferences. Some meetings were held at Norham, some at Upsettlington on the Scots side of the Tweed, immediately opposite. King Edward gave an undertaking that the award of the Crown would be made within the kingdom of Scotland, *Foedera*, i, 756.

60. Stevenson, *Documents*, i, no.137 [May 10th]; repeated on May 31st, *Foedera*, i, 755. Where the Latin text of May 10 speaks of 'bishops, nobles and magnates coming as far as Norham', the French text of May 31st has *les haus hommes et une partie de la communaute de mesme le reaume* coming 'this side of the River Tweed'. From here to p.68 references to primary documentary sources are, wherever practicable, to the texts edited in Stones and Simpson, *Great Cause*.

61. *Ibid.*, ii, 14-19.

62. *Ibid.*, ii, 16-20; i, 175-6.

63. E. L. G. Stones, *SHR*, xxxv, 89-109, the reply itself being printed on pp.108-9. The reply is summarized in *Chron. Rishanger*, 124-5, where it is said to have been *followed* by Edward's guarantee with regard to crossing the Tweed, dated May 31st. See also Stones, *Documents*, no.16;

Stones and Simpson, *Great Cause*, ii, 30-31.

64. The oath of April 1286, to keep the peace and guard the realm on Queen Margaret's behalf, Palgrave, *Docs. Hist. Scot.*, 42.

65. Stones and Simpson, *Great Cause*, ii, 31, referring to the Treaty of Birgham, ratified at Northampton.

66. *Ibid.*, ii, 36.

67. 'Nothing at all proposed, exhibited or shown by the bishops, prelates, earls, barons, magnates and nobles', *ibid.*, *loc. cit.*

68. *Ibid.*: *nihil tamen efficax.*

69. E. L. G. Stones, *SHR*, xxxv, 107.

70. *Chron. Rishanger*, 124-5.

71. J. H. Burton, *History of Scotland* (2nd ed, 1873), ii, 120.

72. *SHR*, xxxv, 89-109.

73. *Cal. Docs. Scot.*, ii, nos. 482, 483, 488, 489.

74. Stones and Simpson, *Great Cause*, ii, 74 n.1. express surprise that other historians have believed that the competitors themselves granted possession to Edward I although they did not have it to grant; but King Edward was under the same misapprehension, for he twice declared that the competitors had done just that: *ibid.*, 88, line 10 of text, 98, line 10 of text.

75. *Ibid.*, 88, 98-9 (6th and 12th June). See below, pp.58-9.

76. *Chron. Bower*, ii, 146.

77. P. Linehan, 'A fourteenth-Century History of Anglo-Scottish relations in a Spanish Manuscript', *BIHR*, xlviii, 106-22. See especially p.120.

78. Stones and Simpson, *Great Cause*, ii, 111.

79. *Ibid.*, 97.

80. *Cal. Docs. Scot.*, ii, nos. 496, 499; Stones and Simpson, *Great Cause*, ii, 90-92.

81. Stevenson, *Documents*, i, nos. 156, 219.

82. *Ibid.*, no.208, shows that the common seal was not available on February 28th, 1292.

83. *Chron. Rishanger*, 363.

84. Stones and Simpson, *Great Cause*, ii, 105.

85. *Ibid.*, 100-101.

86. *Ibid.*, 91, 100.

87. *Ibid.*, i, 120-2.

88. *Ibid.*, ii, 105; cf. pp.112-13.

89. *Ibid.*, 97.

90. *Ibid.*, 88.

91. *Ibid.*, 98-9.

92. *Ibid.*, 24.

93. *Ibid.*, 97.

94. *Ibid.*, 99.

95. Compare 'nullam literam jus commune vel gratiam continentem' in the Latin text of Birgham (Stevenson, *Documents*, i, 169) with 'litteris gracie' in the oath taken by the new chancellor of Scotland in 1291, Stones and Simpson, *Great Cause*, ii, 96.

96. See p.49.

97. *Instrumenta Publica*, 7-9; Stones and Simpson, *Great Cause*, ii, 104.

98. *Instrumenta Publica*, 10-21; *Cal. Docs. Scot.*, ii, no.508; Stones and Simpson, *Great Cause*, ii, 366-70. No.67 is better read as Arderye, i.e. Airdrie in Crailshire, and no.69 is Simon 'of Farsley', a tenant in chief for land near Crail. The names of the two laymen Guardians, Comyn of Badenoch and James Stewart, are unaccountably omitted from this list.

CHAPTER THREE
Bruce versus *Balliol*

1. Palgrave, *Docs. Hist. Scot.*, Illustrations, no.11, 5 June, 1291.

2. G. Neilson, *SHR*, xvi, 1-14; for a contrary view see Stones and Simpson, *Great Cause*, ii, 371-2. They seem to underestimate the degree of coincidence involved in devising a court of 105 entirely without reference to the Roman precedent.

3. See Genealogical Table 1. For Count Florence, the authoritative account is given by G. G. Simpson, 'The claim of Florence, count of Holland, to the Scottish throne, 1291-2', *SHR*, xxxvi, 111-24. There is a useful comment on this by Mme J. Kossmann-Putto, *Revue du Nord*, xl, 541-2.

4. *SHR*, xxxvi, 114.

5. *Chron. Melrose*, 36.

6. Margaret after her father's paternal grandmother. Ada after her mother, or more probably, after her mother's

maternal grandmother. *Ibid.*, 36, calls Ada *alia soror*, implying juniority.

7. *Complete Peerage*, iv, Appendix H, Chart I (669).

8. *Chronica Mag. Rogeri de Houedene* (ed. Stubbs), iii, 298-9.

9. *Chron. Rishanger*, 309-39, esp. 315-6, 'though the land of Scotland be called a 'kingdom', the land itself is only a lordship, like Wales, the earldom of Chester or the bishopric of Durham'; and cf. 329-30.

10. Lists of the auditors are printed in (1) Palgrave, *Docs. Hist. Scot.*, Illustrations, no.11, sections 3 and 4; (2) *Chron. Rishanger*, 262-5. The best edition, however, is Stones and Simpson, *Great Cause*, ii, 80-5, who print all known versions.

11. A brief but instructive analysis of Balliol's auditors, showing close relationship with the Comyns, is given by N. H. Reid, 'The Political Role of the Monarchy in Scotland, 1249-1329' (unpublished PhD thesis, Edinburgh University, 1984), 464-7.

12. The best review of the conflicting claims from a legal standpoint is by Barnaby C. Keeney, 'The medieval idea of the state: the Great Cause, 1291-2', *University of Toronto Law Journal*, viii, 48-71. My account owes much to this lucid and masterly article. For the pleadings themselves see Stones and Simpson, *Great Cause*, ii, *passim* (including Appendix B). Readers may still find it useful to be referred also to Palgrave, *Docs. Hist. Scot.*, Illustrations, no.III, section 12, no.IV, sections 8-20, and pp.39-51 (fragmentary); *Chron. Rishanger*, 257 and 309-42, in rebuttal of the Hastings claim; and Palgrave, *Docs. Hist. Scot.*, Illustrations, no.III, section 13, and no.IV, sections 3-7, and pp.23-34. 'Imperial laws' are referred to, *ibid.*, 20 and *Chron. Rishanger*, 345, 349. Bruce's early pleadings made frequent reference to what was called 'the law by which kings reign'.

13. Palgrave, *Docs. Hist. Scot.*, 19-20, 29-30.

14. *Ibid.* The Appeal of the Seven Earls seems to owe most to the earl of Mar, but Mar and Bruce were closely associated at this period.

15. Edgar, a younger son, gained the throne only with the help of armed intervention by William Rufus of England, but after Edgar each successive Scottish sovereign had been the senior available heir, in marked contrast with the English succession in the same period.

16. *Chron. Rishanger*, 342-50 *and* 272; Stones and Simpson, *Great Cause*, ii, 233, 336.

17. *Ibid.*, 240.

18. G. G. Simpson, *SHR*, xxxvi, 115.

19. Palgrave, *Docs. Hist. Scot.*, 20-1; cf. *Chron. Holyrood*, 130.

20. PRO, D.L.36/111/152.

21. Mar's lands lay to the south and west of the Garioch. To the north-west lay Strathbogie, the patrimony of another Bruce partisan, John earl of Atholl.

22. Alexander, earl of Crawford and Balcarres, *The earldom of Mar in sunshine and in shade* (1882), i, 173, states this without citing an authority. Perhaps Lord Crawford had in mind the later grant of the Garioch to Christian Bruce on her (third) marriage to Andrew Murray, for which see below, p.396; but he distinctly says that her first husband received Garioch with her.

23. Palgrave, *Docs. Hist. Scot.*, 14-21. The document (PRO, E.39/89) consists of two separate membranes of the same width, one slightly shorter than the other. Palgrave thought they appeared to have been originally attached together at the bottom. There is no sign that either bore a seal. Membrane 1 is composed of three clearly separated paragraphs of closely-spaced writing (Palgrave's paras 1-3); membrane 2 has one similarly written closely-spaced paragraph (Palgrave's para 4) and two shorter paragraphs much more widely spaced, as though they had not formed part of the document as at first written out (Palgrave's paras 5 and 6). It is much harder to read the document now than in Palgrave's time, for on being repaired in 1950 it was faced with muslin and backed with fresh vellum, obscuring the endorsement. The document is a transcript, or a draft, or the transcript of a draft. See Stones, *Relations*, no.14, which gives only the first membrane. There is a close connexion between the contents of the first and second membranes.

24. As by F. M. Powicke, *The Thirteenth Century*, 601, no.2. It is not clear why Sir Maurice Powicke would exclude Buchan and Fife, the latter explicitly mentioned in the 'Appeal' (Palgrave, *Docs. Hist. Scot.*, 15). Keeney, op. cit., 51, tentatively includes Bruce himself, but this is clearly out of the question.

25. P. E. Schramm, *A History of the English Coronation*, 157.

26. K. J. Leyser, 'A recent view of the German college of electors', *Medium Aevum*, xxiii, 76-87.

27. Palgrave, *Docs. Hist. Scot.*, 29.

28. For example, the *De situ Albanie* of *c.* 1166 gives the seven divisions as 'Angus with Mearns', 'Atholl with Gowrie', 'Strathearn with Menteith', 'Fife with Fothrif', 'Mar with Buchan', 'Moray with Ross' and 'Caithness'. On this see M. O. Anderson, *Kings and kingship in early Scotland* (1973), 139-45.

29. Palgrave, *Docs. Hist. Scot.*, 16, 'they have cruelly slain as many men, women and little children as they could reach'.

30. W. F. Skene, *Celtic Scotland*, iii, 441-7.

31. *SHR*, xxxvi, 124; Stones and Simpson, *Great Cause*, ii, 150-1.

32. *Ibid.*

33. Compare *Ibid.*, p.312 with pp.150-1.

34. Its authenticity is refuted by the style ascribed to Earl David, the language of the text, and the impossibly anachronistic eschatocol *in cuius rei testimonium sigillum meum presenti scripto est appensum*. It should now be compared with the genuine acts of Earl David, collected and edited by K. J. Stringer, *Earl David of Huntingdon*, 220-68.

35. Stevenson, *Documents*, i, no.255.

36. Stones and Simpson, *Great Cause*, i, 184, D76(A), para. (e).

37. *Ibid.*, ii, 216-21; cf. Keeney, *Univ. of Toronto Law Journal*, viii, 60,n.33.

38. Cotton Charter, xviii, 48; Stones, *Documents*, no.18.

39. *APS*, i, 449.

40. Stones and Simpson, *Great Cause*, ii, 336.

41. *Ibid.*, 331-3, 323-5.

42. *SHR*, xxxvi, 117-8. Mme Kossmann, *Revue du Nord*, xl, 542, considers it likely that Balliol did bribe Count Florence.

43. Stones and Simpson, *Great Cause*, ii, 316-17.

44. F. M. Powicke, *King Henry III and the lord Edward*, ii, 790.

45. *Foedera*, i, 785.

46. On the authority of Wyntoun (*Chron. Wyntoun* [Laing], ii, 311-12), modern historians usually call this John Comyn the 'Black Comyn' and his father and son the 'Red Comyn', as though these sobriquets had been used to distinguish three successive heads of the family named John. Contemporary evidence, however, proves that the John Comyn who was Balliol's brother-in-law and a competitor for the throne in 1291 was himself called the 'Red Comyn'. This, and the fact that the description could be written as one word, support the statement in the text that the title 'Red Comyn' was generally applied to the head of the senior branch of the Comyns, being comparable to the titles of Red and Black Douglas. Cf. *Cal. Docs. Scot.*, ii, nos. 678, 822 (p.189).

47. *Rotuli Scotiae*, i, 12a.

48. *Medieval archives of the University of Oxford*, ed. H. E. Salter, i (1920), 32. Presumably Thomas was a kinsman of Mr Richard of Hunsingore of the diocese of Glasgow, a considerable benefactor of Balliol College; Frances de Paravicini, *Early History of Balliol College* (1891), *passim*. Hunsingore is near Wetherby in the West Riding.

49. *Holyrood Liber*, no.91 (81-2); *Reg. John de Halton, bishop of Carlisle* (1913), i. 34.

50. *Foedera*, i, 757.

51. Stevenson, *Documents*, i, no.305.

52. *Rotuli Scotiae*, i, 172. Philip of Rydale was mayor of Berwick in 1291, *Instrumenta Publica*, 12.

53. *Foedera*, i, 785 (Original edn., ii, 596-7).

54. *Ibid.* (Original edn, ii, 597).

55. *Ibid.* (Original edn., ii, 597-600).

56. *Chronica Mag. Rogeri de Houedene* (ed. Stubbs), i, 211; *Chron. Stephen etc.*, i, 105.

CHAPTER FOUR
A Lamb among Wolves

1. An interesting precursor of appeals from King John to Edward I was the

appeal made to Henry III in 1242 by Walter Bisset, the murderer of Patrick earl of Atholl, against the judgement of Alexander II, on the grounds that Alexander was Henry's liege vassal, Matthew Paris, *Chronica Majora* (ed. Luard, Rolls Series), iv, 201-2. The king of Scotland ignored this appeal.

2. *APS*, i, 447.

3. A. A. M. Duncan and A. L. Brown, 'Argyll and the Isles in the earlier middle ages', *Proc. Soc. Antiq. Scot.*, xc, 192-220. The quotation in the text is from p.217.

4. *Ibid.*, 220, no.VI.

5. For examples of the creation of military fiefs in Argyll by Alexander II and Alexander III, cf. *Highland Papers* (SHS), ii, 121 and i, 107; Barrow, *Anglo-Norman Era*, 137-41.

6. Stevenson, *Documents*, i, nos. 53, 84.

7. The abbot of Reading's case may be followed in *APS*, i, 445-6; *Rotuli Scotiae*, i, 19; *Proc. Soc. Antiq. Soc.*, xc, 61-4 (the best survey, with a full account of the background).

8. Berwick on the strength of a charter of King Edgar of 1095, yet the bishop of Durham had not held Berwick since before 1100. Bek claimed Haddington under the impression that 'Haedynton' (etc.) appearing in some early charters in favour of his predecessors stood for Haddington, whereas the place intended was Edington. Cf. A. A. M. Duncan, 'The earliest Scottish charters', *SHR*, xxxvii, 103-35, esp. 110-13.

What looks like the first stage of a further appeal by a non-Scottish appellant (not mentioned by H. G. Richardson and G. O. Sayles in 'The Scottish parliaments of Edward I,' *SHR*, xxv, 300-17) may be found in the complaint made to Edward I in 1294 by John de Lisle of Northumberland, to whom Balliol had granted Whitsome in Berwickshire, that the king of Scots had refused him free possession, *Foedera*, i, 803, June 26th, 1294.

9. *Ibid.*, 761.

10. Alexander Macdonald's case can be traced in *ibid.*, 761; *Rotuli Scotiae*, i, 21b.

11. *Cal. Docs. Scot.*, ii, 209, 'Mauculom le Engleys del counte de Perth'; cf. *ibid.*, 225. *Rotuli Scotiae*, i, 22-3, prints letters from Edward I to Alexander Macdonald of Islay (Berwick, April 15th, 1296)

appointing him king's bailie, empowering him to take Kintyre into his own hands, and commanding him to put Malcolm le fiz Lengleys in sasine of Kintyre. G. G. Simpson has discovered Alexander's reply to a contemporary and related letter from Edward, PRO, S.C.1/18/147.

The identity of Malcolm le fiz Engleys is not clear. The view taken here is that he may perhaps be identified with Malcolm MacCulian (for whom see below, p.149), who held land in Kintyre in 1306, who had apparently been put in possession of Dunaverty by Edward I without lawful inquest, and who was evidently killed in 1307. The view that he may have belonged to the MacQuillans of Antrim, for whom see E. Curtis, *Proc. Roy. Irish Academy*, xliv, 99-113, has not been verified: K. Nicholls, *Gaelic and Gaelicized Ireland in the Middle Ages* (1972), 134.

12. *Scots Peerage*, vi, 130-1; cf. *APS*, i, 447; A. McKerral, *SHR*, xxx, 5-6.

13. *Cal. Docs. Scot.*, ii, no.1255; *Rotuli Scotiae*, i, 90.

14. Stevenson, *Documents*, ii, no.597.

15. *Rotuli Scotiae*, i, 18b.

16. *APS*, i, 446; *Rotuli Scotiae*, i, 19-20.

17. Sir David Dalrymple, Lord Hailes, *Annals of Scotland*, i (1776), 225; cf. index entry '[ ] Macduff' in J. H. Ramsay, *Dawn of the Constitution* (1908), 576. For the Macduff case see *APS*, i, 445; *Rotuli Scotiae*, i, 18, 20; *Rot. Parl.*, i, 110-11; *Foedera*, i, 788.

18. Stevenson, *Documents*, ii, no.462; *Rotuli Scotiae*, i, 42b.

19. *Chron. Fordun*, i, 330.

20. *Cal. Docs. Scot.*, ii, nos. 685, 686.

21. *Rot. Parl.*, i, 110-11.

22. *Ibid.*

23. *Cal. Docs. Scot.*, ii, nos. 687, 688.

24. Palgrave, *Docs. Hist. Scot.*, 138-41.

25. *Rot. Parl.*, i, 112-3; see also Stones, *Relations*, no.21.

26. *Rot. Parl.*, 113.

27. *Chron. Guisb.*, 264.

28. *Ibid.*, 264. Elsewhere, 'treacherous', *ibid.*, 294.

29. M. Dominica Legge, *SHR*, xxxviii, 110-11.

30. *APS*, i, 445.

31. *Chron. Rishanger*, 263-4. For Master Nicholas, cf. Barrow, *Kingdom*, 245-7; Watt, *Graduates*, 23-5.

32. *Glasgow Registrum*, no.239. *Ibid.*, no.238, shows that Master William Lamberton, future bishop of St Andrews, Master Thomas of Dundee, future bishop of Ross, and Master William of Eaglesham, future Scottish envoy to the papal curia in 1301, were also present at Scone at the time of King John's first parliament.

33. *The Thirteenth Century*, 610.

34. *Scalacronica*, 123, confirmed in part by *Rotuli Scotiae*, i, 35a, instructions to obey Warenne, dated at Morpeth, September 29th; cf. *Cal. Close, 1288-96*, 492.

35. *The Thirteenth Century*, 611 and no.2, the description of the Arbroath Declaration being cited from T. M. Cooper, Lord Cooper, *Supra Crepidam* (1951), 59.

36. *Chron. Picts-Scots*, 216-21, Anagni, June 27th; Stones, *Relations*, no.28.

37. The detailed account in *Scimus, fili* of the transactions of the period 1286-92 and later shows that the information on which the letter was based must have been supplied by Scottish informants. The grounds for believing that *Scimus, fili* was nevertheless somewhat out of date by June 1299 are that the letter, having referred to the imprisonment of Bishop Wishart of Glasgow (1297) and of Bishop Mark of Sodor (at an unknown date), speaks of them as still in prison. But Wishart was released on parole in the spring of 1298 (Palgrave, *Docs. Hist. Scot.*, 344), was evidently free in October 1299 (*Cal. Docs. Scot.*, ii, no.1105), and is not known to have been imprisoned again till 1306. There seems to be no record of Bishop Mark's movements between August 29th, 1296, when King Edward's bailie of Dumfries was ordered to bring him to the king at Berwick, presumably to do homage (*Rotuli Scotiae*, i, 24), and February 7th, 1302, when he was at Rushen (*Register of St Bees*, ed. J. Wilson (1915), no.46). There is no record of the bishop's homage in 1296, and perhaps the reason for his imprisonment was his failure to perform it.

38. Probably a reference to Edward I's appointment of Anthony Bek as lieutenant in Scotland, August 1290; see above, p.42.

39. This expression, derived from Roman Law, was a commonplace way of excusing acts committed under improper compulsion or duress; cf. *Collected Papers of T. F. Tout*, ii, 285-7; *Bracton on the laws and customs of England*, ed. S. E. Thorne (1968), ii, 296.

40. *Chron. Rishanger*, 371.

41. *Foedera*, i, 801.

42. *Ibid.*, i, 804.

43. *Handbook of British Chronology* (2nd edn, 1961), 511; *Chron. Guisb.*, 243.

44. *Ibid.*, 280; and see *Foedera*, i, 811 and *Reg. Johannis de Pontissara episcopi Wyntoniensis, 1282-1304*, ed. C. Deedes (Canterbury and York Society, 1915-24), 510-12, for Pope Celestine's letter of October 1294 admonishing Edward I not to wage war on the French.

45. Stevenson, *Documents*, ii, no.334.

46. *Ibid.*, no.335.

47. *Chron. Guisb.*, 264 (Scone); *Chron. Lanercost*, 161-2 (Stirling); *Chron. Fordun*, i, 327 (Scone), wrongly placed after instead of before the campaign of 1296). Though two chronicles give Scone, the true place and date of the parliament are shown to have been July 5th, 1295, at Stirling, by King John's letters to King Philip IV, *APS*, i, 453 and his charter for Bishop Bek (*Cal. Docs. Scot.*, ii, no.872). Cf. *SHR*, xxv, 304, n.5.

48. *History of England, 1216-1377*, 194.

49. In *Chron. Fordun*, i, 328, the twelve are actually called Guardians.

50. *Littere Wallie*, ed. J. G. Edwards, 184. Admittedly, this was only a section of the baronage.

51. *APS*, i, 453; and for their arrival in France, *Chron. Lanercost*, 166, where the year should be 1295, not 1294.

52. See below, p.91.

53. For John de Soules see M. McMichael, 'The feudal family of de Soulis', *Dumfriesshire Trans.*, 3rd ser., xxvi, 163-93, esp. 174-81.

54. J. Hodgson, *History of Northumberland*, II, i, 31, n.b; *Cal. Docs. Scot.*, ii, nos.1060, 1696; W. Percy Hedley, *Northumberland Families*, i (1968), 211.

55. *APS*, i, 451-3.

56. *Ibid.*, 453b.

57. Ranald Nicholson, 'The Franco-Scottish and Franco-Norwegian treaties of 1295', *SHR*, xxxviii, 114-32.

58. *Cal. Docs. Scot.*, ii, 148 (no.635), where the year should be 1293; cf. *ibid.*, no.675.

59. J. Dowden, *Bishops of Scotland*, 359-60, surnamed from the village of Great Dalton in Annandale. He was also known as Thomas 'of Kirkcudbright'. Cf. Watt, *Graduates*, 308-10.

60. For what follows, see R. Brentano, *York Metropolitan Jurisdiction* (1959), 94-108, esp. 98-108.

61. Stones and Simpson, *Great Cause*, ii, 84.

62. *APS*, i, 449.

63. *Chron. Lanercost*, 169; *monstratis armis*, felicitously 'wapinschaw' in H. Maxwell's translation, *The chronicle of Lanercost* (1913), 129; *Chron. Guisb.*, 269. Cf. the phrase *armorum ostensio*, *Melrose Liber*, no.396.

64. *Chron. Stephen etc.*, iii, 242-3; likewise Alexander II in 1244, *Chron. Bower*, ii, 74.

65. *Formulary E*, ed. A. A. M. Duncan, no.89. For a description of the Scots army in 1244, see Matthew Paris, *Chronica Majora* (ed. Luard, Rolls Ser.), vi, 518, n. 1: '500 knights and 60,000 foot. The foot were lightly armed and suitably equipped with weapons, viz., axes sharpened to a point, spears and bows.' Cf. the Dürer drawing of 1521 reproduced in *SHR*, xxx, facing 9.

66. *Chron. Guisb.*, 269. But if the summons preserved as no.86 of *Formulary E* belongs to February 1296, a fairly general call up seems indicated.

67. *Chron. Guisb.*, 270.

68. *SHR*, xli, 5-6 and n.1.

69. Stones and Simpson, *Great Cause*, i, 9; *Chron. Bower*, ii, 109; *Northumberland Pleas, 1198-1272* (1922), no.776 = *Cal. Docs. Scot.*, i, no.2452; cf. Fraser, *Douglas*, i, 58-61.

70. *Chron. Guisb.*, 325-6.

71. *Ibid.*, 270, where (as the editor points out) Edinburgh is a mistake for Jedburgh, *Foedera*, i, 829 (= *Rotuli Scotiae*, i, 22b, cf. *ibid.*, 21b), October 16th, 1295. Professor Rothwell, however, was not justified in speaking of an 'agreement' to surrender the castles, despite the wording

of the letters. Walter of Guisborough is clearly right in stating that the Scots refused to yield them, and in fact Edward I ordered the seizure of the English property of Scotsmen by writs of the same date, October 16th; Stevenson, *Documents*, ii, no.342.

72. *Chron. Guisb.*, 270.

73. *Parl. Writs*, i, 275-7 (December 16th, 1295), the recruiting expedited by instructions of February 23rd, 1296, *Cal. Docs. Scot.*, ii, no.727. A very large force of infantry was called up in addition to the feudal levies, for 60,000 foot were to be in pay at Newcastle at the beginning of March (PRO, E.159/69, m. 11d. I owe this reference to Dr. E. B. Fryde). The earl of Ulster with a considerable force of Irish was ordered to be at Whitehaven on March 1st (*Parl. Writs.*, i, 277), and *Chron. Guisb.*, 279, says the earl with 400 horsemen and '30,000' foot from Ireland joined King Edward at Stirling (June 1296). The truth, elucidated by Professor J. F. Lydon, 'An Irish army in Scotland, 1296', *The Irish Sword*, v (1962), 184-90, seems to be that 3157 Irish troops, an impressive total, joined Edward I at Roxburgh on May 13th and stayed in Scotland till August, being used to flush out Scots resisters in hill country. The cost of this Irish contingent was approximately £8000.

CHAPTER FIVE
Two Kinds of War

1. *Chron. Guisb.*, 279, 275.

2. *Cal. Docs. Scot.*, ii, 173. Adderston in Cavers, a Balliol lordship.

3. *Ibid.*

4. *Chron. Guisb.*, 271-2. *Chron. Guisb.*, and *Chron. Lanercost* are the basis of the narrative that follows. On nationality, see *Memoranda de Parliamento* (ed. Maitland), pp.192-3; G. W. S. Barrow, *The Anglo-Norman Era in Scottish History*, 145-56. H. Summerson, 'Crime and Society in medieval Cumberland', *CWAAS Trans.*, lxxxii (1982), 113-16, has illuminating evidence on this topic, chiefly for the fourteenth century, which seems to prove that distinctions of nationality were in fact well understood.

5. *Spalding Club Miscellany*, ii, 314.

6. *Chron. Guisb.*, 275.

7. *Chron. Lanercost*, 173; Stevenson, *Wallace Docs.*, 3.

8. Palgrave, *Docs. Hist. Scot.*, 149: 'they burned about 200 little scholars who were in the school at Corbridge learning their first letters and grammar, having blocked up the doors and set fire to the building.' This instrument (or draft) seems to have been prepared for the benefit of King Philip IV in order to demonstrate how unjust and ill-founded was his alliance with the Scots. Corbridge must be an error for Hexham. *Chron. Lanercost*, 174, says 'they collected a crowd of young schoolboys in Hexham school and, blocking the doors, set fire to the building and its inmates innocent in the sight of God.'

9. *Chron. Guisb.*, 277. That the Scots burned the priory and town of Hexham and many other towns and villages is not in doubt, but there seems to be some uncertainty about the story of the schoolboys.

10. *Cal. Docs. Scot.*, ii, 225. For the rehabilitation of Berwick, cf. Stevenson, *Documents*, ii, nos. 356, 392, 406, 407, 416, 417, 418, 422, 426.

11. Stevenson, *Documents*, ii, 26.

12. *Chron. Guisb.*, 277-8. For Earl Patrick, cf. Stones, *Relations*, no.22.

13. *Chron. Guisb.*, 278; Stevenson, *Documents*, ii, 26.

14. Bartholomew Cotton, *Historia Anglicana* (ed. Luard, Rolls Series), 312, says the dead were, on King Edward's orders, counted under the supervision of Earl Patrick of Dunbar and Sir John Benstead, and numbered 10,052 (surely an exaggeration).

15. The 'battle' of Ramsey, I.O.M., 1275, can hardly be reckoned a major engagement.

16. *Chron. Lanercost*, 178-9; *Chron. Guisb.*, 279; Stevenson, *Documents*, ii, 28.

17. J. F. Lydon in *The Irish Sword*, v, 187-8.

18. *Chron. Guisb.*, 280.

19. G. Watson, 'The Black Rood of Scotland', *Transactions of the Scottish Ecclesiological Society*, ii, I, 27-46, esp. 37-40.

20. M. Dominica Legge, 'La piere d'Escoce', *SHR*, xxxviii, 109-13.

21. *Political Songs of the English Nation*, ed. T. Wright (Camden Society, 1839), 307.

22. *SHR*, xxxviii, 109-10.

23. *Chron. Bower*, ii, 166.

24. For the terms of this more honourable submission, presumably the first 'form of peace' mentioned in *Chron. Guisb.*, 280, see E. L. G. Stones and M. N. Blount, in *BIHR*, xlviii, 95-6, 104-5.

25. *Cal. Docs. Scot.*, ii, no.754.

26. Stevenson, *Documents*, ii, no.372 (p.60).

27. Stones and Blount, *BIHR*, xlviii, 99.

28. *Chron. Wyntoun* (Laing), ii, 337, 'the pelure thai tuk off hys tabart (Twme-Tabart he wes callyt efftyrwart)'.

29. *Cal. Docs. Scot.*, ii, no.1027 (p.256), and no.854.

30. *Ibid.*, nos. 839, 848; *Chron. Guisb.*, 284.

31. *Cal. Docs. Scot.*, ii, no.742. A considerable number of other documents calendared by Bain in this volume also deal with Scots made prisoner in 1296.

32. *Moray Registrum*, p.xxxvii; *Cal. Docs. Scot.*, ii, pp.xxix-xxx.

33. *Chron. Bower*, ii, 148; *Family of Rose*, 29.

34. *Cal. Docs. Scot.*, ii, 177.

35. *Ibid.*, *passim* between nos. 747 and 803.

36. Stevenson, *Documents*, ii, 28-9. During his stay of five days at Aberdeen the king seems to have gone out to Lumphanan (*Cal. Docs. Scot.*, ii, no.787), though the fealty sworn there is puzzlingly dated July 21st. If the fealty was taken by proxy, this would affect our view of many of the fealties said to have been sworn to the king during his tour.

37. Stevenson, *Documents*, ii, 29; under Sir John de Cantilupe, Sir Hugh Despenser and Sir John Hastings of Abergavenny.

38. Comyn's lordship of Lochaber appears in Stevenson, *Documents*, ii, 190; note that an agreement of 1234 to which Walter Comyn lord of Badenoch set his seal was witnessed by Farquhar steward of Badenoch and Edward steward of Lochaber, *Moray Registrum*, no.86.

39. A minuscule hamlet at which at least one privy seal writ was dated: *Yorkshire*

Inquisitions, iii, ed. W. Brown (Yorks. Archaeological Soc., 1902), 39-40n.

40. Stevenson, *Documents*, ii, 29-30. This contemporary journal (also printed in *Instrumenta Publica*, 177-83, and in an early translation, P. Hume Brown, *Early Travellers in Scotland* (1891), 2-6) states that the king stayed from July 31st to August 2nd at Kildrummy, a castle of the earl of Mar (cf. *Cal. Docs. Scot.*, ii, 196 and no.800). The writer's form for this name, Kyndrokyn (*Instrumenta Publica*, 179), instead of Kyndromyn, suggests a confusion with Kindrochit, explicable if he had heard that the bishop of Durham had come south through the Braes of Mar and stayed at Kindrochit.

41. *Rotuli Scotiae*, i, 27b; Stevenson, *Documents*, ii, 31-2; *Chron. Guisb.*, 281, 284.

42. *Cal. Docs. Scot.*, ii, no.853.

43. *Ibid.*, no.264. William de Rue seems to have become something of a specialist in Scottish administration.

44. PRO, E.159/71, rot.30d; above, p.10.

45. *Instrumenta Publica*, 60-174; *Cal. Docs. Scot.*, ii, no.823.

46. *History of England, 1216-1377*, 198.

47. *Cal. Docs. Scot.*, ii, 196. So in 1291: Glasgow Univ. Lib. MS Gen. 1053, fo.19v.

48. *Cal. Docs. Scot.*, ii, 196.

49. *Ibid.*, 200.

50. *Ibid.*, 204.

51. *Ibid.*, 196; *Historiae Dunelmensis Scriptores Tres* (ed. J. Raine, Surtees Soc.), 84.

52. *Cal. Docs. Scot.*, ii, 211; cf. A. I. Dunlop, 'Bagimond's Roll', in *Miscellany* (SHS), vi (1939), 6-10.

53. Stevenson, *Documents*, ii, 31. The local inquests held at Berwick at the time of parliament, given in *Cal. Docs. Scot.*, ii, no.824, prove that a fair number of gentry from the southern sheriffdoms of Wigtown, Ayr, Dumfries, Fife, Lothian and Berwick were present personally. In 1291 fealties were taken by sheriffdoms and the sheriff had discretion as to which freeholders should take the oath. The clerks clearly thought it odd that in the Merse Edmund of Bundington had taken the oath though only a 'simple countryman' (*simplex patriota*): Glasgow

Univ. Lib. MS Gen. 1053, fos. 10-11; Stones and Simpson, *Great Cause*, ii, 368, no.60.

54. *Cal. Docs. Scot.*, ii, 193, 199, 203.

55. *Ibid.*, 213.

56. *Chron. Guisb.*, 294.

57. *Ibid.*

58. *Ibid.*, and 303, and references, *passim*, in *Cal. Docs. Scot.*, ii (esp. no.951), and in Stevenson, *Documents*.

59. *Chron. Guisb.*, 302; *Cal. Docs. Scot.*, ii, no.951.

60. *Chron. Guisb.*, 303. The pun doubtless sounded less forced in French, but it could hardly have been a piece of popular humour.

61. F. W. Maitland, *Memoranda de Parliamento* (Rolls Series, 1893), 184, referring to 1296-7; *Rot. Scot.*, i, 40b (Ayr merchants to send their wool to Berwick).

62. *Cal. Docs. Scot.*, ii, 196.

63. *Ibid.*, no.839, a protection for the bishop for two years from September 8th, 1296, suggests that he was in the king's peace then.

64. He had failed to appear in time for the Berwick parliament (*Rotuli Scotiae*, i, 24), and later was put in prison.

65. On this in general, see Barrow, *Kingdom*, 233-54.

66. Evan Macleod Barron, *The Scottish War of Independence* (London: James Nisbet, 1913). In this work I have used the second edition (Inverness: Robert Carruthers, 1934).

67. Edition of 1945, 218 (my italics).

68. P. Fraser Tytler, *The History of Scotland from the accession of Alexander III to the Union* (4 vols, Edinburgh, 1882), i, 60; elaborated and generalised by Joseph Stevenson half a century later: Stevenson, *Documents*, i, pp.lii-liii.

69. Dowden, *Bishops*, 21, Fordun's 'Aytuil' doubtless for Auteuil. Fraser was buried in the Dominican Priory in Paris. *Cal. Docs. Scot.*, ii, 265, shows that the bishop was against King Edward's peace in November, 1296.

70. *Chron. Lanercost*, 168-9, says that the bishops of St Andrews and Dunkeld remained in France, but the knights and esquires associated with them had to beg a lift home in a German ship trading to Scotland. Ingram de Umfraville certainly

returned and did homage to Edward I (*Cal. Docs. Scot.*, ii, 199, 224), but there is no record of any homage by or restitution to John de Soules. Moreover, a letter of Philip IV of February 25th, 1298, is evidence of continued Scottish representation at Paris cf. *Foedera*, i, 861 and G. P. Cuttino, ed., *Gascon Calendar of 1322* (1949), p.41, no.420. A receipt dated Paris, February 10th, 1298 (meaning that year or perhaps 1299) bore the seal of John de Soules: M. Demay, *Inventaire des sceaux de la collection Clairambault* (1885), no.8684.

71. Barrow, *Kingdom*, 239-40, and for what follows, 241-3. See also Watt, *Graduates*, 585-90.

72. M. Ash, in *The Scottish Tradition* (ed. G. W. S. Barrow), 44.

73. Barrow, *Kingdom*, 242; Stevenson, *Documents*, ii, 61.

74. *Chron. Guisb.*, 299; on James and his career see G. Barrow and A. Royan, 'James fifth Stewart of Scotland, 1260(?)-1309', in *Essays on the Nobility of Medieval Scotland*, ed. K. J. Stringer (1985), 166-94.

75. *Kingdom of the Scots*, 347, 349-50, 352-3.

76. *Chron. Lanercost*, 190; cf. also *Chron. Guisb.*, 296, calling the bishop of Glasgow and the Stewart the authors of the revolt. So also Boniface VIII, writing in 1302, *Foedera*, i, 942.

77. *Chron. Guisb.*, 299. A letter of July 23rd, 1297, probably written by Cressingham, told Edward I that Wallace lay in Selkirk Forest with a large company, Stevenson, *Documents*, ii, no.453. The raid on the *domus episcopi*, probably the bishop's palace at Ancrum on the edge of the Forest (although the episcopal residence at Stobo is a possibility), would have taken place a few weeks later.

78. *Chron. Guisb.*, 314.

79. *Rotuli Scotiae*, i, 40.

80. *Ibid.*, i, 42b; Stevenson, *Documents*, ii, no.437. The Lancashire sheriff of Aberdeen, Henry of Lathom, went over to the Scots, *Cal. Docs. Scot.*, ii, no.972.

81. Stevenson, *Wallace Docs.*, 191; *Cal. Docs. Scot.*, ii, no.418; *Chron. Fordun*, i, 328; *Chron. Bower*, ii, 170; *Scalacronica*, 123. Sir Thomas Grey, of Heaton on the Till, no doubt preserves the true form of the sheriff's name, William de Hesilrig. A father and son of this name witness *Laing Chrs.*, no.16 (*c.* 1292-5) and occur in another north Northumberland document, *ibid.*, no.14. Hesilrig is Hazelrigg, in Chatton, north Northumberland, a few miles from Heaton. Joseph Bain, in an unhappy passage (*Cal. Docs. Scot.*, ii, pp.xxvii-xxviii), argues that the English sheriff of Lanark or Clydesdale was really a Scot, Sir Andrew Livingstone, who was sheriff of Lanark for the financial year ending November 1296. There is no reason to doubt that Wallace slew an English sheriff named William Hesilrig.

82. *Chron. Guisb.*, 295.

83. *Cal. Docs. Scot.*, ii, nos. 357, 358, 365, 429, 431, 468.

84. *APS*, i, 449.

85. *Ibid.*, i, 448.

86. *Chron. Guisb.*, 295.

87. Henry Percy the elder, grandson of John de Warenne, earl of Surrey, succeeded his brother, *c.* 1293, and played a prominent part in the Scottish wars of Edward I and Edward II until his death in October 1314. He was succeeded by a son of the same name.

88. Robert Clifford, son of Roger Clifford and Isabel de Vieuxpont, an heiress of the great northern landowning family of Vieuxpont of Brougham, Westmorland. Like Henry Percy, Robert Clifford played a major part in Anglo-Scottish history, until his death at Bannockburn.

89. *Chron. Guisb.*, 297-8.

90. Stevenson, *Documents*, ii, no.467, shows that Wishart, Bruce and the Stewart had not come to confirm the peace by August 5th. For the course of the negotiations, see *ibid.*, nos. 447, 452, 453, 454, 462, 464; Palgrave, *Docs. His. Scot.*, 197-200. *Ibid.*, 199-200, shows that a condition of Bruce's submission was the surrender as hostage of his only child Marjorie, who can only have been a few years old at most. *Cal. Docs. Scot.*, ii, 247, shows that Bruce had not submitted by early November 1297, and it is virtually certain that he neither submitted nor surrendered his daughter.

91. Stevenson, *Documents*, ii, no.447: '[a] Robert, counte e James Seneschal e a tuite la comunaulte du royaume de Escoce', the context making it probable that in this

phrase the English leaders were replying in the terms used by their Scots opponents. If 'Robert' refers to Bruce, the whole of Wishart's name has been lost through injury to the parchment.

92. *Chron. Guisb.*, 299; Stevenson, *Documents*, ii, no.452.

93. PRO, E. 159/70, rot.29d. This letter may be said to carry even greater weight than the better-known one mentioned in the next note, for it was a private letter from one financial official to another.

94. Stevenson, *Documents*, ii, no.455.

95. *Ibid.*, no.453.

96. *Chron. Bower*, ii, 171.

97. *Chron. Guisb.*, 299.

98. *Scottish War of Independence*, 32-57.

99. *Cal. Docs. Scot.*, ii, nos. 921, 922, 923.

100. *Chron. Guisb.*, 297, *ambos illos comites Johannem de Badenaughe et Johannem de Bughan*. Badenoch was not an earl, but Guisborough seems to have thought he was, cf. *ibid.*, 366.

101. Stevenson, *Documents*, ii, nos. 456-60. For the name Gartnait in early Pictish history, cf. Anderson, *Early Sources*, references in index.

102. *Chron. Guisb.*, 297.

103. Stevenson, *Documents*, ii, no.467.

104. *Ibid.*, no.462.

105. *Ibid.*, no.467, p.226.

106. *Chron. Guisb.*, 301, gives English strength as 1,000 cavalry and 50,000 foot, against a Scottish force of 180 horse and 40,000 foot. The numbers of both foot and horse are doubtless exaggerated.

107. J. H. Ramsay, *Dawn of the Constitution*, 453. *Dunfermline Registrum*, no.216, shows that the lands of Cornton, just west of the Causeway, paid teinds in oats, *c.* 1218. This record speaks of teinds of corn and fish of Airthrey and Cornton 'west of Causewayhead [*a capite de la chaucee*] next beside the Spittal as far as the peatary of Airthrey'. There was also north of the Forth an area called the 'burgh grieve's flat', part of which at least, in the direction of Airthrey and of Stirling Bridge, was regularly ploughed.

108. *Chron. Guisb.*, 300. The certainty of *Chron. Lanercost*, 190, that the Stewart had treacherously led the English to destruction surely exaggerates his

influence with Warenne and Cressingham, of whom he was virtually a prisoner.

109. *Chron. Guisb.*, 300.

110. *Ibid.*, the *vadum non longe ab hinc* was obviously at Drip, the highest ford over the combined Teith and Forth, referred to as a crucial crossing in 1304, *Cal. Docs. Scot.*, ii, nos. 1462, 1470.

111. *Ibid.*, p.xxx.

112. *Ibid.*, iv, no.1835.

113. *Chron. Guisb.*, 303. For the 'polles', see below, pp.211-12.

CHAPTER SIX
Experiments in Guardianship

1. As shown by letters issued on November 7th, *Chron. Guisb.*, 306, although Murray might by then have been dead without Wallace's knowledge. An inquest of 1300 (*Cal. Docs. Scot.*, ii, no.1178) says that Andrew Murray was killed at Stirling against the king (of England), but probably he was mortally wounded in the battle and died some two months later. His posthumous son, the future Guardian, was not born till Whitsun, 1298.

2. Stevenson, *Wallace Docs.*, 159 (with facsimile as frontispiece); also in K. Höhlbaum, *Hansisches Urkundenbuch*, Bd. i (Halle, 1876), no.1251 (422). This letter may have been destroyed during the second world war; at any rate, its whereabouts is not known.

3. Stevenson, *Wallace Docs.*, 191-2.

4. This is shown by the uniformity of the style used, by the traditional address of the only surviving charter, *omnibus probis hominibus*, and by the formulae and phraseology of the documents, which conform closely (making allowance for the unprecedented situation) with productions of the chapel during the later thirteenth century.

5. *Chron. Guisb.*, 306.

6. Anderson, *Diplomata*, Pl.XLIII. This original is also lost, so that we now possess no original document issued by Wallace.

7. Stevenson, *Wallace Docs.*, 191. The Lübeck letter from Murray and Wallace was exhibited at the Glasgow Exhibition of 1911. It bore two seals, presumably of Murray and Wallace in their official capacity. Only the upper seal (Murray's?)

survived in 1911, with the royal arms of Scotland on the obverse, and on the reverse possibly a personal device; compare de Soules's seal of guardianship (Stevenson and Wood, *Seals*, 25 and no.22).

8. *History of England* (3rd edn, 1945), 218.

9. *Chron. Guisb.*, 303-7; *Chron. Lanercost*, 190-1; and see p.93 below.

10. *Cal. Docs. Scot.*, iv, no.1835. Sir Richard Waldegrave, constable of Stirling in 1297, together with most of the garrison, was slain at Stirling Bridge. The castle was entrusted by Warenne to William Fitz Warin and Marmaduke Tweng, who were joined by William de Ros, brother of Robert de Ros of Wark, who had joined the Scots. They were soon forced to surrender from want of provisions. Wallace spared Ros's life because of his brother, but imprisoned him in irons in Dumbarton castle; Wallace also spared the lives of Tweng and Fitz Warin.

11. *Chron. Guisb.*, 307.

12. *Ibid.*, 305-6.

13. John of Hexham, in *Symeonis Monachi Opera Omnia* (ed. Arnold, Rolls Series), ii, 290; and cf. *Chron. Stephen etc.*, ii, 153.

14. V. H. Galbraith, in *EHR*, lviii, 67 and n.7, 68; and *The Chronicle of Bury St. Edmunds, 1212-1301*, ed. Antonia Gransden (1964), 142.

15. *Chron. Guisb.*, 273; W. P. Hedley, *Northumberland Families*, i (1968), 38-9; *Scots Peerage*, viii, 246-7.

16. *Ancient Petitions relating to Northumberland*, ed. C. M. Fraser (Surtees Soc., 1966), 22.

17. Stevenson, *Wallace Docs.*, 191.

18. *Chron. Bower*, i, 362.

19. For him, see Stevenson, *Documents*, no.512; *Cal. Docs. Scot.*, ii, nos. 778, 1017, 1574, 1822.

20. Barrow, *Kingdom*, 212-32.

21. Dowden, *Bishops*, 21.

22. Palgrave, *Docs. Hist. Scot.*, 332, 339.

23. *Chron. Guisb.*, 297, says that when the earl was sent to pacify the north (July 1297) 'at first he pretended to repress rebellion, but in the end changed sides and became a thorn in our flesh'. *Rotuli Scotiae*, i, 50b, shows that on September 26th, 1297, the regency in London still believed that the earl was loyal, but as they held the same belief with regard to the Stewart and the earl of Lennox, who joined Wallace openly on September 11th, this is no evidence that Buchan was on the English side as late as this date. *Cal. Docs. Scot.*, ii, no.963, orders the king's bailiff of Tynedale to resume into his own hands the lands of John Comyn (the elder) of Badenoch, November–December 1297.

24. *Cal. Docs. Scot.*, ii, no.1017. Stevenson, *Documents*, no.512, suggests that, in May 1298, William Comyn was not opposed to the election of Lamberton as such, but only to his own exclusion from participation in the election.

25. Theiner, *Monumenta*, no.362; Dowden, *Bishops*, 21-2.

26. *Cal. Docs. Scot.*, ii, no.1071, shows that it was reported in England in July 1299 that the bishop of St Andrews, the abbots of Jedburgh and Melrose, and Sir John de Soules were waiting for a passage to Scotland at Damme, by Bruges. Soules was in France in 'February 1298', possibly meaning 1299, *SHR*, xxvii, 139. In April 1299 King Philip had received as envoys from the Guardians in Scotland the abbot of Jedburgh and Sir John Wishart, *Cal. Docs. Scot.*, ii, 535 (for the correct dating, see Barron, *Scottish War of Independence*, 132).

27. *Chron. Rishanger*, 185; *Foedera*, i, 897.

28. Stevenson, *Documents*, ii, no.574; *Cal. Docs. Scot.*, ii, nos. 1079, 1080.

29. Stevenson, *Documents*, ii, 382-3.

30. *Chron. Picts-Scots*, 126; Stones, *Relations*, no.28; Stevenson, *Documents*, ii, no.569.

31. *Cal. Docs. Scot.*, ii, 535 (see above, n.26).

32. Stevenson, *Wallace Docs.*, 145.

33. *Chron. Guisb.*, 307-8.

34. *Ibid.*, 314.

35. *Ibid.*, 315.

36. *Ibid.*, 328.

37. Wallace spent some time early in 1298 besieging Roxburgh, *Chron. Rishanger*, 184; his charter to Alexander Scrimgeour, March 29th, 1298, was issued at Torphichen.

38. *Ibid.*, 384; the earl is not named, but his description as *de illa natione praecipuus* suggests a prominent earl such as Strathearn, Carrick or Lennox. For

reasons given below, n.41, it could hardly have been Atholl or Menteith.

39. Anderson, *Diplomata*, Pl.XLIII.

40. *Cal. Docs. Scot.*, ii, nos. 937, 939, 940, 942, 944, 948, 950, 952, 953.

41. N. Trivet, *Annales* (ed. T. Hog), 371; *Chron. Rishanger*, 185. Edward I was still at Ghent on February 25th, and at Sluys, on the point of embarking for England, on March 12th, *Cal. Chancery Warrants*, i, 90-91. Aardenburg, between Ghent and Sluys, was then a town of some importance (*Annales Gandenses*, ed. H. Johnstone, *passim*). We may put the date of the Scottish 'defection' about March 9th (*Gascon Calendar of 1322*, p.39). Langtoft names the leaders of the party, who he says went to Paris to plead for King Philip's aid against the English, as the earls of Atholl and Menteith, and John Comyn the younger of Badenoch, the future Guardian, Stevenson, *Wallace Docs.*, 72-3. Most of the Scots in Flanders were in the 'meinie' or following of one or other of these great men. Langtoft says that they were rebuffed by Philip IV, quickly took ship for Scotland, and reached home without being intercepted. In *Cal. Docs. Scot.*, ii, 253, Edward I refers in a letter to Philip IV to the Scots who were in his service (in Flanders) and have deserted him.

42. *Moray Registrum*, 470. The earl's wartime activity began with the raid on northern Cumberland in March 1296 and, as we have seen (above, p.93), may have involved participation with Wallace in the raid of September-November 1297.

43. *Yorkshire Inquisitions*, ii, ed. W. Brown (1898), 1-2; *Cal. Inquis. Misc.*, i, no.1090. This inquisition has been wrongly filed under 5 Edward I instead of 5 Edward II (i.e. 29 March 1312).

44. J. E. Morris, *The Welsh Wars of Edward I* (1901), 286-92, 313-4, gives details of the Falkirk army. Apropos his statement, *ibid.*, 314, that new evidence divides the cavalry into four brigades, it may be noted that Bartholomew Cotton, *Historia Anglicana* (ed. Luard, Rolls Series), 343-4, also gives four brigades.

45. For the Irish contingent, insignificant despite *Chron. Guisb.*, 324, see J. J. Lydon, 'Irish levies in the Scottish Wars, 1296-1302', *The Irish Sword*, v, 207-8.

46. *Chron. Lanercost*, 190; *Flores Historiarum* (Rolls Series), iii, 123, 321; *Chron. Rishanger*, 385-6.

47. *Ibid.*, 186; *Parl. Writs*, i, 314b-15b, writs of summons for Welsh foot to reach Carlisle, and for English foot to reach Roxburgh, on Wednesday, June 25th. *Parl. Writs*, 316, alters summons so that cavalry shall gather on June 23rd; and there is also a summons for cavalry on June 25th.

48. *Chron. Guisb.*, 324. King Edward took the banner of St John of Beverley with him on the campaign, *Cal. Docs. Scot.*, ii, no.1177.

49. *Cal. Chancery Warrants*, i, 94-5, shows the king at Lauder, July 9th, Fala and Dalhousie, July 10th. This route became by far the commonest to be used by large forces invading Scotland from the south.

50. *Cal. Docs. Scot.*, ii, no.998.

51. *Chron. Guisb.*, 324; *Chron. Rishanger*, 186; A. Macdonald, *Place-Names of West Lothian*, 39. Edward I's nephew Thomas earl of Lancaster dated a letter of safe conduct at Temple Liston on July 16th: Univ. of London Library, MS Fuller 35/2.

52. *Chron. Guisb.*, 325.

53. *Ibid.*, 324.

54. *Ibid.*, 324-5. There seems to be no record of Tantallon before the fourteenth century, though the name is ancient.

55. PRO, E.159/71, rot. 118v.

56. *Chron. Guisb.*, 326. Umfraville was of course an Englishman, lord of Prudhoe, Redesdale and Coquetdale.

57. *Ibid.*, 326; *in mora citra Linlyscoch.*

58. Stevenson, *Wallace Docs.*, 145.

59. Morris, *Welsh Wars*, 256-8; J. G. Edwards, *EHR*, xxxix, 1-12; *ibid.*, xlvi, 262-5.

60. *Chron. Guisb.*, 327. The *foresta de Selkyrke*, *ibid.*, 326, is either a slip for *foresta de Falkirk*, i.e., Callendar Wood, or simply a mistake. There is remarkably complete agreement among contemporary or nearly contemporary record and chronicle sources that the battle of Falkirk was in fact fought at or beside Falkirk ('this side of Falkirk', i.e., east, *Scalacronica*, 125). One of the earliest references to the battle by name calls it *bellum varie capelle*, i.e. the battle of Falkirk (*SHR*, v, 24, a record of 1354

supplied with misleading commentary by John Edwards). Cf. also *Cal. Docs. Scot.*, ii, nos. 1007, 1011.

61. No doubt the earls of Atholl and Menteith, who had come home from Flanders earlier in the year, together with the Stewart, the earls of Buchan, Strathearn, Lennox and Carrick and Comyn the younger of Badenoch, were the principal nobles contributing to the Scottish army (cf. *Chron. Rishanger*, 414).

62. *Chron. Guisb.*, 328. Stevenson, *Documents*, ii, no.529, shows Edward I granting away property forfeited by James 'late' Stewart of Scotland, on August 31st, 1298.

63. G. W. S. Barrow, 'Lothian in the first War of Independence', *SHR*, lv (1976), 155-7.

64. *Cal. Docs. Scot.*, ii, no.1009; BL, MS Add.28024, fo.180; *Register and Records of Holm Cultram*, ed. F. Grainger and W. G. Collingwood (Cumberland and Westmorland Antiquarian and Archaeological Soc., Record Series, 7, 1929), 60 (misdated 1292). Megget was among Hay's forfeited lands; for the Hays at Megget cf. *Origines Parochiales*, i, 223; *Melrose Liber*, no.264. Others known to have been forfeited at this time include Nicholas de Soules, David of Brechin, Neil Cockburn, John Marischal, John of St Michael, Roger of Ale Moor, Alexander Lindsay, Agnes de Vescy, Thomas Randolph, Herbert Maxwell, Richard of Glen, Patrick the Archer, Gilbert Macculloch(?), Robert of Moffat, Gilbert 'Mackinoluagh', Cuthbert MacGilwini and his son, Alexander Fraser and John of Luss. Cf. G. W. S. Barrow, 'The aftermath of war: Scotland and England in the late thirteenth and early fourteenth centuries', *Trans. Roy. Hist. Soc.* 5th ser., xxviii (1978), 116-19.

65. *Chron. Guisb.*, 327. The account in the text is chiefly based on this source, which gives much the fullest account evidently composed by an eyewitness or from information supplied by one.

66. *Chron. Fordun*, i, 330.

67. *Ibid.*

68. *Chron. Rishanger*, 187, gives what is probably one of the earliest and most authentic reports of this remark: 'I have browghte ȝowe to the ryng, hoppe ȝef ȝe kunne'. There seems no reason to doubt

either that Wallace spoke, or that the greater part of his force at Falkirk would understand, the Middle English speech which developed into Scots.

69. *Cal. Docs. Scot.*, ii, nos. 1007, 1011.

70. *Chron. Rishanger*, 188; *Cal. Docs. Scot.*, ii, 147, 202; for Jay see *SHR*, v, 23-4.

71. *Chron. Rishanger*, 387; cf. Bartholomew Cotton, *Historia Anglicana*, 344.

72. *Chron. Guisb.*, 328.

73. *Ibid.*, (severely damaging Scone Abbey, *Scone Liber*, no.124). *Chron. Guisb.*, shows that Edward wished to proceed to Galloway but was deterred by shortage of food; Cotton (*loc. cit.*) says that many Scots with their forces gathered in Galloway; Bruce was well placed to lead this rallying of forces which, presumably, had had no hand in the battle of Falkirk.

74. Stevenson, *Documents*, ii, 413-4.

75. *Cal. Docs. Scot.*, ii, no.1009; BL, MS Add.28024, fo.180.

76. *Chron. Rishanger, 388.*

77. SRO, Dudhope Muniments, Box 40, bdle 1, no.311.

78. *Chron. Rishanger*, 188. Cal. Docs. Scot., iv, Appendix I, no.7, suggests strongly that Lochmaben castle was in the younger Bruce's hands in May 1298.

79. SRO, Dudhope Muniments, Box 40, bdle 1, no.311.

80. *Cal. Docs. Scot.*, ii, 535.

81. SRO, Dudhope Muniments, Box, 40, bdle 1, no.311; *APS*, i, 454; *Hist. MSS. Comm., 5th Report* Appendix 612.

82. Sir Walter Scott, *Minstrelsy of the Scottish Border* (ed. T. Henderson, 1931), 616; *Hist. MSS. Comm., 5th Rep.*, App. 612; *Kelso Liber*, no.397.

83. *Arbroath Liber*, i, no.231.

84. *SHR*, xxiv, 325.

85. *Arbroath Liber*, i, no.231; *Cal. Docs. Scot.*, ii, 439; *Laing Chrs.*, no.18; *Kelso Liber*, no.193; *Cal. Docs. Scot.*, ii, no.1978. It is noteworthy that the sheriff of Lanark in 1301, Walter Logan, was out with Bruce in 1306. Apparently Logan was a tenant and vassal of Bruce, *Cal. Docs. Scot.*, iv, 387-8.

86. See, e.g., the reasonably orderly accounts rendered for the years 1302-4,

Cal. Docs. Scot., ii, no.1608, implying the existence of an established revenue system.

87. *Newbattle Registrum, passim*, contains several documents from which the descent of the Malherbe-Morham family may be traced, and refers to the property in the Carron valley which they inherited from the Colvilles.

88. *Ibid.*, nos. 216-19; *Cal. Docs. Scot.*, ii, no.1066.

89. *Ibid.*, 1949 (519).

90. *Ibid.*, no.1066.

91. *Ibid.*, nos. 1066 and 1108.

92. *Laing Chrs.*, no.18.

93. *Cal. Docs. Scot.*, ii, no.1949.

94. *Flores Historiarum*, iii, 113. It is not certain that Olifard was the first commander appointed by the Scots after they recaptured Stirling.

95. *Cal. Docs. Scot.*, ii, no.1517.

96. *Ibid.*, iii, 433, seems to show that in 1311-12 Gilbert Malherbe, though not then sheriff of Stirling, had held the office recently. For his subsequent career, cf. *Reg. Mag. Sig*, i, Appendix 2, no.516; *Chron. Fordun*, i, 348; Barbour, *Bruce*, 338.

97. Stevenson, *Documents*, ii, no.527, a letter written by Sir John Kingston, commander of Edinburgh Castle, dated August 9th. The year must be 1299, as noted by F. M. Powicke, *The Thirteenth Century*, 696, n.1. Kingston's news was that the earl of Buchan, the bishop of St Andrews and the earls and magnates of Scotland were taking part personally in the raid.

98. Stevenson, *Documents*, ii, no.527.

99. PRO, C.47/22/8 (calendared somewhat misleadingly by Bain, *Cal. Docs. Scot.*, ii, no.1978; there is a facsimile in *Nat. MSS. Scot.*, Pt. II, no.8). In this document, partly illegible, the list of earls runs 'le counte de Carrik' le counte de Boghan le counte [   ]le le counte de Menethet3.' Atholl was the only earldom for which the thirteenth-century form might end in the letters 'le'.

100. PRO, C. 47/22/8. *Cal. Docs. Scot.*, ii, no.1978, omits this significant fact.

101. Stevenson, *Documents*, ii, no.527.

102. *Cal. Docs. Scot.*, ii, no.1978; Stevenson, *Documents*, ii, no.527.

103. See above, n.99. For Wallace's visit to France, see below, p.110.

104. Stevenson, *Documents*, ii, no.445. The 'Laclan' or 'Lohlan' 'Macrogri' of this memorandum, and his brother Roderick, are the Rolandus filius Alani and his brother Roderick of the preceding document, *ibid.*, no.444, and also the 'sons of Roderick' of *ibid.*, no.615. Lachlan and Roderick were sons of Alan son of Roderick (son of Reginald son of Somerled); hence they were 'Macalans', but also, by line, 'Macruaries'. The name Macruarie has usually been given to the family here. For Lachlan's career see Barrow, *Kingdom*, 381-2, and *Memoranda de Parliamento*, 191.

CHAPTER SEVEN
The King over the Water

1. *APS*, i, 454. Contact between Scotland and France was evidently maintained by the bishop of Dunkeld (for whom see below, p.350) and John de Soules, who received payments at the French court in February and May, 1299, the former by the hand of Patrick of 'Auroacin in Scotland' ('Over Ayton, Berwickshire?), knight: *Les journaux du trésor de Philippe IV le Bel*, ed. J. Viard (1940), nos. 2118, 2539.

2. *Ibid.*

3. This is not given in the printed text, but may be seen on the original, PRO, E.39/14/14; cf. *Foedera*, i, 915.

4. It was still holding out in August 1299, Stevenson, *Documents*, ii, no.527, but had submitted by the end of the year when the garrison was faced by starvation, *Chron. Rishanger*, 402. They were allowed to return to England unharmed, *Flores Historiarum*, iii, 133, 310. Cf. also for this episode, *Chron. Guisb.*, 332.

5. Stones, *Relations*, no.27.

6. *Les journaux du trésor*, ed. Viard, nos.3901, 3908, 3504: the surname forms being Li Galoys (Wallace), Moubray, Fressel (Fraser), Viezpont (Vieuxpont), Letcham (Leitholm), Fondrin (*sic*, for Foudrin', i.e. Fotheringay).

7. *Cal. Docs. Scot.*, ii, nos. 171, 172. *Yester Writs*, no.18, is a charter issued by Hugh of Fotheringay who may be the knight in Wallace's company or perhaps his son.

8. Stones and Simpson, *Great Cause*, ii, 85.

9. Assuming that this Roger Moubray belonged to the Scottish branch of the family whose chief member in this period was Sir Geoffrey Moubray justiciar of Lothian, 1294-6. The personal name Roger was used by the Scottish Moubrays: Barrow, *Anglo-Norman Era*, 186.

10. Stevenson, *Documents*, ii, 94.

11. PRO, S. C.1/61/32.

12. Some versions of Bower's *Scotichronicon* have an account, perhaps somewhat exaggerated, of Wallace's reception at the court of Philip IV. He was, we are told, held in the highest honour by the king, who was reluctant to allow him out of his company: *Chron. Bower*, ii, 176 n.

13. *SHR*, xxiv, 246.

14. *Chron. Lanercost*, 177; cf. *Cal. Docs. Scot.*, ii, nos. 728, 729.

15. *Ibid.*, no.728. The Gallovidians' petition to Edward I to be relieved of the burden of 'surdit de sergaunt' (for which see *SHR*, xxxix, 170-5), may belong to this period; *Cal. Docs. Scot.*, ii, no.1874.

16. *SHR*, xxiv, 246.

17. Morris, *Welsh Wars*, 298; *Chron. Guisb.*, 334, *Chron. Lanercost*, 194; *Cal. Docs. Scot.*, ii, no.1136.

18. *Liber quotidianus contrarotulatoris garderobae anno regni Edwardi Primi vicesimo octavo* (Soc. Antiquaries of London, 1787), 120, 123; *Cal. Docs. Scot.*, ii, 284-5; *Chron. Rishanger*, 439. Malcolm le fiz Lengleys was empowered to attack the Scots by sea in July 1300, Stevenson, *Documents*, ii, no.597.

19. 'Edward I's pele at Lochmaben', *Dumfriesshire Trans.*, 3rd Ser., xxxi, 64, n. 36. Bruce had attacked Lochmaben and threatened Annan after the Peebles meeting in August 1299, *Cal. Docs. Scot.*, ii, 283-4.

20. *Ibid.*, no.1101.

21. *Chron. Rishanger*, 440.

22. *Ibid.*, 440; *Siege of Carlaverock* (ed. N. H. Nicolas, 1828), 82-5. The writer of the ballad on the siege says that the king spared the lives of the garrison, who numbered about sixty, *ibid.*, 86-7. *Cal. Docs. Scot.*, ii, nos.1162, 1196, show that the constable and twenty-one of the

garrison were spared and imprisoned at Newcastle and Appleby. The more laconic account in *Chron. Lanercost*, 194, says that many found in the castle were hanged.

23. *Chron. Rishanger*, 440.

24. *Ibid.*, where Twynam should be read for Swynam; cf. *Cal. Docs. Scot.*, ii, nos.1147-50.

25. *Chron. Rishanger*, 441 and n. 1. The MS. reads *qrend'* (British Library, MS. Cotton Claudius D vi, fo. 175v); there is no doubt that this is a mistaken form of 'Crith', i.e. the River Cree; cf. *Chron. Lanercost*, 194, *usque ad aquam de Grithe* (*recte* Crithe).

26. *Chron. Rishanger*, 442, where the editor's marginal note is certainly an error.

27. *Ibid.*, 441-2; *Cal. Docs. Scot.*, ii, nos. 1147, 1148, 1159.

28. *Foedera*, i, 924; *Chron. Guisb.*, 334; *Chron. Fordun*, i, 331.

29. *Chron. Rishanger*, 447.

30. *Ibid.*, 447. The Scots retorted that they for their part would fight to the last to resist King Edward's schemes.

31. Theiner, *Monumenta*, no.368; *Cal. Papal Letters*, i, 590.

32. *Ibid.*, December 18th, 1300, is the last known document in which they appear as Guardians. The earliest known document in which Soules appears as Guardian is that recorded by *Chron. Fordun*, i, 332, under 1300 by mistake for 1301. The statement in one MS. of Fordun that Soules acted as 'one of the Guardians of Scotland making no mention of the other' may be explained by reference to Fordun's earlier statement (ibid., 331) that John Comyn remained Guardian continuously from 1298 to 1304. But the other MSS. merely have 'John de Soules Guardian of the kingdom of Scotland'; and the statement about Comyn may be wrong.

33. *Chron. Fordun.*, i, 331.

34. *Cal. Docs. Scot.*, ii, no.1452.

35. *APS*, i, 445; for identification of 'Ardrossan', cf. *Dumfriesshire Trans.*, 3rd Ser., xxvi, 174-81.

36. *Cal. Docs. Scot.*, ii, 296.

37. *Chron. Fordun*, i, 331.

38. N. H. Reid, 'The Political Role of the Monarchy in Scotland, 1249-1329'

(unpublished Edinburgh PhD thesis, 1984), 180-8. It is not possible to do justice to Dr. Reid's closely-argued reconsideration of the evidence in a brief summary.

39. *Foedera*, i, 926; on the manner in which the barons were required, after the letter had been engrossed, to affix their seals, cf. *The Ancestor*, no.6 (1903), 188-90.

40. *Chron. Rishanger*, 451.

41. *Cal. Docs. Scot.*, iv, 449; cf. T. F. Tout, *Chapters in Administrative History*, ii, 70, n.

42. *Chron. Picts-Scots*, 221-31; Stones, *Documents*, no.30.

43. *Cal. Docs. Scot.*, ii, no.1167, which belongs to 1301, not 1300; cf. *SHR*, xxxiv, 130 and n.5.

44. *Chron. Picts-Scots*, 216-21; Stones, *Documents*, no.28.

45. Dowden, *Bishops*, 151; Theiner, *Monumenta*, no.364. Instituted rector of Lilford, Northamptonshire, 1282, on presentation of Sir William Murray; resigned next year, succeeded by John Murray (*Rolls and Register of Bishop Oliver Sutton*, ed. R. Hill (Lincoln Record Soc.), ii, 16, 26). Rector of Bothwell (the principal seat of Sir William Murray of Bothwell) in 1296, *Cal. Docs. Scot.*, ii, 212.

46. E. M. Barron, *Scottish War of Independence*, 204-5; his presentation to Lilford rectory (see previous note) would fit in well with the suggested relationship.

47. Stevenson, *Documents*, ii, no.569.

48. Stevenson, *Wallace Docs.*, 163 (= PRO, S. C.1/30/81). Professor Robert Fawtier kindly informed me that Philip IV was at Pierrefonds on November 3rd, 8th and 9th. Among the documents found in Wallace's possession at the time of his capture in 1305 were safe-conducts issued by King Philip and King Hakon of Norway: F. Palgrave, *The Antient Kalendars and Inventories of the Treasury of His Majesty's Exchequer, etc.* (1836), i. 134.

49. *Chron. Rishanger*, 451. Rishanger adds the name of the 'chancellor of Gascony', but I am assured by Dr Pierre Chaplais that there was no such official in 1300. Perhaps the third member of the English mission was Edward I's friend Otto de Granson.

50. *Chron. Picts-Scots*, 232-71 (*Instructiones*); 271-84 (*processus* of Master Baldred Bisset). The date is deduced from *ibid.*, 271, 'soon after Whitsun last past'. These Latin texts apparently survive only in *Chron. Bower* (where they were taken from a lost work attributed to Master Alan of Montrose). A very full contemporary summary in French is in British Library, MS. Cotton Vespasian F. vii, fo.15 (Stones, *Relations* no.31).

51. *Chron. Rishanger*, 451.

52. *Chron. Picts-Scots*, 239-40.

53. British Library, MS. Cotton Vespasian F. vii, fo.16.

54. *Chron. Fordun*, i, 332, where the year should be 1301. For the date being after Whitsun, cf. *Chron. Picts-Scots*, 271.

55. For these men's careers see Watt, *Graduates*, 49-51, 176-7, 206-7.

56. *Chron. Wyntoun (Laing)*, ii, 351.

57. *Cambuskenneth Registrum*, no.3; cf. *Newbattle Registrum*, no.59; *Historiae Dunelmensis Scriptores Tres* (ed. J. Raine, Surtees Soc., 1839), 93; R. Brentano, *York Metropolitan Jurisdiction*, 126, 159.

58. *Nat. MSS. Scot.*, ii, Pl.XII; NLS, MS. Adv.15.1.18, no.43 (Sept. 1289).

59. *Ibid.*; cf. *Cal. Docs. Scot.*, ii, references in index s.v. Dunwich.

60. *Nat. MSS. Scot.*, ii, Pl.XII. Uberto was bishop of Bologna from 1302 to 1322 Baldred Bisset, 'scozzese', doctor of laws, was acting at Bologna as vicar of Bishop Uberto in an arbitration of April 15th, 1305, G. C. Trombelli, *Memorie istoriche concernenti le due canoniche di Santa Maria di Reno e di San Salvatore insieme unite* (Bologna, 1752), 71.

61. PRO, S. C.1/21/166, summarized in *Cal. Docs. Scot.*, ii, no.1431. Probably 1302 is the right year, if the letter of Philip IV was brought back to Scotland by Lamberton after his visit to France in 1301, referred to in *APS*, i, 454.

62. *Chron. Picts-Scots*, 283.

63. Stevenson, *Documents*, ii, nos. 579, 586.

64. *Ibid.*, no.603. 'Castrum Jeuriaci in Montana', diocese Langres, belonging to the abbot of Cluny, is to be identified with the illustrious Château Gévrey-Chambertin. Cf. A. I. Cameron in *Papers of the British School at Rome*, xii (1932), 36 and n.1.

65. *SHR*, xxiv, 130-1. Stevenson, *Documents*, ii, nos. 579-80, 586, 603.

66. *Ibid.*, nos. 579-80, 586, 603.

67. A list of these acts has been made by G. G. Simpson, *Handlist of the Acts of Alexander III, the Guardians and John* (*Regesta Regum Scottorum*, 1960, duplicated), Appendix, nos. 417-22.

68. SRO, Dudhope Muniments, Box 40, bdle 1, no.309.

69. J. H. Stevenson and M. Wood, *Scottish Heraldic Seals*, no.22.

70. NLS, Chr.4793.

71. *St Andrews Liber*, 120.

72. As 'Master N. de Sancto Andrea', *Chron. Rishanger*, 263; Barrow, *Kingdom*, 245-7.

73. *Glasgow Registrum*, no.239.

74. *Chron. Bower*, i, 362.

75. BL, MS. Add.33245, fo.86v.

76. *Foedera*, i, 925.

77. *Cal. Docs. Scot.*, ii, no.1244 (where Balnul is in error for Balmil).

78. *Ibid.*, no.1191.

79. *Ibid.*, no.1220; Stevenson, *Documents*, ii, no.612.

80. *Ibid.*, no.611. 'Stanhouse' is clearly Stonehouse near Strathaven. Simon Fraser had been at least nominally on the English side until the capture of Caerlaverock, where he was present in the meinie of the earl of Dunbar (*Siege of Carlaverock*, ed. N. H. Nicolas, 36; 'laonis' is of course 'Lothian', sometimes used for the title of the earls of Dunbar or March, not 'Lennox' as supposed by Nicolas). Fraser must have gone over to the Scots about the turn of the years 1300 and 1301, while at Wark on Tweed; he carried off the horses and armour of Sir William Durham, *Cal. Docs. Scot.*, ii, no.1317. *Ibid.*, no.1121, reporting that 'the Guardian of the realm of Scotland' had entered Cunningham, probably belongs to this period.

81. *Ibid.*, iv, 449; cf. *ibid.*, ii, no.1235.

82. *Ibid.*, ii, nos. 1224-5, 1233, 1235-6, 1239-40.

83. J. F. Lydon, 'Irish levies in the Scottish Wars', *The Irish Sword*, v (1962), 212-3.

84. *Cal. Docs. Scot.*, ii, no.1282; for the peace of Asnières, cf. *Treaty Rolls*, i (ed.

P. Chaplais, 1955), 149-52; English draft in Palgrave, *Docs.*, 241-7.

85. *Ibid.*, iv, 451: the news of the surrender of Turnberry reached Edward while still at Bothwell, i.e. before September 27th, and the surrender may have occurred by the beginning of September, *ibid.*, 448.

86. *Ibid.*, ii, no.1236.

87. N. Trivet, *Annales* (ed. T. Hog), 397, n.7. For John de St John's wardenship of Galloway in 1301 and lieutenancy in Scotland in 1302 see *Cal. Close R.*, *1296-1302*, 421, 540.

88. Illegible in MS. In the second lacuna some words following *pouer*, 'force', cannot be read.

89. *SHR*, xxxiv, 131-2; Stones, *Relations*, no.32.

90. *Ibid.*, 343.

91. J. F. Lydon, in *The Irish Sword*, v (1962), 209-10; G. H. Orpen, *Ireland under the Normans*, iv, 144.

92. *Melrose Liber*, i, no.351.

93. *APS*, i, 454. *Treaty Rolls*, i, (ed. P. Chaplais, 1955), 149-52, gives the English and French versions of the agreement.

94. There is no evidence of his presence in Scotland in the intervening years, a long period for one of the principal bishops to have left no record of his presence. The dean of Dunkeld (Master Hervey of Crambeth) is found acting in place of the bishop in a transaction of 1303, in association with John Comyn of Badenoch (either the Guardian or less probably his father), the bishops of Glasgow and Ross, and the abbot of Scone, *Coupar Angus Chrs.*, i, nos. 69, 73. The dean of Dunkeld was functioning as Bishop Crambeth's vicar-general in 1300 and in 1302, *ibid.*, nos.66, 72. French financial record shows Bishop Crambeth ('Sir Matthew bishop of Dunkeld in Scotland') receiving an annual pension of 200 *livres tournois* from September 1298 to October 1301: *Les journaux du trésor*, ed. Viard, nos. 1106, 2640, 3520, 4138, 4149, 4823, 5322. Unfortunately, the record is missing for subsequent years.

95. *Chron. Fordun*, i, 333, 336. *Ibid*, 331, says Comyn was Guardian continuously from 1298 to 1304, but we have seen reasons to suggest that he was not in office in 1301 or 1302. One must, however, note

Cal. Docs. Scot., iv, no.1827 (= PRO, C.153/1, fo.140), which, if the regnal year is correctly stated as 31st, shows that John de Soules was believed by an Aberdeen jury to have still been 'Guardian of the land of Scotland on behalf of the community of that land' on November 11th, 1303. If, however, the regnal year should be xxx instead of xxxi, this would make Soules Guardian in November 1302, and this would square well with our other evidence of his term of office. The apparent date of this record supports the suggestion of Dr Norman Reid (above, p.115) that Soules and Comyn were joint (senior and junior) Guardians from 1301 to 1304.

96. *Chron. Rishanger*, 213.

97. *Chron. Fordun*, i, 333-5, where *Marcii* should be read for *Augusti* in line one of 333, i.e., February 24th, 1303, Quadragesima Sunday. Cf. *Chron. Guisb.*, 351-2.

98. H. M. Colvin and R. A. Brown, *The History of the King's Works* (1963), i, 415. Possibly the Scots even seized Edinburgh castle in June, 1302 (BL, MS. Cott. Cleop. D iii, fo.52v).

99. For the Irish element in the invasion of 1303-4, at 3457 men the largest ever brought from Ireland to serve in Edward I's Scottish wars, see J. F. Lydon, 'Edward I, Ireland and Scotland, 1303-1304', in *England and Ireland in the later middle ages*, ed. J. F. Lydon (Blackrock, 1981), 43-61.

100. *Flores Historiarum*, iii, 113-4; *Cal. Docs. Scot.*, ii, nos. 1687, 1386.

101. Cf. Barron, *Scottish War of Independence*, 192-3.

102. Typescript Itinerary of Edward I, PRO, Literary Search Room, Press Mk.15/79C, Lochindorb, September 24th-25th, Gartenrothe (Castle Roy?), September 28th-October 2nd; to which add privy seal writ dated Lochindorb October 1st, *Yorkshire Inquisitions*, ed. Brown, iii, 72n.

103. *Cal. Docs. Scot.*, ii, no.1432, and *ibid.*, iv, 474.

104. Stevenson, *Documents*, ii, no.645; J. F. Lydon, *England and Ireland in the later middle ages*, 50.

105. *APS*, i, 454-5. Professor Stones has kindly pointed out that it is possible that this letter never reached the Scottish

leaders at home, for the only extant version was intercepted. But we cannot be sure that no other copy got through.

106. Cf. Galatians, II, 2.

107. Palgrave, *Docs. Hist. Scot.*, 333.

108. *Flores Historiarum*, iii, 118.

109. *Ibid.*, 113; *Chron. Rishanger*, 388, 402.

110. *Flores Historiarum*, iii, 118.

111. *Ibid.*, 319-20.

112. *Cal. Docs. Scot.*, ii, no.1668.

113. *Ibid.*, no.1560; PRO, E.101/12/25.

114. *Foedera*, i, 966.

115. *Scalacronica*, 127.

116. *Cal. Docs. Scot.*, iv, no.1827.

117. *Ibid.*, ii, no.1455. No.1848 is a safe-conduct for Master Baldred (Bisset) 'the Scot', but it seems unlikely that Bisset came to Scotland. By 1310 he was busy defending the late Pope Boniface VIII at Avignon (*Innes Review*, xxv, 147, n.306).

118. Palgrave, *Docs. Hist. Scot.*, 279-285.

119. PRO, C.47/22/4. These are draft peace terms, extremely fragmentary and largely illegible. They begin '*Les messages qui furent enuiez de part la comunaute descoce*'. They ask for Sir John de Soules to be received into King Edward's peace and faith, and the king's answer begins, '*A ce le Roi respont qe endroit du dit Johan il ne vuet suffrir qe ...*' There can be little doubt that some particular stiffness of Edward I towards Soules lay behind his conduct as reported by Grey, *Scalacronica*, 127, 'Sir John refused the conditions, left Scotland and died in France.' But it seems most unlikely that Soules ever returned to Scotland.

120. Palgrave, *Docs. Hist. Scot.*, 287.

121. *Cal. Docs. Scot.*, ii, no.1741; *Rotuli Parliamentorum*, i, 212-3.

122. *The Gascon Calendar of 1322*, ed. G. P. Cuttino (Camden Third Series, lxx, 1949), no.437 (September, 1304).

123. *Ibid.*; cf. *Foedera*, i, 974-5, the terms as modified (and largely moderated) by October 1305.

124. Stevenson, *Documents*, ii, no.471. Cf. Palgrave, *Docs. Hist. Scot.*, 284. For the contrast between 'will' and 'grace', see *Flores Historiarum*, iii, 320. The provision in the treaty of February 1304: 'as for Sir William Wallace, it is agreed that he may

place himself in the will and in the grace of our lord the king, if it shall seem good to him [Wallace] to do so' is presumably the authority for Sir Maurice Powicke's statement that 'Wallace might have made his peace if he had wished' (*The Thirteenth Century*, 333). But although it may seem to contrast with the king's other provisions regarding Wallace (especially Stevenson, *Documents*, ii, no.471; Palgrave, *Docs. Hist. Scot.*, 284), this provision can hardly be taken to mean that Edward I would have extended his *peace* to Wallace. The indictment against Wallace at his trial declares that the king offered him peace, but this document can hardly be trusted on such a point, Stevenson, *Wallace Docs.*, 192.

125. Palgrave, *Docs. Hist. Scot.*, 276.

126. *Ibid.*

127. *Ibid.*, 323-4.

CHAPTER EIGHT
Defeat

1. Palgrave, *Docs. Hist. Scot.*, 286-7.
2. For the authorities for the St Andrews parliament, see *SHR*, xxv, 311, n., and see especially Stevenson, *Documents*, ii, 471, n.1.
3. Palgrave, *Docs. Hist. Scot.*, 194-7.
4. *Ibid.*, 299-301. *Foedera*, i, 955, assigns this to 1306, an impossible year.
5. Palgrave, *Docs. Hist. Scot.*, pp.ccxxii-cxxiii.
6. *Cal. Docs. Scot.*, ii, pp.xxii-xxiii, and no.730.
7. *Ibid.*, p.xxiii.
8. Cremannan, whose name survives only on the large-scale maps, was a considerable barony in Balfron, Stirlingshire. For Sir Thomas of Cremannan's grant of the patronage of Balfron church to Inchaffray abbey see *Inchaffray Chrs.*, no.119.
9. *Cal. Docs. Scot.*, ii, no.1481. See above, p.151.
10. Palgrave, *Docs. Hist. Scot.*, 288, where the editor prints 'Glames' (!) for 'Slanes', i.e. Old Slains. 'Morthelagh' represents Mortlach or Balvenie, in Banffshire.
11. *Cal. Docs. Scot.*, ii, no.1529.
12. *Ibid.*, nos. 1528 and 1530 (= PRO, E.39/100, 132 B, from which it appears that the name of the canon of Elgin, prebendary of Inverkeithney, was Master

Geoffrey of [Dol] bodlech, i.e. Dunballoch, in Kirkhill).
13. *Ibid.*, nos. 1543, 1496, 1506.
14. *Ibid.*, no.1713.
15. F. W. Maitland, *Memoranda de Parliamento* (Rolls Series), 14. Wishart's journey south can be traced from an indulgence issued at Torksey in Lincolnshire, February 18th, 1305, and from his witnessing, with Robert Bruce earl of Carrick, Edward I's charter of confirmation for Coldingham Priory, Westminster, March 20th: *Registrum Antiquissimum of Lincoln*, ii (ed. C. W. Foster, 1933), no.423; J. Raine, *History of North Durham*, Appendix no.437.
16. *APS*, i, 119-20; *Memoranda de Parliamento*, 293; cf. *ibid*, 178.
17. *APS*, i, 119 shows that Patrick earl of Dunbar (or March) failed to serve on the commission, and his place was taken by Sir John Menteith. The earl was at Dunbar on February 24th, 1305: *Kelso Liber*, no.307. Cf. *Cal. Docs. Scot.*, ii, no.1244, for Adam Gordon and John of Inchmartin. Under the Ordinance of 1305, Adam Gordon was to be one of the justices of Lothian and John of Inchmartin was to be sheriff of Perth.
18. *APS*, ii, 119; *Handbook of British Chronology* (2nd edn). 513.
19. E. M. Barron, *Scottish War of Independence*, 175-8. It should be noted that *Flores Historiarum*, iii, 124, says that the two Scottish bishops at the September parliament were St Andrews and Glasgow; but according to *APS*, i, 119, they should have been St Andrews and Dunkeld, and the name in *Flores Historiarum* may be a mistake. The bishops of St Andrews and Glasgow were at Melrose on Thursday, November 4th 1305: *Melrose Liber*, no.349.
20. *APS*, i, 119-22; Stones, *Relations*, no.33; summarized, *Cal. Docs. Scot.*, ii, no.1691.
21. The Ordinance is written in French, and gives the geographical limits as 'entre la rivere de Forth et les Montz' and 'dela les Montz'. Clearly, 'les Montz' is both a translation and an etymological equivalent of 'le Moneth', the Mounth, the ancient name given to the hills stretching from Loch Ericht to the sea between Aberdeen and Stonehaven (Barrow, *Kingdom*, 137-8).

22. Palgrave, *Docs. Hist. Scot.*, 292-3. This council included all the ten commissioners elected at the Scone parliament of May 1305, including the earl of Dunbar who had failed to serve on the commission.

23. *Ibid.*, 293.

24. Powicke, *The Thirteenth Century*, 711.

25. Stones, *Relations*, p.251.

26. *Ibid.*, p.251, 'l'usage de Scot' et de Bret' desorendroit soit defendu.'

27. E. M. Barron, *Scottish War of Independence*, 210, followed by A. M. Mackenzie, *Robert Bruce, King of Scots* (1934), 139; cf. the latter's *Scottish Pageant* (1946), 173-4.

28. *APS*, i, 633-5. It may have been to this 'usage of Scots and Brets' that *Flores Historiarum*, iii, 124, refers in saying that when Edward I approved the Ordinance in the September parliament 'he completely annulled only one single article, concerning a certain (native) Scottish judgement (*de quodam judicio Scotico*)'.

29. Cf. K. H. Jackson, 'The Britons in Southern Scotland', *Antiquity*, xxix, 88.

30. Palgrave, *Docs. Hist. Scot.*, 276, 284, 295; Stevenson, *Documents*, ii, no.633.

31. *Cal. Docs. Scot.*, iv, 477.

32. Stevenson, *Wallace Docs.*, 101-2, 147. Palgrave, *Docs. Hist. Scot.*, 295, has an entry 'Of land, that is £100 (worth) by [*par*, taken by the editor to mean *pour*] John Menteith', usually understood to mean that this was Mentcith's reward for Wallace's capture. It is not clear beyond cavil that the entry has this meaning.

33. Stevenson, *Documents*, ii, 453, shows Menteith still Scottish in September 1303, while *Cal. Docs. Scot.*, ii, no.1474 shows him in King Edward's peace and confidence by March 1304.

34. The exceptional trust reposed in Menteith by Edward I is shown by the fact that Dumbarton castle, burgh and sheriffdom were put in his charge.

35. Stevenson, *Wallace Docs.*, 147, 189; also in *Annales Londonienses*, in *Chronicles of the Reign of Edward I and Edward II*, ed. Stubbs, i, 139-42. For William de Leyre, alderman of Baynard's Castle Ward, 1298-1319, sheriff in 1290, and several times MP, cf. E. Ekwall, *Two early London Subsidy Rolls* (Lund, 1951), 163, 275.

36. M. H. Keen, 'Treason trials under the law of arms', *TRHS*, 5th Ser., xii, 87, 93, 103, seeks to show that Wallace's trial followed the normal pattern of treason trials under the law of arms, but his argument is unconvincing. There is no evidence that Wallace's trial was under the 'law of arms'; it was held by justices (including common law judges) acting on a commission of gaol delivery 'according to the law and the usage of our realm' (Stevenson, *Wallace Docs.*, 187). Moreover, Mr Keen ignores the principal objection to the trial, which was that Wallace was not one of King Edward's lieges, as Wallace himself was able to declare at his trial.

37. Stevenson, *Wallace Docs.*, 189.

38. *Ibid.*, 193. These four towns are named in what seem to be the most authoritative sources; *Chron. Lanercost*, 203, has Newcastle, Berwick, Perth and Aberdeen.

39. J. G. Bellamy, *Law of treason in England in the later Middle Ages* (1970), accepts the charge of treason apparently on the ground that King John's submission of 1296 was lawfully valid and must have bound all Scots. Had the law concerning fealty and treason already been so clear cut in the period it would be impossible to explain why Edward I found it necessary to receive so many individual fealties as he did in 1291, 1296 and 1304.

40. Wyntoun, *Original Chronicle* (Laing), 348-9.

41. Stones, *Relations*, p.255. The words themselves do not necessarily imply mistrust, since *ibid.*, 121, tells the chamberlain (whose loyalty was not in question) to commit the sheriffdom of Berwick to a man 'for whom he shall be willing to answer'.

42. *Scottish War of Independence*, 172.

43. F. Palgrave, *Antient Kalendars and Inventories*, i (1836), 134.

44. PRO, C.47/22/8. See above, p.107.

45. *Cal. Docs. Scot.*, ii, no.1745.

46. *Ibid.*

47. Barbour, *Bruce*, 14-20; *Chron. Fordun*, i, 337-40; Wyntoun, *Original Chronicle* (Laing), 364-8.

48. *Handbook of British Chronology* (2nd edn), 513, gives no parliament between September 1305 and May 1306.

49. *Chron. Guisb.*, 366-7; *Scalacronica*, 129-30.

50. Palgrave, *Docs. Hist. Scot.*, 335.

51. Above, p.60, n.2.

52. The English proposal of July, 1297 that Marjorie Bruce should be a hostage (Palgrave, *Docs. Hist. Scot.*, 199) seems to be the earliest mention of her in record.

53. *Cal. Docs. Scot.*, ii, 340-1.

54. *SHR*, xxxiv, 127-8.

55. *Cal. Docs. Scot.*, ii, nos. 1420, 1437, 1658.

56. *Ibid.*, no.1356, given in full (with material omitted by Bain), Stevenson, *Documents*, ii, no.438, where it is misdated 1297. Cf. *Scottish War of Independence* 126-8.

57. *Cal. Docs. Scot.*, ii, no.1385. Botetourte's relationship to King Edward appears in the Hailes Abbey chronicle (BL, MS. Cott. Cleop. D iii, fo. 51) in an otherwise correct and detailed genealogical table. This chronicle takes the closest interest in the Plantagenet royal house and is well-informed about its relationships.

58. *Cal. Docs. Scot.*, ii, no 1374.

59. *Ibid.*, no.1437.

60. *Ibid.*

61. *Ibid.*, no.1465; cf. *ibid.*, no.1432 and iv, 474.

62. His use of the title is shown by documents at the Essex Record Office, D/DBa T4, D/DBa T1/4.

63. Guisborough Priory obit 'XI Kal. May'; died 'shortly after Easter' (March 29th), buried at Holm Cultram: *Yorks. Arch. Journal*, xiii, 255n.; *Chron. Guisb.*, 363. *Cal. Docs. Scot.*, ii, nos.1493, 1495 are misdated by Bain; they refer to Bruce's grandfather and belong to April 1295.

64. Stevenson, *Documents*, ii, no.641.

65. *Ibid.*, nos. 1540, 1546.

66. *Ibid.*, nos. 1588, 1604. *Ibid.*, iv, no.1818, seems to refer to Bruce's father, and therefore to belong to c. 1302.

67. *Ibid.*, ii, no.1606 (10).

68. *Ibid.*, nos. 1708, 1736. Longmorn ('Launde Morgan') was a small forest south of Elgin.

69. *Ibid.*, no.394.

70. On this, see Ruth Crosby, 'Robert Mannyng of Brunne: a new biography', *Publications of the Modern Language Association of America*, lvii (1942), 15-28, esp. 22-4. It should be added that Robert Bruce the future king cannot have been at Cambridge between May 1297 and the beginning of 1302, and he is unlikely to have been able to visit Cambridge before October 1302.

71. *Letters from Northern Registers* (ed. J. Raine, Rolls Series), no.103 (which must date not later than February 25th, 1304; cf. *ibid.*, no.104).

72. *The Story of England by Robert Manning of Brunne* (ed. F. J. Furnivall, Rolls Series), i, 12-13; A. B. Emden, *A biographical register of the University of Cambridge to 1500* (Cambridge, 1963), 99-100.

73. It seems most improbable that Bruce was in the south as early as the spring of 1302; while his visit can hardly have been as late as 1305, since the poet Robert Manning was evidently present at the feast, and there is evidence which makes it unlikely that Manning was at Cambridge as late as that year. Bruce is not likely to have been in the south of England in 1304 before the Long Vacation.

74. Alexander Bruce is called 'dean of Glasgow' in the accounts of his death. Probably he was made dean with the approval of Wishart either at the end of 1305 or in the first half of 1306; indeed, his appointment may have been in consequence of his brother's coronation.

CHAPTER NINE
Revolution

1. *Hist. MSS. Comm. 14th Report, Strathmore and Kinghorne*, Appendix 177 (wrongly attributed to the future king's father). The original bears an endorsement relating to Greenan in Carrick, not under the elder Bruce's control; the clerk evidently changed his mind and used the parchment thus endorsed for Longforgan instead. The charter must date between April 21st 1304 and March 25th 1306 and probably belongs to 1304 or 1305. Cf. *Cal. Docs. Scot.*, ii, 202. It might be tempting to re-date to this period a suspiciously 'baronial' charter purporting to be issued by King Robert I (*RRS*, v, no.387; *HMC*

15th Rep., pt.8, 41, no.74), but its witnesses suggest rather a date of *c.* 1312.

2. *Scalacronica* (Maxwell), 28.

3. Wishart and Lamberton were together at Melrose on November 4th (*Melrose Liber*, no.349).

4. *Chron. Guisb.*, 367.

5. Best edited in Stones, *Relations*, no.34. First edited, very badly, by H. T. Riley, *Registra Johannis Whethamstede etc.*, (Rolls Series) ii, 347-53. Although commented upon by Charles Johnson, *EHR*, xxxiii, 366-7, this highly important document was in effect rediscovered by Professor Stones. A clue to the explanation of why the newsletter was copied into the register of Abbot John Whethamstede of St Albans may be found in the next document copied into the MS, in the same handwriting (BL, MS. Cott. Tiberius E vi, fo.202r). This is a letter from Walter of Gloucester, king's escheator south of Trent (1298-1311) to his sub-escheator Nicholas of Wheathampstead, dated Westminster, March 15th, 1306, and referring to a royal writ dated February 17th/18th, 1306. Perhaps Walter was the friend addressed by the anonymous writer of the letter, and perhaps Nicholas, to whom it (or a copy) may have been sent for information, was an ancestor of Abbot John. There are references to Nicholas between 1301 and 1313 in *Cal. Close Rolls, 1296-1302*, 490, *1307-1313*, 132 and *Cal. Pat. R., 1307-13*, 584.

6. Rothesay belonged to James the Stewart, with whom Boyd seems to have had some connexion; G. Crawford, *History of the shire of Renfrew* (1710), 44. Inverkip was also in the Stewart's lordship, but whether held in demesne or not is uncertain.

7. Palgrave, *Docs. Hist. Scot.*, 315; *Cal. Docs. Scot.*, ii, no.1834.

8. *Macfarlane's Geographical Collections* (SHS), 187. There is little to be seen of the castle today, and the 1-inch Ordnance Survey Map does not indicate its site.

9. Stones, *Relations*, p.260: 'chastel Dananerbi (de Ananorbi)', for which I should propose to read 'Donauerthi', i.e. Dunaverty. In *ibid*, line 13, I read (in the MS) 'ly', and would reconstruct 'en lyle de Kentir'. I suppose also that 'Mac' should be supplied before 'Coyllan' in line 15.

10. For this identification, see above, p.58, n.11. The evidence that Malcolm le Fiz Lengleys was put in possession of Kintyre by King Edward without due process of law is to be found in *Rotuli Scotiae*, i, 22-3; PRO, S. C.1/18/147.

11. Stones, *Relations*, no.34, p.130.

12. *Ibid.*, no.34, pp.266-9.

13. *Ibid.*, p.263. The newsletter gives yet another example of Barbour's uncanny accuracy in detail, for he says that after Comyn's murder 'the lord of the Bruce to Glaskow raid', Barbour, *Bruce*, 24.

14. *Paisley Registrum*, 373-4, shows the bishop's presence at Glasgow on February 6th, 1306. It does not seem rash to guess that Wishart knew in advance approximately when the *coup* was to be carried out.

15. Palgrave, *Docs. Hist. Scot.*, 348; see also below, p.186, n.112.

16. Stevenson, *Documents*, i, 169-70.

17. *Paisley Registrum*, 204 (January 18th, 1297).

18. It is possible that he was referring to Edward I's undertaking of June 1291 (of which Wishart himself had issued an inspeximus) to protect the liberties and privileges of holy church in Scotland. But the reign of King John had intervened since that date, and Edward had not renewed his undertaking after conquering Scotland in 1296.

19. Palgrave, *Docs. Hist. Scot.*, 335-6. Barbour, *Bruce*, 21, says that Bruce at once sent a letter to Lamberton telling him of the murder of Comyn; this may be true, for it would be in accord with their mutual band of June 1304.

20. Stones, *Relations*, no.34, p.267.

21. *Ibid.*, 'il se defendroit de plus long bastoun q'il eust'.

22. *Chron. Guisb.*, 367.

23. Marquess of Bute, 'Notice of a manuscript of the later part of the fourteenth century etc.', *PSAS*, New Ser., vii (1884), 166-92; Judges, ix, 8-15.

24. It may have been after Robert I's inauguration that Edward I granted Inchcolm, valued at £200 *p.a.*, to Newminster Abbey in Northumberland, ostensibly to compensate Newminster for its losses at the hands of the Scots (*Ancient Petitions relating to*

Northumberland, ed. C. M. Fraser, 194-5, 201).

25. *Cambuskenneth Reg.*, pp.lii-liii; A. A. M. Duncan, *SHR*, xlv (1966), 199.

26. *Foedera*, i, 1003. The abbey, Edward declared, was 'situated in the midst of a perverse nation'.

27. Palgrave, *Docs. Hist. Soc.*, 319.

28. *Flores Historiarum*, iii, 129-30; *Proc. Soc. Antiq. Scot.*, New Ser., vii, 172. *Scots Peerage*, ii, 258 and iv, 11 (and other authorities) are evidently in error in making Isabel daughter of Earl Duncan III rather than of Earl Colban (d. 1270). Earl Duncan IV is called her nephew by Robert Keith in a letter to Edward II of *c.* 1307: PRO, S. C. 1/37/107.

29. The sources mentioning the countess are *Chron. Guisb.*, 367; *Scalacronica*, 130; *Flores Historiarum*, iii, 324; and *Proc. Soc. Antiq. Scot.*, New Ser., vii, 172.

30. *St Andrews Liber*, 398 (*c.* 1287-95), probably north west of Balmullo; an estate later found as belonging to the earldom of Fife.

31. *Scalacronica*, 130. Cf. J. Nichols, *The History and Antiquities of the County of Leicester* (reprint edn., 1971), iii, pt.1, 129; pt.11, 1112-13. Earl John had Whitwick by the gift of his father Earl Alexander, who inherited it from Roger de Quincy earl of Winchester. Stones, *Relations*, p.262, suggests, surprisingly, that the earl of Buchan was with the earl of Atholl and in touch with Berwick at this point, but the source may not be completely reliable here.

32. *Chron. Guisb.*, 367.

33. This is the definitive conclusion reached by Professor Duncan after a careful study of Robert I's surviving acts: *RRS*, v, Introduction.

34. Information available to the authors of *Chron. Lanercost*, *Chron. Guisb.*, and *Scalacronica* (in the case of the last two, and possibly all three authorities, this was a single source) makes it plain that the act of making Bruce king was performed by the countess of Buchan on March 25th. Moreover, the weight of evidence supports the belief that the countess placed a coronet on the new king's head: *Chron. Guisb.*, 367; *Scalacronica*, 130; *Proc. Soc. Antiq. Scot.*, New Ser., vii, 175.

35. Stones, *Relations*, no.35, p.138; cf. M. Ash, 'William Lamberton, Bishop of St

Andrews', in *The Scottish Tradition*, ed. G. W. S. Barrow (1974), 48.

36. *Cal. Docs. Scot.*, ii, no.1914 (the coronet was stolen by Geoffrey de Coigners, but the theft was discovered and pardoned).

37. Stones, *Relations*, p.276.

38. The English charge against Lamberton says that Bruce was 'crowned and also proclaimed king of Scotland': Stones, *Relations*, p.276. Palgrave, *Docs. Hist. Scot.*, 319, mentions a letter sent by Bruce to the earl of Strathearn within a few days of his coronation. The earliest known official document whose text has survived is a charter of inspection for Sir John of Luss, dated Inchmahome, September 28th, 1308 (*RRS*, v, no.1).

39. Palgrave, *Docs. Hist. Scot.*, 348-9.

40. Evidence of King Robert's movements between his coronation and the battle of Methven is to be found in Palgrave, *Docs. Hist. Scot.*, 319-21 and *Chron. Lanercost*, 203-4. Barbour, *Bruce*, 24, is presumably covering up ignorance in saying 'and syne went our all the land, frendis and frendschip purchesand'.

41. *Chron. Lanercost*, 203-4. It is conceivable that this expedition to Galloway is identical with that carried out by Bruce *before* his coronation, for which see Stones, *Relations*, p.261.

42. *Cal. Docs. Scot.*, ii, nos. 1747, 1748.

43. *Ibid.*, no.1754.

44. Barbour, *Bruce*, 24.

45. *Cal. Docs. Scot.*, ii, nos. 1782, 1790. Cf. also *ibid.*, no.1755.

46. *Nat. MSS, Scot.*, ii, Pl.14 (*Cal. Docs. Scot.*, ii, no.1787).

47. *Cal. Docs. Scot.*, ii, no.1781.

48. Palgrave, *Docs. Hist. Scot.*, 328-9, 336-7.

49. *Cal. Docs. Scot.*, ii, nos. 1786, 1813, 1815, 1824.

50. *Ibid.*, no.1786.

51. *Chron. Guisb.*, 368; Barbour, *Bruce*, 27-31. Palgrave, *Docs. Hist. Scot.*, 321, shows that before Methven Bruce was at Callander, north of Crieff, and then at Kenmore (a resort of the earls of Strathearn perhaps opposite St Fillans, perhaps an island (now submerged) by Edinample: *Inchaffray Chrs.*, nos.87, 118; *Macfarlane's Geog. Coll.*, ii, 565, '. . . Na

Keandmoir with a house on it'; A. A. M. Duncan, *Scotland: the Making of the Kingdom* (1975), 441). Some sources give the date of the battle of Methven as June 26th, other sources as June 19th. In *Chron. Holyrood*, 179, no.2, Mrs Anderson decided in favour of June 26th, chiefly on the strength of *Cal. Docs. Scot.*, ii, no.1811. But there is proof that the true date was June 19th. Malise earl of Strathearn issued an indemnifying letter for Gilbert of Glencarnie at Perth on June 26th, Fraser, *Grant*, iii, no.12. Apart from the improbability of this letter's being issued on the day of the battle, it is clear from the account of the earl's movements in *Cal. Inqu. Misc.*, i, no.2029, that he left his refuge at Kenmore and joined Valence only after he had heard the result of Methven. John Sandal's Account Book for 1306-7, *Cal. Docs. Scot.*, v, no.492, gives June 19th as the date of Methven.

52. *Scottish War of Independence*, 224-35. See Appendix, below, for a list of Scottish landowners forfeited for supporting Bruce.

53. For the preceding see G. W. S. Barrow, *Robert Bruce and the Scottish Identity* (1984), 7; idem, *The Anglo-Norman Era in Scottish History* (1980), 149-52; idem in *TR Hist S*, 5th Ser., xxviii (1978), 116; and Barrow, *Kingdom*, 251-2.

54. *Chron. Fordun*, i, 331; *Scalacronica*, 127; *Melrose Liber*, i, no.391; *Dumfriesshire Trans.*, 3rd Ser., xxvi,.

55. *Cal. Docs. Scot.*, ii, no.1857.

56. *Ibid.*, nos. 1843, 1857; cf. iii, no.56.

57. *APS*, i, 459; James the Stewart died on July 16th, 1309: *Chron. Bower*, ii, 242.

58. *Foedera*, i, 974-5.

59. Stones, *Relations*, p.255, of September, 1305, must be compared with *Foedera*, i, 974-5. Sir Maurice Powicke (*The Thirteenth Century*, 713) believed that the later document rescinded Fraser's sentence of exile. But although it explicitly remitted the sentence of exile passed on John Comyn of Badenoch, David Graham and the bishop of Glasgow, it said nothing explicitly of any similar remission in favour of Fraser, merely that in respect of redemption of his lands and amends for wrongdoing he must pay three years' value, like Comyn.

60. Stones, *Documents*, p.132.

61. *Flores Historiarum*, iii, 133-4. *Proc. Soc. Antiq. Scot.*, New Ser., vii (1884-5), 177-8, says that he was captured at Linlithgow. His capture was the occasion of the most sickening of the many killings ordered by King Edward in 1306. Young Herbert Morham, son of Sir Thomas Morham, who had commanded the Scots besieging Stirling in 1299 and had subsequently been taken prisoner with his father and lodged in the Tower, was (along with his father) excepted from the terms of surrender in 1304, Palgrave, *Docs. Hist. Scot.*, 281. Herbert had foolishly wagered his head that Fraser would never be captured. On September 7th, 1306, shortly before Fraser met his death, Herbert Morham and his esquire, Thomas du Boys, were beheaded. Herbert Morham had the name for being the tallest and most handsome knight in Scotland; cf. *Proc. Soc. Antiq. Scot.*, New Ser., vii, 190-2.

62. Inherited through descent from David, son of Duncan II earl of Fife. Cf. *Moray Registrum*, nos.16, 30, 62; *Scots Peerage*, iv, 8; *Northern Notes and Queries* iv (1890), 146-7.

63. *Arbroath Liber*, i, no.231.

64. *Cal. Docs. Scot.*, ii, no.1646.

65. *Ibid.*, no.1633.

66. *Ibid.*, no.1849.

67. Palgrave, *Docs. Hist. Scot.*, 319 ff, and *Cal. Inqu. Misc.*, i, no.2029, give an exceptionally full account of the earl of Strathearn's conduct. See now C. Neville, 'The Political Allegiance of the earls of Strathearn during the war of independence', *SHR*, lxv (1986), 133-53.

68. *Cal. Docs. Scot.*, ii, no.1854.

69. *Ibid.*, nos. 960, 1054, 1055. William Douglas was imprisoned in Berwick castle in July 1297, where he was reported 'mout sauvage e mout araillez', 'very savage and very angry', Stevenson, *Documents*, ii, 205.

70. *Cal. Docs. Scot.*, iii, no.682; Barbour, *Bruce*, 9, 22-3.

71. *Ibid.*, 421. The name James was probably used in the Stewart family because their abbey of Paisley was dedicated to St James the Great (as well as to Mirren and Milburga of Wenlock).

72. Barbour, *Bruce*, 23.

73. *Cal. Docs. Scot.*, ii, no.730. Cf. nos. 704, 861, 1670 (which shows that Sir John of Cambo had rented the fishing rights of Crail for a year prior to February 1296). Crail was inherited from Richard de Beaumont, kinsman of Ermengarde de Beaumont queen of William the Lion, to whom Alexander II seems to have granted Crail early in the thirteenth century: NLS, MS.8487. From Agnes de Beaumont the barony passed to her daughter Isabel who married John de Vesci the elder: *Cal. Close R., 1296-1302*, 10.

74. *Ibid.*, no.1676.

75. *Ibid.*, no.1811.

76. *Ibid.*, no.730.

77. *Ibid.*, iv, no.1827.

78. F. W. Maitland, *Memoranda de Parliamento*, nos. 353, 381, 387.

79. Palgrave, *Docs. Hist. Scot.*, 314. Lindsay had been a leader of the revolt in 1297 (Stevenson, *Documents*, ii, no.454), but seems to have been briefly in Edward I's peace after Falkirk (*ibid.*, no.529), but soon forfeited (*Cal. Docs. Scot.*, iii, no.258). In 1305 he was regarded by Edward as having been a prominent enemy, Stones, *Relations*, p.253, and he was among those who were present with Bruce when Comyn was murdered on February 10th 1306: *Cal. Docs. Scot.*, v, p.204.

80. *Cal. Docs. Scot.*, ii, no.1811. Some Annandale tenants were opposed to Bruce. The family of Torthorald was anti-Bruce (*Reg. Mag. Sig.*, i, no.30; *Cal. Docs. Scot.*, iii, *passim*), but it is not clear that Torthorald formed part of the lordship of Annandale. PRO, D. L.36/3, fo.87, no.1, speaks of tolls levied 'between the barony of Annandale and the tenement of Torthorald', which suggests that Torthorald was separate. *Cal. Docs. Scot.*, i, no.1683, renders this document incorrectly.

81. Palgrave, *Docs. Hist. Scot.*, 301; *Cal. Docs. Scot.*, ii, no.1842.

82. Palgrave, *Docs. Hist. Scot.*, 359-60; *Cal. Docs. Scot.*,ii, nos. 1839, 1840.

83. *Ibid.*, 194-7, 299-301.

84. Both William Fenton and his son John figure on the roll of forfeited landowners, below, Appendix. *Coupar Angus Chrs.*, i, no.71, mentions three generations of the family, Sir William, his father John, and his son and heir John.

85. Alan Murray, kinsman of Sir William Murray of St Fort, was no doubt Alan Murray of Culbin, since he is said to have held lands in the sheriffdoms of Fife and Forres, Palgrave, *Docs. Hist. Scot.*, 299, 307.

86. Compare *ibid.*, 195 with *ibid.*, 313. For Thomas of Cremannan, cf. *Lennox Cartularium, passim*.

87. Palgrave, *Docs. Hist. Scot.*, 302.

88. *Ibid.*, 308. Earl Malise of Strathearn's indemnification of Gilbert of Glencarni the elder, June 26th, 1306 (Fraser, *Grant*, iii, no.12) provides an excellent illustration of a lesser baron attaching himself to a great magnate. Whereas Gilbert has, contrary to the tenor of his charter of Glencarnie, rendered the earl personal service in the war of Scotland, adhering to the earl with his forces and his power, the earl declares that this service shall not form a precedent or redound to the prejudice of Gilbert and his heirs. It may be noted, similarly, that Walter Logan, lord of Hartside, who was sheriff of Lanark in 1301, had a grant of Luce in Annandale from Robert Bruce in 1298 and called Bruce his lord. Logan figures on the roll of forfeited landowners in 1306. Cf. *Cal. Docs. Scot.*, iv, 387-8; *Kelso Liber*, no.193; below, Appendix.

89. *Rotuli Scotiae*, i, 27a, shows Robert Cameron of Baledgarno a tenant of the earl of Atholl (although for Baledgarno itself, in the Braes of the Carse of Gowrie, he was a tenant-in-chief of the Crown, *ibid.*, 29a). Sir John Cameron, probably of Baledgarno, is among the knights mainperned in August 1297 by the earl of Atholl, Sir John of Inchmartin and Sir Alexander Menzies, *Cal. Docs. Scot.*, ii, no.942. John of Inchmartin, who played a very prominent part in the war against England down to 1304, was also both a tenant-in-chief in his own right and a tenant of the earl of Atholl, Scottish Record Office, Register House Charters, no.67; cf. *Coupar Angus Chrs.*, i, 160-1. His son David was executed in 1306, *Cal. Docs. Scot.*, ii, no.1811; *Proc. Soc. Antiq. Scot.*, New Ser., vii, 173. For a charter in which are associated John of Strathbogie earl of Atholl, Alexander Menzies, John of Inchmartin, John Cameron, Laurence of Strathbogie, and Robert Cameron of Balnely, cf. J. A. Robertson, *Comitatus de Atholia etc.* (privately printed, 1860), 38.

90. For Ewen Mackessan or MacCassen, of Garchell, cf. *Lennox Cartularium*, 22, 32, 46, 47, 82, 83; Fraser, *Lennox*, ii, 406, no.209. This is probably the person appearing on the roll of forfeited landowners as 'Coweyn Mackassen in the county of Stirling', Palgrave, *Docs. Hist. Scot.*, 313.

91. *Cal. Docs. Scot.*, ii, no.742; mainperned by the earl of Atholl and others, 1297, *ibid.*, no.942.

92. Palgrave, *Docs. Hist. Scot.*, 306; cf. *Cal. Docs. Scot.*, ii, no.857.

93. For the part played by Sir Malcolm in Bruce's dealings with the earl of Strathearn, see Palgrave, *Docs. Hist. Scot.*, 320-1. His forfeiture is recorded *ibid.*, 311 (mis-spelt Everph'me). Cf. *Cal. Docs. Scot.*, ii, no.1858.

94. See G. W. S. Barrow, 'Lothian, 1296-1328', *SHR*, lv (1976), 151-71.

95. *Inchaffray Chrs.*, xlv and n.2.

96. *Reg. Mag. Sig.*, i, Appendix 1, no.77, Abbot Maurice of Inchaffray a witness to a charter dating from the period when Alexander Abernethy was warden of Scotland between Forth and the Mounth and Matthew of Kinross was dean of Dunkeld. Abernethy was appointed warden at Michaelmas 1303 (*Cal. Docs. Scot.*, 11, no.1694), but Matthew of Kinross was not dean of Dunkeld until 1304 (*ibid.*, no.1473, 1573). Abbot Maurice was active on Bruce's behalf at the time of his coronation, Palgrave, *Docs. Hist. Scot.*, 319, attempting to win the earl of Strathearn's support.

97. *Cal. Docs. Scot.*, ii, nos.1592, 1689. Patrick and Malcolm of Glendochart did homage in 1296 (*ibid.*, 199, 200), as did Conan of Balquhidder (*ibid.*, 200).

98. *Reg. Mag. Sig.*, i, Appendix 11, nos. 476, 652.

99. Barbour, *Bruce*, 35ff. (at 'the hed of Tay'); *Chron. Fordun*, i, 342. Dail Righ means the king's meadow, but it is not certain, and seems a little improbable, that the place got its name from Bruce and his battle; it is surely older. Beside Dail Righ is the little Lochan nan Arm, 'tarn of the weapons'. The battle is wrongly located by F. M. Powicke, *The Thirteenth Century*, 716, at Dalry in Ayrshire.

100. Barbour, *Bruce*, 44; *Cal. Docs. Scot.*, ii, no.1829. *Chron. Fordun*, i, 342.

101. *Cal. Docs. Scot.*, ii, no.1810. A further contribution to the evidence for the events of the summer of 1306 is provided by *Cal. Inqu. Misc.*, i, no.2029, which says that some time after the battle of Methven the earl of Strathearn sent his son with his own forces beyond the Mounth in aid of King Edward's expedition. John Sandal's Account Book 356, n.51 refers to an engagement by Loch Tay, presumably soon after Methven: *Cal. Docs. Scot.*, v, p.213.

102. Barbour, *Bruce*, 45; *Chron. Fordun*, i, 342.

103. *Cal. Docs. Scot.*, ii, no.1829; Barbour, *Bruce*, 59-60.

104. *Ibid.*, 57-8. Barbour says that Atholl stayed at Kildrummy. I have inferred that he accompanied the queen from the penalty which King Robert afterwards imposed on Earl William of Ross of maintaining chaplains in the church of Tain to say mass for the earl of Atholl. See below, p.318. Good sources say that the earl was taken 'in flight', *Flores Historiarum*, iii, 134; *Proc. Soc. Antiq. Scot.*, New Ser., vii, 181. The omission of the earl's name from the Kildrummy prisoners listed in Sandal's Account Book confirms that he was elsewhere.

105. Barbour, *Bruce*, 47; *Chron. Fordun*, i, 342.

106. Fraser's capture and execution aroused enormous interest in southern England, to judge from the widespread accounts which still survive. See, *inter alia*, *Siege of Carlaverock*, 217-20. The remains of his body, together with the gallows on which he had been hanged, were afterwards burned on King Edward's orders, *Annales Londonienses*, 149. In this context the verb 'to draw' has its normal thirteenth-century meaning of 'to drag to the place of execution by means of horses, usually on a hurdle'.

107. *Complete Peerage*, i, 305.

108. *Chron. Guisb.*, 369; *Flores Historiarum*, iii, 134-5; *Annales Londonienses*, 149-50; *Scalacronica*, 131.

109. *Chron. Fordun*, i, 342; *Flores Historiarum*, iii, 135; *Scalacronica*, 131.

110. *Chron. Guisb.*, 369 (reading 'Lochdon' for 'Lochdor'); *Chron. Lanercost*, 204; cf. *Reg. Mag. Sig.*, i, no.510.

111. *Cal. Docs. Scot.*, ii, no.1811.

112. *Ibid.*

113. *Highland Papers* (SHS), ii, 125; Anderson, *Diplomata*, Pl. XLIII. Cf. G. G. Simpson, *Handlist of the Acts of Alexander III, etc.*, nos. 413, 418, 422.

114. Palgrave, *Docs. Hist. Scot.*, 357.

115. *Cal. Docs. Scot.*, ii, no.1910.

116. Palgrave, *Docs. Hist. Scot.*, 358–9; *Proc. Soc. Antiq. Scot.*, New Ser., vii, 175-6 (an eight foot cube, in the shape of a little house, to be an iron crown in punishment for Countess Isabel's share in Bruce's inauguration); *Flores Historiarum*, iii, 324; *Chron. Guisb.*, 367; *Scalacronica*, 130, 'the countess, . . . by command of King Edward of England, was placed in a little house of timber in a tower in the castle of Berwick, the sides latticed so that all there could gaze on her as a spectacle.' *Chron. Rishanger*, 229, says '[the countess] was placed in a little wooden house on the wall of Berwick castle, so that passers-by might gaze on her.'

117. G. Villani, *Istorie fiorentine*, ii (Milan, 1802), 111; S. Battaglia, *Grande Dizionario della lingua italiana* (Turin, 1961), s.v. *gabbia*, 2. These Italian references are due to the kindness of Mrs Margaret Burns.

118. Palgrave, *Docs. Hist. Scot.*, 358; *eesement de chambre cortoise*. This was, however, to be constructed very carefully so that there was no danger of the prisoner escaping or being rescued by way of the privy.

119. *Rotuli Scotiae*, i, 85b.

120. *Cal. Docs. Scot.*, iii, nos. 131, 227, 244, 248, 340.

121. Palgrave, *Docs. Hist. Scot.*, 359.

122. *Chron. Guisb.*, 369; *Cal. Docs. Scot.*, ii, no.1910.

123. *The Thirteenth Century*, 716.

124. W. D. Lamont, 'Alexander of Islay, son of Angus Mór', *SHR*, lx (1981), 160-169, who discounts the late and poor tradition that Alexander Macdonald was opposed to Bruce, suggests that in any case Alexander was probably dead by 1301, and argues, not quite convincingly perhaps, that the references in contemporary documents to a 'Donald of Islay' actually refer to Angus Og (cf. *Cal. Docs. Scot.*, iv, no.1822, perhaps of 1306;

APS, i, 459 and *Melrose Liber*, ii, no.376, dating to March 1309).

125. R. Greeves, 'The Galloway Lands in Ulster', *Dumfriesshire Trans.*, 3rd Ser., xxxvi; R. Frame, in *Irish Hist. Studies*, xix, 17, n.60. See above, p.331, nn.27-28.

126. *RSS*, v, no.355 (Dudhope Charters); cf. *SHR*, xxxii (1953), 38.

127. Stevenson, *Documents*, ii, no.401. It was from the mouth of the Roe that the Easter Ross family of Munro (Mun-rotha) are held to have migrated to Scotland about this time.

128. Barbour, *Bruce*, 45-53. The rock called Clach nam Breatann, an ancient boundary mark above the Falls of Falloch, a few miles north of the head of Loch Lomond, is locally believed to have been one of Bruce's hiding-places at this period.

129. *Cal. Docs. Scot.*, ii, nos. 1833, 1834.

CHAPTER TEN
A King in Search of his Throne

1. E.g., *Reg. Mag. Sig.*, i, nos. 12, 13, etc.

2. Barron, *Scottish War of Independence*, 252ff., citing a St Albans writer, as well as Fabyan and Rastell; on all of which see T. F. Tout, *EHR*, xxix, 756.

3. *Chron. Guisb.*, 368.

4. *Chron. Lanercost*, 205, *in remotis insulis Scotiae*. (Orkney and Shetland, of course, were not part of Scotland at this date).

5. *Cal. Docs. Scot.*, ii, nos. 1888, 1889.

6. Barbour, *Bruce*, 55, 65.

7. *Reg. Mag. Sig.*, i, Appendix I, no.10: *ita tamen quod carte si quas habet episcopus de dictis tribus celdris . . . vel de centum solidis ex donatione antecessorum nostrorum seu nostra de cetero nihilum obtineant firmitatem; RRS*, v, no.Ra 10.

8. *Cal. Pat., 1292-1301*, 69.

9. Palgrave, *Antient Kalendars and Inventories*, i, 134.

10. *Chron. Guisb.*, 329.

11. *Cal. Docs. Scot.*, ii, nos. 1253-55. The Bissets nursed an old claim to Arran: Barrow, *Anglo-Norman Era*, 16, 68.

12. *Cal. Docs. Scot.*, ii, no.1888, cf. no.1941.

13. Barbour, *Bruce*, 248.

14. *Cal. Docs. Scot.*, iii, no.632. On the confused situation in Ulster, see R. Frame, *Irish Hist. Stud.*, xix, 29-30.

15. A. McKerral, *SHR*, xxx, 7-8. A prominent Macdonald (a son of Angus Og ?), fighting in Edward Bruce's army, was killed at the battle of Dundalk in 1318: *Annals of Ulster*, ii, 433.

16. *Chron. Guisb.*, 370. Perhaps Michaelmas is a mistake for Candlemas, February 2nd, 1307

17. *Ibid.*

18. *Chron. Lanercost*, 205. The Irish sub-king and the large force of Irishmen point to close links between Bruce and Ireland during the winter. Their presence also tends to support the suggestion, although it has been controverted, that Malcolm MacQuillan was of the MacQuillans of Antrim. See *Flores Historiarum*, iii, 136, 327; *Proc. Soc. Antiq. Scot.*, New Ser., vii (1884-5), 184. The forms of Malcolm's surname here are Makayle and Makaillis (probably a mistake for Makaill'). Macaill, in the index to *Flores Historiarum*, is perhaps a variant reading in one of the MSS., although the editor does not say so.

19. Barbour, *Bruce*, 65-74, 78-81.

20. John Hastings, who had failed to get one third of the kingdom of Scotland as a competitor in 1291, had a grant of the earldom of Menteith (which included Arran), 'forfeited' by Earl Alan, in 1306, save for lands already given to his younger brother Edmund Hastings (for whose holding of, or claim to, Inchmahome, capital messuage of the earldom, in the period 1296-1301, in right of his wife Isabel daughter of Isabel countess of Menteith, cf. *The Ancestor*, viii (1904), 101); *Cal. Docs. Scot.*, ii, no.1771.

21. *Chron. Fordun*, i, 343.

22. *Cal. Docs. Scot.*, ii, 184, 200, where the homage is recorded in 1296 of Christian, wife of Duncan of Mar, of the county of Inverness ('widow', *ibid.*, is an error). *Ibid.*, 200, records the homage of Duncan, son of the earl of Mar, doubtless Christian's husband. Cf. *Inchaffray Chrs.*, 299-300.

23. See Genealogical Table 11.

24. *Inchaffray Chrs.*, nos. 142, 143.

25. *The Story of England by Robert Manning of Brunne* (ed. F. J. Furnivall, Rolls Series), i, 12-13. Cf. *Chron. Lanercost*, 205-6; *Chron. Guisb.*, 370. The heads of the Irish sub-king, Malcolm MacQuillan, Alexander Bruce and Sir

Reginald Crawford were fixed to the three gates of Carlisle; Thomas Bruce's head was placed above the castle keep.

26. Barbour, *Bruce*, 81. That this lady, who was marvellously happy at Bruce's return, had at one time been his mistress may be suggested by the fact that Bruce had natural children called Neil of Carrick (killed at Neville's Cross, 1346) and Christian of Carrick.

27. *Ibid.*, 82.

28. *Cal. Docs. Scot.*, ii, nos. 1957, 1961.

29. *Ibid.*, no.1896.

30. *Ibid.*, no.1942 (referring to April, not June); and see 512; Barbour, *Bruce*, 129.

31. *Ibid.*, 129-33.

32. *Ibid.*, 136-42. For the site, beside the farmstead of Allantonplains, cf. *Ayrshire Archaeological and Natural History Collections*, vi (1961), 241.

33. *Chron. Guisb.*, 378.

34. *Cal. Docs. Scot.*, ii, no.1926.

35. *Chron. Guisb.*, 378.

36. *Chron. Lanercost*, 207.

37. *Cal. Docs. Scot.*, ii, no.1909.

38. *Chron. Lanercost*, 207; *Flores Historiarum*, iii, 327.

39. *Cal. Docs. Scot.*, ii, no.1908 (= Palgrave, *Docs. Hist. Scot.*, 361-3).

40. PRO, E.101/373/23.

41. *Cal. Docs. Scot.*, iii, no.14.

42. *Ibid.*, no.12. *Ibid.*, no.13.

43. *Ibid.*, no.14. For Douglas in Paisley Forest, September 1307, cf. PRO, E.101/373/23.

44. Barbour, *Bruce*, 145-7. In this expedition Douglas, presumably in accordance with Bruce's firm policy, destroyed his own castle of Douglas. This was not the occasion of the famous 'Douglas Larder', when Douglas took his own castle by a stratagem, killed Clifford's English garrison and threw the bodies down the well. According to Barbour, *Bruce*, 85-90, this exploit was carried out early in 1307.

45. Theiner, *Monumenta*, no.386; Dowden, *Bishops*, 201; see above, pp.119-120. One of Nicholas's first achievements was to secure a reduction in the taxation due to the papacy on his promotion from either 160 or 100 merks to only 60 merks, on this occasion only, 'on account of the

notorious desolation of the whole of (?) Scotland' by war; *Regestum Papae Clementis V*, Appendix I (Rome, 1892), 217, no.67. I am grateful to the Rev. Charles Burns for checking this reference for me against the MS. register, and also against the printed volume, from which the entry is cited briefly in W. E. Lunt, *Financial Relations of the Papacy with England to 1327*, 469.

46. Text in *SHR*, xlix, 57-59.

47. Inverlochy was taken on or about the feast of some virgin whose name is illegible in Duncan's letter. Female saints whose feasts would have been familiar to a Scots letter-writer included Triduana, Findoca, Ursula and 11,000 (!) virgins, Kennere and Begha (October 8th, 13th, 21st, 29th and 31st respectively).

48. *Cal. Docs. Scot.*, iv, no.1837 (full text, *ibid.*, 399, where, among other *corrigenda*, substitute for *nous ounes, nous oimes*, 'we heard'; for *a vuer, avuer*, 'call up'; for *afraunce, afiaunce*, 'trust'; for *de mene, demene*, 'own').

49. *Ibid.*, iii, no.43.

50. *Ibid.*, no.47 (August, 1308; J. R. Maddicott, *Thomas of Lancaster*, 109 n.2).

51. Barbour, *Bruce*, 156: 'And heryit thame on sic maneir, / That eftir that weile fifty yhier / Men menyt the heirschip of Bouchane.'

52. *Cal. Docs. Scot.*, iv, p.400.

53. *APS*, i, 477.

54. *Scottish War of Independence*, 295-8.

55. Palgrave, *Docs. Hist. Scot.*, 330.

56. *Cal. Docs. Scot.*, ii, no.1907; PRO, C.47/22/4, no.77 = *Cal. Docs. Scot.*, iv, 400, where the first sentence of the third item should read: *Fete a sauoir que le Euesqe de Moref feut un an ore de vostre reaume Descoce encontre vestre fey.*

57. Barbour, *Bruce*, 156.

58. His earliest appearance is as witness to a royal mandate dated October 14th, 1308, *RRS*, v, no.4.

59. It has long been usual to identify Chancellor Bernard with Bernard 'de Lyntone', parson of the parish church of Mordington near Berwick in 1296 (*Cal. Docs. Scot.*, ii, 207). The identification is not supported by any positive evidence and there seems little doubt that the chancellor was a Tironensian monk who had earlier been abbot of Kilwinning in

Ayrshire, as established by Professor Duncan: *RRS*, v, Introduction.

60. It looks as though Robert I secured the supersession of Abbot John (who was pro-English, *Cal. Docs. Scot.*, iii, no.158) by Bernard either in 1310 or 1311; cf. *Arbroath Liber*, i, no.332. I am indebted to Professor Duncan for valuable notes on Bernard's appointment as abbot of Arbroath.

61. PRO, C.47/22/6, no.4, summarized unsatisfactorily, *Cal. Docs. Scot.*, iii, no.80.

62. *Cal. Docs. Scot.*, iii, no.80 and pp.xiii-xiv; Barron, *Scottish War of Independence*, chap.29; Colin MacDonald, *History of Argyll* (no date), 134.

63. The crucial opening words, which Bain, probably correctly, took to give the date at which John Bacach received Edward II's letter, run as follows: *Litteras vestras ultimo directas xi° die mensis marcij percepimus, de quarum tenore vestre Regalitati multipliciter regraciamur.* Although it might seem logical for the writer of a letter to identify his correspondent's last letter by its own date, thirteenth-and fourteenth-century usage supports the belief that the date given is that of receipt.

64. Probably the three castles were Fraoch Eilean, Fincharn and Inchchonnell on Loch Awe. I have greatly benefited from correspondence with Dr Hugo Millar of the Glasgow Archaeological Society who has made a study of the castles of Loch Awe. One should note the striking resemblance between John of Lorn's statement about castles and loch and the geographical information in *Chron. Bower*, i, 46: 'Loch Awe, 24 miles, where are three castles.'

65. *History of Argyll*, 133.

66. By March 1309, Robert I's first parliament was attended by 'the barons of all Argyll and the Hebrides', including Gillespie MacLachlan, who less than three years earlier had been asking Edward I to grant him the lands of one of Bruce's first adherents (*APS*, i, 459; Palgrave, *Docs. Hist. Scot.*, 318).

67. *Chron. Fordun*, i, 345.

68. *Chron. Guisb.*, 384 (surviving manuscripts have 'Jacobus' instead of 'Robertus'; the context makes it clear that the writer could not have been referring

to Edward Bruce, although a conflation of Robert Bruce and James Douglas is conceivable).

69. Barbour, *Bruce*, 169-70, writes 'a sheer crag, high and hideous, reached to the sea [raucht till the se],' from where John of Lorn witnessed the fighting. Barbour's 'sea' must mean Loch Awe, not Loch Etive, from the surface of which a battle on the slopes of Cruachan could not be seen.

70. Barbour, *Bruce*, 170, 170.

71. *Chron. Fordun*, i, 345.

72. Barbour, *Bruce*, 172.

73. This is the view of Dr Hugo Millar, *per litt.*

74. *Rotuli Scotiae*, i, 58a.

75. *Cal. Docs. Scot.*, iii, no.80.

76. *APS*, i, 459.

77. Cal. Docs. Scot., iii, 23.

78. *Ibid.*, no.191.

79. For a different reconstruction, cf. R. Nicholson, *Scotland : the Later Middle Ages* (1974), 79-80.

80. Barbour, *Bruce*, 161-6; *Chron. Lanercost*, 212 (which says that the leaders were Edward Bruce, Alexander Lindsay, Robert Boyd and James Douglas, and that their forces came from the outer isles); *Chron. Fordun*, i, 345.

81. Barbour, *Bruce*, 162. His form 'Cre' is anachronistic, the fourteenth-century forms being Crith(e), Crich(e) etc., i.e. 'boundary'. The Dee would have been almost within sight of Buittle castle (Book IX, lines 533-5), the Cree far out of sight.

82. *Rotuli Scotiae*, i, 66, 80a.

83. *Ibid.*, 80.

84. *APS*, i, 459.

85. Barbour, *Bruce*, 156; *Chron. Holyrood*, 179.

86. *RRS*, v, no.4.

87. Barbour, *Bruce*, 172.

87a. English record dates the forfeiture of Alexander Stewart (for Uldale in Cumberland) only from 7 May 1314; PRO, E.372/160, m.50.

88. *Cal. Docs. Scot.*, iii, no.1786, ii, no.423. Knapdale had been seized on behalf of John Menteith by John of Lorn in 1301, *ibid.*, ii, no.1255. The history of Arran is obscure in this period. It seems to have gone with the earldom of

Menteith. John Menteith's son and heir emerges in the middle of the fourteenth century as lord of both Knapdale and Arran, and the probability is that his father was confirmed in these lordships by Robert I; cf. *RMS*, i, App.II, no.1495 (Index B).

89. Barbour, *Bruce*, 168.

90. *Rotuli Scotiae*, i, 61b. See above, p.110.

91. *Chron. Guisb.*, 384.

92. *APS*, i, 459; cf. *ibid.*, 71. The parliament alleged to have been held by Bruce at Scone Abbey, referred to in *SHR*, xxv, 315, n.1, may perhaps have been the coronation assembly.

93. *Les journaux du trésor*, ed. Viard, no.5917.

94. *Gascon Register A*, ed. G. P. Cuttino with the collaboration of J.-P. Trabut-Cussac (British Academy, 1975), ii, 354, no.71.

95. *APS*, i, 459. An English contemporary says that Philip IV's letter to Robert I did not give him his royal title but addressed him as his 'dear friend' (*Annales Londonienses*, 226). But perhaps this was only in a copy which was 'edited' for safe passage through England.

96. *Foedera*, ii, 63; *Rotuli Scotiae*, i, 59-60.

97. *RRS*, v, no.5; cf. the undated confirmation also issued on this occasion for Melrose Abbey, *RRS*, v, no.385.

98. BL, MS. Harl. 4694, fos. 5-6, 35-6 (a manuscript of Sir James Balfour of Denmilne, Lord Lyon King of Arms.)

99. *APS*, i, 289, paragraph beginning 'In a MS. which belonged to Mr J. Anderson . . .'

100. Serious errors make the editorial comment in *APS*, i, 289, misleading. BL, MS. Harl. 4694, fos. 5-6, 35-6, contains copies of two separate versions of an identical document, whose text may be found in *APS*, i, 460, cols. 1-2. Unlike the versions there printed the Harleian versions are both dated at St Andrews: (1) *Datum in parliamento tento Apud Sanctum Andream in Scotia xvii die Martij Anno Gratie Millesimo Trecentesimo octavo*, of which Balfour notes 'ther is onlie tuo sealls left of this declaratione, viz. Sigillum Episcopi St Andreae, et Dunkeldensis. and .6. uthers broken from it;' (2) *Datum in parliamento tento Apud*

Sanctum Andream in Scotia 17 *die Martij Anno Gratie* M⁰. CCC⁰. VIII⁰ To which is added (by Balfour or another?) *Sex sigilla cere viridis Episcoporum sunt appensa.*

101. *APS*, i, 460, col.2, lines 2-6.

102. *Ibid.* The 'documents sealed in the past' would no doubt have special reference to the records of homages to Edward I in 1291, 1296 and 1304.

103. *Chron. Picts. Scot.*, 280.

104. Cp. *ibid.*, 218 (= Stones, *Relations*, 169), *per vim et metum qui cadere poterat in constantem* and *Chron. Picts-Scots*, 277, *per vim et metum qui cadere poterant in constantes* with *APS*, i, 460, col.2, *per vim et violentiam quibus non poterat tunc resisti et metus multiplices cruciatus corporum ac terrores varios qui sensus perfectorum et animos avertere poterant et cadere in constantes.* The elaboration of the 1309 document is partly due to its author's desire toemploy the *cursus*; see below, p.306. For the phrase itself, see above, p.338, n.39.

105. BL, MS. Harl. 4694, fo.6.

106. *Ibid.*, fo.36. It is hard to explain the affixing of a seal by the bishop of Glasgow, a prisoner in England, except on the assumption that he was, with or without his knowledge and consent, 'represented'. Lamberton may have been present in person even though he was technically in Edward II's peace: *Foedera*, ii, 68, and see below, p.374, n.7.

107. *APS*, i, 289, col.1, at foot. There is obviously an error or a muddle in the list of signatories, but it may be suggested that seals were placed by Ross, Lennox and Edward Bruce, and by representatives of the 'communities' of the earldoms of Fife, Menteith, Mar and Buchan, as in *ibid.*, 459. In the opinion of Dr Norman Reid the document of which an abstract from James Anderson's papers is printed in *APS*, i, 289, col.1 was in fact the Scots barons' letter to Philip IV ('Political Role of the Monarchy', 344, n.151). But the phrases dealing with Bruce's rightful claim to the throne find no place in that letter and closely resemble the corresponding phrases of the declaration.

108. *Ibid.*, 289.

109. BL, MS. Harl. 4694, fo.35r.

110. The following list is derived from *APS*, i, 459 and 289; the name of John

Fenton is added from the original letter (SRO, S. P.3), where it appears, with that of Alexander Fraser, on one of the seal tags (no.12), but was missed by the editors of *APS*. The tags themselves appear to have been cut from a draft of the final version of the document, since some of its phraseology may be read on tags 5 and 10. The document is not wholly legible, and probably some three or four names are lost. In particular, there is room for at least two names in the text on line 3 after *comit* [*is Rossie*] and on line 4 after *Alexander d*[*e* . . .].

111. *Rotuli Scotiae*, i, 77b.

112. It was a mark of the king's achievement that by July 23rd, 1310 he had secured papal absolution from the sin of homicide, as a private man ('Robert de Bruyss, layman of Carrick, diocese of Glasgow'): H. J. Lawlor, in *SHR*, xix, 325-6.

CHAPTER ELEVEN
The Turn of the Tide

1. *Cal. Docs. Scot.*, iii, no.202.

2. T. Wright, *Political Songs of England* (Camden Soc., 1839), 216: 'Now Kyng Hobbe in the mures gongeth / For te come to toune nout him ne longeth.' The news of Bruce's rising and of his flight in the heather quickly reached Italy, for Villani refers to Edward I's failure to subdue 'Ruberto di Busoo' who with his followers had fled to the bogs and wild mountains of Scotland; G. Villani, *Historie universali de suoi tempi* (Florence, 1570), 340-1.

3. *Rotuli Scotiae*, i, 61 (for 'Landyan' read 'Laudyan', Lothian).

4. *Chron. Lanercost*, 214.

5. *Rotuli Scotiae*, i, 61b; *Cal. Docs. Scot.*, iii, no.245.

6. *Ibid.* no.186 (= PRO, Ancient Petitions 7743). It is clear from the original that Bain's dating is wrong, and that this belongs to 1312, and refers to the truce mentioned in *Rotuli Scotiae*, i, 111. Bain's summary is misleading and inadequate.

7. *Rotuli Scotiae*, i, 111: *illorum qui ex parte predicti Roberti se tenent*; PRO, Ancient Petitions 7743, para. 2: *les gentz del enemiste.*

8. *Chron. Lanercost*, 217.

9. *Ibid.*, 217. This is borne out by surviving letters of Sir John Graham

referring to Eskdale in 1309 (*Melrose Liber*, nos. 378-80).

10. For an assessment of the position of the inhabitants of south-eastern Scotland in this period, cf. G. W. S. Barrow, 'Lothian in the first War of Independence', *SHR*, lv (1976), 151-71; *idem*, 'The Aftermath of War: Scotland and England in the late thirteenth and early fourteenth centuries,' *Transactions of the Royal Historical Society*, 5th Ser., xxviii (1978), 103-25.

11. Fraser, *Grant*, iii, no.11. For a tradition concerning the lordship and name Glencarnie (Glenchernich), whose seat was where Boat of Garten now is, see L. Shaw, *History of the Province of Moray* (1775), 39n. The lands of Glencarnie were held of the earls of Strathearn.

12. A charter of August 8th, 1309, preserved at Cawdor Castle, is dated 'Loch Bren', i.e. Loch a 'Bhraoin, now in Scots Loch Broom; another, of October 20th, 1309, is dated at Dunstaffnage: *RRS*, v, nos. 9, 10.

13. *Chron. Guisb.*, 385-6: the English burned and laid waste, and the Scots lurked in hills and boggy places. *Rotuli Scotiae*, i, 80 and *Cal. Docs. Scot.*, iii, no.218 are the chief authorities here.

14. *Cal. Docs. Scot.*, iii, no.221.

15. *Rotuli Scotiae*, i, 80.

16. *Ibid.*

17. *Ibid.*, 60a; Barbour, *Bruce*, 190.

18. *Rotuli Scotiae*, i, 106.

19. *Cal. Docs. Scot.*, iii, no.304; cf. no.279.

20. *Ibid.*, no.218.

21. *Rotuli Scotiae*, i, 86.

22. *Ibid.*, 99b; cf. 90a, 93b.

23. *Ibid.*, 90b.

24. *Ibid.*, 96.

25. *Chron. Lanercost*, 210.

26. *Chron. Man*, 233-4; *Rotuli Scotiae*, i, 96, 107a; *Cal. Docs. Scot.*, iii, no.481.

27. *Ibid.*; cf. nos. 277, 391.

28. *Ibid.*, nos. 307, 391. Simon Montague's involvement in Man seems to have gone back as early as 1305 (*Chron. Man*, 233).

29. *Chron. Man*, ed. P. A. Munch (Christiania, 1860), 27-8.

30. *Cal. Docs. Scot.*, iii, *passim*, references in index. In 1317 Dungal supervised the funeral in London of John Macdougall of Lorn who died at Ospringe in Kent while on pilgrimage to Canterbury; Dungal may have regarded the lord of Argyll as his kinsman: *Cal. Docs. Scot.*, v, pp.230-1.

31. *Ibid.*, iii, no.420; J. R. S. Phillips, 'The Mission of John de Hothum to Ireland, 1315-1316' in *England and Ireland in the later middle ages*, ed. J. F. Lydon, 62.

32. *Cal. Docs. Scot.*, no.562.

33. *Ibid.*, no.451.

34. Barbour, *Bruce*, 257; *Cal. Docs. Scot.*, iii, no.562.

35. *Chron. Lanercost*, 220.

36. *Ibid.*, 214; *Chron. Guisb.*, 386.

37. *Cal. Docs. Scot.*, iii, 425-7.

38. *Ibid.*, no.45; *Rotuli Scotiae*, i, 61b.

39. *Ibid.*, 105b.

40. Barbour, *Bruce*, 158.

41. *Ibid.*, 160; but cf. *Chron. Fordun*, i, 346; *Chron. Lanercost*, 221-2.

42. Barbour, *Bruce*, 191.

43. *Ibid.*, 192.

44. *Chron. Holyrood*, 180; Barbour, *Bruce*, 178-82.

45. *Ibid.*, 179, Sym of the Ledows. Ledhous (Leidhous, etc.) was the name of some lands beside Crossford in Lesmahagow parish, the next parish north of Douglas.

46. *Ibid.*, 181; *Chron. Lanercost*, 223; *Cal. Docs. Scot.*, iii, 406 and elsewhere *passim*; *Scalacronica*, 140, reading *de* for *et* before Burglioun. Bouglon is in dép. Lot-et-Garonne, arr. Marmande.

47. Barbour, *Bruce*, 182-90; *Chron. Holyrood*, 180.

48. *Reg. Mag. Sig.*, i, Appendix II, nos. 285, 373.

49. *Chron. Lanercost*, 223, perhaps meaning 'east' port, not 'south'.

50. *Ibid.*

51. J. F. Willard, 'The Scotch raids and the fourteenth-century taxation of northern England', *University of Colorado Studies*, v (1907-8), no.4, 237-42; Jean Scammell, 'Robert I and the north of England', *EHR*, lxxiii, 385-403.

52. *Cal. Docs. Scot.*, iii, no.337.

53. *Chron. Lanercost*, 216.

54. *Ibid.*, 220; *Historiae Dunelmensis Ecclesiae Scriptores Tres* (ed. J. Raine, Surtees Soc.), 94.

55. *Ibid.*; Stones, *Relations*, no.37; *RRS*, v, no.21.

56. *Chron. Lanercost*, 224.

57. PRO, D. L.36, iii, fo.12, 3rd doc.; *Cal. Docs. Scot.*, i, no.321; iii, no.413.

58. *Chron. Lanercost*, 230; cf. also *Cal. Docs. Scot.*, iii, nos.602, 631, 648, the last two referring to the capture of a Scottish ship at or off Hartlepool early in 1319.

59. J. Scammell, *art. cit.*, 386.

60. *Cal. Docs. Scot.*, ii, no.1479.

61. *Ibid.*, no.1639 and 443.

62. *Rotuli Scotiae*, i, 78b.

63. W. Stanford Reid, 'Trade, traders and Scottish independence', *Speculum*, xxix, 217, citing H. J. Smit, *Bronnen tot Geschiedenis van den Handel med Engelond etc.* (The Hague, 1928), i, 214. The whole of Reid's article, and also that by Jas. W. Dilley, 'German merchants in Scotland, 1297-1327' *SHR*, xxvii, 142-55, should be read for a survey of the evidence on trade between Scotland and the continent in this period.

64. *Cal. Docs. Scot.*, iii, nos. 252, 679.

65. Jas. W. Dilley, 'Scottish-German Diplomacy', *SHR*, xxxvi, 83.

66. *Ibid.*, 85.

67. W. Stanford Reid, *art. cit.*, 422.

68. Reid, *art. cit.*, stresses the importance of smuggling for the Scots in this period.

69. *Rotuli Scotiae*, i, 59-60; 107-8.

70. *Cal. Docs. Scot.*, iii, no.300; cf. *Rotuli Scotiae*, i, 112.

71. *Ibid.*; *Cal. Docs. Scot.*, iii, no.346.

72. *APS*, i, 461-4.

73. *Cal. Docs. Scot.*, iii, no.500.

74. *Ibid.*, ii, no.927. Farquhar Bellejambe had been a canon of Aberdeen.

75. *RRS*, v, Introduction.

76. *Arbroath Liber*, i, no.332.

77. *Ibid.*, no.360.

78. *RRS*, v, nos. 17, 18.

CHAPTER TWELVE
Bannockburn

1. *Rotuli Scotiae*, i, 118, 119b, etc.

2. *Chron. Lanercost*, 219.

3. *Rotuli Scotiae*, i, 119a.

4. *Vita Edwardi*, 43.

5. *Rotuli Scotiae*, i, 113-4.

6. *Ibid.*, 114b.

7. *Cal. Close Rolls, 1313-18*, 86.

8. *Cal. Chancery Warrants*, i, 395 (February 26th), 398 (April 20th); cf. *Rotuli Scotiae*, i, 120a.

9. See J. E. Morris, *Bannockburn* (1914), 40-1; and *Rotuli Scotiae*, i, 115ff.

10. Morris, op. cit., 35; *Complete Peerage*, xi, Appendix B, 11. M. McKisack, *The Fourteenth Century*, 35, speaks of 'possibly, some Irish'.

11. *Cal. Pat. Rolls, 1313-17*, 121; *Cal. Chancery Warrants*, i, 402.

12. Barbour, *Bruce*, 194.

13. Morris, *Bannockburn*, 40; *Rotuli Scotiae*, i, 120b.

14. *Ibid.*, 120b and 126-7.

15. Morris, *Bannockburn*, 41.

16. See above, p.96, n. 4.

17. *Complete Peerage*, xi, Appendix B.

18. Morris, *Bannockburn*, 34.

19. *Vita Edwardi*, 49-50; *Chron. Lanercost*, 224.

20. Morris, *Bannockburn*, 34-5, makes the total of protections 830. My own count is about 890. The source is the *Rotulus Scotiae* for 8 Edward II, PRO, C.71/7, m.1, m.5.

21. Morris, *Bannockburn*, 35.

22. *Cal. Close Rolls, 1313-18*, 76.

23. Barbour, *Bruce*, 234-5. He had fought at Methven in 1306, *Cal. Docs. Scot.*, v, no.492.

24. *Vita Edwardi*, 50.

25. *Chron. Bower*, ii, 248.

26. Barbour, *Bruce*, 194.

27. Morris, *Bannockburn*, 49.

28. Above, p.94, n.2.

29. *Chron. Lanercost*, 214.

30. Barbour, *Bruce*, 194, 198: 100,000 English to 30,000 Scots.

31. T. M. Cooper, Lord Cooper in *SHR*, xxvi, 2-9; cf. the same author's *Supra Crepidam*.

32. Barbour, *Bruce*, 197.

33. *RRS*, i, no.46.

34. *APS*, i, 454; cf. Stevenson, *Documents*, nos.632, 634; *Cal. Docs. Scot.*, ii, no.1432; *Chron. Lanercost*, 225.

35. *Rotuli Scotiae*, i, 126-7.

36. *Vita Edwardi*, 50.

37. *Ibid.*, where the writer also says: 'All who were present agreed that never in our times has such an army gone forth from England.'

38. *Cal. Docs. Scot.*, iii, no.365.

39. *Vita Edwardi*, 51.

40. Barbour, *Bruce*, 201, 204.

41. *Ibid.*, 200-1.

42. *Ibid.*, 200, 226. It is strange that James Douglas was knighted only on the eve of Bannockburn, *ibid.*, 211. A French account, characterized by a mixture of gross error and accurate detail, says that on the eve of the battle Robert I knighted his bastard son (Robert Bruce of Liddesdale?), his brother Edward Bruce, (Walter) the Stewart, the earl of Moray and Sir John [*sic*] Douglas: *Chronographia Regum Francorum*, ed. H. Moranvillé (Paris, 1891-3), i, 182-3.

43. *Ibid.*

44. Again strange, since Bute was in the Stewart's lordship.

45. *Ibid.*, 201-2.

46. T. Miller, *The site of the battle of Bannockburn* (Historical Association, 1931); R. A. Carruthers, 'The site of the battle of Bannockburn', *Chambers Journal* (February 1933), reprinted as an appendix to Barron, *Scottish War of Independence*.

47. W. Mackay Mackenzie, *The Battle of Bannockburn: a study in mediaeval warfare* (1913); his hypothesis being first adumbrated in a paper in *Proceedings of the Glasgow Archaeological Society* for 1908-9. See also his sadly crotchety *The Bannockburn Myth* (Edinburgh, 1932), a reply to Miller.

48. P. Christison, 'Bannockburn – 23rd and 24th June, 1314. A study in military history', *Proc. Soc. Antiq. Scot.*, xc (1956-7, pub. 1959), 170-9; subsequently republished in a revised form as *Bannockburn: the story of the battle* (National Trust for Scotland, revised edn, 1962).

49. Authorities of the Geological Survey are quoted as saying that the peat had been removed from the Carse of Stirling long before 1314; but documentary evidence of the fourteenth and sixteenth centuries shows that peats were still being cut then in parts of the Carse.

50. All these are on the 1-inch Ordnance Map, except for Pelstream, taken from the article by General Christison, above, n.48.

51. Stevenson, *Documents*, nos.632, 634; *Chron. Guisb.*, 303: *iuxta polles, ad polles*.

52. Mackenzie, *Battle of Bannockburn*; Barron, *Scottish War of Independence*; J. D. Mackie, *SHR*, xxvi, 189-90. Sir Herbert Maxwell, in one of his rare flights of accuracy, saw that Barbour's *pollis* must be the Scots 'pows' or sluggish streams with which he was familiar in Galloway and elsewhere, and that the makeshift bridging would obviously be required for streams, not for pools, *SHR*, xi, 246, n. 1. But Sir Herbert did not realize that the whole region of the Carse was known as 'the Pows'; and in any case his own suggested site for the battle is quite unacceptable.

53. *Exch. Rolls*, i, 24, 38; cf. *Dunfermline Registrum*, no.215 (1215) and F. W. Maitland, *Memoranda de Parliamento*, 212 (1305), which show the king's serjeants holding or claiming land, rights, etc., in Skeoch and in the Old and New Parks.

54. See the map attached to his *Site of the battle of Bannockburn*.

55. *Dunfermline Registrum*, no.215. The ancient name of Balquhiderock would hardly have survived continuously as a farm-name had this area been out of cultivation for a long stretch.

56. Watson, *Celtic Place-Names of Scotland*, 195-6. Probably Bannok was a vestigial district name, from a Celtic word, *bannauc* or *bannog* meaning 'peaked', 'having peaks'.

57. The canon of Bridlington (*Gesta Edwardi de Carnarvan*, ed. Stubbs, 46) and John de Trokelow (*Annales*, ed. Riley, 124), both English writers, seem to be the earliest to use the name Bannockburn apparently for the place. But see the story told in *Chron. Bower*, ii, 247-8; cf. also *Cal. Docs. Scots.*, ii, no.1636.

58. Chronicles use Bannockburn for the place sooner than formal title-deeds. The authorities for the statement in the text are as follows. (1) Scottish Chronicles and comparable sources: *Chron. Holyrood*, 180; *Chron. Fordun*, i, 342, 346; *Chron. Bower*, ii, 243, 245, 246, 247-8, 251, 254, 255; *Chron. Pluscarden*, i, 237, 240;

Chron. Wyntoun (Laing), ii, 312, 403, iii, 336; *Glasgow Registrum*, no.327. (2) Scottish Record sources: *Dunfermline Registrum*, no.215; *Cambuskenneth Registrum*, no.210; *Reg. Mag. Sig.*, i, nos.464, 357, 759, Appendix ii, nos. 237-9, 580-1, 1643; ii, nos. 1879, 1960, 3363, 3494; iv, nos. 1799, 1973, 1630; vi, nos. 1162, 1243; *Retours*, Stirling, nos. 121, 215, 236, 255, 257, 261, 331, 361.

59. *Dunfermline Registrum*, no.215; *Cambuskenneth Registrum*, no.210; *Reg. Mag. Sig.*, i, nos. 357, 759, and many other references passim. The identity of Ochtirbannok and Milton is shown by a charter of 1660 whereby John Murray of Touchadam granted land in Balquhiderock to James Greinnock, smith in Bannockburn, referring to 'Overbannockburn commonly called the Mylntoune' (ex inf. A. A. M. Duncan).

60. *Dunfermline Registrum*, no.215.

61. J. M. Mackinlay, *Ancient Church Dedications in Scotland*, ii, (Non-Scriptural), 503; cf. the same author's *The Influence of the Pre-Reformation Church on Scottish Place-Names* (1904), 25-6.

62. *Reg. Mag. Sig.*, ii, no.3494.

63. *Ibid.*, iv, no.1630; *Retours*, Stirling, no.121, etc.

64. *Dunfermline Registrum*, no.215.

65. *Reg. Mag. Sig.*, ii, no.1960, thereafter many references, e.g., *Retours*, Stirling, no.236.

66. *Dunfermline Registrum*, no.215.

67. Trokelow, *Annales* (ed. Riley), 83; *Annales Londonienses* (ed. Stubbs), 231; *Annales Paulini* (ed. Stubbs), 276.

68. *Cal. Docs. Scots.*, iii, nos.626, 627, 682. Cf. *Henry of Pytchley's Book of Fees*, ed. W. T. Mellows, Northants Record Society (1927), 91; 'Gilbert de Clare died killed in battle in Scotland at Stirling.'

69. *Chron. Holyrood*, 180; *Chron. Fordun*, i, 342; *APS*, i, 682b.

70. *Chron. Bower*, ii, 243, 245, 254.

71. Trokelow, *Annales*, 124 (for *Baumkesburne* read *Bannukesburne*); *Gesta Edwardi de Carnarvan*, 46.

72. *Cal. Docs. Scot.*, iii, no.1636.

73. *Chron. Fordun*, i, 346; *Chron. Bower*, ii, 246 etc.; *Chron. Pluscarden*, i, 237, 240; *Chron. Wyntoun* (Laing), ii, 312, 403.

74. Trokelow, *Annales*, 86.

75. *Brut y Tywysogion, Peniarth MS. 20* (ed. T. Jones, Cardiff, 1941), 231; cf. Translation, T. Jones, *Brut y Tywysogion or The Chronicle of the Princes, Peniarth MS. 20 version* (Cardiff, 1952), 123, 219.

76. *Chronica monasterii de Melsa* (ed. Bond), ii, 331.

77. *Chronicon Galfridi le Baker de Swynebroke*, ed. E. M. Thompson, 7.

78. *Chron. Bower*, ii, 247-8.

79. *Ibid.*, 248: *Bannokburn . . . qui locus [al. campus] est . . . juxta burgum regium de Strivelyn in Scotia.*

80. *SHR*, xxvi, 190.

81. Barbour, *Bruce*, 199-200.

82. *Ibid.*, 137-8.

83. *Ibid.*, 202.

84. *Ibid.*, 199-200.

85. *Flores Historiarum*, iii, 158. N. Denholm Young dismisses this as 'surely rubbish' (*Vita Edwardi*, 27) and prefers that work's explanation that the earls' quarrel over supremacy in leading the van arose because Hereford claimed in right of being Constable and Gloucester claimed by hereditary custom (*Vita Edwardi*, 53). There is no doubt that the two earls were jointly in command of the van, and neither explanation of their quarrel is flattering to King Edward's good sense.

86. *Scalacronica*, 141.

87. *Vita Edwardi*, 51.

88. *Ibid.*; Barbour, *Bruce*, 211; cf. Morris, *Bannockburn*, 66-7.

89. Barbour, *Bruce*, 211.

90. *Vita Edwardi*, 51; Morris, *Bannockburn*, 67.

91. *Scalacronica*, 141; *Chron. Lanercost*, 225; Barbour, *Bruce*, 206ff. (who puts the episode before Gloucester's advance). *Vita Edwardi*, 51, confuses the separate advances of Gloucester and Clifford.

92. *Scalacronica*, 141.

93. Barbour, *Bruce*, 206.

94. *Ibid.* Perhaps Barbour implies that Beaumont was one of the three bannerets.

95. Barron, *Scottish War of Independence*, 504.

96. *Vita Edwardi*, 51.

97. *Chron. Lanercost*, 225.

98. Barbour, *Bruce*, 206.

99. *Ibid.*, 206-7.

100. *Ibid.*, 207.

101. *Ibid.*, 204, 207, 'the way' being the high road leading past St Ninians kirk towards Stirling.

102. *Scalacronica*, 141.

103. Barbour, *Bruce*, 209.

104. *Chron. Lanercost*, 225; *Scalacronica*, 142; Barbour, *Bruce*, 214, 219-20. *Vita Edwardi*, 51-2, speaks of the caution engendered among the English leaders because of their toil on June 23rd.

105. Barbour, *Bruce*, 220-1.

106. *Scalacronica*, 141-2.

107. The MS reads as follows: 'al ost le Rey . qy ia auoint gerpy la voy du boys . estoint uenuz en un plain deuers leau de Forth . outre Bannokburn . un mauueis parfound Ruscell' marras.' (Cambridge, Corpus Christi College MS. 133, fo.205r, col.2). Since both *ruscell* and *marras* are masculine nouns, it is not clear which is qualifying which.

108. *Chron. Lanercost*, 226; *Vita Edwardi*, 54.

109. *Chronicon Galfridi le Baker*, ed. Thompson, 7.

110. *Scalacronica*, 142.

111. *Ibid.*

112. NLS, MS Adv.35.3.7, p.318; Mackenzie, *Writers*, iii, 210; A. A. M. Duncan, in *SHR*, xlv, 199. Thomas Hay of Lochwharret (now Borthwick, south of Edinburgh) had joined Bruce by Christmas, 1308; *Cal. Docs. Scot.*, iii, no.245.

113. Above, p.87; below, p.307.

114. Barbour, *Bruce*, 214-15.

115. Information kindly supplied by Professor H. A. Brück, Astronomer Royal for Scotland, *per litt.*, June 14th, 1962.

116. Barbour, *Bruce*, 221.

117. *Ibid.*, 222 (lines 447, 457).

118. *Ibid.*, line 437.

119. *Chron. Bower*, ii, 252.

120. T. Miller, *Site of the battle of Bannockburn*, 6 n., 15 n.

121. As suggested by Barron, *Scottish War of Independence*, 464.

122. Barbour, *Bruce*, 221.

123. *Arbroath Liber*, i, Preface, p.xxiii; F. C. Eeles, 'The Monymusk Reliquary or Brecbennoch of St Columba', *Proc. Soc. Antiq. Scot.*, lxviii (1933-4), 433-8.

124. *Chron. Bower*, ii, 249-50.

125. See p.367 and n. 42.

126. Barbour, *Bruce*, 223.

127. *Chron. Lanercost*, 225.

128. *Ibid.*, 226; *Vita Edwardi*, 53-4.

129. Barbour, *Bruce*, 231.

130. *Ibid.*, 229.

131. *Ibid.*, 227.

132. *Ibid.*, 229. Once Bruce's brigade or 'battle' was fully engaged (Barbour says) all four 'battles' were fighting on one front, *ibid.*, 231.

133. *Ibid.*, 230.

134. *Ibid.*, 232.

135. *Ibid.*, 233.

136. *Ibid.*, 203, line 426; cf. 233, line 230. They were within the New Park.

137. *Scalacronica*, 142; Barbour, *Bruce*, 196.

138. *Ibid.*, 234; *Scalacronica*, 142-3; Thomas Walsingham, *Historia Anglicana* (ed. H. T. Riley), 141.

139. *Scalacronica*, 143; Barbour, *Bruce*, 235.

140. *Ibid.*, 235.

141. *Scalacronica*, 142.

142. Although Mackenzie took this as evidence for his suggested site of the battle, it is not certain that the writer meant that the tidal reaches were in the battle zone, or that he was correctly informed, and it is possible that many of the English troops fleeing after the battle were drowned or bogged down in this part of the burn.

143. *Chron. Lanercost*, 226.

144. *Vita Edwardi*, 54.

145. T. Walsingham, *Hist. Angl.*, 141, and information kindly given by Professor A. A. M. Duncan.

146. *Ibid.*, 142; Barbour, *Bruce*, 240. The earl is buried in Tewkesbury Abbey.

147. *Annales Londonienses*, 231, to whose list add the name of John de Grey from *Gesta Edwardi de Carnarvan*, 46. Cf. BL, MS. Cott. Cleop. D iii, fo.56v. The Pipe Roll for 8 Edw. II (PRO, E.372/160, m.50) gives the names of Edmund Comyn, Nicholas de Vieuxpont, Robert Clifford, Robert Bertram and William de Vesey of Kildare.

148. *Ibid.*, 46–7; Barbour, *Bruce*, 236; *Vita Edwardi*, 54.

149. Barbour, *Bruce*, 236–7. *Scalacronica*, 143, actually says that the king's party rode round the outside of the Torwood (i.e., to the west), before reaching the plain of Lothian. But they would scarcely have had time for such a lengthy detour. *Chron. Lanercost*, 227, says that the king's party included Hugh Despenser the younger and Sir Henry Beaumont. J. R. S. Phillips, *Aymer de Valence, earl of Pembroke, 1307–1324* (Oxford, 1972), 75, gives evidence to show that Pembroke was also with King Edward.

150. Barbour, *Bruce*, 237, 241–3.

151. He figures on a list entered on the Pipe Roll for 8 Edward II (PRO, E 372/160, m.50).

152. *Ibid.*, 237; *Chron. Lanercost*, 228; *Chronographia Regum Francorum*, ed. Moranvillé, 182–3, Hereford captured fleeing to 'an old castle'.

153. *Chron. Lanercost*, 228; *Vita Edwardi*, 55.

154. Barbour, *Bruce*, 245; *Cal. Docs. Scot.*, iii, no.393. It was intended that the young earl of Mar, Bruce's nephew, should be repatriated at this time, but when he reached Newcastle he refused to go any further and chose to remain with King Edward, to whom he was closely attached, *Chron. Lanercost*, 229, and below, p.274.

155. Barbour, *Bruce*, 240–1.

156. T. Walsingham, *Hist. Angl.*, 141, 'because of some close friendship with the Scottish king, which some time before had chanced to develop at the English king's court'.

157. Above, p.139–40.

158. T. Walsingham, *Hist. Angl.*, 141–2.

159. *Chron. Lanercost*, 228; Barbour, *Bruce*, 238; *Annales Londonienses*, 231.

160. T. Jones, *Brut y Tywysogion* (1952), 48–9 and 62–3.

161. Dunbar seems to have made his peace with Robert I as soon as he had seen Edward II safely out of his sight (PRO, E.372/160, m.50).

CHAPTER THIRTEEN
War and Peace

1. On Clement see *EHR*, lxxxiii, 303ff.

2. Apart from Englishmen who became 'Scottish', the following Scots holding land in northern England are recorded as being forfeited for 'rebellion' as from June 25th 1314, the day after the battle: Earl Patrick of Dunbar (Beanley), John Wishart (Monylaws), Henry Prendergest (Akeld), all Northumberland, and Walter Curry (Kirklinton, Cumberland), while Roger de Moubray, lord of Bolton in Allerdale, Cumberland, was forfeited from either July 12th or September 29th; PRO, E.372/160, m.50.

3. Jean Scammell, *EHR*, lxxiii, 402.

4. J. F. Lydon, 'The Hobelar: an Irish contribution to medieval warfare', *The Irish Sword*, ii (1954–6), 12–16.

5. Le Bel, *Chroniques*, 47–8.

6. *Chron. Lanercost*, 233. In one of those graphic touches by which Barbour creates the illusion of having been present at the events he describes, he says of the Scots withdrawing from Stanhope Park (over Wolfcleugh Common?) in 1327: 'And tynt bot litill off thar ger /   Bot gyf it war ony summer [sumpter] / that in the mos wes left liand' (Barbour, *Bruce*, 358).

7. *Dumfriesshire Trans.*, 3rd Ser., xxvi, 186.

8. *Chron. Lanercost*, 228–9.

9. *Ibid.*, 229. Confirmed by evidence discussed in *Arch. Æliana*, 5th ser., ii, 149–52.

10. J. Hodgson, *History of Northumberland*, pt. III, ii, 390; *Rot. Parl.*, i, 293.

11. *Chron. Lanercost*, 230.

12. *Ibid.*, 232.

13. *Ibid.*, 233.

14. Barbour, *Bruce*, 270–3; *Scalacronica*, 143; particulars of a Gascon knight and seven horses lost at Simprim, February 14th, 1316, in *Gascon Rolls*, ed. Y. Renouard (1962), no.1749.

15. *Scalacronica*, 143; Barbour, *Bruce*, 287–91.

16. *Ibid.*, 187–91; *Scalacronica*, 143.

17. Barbour, *Bruce*, 278. Moray was at Lauder on Dec. 6th, 1316; SRO, Reg. Ho. chrs., no.83.

18. Barbour, *Bruce*, 292–6; *Chron. Bower*, ii, 259.

19. Barbour, *Bruce*, 293; see below, p.391.

20. *Ibid.*, 295.

21. *Ibid.*, 297ff. Keith of Galston was afterwards to bring the body of Douglas home from Spain, *ibid.*, 376.

22. *Ibid.*, 298; *Chron. Lanercost*, 234-5; *Scalacronica*, 144. According to John of Tynemouth, Peter was bribed with £800 by Douglas, but afterwards executed on a false charge of plotting against the king's life (Stevenson, *Illustrations*, 5).

23. Lord Hailes (Hailes, *Annals*, ii, 77n.) proposed over-ingeniously to substitute 'the Marche Earl' (i.e. Patrick earl of Dunbar) for 'the marschall' of Barbour, *Bruce*, 297, on the grounds that (1) Keith lived far from Berwick; (2) was not likely to have been sheriff of Lothian; (3) Grey (*Scalacronica*, 144) says that Spalding and the earl of March helped to procure the fall of Berwick. But in an undated charter of this period Keith is styled warden of Berwick, and he may well have had some interest in the burgh; *Melrose Liber*, no.372.

24. Barbour, *Bruce*, 302, says 'six days', but see *ibid.*, 464-5.

25. *Chron. Lanercost*, 235.

26. G. W. S. Barrow, 'A note on Falstone', *Arch. Æliana*, 5th Ser., ii, 149-52. This may have been before February 1317, by which date Richard of Middleton was reported to have been captured and delivered to Edward 11: *Cal. Docs. Scot.*, iii, no.539. Harbottle seems to have been recaptured by the English before 1320: *ibid.*, no.686.

27. *Chron. Lanercost*, 235-6; *Cal. Docs. Scot.*, iii, nos. 707, 858.

28. Barbour, *Bruce*, 304-10.

29. For Archbishop Melton's handling of the situation caused by the war see Rosalind Hill, 'An English archbishop and the Scottish War of Independence', *Innes Review*, xxii, 59-71.

30. Gilsland suffered severely from the Scottish raids. A schedule of assized rents due from the Gilsland farms of Wetheral Priory for the Whitsun and Martinmas terms, 1327, shows rents in arrears for periods of 2, 9, 10, 12 and in one case even 20 years. Yet the schedule also proves that after a few years' truce recovery could begin and that the district cannot have been totally depopulated. (Dean and Chapter of Carlisle, MS. Cartulary of Wetheral Priory, schedule bound in at the end of the volume.)

31. *Chron. Lanercost*, 240.

32. *Foedera*, ii, 404, safe-conduct for 12 Scots to come to Newcastle, valid till January 13th, 1320; *ibid.*, 412 (= *Cal. Pat. R.*, *1317-21*, 414), where twelve Scots are named, with safe-conduct to discuss King of Scots' business with Edward 11, valid for duration of truce. The second safe-conduct, dated January 7th 1320, was presumably a renewal of the October letter and for the same persons.

33. Below, pp.303-9.

34. The authorities for what follows are: *Foedera*, ii, 1, 441, 450; Stones, *Relations*, 292-307; P. A. Linehan, 'A fourteenth-century history of Anglo-Scottish relations in a Spanish manuscript', *BIHR*, xlviii (1975), 106-22; *Les journaux du trésor de Charles IV le Bel*, ed. J. Viard (Paris, 1917), nos.396, 512, 3230, 3920, 4015, 5016, 6262 (expenses of French envoys); Watt, *Dictionary*, 176-7, 299-301.

35. *BIHR*, xlviii, 121.

36. Stones, *Relations*, 305.

37. *BIHR*, xlviii, 116.

38. *Cal. Docs. Scot.*, iii, no.764 (summarizing *Foedera*, ii, 463, 472, 474). On this see J. R. Maddicott, *Thomas of Lancaster* (1970), 301-3; *Formulary E*, ed. A. A. M. Duncan (1976), no.55 and comment.

39. *Chron. Lanercost*, 241-2.

40. J. E. Morris, *Bannockburn*, 94-5; *EHR*, xix, 711-13.

41. *Chron. Lanercost*, 246 (for Lenyn read Leuyn, i.e. River Leven).

42. M. R. Powicke, in *Speculum*, xxxv, 561.

43. Barbour, *Bruce*, 330.

44. *Foedera*, ii, 496, shows that by September 27th, 1322, men were fleeing from the North Riding into County Durham with their cattle.

45. *Chron. Lanercost*, 247; *Foedera*, ii, 497 (from which it appears that the encounter upon 'Blakhoumor' was not fortuitous). For the identification of 'Blakehoumor' see A. H. Smith, *Place-Names of the North Riding of Yorkshire*, 197, where the references to *Yorkshire Lay Subsidy* (Yorks. Arch. Soc., 1897), 56, and to *Yorkshire Deeds* (Yorks. Arch. Soc., 1924), iv, 85, certainly refer to a locality in the region of Old Byland. The account in the text is based on the assumption that when contemporary sources use the name Byland they mean Old Byland; and that

in Barbour, *Bruce*, 332, line 368, 'Bilandis abbay' is a mistake arising from confusion between Old Byland (close to Rievaulx Abbey) and [New] Byland Abbey.

46. *Cal. Docs. Scot.*, iii, nos. 790, 791; *Chron. Lanercost*, 247; *Scalacronica*, 149.

47. Barbour, *Bruce*, 332 and *Chron. Lanercost*, 247, agree on the nature of the terrain, and their accounts will fit only Sutton Bank and Roulston Scar.

48. *Gesta Edwardi de Carnarvan*, 79-80 (which says wrongly that Edward was at Byland Abbey instead of Rievaulx); *Chron. Lanercost*, 248.

49. *Ibid.*; *Cal. Docs. Scot.*, iii, no.791; *Foedera*, ii, 498.

50. *Ibid.*, ii, 511.

51. A French knight Raoul Silvani or de Jouy was an envoy from Charles IV to Robert I in 1322 or 1323, but the purpose of his mission is not known: *Les journaux du trésor*, ed. Viard, nos. 2404, 2933.

52. Stubbs, *Select Charters* (9th edn), 460.

53. *Ibid.*, 480.

54. Barbour, *Bruce*, 294. See below, p.266.

55. *Cal. Docs. Scot.*, ii, 536.

56. Hailes, *Annals*, ii, 74.

57. *Foedera*, ii, 340.

58. *Cal. Papal Letters*, ii, 191-2, 199. Sir Gilbert Middleton and his brother Richard, implicated in the kidnapping of the cardinals, were captured, in Tynedale and at Mitford respectively, and executed before March 1st 1318: *Cal. Pat. R.*, *1317-21*, 112; *Cal. Docs. Scot.*, iii, no.539.

59. Above, pp.240-1.

60. *Chron. Lanercost*, 248; cf. *ibid.*, 251.

61. *Proc. Soc. Antiq. Scot.*, iii (1857-60), 458-61; cf. *RRS*, v, no.215.

62. The best version of these is probably that found on an Exchequer Memoranda Roll (PRO, E.159/96, m.70), summarized *Cal. Docs. Scot.*, iii, no.803. This is printed in Stones, *Relations*, no.39, which see for the various chronicle versions.

63. *Foedera*, ii, 521, 524.

64. *Ibid.*, 595.

65. *Ibid.*, 541ff.

66. *Ibid.*, 542, *Responsiones Papae ad articula*, 2, 3.

67. *Foedera*, ii, 613.

68. *Ibid.*, 541.

69. *Ibid.*, 558; repeated August 20th, *ibid.*, 567.

70. *APS*, xii, 5-6; *RRS*, v, no.299. See R. Nicholson, *Scotland: the later Middle Ages*, 117.

71. Vatican Archives, Instrumenta Miscellanea 944. I am indebted to Fr Charles Burns for providing me with information about this letter, together with a photostat.

72. *Chron. Lanercost*, 258-9.

73. *Foedera*, ii, 689 (*Cal. Docs. Scot.*, iii, no.907).

74. *Ibid.*, 696 (*Cal. Docs. Scot.*, iii, no.914).

75. *Chron. Fordun*, i, 351.

76. Barbour, *Bruce*, 343; *Cal. Docs. Scot.*, iii, nos. 853, 887, 888, 889, 965. On October 2nd, 1323, Edward II ordered the wardens of the truce on the Marches to arrest all Scots residing in England, *ibid.*, no.827. It was alleged in April 1326 that there had been 'unofficial' Scottish attempts to surprise the castles of Carlisle, Norham, Wark on Tweed, Dunstanburgh and Alnwick, *ibid.*, nos. 882, 883. Edward II seems to have made some attempt to discuss points of the truce with Robert I in June, 1326, *Foedera*, ii, 631.

77. *Cal. Docs. Scot.*, iii, no.922; R. Nicholson, 'The last campaign of Robert Bruce', *EHR*, lxxvii, 242.

78. *Chron. Lanercost*, 259. *Chron. Fordun*, i, 352, speaks of two incursions, one on June 15th, one in August. The place of entry in June is suggested (1) by Le Bel's remark that the Scots came in so quietly that no one in Carlisle or Newcastle got wind of them, Le Bel, *Chroniques*, i, 46; (2) by the fact that Weardale was their first objective.

79. See R. Nicholson, *EHR*, lxxvii, 233-4.

80. Edward III lodged the second night 'in the mean hall of an abbey which was there', Le Bel, *Chroniques*, i, 50. Only Blanchland, a remote Premonstratensian house on the upper Derwent, will fit.

81. Barbour, *Bruce*, 345. The suggestion that this was the Gaunless valley would fit in with Grey's statement that Archibald Douglas's party fell upon and massacred a large gathering of peasants *near* Darlington (*Scalacronica*, 154).

82. *Ibid.*, says that the English army marched to Haydon Bridge by way of

'Anandredalle', clearly not Annandale but Allendale. East Allendale would lie on their natural route south-eastward from the neighbourhood of Haltwhistle, where they forded the Tyne, to Blanchland.

83. There is an unusually serious conflict of evidence among the most nearly contemporary authorities for the Stanhope Park affair. This probably reflects a genuine confusion and uncertainty on the part of the eye-witnesses from whom our accounts, directly and indirectly, are derived. The conflict is impossible to resolve, and the account in the text can be no better than an approximation, based on Le Bel, *Chroniques*; Barbour, *Bruce*; *Scalacronica*; *Chron. Lanercost*; *Cal. Docs. Scot.*, iii, nos. 929, 933.

W. M. Mackenzie's notes (Barbour, *Bruce*, 482ff) are valuable, but his argument that the Scots were always on the north bank of the Wear needs modifying in view of the clear implication in Le Bel, *Chroniques*, i, 62, that when the English first approached they found the river between them and the Scots. Since the English were coming from Blanchland, they can hardly have been on the south side of the river, while the Scots were strongly positioned on a steep hillside, presumably the hill opposite Stanhope.

84. *Foedera*, ii, 712.

85. See R. Nicholson, *EHR*, lxxvii, 242-5.

86. *Rotuli Scotiae*, 221b. Compare Barbour, *Bruce*, 361: 'The landis of Northumbirland, / That next Scotland thar wes liand, / In fe and heritage gaf he / and thai payit for the selys fee' with the record of the king's grant of part of Belford (formerly a Graham, before that a Muschamp barony) to a Scrymgeour, September 4th, 1327, *RRS*, v, no.324.

87. *Rotuli Scotiae*, i, 221-3.

88. The essential guide here is E. L. G. Stones, 'The Anglo-Scottish negotiations of 1327', *SHR*, xxx, 49-54. William is said (see Stones, *Relations*, 289, n. 3) to have been a local clerk, taking his surname from Deanham beside Wallington, Northumberland.

89. *SHR*, xxx, 51, 53-4; cf. Stones, *Relations*, no.40.

90. *SHR*, xxx, 51.

91. The phrase is to be found in the preliminaries and final text of the treaty of Birgham (1290), echoed in *Scimus, fili* (1299), and repeated (as a false attribution to Richard I) in the Bamburgh brief (1321): Stevenson, *Documents*, i, 160-167; Stones, *Relations*, 167; *BIHR*, xlviii, 117.

92. Stones, *Relations*, no.41a. (My italics.)

93. See *SHR*, xxix, 27-8 and n. It must be emphasized that the main body of the treaty itself refers to the possibility of revolt 'in the Isle of Man or in the other isles of Scotland' (Stones, *Relations*, no.41c) thus implying, as Professor Stones noted, English recognition of Scottish possession of Man and the isles.

94. E. L. G. Stones, 'The English mission to Edinburgh in 1328', *SHR*, xxviii, 121-32.

95. *SHR*, xxix, 48.

96. The text of the brieve of summons to this parliament has survived and is edited by A. A. M. Duncan in *SHR*, xlv (1966), 52 and *Formulary E* (1976), no.77. Cf. *RRS*, v, no.563.

97. Successor to David Murray, Bishop John, son of a Dundee burgess, may have been kinsman (nephew?) of John of Pilmuir monk of Coupar Angus who was envoy from Robert I to England in January 1321: *Cal. Docs. Scot.*, iii, no.718. See also *Les journaux du trésor de Philippe IV le Bel*, ed. Viard, no.3520, for Brother John of Coupar at Paris in 1299.

98. Statements about those present are taken from the records of the Treaty of Edinburgh and from charters and other acts of the king dating from this parliament (*RRS*, v, nos. 335-41, 346-7).

99. Stones, *Documents*, 341.

100. *RRS*, v, no.563.

101. See E. L. G. Stones, 'An addition to the Rotuli Scotiae', *SHR*, xxix, 42-50, nos. 21, 23-6.

102. It should be made clear that these lords were not under threat of total disinheritance merely on the score of their allegiance. The choice before them was to swear allegiance *either* to the English king and recover their lands in England *or* to the Scottish king and recover their lands in Scotland.

103. Jean Scammell, *EHR*, lxxiii, 402.

104. *SHR*, xxix, 30-1.

105. Queen Joan lived until 1362, dying at Hertford Castle and being buried in the Greyfriars church in London, in the middle of the choir, at the head of the alabaster tomb of her mother Queen Isabella: *Scalacronica*, 202; J. G. N[ichols] in *Collectanea Topographica et Genealogica*, v (1838), 278-9.

106. *SHR*, xxiv, 33; *History*, xxxviii, 56-8. On the English failure to restore the Black Rood (despite the report in *Chron. Lanercost*, 261), cf. E. L. G. Stones, *SHR*, xxxviii, 174-5.

107. *Ibid.*, xxix, 34-5; Stones, *Relations*, no.42; *RRS*, v, no.353, which is carefully worded to restore to Henry Percy property truly inherited or held by just title and to empower him to claim property or rights in the king's or any lower court if he believes he has a right to them. The charter restores no land specifically named.

108. *History*, xxxviii, 61.

CHAPTER FOURTEEN
Good King Robert

1. Barbour, *Bruce*, 285-6.

2. *Cal. Docs. Scot.*, iii, no.194; *Foedera*, ii, 126. Unless otherwise noted, statements about episcopal appointments and careers are based on Dowden, *Bishops*, Watt, *Fasti*, and Watt, *Graduates*.

3. *Cal. Docs. Scot.*, iii, no.207.

4. *Glasgow Registrum*, no.258; *St Andrews Liber*, 120, where for 'Domdouyr' read 'Donidouyr'.

5. *Cal. Docs. Scot.*, iii, no.50.

6. Paris, Bibliothèque Nationale, MS latin 10919, modern foliation 238v-239r. I am grateful to M. J-P. Genet for kindly locating this document and providing me with a transcript. Summarized briefly in F. Michel, *Les écossais en France, les français en Ecosse* (1862), i, 43-4, the text survives only in a copy which unfortunately lacks the date. The MS in which it is copied is an official contemporary register of Philip IV's correspondence and state papers, and the inclusion of Lamberton's letter is remarkable.

7. *Foedera*, ii, 68. In view of its date (March 4th, 1309), we might infer from this safe-conduct that Bishop Lamberton was present, or thought to be present, at the St Andrews parliament. On August 15th, 1309, Lamberton was at Durham,

Raine, *North Durham*, Appendix, no.488. For further details see Watt, *Graduates*, 322.

8. *Rotuli Scotiae*, i, 80.

9. *Lindores Liber*, no.10 (February 19th, 1310).

10. Raine, *North Durham*, Appendix, no.489; the details are given in the original document, Durham, Dean and Chapter Muniments, Misc. Charter no.1351.

11. *RRS*, v, nos. 18, 19.

12. *Foedera*, ii, 363-4, 406.

13. *Chron. Bower*, ii, 271.

14. On Lamberton and his career see M. Ash, 'William Lamberton, Bishop of St Andrews, 1297-1328', in *The Scottish Tradition*, ed. G. W. S. Barrow (1974), 44-55.

15. *Cal. Docs. Scot.*, iii, no.301.

16. *RRS*, v, nos. 17, 19.

17. *Aberdeen Registrum*, i, 44-5, of date December 5th, 1318, records a remission of rancour and restoration of revenues to Bishop Cheyne of Aberdeen, purporting to have been granted at the Scone parliament of December 3rd, 1318. This parliament did in fact meet, but the remission cannot be authentic as it stands, for one witness is Murdoch earl of Menteith (not earl before 1320). See *RRS*, v, no.140, comment.

18. *Cal. Docs. Scot.*, iii, no.355. By November 1314 Bishop Andrew had come into King Robert's peace, *APS*, i, 289, last item in col.2.

19. *Cal. Docs. Scot.*, iii, no.718; *Moray Registrum*, 14 and nos. 117, 277. The bishop was an envoy to the Roman Curia in 1329, presumably to negotiate for the rite of anointing to be included in David II's coronation, *Exch. Rolls*, i, 211, and thus a colleague of Mr. Alexander Kinninmonth who may have acted as a Scottish envoy in 1321 with the bishop's uncle and namesake (above, p.373, n.97).

20. Dowden, *Bishops*, 360-1; G. Donaldson, *Dumfriesshire Trans.*, xxvii, 132.

21. Based on Sarti and Fattorini, *De claris archigymnasii Bononiensis professoribus* (2nd edn, C. M. Foroliviensis and C. A. Ravennas, 1888-96), ii, 307-31.

22. *Ibid.*, 327-30; G. C. Trombelli, *Memorie istoriche concernenti le due*

canoniche di S. Maria di Reno e di S. Salvatore insieme unite (Bologna, 1752), 71; R. J. Brentano, *York Metropolitan Jurisdiction*, 126, 144, 159; *Nat. MSS. Scot.*, ii, Pl. XII; D. McRoberts, *The Medieval Church of St Andrews* (1976), 114 and n.306.

23. Thanks to the high proportion of university graduates among them, the careers of most of these clerics may be studied in Watt, *Graduates, passim*.

24. SRO, State Papers, no.4 (written in a chancery hand of the earlier fourteenth century).

25. BL., MS. Harl. 4694, fos. 5-6, 35-6; see above, p.363 and n.100.

26. D. Hunter Marshall in *SHR*, xxiii, 280-93. In *Coupar Angus Chrs.*, no.105 (1325), *concilium Scoticanum* is the equivalent of *concilium provinciale*, both referring to a provincial council of the Scottish Church.

27. A laborious search of all the surviving record might throw some light on the question of which clergy were available to meet at Dundee on February 24th, 1310. Bishop Lamberton of St Andrews and his Official, Master William of Eaglesham, were evidently present at a justiciary court at Lindores on February 19th, 1310 (*Lindores Liber*, no.10), and Bishop Lamberton held synods at St Andrews and (possibly) at Holyrood in this year (Raine, *North Durham*, Appendix, no.489). Bishop Murray of Moray was at Elgin on March 23rd, 1310 (*Moray Registrum*, nos. 135-6).

28. SRO, State Papers, no.5, in a chancery hand closely similar to but not identical with that of the 'Dundee Declaration'.

29. Above, p.374, n.18.

30. See *RRS*, v, no.140, comment, for Bishop Cheyne of Aberdeen.

31. Most of this section is based on *Reg. Mag. Sig.*, i; *RRS*, v, and standard works such as the *Scots Peerage*. To these sources references are given only where necessary for clarity or because of conflicting evidence.

32. The date of the Cambuskenneth parliament in which it was enacted that all who were against the king's peace should be forfeited, *APS*, i, 464; *RRS*, v, no.41. Barbour, *Bruce*, 246, says that a year's grace was allowed to those concerned, and although the act as we have it mentions no

period of grace, Barbour's statement seems borne out by the dates at which several magnates changed sides after November 1314.

33. This did not stop her styling herself countess of Buchan and *constabulatrix Scotie* in a confirmation to the monks of Garendon partly for the soul of her uncle John Comyn, earl of Buchan: J. Nichols, *Hist. and Antiqu. of the County of Leicester*, iii, pt.11, (1804), p.834, col.1.

34. R. Nicholson, *EHR*, lxxvii, 234.

35. For his relationship to the earl of Angus, cf. Hodgson, *History of Northumberland*, 11, i, 31, n.(b).

36. First recorded as earl in a charter of June 1329; but Barbour, *Bruce*, 359, and *Scalacronica*, 155, call him earl of Angus in their accounts of the Stanhope Park campaign in 1327.

37. *Scalacronica*, 140.

38. Barbour, *Bruce*, 239-40, apparently meaning the night of June 23rd-24th.

39. *RRS*, v, no.490.

40. *Scots Peerage*, viii, 249; 251 and n.2.

41. *RRS*, v, no.112.

42. This is shown by *Cal. Docs. Scot.*, iii, no.410, and by a document discovered by Professor Duncan in the MS. Morton Cartulary (omitted from the printed edition), now *RRS*, v, no.72.

43. Based on evidence provided by Professor Duncan. *Scalacronica*, 144, says that Murdoch of Menteith became earl of Menteith through his niece's resignation.

44. *Reg. Mag. Sig.*, i, Appendix 11, nos. 263, 384, 514; *The Scottish Tradition*, ed. Barrow, 40.

45. *Lennox Cartularium*, 1-2.

46. See Genealogical Table 11.

47. The earl was deemed to have forfeited Beanley in Northumberland from 25 June 1314; PRO, E.372/160, m. 50. He attended Robert I's Ayr parliament of May 1315; *Melrose Liber*, nos.416, 417. It has been denied that this was a parliament, and perhaps it should be called a council, although *Chron. Bower*, ii, 256, says *parliamentum statuit apud Ayre*. See *RRS*, v, nos. 58-68.

48. *Reg. Mag. Sig.*, i, Appendix 1, no.31; *Moray Registrum*, no.264. The latter, undated, text may be the original version, and Randolph appears as earl of Moray in October 1312, *APS*, i, 463.

49. *Moray Registrum*, no.264; cf. Stevenson, *Documents*, ii, 190.

50. See G. W. S. Barrow, 'Some problems in 12th and 13th century Scottish history – a genealogical approach', *The Scottish Genealogist*, xxv, no.4 (1978), 104-5.

51. See *RRS*, v, no.72, comment.

52. National Library of Scotland, MS. 72, fo.10r; *RRS*, v, no.72.

53. The exact relationship is unknown, but see *The Scottish Tradition* ed. Barrow, 40.

54. *Reg. Mag. Sig.*, i, Appendix I, no.68.

55. J. W. Buchan and H. Paton, *History of Peeblesshire*, iii, 544; *Reg. Mag. Sig.*, i, Appendix I, nos. 95, 96; *RRS*, v, nos. 5, 60.

56. *RMS*, i, App.1, no.96.

57. *Cal. Docs. Scot.*, ii, no.1452; *RRS*, v, nos. 94, 166, 184, 200, 392.

58. Dowden, *Bishops*, 311-12; *RRS*, v, no.166.

59. *Ibid.*, no.184.

60. *Ibid.*, no.198.

61. Above, pp.83, 158; *Cal. Docs. Scot.*, v, p.204, col.2.

62. *Reg. Mag. Sig.*, i, no.24.

63. *Ibid.*, Appendix I, no.6.

64. Appears as lord of Nithsdale in March 1309, *APS*, i, 459, and in February 1310, *Lindores Liber*, no.10.

65. *RRS*, v, no.409 (probably dating 1318-20).

66. Palgrave, *Docs. Hist. Scot.*, 302.

67. *RRS*, v, no.150 (May 1st, 1319).

68. *Reg. Mag. Sig.*, i, Appendix I, no.80, King Robert died in debt to Sir William Blount, *Exch. Rolls*, i, 285, 404.

69. *Chron. Lanercost*, 250.

70. *Ibid.*, 250.

71. Barbour, *Bruce*, 197, 'bot ane berdlas hyne'; for Andrew, see *Cal. Docs. Scot.*, v, nos. 486, 513.

72. *RRS*, v, no.391.

73. Hermitage castle, recorded in 1296 and 1300 (Stevenson, *Illustrations*, 49; *Cal. Docs. Scot.*, ii, no.1165), was first built in the 1240s, being the castle in 'Lothian' which, with another in 'Galloway', probably Caerlaverock, excited the suspicions of Henry III of England: Matthew Paris, *Chronica Majora* (Rolls Ser.), iv, 380; *Chron. Fordun*, i, 291.

74. *Chronica Magistri Rogeri de Houedene* (ed. Stubbs), iii, 308.

75. It is not certain, but seems probable, that Carmichael, like Douglasdale, was the inheritance of the lords of Douglas, *Origines Parochiales*, i, 151; *Reg. Mag. Sig.*, i, no.77 and Appendix I, no.35. For other grants, see *RRS*, v, *passim*, including nos.166, 167, 267.

76. PRO, S. C. 1/37/107; *Cal. Docs. Scot.*, ii, no.1406 and p.425. That the Keiths had some link with the Campbells seems to be shown by the fact that Edward Keith's seal was fixed to the same tag as those of Donald and Arthur Campbell on the SRO 'original' of the letter to the pope of 1320: A. A. M. Duncan, in *The Study of Medieval Records* (1971), 184.

77. *Lindores Liber*, no.10.

78. SRO, Lindsay Collection, Box 19, no.6.

79. *RRS*, v, nos. 42, 155.

80. *Ibid.*, no.67.

81. *Foedera*, ii, 412; *Cal. Pat. R., 1317-21*, 414.

82. *Cal. Pat. R., 1317-21*, 414; *Foedera*, ii, 412, 521, 524; Stones, *Documents*, 170. Cf. *The Scottish Tradition*, 54-5.

83. *RRS*, v, no.239. 'Aulesai' is unidentified, but likely to be Ailsa, although this famous rock was historically in Dailly parish, Ayrshire.

84. *Foedera*, ii, 524. Menteith had helped to negotiate the truce; *RRS*, v, no.232.

85. *Reg. Mag. Sig.*, i, Appendix I, no.95; Buchan and Paton, *Peeblesshire*, iii, 544; *RSS*, v, no.5.

86. *Reg. Mag. Sig.*, i, nos.7, 8; *Rotuli Scotiae*, i, 22.

87. *Reg. Mag. Sig.*, i, no.11; and Appendix II, no.286 and n.; *RRS*, v, no.276. Cessford was an estate comparable to Eckford, Caverton etc., held by knight-service, and it seems probable that all these estates contributed to the castle ward of Roxburgh. *RRS*, v, no.414.

88. *Ibid.*, no.152; Fraser, *Southesk*, ii, 478.

89. *Reg. Mag. Sig.*, i, nos.56, 58, 71 and Appendix I, no.45; *RRS*, v, no.177.

90. *Lindores Chartulary*, no.1; *RRS*, v, no.371.

91. J. A. Robertson, *Comitatus de Atholia etc.* (1860), 9-10, a grant by David of Strathbogie earl of Atholl to Robert Menzies of the thanage of Cranach for one archer (*c.* 1312-14).

92. *Reg. Mag. Sig.*, i, Appendix I, nos.100, 101, 102.

93. *Cal. Docs. Scot.*, ii, no.824 (6).

94. *Ibid.*, no.824 (2).

95. *Reg. Mag. Sig.*, i, Appendix I, nos. 5, 81. Another good illustration of the confirmation of a holding of ancient type is seen in Robert I's charter (Loch Broom, August 8th, 1309) to William, thane of Cawdor, of the thanage of Cawdor in feuferm for 12 merks a year: *Cawdor Bk.*, 3-4.

96. Palgrave, *Docs. Hist. Scot.*, Illustrations, no.II, p.v.; *Foedera*, i, 767 (where Nicolaus and Colinus were probably not father and son, but refer to the father only); *Chron. Rishanger*, 365. On the Campbells, see W. D. Sellar, *Scottish Studies*, 17 (1973), 109-25.

97. *Rotuli Scotiae*, i, 32a.

98. *RRS*, v, no.46.

99. *Reg. Mag. Sig.*, ii, no.3136 (1304; or 1302, cf. *Proc. Soc. Antiq. Scot.*, xc, 204)).

100. *Reg. Mag. Sig.*, i, Appendix I, no.105.

101. Palgrave, *Docs. Hist. Scot.*, 318; see Appendix below.

102. *APS*, i, 459; *RMS*, i, Appendix II, no.654. In 1296, Gillespie Maclachlan had sent in his homage in common with the other freeholders; *Cal. Docs. Scot.*, ii, 209, 'Gilascopc fiz Rouland' of the county of Perth.

103. *Reg. Mag. Sig.*, i, Appendix I, no.9. It may be noted that according to the *Annals of Ulster*, ed. B. MacCarthy (1893), ii, 433, *Annals of Loch Cé*, ed. W. M. Hennessy (Rolls Series, 1871), i, 595, and *Annals of Clonmacnoise*, ed. D. Murphy (1896), 281, one 'MacRory, king of the Hebrides' fell at Dundalk in 1318, probably Ruairi Macruarie, Lachlan's brother.

104. *Reg. Mag. Sig.*, i, Appendix II, nos.56-8. For Cenel Badin (Cineal Bhaodain), one of the most ancient district names in the Highlands, cf. Watson, *Celtic Place-Names of Scotland*, 122.

105. Barbour, *Bruce*, 269-70. In general, see Barrow, *Kingdom*, 362-83.

106. *Chron. Pluscarden*, i, 251.

107. *APS*, i, 464-5. For its status as a 'parliament', see above, p.389, n. 3. An impressive list of those present is given in *APS*, i, 290. Seals were affixed to the document recording the tailzie of the Crown by 'the prelates, earls, barons and greater men (*maiores*) of the community'.

108. NLS, MS. 72, fo.93, Morton Chartulary (omitted from the published edition); *RRS*, v, no.101.

109. *APS*, i, 465-6.

110. *Ibid.*, Pt.2, 628, 664; cf. *ibid.*, i, 546. For other record of the Cambuskenneth parliament of July, 1326, see *ibid.*, i, 475-476.

111. Apologies for David II are sustained by Bruce Webster, *TRHS*, 5th ser., xvi, 115-30 and R. Nicholson, *SHR*, xlv, 59-78; *Scotland: the Later Middle Ages*, chaps. 6 and 7.

112. *Reg. Mag. Sig.*, i, no.84; Appendix I, no.67; Appendix II, nos. 43, 69.

113. *Lindores Liber*, no.10. Cf. *Historiae Dunelmensis Scriptores Tres*, Appendix no.94, which shows that Thomas Randolph was acting as lieutenant of Robert I in 1314. As early as 1309, Randolph was warden this side (north?) of Forth: *St And. Lib.*, xxxi.

114. Barbour, *Bruce*, 278.

115. Information from Professor Duncan.

116. A. A. M. Duncan, 'The *acta* of King Robert I', *SHR*, xxxii, 1-39, gave the first serious study of this aspect of Robert I's reign. The same scholar's Introduction to *RRS*, v, is much fuller in its scope and provides an authoritative and comprehensive analysis of the operation of the royal writing-office.

117. *APS*, i, 466ff.

118. PRO, S. C.1/18/147 (Ancient Correspondence), a letter discovered by G. G. Simpson, shows Alexander of Islay telling King Edward I that 'many people say that according to the law of England and Scotland no one ought to lose his heritage unless he be first impleaded by writ and named in the writ by his own name': for the text see *SHR*, l (1971), 16-17.

119. *APS*, i, 752.

120. *Reg. Mag. Sig.*, i, Appendix 1, no.59; on this cf. W. C. Dickinson, 'Surdit de Sergaunt', *SHR*, xxxix, 172. I have been helped on this point by Dr Hector Macqueen.

121. *SHR*, xxxix, 172-3.

122. *Formulary E*, ed. Duncan, no.83.

123. The formularies are the Ayr and Bute MS formularies edited by Lord Cooper (*Register of Brieves*, ed. T. M. Cooper, Stair Society, 1946) and Edinburgh University Library, MS. 207, published as *Formulary E*, ed. A. A. M. Duncan (1976).

124. The date is determined partly by the available evidence on when this disease, which spread from the south, reached Scotland; partly by evidence suggesting that the king's enactment shortly preceded the parliament of August 1320. *Chron. Lanercost*, 240, reports the onset of the disease in northern England early in 1320; *Chron. Fordun*, i, 349, says that almost all beasts in Scotland died in the severe winter of 1320-1 (following the disease?).

125. See above, p.375, n.32.

126. *Reg. Mag. Sig.* i, no.510.

127. *Aberdeen Registrum*, i, 44-5.

128. A. A. M. Duncan, 'The early parliaments of Scotland', *SHR*, xlv (1966), 49. Into this article (pp.36-58) the author distils most of what is known of Scottish parliaments in the thirteenth and earlier fourteenth century.

129. *RRS*, v, nos. 17, 18.

130. '[Freeholders] were present and therefore had been summoned . . . and the documents suggest that the reason was the king's need for wide political support in the struggle for independence and in important, even revolutionary, decisions such as those of 1314, 1315 and 1318': A. A. M. Duncan, *SHR*, xlv, 54.

131. *Formulary E*, ed. Duncan, no.77.

132. *APS*, i, 475-6.

133. *Exch. Rolls*, i, 110-11.

134. Barbour, *Bruce*, 322; *Reg. Mag. Sig.*, Appendix 1, no.17.

135. *Percy Chartulary*, ed. M. T. Martin (Surtees Society, 1911), 437-440; *RRS*, v, no.163.

136. *APS*, i, 681b; *Reg. Brieves*, 56; *Formulary E*, ed. Duncan, no.60. The farm actually levied was only 400 merks (*Exch. Rolls*, i, 311-2), but that may have been a deliberately reduced farm to favour Sir Alexander Seton, the farmer in 1328. The same farm, however, was rendered to the crown in 1329 and 1330 by the ordinary aldermen.

137. G. W. S. Barrow, in *T. R. Hist. S*, 5th Ser., xxviii, 106-8.

138. J. Donnelly, 'Thomas of Coldingham, merchant and burgess of Berwick upon Tweed (died 1316)', *SHR*, lix (1980), 105-25.

139. *Exch. Rolls*, i, 173.

140. *Cal. Docs. Scot.*, iii, 343-4; PRO, E.122/193/8 and 9.

141. *Cal. Docs. Scot.*, iii, no.1524.

142. *Foedera*, ii, 363-4, June 1st 1318 (in violent language); 406, November 5th 1319.

143. *Cal. Papal Letters*, ii, 191.

144. *Ibid.*, 199.

145. For what follows on the Declaration of Arbroath detailed references may be found in the literature here listed. G. W. S. Barrow, *Robert the Bruce and the Scottish Identity* (Saltire Society, Saltire Pamphlets, New Series no.4, 1984); *idem*, 'The idea of freedom in late medieval Scotland', *Innes Rev.* xxx (1979), 26-32; T. Cooper, *Supra Crepidam* (1951), 48-59; G. Donaldson, 'The pope's reply to the Scottish Barons in 1320', *SHR*, xxix, 119-20; A. A. M. Duncan, *The nation of Scots and the Declaration of Arbroath (1320)*, (Historical Association, 1970); *idem*, 'The making of the Declaration of Arbroath', in *The Study of Medieval Records: Essays in honour of Kathleen Major*, ed. D. A. Bullough and R. L. Storey (1971), 174-88; J. Fergusson, *The Declaration of Arbroath* (1970); G. G. Simpson, 'The Declaration of Arbroath revitalized', *SHR*, lvi (1977), 11-33; A. Theiner, *Vetera Monumenta Hibernorum et Scotorum historiam illustrantia* (Rome 1864), nos. 430-437.

146. Theiner, *Monumenta*, nos. 431-3. The pope's letter to Edward II (ibid., no.430), which quotes almost *verbatim* from the Scots barons' letter, shows that it had reached the curia by July 29th, no doubt several weeks earlier at least.

147. *The Ancestor*, vi (1903), 185-90.

148. The pope's reply to Robert I's letter (Theiner, *Monumenta*, no.431) says that the king excused the delay in writing to the papacy but since the king's letter is lost we do not know what explanation he gave.

149. Above, p.241.

150. Ben was a Scots envoy for the truce negotiations of December 1319: *Cal. Pat. R., 1317-21*, 414; cf. *Foedera*, ii, 404.

151. Theiner, *Monumenta*, no.435.

152. For a recent discussion of Scottish origin legends see E. J. Cowan, 'Myth and identity in early medieval Scotland', *SHR*, lxiii (1984), 111-35, especially pp.116-20.

153. The late draft of the 1320 letter preserved in Bower's *Scotichronicon* (*Chron. Bower*, ii, 286) has a better reading here than the SRO 'original': J. Fergusson, *Declaration of Arbroath*, 20, 35, 51.

154. The translation is that of Sir James Fergusson, *op. cit.*, p.9.

155. Sir Roger Kirkpatrick is named third among five knightly envoys at the truce negotiations of December 1319: *Cal. Pat. R., 1317-21*, 414. His presumed kinsman Humphrey Kirkpatrick, prominent in financial administration at the end of Robert I's reign, had an English safe-conduct in December 1332 (*Cal. Docs, Scot.*, iii, no.1067) and escorted the young king and queen of Scots safely to France in 1334: *Exch. Rolls*, i, refs. in index; *Chronique de Richard Lescot, religieux de Saint-Denys, 1328-44*, ed. J. Lemoine (Paris, 1896), 35.

156. Above, p.282.

157. Duncan, in *The Study of Medieval Records*, 186.

158. *Cal. Pat. R., 1317-21*, 414; R. E. Latham, *Revised Medieval Latin Word-List* (1980 reprint), s.v. *valettus*.

159. Duncan, *op. cit.*, 183.

160. *Cal. Pat. R., 1317-21*, 414.

161. Stevenson, *Illustrations*, 10; *Scalacronica*, 144; G. W. S. Barrow (ed.), *The Scottish Tradition* (1974), 39-40.

162. *Scalacronica*, 144; Barbour, *Bruce*, 338-9.

163. *APS*, i, 415; W. C. Dickinson, *SHR*, xlii, 84-5.

164. *Chron. Fordun*, i, 349.

165. *Chron. Bower*, ii, 274-5; Stevenson, *Illustrations*, 10.

166. Above, p.105-6.

167. *Cal. Docs. Scot.*, iii, no.410; cf. Palgrave, *Docs. Hist. Scot.*, 302, for Gilbert Malherbe's demand for the wardship of the son of Malise Logie in 1306.

168. Barbour, *Bruce*, 339-41.

169. Safe-conducts for Sir Ingram de Umfraville of Scotland with a sizeable retinue, passing through England to overseas parts, were issued on January 26th, 1321, and in February Sir Ingram issued a release of the manor of Stebbing in Essex: *Cal. Pat. R., 1317-21*, 555; Hist. MSS. Comm., *Report on Various Collections*, vii, 313.

CHAPTER FIFTEEN
In Search of Robert Bruce

1. Barbour, *Bruce*, 160.

2. *Ibid.*

3. *Ibid.*, 340-1.

4. *Ibid.*, 212.

5. T. Wright, *Political Songs of England*, 216.

6. G. Villani, *Historie universali de suoi tempi* (Florence, 1570), 340-1.

7. Barbour, *Bruce*, 368.

8. *The Liber Epistolaris of Richard de Bury*, ed. for the Roxburghe Club by N Denholm Young (Oxford, privately printed, 1950), 325-6, no.463; *RRS*, v, no.569.

9. *Formulary E*, ed. Duncan, no.94; R. Nicholson, *SHR*, xlii, 38-9. One might expect 'your' instead of 'our' after 'God's will,' for Bruce's Scotland was already free, Ireland still under the heel of the conqueror. But the scribe of this MS (Edinburgh University Library, MS.207, fo.150v) carefully distinguishes initial 'n' from 'v', so 'nostra nacio' must be read. Thus Bruce is boldly speaking of a *single* Scottish nation dwelling in both Ireland and Scotland.

10. Cf., e.g., A. L. Poole, *From Domesday Book to Magna Carta* (1951), 317: 'The beginnings of a settled state . . . survived for a century until Edward Bruce with his army, flushed with his [*sic!*] victory at Bannockburn, entered Ireland and began the process of disintegration which

reduced most of the country once more to chaotic independence.'

11. The phrases in King Robert's letter find a contemporary echo in the protest against English rule sent to the pope by certain Irish kings and notables in 1317, *Chron. Bower*, ii, 267, 'the kings of lesser Scotia [i.e., Scotland] have all taken the origin of their race from our greater Scotia [i.e., Ireland], retaining in some sort our language and our ways of life.' This is close in sense to the 'our nation' of Bruce's letter.

12. The passage which follows owes much to the important article by Dr. Robin Frame, 'The Bruces in Ireland, 1315-18', *Irish Historical Studies*, xix (1974), 3-37. To the full review there cited of the literature prior to that date, may be added J. R. H. Greeves, 'Robert I and the De Mandevilles of Ulster' in *Dumfriesshire Trans.*, 3rd ser., xxxiv, 59-73.

13. above, pp.293-4.

14. Frame, *art. cit.*, 32-4; J. R. S. Phillips, 'Documents on the early stages of the Bruce invasion of Ireland, 1315-1316', *Proceedings of the Royal Irish Academy*, lxxxix (1979), C, no.11, 247-70.

15. Frame, *art. cit.*, 29-30.

16. *Ibid.*, 24.

17. Edward Bruce seems to have tried to involve the Welsh in his campaign aimed at ejecting the English from Ireland, by offering military help, perhaps in 1316, to eject them from Wales also. See what may be a genuine letter from him, edited by J. B. Smith, *Bulletin of the Board of Celtic Studies*, xxvi (1976), 478.

18. Frame, *art. cit.*, 15.

19. *Chron. Pluscarden*, i, 250; possibly based on Barbour's account (xviii, lines 31-6) that John Stewart told Edward Bruce at Faughart that his brother (Walter the Stewart) would shortly come with fifteen hundred men.

20. On the relations between Scotland and Ireland between 1315 and 1329 see R. Nicholson, 'A sequel to Edward Bruce's invasion of Ireland', *SHR*, xlii (1963), 30-40. King Robert's visits to Ulster are dealt with on pp.32-4 and 36-7 (to the references cited for the second visit add *SHR*, xxxii (1953), 38, a mandate of the king dated at 'Wlryngfrith', i.e. Larne, on August 13th, 1328 = *RRS*, v, no.355).

21. *Inchaffray Chrs.*, 44-5.

22. *Chron. Bower*, ii, 271-2.

23. Raine, *North Durham*, Appendix, nos. 79, 80.

24. *Cal. Docs. Scot.*, iii, no.984 (Cardross, May 3rd, 1329).

25. *Coupar Angus Chrs.*, no.100 (February 8th, 1319).

26. *RRS*, v, no.196.

27. *Ibid.*, no.Ra61.

28. *Ibid.*, no.356.

29. G. Neilson, *The Scottish Antiquary*, xiii (1898), 49-54. Houses were built at Inchmichael in 1329, presumably for the king's stay, *Exch. Rolls*, i, 152.

30. The position of the medieval village of Cardross is indicated today by the remains of the parish church in the Levengrove Park, and by the name Kirkton, still applied to the area a little to the west of the ruins. The modern village of Cardross four miles to the west dates from a much later period.

31. *Reg. Mag. Sig.*, i, no.90. A ploughgate would be 104 Scotch acres of arable, but might well have included a much larger area of uncultivated ground.

32. *Hist. MSS. Commission, 2nd Report*, Appendix, 167; *RRS*, v, no.294; cp. nos. 292, 293.

33. The following passage is based on *Exch. Rolls*, i, 56, 118, 123-36.

34. D. Murray, *Old Cardross* (Glasgow, 1880); also in letters in *The Glasgow Herald*, June 12th and 15th, 1928. Cf. Eunice Murray, *The church of Cardross and its ministers* (Glasgow, 1935), 6-8.

35. *Reg. Mag. Sig.*, i, no.117.

36. The copy I have consulted is in Dumbarton Public Library, Murray Collection, iii.

37. Cf. W. P. (afterwards Sir William) Macarthur, 'Some notes on old-time leprosy: the case of King Robert the Bruce,' *Journal of the Royal Army Medical Corps*, xlvi, 321-30 esp. 326 and n.1.

38. *Chron. Lanercost*, 259, 264; *Scalacronica*, 159.

39. Le Bel, *Chroniques*, i, 33, 48.

40. *SHR*, xlii, 34.

41. *Ibid.*, 36; *RRS*, v, no.355.

42. Barbour, *Bruce*, 362.

43. In this connexion, too much should not be made of the fact that Queen

Elizabeth died at Cullen (October 26th, 1327) and that young David Bruce was established in the bishop of St Andrews' house at Inchmurdo near Boarhills.

44. Barbour, *Bruce*, 376 and notes, esp. 490-1; A. A. M. Duncan, in *SHR*, xxxii, 18-22; *RRS*, v, no.380.

45. *Moray Registrum*, 291-3. John of Pilmuir, son of a burgess of Dundee, had spent many years in France and had acted as vicar in spirituals to Clement VI when he had been archbishop of Rouen: Dowden, *Bishops*, 153. It is a most unusual feature of the bishop's provision that the annual revenues of the three churches concerned are calculated in 'little' *livres tournois*.

NOTES TO APPENDIX

1. Formerly granted to William Latimer, deceased.

2. Possibly comprehended in the Stewart's lands already forfeited and granted to the earl of Lincoln.

3. Together with custody of castle and sheriffdom of Dumbarton.

4. Subsequently restored.

5. Yeoman of William Latimer, fought at Methven and brought news of that encounter to king.

6. Formed dowry of Mary sister of Robert I.

7. Richard and Robert had petitioned Robert I for John Comyn's lands.

8. Roland Askeloc appears as a landowner at Borgue in the Stewartry in Marquess of Bute muniments, Dumfries House, Loudoun charters no.7, granting Borness to Duncan son and heir of Donald Campbell. In 1296 homages are recorded of Hector Askeloc and Roland MacGachen ('Hector's son'), and in that year Roland Askeloche and his son Hector were jurors, all referring to Wigtownshire: *Cal. Docs. Scot.*, ii, 198, 202, 215.

9. At capture of Simon Fraser, news of which he brought to king.

10. In Durisdeer.

11. Cancelled.

12. Same person as preceding?

I. The succession, 1290–92.

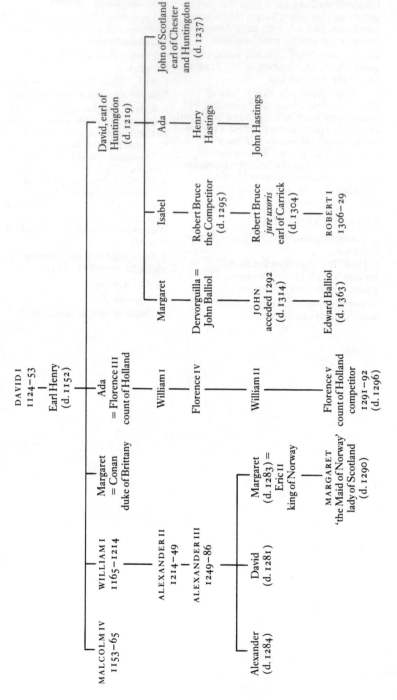

II. Some of the family relationships of King Robert I.

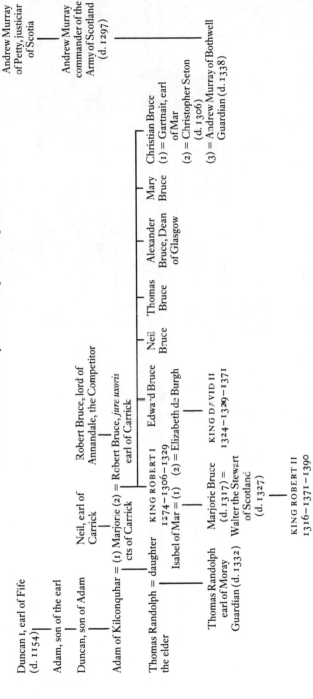

II. Some of the family relationships of King Robert I — *contd*

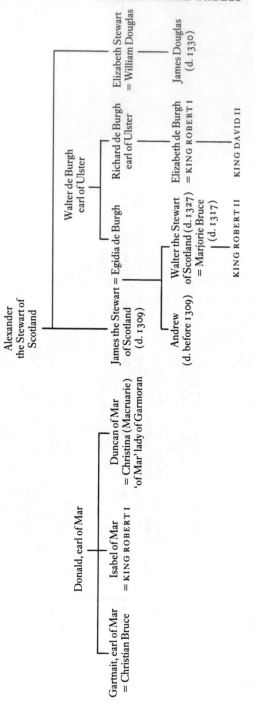

Table of Dates

1286	March 18th-19th	Death of Alexander III, king of Scots.
	c. April 28th	Parliament at Scone. Election of Guardians.
	September 15th	Scots mission finds Edward I at Saintes.
1289	November 6th	Treaty of Salisbury.
1290	July 18th	Treaty of Birgham
	(August 28th	ratified at Northampton).
	c. September 26th	Death of Queen Margaret, 'the Maid of Norway'.
	October 7th	Bishop Fraser requests Edward I to intervene.
1291	c. May 10th	Edward I reaches Norham. Anglo-Scottish parliament. Edward I declares his right to over-lordship over Scottish realm.
	c. May 31st	Community of the realm of Scotland reply to Edward's demand for recognition as overlord.
	June 3rd	English host assembles at Norham.
	June 4th	Competitors put Edward I in possession of kingdom and royal castles. Edward I promises to restore these to rightful king within two months of accession, and thereafter to demand nothing more than homage and its attendant rights.
	June 11th	Guardians resign their authority and are re-appointed.
	June 13th	Guardians and magnates swear fealty to Edward I as superior lord of Scotland. Commencement of *Rotuli Scotiae* in English chancery.
1291-1292	August-June-November	Court of claims to determine succession to Scottish throne.
1292	November 7th	Bruce the Competitor resigns claim to seek the Scottish throne to his son and heirs.
	November 9th	Bruce the Competitor's son resigns earldom of Carrick to his own son, the future king.
	November 10th-14th	Count Florence V of Holland presses his claim to Scottish throne.
	November 17th	Court pronounces judgement in favour of Balliol.
	November 30th	King John enthroned and crowned at Scone.

	December 22nd	Edward I gives judgement in case of Roger Bartholomew.
	December 31st	Edward I repudiates all promises and obligations made during the interregnum.
1293	January 2nd	King John declares null the Treaty of Birgham and all Anglo-Scottish agreements made during the interregnum.
	After September 29th	King John protests against Edward I's claim to hear appeals; withdraws his protest, and submits as Edward's liege vassal.
1294	June	War between Edward I and Philip IV over Gascony. King John and Scottish magnates summoned for military service overseas.
	September	Revolt in Wales.
	Before December	Scots obtain absolution from Pope Celestine V from oaths taken under duress.
1295	July 5th	Stirling parliament; election of council of twelve.
	October 23rd	Franco-Scottish treaty.
1296	March	War between Edward I and John Balliol.
	March 30th	Capture and sack of Berwick.
	April 27th	Battle of Dunbar.
	July 2nd-10th	King John submits to Edward I, renounces French treaty and abdicates, resigning kingdom of Scotland to Edward I.
	August 28th	Berwick parliament; Edward I receives homages and fealties of some 2,000 freeholders in Scotland.
	c. September 29th	Edward I commits government of Scotland to John earl Warenne.
1297	Before May	Disturbances in west highlands, Aberdeenshire and Galloway.
	May	Wallace slays sheriff of Lanark. Wallace and William Douglas attack the justiciar at Scone. Robert Bruce, earl of Carrick, heads revolt in Carrick.
	June-July	The Stewart, the bishop of Glasgow and Bruce confront Clifford and Percy at Irvine and capitulate.
	Summer	Rising in Moray under Andrew Murray.
	August 22nd	Edward I sails for Flanders.
	c. August 31st	Murray and Wallace join forces at Stirling Bridge.
	September 11th	Warenne's army destroyed at Stirling Bridge. Wallace and Murray liberate Scotland.
	October-November	Wallace raids northern England.
	November 3rd	William Lamberton elected bishop of St Andrews.

1298	Before March	Wallace appointed Guardian.
	Late February–Early March	Scots magnates and their followers with Edward I in Flanders leave him at Aardenburg (Netherlands) and sail to Scotland.
	March 14th	Edward I returns to England.
	July 1st	English army, assembled at Roxburgh, advances into Scotland.
	July 22nd	Battle of Falkirk.
	Between July and December	Wallace resigns guardianship; Bruce and Comyn the younger of Badenoch elected joint-Guardians.
1299	July	John Balliol transferred from England to papal custody near Cambrai.
	August	Scots magnates raid The Forest. Bishop Lamberton made chief Guardian with Bruce and Comyn.
	Late summer–autumn	Wallace goes to French court with five other Scots knights.
	Before December	Scots take Stirling castle.
1300	May 10th	Rutherglen parliament. Ingram de Umfraville appointed Guardian *vice* Bruce, resigned.
	July–August	Edward I's campaign in Galloway.
	October 30th	Truce for seven months.
	November	Philip IV issues letter recommending Wallace to pope.
1301	Beginning of year	John de Soules appointed sole Guardian.
	May 7th	Edward I's letter to pope, defending his policies in Scotland.
	May–June	Scottish delegation at papal curia defending Scottish independence.
	Summer	John Balliol transferred from papal custody to his own castle of Bailleul-en-Vimeu.
	July–September	Edward I and Edward of Caernarvon campaign in south-western Scotland.
	c. September 24th	Edward I takes Bothwell castle.
1302	January 26th	Truce for nine months.
	c. January 26th (before February 16th)	Bruce submits to Edward I and comes into his peace. Bruce marries Elizabeth de Burgh.
	July 11th	Battle of Courtrai.
	Autumn	Scottish delegation at Paris.
1303	February 24th	Battle of Roslin.
	May	Edward I's expedition to Scotland.
	May 20th	Peace between France and England, excluding the Scots.
1304	February 9th	Comyn and other Scots magnates submit to Edward I.

	March	St Andrews parliament; Scots freeholders submit to Edward I and have their lands restored.
	April 21st	Robert Bruce of Annandale, father of the future king, dies in England.
	May-July	Siege of Stirling castle.
	June 11th	Secret band between Bruce and Bishop Lamberton.
	July 20th	Fall of Stirling.
1305	February	Westminster parliament; new constitution ordered for Scotland.
	May	Scottish parliament to advise on new constitution.
	August 3rd	Wallace captured.
	August 23rd	Wallace executed.
	September 15th	Westminster parliament; Ordinance for the Government of Scotland promulgated.
1306	February 10th	Bruce murders Comyn at Dumfries.
	March 25th	Bruce enthroned and crowned at Scone by Isabel of Fife, countess of Buchan.
	March 27th	Bishop Lamberton celebrates pontifical high mass at Scone.
	June 19th	Battle of Methven.
	August 11th (really July?)	Battle of Dail Righ.
	September	Bruce flees from Dunaverty to Rathlin.
1307	February	Bruce returns to Carrick.
	April	Ambush at Glen Trool.
	c. May 10th	Battle of Loudoun Hill.
	July 7th	Death of Edward I.
	December 25th-31st	Encounter at Slioch near Huntly.
1308	May 23rd	Battle of Inverurie (?).
	c. June 24th	Galloway campaign (and raids on northern England?)
	August 15th or later	Battle of Brander.
	October 31st	Earl of Ross submits.
1309	March 16th-17th	St Andrews parliament.
	August-October	Bruce on western expedition.
1310-1311	September-August	Edward II's campaign in Scotland.
1312	August	Bruce raids northern England.
	October 29th	Scoto-Norwegian Treaty of Inverness.
1313	January 7th-8th	Bruce takes Perth.
	February 7th	Bruce takes Dumfries.
	May 18th-June 12th	Bruce takes Isle of Man.

	June 23rd	Edward Bruce gives one year's respite to Stirling Castle.
1314	February 19th-20th	Douglas takes Roxburgh castle.
	March 14th	Randolph takes Edinburgh castle.
	June 23rd-24th	Battle of Bannockburn.
	November	Cambuskenneth parliament; forfeiture of Bruce's opponents.
1315	April 27th	Succession to Scottish throne settled on Edward Bruce, failing male heirs to Bruce.
	May	Edward Bruce's expedition to Ireland.
1316	May	Edward Bruce crowned king of Ireland at Dundalk.
	(November 26th?)	Death of Robert Wishart bishop of Glasgow.
1317	January-May	Bruce in Ireland.
1318	April 1st-2nd	Capture of Berwick.
	October 14th	Death of Edward Bruce near Dundalk.
	December 3rd	Succession to Scottish throne settled on Robert Stewart, failing male heirs to Bruce.
1319	July	Edward II besieges Berwick.
	September 20th (?)	Battle or 'Chapter' of Myton.
	December 25th	Two-year truce.
1320	March	Great council at Newbattle Abbey.
	April 6th	Declaration of Arbroath (letter of Community of the Realm of Scotland to Pope John XXII).
	August 4th	Scone parliament; trial of Soules conspirators.
	August 26th	John XXII replies to barons' letter.
1321	March-April	Abortive Anglo-Scottish peace talks at Bamburgh.
1322	March 16th	Battle of Boroughbridge.
	August-September	Edward II's last expedition to Scotland.
	October	Bruce leads raid into north Yorkshire.
	October 20th	Battle of (Old) Byland.
1323	January 3rd	Bruce-Harcla 'treaty'.
	May 30th	Thirteen-year truce.
1324	January	Papacy recognizes Bruce's title as king of Scotland.
1326	April	Franco-Scottish treaty of Corbeil.
	July 15th	Succession to Scottish throne settled on David Bruce, remainder to Robert Stewart.
1327	January 20th	Deposition of Edward II.

	February 1st	Coronation of Edward III. Scots break truce with attack on Norham.
	June 15th	Scots raid Co. Durham.
	July 18th	Edward III and his army at Durham.
	July 31st	Edward III in Allendale.
	August 1st–5th	English and Scots confront each other at Stanhope Park.
	c. August 7th	Edward III withdraws to York.
	August–September	Bruce invades Northumberland.
	October–December	Peace negotiations.
1328	March 17th (May 4th	Treaty of Edinburgh ratified at Northampton).
	May 20th	Death of William Lamberton bishop of St Andrews.
	July 12th	Marriage between David Bruce and Joan of the Tower.
1329	June 7th	Death of Bruce.
1330	March 25th	Death of Douglas in Spain.

Index

Aardenburg, Netherlands, Scottish magnates
    leave Edward I at (1298), 98
Abbey Craig, in Logie, Stirling, 86-7, 88, 101,
    223
Aberdeen, 9, 75, 105, 161, 199, 266, 300,
    353,n.38
    castle, 156, 178, 180, 266
    bishops of, see Cheyne
    dean of see Crambeth
    sheriff of, 105 see also Atholl, Comyn,
    Lathom
Aberdeenshire,39, 83
Abernethy, Alexander (lord of), 121, 166, 172,
    186, 190, 359,n.96
Abernethy, William (lord of), 309
Abernethys, the (Patrick and William), 26
Abernethy, Perth, 136
Aboyne castle, Aberdeen, 156
Ada of Scotland, countess of Holland, daughter
    of Henry, earl of Northumberland, 39-40,
    45-6
Adam the marischal, 278
Adderaton, Henry of, rector of Benington, 69
Affrica of Man, 58
Agricola, Cn. Julius, 75
Aird, The, Inverness, 74
Airth, William of, 275
Airthrey, in Logie, Stirling, 343,n.107
Alan (of St Edmund), bishop of Caithness
    (1282-91), 37
Alan, bishop of Sodor and Man (1305-1321),
    266
Alan, Adam son of, constable of Cardross, 320
Aldgate, 137
Ale Moor, Roger of, forfeited, 346,n.64
Alexander I, king of Scots (1107-24), 165, 322
Alexander II, king of Scots (1214-49), 5, 23,
    39-40, 42, 56, 72, 78, 294, 336,n.1,
    337,n.73
    marriages, 12
Alexander III, king of Scots (1249-86), 1, 18,
    32, 34, 49, 56, 57, 58, 59, 130, 132, 166,
    214, 246, 249, 256, 302, 322, 332,n.30,
    337,n.5
    inauguration of, 5
    government of, 7-9
    council, 6
    relations with English Crown, 11-12, 202

annexation of Hebrides, 11
    marriages, 13-15, 64
    suppresses Manx revolt, 28
    regarded as Robert I's last lawful predeces-
    sor, 166, 185, 294-5
    last day and death, 1-2
    funeral, 15
Alfonso XI, king of Castile and Leon, 323
Alfonso, son and heir of Edward I (d. 1284), 27
Allanton Plains farm, in Galston, Ayr, site of
    battle of Loudoun Hill (1307), 361,n.32
Allendale, Northumberland, 253
Alnwick castle, Northumberland, 92, 254,
    372,n.76
Alnwick, abbot of, 77
Alpin, archdeacon of St Andrews, 267-8
Alpin, Mr, treasurer of Scotland (identical with
    Alpin, archdeacon of St Andrews, and
    with Mr Alpin of Strathearn, bishop of
    Dunblane, 1296?), 50, 267-8
Altyre, Moray, 324
Alvie, Inverness, surplus kirk revenues devoted
    to the celebration of masses for the souls
    of Bruce and Randolph, 324
Alyth, Walter of, 133, 158, 327
Amersham, Walter of, chancellor of Scotland
    for Edward I, 75
Amiens, France, 265
Amounderness, Lancashire, 237
Ancrum, Roxburgh, bishop of Glasgow's
    palace, 83
Andrew, bishop of Argyll (1300-42), 174, 266,
    269
Andrew, Saint, patron of Scotland, 7, 17, 225,
    306, 318
Anelf, son of, see Macaulay
Anglesey, 56, 193
    Holyhead in, 193
Anglo-French Treaty of Paris (1303), 124,
    127-8
Angoulême, Hugh of, papal nuncio to Edward
    II, 251
Angus, 6, 133, 158, 174, 336,n.28
    earldom of, 258, 274
Angus, Gilbert de Umfraville, earl of (1267-
    1307), 37, 45, 64, 100, 156, 274
Angus, Robert de Umfraville, earl of (1307-
    c.1321), 186, 231, 274

Angus, John Stewart of Bunkle, earl of (?1328-31), 274, 282
Angus, Laurence of, 327
Angus, mormaer of Moray (d. 1130), 277
Annan, Robert of, 146
Annan, 20, 112
  mote of, 21, 25
Annandale, 17, 20-25, 47, 66, 67, 69-71, 74, 84, 96, 108, 123, 142, 158, 277, 281, 288, 321
  to be held in regality, 283
  lords of, see Bruce, Randolph
  knights or gentry of, 21, 84, 110, 158
Antrim, 26, 163, 252, 317
Appleby, Westmorland, 237, 348,n.22
Aquitaine, duchy of, 54-5, 62 see also Gascony
Aragon, 62
Arbroath Abbey, Angus, 120, 134, 178, 304, 318
Arbroath, Declaration of (1320), 61, 223, 240, 241, 268, 302-9, 315, 378,n.145
  authorship, 308
  date of, 304-5
  list of names, 308-10
(Arbuthnot?), Duncan of, 326
Archibald, bishop of Moray (1253-98), 46, 79
Arderye (Airdrie), Crail, 334,n.98
Ardnamurchan, Argyll, 55, 291
Ardross, Fife, 115
Ardrossan, Fergus of, 284, 308
Ardscull, Co. Kildare, 316
Ardskeodnish (also Kilmartin parish), Argyll, 289
Ardstaffnage see Dunstaffnage
Argentan, Giles d', 207, 229
Argyll, 56, 58, 160, 182, 187, 192, 289-90
  barons of, 56, 178-9, 180, 186, 289-90
  campaign of Robert I in, 178-81, 183, 321
  men of, 192, 210, 243
  sheriffdom of, created under Robert I, 295
  bishops of, see Andrew, Laurence
  lords of, see Macdougall
Argyllshire, 55
Arnold, bishop of St Andrews (1160-1162), 266
Arran, Isle of, 56, 168, 361,n.20
  lordship of, 183
  vicar of, 26
Arthur, duke or count of Britanny, 49
'Arthur, King' (code name for Thomas, earl of Lancaster, q.v.), 242
Arthur, John, of Caen, notary, 35
Arthuret, Cumberland, 69
Artois, Robert, count of, 68
Askeloc, Roland, 158, 326, 381,n.8
Asnières, provisional peace of, 121-2
Athelstan, king of the W. Saxons (924-939), imitated by Edward I (1298), 99

Atholl, 3, 145, 160, 174, 258, 274-5, 336,n.28
Atholl, earl of, 3, 23, 50
Atholl, John of Strathbogie, earl of (d. 1306), 29, 37, 65, 74, 106, 112, 153, 156, 159, 160-1, 335,n.21, 344,n.37, 345,n.41, 346,n.61
  sheriff of Aberdeen, 156
  warden between Forth and Spey (1304), 156
  marries Marjorie, daughter of Earl Donald of Mar, 274
  approved Bruce's bid for throne, 151
  present at Robert I's coronation, 151
  supports Robert I, 156, 274
  forfeited by Edward I, 325, 326
  captured and executed, 161
Atholl, David of Strathbogie, earl of (d. 1326), 171, 176, 186, 191, 274-5
Atholl, John Campbell, Neil Campbell, earl of, see Campbell
Atholl, Patrick, earl of, 333,n.1
Auchrannie, in Glenisla, Angus, 134
Auchterarder, sheriff of, 159
Auldearn castle, Nairn, 177
Auroacin (Over Ayton, Berwick?), Patrick of, 347,n.1
Auteuil, Paris ('Aytuil'), 80
Avenel, Robert, 20
Avignon, 303-6, 324
Avoch, Ross, 74
Ayermin, William, bishop of Norwich (1325-36), 257
Aymer, laird of Hadden, 93
Ayr, 9, 38, 84, 103, 169, 172, 341,n.61
  sheriff of, see Robert Bruce
  sheriffdom of, 141
  castle, 103, 121, 142, 148, 171, 182, 191
  parliament at (1312), 202; (1315), 293, 375,n.47
Ayrshire, 121, 188

Baddeby, Alexander, 278-9
Badenoch, 75, 145, 159, 277
  Farquhar, steward of, 340,n.38
  lords of, see Comyn; Randolph
Badlesmere, Bartholomew, 240
Bailleul-en-Vimeu, Picardy, dép. Somme, 119, 251
Bain, Joseph, 133, 342,n.81, 362,n.63
Baird, Robert, of Strathaven, 113, 237
Balcaskie (Fife), Thomas of, 158, 326
Baldock, Robert, 240
Baledgarno, in Inchture, Perth, 358,n.89
Balfron, Stirling, 352,n.8
Ballencrieff, E. Lothian, 159
Balliol, family of, 64 see also Dervorguilla, John Balliol, king of Scots
Balliol, Alexander, of Cavers, chamberlain of Scotland, 37, 65, 126
  forfeited, 279

Balliol, Edward, son and heir of King John (d.
    1364), 166, 279, 294, 322
  betrothed to Jeanne de Valois, 65
  rights to throne to be recognised by Edward
    I (1300), 113
  treated as heir by de Soules (1301), 114, 119
  possibility of his gaining the Scottish throne
    (1301-2), 122-3
  brought from Picardy to England, 251
Balliol, Eleanor, wife of John Comyn, 49
Balliol, Henry, granted Branxholm, 279-80
Balliol, Hugh, eldest son of John Balliol of
    Barnard Castle, 23
Balliol, John, of Barnard Castle (d. 1268), 5-6,
    26, 42
  see also Dervorguilla
Balliol, John, of Barnard Castle, lord of Gallo-
    way, king of Scots (1292-1306), 6, 15-16,
    17, 29-30, 33, 37, 39, 40-4, 45-6, 49-50,
    51-2, 131, 155, 184, 223, 256-7, 265,
    284,307, 308, 309
  as 'heir of Scotland', 29
  his claim to the throne, 36, 39, 40-4, 45-6,
    47-8
  accession and inauguration, 50
  his active reign as King John, 54-74 passim
  homage and fealty to Edward I, 51, 59
  his submission and enforced abdication, 73,
    74
  treated as king in absentia by Scots, 90-1, 95,
    104, 109, 110, 118-19, 143-4, 166
  his transference from English to papal
    custody, 95
  his sojourns at Malmaison, Château Gévrey-
    Chambertin and Bailleul-en-Vimeu, 119
  attempts to have him restored to the Scottish
    throne, 95, 113, 118-20, 121-3
  and John de Soules, 114-5
  lands forfeited by, 279, 280
Balliol, Richard, of Yetholm, forfeited, 279
Balliol, William, 106
  envoy at Paris (1302), 124
Balmullo, Fife, 151-2, 356,n.30
Balmyle, Mr Nicholas of (alias 'of St And-
    rews'), 60, 94, 268, 305
  chancellor of Scotland (1301), 119-20, 178
  bishop of Dunblane (1307-19), 174, 185,
    263, 267
Balquhidder, Perth, Gilchrist and Henry of,
    160
Balquhidder, Perth, Conan of, 359,n.97
Balquhiderock, in St Ninians, Stirling, 214,
    215, 219, 227
  Carse of, 211, 216, 224-5
  Dryfield of, 211, 216, 224-5
Balvenie (alias Mortlach) castle, Banff, 134,
    176
Bamburgh, Northumberland,

castle, 231, 236, 277
  peace talks (1321), 240-1, 247, 249
Banff, 75, 176
  castle, 86, 175, 178, 180, 182, 190-1
Bannock (Bannok, afterwards Bannockburn),
    location in St Ninians, Stirling, 214, 224,
    229
Bannock Burn, Stirling, 209-15, 216, 218-9,
    221-2, 224, 227, 229-30
Bannockburn, battle of (June 1314), 187,
    233-6, 302
  general account of, 203-32
  preparations for, on English side, 203-4; on
    Scottish side, 207-9
  troop movements on eve of battle, 209-10
  site and topography of, 211-17, 224-5
    four different sites suggested, 211
    three distinct zones radiate from Stirling,
      211-2
    presence and significance of the 'pows',
      211-2
    position and character of New Park, 212-3
    ancient locality of Bannock, 214-5
    different names given to the battle and
      reasons for them, 215-6
    conclusion: the battle on June 24th fought
      on the Dryfield of Balquhiderock, 216
  events of June 23rd, 216-23
    advance of Hereford and Gloucester, 217
    Robert I fells Sir Henry de Bohun, 218
    advance of Clifford and Beaumont, 219-20
    repulse of Clifford, 220-1
    how the English cavalry spent the night of
      23rd-24th, 221-2
    Seton crosses over to Robert I's camp, 223
  events of June 24th and after, 223-32
    speech of Robert I, 225
    the Scots attack, 225-6
    the English horse fail to break the Scottish
      line, 226-7
    the English archers are brought up, 227; and
      repulsed by Keith, 227
    King Robert's brigade is engaged, 227-8
    the English are thrown back, 228-9
    King Edward leaves the field, 229
    the English army is smashed, 229-30
    English losses, 230
    Edward II escapes, 230-1
    many English magnates captured, 231
    consequences of battle, 232-3
Bannok see Bannock
Barbour, John, archdeacon of Aberdeen,
    historian, 312-3
  on Robert Bruce's coup (1306), 139, 146,
    231
  on James Douglas, 157
  on Robert I's movements in 1306-7, 161
  on Robert I's movements in 1308, 182
  on Bannockburn, 217, 219, 222, 224-30

Barclay, David, 178, 186, 258
Barclay, Walter, sheriff of Aberdeen, 310, (of Monykebbuck), 328
Barclay, Walter (of Kercock), 133, 178, 274, 328
Bard, Peter, naval leader, 204
Barkston, Yorks., W.R., Walter of, 155
Barnard Castle, Co. Durham, 5, 112
'barony', concept of, under Robert I, 292
Barra, Isle of, 55, 170
Barron, E. M., 79, 85, 134, 139, 154-5
Bartholomew, Mr. Roger, burgess of Berwick, 51-2, 55, 58
Bassett, Ralph, lord of Drayton, 102
Beauchamp, Guy de, earl of Warwick (1298-1315), 104, 203, 206
Beaumont, family of, 358,n.73
Beaumont, Ermengarde de, queen of William I, the Lion, King of Scots (1165-1214), 358,n.73
Beaumont, Henry de (cousin of Edward II), 157, 162, 192-3, 207, 246, 271
    at Bannockburn, 218-20, 221, 370,n.149
    one of the disinherited, 259, 260
Beaumont, Lewis, bishop-elect of Durham, 246-7
Beaumont, Richard de, 358,n.73
Bek, Anthony, bishop of Durham (1283-1311), 29, 30, 57, 73, 74, 75, 192, 329,n.23
    lands raided, 93
    on the Falkirk campaign (1298), 99, 100, 102
    releases Thomas of Galloway (1296), 112
Bel, John le, 252
Belford, Northumberland, 373,n.86
Bellejambe, Farquhar, bishop of Caithness (1304-27), 174, 201
Ben, James, bishop of St. Andrews (1328-32), 240, 251, 305, 379,n.150
Ben, Robert, 326
Benington, Herts., Scots colony at, 69
Benstead, John, 76, 340,n.14
Berefrey, siege-engine at Stirling, 129
Bergen, Norway, 29, 168
    Narfi, bishop of, 333,n.49
Berkeley, Maurice, lord of, 207, 231
Bermingham, John, 317
Bernard, chancellor of Scotland, 178, 186, 201-2, 296
    abbot of Kilwinning, later abbot of Arbroath, 178, 201, 225, 257, 264, 268-9
    bishop of Sodor and Man, 268
    and the Declaration of Arbroath, 304, 308
Berwick on Tweed, 7, 9, 38, 51, 57, 59, 64, 68, 69-71, 75, 76-7, 101, 120, 137, 148, 150, 156, 181, 191, 201, 203-4, 207, 209, 230-1, 236, 238, 239, 247, 249, 260, 266,

300, 301-3, 329,n.23
    Red Hall at, 9-10, 71
    White Hall at, 10
    sack of by Edward I (1296), 61-2, 71
    rebuilding of by Edward I, 71
    its headquarters role in 1305, 135
    captured by Scots (1318), 238-9
    burgesses of, 38, 71, see also Bartholomew, Rydale, Spalding
    castle, 68, 69, 92, 96, 152, 162, 188-9, 191, 357,n.69 Scots attempt on (1312), 191-3, 236, 238, 240 captured by Scots (1318), 239, 251, 265
Berwick, John of, parson of Renfrew, 268
Berwickshire (also The Merse), 74, 85, 159, 188-9, 238, 341,n.53
Bethoc, daughter of King Donald Bán, 145
Bevercotes, William of, chancellor of Scotland for Edward I, 134
Beverley, Yorks, 244
    shrine of St John at, 99
Bickerton, Walter of, laird of Kincraig, Fife, 133, 158, 325
Biggar, Lanark, 126
Biggar, Lanark, family of, 50
Biggar, Nicholas (lord of), 43-4, 47
Bigod, Roger, earl of Norfolk (d. 1306), 90, 102
Birgham, Berwick, 43
    Treaty of (1290), 13, 17, 27-8, 29, 31, 34, 36, 37, 51, 52, 59, 61, 65, 117, 129, 132, 149, 261, 304
Birnie, Moray, 324
Bishop, Andrew, 327
Bishopthorpe, York, truce of (also 'Thirteen Year Truce', 1323), 249-50, 252
Bisset of the Glens of Antrim, family of, 168-9, 316
Bisset, Mr Baldred, 174, 185, 268, 349,nn50,60, 351,n.117
    pleads the Scottish cause at the papal curia (1301), 118-9, 241, 306
    connexions with Bologna, 268
Bisset, Hugh, of Antrim, 168-9
Bisset, Thomas, of Antrim, 168
Bisset, Walter, 336,n.1
Bisset, William, keeper of Stirling castle (1305), 135
Blair, Brice, 158, 327
Blakehoumor (Sutton Bank), Yorks, 243
Blanchland Abbey, Northumberland, 252-3
Blaye, dép. Gironde, 110
Blount, William (of Esbie?), 281
Bogie, in Kirkcaldy, Fife, 134
Boharm, Banff, 74
Bohun, Henry de, 218, 313
Bohun, Humphrey de, earl of Hereford (d. 1298), 40, 90, 102

Bohun, Humphrey de, earl of Hereford (1299-1322), 113, 158, 203, 206, 207, 242, 264
    at Bannockburn, 217-19, 221
Bolhope, William of, 154
Bologna, Uberto, bishop of (d. 1322), 118, 349,n.60
Bologna, 118
    university of, 267-8
Bolton, Northumberland, 85
bone gent, bones genz, bona gens, 27, 32, 34, 52, 130, 133 *see also probi homines*
Boneville, John de, 274
Boniface, Mr Bertrand, 240
Boniface VIII, Pope (1294-1303), 61, 95, 113-4, 128, 185, 236, 263, 268, 303, 342,n.76, 351,n.117
    his attitude in 1300 and 1301, 114, 116, 124, *see also Scimus, fili*
Bordeaux, 57, 110 *see also* Mazun
Border, 27, 55, 67, 68, 69, 92, 190, 196, 197, 233-6, 242, 243, 249-50, 252, 329,n.23, 330,n.37
    West March, 20, 195
Borestone, in St Ninians, Stirling, 211, 214, 225
Boroughbridge, Yorks., 239, 242
Botetourt, John de, 142, 164, 171
Bothwell castle, 120-1, 172, 190, 191, 231, 350,n.85 *see also* Murray, Oliphant
Bothwell, Eustace of, 328
Bouglon, dép. Lot-et-Garonne, 365,n.46
Bower, Walter, 33-4
Boyd, family of, 285, 308
Boyd, Robert, of Noddsdale in Cunningham, 146, 148, 156, 158, 160, 186, 193, 280, 285, 328, 363,n.80
Boys, Thomas de, 326, 357,n.61
Boys, Walter de, 326
Boyville, William de, 38
Brabant, 62
Braemar, Aberdeen, *see* Kindrochit
Braid, Midlothian, 99
Brander, Pass of, Argyll, battle of, 179-81 *passim*, 321
Breadalbane, Perth, 160
Brecbennach of St Columba (Monymusk Reliquary), 7, 225
Brechin, 26, 127
    cathedral church of, 127
    castle, 73, 74, 127
    bishops of, *see* Comyn, Kinninmonth
Brechin, David of, 106, 186, 309, 310, 313
    forfeited, 346,n.64
Brets and Scots, usage of, 135-6
Brewster, Thomas, 78
Bridge of Dee, Kirkcudbright, 113
Bristol, 113, 204

Brittany, John of (d. 1334), lieutenant of Scotland (1305, 1307), earl of Richmond, 68, 134, 173, 243
Brittany, 10
    counts or dukes of, *see* Arthur, Conan
Brix (Bruis), dép. Manche, 20
Brodick castle, Arran, 169
Brotherton, Thomas of, earl of Norfolk (1312-38), 206
Brough-under-Stainmore, Westmorland, 237
Broun, Godfrey, of Colston, 188
Brown, Richard, 310
Bruce, family of, 20, 22, 67, 138
Bruce, Adam, lord of Cleveland, 21
Bruce, Alexander, dean of Glasgow (d. 1307), 143, 169, 171
Bruce, Alexander, earl of Carrick (d. 1333), 277
Bruce, Christian, 44, 141, 148, 162, 282
Bruce, David II, king of Scots (1329-71), 254-5, 258-60, 277, 293, 294
Bruce, Edward, king of Ireland (d. 1318), 143, 193, 196, 293-4, 315-7, 380,n.19
    campaign in Galloway (1308), 181-2
    lord of Galloway, 185
    takes Bothwell and Rutherglen (1314), 191
    besieges Stirling and allows Moubray a term, 195
    raids Cumberland, 198
    at Bannockburn, 210, 216, 218, 225-7, 229
    knighted, 367,n.42
    raids northern England, 237
    his Irish expedition, 238, 314-17
    his death at Dundalk, 238
Bruce, Isabel, queen of Norway, 65-6, 161, 168
Bruce, Marjorie, daughter of King Robert I (d. 1317), 141, 160-1, 162, 196, 231, 282, 293-4, 342,n.90
    marries Walter the Stewart of Scotland (1315), 282
Bruce, Mary, 231, 275, 281, 289
    imprisoned in a cage (1306), 162, 360,n.118
Bruce, Maud, 275, 282
Bruce, Neil, 160, 161, 318-9
Bruce, Robert, lord of Annandale (d. 1142), 20-1
Bruce, Robert, lord of Annandale (d. 1190), 20-1, 288
Bruce, Robert, lord of Annandale (d. 1245), 23, 331,nn7,8
Bruce, Robert, lord of Annandale, the 'Competitor', the 'Noble' (d.1295), 15-16, 17, 26, 29, 33, 37, 39, 50, 62, 65-6, 80, 266
    sketch of his career, 22-5
    his claim to the Scottish throne, 39-48 *passim*, 184
    his death, 65-6

Bruce, Robert, lord of Annandale, earl of
    Carrick, *jure uxoris* (d. 1304), 17-18, 23,
    24, 25, 26, 37, 48, 65-6, 69-71, 73-4, 77,
    79, 84, 110, 142-3, 331,n.24
Bruce, Robert, earl of Carrick (1292-1309),
    Guardian of Scotland (1298-1300), king
    of Scots (1306-29), 68, 79, 109, 110, 112,
    114, 138, 153, 156, 157, 159, 161-2, 173,
    178, 181, 191, 203, 207, 238, 242, 256,
    302, 303, 306, 307, 308, 358,n.88
  Character: 165, 194-5, 196, 312-3
  religious devotion, 317-9; last pilgrimage,
    319
  a potentate of the Western Gaidhealtachd,
    321
  Military principles: 183, 187, 194-5
  tactics, 192, 317, 321; at Bannockburn,
    216-7, 220, 225, 226-8
  Achievement: 164-6, 187-8, 196, 202, 230,
    232, 260-1, 262-3
  Government of Scotland under: 294-302
  administrative machinery, 294-7
  justiciars, 295
  sheriffs, 295
  chapel or chancery, 295-6
  legislation, 296-9
  parliaments, 299-300
  burghs, 300-2
  his relations with the Church and clergy,
    262-9
  his relations with the nobility as a whole,
    269-92
  his relations with the earls, 270-8
  his relations with the remaining nobles,
    278-86
  his relations with the community of the
    realm, 302
  his treatment of feudal tenure and military
    service, 286-9
  his relations with the barons of Argyll and the
    Isles, 289-92
  policy towards forfeiture of opponents, 270,
    278-82
  his policy towards 'regalities' and 'baronies',
    282-3, 292
  and the succession problem, 293-4
  Life and career:
  his birth and upbringing: 26, 321
  his family background, 22-6, 321
  succeeds to earldom of Carrick (1292), 66
  his first marriage, to Isabel, daughter of the
    earl of Mar, 141, 293
  his position in 1295-6, 67, 69-71
  fealty and homage to Edward I (1296), 76-7
  becomes a leader of the national rising of
    1297, 83-4
  refuses to submit to English, 84
  leads out 'army' of Carrick, 86

was he the earl who knighted William
    Wallace?, 96, 344,n.37
jealousy between him and the Red Comyn,
    98
probably contributes cavalry to Wallace's
    army at Falkirk, 346,n.61
burns castle of Ayr, 103
his suggested movements after Falkirk, 103
appointed joint-Guardian with the Red
    Comyn (1298), 104
confirms an act of Wallace's guardianship,
    104
his style as Guardian, 105
difficulty of co-operating with the Red
    Comyn, 106
takes part in the Forest Raid (August 1299),
    106-8
involved in a *fracas* with the Comyns at
    Peebles, 107
attacks Lochmaben castle, 108, 112
besieges Stirling castle, 109
instrumental in appointment of David
    Murray to see of Moray, 116
resigns guardianship (? early 1300), 112
his military activity for the patriots, 121, 124
deserts the patriots and submits to Edward I
    (1302), 114, 121-4
his fears in the event of a Balliol restoration,
    121-3
the wardship and marriage of Donald, son
    and heir of Earl Gartnait of Mar, granted
    to him, 122
his second marriage, to Elizabeth de Burgh,
    123-4, 141, 293
makes a secret 'band' with William Lamber-
    ton (1304), 131, 142
his role in the settlement of Scotland (1305),
    134, 135, 352,n.15
his entourage in 1305-6, 145-6
probably remains in Scotland, 134, 139
his conditional retention of Kildrummy
    castle, 139
did Edward I lose confidence in him during
    1305?, 139-40
has Malcolm Wallace in his following
    (1299), 139
stories explaining his murder of the Red
    Comyn, 140-1
his friendship with Raoul de Monthermer,
    140, 231
attends English parliament (October 1302),
    141
sheriff of Ayr and Lanark, 141
his military activity on behalf of Edward I,
    141-2
settles his affairs on his father's death, 131,
    142
relations with Edward of Caernarvon, 143

Bruce, Robert, earl of Carrick—*contd*
his family, 143
his prosperity and prospects (1305), 142-4
his claim to the Scottish throne, 36, 143, 146
discusses revolt with Lamberton and
  Wishart, 146
seeks conference with the Red Comyn, 146
murders the Red Comyn at Dumfries
  (February 10th, 1306), 146-8
his movements after the murder, 148-50
seizes castles, including Dunaverty, 148
close relations with Bishop Wishart, 149-50
his oath to abide under the direction of the
  Scottish clergy, 149-50
declares his claim to the throne to the
  English, and his intention of defending
  himself with a 'long stick', 150, 196
his bid for the throne supported by influential
  people, 150-1
his inauguration and coronation at Scone,
  150-2, 265
his activity after the coronation, 152-3,
  356,n.51
routed at Methven near Perth (June 19th,
  1306), 153-4
his supporters in 1306, 154-9, 325-8
his opponents in 1306, 156-7
forfeited by Edward I, 325, 326
the men in his sphere of influence, *see* his
  flight to Drumalban, 160
worsted by John Macdougall at Dáil Righ,
  160
reduced to life of a fugitive, 160-1, 163-4
finds safety in the Lennox, 163
reaches Dunaverty and flees to Rathlin,
  163-4
mystery of his whereabouts (September
  1306-February 1307), 166-71
probably in northern Ireland and the southern Hebrides, 169-71
his dependence on Christina Macruarie, 170
receives help from Christian of Carrick, 171
his military activity, 171-2
ambushes English in Glen Trool, 172
routs Valence at Loudoun Hill (*c.*May 10th,
  1307), 172
enjoys popular support, 172-3
raids Galloway, 173, 174
attacks earl of Buchan, 174-5
recovers from his sickness, 180
routs Buchan at Barra Hill, 176
orders the 'Herschip of Buchan', 177
attacks the earl of Ross, 177
his success by spring, 1308, 178
attacks the Macdougalls of Lorne, 178-81
wins battle of the Pass of Brander, 180-1
turns to routine of administration, 182
gains new adherents, 182-3

holds first parliament (St Andrews, March,
  1309), 183-6
manifesto in his favour, 184-5
his chief supporters in 1309, 185-6 his
  opponents, 186, 190
his position in 1309, 186-8
draws support from a variety of regions,
  188-9
his western tour (1309), 190
receives Dumbarton (1309?), 191, and
  Dumfries (1313), 191
threatens Man (1310), 192
captures Man (1313), 193
attacks Berwick castle, 193
captures Perth (1313), 194
rebukes Edward Bruce for granting a term to
  Stirling castle, 195
has Edinburgh and Roxburgh castles razed,
  196
raids northern England, 197-8
his system of blackmail, 197-8
his apparent vindictiveness towards Hartlepool, 198
his relations with continental cities and
  rulers 199-200; and with the French
  kings, 200
makes treaty with Norway (1312), 201-2
his reliance on Bernard the chancellor,
  201-2
his army at Bannockburn, 207-9
his dispositions before the battle, 209-10,
  216-17
slays Henry de Bohun in single combat, 218
laments his broken axe-shaft, 218
warns Moray of Clifford's advance, 220
restrains Douglas, 221
decides to withdraw to Lennox but is dis-
  suaded by Alexander Seton, 222-3
addresses the army, 225
orders Keith to attack English archers, 227
brings up his own brigade, 227-8
and the 'lesser folk', 228
his clemency and generosity, 230-1
vindicates his claim to the throne, 232
his policy after Bannockburn, 233-6
his raids and levies of blackmail, 236-8
resumes lordship of Tynedale (1314), 237
his expedition to Ireland to help Edward
  Bruce, 238, 314-7
directs capture of Berwick, 239
and Earl Thomas of Lancaster, 242
raids Lancashire, 243
withdraws main army to Culross, 243
pursues Edward II to North Yorkshire, 243
routs Richmond near Old Byland (1322), 243
negotiates with help of Henry de Sully, 244-5
his relations with papacy, 245-7, 250-1, 302,
  306

Bruce, Robert, earl of Carrick—*contd*
  rebukes papal legates, 247
  negotiates with Andrew Harcla, 248-50
  concludes thirteen-year truce (May 1323),
    249-50
  resumes Franco-Scottish alliance (1326),
    251
  breaks truce in 1327, 251-2
  crosses to Ulster, 252, 316-17, 380,n.20
  invades Northumberland, 253-4 believed to
    plan annexation of county, 254
  negotiates for final peace, 254-5
  his title recognized by Edward III, 256
  concludes Treaty of Edinburgh (1328),
    257-61
  present at Holyrood abbey, 257
  agrees to marriage of his son David with Joan
    of the Tower, 258-9
  and the Declaration of Arbroath (1320),
    304, 306
  and the Soules conspiracy, 240, 309
  his policy towards Ireland, 317
  his retirement at Cardross, 319-22
  his disease, 317, 322-3
  his death, 322-3
  his burial at Dunfermline, 323
  his heart carried to Spain, 323-4
  and brought back to Melrose, 324
  requiem mass celebrated for his soul at Elgin
    cathedral, supported by revenues of Alvie,
    Birnie and Altyre, 324
Bruce, Robert, lord of Liddesdale, bastard son
    of Robert I, 282-3, 318
  knighted, 367,n.42
Bruce, Thomas (d. 1307), 169, 170-1
Bruges, 9
  and Robert I, 199
Bruning, John (son of Adam), 295
Brunne, Robert of, *see* Manning
Brunswick, *see* Otto IV
Buchan, 4, 159, 177, 182, 187, 271
  earldom of, 185, 258, 259, 270-1
  earls of, 336,n.24
  herschip of, 177, 362,n.51
Buchan, Alexander Comyn, earl of (d. 1289),
    Guardian of Scotland, 15-16, 26,
    330,n.37
  justiciar of Scotia, 332,n.34
Buchan, John Comyn, earl of (1289-1308), 37,
    45, 52, 60, 65, 67, 69, 73, 74, 76, 80, 101,
    145, 150, 151, 156, 271, 375,n.33
  sent to quell the Moray rising, 86
  joins the Scots, 86, 94
  contributes cavalry at Falkirk, 101
  justiciar of Scotia, 105
  sheriff of Wigtown, 110
  campaigns 1299-1300, 106-8, 110-14,
    347,n.97

compaigns with de Soules, 121
an envoy at Paris (1302), 124
lands restored (1304), 133
on council of 1305, 135
holds Buchan against Robert I (1307-1308),
    176-7
defeated near Inverurie, 176-7
lands forfeited by, 279, 280-1
his wife, *see* Fife, Isabel of
Buittle castle, Kirkcudbright, 17, 66, 182, 191,
    194, 280
Bundington, Edmund of, 341,n.53
Bunkle, Berwick, *see* Stewart
Bunkle, Alexander of, 120
Bunkle, Mr Thomas of, clerk of Dunkeld, 120
Burdon, Walter, 37 *see also* Burradon
Burgh-on-Sands, Cumberland, 173
Burgh, Elizabeth de, queen of Scots (d. 1327),
    160-1, 162, 231, 293
  marriage to Robert Bruce, 123-4, 141
Burgh, Gelis (Egidia) de, daughter of Walter,
    earl of Ulster, 81, 141
Burghersh, Henry, bishop of Lincoln (1320-
    40), 257
burghs, 8-9
  under Robert I, 300-2
Burradon, William of, 155 *see also* Burdon
Burstwick, Yorks, 162
Burton, J. Hill, 32
Bury St Edmunds, East Anglia, 93
Bute, 56, 81
  lords of, *see* Stewart
  men of, 210, 243
Butler, Edmund, justiciar of Ireland, 316
Butterwambe, Henry, 288
Byland abbey and Old Byland, Yorks., 244,
    371,n.45

Caddonlee, Selkirk, 67
Caddon Water, 67
Caerlaverock, Dumfries, barony of, 318
Caerlaverock castle, 112, 113, 350,n.80,
    376,n.73
  taken by Edward I (1300), 112-3
  held against Bruce, 182
  regained by Scots, 191, 194
Caernarvon, Edward of, *see* Edward II
Caernarvon, 56, 63
Cairn o' Mount, Mearns, 75
Caithness, 336,n.28
  earldom of, 175, 185, 270-1
  earl of, 156; *see also* Magnus
  bishops of, *see* Alan, Bellejambe
Caldecote, Robert, son of Geoffrey of, 326
Calhau, Raymond de, 238
Callendar, Wood of, in Falkirk, Stirling, 100,
    101
Cambo (Fife), John of, 133, 157

Cambridge, university of, 143
Cambuskenneth abbey, Stirling, 131, 275
    parliament at (1314), 270, 275
    parliament at (1326), 294, 300, 301
Cameron, John, of Baledgarno, 133, 158, 159,
    325
Cameron, John, of Balnely, 159, 326
Cameron, Robert, of Baledgarno, 358,n.89
Cameron, Robert, of Balnely, 358,n.89
Campbell, family or clan of, 186
    lands granted to, 275, 281, 289-90
Campbell, Colin, the elder, of Lochawe, 289
Campbell, Colin, the younger, of Lochawe, 289
Campbell, Arthur, 290, 308 (?Martin),
    376,n.76
Campbell, Donald, 163, 284, 290, 308, 327,
    376,n.76
Campbell, Dugald, 290
Campbell, Duncan, 290
Campbell, Duncan, son of Thomas, 290
Campbell, John, earl of Atholl (d. 1333), 281,
    299
Campbell, Neil, of Lochawe, 151, 156, 163,
    223, 281, 284, 289, 327
Campbell, Mr Neil (1291), 289
Canterbury, 116
    peace negotiations at (1301), 120
    archbishops of, see Thomas, Stratford,
        Winchelsey
Cantilupe, John de, 75
Cardross, Dunbarton, 319
    Robert I's house at, 319-21
    Mains of, 320-1
Carinish, N. Uist, 170
Carlisle, 69, 92, 99, 104, 112, 120, 171, 231
    castle, 23, 69, 236, 237, 361,n.25, 372,n.78
    bishops of, see Halton
Carnemoel see Kirkinner
Carnwath, Lanark, 158
Carrick, Duncan, earl of, 26, 321, 331,n.26
Carrick, Marjorie, countess of (d. 1292), 17,
    25-6, 48, 65, 141, 321
Carrick, Neil, earl of (d. 1256), 25, 321
Carrick, earls of, see also Bruce, Kilconquhar
Carrick, Christian of (Kennedy?), 171
Carrick, Christian of, bastard daughter of
    Robert I, 361,n.26
Carrick, Gilbert of, great great grandfather of
    Robert I, 26, 321
Carrick, Gilbert of, 327 see also Roland, Gilbert,
    son of
Carrick, Neil of, bastard son of Robert I (d.
    1346), 361,n.26
Carrick, 17, 25-6, 84, 103, 110, 121, 158, 316
    earldom of, 48, 65, 66, 121-4, 141-2, 276-7,
    321
    men of, 122, 124, 142, 210
    Robert I active in, 168, 169-72

Carron, River, Stirling, 105, 209, 210, 211-2
Carruthers, R. A., 211
Castlehill, Dumbarton, 320
Castlerankine, in Denny, Stirling, 105
Causewayhead, in Logie, Stirling, 343,n.107
Cavers, Roxburgh, strongpoint at, 191
Cawdor, Nairn, William, thane of, 377,n.95
Celestine V, Pope (1294), 63, 116, 338,n.44
Cessford, Roxburgh, 287
Chamberlain, 7-8 see also Dunnideer
Champneys, Mr Peter de, vicar-general of
    bishop of St Andrews, 67
Chancellor, 7-8, 119-20, 178, 201-2, 296 see
    also Balmyle, Bernard, Hunsingore,
    Kennedy, Twynholm
chapel, king's (royal writing office), 8, 28, 91,
    119, 178, 295-6, 304, 306
Chapeu, Adam, 327
Charles IV, king of France, 245, 251
Charteris (de Carnoto), Andrew, 102
Chester, earl of, see John of Scotland
Chester, earldom and honour of, 335,n.9
Chester castle, 75
Cheviot Hills, 71
Cheyne, Henry, bishop of Aberdeen (1282-
    1328), 41, 65, 79, 86, 134, 174, 266, 299,
    302, 375,n.30
Cheyne, Reginald, the elder, of Inverugie and
    Duffus, 172, 175, 266
    as warden of Moray (1308), 176
Cheyne, Reginald, the younger, of Inverugie
    and Duffus, 266, 309
Chilham, Isabel of, 161
Christison, P, 211
Church in Scotland
    conflict with Pope John XXII, 302-3
    its antiquity, 5
    its representation in the guardianship of
        1286-91, 15; and in later guardianships,
        63-4, 84, 107, 114
    represented at King Robert's inauguration,
        151-2
    freedom of clerical elections in, 28
    special character of, 93, 268
    its liberties, 149-50
    its role in pleading the Scottish case at the
        papal curia, 118
    its position and fortunes under Robert I, 263-9
    its public support of Robert I in 1309, 184-5;
        in 1310(?), 268; in 1314-1316, 268-9
Clackmannan, 16
Clackmannan, sheriff of, 159
Clairvaux abbey, 24-5, 318
Clare, Gilbert de, earl of Gloucester (1263-
    95), 48
Clare, Gilbert de, earl of Gloucester (1307-
    14), 183, 203, 206-7, 226, 230, 231
    at Bannockburn, 217-9, 221

Clare, Isabel de, 23
Clare, Joan de, countess-dowager of Fife, 105
Clare, Thomas de, 18
Cleish Hills, 64
Clement V, Pope (1305-14), 233, 245, 263
Clement VI, Pope (1342-52), 324
Clennell, Thomas, 155
Cleveland, Yorks., 21, 242, 254
Clifford, Robert (d. 1314), 84, 96, 120, 142,
    157, 171, 230, 231, 338,n.88
  given lordship of Douglas, 157
  his garrison thrown into well, 361,n.44
  at Bannockburn, 207, 217-19, 226
Closeburn, Stephen of, 158, 325
Clyde, River, 5
  Firth of, 149, 188, 321
Clydesdale, 6, 43, 108, 120, 158, 173, 174
Cobham, Ralph, 243
Cockairney, in Kinross, 134
Cockburn, Neil, forfeited, 346,n.64
Cockburn, Peter, 326
Cockermouth, Cumberland, 92
Cockfield, Co. Durham, 253
Cokdaill (Cockdale), possibly Gaunless valley,
    Co. Durham, 252-3
Cokyn, John, 327
Coldingham, Berwick
  freeholders of, 101
  prior of, 77
  priory, 352,n.15
Cologne, 10
  merchants of, 10
  schools of, 267
Columba, Saint (Columcille), 7
  his reliquary, the Brecbennach, 7, 225
Colville, family of, 347,n.87
Comlongon, Ayr, laird of, 326
Community of the realm of Scotland, 16-17,
    18, 27-8, 31-8, 44, 53, 64, 67, 81, 84, 89,
    91, 98, 118, 127-30, 132, 134, 138,
    143-4, 145, 146, 155, 166, 178, 183-6,
    232, 240, 246, 262-3, 292-311 passim,
    306, 307, 308
  and the Declaration of Arbroath, 302-3,
    310-11
Comyn, family of, 49-50, 57, 78, 138, 145, 166
  in the north of Scotland in later middle ages,
    279-80
  Red Comyns (senior or Badenoch line), 49
Comyn, Alexander, brother of Earl John of
    Buchan, 107, 156, 177
  sheriff of Aberdeen, 156
Comyn, Alice, 271, 375,n.33
Comyn, Edmund, of Kilbride, his widow, 280
Comyn, John, lord of Badenoch, the 'Red
    Comyn', (d. c.1274), 336,n.46
Comyn, John, lord of Badenoch, the 'Red
    Comyn', justiciar of Galloway, Guardian

of Scotland, 1286-1292 (d. 1303), 15-16,
    27, 38, 44-5, 49, 56, 65, 73, 74, 75, 76, 80,
    107, 329,n.7, 332,nn.30,36, 334,n.98
  sent to quell the Moray rising, 86
  joins the Scots, 344,n.22
  contributes cavalry at Falkirk, 101
  mentioned in 1303(?), 351,n.98
Comyn, John, lord of Badenoch, the 'Red
    Comyn', Guardian of Scotland, 1298-
    1301, 1303-4 (d. 1306), 69, 74, 142, 149,
    150, 161, 186, 246, 289, 336,n.46,
    357,n.59
  probably contributes cavalry at Falkirk,
    345,n.60
  elected joint-Guardian (1298), 104
  as joint-Guardian, 106-8, 109-14
  as sole Guardian, 124-8
  conducts surrender negotiations, 129-30,
    132-3
  required by Edward I to capture Wallace, 130
  on council of 1305, 135
  events leading to his murder, 139-41, 145-8
  his murder (February 10th, 1306), 146-8
  his career, 145
  lands forfeited by, 279-81
Comyn, John, titular lord of Badenoch (d.
    1314), 226, 230
Comyn, Margaret, 271
Comyn, Robert (d. 1306), 148, 161, 246
Comyn, Walter, earl of Menteith, lord of
    Badenoch (d. 1258), 340,n.38
Comyn, Walter, granted land by Robert I, 280
Comyn, William, O.P. (also William of Kilcon-
    quhar), bishop of Brechin (1275-?95), 16
Comyn, William (of Kirkintilloch?), 37
Comyn, Mr William, provost of chapel-royal of
    St Mary of the Rock, St Andrews, 94
Conan, duke or count of Brittany (d. 1171), 40
Constantinople, emperors and empress of, 207
Conveth, Mearns (Laurencekirk), 80, 264
Coquetdale, Northumberland, 71, 197
Corbeil, dép. Seine-et-Oise, Treaty of (1326),
    251, 259
Corbridge, Northumberland, 71, 197
Cornton, in Logie, Stirling, 343,n.106
Cornwall, 193
Corry, Nicholas, 326
Couci, dép. Aisne, 12, 279
Couci, Alice de, 13
Couci, Enguerand, lord of, 12-13 see also Guines
Couci, Marie de, queen of Scots, 12-13, 42
Council, 16-17
  Council in 1278, 12
  Council (1286-91), 332,n.27
  Council of Twelve (1295-96), 63-6, 67, 73
  Council in 1305, 135
  Council at Newbattle (1320), to discuss
    policy over Declaration of Arbroath, 303,
    304

Coupar Angus abbey, Perth, 267, 318, 332,n.33
Coupland, 197
Courtrai, Belgium, battle of (1302), 88, 124, 227
Cowie Mounth, Mearns, 75
Crail, Fife, 157, 358,n.73
Crambeth, Fife and Kinross, barony of (now Dowhill), 64, 134
Crambeth, Mr Hervey of, dean of Dunkeld, 350,n.94
Crambeth, Matthew (of), dean of Aberdeen, bishop of Dunkeld (1288-1309?), 27, 34, 41, 64, 65, 79, 80, 95, 120, 185, 263, 266
  Scottish representative at French court (1295-1304?), 124-6, 347,n.1
  returns to Scotland, 129
  his lands restored, 134
  at English parliament, September 1305?, 352,n.19
  supports Robert I, 174, 263
Crawford, family of, 308
Crawford, Alexander, 284
Crawford, Alice, 284, 289
Crawford, Ralph, 37
Crawford, Reginald (d. 1307), 146, 158, 169, 325
Crawford, Susan, 284, 290
Cree, River, 113
  Scots suffer reverse at (1300), 113
  battle beside (probably beside River Dee, q.v., 1308), 182
Creetown, Kirkcudbright, 113
Creich, Fife, 58
Creich (alias Ferincoskry), Sutherland, 177
Cremannan, in Balfron, Stirling, 352,n.8
Cremannan, John of, 134, 158
Cremannan, Thomas of, 158, 159, 327, 328, 352,n.8
Cresseville, Simon de, of Attercliffe nr. Sheffield, 155
Cressingham, Hugh, treasurer of Scotland, 71, 75, 78, 85, 86, 87, 342,n.77
  slain at Stirling Bridge, 88
Crichton, Midlothian, 278
cro, see wergild
Cromarty, burgh and sheriffdom of, 271
Cromarty castle, 127
Crosbie, family of, 21
Cruachan, Argyll, 180
Cruggleton, Wigtown, 110
'Culdees' of St Andrews, 94
Cullen, Banff, 75, 380,n.43
Culross, Fife, 243
Cumberland, 20, 53, 67, 142, 188, 190, 237, 254, 345,n.41
  Scottish raids in, 197-8, 240
Cumbraes, the, 56

Cumnock, Ayr, 141, 173
Cunningham, Ayr, 20, 121, 141, 280
Cunningham, Robert, constable of Caerlaverock, 112
Cunningham, Robert of, 326, 328
Cupar, Fife, castle, 152, 190
Curry, Walter, forfeited, 370,n.2

Dail Righ (Dalry), in Killin, Perth, fight at (1306), 160-1
Dalhousie, Midlothian, 345,n.49 see also Ramsay
Dallas, Thomas of, 327
Dalmeny, W. Lothian, 1
Dalqueich, in Orwell, Kinross, 134
Dalswinton, Dumfries, estate of Comyn of Badenoch, 121, 140, 146, 148, 182, 191, 280, 285
Dalton, Dumfries, 339,n.59
Dalton, Thomas of (also of Kirkcudbright), bishop of Galloway (1294-1319), 66, 79, 174, 266
  attempts to mediate between Edward I and the Scots (1300), 113
Damme, Flanders, 95
Dampierre, Guy de, count of Flanders, 62, 90
Darlington, Co. Durham, 242, 372,n.81
Darnaway forest, Moray, 143
David I, king of Scots (1124-53), 6, 7, 20-1, 27, 53, 56, 92-3, 165, 274
  his laws, 135
David, lord of Strathbogie, son of Earl Duncan II of Fife, 357,n.59
David of Scotland, earl of Huntingdon (d. 1219), 23, 39-40, 41-2, 43, 46, 48, 310
Deanham, Northumberland, 373,n.88
Dee, River, Aberdeen and Mearns, 85
Dee, River, Kirkcudbright, battle beside (1308), 182
Deeside, Aberdeen, 75
dempster (judge, doomsman), 3
Dempster, Andrew (le Jugeor), of Angus, 133, 158, 326
Denmark, 10
Denum, William of, 254
Dervorguilla, lady of Galloway (d. 1290), 5, 26, 29, 41, 42, 50, 60, 110
Despenser, Hugh, the elder, 116, 242-3, 340,n.37
Despenser, Hugh, the younger, 207, 242-3, 370,n.149
Deveron, River, 75
Devon, 193
Deyncourt, William, 220
Dingwall, Ross, 177, 271
  sheriffdom of, 271
Dinwiddie, family of, 21
Dirleton castle, E. Lothian, 99-100, 191

'disinherited, the', problem of, 255, 259, 260, 270

Dol (dép. Ille-et-Vilaine), 20-1

Don, River, Aberdeen, 75

Donald Bán, king of Scots (1093-7), 145, 146

Douglas, Archibald, 252, 372,n.81
   lands granted to, 271-4

Douglas, Archibald the Grim, earl of, 324

Douglas, James, lord of (also the Black Douglas, the Good Douglas) (d. 1330), 156, 157, 158, 169, 193, 195-6, 208, 240, 288, 304, 312
   recovers Douglasdale, 174
   and the 'Douglas Larder', 356,n.44
   and the battle of Brander, 180-1
   in Galloway campaign (1308), 358,n.80
   at St Andrews parliament (1309), 186
   takes Roxburgh castle (1314), 195
   sacks Hartlepool, 198
   at Bannockburn, 209-10, 216-7, 221, 225, 226-7, 230-1
   knighted, 367,n.42
   his role in the succession arrangements, 294
   as king's lieutenant, 295
   leads raids on northern England, 236-8, 239-40, 243-4, 252-4
   activity in 1316-17, 238
   takes Berwick, 238-9
   attacks English at Melrose, 243
   present at Treaty of Edinburgh, 257
   lands and rewards granted to, 280, 284
   takes Bruce's heart to Spain, and is killed in Granada bearing it into battle, 323-4

Douglas, William, lord of (d. c.1299), 69, 71, 83, 84
   his son found at Stebbing (1296), 69
   joins forces with Wallace, 83
   imprisoned (1297), 85, 157
   his death in the Tower of London, 157, 357,n.69

Douglas, Lanark, parish kirk of, 324

Douglas castle, Lanark, 83

Douglasdale, 84, 174, 284

Dover, 95

Dowhill, Kinross, see Crambeth

Down, Co Down, 317

Draffan, Clydesdale, 284

Dreux, Robert I, count of, 15

Dreux, Yolande of, queen of Scots, afterwards duchess of Brittany, 1, 13-16, 18
   marriage to king Alexander III, 13, 64

Drip, fords of, in Kincardine-in-Menteith, Perth, 87

Drogheda, 192

Droxford, John, Keeper of the Wardrobe, 76

Dru (de Rue), William 75-6

Drumalban, 55, 64
   Robert I's refuge in 1306, 160

Drymen, Stirling, 127

Dublin, 192

Duf, king of Scots, 58

Duffus castle, Moray, 175-6

Dumbarton, burgh, 319
   castle, 135, 149, 191, 319, 344,n.10, 353,n.34

Dumfries, 9, 18, 20, 114, 161
   bailie of, 338,n.37
   castle, 17, 146, 148, 182, 191, 194
   Greyfriars of, 140, 145-8

Dumfriesshire, 6, 121, 341,n.53

Dun, Thomas, pirate, 193

Dunaverty castle, Kintyre, 148, 163-4, 168, 170, 337,n.11

Dunballoch (Dolbodlech), Mr Geoffrey of, canon of Elgin, 352,n.12

Dunbar, E. Lothian
   battle of (1296), 72, 88, 155, 189
   castle, 72, 74, 191, 231
   earldom and earls of, 50, 72, 185, 197, 203
   see also March

Dunbar or March, countess of, 72, 151

Dunbar, Gilbert of, 51

Dunblane
   bishopric of, 174
   bishops of, see Balmyle, William

Duncan, A. A. M., 339,n.65

Dundalk, Ireland, 315, 361,n.15

Dundarg castle, Aberdeen, 174

Dundee, 9, 10, 23, 76, 268-9, 300-1
   castle, 85, 190-1, 265
   constableship of, 104, 119
   Greyfriars of, council held at, 268-9

Dundee, Mr Hervey of, bishop-elect of Caithness, 267

Dundee, Mr Michael of, 267

Dundee, Mr Ralph of, clerk of Alexander III, Crown tenant in Angus and Argyll, 80, 133, 158, 267, 327

Dundee, Thomas of, bishop of Ross (1295-1321), 80, 174, 177, 178, 185, 201, 263, 267, 338,n.32, 350,n.94

Dunfermline, 38, 142
   abbey of, 7, 12, 127

Dunfermline, Ralph of Greenlaw, abbot of, 41

Dunfermline, abbot of, 299

Dunipace, Stirling, 105

Dunkeld, 182
   diocese and see of, 64, 94
   bishops of, see Crambeth, Sinclair

Dunnideer, Mr Stephen of, bishop-elect of Glasgow, chamberlain of Scotland, 264

Dunollie castle, Argyll, 290

Duns Scotus, 268

Dunstaffnage, Argyll, also Ardstaffnage, 55, 179-81, 183, 190, 290

Dunstanburgh castle, Northumberland, 372,n.76
Dunwich, Peter of, 75, 118
Dupplinmuir, Perth, battle of, 282
Durand, Guillaume, bishop of Mende, 240
Duraunt, John, 308
Durham, William, 350,n.80
Durham, 197, 252
　castle, 92
　County of, 21, 92, 188, 237, 371,n.44 (see also palatine bishopric of)
　palatine bishopric of (also St Cuthbert's Land), 75, 92, 197-8, 254, 335,n.9
　prior of, 77
　bishops of, see Beaumont, Bek, Kellaw
Durward, Alan, of Fichlie, 159, 161, 328

Eaglesham, Mr William, archdeacon of Lothian, 118, 120, 174, 241, 305, 338,n.32, 375,n.27
earls of Scotland (formerly mormaers), 3, 8, 45, 69
　'Seven earls', 44-6
　and the Declaration of Arbroath, 302-3
　sealed Declaration of Arbroath, 304
　earls' conduct in 1297, 86; in 1299, 106-8
　the earls under Robert I, 270-8
Earnside, Perth, 136
East Lothian, 280
Ebchester, Co. Durham, 290
Edgar, king of Scots (1097-1107), 42, 50, 146
Edinample, Perth, 357,n.51
Edinburgh, 6, 38, 56, 59, 63, 73, 100, 106, 304
　castle, 1, 13, 39, 73, 96, 152, 188-9, 191, 339,n.71, 351,n.98; taken by Randolph (1314), 196
　sheriffdom of, 135, 188-9
　parliament at (1328), 300, 301
　treaty of (1328), 233, 299 see also Holyrood
　negotiations for, 254-6
　conclusion of, 255-60
　ratified at Northampton, 260
　merits of, 260-1
Edinburgh, Thomas, a priest of, 154
Edington, Berwick, 337,n.8
Edmund, earl of Cornwall, 24
Edward the Confessor, king of England (1042-66), 3, 73
Edward I, king of England (1272-1307), 3, 10, 16, 17, 24, 26, 27-40, 42, 57, 58, 59-60, 65-6, 68, 78-9, 80, 81, 83-4, 85, 94, 95, 106, 109, 110, 115-17, 118, 121, 123-4, 126, 128-9, 130-1, 136, 138-40, 143, 145-6, 148, 150, 152, 154, 155, 156, 157, 158-9, 160, 162, 163, 165, 166-9, 171, 183, 184, 186, 199, 201, 209, 231, 233, 241, 246, 257, 268, 283, 284, 286, 290, 294, 296, 298, 301, 303, 330,n.37, 358,n.79

　presides over court of claims, 1291-1292, 38, 39-50 passim
　and Bartholomew's appeal, 51-2
　and Scottish appeals in general, 52-3, 54-5, 57-60
　Welsh Wars of, 68
　his attitude towards Scotland, 11-12, 59-60, 61, 68, 73-4, 78-9
　takes advantage of Scottish situation, 61-2
　his war with France, 62-3, 68
　orders Scots to perform military service overseas, 62-3
　faces revolt in Wales, 63
　conducts war against Scotland (1296), 69-75
　sacks Berwick, 71
　removes Scottish regalia to London, 73
　advances to Elgin, 75
　holds parliament at Berwick, 75-6
　receives Scottish homages, 76-8
　sends the senior Comyns to the north of Scotland, 86
　his sojourn in Flanders (1297-8), 90, 98
　his conduct of the Falkirk campaign (1298), 95-6, 98-104
　invades Scotland by East March, 99
　decides to withdraw, 100
　advances to Falkirk, 100
　at the battle, 102-3
　tours the south-west, 103
　grants land 'forfeited' by Scots, 104, 346,n.61
　leaves Scotland, 104
　leads Scottish expedition by West March (1300), 112-14
　captures Caerlaverock, 112-13
　routs Scots at the Cree, 113-14
　makes truce, 113-14
　and a possible Balliol restoration, 118-19, 122-3
　his campaign of 1301, 120-1
　receives Bruce's submission, 121-3
　invades Scotland by East March (1303), 127
　besieges and captures Stirling (1304), 128-9
　receives general Scottish submission, 129-30
　his vindictiveness towards Wallace, 130, 136-7
　his resettlement of Scotland (1304-1305), 132-6
　his Ordinance (1305), 134-6
　his relations with Bruce, 139-40, 141-2
　shows favour to Alexander Bruce, 143
　his reaction to Bruce's coup, 153
　his savage punishments, 161-2, 169
　his anxiety to capture Bruce, 172
　his lack of success against Bruce noted in Italy, 364,n.2

Edward I, king of England—*contd*
  his authority in Scotland diminished, 172-3
  his death at Burgh-by-Sands, 173
Edward II, king of England (1307-27) (*also*
    Edward of Caernarvon, prince of Wales),
    27, 176, 180, 193, 198, 200, 202, 233,
    238, 239, 240, 241, 242-3, 245, 247,
    248-9, 284, 315, 332,n.30
  campaigns in Scotland before his accession,
    120-1, 161
  relations with the Bruces (1304), 143
  succeeds Edward I, 173
  appealed to by Earl William of Ross, 175, 177
  appealed to by John Macdougall, 179
  hears news of Macdougall, 181
  receives Scottish petition (1309), 186
  military activity in Scotland before Bannock-
    burn, 188, 190, 202, 203
  his supporters in Lothian, 189
  his struggle with the English barons, 195
  his preparations for Bannockburn, 203-8
  conduct during battle, 217, 219, 222, 225-7,
    229
  escapes to England, 230-1, 277
  military activity in Scotland after Bannock-
    burn, 239-40, 243
  narrowly escapes capture (1322), 243-4
  policy towards Scotland, 233, 240-1, 244-5,
    249-51, 372,n.76
  deposition, 251
  and Earl Donald of Mar, 274-5
  policy towards Scottish church, 263-6, 268
Edward III, king of England (1327-77), 294,
    317, 318
  coronation, 251
  in the campaign of Stanhope Park, 252-3
  and the peace negotiations of 1327-1328,
    254-6
  and the Treaty of Edinburgh, 255-7, 258-60
  ratifies the Treaty at Northampton, 260-1
Effie (Euphemia), countess of Ross, 86
Egglescliffe, John of, bishop of Glasgow, 250,
    264
Elderslie, Renfrew, 77
Elgin, 75
  castle, 86, 175-7
  cathedral church of, 324
  cathedral clergy of, 178
Elias, Mr, royal harper, 5, 329,n.2
Ellon castle, Aberdeen, 174
Ely, bishop of *see* Hothum
English language, 4, 6-7 *see also* Scots language
Eric II, king of Norway, 9, 65-6
  claims the Scottish throne, 39-43, 65
Errol, Perth, 285
Eskdale, Dumfries, 20, 115, 364,n.9
Essex, sheriff of, 69
Esticroft in Annandale, 331,n.23

Ettrick, *see* Forest
exchequer of Scotland (at Berwick), 71

Fala, Midlothian, 345,n.48
Falkirk, 68, 210
  battle of (1298), 58, 62, 88, 93, 100-4
Falstone, fortalice of, 239, 371,n.26
Farsley, Geoffrey, 188
Farsley, Simon of, 334,n.98
Faughart, Co. Louth, 317, 380,n.19
Felton, Robert, constable of Lochmaben, 112
Fenes, Guillemin de, commander of Roxburgh
    castle, 195
Fenton, John (father of William), 358,n.84
Fenton, John (son of William), 178, 186, 328,
    358,n.84, 364,n.110
Fenton, William, 133, 158, 326, 358,n.84
Ferrers, Eleanor, abducted by William Doug-
    las, 83
Ferrers, William, lands forfeited by, 279, 280
feudal tenures, under Robert I, 286-92
  archaic tenures (including thanage), 288-9
Fife, 133, 238, 280, 336,n.28, 341,n.53
  earldom of, 76, 174, 185, 277-8, 364,n.107
  earls of, 3, 23, 58, 76, 331,n.25, 336,n.24
  men of, 102, 210
  sheriff of, 238
Fife, Duncan III, earl of (d. 1289), Guardian
    of Scotland, 15, 26, 332,n.33
Fife, Duncan IV, earl of (d. 1353), 45, 50, 151,
    156, 238, 258, 275, 278, 304
  lands restored to, 278
Fife, Isabel of (aunt of Earl Duncan IV, q.v.),
    countess of Buchan, 278
  takes part in Robert I's inauguration, 151,
    356,n.34
  imprisoned in a cage (1306-10), 162, 284,
    360,nn.116,118
Filey, Yorks, 199
Fillan, Saint, of Glendochart, 160, 318
Fincharn castle, Argyll, 362,n.64
Finchley, Middx, 78
Fitz Alan, Brian, of Bedale, Guardian of
    Scotland, 35, 38, 77
Fitz Alan, Edmund, earl of Arundel (1306-26),
    206, 238
Fitz Marmaduke, John, vassal of the bishop of
    Durham, 99
Fitz Warin, William, 88, 344,n.10
Flanders, 9-10, 13, 62, 78, 98, 199, 202
  merchants of, 9-10, 68
  rising against the French (1302), 124
  count of, 199 *see also* Dampierre
Fleming, Malcolm, 280, 288
Florence III, count of Holland, 40
Florence V, count of Holland, 146
  claims the throne of Scotland (d. 1296),
    39-49 *passim*

Folkard, Alexander, of Folkerton, Lanark, 158, 327

Forbes, John, 327, 328

Fordoun, Mearns, 318

Fordun, John, chronicler, 102
on John de Soules, 114
on Robert Bruce's *coup* (1306), 139-40
on battle of Dail Righ, 160
on Robert I's whereabouts (1306-7), 170
on Robert I's Argyll campaign, 180

Forest, The (*also* Forest of Selkirk, Forest of Ettrick), 6, 96, 120, 126-7, 142, 174, 188, 243
archers of, at Falkirk, 96, 101, 102
Scots magnates in (1299), 106-7

Forfar
castle, 182
sheriff of, 105

Forth, River, 5, 86-8, 103, 107, 135, 150, 190-1, 211-2, 228-9
floating bridges across, 127
'earls' ferry' over, 150

Fotheringay, Hugh of, 110, 347,n.7

Fothrif (West Fife), 336,n.28

Foudland, Hills of, Aberdeen, 175

France, 10, 64, 79, 80, 94, 95, 187, 202
king of, 54-5, 200
kings of, *see* Charles, Louis, Philip

Francis, William, 195-6

Franco-Norwegian Treaty (1295), 65

Franco-Scottish Treaty of Paris (1295), 63-5, 66, 68, 73, 90, 93, 95, 128, 137, 300
and Franco-Scottish alliance, 183, 200, 254, 259 *see also* Corbeil

Fraoch Eilean castle, Argyll, 362,n.64

Fraser, Alexander, forfeited, 346,n.64 (same as following?)

Fraser, Alexander, of Touch Fraser, 186, 258, 281, 325, 326, 328, 364,n.110

Fraser, John, archdeacon of St Andrews, 94

Fraser, Richard, 110, 325, 326

Fraser, Simon, the elder, of Oliver Castle (d. 1291), 64

Fraser, Simon, the younger, of Oliver Castle (d. 1306), 121, 138, 142, 158
relations with Scots magnates in 1299, 106
present at siege of Caerlaverock (1300), 350,n.80
joins Scots, 350,n.80
fights at Roslin, 126
at Happrew, 127
required by Edward I to capture Wallace, 130
animosity of Edward I towards, 130, 138, 155-6
his lands devastated, 153
supports Robert I and is executed, 156, 161, 359,n.106

Fraser, Thomas, 158, 325, 327

Fraser, William, bishop of St Andrews (1279-97), Guardian of Scotland, 15, 27, 30, 38, 41, 44, 45, 52, 57, 59, 60, 64, 65, 67, 76, 79, 80, 93, 330,n.37, 332,n.36
death of, at Auteuil, 80

Fraser Tytler, Patrick, 80

Frederick II, emperor, 162

Frendraught, Duncan of, 172, 175, 176, 190

Frere, Mr William, archdeacon of Lothian, 94, 118, 120, 174

Fryde, E. B. 339,n.73

Furness, Lancashire, 237, 238, 243

Fyvie, Aberdeen, 75, 175

Gaelic language, 4, 6, 321

Gainsborough, Brother William of, O.P. (afterwards bishop of Worcester), 116

galloglasses (*gallóglach*), Hebridean mercenaries, 57, 107, 169

Galloway, 17, 20, 49-50, 83, 108, 121, 135, 142, 159, 169, 178, 181-2, 188, 192, 210, 298, 316, 346,n.72
campaign in (1300), 109-14
campaign in (1308), 181-2
special laws of, 3, 136
its separatism, 109-12
lords of, 66, 182
lordship of, 276-7, 280
men of, 92-3, 156, 174, 181-2, 197
Robert Bruce's movements in (1306), 152
Robert Bruce's movements in (1307), 169, 170-1, 173-4
castles of, held against Bruce, 182, 191
taken by Bruce, 194
chiefs of, 178, 181-2

Galloway, see of (*also* Whithorn), 66
bishops of, *see* Dalton, Henry, Wedale

Galloway, Alan, lord of, 5

Galloway, Fergus of, 26, 321, 331,n.26

Galloway, Gilbert of, 26, 331,n.26

Galloway, Thomas of, 5-6, 112

Galloway, Uhtred of, 26, 331,n.26
see also Balliol, Bruce, Dervorguilla

galnis, see wergild

Garchell, in Drymen, Stirling, 159

Garioch, 23, 39, 43-4, 46, 47-8, 141, 142, 159, 176

Garioch, James of, 158

Garmoran, lordship of (Knoydart, Moidart, Arisaig, Rum, Eigg, Uist, Barra and Gigha), 170, 290-1, 321

Garten, Strathspey, 127, 351,n.102

Garth, in Denny, Stirling, 105

Gartnait (*also* Gratney), earl of Mar (d. before 1305), 86

Gascony, 1, 57, 62, 63, 68, 305, 332,n.36
bastides in, 71
knights from, at Bannockburn, 207

Gaucelin, Mgr John, papal legate (1317), 246
Gaveston, Piers, earl of Cornwall (d. 1312),
    180, 188, 190, 192, 203, 238
Gelders, 62
Genoa, 24, 65, 207
    firms in, 199
Germany ('Eastland'), 62
    merchants of Hanse, 'eastlanders', 10, 199
Gévrey-Chambertin, château of, dép. Côte
    d'Or, 119, 349,n.64
Ghent, 345,n.40
Gilbert, Walter son of, commander of Bothwell,
    191, 231
    lands granted to, 280
Gildas, Prophecies of, 34, see also Merlin
Gillis the hunter, 319
Gilsland, Cumberland, 240
Girthon, Kirkcudbright, 113
Girvan, Ayr, 319
Glasgow, 9, 106, 136, 149
    bell tower of, 152
    cathedral church of St Kentigern (Mungo)
        of, 50
    dean of, see Bruce, Wishart,
    diocese and see of, 21, 64, 94, 117, 263-4,
        303
Glen, Richard of, forfeited, 346,n.64
Glen, in Falkirk, Stirling, 101
Glenarm, Antrim, 163
Glencarnie, in Duthil, Inverness, 190, 358,n.88
Glencarnie, Gilbert of, the elder, 159, 172,
    190, 356,n.51
Glencarnie, Gilbert of, the younger, 190
Glendochart, Perth, 160
Glendochart, Malcolm of, 359,n.97
Glendochart, Patrick (Macnab) of, 160
Glendun, Antrim, 252
Glenluce abbey, Wigtown, 319
Glen Trool, Kirkcudbright, 172
Glenurquhart, Inverness, 74
Gloucester, earls of, 113 see also Clare, Mon-
    thermer
Good King Robert's Testament, 187
good men, see probi homines
Gordon, Berwick, 189
Gordon, Adam (lord of), 120, 134, 166, 186,
    189, 203, 275, 305
Gourlay, William, 133, 157
Govan, Lanark, 104
Gowrie, 86, 336,n.28
Graden, Berwick, Peter of, 146, 328
Graham, David, 74, 106-7, 309, 319, 357,n.59
    required by Edward I to capture Wallace, 130
Graham, Patrick, the elder (d. 1296), 37, 52,
    58, 60, 72
Graham, Patrick, the younger, 133, 290, 310,
    327
Granson, Otto de, 349,n.49

Great Dalton, Dumfries, 339,n.59
Great Glen, 55
Greenan, Carrick, 354,n.1
Greenlaw, Ralph of, abbot of Dunfermline, 12
Greinnock, James, of Touchadam, 368,n.59
Gretna, Dumfries, 20, 21
Grey, Thomas, the elder, of Heaton on Till,
    219, 220
Grey, Thomas, the younger, of Heaton on Till,
    chronicler, on William Oliphant, 129, 309
    on Robert Bruce's coup (1306), 140-1, 146,
        152
    on Bannockburn, 219, 222-3
Grimaldi, Rainier de, 305
guardianship of Scotland, and rule of Guar-
    dians, 15-17, 26-38, 54, 63-4, 67, 127-8,
        178, 223, 246, 324
    approximation to in 1297, 84
    under Wallace, 90-1, 96
    joint guardianship from 1298 to 1301,
        104-8, 109-14
    under John de Soules, 114-15, 119-20
    its failure (1304), 132, 143
Guienne (Aquitaine), 100 see also Gascony
Guines, Enguerand de (lord of Couci), 13, 115
    lands forfeited by, 279, 280
Guines, Pas de Calais, 13
Guisborough, Yorks.
    priory of, 21, 67, 180
Guisborough, Walter, canon of, chronicler,
    on the Scots' yoke of servitude, 60
    on their treachery and instability, 60
    on the Scottish council of 1295, 63
    elsewhere cited or quoted in text, 67, 71, 78
    on Scottish nobles' attitude to Edward I, 81,
        85, 86
    on Robert Bruce, the future king in 1297, 84
    on Wallace, 85, 92 on the Scottish schiltrom,
        101
    on Robert Bruce's coup (1306), 140-1
    on Comyn's murder, 148
    on Robert I's coronation, 150-2
    on Robert I's whereabouts (1306-7), 166,
        169
    on Edward I and the Scots, 173

Hadden, Aymer of, 93, 188
Hadden, Ralph of, 37
Haddington, 9, 57, 90, 285, 337,n.8
    constabulary of, 135
    strongpoint at, 191
    east mill of, 285
Hague, The, 46
Hailes, David Dalrymple, lord, 246
Hainault, 199
    troops from, 252-4
    John of, 252
    Philippa of, queen of England, 252

Hakon v, King of Norway, 168, 201, 349,n.48

Halidon Hill, battle of (1333), 322

Hallyards, Midlothian, see Temple Liston

Halton, John, bishop of Carlisle (1292-1324), 84, 240

Haltwhistle, Northumberland, 134, 372,n.82
church of, 318

Hambleton Hills, Yorks., 243, 318

Hamburg, 10, 90

Hamilton, family of, 191

Hanse, 199, 202 see also Germany, merchants

Harbottle castle, Northumberland, 239

Harcla, Andrew, earl of Carlisle (1322-1323), 238, 242, 281, 332,n.30

Harcla treaty (1323), 248-50, 255, 259, 281

Harden, Roxburgh, 158

Hartlepool, Co. Durham, 198, 242

Hastang, Robert, constable of Roxburgh, 106
his spy's report (1299), 107

Hastings, Edmund, younger son of John
Hastings of Abergavenny, 230, 280, 361,n.20

Hastings, Isabel, 361,n.20

Hastings, John, of Abergavenny, 39, 40-1, 43-4, 75, 169, 335,n.12, 361,n.20

Hatfield Broadoak, Essex, 331,n.8

Hattele, Alexander of, 328

Hay, Gilbert (de la), laird of Errol, constable of
Scotland, 153, 156, 157, 237, 258, 275, 284-5, 325, 327, 328
attends St Andrews parliament (1309), 186
specially favoured by Robert I, 284-5
lands granted to, 271, 275

Hay, John (de la), 133, 328

Hay, Thomas (de la), of Borthwick, Lothian, 151, 188, 223

Hay, William (de la), of Lochwarret (or
Lochwharret, now Borthwick), 102

Hay, William (de la), north-country landowner, 178

Haydon Bridge, Northumberland, 253

Hazelrigg, in Chatton, Northumberland, 342,n.81

Heaton on the Till, Northumberland, 342,n.81

Hebrides (also Outer Isles, Western Isles), 55, 256, 259
probable refuge of Robert I among (1306-7), 166-70 passim
chiefs and men of, 289-92
men of, 192, 210, 243-4

Hendon, Middlesex, 78

Henry, abbot of Scone, 350,n.94
approves Bruce's bid for throne, 151
participates in Bruce's coronation, 151
imprisoned in England, 153

Henry, archdeacon of Galloway, 66

Henry, bishop of Galloway (1255-93), 38, 66

Henry I, king of England (1100-35), 20, 21, 25

Henry II, king of England (1154-89), 11, 53, 62, 331,n.26

Henry III, king of England (1216-72), 11-13, 24, 63, 336,n.1

Henry, son of king David I, earl of North-
umber-land (d. 1152), 39
called 'earl of Huntingdon', 46

Hereford, earls of, see Bohun

Hermitage castle, Roxburgh, 115, 283, 376,n.73

Heron, Robert, comptroller of chamberlain of
Scotland, 134-5

Herries, family of, 21

Herries, Ralph, 158

Hertford, 74

Hesilrig, William, sheriff of Lanark, killed by
Wallace (1297), 83, 137, 342,n.81

Hexham, 197, 340,n.8
priory ('abbey') of, 91, 92-3, 340,n.9
school at, 340,n.8

Hingham, William, lord of, 230

Hitchin, Herts, 74

Hoddam, Annandale, 146

Holderness, 3, 237

Holland, 10, 62

Holland, count of, 199, see also Florence,
William

Holm Cultram, abbey of, Cumberland, 142, 197

Holyrood, abbey of, Midlothian, 6, 243, 257, 265, 375,n.27

Hothum, John de, bishop of Ely, 240

Houxty, Northumberland, 239

Hunsingore, Yorks, W.R., 336,n.48

Hunsingore, Mr Richard of, 336,n.48

Hunsingore, Mr Thomas of, chancellor of
Scotland, 50, 81, 336,n.48

Huntercombe, Walter, 28

Huntingdon, Honour of, 23, 47, 321

Huntingdon, earl of, see David, John of Scotland

Inchaffray abbey, Perth, 17, 105, 160, 170, 318, 352,n.8
abbot of, see Maurice

Inchchonnell castle, Argyll, 181, 362,n.64

Inchcolm, Fife
abbey of, 355,n.24
abbot of, 151

Inchmahome, Perth, 182, 356,n.38, 361,n.20

Inchmartin, David, son of John, executed for
supporting Bruce (1306), 358,n.89

Inchmartin, John of, 74, 120, 134, 358,n.89

Inchmichael (now Lochinch), Wigtown, 319

Inchture, Perth, parliament at (1312), 202, 266, 300

Inchture, Robert of, 327

Inglewood, Forest of, Cumberland, 174, 197

Innerpeffray, Malcolm of, 159, 327
Invercharach, Banff, 75
Inverkip castle, Renfrew, 121, 126, 148
Inverlochy castle, 175, 321
Inverness, 9, 38, 86, 201-2, 300
  sheriff of, 38
  castle, 86, 175, 196
  Treaty of (1312), 200-2
Inverurie, Aberdeen, 176
Iona, 5, 7
Ireby, Christian, wife of Bruce the Competitor, 25
Ireby, William, 25
Ireland, 11, 25-6, 131, 149, 163, 168-9, 181,
  192-3, 236, 255, 259, 262, 292, 293, 306,
  314-7, 321, 339,n.73
  crown of, 293-4
  kings of, 169
  sub-kings of, 169
  kings and people of, 314, 316
  northern Ireland, 81, 141, 170, see also Ulster
  Scottish expedition to (1315), 169
Irish troops in Scotland
  on the English side, 73, 121, 126, 127, 204,
    339,n.73
  on the Scottish side, 169
  first on Scottish then on English side, 168-9
Irvine, Ayr, 9, 84, 280, 288
  capitulation of, 84-5
Isabel, daughter of Earl David of Huntingdon,
  23, 331,n.11
Isabella of France, queen of England, 239, 245,
  252, 254, 260, 374,n.105
Islay, 55, 163, 291
  lords of, see Macdonald
Islay, Ruairi of, 299
Isles, Christiana of the, see Mar, Christina of
  Italy
  news of Robert I in, 364,n.2
  cages used in, 162

Jardine, family of, 21
Jay, Brian le, Master of the Temple in England,
  99
  slain at Falkirk, 103
Jedburgh, 71
  castle, 68, 103, 135, 188-9, 191
  abbot of, see Morel
Joan of England, queen of Scots (d. 1238), 12
Joan of the Tower, queen of Scots (d. 1362),
  254-5, 258-60, 374,n.105
John, abbot of Arbroath, 362,n.60
John, king of England (1199-1216), 11, 49,
  331,n.26
  and Magna Carta, 22
John, king of Scots, see Balliol
John, the nephew, Mr, clerk of Galloway
  (Johannes Nepos), 66

John XXII, Pope (1316-34), 240, 241, 245-50,
  264, 275, 302-3, 305, 308, 309
John of Scotland, earl of Chester and Huntingdon (d. 1237), 23, 42
Johnstone, family of, 21

Keith, family of, 271
Keith, Alexander, 146
Keith, Bernard, 328
Keith, Edward, 186, 271, 376,n.76
  lands granted to, 271
Keith, Robert, marischal of Scotland, 237,
  271, 284-5, 295
  in the Forest raid (1299), 106
  captured in Galloway (1300), 113
  justice between Forth and the Mounth
    (1305), 284-5
  joint-warden of Scotland (1305-6), 139
  joins Robert I (1308), 188
  attends St Andrews parliament (1309), 186
  at Bannockburn, 208, 217, 227
  and the capture of Berwick, 329
  warden of Berwick, 371,n.23
  lands granted to, 271
Keith, William, of Galston, 239, 324
Kellaw, Richard, bishop of Durham (1311-
  16), 197
Kelso, abbey of, 6
  Richard, abbot of, 41
Kendal, 329,n.27
Kenmore, Perth, 356,n.51
Kennedy, clan of, 299, 308 see also Carrick,
  Roland
Kennedy, Mr Alexander, chancellor of Scot-
  land, 81
Kilconquhar, Fife, 331,n.25
Kilconquhar, Adam of, jure uxoris earl of
  Carrick (d. 1271), 25
Kildrummy castle, Aberdeen, 75, 138, 142,
  159, 160-1, 274, 341,n.40
Killin, Perth, 170
Kilmarnock in Cunningham, Ayr, 280
Kincardine castle, Mearns, 74
Kincardine O'Neil (Oneil), Aberdeen, 74,
  278
Kindrochit (now Braemar), 75
Kinghorn, Fife, 1-2, 13, 118
Kinghorn, Mr William of, vicar-general of
  bishop of St Andrews, 67
King's Lynn, Norfolk, 127
Kingston, John, constable of Edinburgh
  (1299), 106, 139, 347,n.96
Kinloss abbey, Moray, 127
Kinninmonth, family of, 305
Kinninmonth, Mr. Alexander, parson of
  Kinkell, archdeacon of Lothian, bishop of
  Aberdeen (1329-44), 241, 305-6, 308,
  374,n.19

Kinninmonth, John, bishop of Brechin (1298-
    c. 1322), 134, 174, 185, 263, 266, 305
Kinnoull, Perth, 278
Kinross, 64
Kinross, Mr Matthew of, dean of Dunkeld,
    359,n.96
Kinrymont (now St Andrews), 7
Kintail, 55
Kintore, Aberdeen, 75, 142
Kintyre ('the isle of Kintyre'), 56, 58, 148, 163,
    291
    clerk of, 26
    Mull of, 168
Kirkconnel, Robert of, 158, 326
Kirkconnel, Thomas of, 158, 326
Kirkcudbright, 113
    stewartry of, 25
Kirkcudbright, Thomas of, see Dalton
Kirkinner (also Carnemoel), Wigtown, 143
Kirkintilloch castle, Dunbarton, 152, 191, 280,
    288
Kirkliston, in Liston, Mid and W. Lothian, 99
Kirkoswald, 237
Kirkpatrick, family of, 21, 308
Kirkpatrick, Humphrey, 379,n.155
Kirkpatrick, Roger, and the tale of 'I mak
    siccar', 148, 379,n.155
Kirkwall, St Magnus cathedral at, 168
Knapdale, Argyll, 168, 183
Knaresborough, Yorks., 239
Knockdolian, Ayr, John of, 328
Kyle, Ayr, 20, 121, 141
Kyle Stewart (N. Kyle), 81

Lacy, of Meath, family of, 316
Lamberton, William, bishop of St Andrews
    (1297-1328), 80-1, 99, 106-8, 109, 112,
    114, 118, 131, 143, 155, 241, 258, 302-4,
    305, 306, 336,n.32
    his election and consecration, 94-5
    his diplomatic activity, 95, 124, 200, 258
    elected joint-guardian, 107-8
    collaborates with de Soules, 115, 118, 120
    makes secret 'band' with Bruce (1304), 131,
        139, 142
    his close relations with Wallace, 128
    returns to Scotland from France, 129
    lands restored, 129
    at English parliament, September 1305,
        352,n.19
    on council of 1305, 135
    joint-warden of Scotland (1305-6), 139
    charges against in 1306, 140
    part played in Bruce's coup (1306), 145-6,
        150
    his part in Robert I's coronation, 151-2, 263,
        356,nn.35,38
    captured and imprisoned in irons, 153

    his letter to Philip IV (1309), 264-5
    his career under Robert I, 174, 185, 264-6,
        375,n.27
Lammermuir, 72
Lanark, sheriff of, 78, 105 see also Bruce,
    Robert, Hesilrig, Livingston, Logan
Lanarkshire, 188
Lancaster, 243
Lancaster, Henry, earl of (1326-45), 252
Lancaster, Thomas of, earl of Lancaster (d.
    1322), 75, 203, 204, 206, 239-42, 247-8,
    345,n.51
Landun, William of, 240
Lanercost priory, Cumberland, 171
Largs, battle of (1263), 72
Lathom, Henry of, sheriff of Aberdeen, 155,
    342,n.80
Latimer, William, 127, 142
Lauder, Berwick, 280, 288, 345,n.49
Lauder, Robert, the elder, justiciar of Lothian,
    240, 258, 284, 285, 309
Lauderdale, Berwick, 81, 99, 209, 280, 288
    common route for English invasions of
        Scotland, 345,n.49
Laurence, bishop of Argyll (d. c.1299), 26, 79
Laurencekirk, see Conveth
laws of Scotland
    conservation of, 3
    to be preserved (1290), 28
    on royal succession, 42, 293-4
    reviewed in 1305, 135-6
    of King David I, 135
    under Robert I, 295-9
    Celtic law, 135-6
Ledows (Ledhous?), Sim of the, 195
Leinster, North, 316
Leith, 9, 99
Leitholm, Edward of, 110
Lennox, 127, 163, 174, 188, 222, 258
    earldom of, 276
    temporarily granted to John Menteith, 183
    earls of, 50
    dean of Christianity of, 150
Lennox, Malcolm I, earl of (1270-?1290),
    37
Lennox, Malcolm II, earl of (?1290-1333),
    87, 88, 133, 159, 185, 275, 276, 319,
    344,n.23, 344,n.38, 346,n.61, 364,n.107
    present at Robert I's coronation, 151
    his loyal support of Robert I, 151, 156, 163
    lands granted to, 276
Leny, John of, 159, 327
Lenzie, Dunbarton, 288
Lesmahagow, Lanark, 365,n.45
Leven, River, Dunbarton, 319-21
Lewes, Sussex, battle of (1264), 24, 68
Lewis, Isle of, 55
    Butt of, 11

Leyre, William de, alderman of London, 353,n.35
  Wallace lodged with (1305), 136
Libaud, Pierre, commander of Edinburgh castle, 196, 281, 285
Liddesdale, Roxburgh, 20, 69, 115, 142, 197, 282-3
  castle, 115, 283, 376,n.73
Lilford, Northants, 116
Limerick, 315, 316
Lincoln, Henry de Lacy, earl of (d. 1311), 68, 102, 116, 155
Lincoln, 115
Lindsay, family of, 13, 22, 50, 279
Lindsay, Alexander, of Barnweill, 83, 138, 186, 279
  forfeited, 346,n.64
  required by Edward I to capture Wallace, 130
  animosity of Edward I towards, 130, 138, 358,n.79
  supports Robert I, 158, 160
  in Galloway campaign (1308), 363,n.80
Lindsay, Christian, wife of Enguerand de Guines, 13
Lindsay, David, of Crawford, 258
Lindsay, James (son of Walter), 158, 328
Lindsay, John, son of Simon, 279
Lindsay, John, bishop of Glasgow (1323-1335), 257, 264, 265, 279
Lindsay, Philip, chamberlain of Scotland under Alexander III, 264, 279
Lindsay, Simon, forfeited, 279
Linlathen, Angus, 81
Linlithgow, 100, 121, 230
  castle or 'peel' at, 190, 191
  sheriffdom of, 135
Lintalee, Roxburgh, fight at, 238
Linton, Roxburgh, 158
Lisle, John de, 337,n.8
Liston, Mid and W. Lothian, Kirkliston, Temple Liston, 99
Livingston, W. Lothian, 191
Livingston, Archibald, 141
Lochaber, Inverness, 75, 145, 159
  lordship of, 277, 291
  Edward, steward of, 340,n.38
  lords of, see Comyn
Lochalveth, see Alvie
Loch Awe, Argyll, 56, 179, 180, 362,n.64
  castle of, 181, 362,n.64
  lands of, 289
  River Awe, 181
Loch Broom, Ross, 190, 321
Loch Doon castle, Carrick, 149, 161, 182, 191, 299, 318
Lochindorb, Moray, 127, 351,n.102
Loch Lomond, 163

Lochmaben castle, Dumfries, 20, 21, 25, 66, 104, 108, 140, 146, 158, 248
  visited by Edward I (1300), 112
  attacked by Scots (1301), 121
  held against Bruce, 182
  regained by Scots, 191
Lochmartnaham, King's Kyle, Ayr, 284
Loch Ryan, Wigtown, 121
Loch Tarbert, East and West, Argyll, 291
Lochwarret (or Lochwharret) (now Borthwick), Midlothian, 102
Lockhart, Simon, of the Lee, 158, 326
Logan, family of, 316
Logan, Walter, of Hartside, sheriff of Lanark, 105, 146, 324, 325, 328, 358,n.88
Logie, John, 310, 379,n.167
London, 73, 75, 142
  Tower of, 74, 137, 162
  mayor of (1305), 137
  mob of, 260
London Bridge, 137, 161
Longforgan, Carse of Gowrie, Perth, 146, 354,n.1
Longmorn forest, Moray, 143
Lorn, 56, 159 see also Macdougall
Lothian, 6, 81, 96, 127, 135, 152, 159, 341,n.53
  offered to Otto of Brunswick, 283
  attitude of its inhabitants in the Anglo-Scottish war, 159-60, 197
  archdeacons of, see Eaglesham, Frere
  position of, before Bannockburn, 187-9, 197
Loudoun, Cunningham, Ayr, 121, 284
Loudoun Hill, battle at (1307), 172, 208, 217
Louis VI, king of France, 12, 15
Louis X, king of France, 245
Lovel, family of, 281
Lovel, Hugh, of Hawick, 158, 326, 327
Lovel, John, 'the rich', 230
Lovel, Richard, of Hawick, forfeited, 280
Lübeck, 10, 76, 90
  Robert I writes to, 199
Lucy, Anthony de, 231
Luffness, E. Lothian, 159
  strongpoint at, 191
Luke, Mgr, papal legate (1317), 246
Lumphanan, Aberdeen, 340,n.36
Lundie, Richard, 84, 87
Luss, John of, 159, 356,n.38
  forfeited, 327, 346,n.64

Macaulay, Duncan ('son of Anelf'), 159, 327
MacCan, family or clan of, 112, 170, 178
MacCan, Gibbon, 142
MacCulian, Malcolm, 58, 149, 169, 327, 337,n.11 see also MacQuillan
McCulloch, family of, 308
McCulloch(?), Gilbert, forfeited, 346,n.64

Macdonald, family or clan of, 289, 291
    member killed at battle of Dundalk, 361,n.15
Macdonald, Alexander, lord of Islay, 57, 107,
    163, 291, 360,n.124, 377,n.118
Macdonald, Angus Mór, lord of Islay, 18, 56,
    57, 163, 360,n.124
Macdonald, Angus Og, lord of Islay, 163,
    168-9, 210, 291, 360,n.124
    could have signed Declaration of Arbroath,
    310
Macdonald, Colin, 179
Macdonald, Donald (lord of Islay?), 163, 186,
    291, 360,n.124
Macdonleavie (Maclay), James and John, 290
Macdouall, family or clan of, in Galloway, 112,
    170, 178, 281
Macdouall, Dungal, 142, 181, 190, 191, 193
Macdougall, family or clan of, 163, 168, 178,
    180-1, 266, 281, 290-1, 361,n.15
Macdougall, Alexander, lord of Argyll and
    Lorn (d. 1310), 41, 56, 57, 73, 107, 156,
    179, 181, 186
    his son Duncan, 107
Macdougall, John (also John of Lorn, John
    Bacach), lord of Argyll and Lorn, 156,
    163, 171, 175, 179-81, 190, 290
    routs Robert I at Dail Righ, 160
    appeals for help to Edward II, 179
    defeated at Brander, 179-81, 321
    leads naval expedition against Robert I, 192
    recovers Man, 193
    funeral, 365,n.30
Macduff, Clan, 58
Macduff, son of earl Malcolm II of Fife (d.
    1298), 57, 58, 86, 102
MacGilwini, Cuthbert, forfeited, 346,n.64
Mackenzie, W. M., 211, 212, 216
Mackessan (alias MacCassen, Mackassen),
    'Coweyn' or Ewen, of Garchell, 159, 328
Mackinoluagh', Gilbert, forfeited, 346,n.64
MacLachlan, Gillespie, 186, 290, 362,n.66
    has grant of Shirvan, Argyll, 290
Macnab, see Glendochart
MacQuillan, family of, in Antrim, 149,
    337,n.11, 361,n.18
    Malcolm (identical with Malcolm 'le fiz le
    Engleys' q.v. s.v. Malcolm), 149, 169
Macruarie, Christina, see Mar, Christina of
Macruarie, Lachlan (also Macalan), son of
    Alan Macruarie, lord of Garmoran, 107,
    156, 177, 290
Macruarie, Roderick (also Ruairi), son of Alan
    Macruarie, lord of Garmoran, 290-1,
    347,n.103
MacSween, family of, 58
    John, 58, 168, 192
    his brothers Murdoch and Toirdelbach, 192
MacTaggart, Farquhar, 271

Madog ap Llywelyn, 63
Maes Moydog, Montgomery, battle of (1295),
    101
Magnus, king of Man (d. 1266), 58
Maitland, F. W., 2-3
Malachy O'Moore, Saint (Maelmaedoc Ua
    Morgair), his curse upon the Bruces, 25,
    318
Malcolm III, Canmore, king of Scots (1058-
    93), 25, 242
Malcolm IV, king of Scots (1153-65), 11, 62
Malcolm 'le fiz le Engleys' ('Lengleys', etc.)',
    58, 149, 348,n.18
    was he the same as Malcolm MacQuillan,
    q.v.?, 58, 149, 337,n.11
Malherbe, family of (also Morham, q.v.), 105-6
Malherbe, Gilbert, 105-6, 310
Malmaison, diocese of Cambrai, King John in
    custody at, 119
Man, Isle of, 28-9, 49, 191, 192-3, 255, 256,
    259, 317, 321
    lordship of, 277, 292
    Calf of, 11
Mandeville family, of Ulster, 26, 380,n.12
Mandeville, Henry de, Seneschal of Ulster,
    252
Mandeville, Thomas de, 26
Manning, Robert of, Bourne (Brunne), poet,
    his knowledge of the Bruces at Cam-
    bridge, 143, 170
Manor, Peebles, 278-9, 287
Manton, Ralph, cofferer of the Wardrobe, 76,
    127
Mar, 336,n.28
    braes of, 75, 160
    earldom of, 45, 185, 274, 364,n.107
    earls of, 23, 45, 50, 75
    family of earls of, 141
Mar, Donald I, earl of, 29, 37, 44, 45-6, 65, 66,
    335,n.14
Mar, Donald II, earl of, 122, 142, 151, 252,
    258, 274
Mar, Gartnait, earl of, 44
    his son and heir entrusted to Robert Bruce,
    122
    marries Christian Bruce, 141
Mar, Morgan, earl of, 45
Mar, William, earl of, 45
Mar, Christina, or Christian of, daughter and
    heir of Alan Macruarie of Garmoran, wife
    of Duncan, son of Earl Donald I of Mar,
    170, 290-1, 321
    her son Ruairi, 291
Mar, Duncan of (son of Earl Donald I of Mar),
    170
Mar, Isabel of, first wife of Robert Bruce, 141,
    293
March, earldom of, 277 (see also Dunbar)

March, Patrick IV, of Dunbar, earl of (1290-1308), 37, 100, 141, 150, 156, 159, 277, 340,n.14, 350,n.80, 353,n.22
forfeited, 370,n.2
March, Patrick V, of Dunbar, earl of (1308-1368), 185, 203, 231, 232, 258, 277, 305, 309, 371,n.23
Margaret of England, queen of Scots (d. 1275), 1, 13
Margaret of Flanders, 119
Margaret of Hungary, Saint, queen of Scots (d. 1093), 7
    Black Rood of, 73, 260
Margaret of Norway, 'the Maid of Norway', lady and queen of Scotland (d. 1290), 1, 13, 15-16, 17, 18, 27, 28-30, 42, 57, 334,n.64
Margaret of Scotland, countess of Brittany, daughter of Henry, earl of Northumberland, 40
Margaret of Scotland, queen of Norway (d. 1283?), 1, 9
Marischal, John, forfeited, 346,n.64
Mark, bishop of Sodor and Man (1275-c.1303), 37, 79, 338,n.37
Marshall, D. H., 33
Maubuisson, Odard de, 305-6
Maule, Thomas (of Panmure), 127
Mauley, Edmund de, 226, 229
Maurice, abbot of Inchaffray, supports Robert I, 151, 160, 200
    participates in election of Nicholas Balmyle to see of Dunblane, 174
    as bishop of Dunblane (1322-47), 258, 267
Maxwell, Eustace, 309, 310, 318
Maxwell, Herbert, 367,n.52
    forfeited, 346,n.64
May (also Pittenweem), priory of, 57
Maybole, Ayr, 124
Mazun, John, wine merchant of Bordeaux, his suit against King Alexander III, 1, 57-9
Mearns (Kincardine), 336,n.28
Megget, Peebles, 346n.64
Meldrum, Philip, lands granted to, 274
Melrose, 352n.19
    abbey of, 6, 243, 324
    its grange of Maybole, 124
    abbot of, see Selkirk
Melton, William, archbishop of York (1316-40), 239
Melville, Mary, widow of William, 93
Melville, William, 327
Menteith, 336,n.28
    earldom of, 174, 185, 276, 361,n.20, 364,n.107
Menteith, Isabel, countess of, 361,n.20
Menteith, Mary, countess of, 276

Menteith, Alan, earl of (c.1306-c.1309), 151, 156, 159, 276, 361,n.20
Menteith, Alan, the younger (never styled earl), 276, 278
Menteith, Alexander, earl of (1296-betw. 1297 and 1306), 74, 106, 108, 276, 310, 344,n.38, 345,n.41, 346,n.61
Menteith, Murdoch, earl of (1318-32), 258, 276, 309-10
Menteith, Walter Stewart, earl of (d. c.1296), 37, 58, 135, 276
    see also Menteith, John
Menteith, John (of), alias John Stewart, keeper of Dumbarton castle (1305-?1308 or 1309), 135, 136, 149, 171, 191, 284, 286, 291, 308
    hands Wallace over to Edward I, 136
    pursues Robert I, 163
    enemy of the Macsweens, 168
    joins Robert I, 183
    at St Andrews parliament (1309), 185
Menzies, Alexander, 74, 146, 158, 160, 325, 358,n.89
Menzies, Alexander, the younger, and his wife Gelis Stewart, 279
Menzies, Robert, 258, 310
Menzies, William, 158, 328
merchants
    of England, 68, 199
    of France, 68
    of Flanders, 9-10, 68, 71, 199
    of Germany, 10, 76, 90, 199, 341,n.70
Merioneth, 56, 63
Merlin, prophecy of (same as Prophecies of Gildas, q.v.?), 172, 317
Methven, Perth, 274
    battle of (1306), 154, 207-8
Middleton, Gilbert of, 236, 239, 246
Middleton, Richard of, 239, 371,n.26
Middleton, William, bishop of Norwich (1278-88), 12
military service, 16, 17, 66-7, 207-8, 337,n.5
    knight service (also 'free service'), 16, 17, 47, 85, 286-9, 290
    Scottish service (also 'common army', 'Scottish army'), 3, 17, 85, 86, 124, 330,n.44
    ship-service, 289-92
    standard bearer's service, 162
    tenure in return for, 286-92
    archer service, 287-9
Miller, T., 211
Milton (of Bannockburn), Stirling, 214-5, 368,n.59
Mitford castle, Northumberland, 239
Moffat, Robert of, forfeited, 346,n.64
Molbride, the younger, 290, 328
Monreith, Wigtown, 319

Montfort, Simon de, earl of Leicester, 24, 216

Montagu, Simon, 192, 365,n.28

Montfort, William, dean of St Paul's (d. 1294), 59

Montgomery, John of, 328

Monthermer, Raoul de, earl of Gloucester (d. 1325), 138
  alleged to have helped Robert Bruce in 1305 or 1306, 172
  worsted by Robert I (1307), 172
  friendship with Robert I, 231

Monthermer, Marie de, countess of Fife, 278

Montrose, 9, 73, 75, 127, 323

Montrose, Mr Alan of, his lost work of history, 349,n.50

Monymusk, Thomas, laird of, 159, 328

Moray, 45, 75, 85-6, 177, 178, 190, 199, 210
  Moray Firth, 177, 178
  earldom of, 270, 277, 283
  bishops of, see Archibald, Murray, Pilmour

Moray, Thomas Randolph, earl of Moray, see Randolph

Moray, Angus, mormaer of, 277

Morel, John, abbot of Jedburgh
  envoy to Edward I (1286), 16
  envoy to the French court (1299), 96, 344,n.26

Morham, E. Lothian, 105

Morham, Herbert, the elder, 105, 357,n.61

Morham, Herbert, the younger, 105, 121, 357,n.61

Morham, Thomas, 105

mormaers, see earls

Morpeth, Northumberland, 61, 338,n.34

Morris, J. E., 206-7

Morrone, Peter, see Celestine V, Pope

Mortimer, Roger, 245, 252, 260, 316

Morton, Dumfries, 280

Morvern, Argyll (also Cenel Badin), 55, 291

Morville, dép. Manche, 20

Morville, family of, 280

Morville, Hugh de, constable of Scotland (d. 1162), 20

Moubray, family of, in Scotland, 281

Moubray, Alexander, 310

Moubray, Geoffrey (de), 16, 102, 330,n.36

Moubray, John (de), 65, 74, 134, 171, 176, 186

Moubray, Philip, commander of Stirling castle for Edward II, 195, 217, 230, 231, 239

Moubray, Roger de, 110, 309, 310, 348,n.9
  forfeited, 370,n.2

Moulin, Perth, 3

Mounth, the (now Grampian Mountains), 85, 135, 172, 178, 182
  Robert I and his followers take refuge in (1306), 160-1, 163

Mowat, Bernard, 161

Mowat, Patrick, 200-1

Mowat, William, 133, 158, 328

Mowbray, Vale of, 237

Muckhart, Perth, fortalice of, 190

Muirton, Stirling, 211, 216

Mull, Isle of, 291

Murray, family of, 22, 83

Murray, Adam, bishop of Brechin (1328-49), 251

Murray, Alan, of Culbin (Moray), 133, 158, 326

Murray, Andrew, of Petty, justiciar of Scotia (d. ?1298), 38, 60-1, 74

Murray, Andrew, commander of the army of Scotland (d. 1297), 67, 75, 90-1, 96, 116
  leads the rising in Moray (1297), 85-6
  joins Wallace, 86
  wins battle of Stirling Bridge (1297), 87-9
  his death, 88, 90

Murray, Andrew, of Bothwell, Guardian of Scotland (d. 1338), 121, 194, 258, 309, 343,n.1

Murray, Austin, 327, 328

Murray, David, bishop of Moray (1299-1326), 155, 163, 177, 201, 263, 266, 302, 373,n.97, 375,n.27
  consecration, 116
  family connexions, 116
  approves Bruce's bid for throne, 151
  present at Robert I's coronation, 151, 263
  flees to Orkney, 168, 177
  supports Robert I, 174
  attends St Andrews parliament?, 185

Murray, John, of Drumsergard, 327

Murray, John, of Touchadam, 368,n.59

Murray, John, parson of Lilford, 349,n.45

Murray, William, of Bothwell, 'le Riche', pantler of Scotland (d. 1300), 61, 74, 116

Murray, William of Drumsargard, 133

Murray, William, of St Fort (Fife), 133, 158, 326, 328

Murray, William, of Tullibardine, 37, 98

Muschamp, Robert de, lord of Wooler, 93

Muschet (de Montefixo), William, of Cargill, 258

Musselburgh, 9

Myton-on-Swale, Yorks., 239

Nairn, burgh of, 271
  castle, 175

National Trust for Scotland and Bannockburn site, 301

Nesbit, Robert, 327, 328

Neville, Robert, of Raby, 126, 238

Newbattle abbey, Midlothian, 303, 304, 309

Newcastle upon Tyne, 51, 68, 92, 113, 137, 157, 158, 161, 162, 206, 240, 255-6, 372,n.78
  castle, 92, 236

Newminster, Northumberland, 61
   abbey, 204, 209, 355,n.24
New Park, Stirling, 210, 212-4, 216-9, 223-5
Newtibber, Richard of, 326
Newton Stewart, Wigtown, 113
Ninian, Saint, 7
   his shrine at Whithorn, 319
Nith, River, 112
Nithsdale, 18, 20, 74, 84, 121, 145, 277
   lordship of, 277 see also Randolph
Norfolk, earls of, see Bigod, Brotherton
Norham castle, Northumberland (formerly
   Co. Durham), 31, 37, 61, 68, 236, 251,
   254, 372,n.76
Norhamshire, 93, 254
Normandy, 65
'Normans', in Scotland and the 'Norman
   Myth', 3-4, 7, 20-2
Northallerton, Yorks., 239, 243
   Allertonshire, 254
Northampton
   treaty of Birgham ratified at (1290), 27, 32
   treaty of Edinburgh ratified at (1328), 260-1
Northburgh, Roger, 229
Northumberland, 53, 71, 109, 180, 188, 190
   men of, 69, 236
   Scottish raids in, 197-8, 236, 237
   Scottish invasions of, 92-3, 253-4
North Tynedale, 239
Norway, 9-10, 27, 65, 168, 169, 202
   Kings of, see Eric, Hakon, Magnus
   see also Scoto-Norwegian treaty
Norwich, bishop of, see Middleton
Nottingham, 24

Oban, Argyll, 180
O'Brien, Muirchertach, 316
Olderfleet (now Larne), 163, 252
Oldhamstocks, Berwick, 50
Oldmeldrum, Aberdeen, 176
Old Montrose, Angus, 319
Olifard, family of (also Oliphant, q.v.), 22,
   121
Oliphant (Olifard), William, 166, 299, 309
   commander of Stirling castle, 106, 109, 127,
   128-9
   commander of Perth for Edward II, 194
Oneil, see Kincardine O'Neil
O'Neill (Ua Neill), Domnall, 316, 332,n.31
Ordainers, Lords, and Ordinances of 1311,
   192, 249
Ordinance for the Government of Scotland
   (1305), 133, 134-6, 138
Orkney, 10, 29, 161, 200
   earldom of, 271
   did Robert I take refuge in (1306-07)?,
   166-8, 169
   seneschal of, 200-1

Ormsby, William, English justice in Scotland,
   75, 83
Ospringe, Kent, 365,n.30
Otto IV, emperor (Otto of Brunswick) (1209-
   18), 40, 283
Outer Isles, 149, 166, 321 see also Hebrides
Oxford, university of, 80

Paisley, 78, 81
   abbey of, 357,n.71
   Forest of, 78
Palgrave, Francis, 44, 133
papacy, 28, 245-7, 262-4, 269, 302, 379,n.148
   papal curia, 79, 93-4, 115-16, 241, 250, 263,
   303, 305, 374,n.19, 378,n.146
   popes, see Boniface, Celestine, Clement
Paris, 63, 64, 80, 94, 115, 116, 124-6, 128, 264
   parlement of, 54
   university of, 267
Paris, Matthew, 9
parliaments, in Scotland, 28, 31, 55, 60-1, 63,
   65, 66, 68, 75, 76-7, 91, 105, 124, 133,
   134, 135, 137, 241, 293, 294, 296,
   299-300, 332,n.58, 338,n.32, 378,n.128
   in the reign of Robert I, 181, 183-4, 202
'Parson', siege-engine at Stirling, 129
Patrick the Archer, forfeited, 346,n.64
Peebles, 107, 142
   castle, 120, 158
   sheriff of, see Tweeddale
   sheriffdom of, 135
Pelstream Burn, in St Ninians, Stirling, 211,
   219, 224
Pembroke earl of, see Valence
Penicuik, Midlothian, 106
Penicuik, Margaret, lady of, 106
Penicuik, Hugh of, 106, 133
Penrith, Liberty of, 16
Percehay, Walter de, 26, 332,n.33
Percy, Henry, the elder (d. 1314), 84, 170,
   171
Percy, Henry, the younger, 123, 254, 257, 259,
   260
Perth (also Saint John's town), 9, 11, 38, 73,
   103, 137, 153-4, 183, 188, 193-5, 300,
   313
   castle, 190-1, 193-5
   Treaty of (1266), 11, 201, 249, 295
Perthshire, 6, 133, 158, 160
Pesshun, Stephen, of Lincolnshire, 155
Peter, Saint, 306
Petty, Inverness, 74
Philip IV, the Fair, king of France (1285-1314),
   60, 62-3, 64-5, 73, 79, 90, 95, 98, 109,
   110, 114, 115, 118, 119, 121, 122, 124,
   127, 128, 183-4, 200, 202, 245-6, 264,
   265, 338,n.47, 340,n.8, 341,n.70,
   349,n.48, 359,nn.95,107

Philip v, king of France (1317-22), 240, 241, 245, 305
Picts, 5, 185
Pictish monarchy, 10
Pierrefonds, dép. Oise, 116, 349,n.48
Pilche, Alexander, 328
Pilmour, John of, bishop of Moray (1326-62), 258, 267, 308, 324, 373,n.97, 381,n.44
Pinkie, Peter of, 188; his tenants, 325
Pinkney, Henry, 37, 159; his tenants, 325
Pitfoddels, Aberdeen (same as 'Macfothel'?), 157
Pitlochry, Perth, 3
Pitpullox, Angus, 26
Platan (alias Plater), Philip the forester of, 182
Pluscarden, Moray, prior of, 46
Poitiers, papal curia at, 174, 263
popes, see Boniface, Celestine, Clement
Ponthieu, crossbowmen of, 101
Portsmouth, 62
Powicke, F. M., 61, 162, 351,n.124
Pows, The (also Les Polles, the Carse of Stirling), 88, 212, 215, 222, 224, 228
Prendergest, Henry, forfeited, 370,n.2
Preston, Lancs., 243
probi homines, see also bone gent, bones genz, 27, 34, 52, 59, 88, 296, 343,n.4
processus (1301), 241, 306

Quinci, de, family of, its Scottish estates, 280, 285

Ragman Roll, 76-8, 115-16, 118
Ramsay, Iole of Man, 340,n.15
Ramsay, Edmund, of Dalhousie, 133, 188
Ramsay, William, of Dalhousie, 102
Randolph, Nicholas, 74
Randolph, Thomas, the elder, of Nithsdale, 37, 52, 60, 110
  forfeited, 346,n.64
Randolph, Thomas, the younger (d. 1332), earl of Moray, Guardian of Scotland, 193, 208, 240, 274, 276, 277, 278, 288, 304, 320, 324
  supports Robert I (1306), 158, 325, 326, 327, 328
  captured by English and serves the English king, 183
  rejoins Robert I, 183
  at St Andrews parliament (1309), as lord of Nithsdale, 186
  takes Edinburgh castle (1314), 195
  made earl of Moray, 196
  granted lordship of Man, 193
  takes Man, 193
  raids Anglesey, 193
  at Bannockburn, 210, 216, 220-1, 225, 226-7
  knighted, 367,n.42
  leads raids on northern England, 236-7, 239-44, 252-4
  on Irish expedition, 315-6
  takes Berwick, 239
  takes Rievaulx abbey, 243-4
  wins recognition of Robert I from Pope John, 250
  negotiates Treaty of Corbeil, 251
  present at Treaty of Edinburgh, 257
  his role in the succession arrangements, 293-4
  lord of Badenoch, 324
  as king's lieutenant, 295
  Guardian (1330), 324
Rathlin, Isle of, Antrim, 164, 166, 169, 170
Rattray, Aberdeen, 271-4
Rattray, Eustace of, 310, 327
Reading, 57
  abbot of, see Sutton
Redden Burn, Roxburgh and Northumberland, 69
Redesdale, Northumberland, 71, 197
regalia of Scotland, 28, 73, 74
  hidden and preserved by Bishop Wishart (1306), 149
'regality', institution of, 282-3
Renfrew, 9
  lordship of, 20, 77, 81
responsible men, see probi homines
Restalrig, Midlothian, 58, 77
Restalrig, John of, 77
Restalrig, Simon of, 58, 77
Rhuddlan, Statute of (also Statute of Wales), 1284, 56, 136
Richard I, Coeur de Lion, king of England (1189-99), 49
  cancellation of submission of Falaise by, 117
Richmond castle, Yorks., 236
Richmondshire, 237, 242, 254
Riel, Henry of, 326
Rievaulx abbey, Yorks., 243-4, 372,n.48
Rigaud of Assier, bishop of Winchester, 240
Ripon, Yorks., 239
Rires, in Kilconquhar, Fife, 58, 331,n.25
Rivers, Thomas, O.S.F., 302
Robert I, king of Scots (1306-29), see under Bruce
Robert II, king of Scots (1371-90), 294
  his birth, 294
  grants to by Robert I, 280, 282, 288
Robert, bishop of Ross (d. c.1291), 267
Roche, Gilbert de la, 316
Rochester, Kent, 156, 174
Roe, The, on Lough Foyle, 163, 169
Rokeby, Thomas, 253

Roland, Gilbert (Kennedy), son of, of Carrick, 158, 299

Rome, 94, 95, 121

Romeyn, John, archbishop of York (1285-96), 66

Ros, Robert de, lord of Wark on Tweed, 69
forfeited, 102

Ros, William de, brother of Robert de Ros of Wark, 344,n.10

Rose Castle, Cumberland, 198

Roslin, Midlothian
battle of (1303), 126, 128

Ross, 176, 178, 187, 336,n.28
bishop of, see Dundee
earldom of, 45, 271
earls of, 55

Ross, Farquhar Mactaggart, earl of (d. 1251), 177

Ross, William II, earl of (d. 1323), 45, 55-6, 74, 150, 156, 161, 163, 175-8, 185, 271, 318, 364,n.107

Ross, Hugh, earl of (d. 1333), 186, 258, 271-4, 288, 289, 291
granted thanage of Glendowachy (The Doune), 288

Ross, John of, 271

Ross, Wester, 55

Rossie, Walter of, 158, 326

Rothbury, Northumberland, Forest of, 92

Rothes, Moray, 75

Rothesay castle, Bute, 126, 148

Rothwell, H., 339,n.71

Roxburgh, 6, 12, 59, 69, 99, 106, 121, 339,n.73
castle, 6, 68, 69, 73, 83, 92, 96, 106, 135, 152, 162, 188-9, 191, 277
taken by Douglas (1314), 195
county and sheriffdom of, 85, 188-9
sheriff of, 105

'royal dignity', of Scotland (regia dignitas), 17, 27, 36, 41, 74, 177, 246, 313-14, 330,n.44

'Roy Coveytous, le', identified with Edward I, 172

Rudby, Yorks., N.R., 7

Rue, see Dru

Rushen, Isle of Man, 193, 338,n.37

Rushyford, Co. Durham, 246

Rutherglen, Lanark, 9, 105, 112, 149, 174
castle, 191

Rydale, Philip of, mayor of Berwick, 52

Rye, Henry of 75

St Andrews, Fife, 7, 38, 103, 105
burgesses of, 200-1
parliament at (1304), 133
parliament at (1309), 181, 183-6 passim, 202, 263, 268
bishop of, 331,n.25 see also Arnold, Ben, Fraser, Lamberton, Wishart

cathedral church of, 94, 263 consecrated, 266
synod held at, 265
diocese and see of, 64, 67, 76, 94, 115, 263, 264-6, 305
prior and convent of, 94
archdeacons of, see Alpin, Fraser

St Andrews, John of Haddington, prior of, 41, 94

St Andrews, Nicholas of, see Balmyle

St Cuthbert's land, see Durham, county and palatine bishopric of

St Fillans, Perth, 356,n.51

St Germain-en-Laye, dép. Seine-et-Oise, 95

St Jean d'Angély, dép. Charente, 330,n.37

St John, Aymer de (kinsman of John de St John), 182

St John, John de, 50, 68, 350,n.87
warden of Annandale and Galloway for Edward I, 121

St Michael, John of, forfeited, 327, 346,n.64

St Ninians, Stirling, Kirk of, 210, 214, 216, 219-20

St Omer, dép. Pas-de-Calais, 199

St Pol, Hugh count of, 9, 13

Saint-Sardos, war of, 245, 251

Saintes, dép. Charente, 16, 330,n.37

Salisbury, treaty of (1289), 65, 332,n.39

Sampson, John, 105-6

Sandal, John, chamberlain of Scotland for Edward I, 76, 134, 139, 356,n.51

Sardinia, Enzo (Henry), King of, imprisoned in an iron cage, 162

Saucier, Alexander le, bailie of Inverkeithing, 1

Sawtry, John of, Master of the Temple in Scotland, slain at Falkirk, 103

Scammell, Jean, 197

Scimus, fili (1299), 61, 116, 185, 241

Scone, Perth, 15, 28, 50, 56, 59, 83, 105, 150-1, 277, 338,nn.32,47
inaugurations at of Alexander III, 5 of John Balliol, 50, 60 of Robert I, 150-2
parliaments at, 15, 16, 294, 296, 310, 363,n.92
abbey of, 150-1, 363,n.92

Scort, Robert, 154

Scotia (Alba, Scotland north of Forth and Clyde), 4, 8, 15, 107

Scotland
character of kingdom, 16-17
early history, 4-5, 306
its independence, 27-8, 187-8, 241, 303, 308, 254-61 passim
Celtic character of, 2-6
clans, 2, 4
law of succession, 41-3
Kings of, as vassals of Kings of England, 11-12

Scotland—*contd*
  Kingdom (regnum) of, 40, 41-3, 49, 54-5, 74, 87, 90, 134, 143-4, 186, 245-6 *see also* Community of the realm, earls, Franco-Scottish Treaty, laws, Scotia
Scotlandwell hospital, Kinross, 153
Scoto-Norwegian treaty (1312), 190, 200-2
Scots language, 6, 346,n.68
Scrope, Geoffrey le, C. J. K. B., 257
Scrymgeour, Alexander, standard-bearer of Scotland, 91, 104, 119, 161-2
Seals, of Guardianship, 17, 27, 28, 35, 96, 343,n.7
Seals, of king of Scotland, 28, 50, 201
Segrave, John, Edward I's lieutenant in Lothian, 126, 127, 134, 142, 231
Segrave, Nicholas, 38
Segrave, Mr Stephen, 263
Selkirk, castle or peel, 120, 126, 158, 191
Selkirk Forest (*see also* Ettrick Forest), 67, 72, 83, 85, 96, 238
Selkirk, Patrick of, abbot of Melrose, Scottish envoy in France, 1298-99, 95
Seton, E. Lothian, 285
Seton, Alexander, crusader, 24
Seton, Alexander, 151, 240, 258, 284-5, 309, 378,n.136
  at Bannockburn, 223
  enjoys Robert I's special trust and is rewarded, 285
Seton, Christopher (d. 1306), 148, 155, 161, 171, 281, 318, 325
Seton, John, 161
Shannon, River, 316
Sheriff, office of, 8, 85, 105
  under Robert I, 295
Sherwood, archers of, 101
Shetland, 10, 200-1
Shielswood, Selkirk, 158
Sinclair, Henry (of Herdmanston?), 37
Sinclair, Henry, of Roslin, 238
Sinclair, William, bishop of Dunkeld (1311-37), 238, 246, 258, 266, 269, 302
Sinclair, William, of Roslin, justiciar of Galloway, 37, 38, 329,n.7
Sinclair, William, of Roslin, 324
Siward, family of, 281
Siward, John, 326
Siward, Richard, of Tibbers, 74
Sixhills, Lincs, 162
Skaithmuir, Berwick, fight at, 238
Skelbo castle, Sutherland, 176
Skene, W. F., 2, 44
Skene, Aberdeen, Patrick of, 146
Skeoch, in St Ninians, Stirling, 214-5, 367,n.53
Skinburness, Cumberland, English supply base, 149, 169

Skipton, Yorks, 239
Skye, Isle of, 55, 177, 289, 291
Slains, Old, castle, Aberdeen, 134, 174, 271
Slegh, Andrew, 327
Slioch, in Drumblade, Aberdeen, 176
Sluys, 9, 345,n.41
Small Isles (Rum, Eigg, Muck and Canna), 55, 170 *see also* Garmoran
Smithfield, London, 136, 137
Sodor and Man, bishops of, *see* Bernard, Mark
Solway Firth, 20, 191
  fords of, 20, 69, 197, 243
  'Solwayland', 112
  advance of Edward of Caernarvon beside (1301), 121
Somerled, lord of Argyll (d. 1164), 56
  his son Reginald and his descendants, 347,n.104
Somervilles, (John, Thomas and William), 158, 325, 326
Soules, family of, 23, 50, 279
Soules, Nicholas de (son of William de Soules the elder), 69
  forfeited, 346,n.64
Soules, John de, Guardian of Scotland (d. 1310), 37, 64, 80, 95, 109, 128, 129, 143, 158, 237, 309, 347,n.1
  as sole Guardian (1301-1302 or 1303), 114-26 *passim*
  envoy at French court (1302-04), 124-6
  refuses surrender terms (1304-05), 129, 130-1
  supports Robert I, 155, 328
  his death in France, 155, 351,n.119
Soules, John de (d. 1318), 237
Soules, Ranulf de, lord of Liddesdale (butler of Scotland), 20, 64
Soules, William de, lord of Liddesdale (butler of Scotland), 37, 64
Soules, William de, younger, lord of Liddesdale, 237, 240, 279, 283, 304, 309
Soules conspiracy, 240, 276, 309-10
Soulles, dép. Manche, 20
South Tynedale, 237
Spalding, Peter of, burgess of Berwick, 239, 281
Spens, Sir Patrick, 9
Spey, River, 75, 85-6
Spottsmuir, in Spott, E. Lothian, 72
Sprouston, Roxburgh, 196, 282-3
Standard, battle of the (1138), 21
Stanhope Park, Co. Durham, 370,n.6
  campaign and engagements of, 252-3
Stebbing, Essex, 69
Stenhouse, Stirling, 105
Stewart, family of, 22-3, 138
  lands granted to, 274, 282
Stewart of Bunkle, family of, 282

Stewart, Alexander, of Bunkle, 183, 363,n.87a

Stewart, Andrew, eldest son of James the Stewart (d. before 1309), 153, 169

Stewart, Elizabeth, 83

Stewart, James the (succ. 1282, d. 1309), Guardian of Scotland, 15-16, 18, 27, 38, 49, 50, 55-6, 62, 65, 66, 69, 73, 77, 81-3, 112, 124, 139, 158, 334,n.98, 344,n.22, 355,n.6

his leadership in the revolt of 1297, 81-5, 87-8

at Falkirk (1298), 102, 346,n.61

in the Forest raid (1299), 106-8, 110

as envoy at Paris (1302), 124

returns to Scotland, 129

surrender terms imposed upon, 130, 357,n.57

lands restored, 134

supports Robert I in 1306, 155

submits to Edward I, 155

rejoins Robert I, 155, 183, 282

present at St Andrews parliament, 185-6

his death, 282

possibly godfather of James Douglas, 157

his connexions with Ireland, 163, 169

Stewart, James, brother of Walter the Stewart, 252, 279, 380,n.19

Stewart, John, of Bunkle, earl of Angus, see Angus

Stewart, John, of Jedburgh (d.1298), brother of James the Stewart of Scotland, 37, 77, 83, 96, 101, 102, 274

Stewart, Robert, see Robert II, king of Scots

Stewart, Walter, son of Alan, the (d.1177), 20

Stewart, Walter the (d. 1327), 141, 196, 288, 293, 304, 308, 380,n.19

at Bannockburn, 210, 225

knighted, 367,n.42

defends Berwick (1319), 239

lands granted to, 280, 282

as king's lieutenant, 295

Stirling, 6, 38, 63, 105, 209, 211, 216, 339,n.73,

castle, 6, 16, 73, 86-7, 88, 92, 96, 120, 127, 128-9, 135, 142, 152, 191, 203, 209, 211, 212, 221, 229, 230, 231, 239 see also Malherbe

taken

by Edward I (1296), 73

by Wallace (1297), 92

by Guardians (1299), 105-6, 109

by Edward I (1304), 73, 129

by Robert I (1314), 195, 231

King's Park at, 212

sheriff of, 105

Stirling, Carse of, 211-2, 215, 221-5, 228-9, see also Pows

Stirling, John, 102, 178

Stirling Bridge, 87-8, 137

battle of (1297), 62, 86-9, 90

Stobo, Peebles, 106, 108, 342,n.77

Stone of Destiny ('Stone of Scotland', 'la pierre d'Escoce'), 73, 151, 260

Stonehouse, Lanark, 121

Stones, E. L. G., 33

Stracathro, Angus, 74

Stralsund, Germany, 199

Stratford, John, bishop of Winchester, archbishop of Canterbury (d. 1348), 250

Stratha'an (alias Strathavon), Banff, 75, 156, 275

Strathbogie, Aberdeen, 156, 275, 335,n.21

castle (afterwards Huntly), 176

Strathbogie, Laurence of, 157, 159, 328, 358,n.89

Strathclyde, 210 see also Clydesdale

Strath Eachaig, in Dunoon, 290

Strathearn, 5, 336,n.28

earldom of, 174, 258, 275-6

earls of, 190, 268

Strathearn, Malise III, earl of (1271-1313), 17, 45, 65, 93, 98, 152, 156, 159, 174, 275-6, 310, 326, 356,n.51, 358,n.88, 359,nn.96,101

Strathearn, Malise IV, earl of (1313-c.1329), 156, 275-6, 310

Strathearn, countess of, 310

Strathfillan, Perth, 160, 170, 318

Strathmore, 210

Strathord, in Kinclaven and Moneydie, Perth, 130

Sturmy, John, naval leader, 204

Sully, Henry, lord of, butler of France, 244

'surdit de sergaunt' (Gallovidian custom), 298, 348,n.15

Surrey, see Warenne

Sutherland, earldom of, 175, 271

Sutherland, William, earl of (1263-c.1307), 38, 156, 163, 185, 270-1

Sutton, William, abbot of Reading, 57

Swinburne, John, 77

tailzies (settlements) of the Scottish Crown, 293-4

Tain, Ross, sanctuary of St Duthac at, 161, 318

Tantallon castle, E. Lothian, 100

Tarbert, Argyll, 295, 320, 321

Tarradale castle, Ross, 156, 176

Tascher, Ferricus, 265

Tay, River, 103, 190, 194

Taylorton, Upper, Stirling, 211, 216

Tees, River, 198

Temple Liston (now Hallyards), in Liston, Midlothian, 9, 345,n.51

Teviotdale, 6, 80, 81, 96, 159, 188, 238

Teviotdale, archdeacon of, see Wishart

Therdonne, archdeacon of, 265

Thomas, a priest of Edinburgh, 154

Thomas (Becket), Saint, archbishop of Canterbury, 225

Thurstan, archbishop of York (1114-1140), 21, 239

Thurston, East Lothian, 158

Tibbers castle, Dumfries, 148, 161, 182, 191

Tiptoft, Pain, 207, 226, 230

Tiree, Isle of, 291

Tong, Mr Andrew of, 35, 115

Toom Tabard, nickname of King John, q.v., s.v. Balliol, 74

Torphichen, W. Lothian, 344,n.37

Torthorald, Dumfries, 358,n.80

Torthorald, family of, 358,n.80

Tor Wood, Stirling (also Keltor, les Torres), 103, 105
    its place in the battle of Bannockburn, 209-10, 212-4, 218, 230

Torksey, Lincoln, 352,n.15

Tottenham, Middx, 142

Toulouse, 62

Touny, Robert de, 104

Tout, T. F., 63, 76

Tranent, E. Lothian, 243, 287

Traquair, Peebles, 158

treasurer of Scotland, under King John, 50

treasurer of Scotland, under Edward I, 75, 78

Trevelyan, G. M., 79-80, 91, 96-8

Troup (Banff), Hamelin of, 133, 157, 158, 310, 328

Turnberry Band (1286), 18, 25-6

Turnberry Castle, Ayr, 18, 26, 121, 170, 171-2

Turnberry Point, 170

Turriff, Aberdeen, hospital of, 319

Tweed, River, 31, 37, 67, 69, 145, 333,n.63

Tweeddale, 6, 96, 120, 188
    sheriffs of (alias Peebles or Traquair), 106

Tweng, Marmaduke, 87-8, 207, 231, 344,n.10

Twynholm, Kirkcudbright, 113

Twynholm, Mr Walter of, chancellor of Scotland, 240, 251

Twynholm, William of, 268

Tyne, River, 197

Tynedale, 71, 145, 197

Tynedale, North, 239; South, 237

Tynedale, Liberty of, 42-3, 48, 237, 344,n.23

Tynedale, Waltheof of (12th century), 145

Tynemouth, John of, chronicler, 310

Tyningham House, E. Lothian, 304

Tyrone, Domhnall, king of, 332,n.31, see also Ireland, kings of

Uhtred, Thomas, 243

Uhtred, see also Galloway

Uist (North and South), 55
    chapel of Holy Trinity of Uist, 170

Uldale, Cumberland, 363,n.87a

Ulster, Richard de Burgh, earl of, 18, 123-4, 126-7, 163, 204, 323, 339,n.73

Ulster, 192, 252, 317

Umfraville, family of, 23, see also Angus, earls of

Umfraville, Ingram de, 37, 64, 80, 166, 171, 186, 274, 309, 310, 313, 379,n.169
    in the Forest raid (1299), 106
    as joint-Guardian (1300), 112, 113-14
    campaigns with de Soules, 121
    envoy at Paris (1302), 124
    returns to Scotland, 129
    submission terms imposed on, 130
    opposes Edward Bruce (1308), 182
    at Bannockburn, 207, 226, 231

Upsettlington, Berwick, 37, 333,n.59

Urquhart, castle, Inverness, 86, 127, 156, 175, 321

Valence, Aymer de, earl of Pembroke (1307-24), 145, 202, 240, 264
    appointed lieutenant in Scotland by Edward I, 154
    wins battle of Methven (1306) 153-4
    pursues Robert I and takes Kildrummy (1306), 160-1
    unable to contain Robert I, 171-2
    defeated by him at Loudoun Hill, 172, 217
    receives orders from Edward I, 171-3
    holds a guardian's court at Rutherglen, 174
    superseded in lieutenancy (1307), 173-4
    his support for Bannockburn campaign, 203, 206-7
    re-appointed warden or lieutenant (1314), 203
    at Bannockburn, 207-8, 229, 370,n.149

Valle Crucis abbey, Denbigh, 231-2

Valognes, Adam de, 133, 158, 326

Valois, Charles, count of, 65, 68, 95, 100

Valois, Jeanne de, 65

Varennes, John, lord of, 240

Veirement (Verment), Mr Richard, 12-13

Vere, Robert de, earl of Oxford (1296-1331), 206

Vermand and Vermandois, dép. Aisne, 12

Vesci, de, family of, 282

Vesci, Agnes de, forfeited, 346,n.64

Vesci, (Isabella), lady de, sister of Sir Henry Beaumont and cousin of Edward II, 157

Vesci, John de, the elder, 358,n.73

Vicenza, bishop of, 95

Vicia, Baiamundo de (Master Bagimond), 77

Vicia, Giacomo de, parson of Idvies, 77

Vieuxpont of Brougham, family of, 342,n.88

Vieuxpont (Vipont), William, of Langton, 110, 183, 188, 230

Wake, Thomas, of Liddel, one of the disinher-
    ited, 259, 260
Waldegrave, Richard, 344,n.10
Wale, Thomas, 116
Wales, prince of, see Edward II
Wales, 10, 60, 63, 74, 242, 317, 335,n.9,
    380,n.17
    rulers of, their agreement with the Scots
        (1258), 64
    Edwardian towns in, 71 see also Welsh
Wallace, family of, 81, 138
Wallace, John, brother of William Wallace, 173
Wallace, Malcolm, brother of William Wallace,
    77, 78, 106-7, 139
Wallace, William, Guardian of Scotland
    (d.1305), 10, 58, 67, 77, 78, 79, 80, 81,
        106-7, 109, 142, 168, 183, 223, 321
    leader of rising of 1297, 81-3, 85, 86
    wins battle of Stirling Bridge (1297), 87-9
    knighted, 96
    made Guardian, 96
    period of his ascendancy, 90-103
    his character, 91-2, 137-8
    raids Northumberland, 91-3
    attempts to restore Franco-Scottish alliance,
        93, 107, 110, 115-16
    Lamberton elected bishop of St Andrews
        through his influence, 93-4
    friendship with Bishop Lamberton, 128
    travels to papal curia, 116
    his military activity, 1303-04, 126-9, 136
    measures taken for his capture, 130
    his capture, 136
    his trial and death (August 1305), 136-7
    Edward I's attitude towards, 136, 137,
        351,n.124
    estimate of his significance and influence,
        137-8
wapinschaw (1296), 66
Warenne, John de, earl of Surrey (also Earl
    Warenne) (d. 1304), 72, 86-7, 338,n.34,
    342,n.87
    appointed lieutenant of Scotland for Edward
        I, 75, 79
    loses battle of Stirling Bridge, 87-8
    counter-attacks, 96
Warenne, John de, earl of Surrey (d. 1347),
    206, 243
Wark on Tweed, Northumberland, 239
    castle, 69, 204, 209, 239, 350,n.80, 372,n.76
Wark on Tyne 237
Warkworth castle, Northumberland, 254
Warwick, earl of, see Beauchamp
'Warwolf', new siege-engine at Stirling, 129
Watton, Yorks, 162
Wauchope, Robert, 328
'Wawayne's Pot', coalpit, E. Lothian, 280
Wear, River, 253

Weardale, Co. Durham, 252-3
Wedale, Simon of, bishop of Galloway (1321-
    55), 258, 267
Welsh, nation, 246
    rising of, against Edward I (1294), 63
    troops in Scotland, 86, 87, 96, 98-100, 102,
        204, 218, 231
Wemyss (Fife), Michael, laird of, 154, 326
Wemyss, David, 309
Wergild (law or usage between Scot and Bret,
    also cro and galnis), 3, 135-6
West Calder, Midlothian, 278
Westerkirk, Dumfries, 115, 279
Westminster Abbey, 73, 151, 260
Westminster Hall, 136-7
    parliament at (1302), attended by Robert
        Bruce, 141
Westmorland, 20, 197, 237, 240, 254, 329,n.27
Westquarter Burn, Stirling, 101
Wetheral priory, Cumberland, 371,n.30
Whitehaven, Cumberland, 339,n.73
Whithorn, Wigtown, 121
    cathedral church of 66
    shrine of St Ninian at, 319
Whitsome, Berwick, 287, 337,n.8
Whitwick, Leics, 152, 356,n.31
Wigtown
    castle, 17
Wigtownshire, 25, 341,n.53
Willard, James, 197
William, bishop of Dunblane (d. 1296),
    formerly abbot of Arbroath, 41
William II, count of Holland, 45
William I, the conqueror, King of England
    (1066-87), 209, 242
William II, Rufus, King of England (1087-
    1100), 335,n.15
William I, the Lion, King of Scots (1165-
    1214), 39, 40, 46, 67, 249, 288
Willoughby, Philip, deputy treasurer (English
    exchequer), 76
    letter to, from Hugh Cressingham, 85
Winchelsey, Robert, archbishop of Canterbury
    (1294-1313), 95, 113, 116
Winchester, bishop of, see Rigaud
Wiseman, William, sheriff of Elgin (1305),
    133, 176, 178, 186
Wishart, family of, 80, 138
Wishart, John, archdeacon of Glasgow, after-
    wards bishop of Glasgow (d. 1338), 80
Wishart, John, of the Carse, envoy to the
    French court (1299), 95, 344,n.26
Wishart, John, forfeits Conveth (1306), 327
Wishart, John, forfeits lands of Monylaws
    (1314), 370,n.2
Wishart, Robert, bishop of Glasgow (1271-
    1316), Guardian of Scotland, 15, 27,
    33-4, 38, 41, 49, 60-1, 64, 65, 78-9, 80-1,

Wishart, Robert—*contd*
  83-5, 96, 107, 110, 139, 143, 155, 174,
    268, 269, 330,n.37, 338,n.37, 350,n.94,
    354,n.74
  his part in the events of 1291, 34
  supports Bruce in the Great Cause, 41, 49
  leader in the rising of 1297, 80-5
  English charges against, at papal *curia*, 115
  submission terms imposed on, 130
  participates in resettlement of 1305, 134,
    352,n.15
  part played in Bruce's *coup* (1306), 146,
    149-50
  approves Bruce's bid for the throne, 151
  assists at Robert I's coronation, 151, 263
  his warlike activity in 1306, 152
  captured and imprisoned in irons, 154
  represented at St Andrews parliament
    (1309)?, 185
  repatriated (1314), 231
  his career in Robert I's reign, 263-4
  death, 264
Wishart, Thomas, dean of Glasgow, 80
Wishart, Mr William, archdeacon of Teviot-
    dale, 80

Wishart, William, bishop of St Andrews
    (1271-79), 80
Wissant, dép. Pas-de-Calais, 95
Wiston, Lanark, 158
Wiston, Lanark, Walter of, 158, 327
Witton, Michael of, 159
wool
  importance of in Scottish economy, 9-10,
    199-200, 302
  seized for Edward I (1296-97), 78
Worcester, bishop of (Thomas Cobham), 240
Wright, Thomas, 78
Writtle, Essex, 331,n.8, 332,n.30
Wyntoun, Andrew, prior of Lochleven,
    chronicler, 118
  on Wallace, 138
  on Robert Bruce's *coup*, 139-40

Yester castle, E. Lothian, 75, 191
Yolande, *see* Dreux
York, 98, 142, 239, 244, 249, 252, 253, 256
  archbishops of, *see* Melton, Romeyn

Zouche, Alan la, lands forfeited by, 279, 280
Zouche, William de la, 257, 259